Strategic Studies Instit

**U. S. ARMY WAR COLLEGE GUIDE
TO NATIONAL SECURITY ISSUES**

VOLUME I:

THEORY OF WAR AND STRATEGY

5th Edition

J. Boone Bartholomees, Jr.
Editor

June 2012

The views expressed in this report are those of the authors and do not necessarily reflect the official policy or position of the Department of the Army, the Department of Defense, or the U.S. Government. Authors of Strategic Studies Institute (SSI) publications enjoy full academic freedom, provided they do not disclose classified information, jeopardize operations security, or misrepresent official U.S. policy. Such academic freedom empowers them to offer new and sometimes controversial perspectives in the interest of furthering debate on key issues.

*****

This publication is subject to Title 17, United States Code, Sections 101 and 105. It is in the public domain and may not be copyrighted.

NOTICE: Further dissemination or distribution of this manuscript or quotation from it is not authorized without permission of the authors.

*****

Comments pertaining to this report are invited and should be forwarded to: Director, Strategic Studies Institute, U.S. Army War College, 47 Ashburn Drive, Carlisle, PA 17013.

*****

All Strategic Studies Institute (SSI) publications may be downloaded free of charge from the SSI website. Hard copies of this report may also be obtained free of charge while supplies last by placing an order on the SSI website. SSI publications may be quoted or reprinted in part or in full with permission and appropriate credit given to the U.S. Army Strategic Studies Institute, U.S. Army War College, Carlisle Barracks, PA. Contact SSI by visiting our website at the following address: *www.StrategicStudiesInstitute.army.mil*.

*****

The Strategic Studies Institute publishes a monthly e-mail newsletter to update the national security community on the research of our analysts, recent and forthcoming publications, and upcoming conferences sponsored by the Institute. Each newsletter also provides a strategic commentary by one of our research analysts. If you are interested in receiving this newsletter, please subscribe on the SSI website at *www.StrategicStudiesInstitute.army.mil/newsletter/*.

ISBN 1-58487-532-1

CONTENTS

Introduction vii
    J. Boone Bartholomees, Jr.

Part I: Strategic Theory

1. Why is Strategy Difficult? 3
    David Jablonsky

2. A Survey of the Theory of Strategy 13
    J. Boone Bartholomees, Jr.

3. Toward a Theory of Strategy: Art Lykke and the U.S. Army War College Strategy Model 45
    H. Richard Yarger

4. The Strategic Appraisal: The Key to Effective Strategy 53
    H. Richard Yarger

5. Managing Strategic Risk 67
    James F. Holcomb

6. Continuity and Change in War 79
    J. Boone Bartholomees, Jr.

7. A Theory of Victory 91
    J. Boone Bartholomees, Jr.

8. Toward a Strategic Theory of Terrorism: Defining Boundaries in the Ongoing Search for Security 107
    Frank L. Jones

9. Thucydides and Contemporary Strategy 119
    R. Craig Nation

10. Eastern Strategic Traditions: Un-American Ways of War 133
    Glenn K. Cunningham

Part II: Instruments and Elements of Power

11. National Power 147
    R. Craig Nation

12. Strategic Communications: Wielding the Information Element of Power 159
    Dennis M. Murphy

13. Diplomacy as an Instrument of National Power 173
    Reed J. Fendrick

CONTENTS

14. Theory and Practice of Modern Diplomacy: Origins and Development to 1914 179
    Louis J. Nigro, Jr.

15. Economic Diplomacy: Views of a Practitioner 193
    Constance Phlipot

16. Economics: A Key Element of National Power 205
    Clayton K. S. Chun

17. Military Power and the Use of Force 217
    John F. Troxell

Part III: Strategic Interests and Considerations

18. Applying Clausewitz and Systems Thinking to Design 245
    Glenn K. Cunningham and Charles D. Allen

19. Intelligence as a Tool of Strategy 257
    John Aclin

20. The Airplane and Warfare: Theory and History 273
    Tami Davis Biddle

21. John Warden's Five Ring Model and the Indirect Approach to War 295
    Clayton K. S. Chun

22. Naval Theory for Soldiers 309
    J. Boone Bartholomees, Jr.

23. On the Theory of Cyberspace 325
    Jeffrey L. Caton

About the Contributors 345

FIGURES - VOLUME I

Chapter 1

Figure 1-1. The Policy Continuum 4

Figure 1-2. The Remarkable Trinity 5

Figure 1-3. The Impact of Technology 5

Figure 1-4. The Continuum of War 8

Figure 1-5. National Strategy: The Horizontal Plane 9

Figure 1-6. National Strategy and the Vertical Continuum of War 9

Chapter 3

Figure 3-1. Strategic and Operational Art 47

Figure 3-2. Comprehensiveness of Strategy 48

Figure 3-3. The Lykke Model 48

Chapter 4

Figure 4-1. Strategic Appraisal Process 54

Figure 4-2. Realms of Strategy 55

Figure 4-3. Levels of Intensity 58

Figure 4-4. Strategic Factors 59

Figure 4-5. Strategic Thinking Competencies 61

Chapter 7

Figure 7-1. Scale of Success 94

Figure 7-2. Scale of Decisiveness 95

Figure 7-3. Scale of Achievement 95

FIGURES - VOLUME I

Chapter 17

Figure 17-1. Components of Security Policy 219

Figure 17-2. Evaluations of Compellent Threats 222

Figure 17-3. Range of Military Operations 224

Figure 17-4. Guidelines for the Use of Force 227

Figure 17-5. Weinburger Doctrine from Vietnam to Iraq 231

Chapter 18

Figure 18-1. The Army Organizational Life Cycle Model 248

Figure 18-2. Characteristics of Centers of Gravity 252

Figure 18-3. Determining Center of Gravity 253

Chapter 19

Figure 19-1. Interaction with the Analysts 266

Chapter 21

Figure 21-1. John Warden's Five Ring Model 299

Chapter 23

Figure 23-1. Cyberspace as Domain and Commons 327

Figure 23-2. Kinetic versus Nonkinetic Means and Effects 329

INTRODUCTION

J. Boone Bartholomees, Jr.

This edition of the *U. S. Army War College Guide to National Security Policy and Strategy* continues to reflect the structure and approach of the core national security strategy and policy curriculum at the War College. The fifth edition is published in two volumes that correspond roughly to the Department of National Security and Strategy's core courses: "Theory of War and Strategy" and "National Security Policy and Strategy." Like previous editions, this one is based on its predecessor but contains both updates and new scholarship. Over a third of the chapters are new or have undergone significant rewrites. Many chapters, some of which appeared for years in this work, have been removed. Nevertheless, the book remains unchanged in intent and purpose. Although this is not primarily a textbook, it does reflect both the method and manner we use to teach strategy formulation to America's future senior leaders.

The book is not a comprehensive or exhaustive treatment of either strategic theory or the policymaking process. Both volumes are organized to proceed from the general to the specific. Thus, the first volume opens with general thoughts on the nature and theory of war and strategy, proceeds to look at the complex aspect of power, and concludes with specific theoretical issues. Similarly, the second volume begins by examining the policy/strategy process, moves to a look at the strategic environment, and concludes with some specific issues. This edition continues the effort begun in the fourth edition to include several short case studies to illustrate the primary material in the volume.

PART I

STRATEGIC THEORY

CHAPTER 1

WHY IS STRATEGY DIFFICULT?

David Jablonsky

Colonel (Ret.) Arthur Lykke has taught an entire generation of U.S. Army War College students that strategy at any level consists of ends or objectives, ways or concepts, and means or resources. This three-element framework is nothing more than a reworking of the traditional definition of strategy as the calculated relationship of ends and means. Yet, the student response is always overwhelmingly favorable, with Lykke's framework invariably forming the structure for subsequent seminar problems on subjects ranging from the U.S. Civil War to nuclear strategy. This is due, in part, to the fact that students weaned on the structural certitude of the five-paragraph field order and the Commander's Estimate naturally find such structure comforting in dealing with the complexities of strategy. But those students also know from their experience in the field that there are limits to the scientific approach when dealing with human endeavors. As a consequence, they can also appreciate the art of mixing ends, ways, and means, using for each element some subjective and some objective criteria of suitability, feasibility, and applicability—the essence of strategic calculation.[1]

The ends-ways-means paradigm also provides a structure at any level of strategy to avoid confusing the scientific product with the scientific process. The former involves production propositions that are logically related and valid across time and space. The search for these immutable principles over the centuries by students of war failed, because they looked at classical strategy as something like physical science that could produce verities in accordance with certain regularities. This was further compounded by military thinkers who made claims for scientific products without subjecting those products to a scientific process. Both Jomini and Mahan, for instance, ignored evidence in cases that did not fit their theories or principles of strategy.[2] The strategic paradigm, then, serves as a lowest common denominator reminder that a true scientific product is not possible from the study of strategy. At the same time, however, that paradigm provides a framework for the systematic treatment of facts and evidence—the very essence of the scientific process. In this regard, Admiral Wylie has pointed out:

> I do not claim that strategy is or can be a 'science' in the sense of the physical sciences. It can and should be an intellectual discipline of the highest order, and the strategist should prepare himself to manage ideas with precision and clarity and imagination. . . . Thus, while strategy itself may not be a science, strategic judgment can be scientific to the extent that it is orderly, rational, objective, inclusive, discriminatory, and perceptive.[3]

All that notwithstanding, the limitations of the strategic paradigm bring the focus full circle back to the art involved in producing the optimal mix of ends, ways, and means. Strategy, of course, does depend on the general regularities of that paradigm. But strategy does not always obey the logic of that framework, remaining, as the German Army Regulations *Truppen-fuhrung* of 1936 described it, "a free creative activity resting upon scientific foundations."[4] The purpose of this chapter is to demonstrate why, despite increasingly scientific approaches to formulation and implementation, strategy remains principally an art rather than a science, and why within that art the "creative activity" of blending the elements in the strategic paradigm has become progressively more difficult over the centuries.

FROM REVOLUTIONS TO TOTAL WAR

In the wake of the Napoleonic Wars, there was a growing recognition of the increased complexity of strategy, summarized in Carl von Clausewitz's warning that "there can be no question of a purely military evaluation of a great strategic issue, nor of a purely military scheme to solve it."[5] At the tactical level, the Prussian philosopher wrote, "the means are fighting forces trained for combat; the end is victory." For the strategic, however, Clausewitz concluded that military victories were meaningless unless they were the means to obtain a political end, "those objects which lead directly to peace."[6] Thus, strategy was "the linking together (*Verbindung*) of separate battle engagements into a single whole, for the final object of the war."[7] And only the political or policy level could determine that objective. "To bring a war, or any one of its campaigns to a successful close requires a thorough grasp of national policy," he pointed out. "On that level strategy and policy coalesce."[8] For Clausewitz, this vertical continuum (see Figure 1-1) was best exemplified by Frederick the Great, who embodied both policy and strategy and whose Silesian conquests of 1741 he considered to be the classic example of strategic art by demonstrating "an element of restrained strength, . . . ready to adjust to the smallest shift in the political situation."[9]

**Figure 1-1.
The Policy Continuum.**

With his deceptively simple description of the vertical continuum of war, Clausewitz set the stage for the equivalent of a Copernican shift in the strategic ends-ways-means paradigm. Now that paradigm was more complex, operating on both the military and policy levels with the totality of the ends, ways, and means at the lower levels interconnected with the political application at the policy level of those same strategic elements. This connection was the essence of Clausewitz's description of war as a continuation of political intercourse (Verkehr) with the addition of other means. He explained that:

> We deliberately use the phrase 'with the addition of other means' because we also want to make it clear that war in itself does not suspend political intercourse or change it into something entirely different.... The main lines along which military events progress, and to which they are restricted, are political lines that continue throughout the war into the subsequent peace.... War cannot be divorced from political life; and whenever this occurs in our thinking about war, the many links that connect the two elements are destroyed and we are left with something pointless and devoid of sense.[10]

THE INDUSTRIAL AND FRENCH REVOLUTIONS

This growing complexity in dealing with the strategic paradigm was compounded by two upheavals. Clausewitz was profoundly aware of one, the French Revolution; he was totally ignorant of the other, the Industrial/Technological Revolution. Prior to the French Revolution, 18th-century rulers had acquired such effective political and economic control over their people that they were able to create their war machines as separate and distinct from the rest of society. The Revolution changed all that with the appearance of a force "that beggared all imagination," as Clausewitz described it:

Suddenly, war again became the business of the people—a people of thirty millions, all of whom considered themselves to be citizens. There seemed no end to the resources mobilized; all limits disappeared in the vigor and enthusiasm shown by governments and their subjects.... War, untrammeled by any, conventional restraints, had broken loose in all its elemental fury. This was due to the peoples' new share in these great affairs of state; and their participation, in its turn, resulted partly from the impact that the Revolution had on the internal conditions of every state and partly from the danger that France posed to everyone.[11]

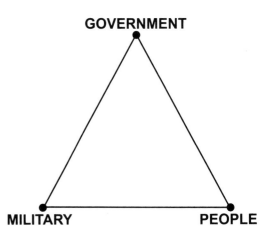

Figure 1-2.
The Remarkable Trinity.

For Clausewitz, the people greatly complicated the formulation and implementation of strategy by adding "primordial violence, hatred and enmity, which are to be regarded as a blind natural force" to form with the army and the government what he termed the remarkable trinity (see Figure 1-2). The army he saw as a "creative spirit" roaming freely within "the play of chance and probability," but always bound to the government, the third element, in "subordination, as an instrument of policy, which makes it subject to reason alone.[12]

It was the complex totality of this trinity that, Clausewitz realized, had altered and complicated strategy so completely.

Clearly the tremendous effects of the French Revolution . . . were caused not so much by new military methods and concepts as by radical changes in policies and administration, by the new character of government, altered conditions of the French people, and the like.... It follows that the transformation of the art of war resulted from the transformation of politics.[13]

But while that transformation had made it absolutely essential to consider the elements of the Clausewitzian trinity within the strategic paradigm, the variations possible in the interplay of those elements moved strategy even farther from the realm of scientific certitude. "A theory that ignores any one of them or seeks to fix an arbitrary relationship between them," Clausewitz warned in this regard, "would conflict with reality to such an extent that for this reason alone it would be totally useless."[14]

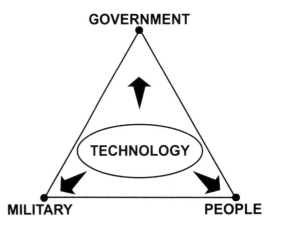

Figure 1-3. The Impact of Technology.

Like most of his contemporaries, Clausewitz had no idea that he was living on the eve of a technological transformation born of the Industrial Revolution. But that transformation, as it gathered momentum throughout the remainder of the 19th century fundamentally altered the interplay of elements within the Clausewitzian trinity, further complicating the formulation and application process within the strategic paradigm (see Figure 1-3).

In terms of the military element, technology would change the basic nature of weapons and modes of transportation, the former stable for a hundred years, the latter for a thousand. Within a decade of Clausewitz's death in 1831, that process would begin in armaments with the introduction of breech-loading firearms and in transportation with the development of the railroads."[15]

Technology had a more gradual effect on the role of the people. There were, for example, the great European population increases of the 19th century as the Industrial Revolution moved on to the continent from Great Britain. This trend led, in turn, to urbanization: the mass movement of people from the extended families of rural life to the "atomized," impersonal life of the city. There, the urge to belong, to find a familial substitute, led to a more focused allegiance to the nation-state manifested in a new, more blatant and aggressive nationalism.

This nationalism was fueled by the progressive side effects of the Industrial Revolution, particularly in the area of public education, which meant, in turn, mass literacy throughout Europe by the end of the 19th century. One result was that an increasingly literate public could be manipulated by governments as technology spawned more sophisticated methods of mass communications. On the other hand, those same developments also helped democratize societies, which then demanded a greater share in government, particularly over strategic questions involving war and peace. In Clausewitz's time, strategic decisions dealing with such matters were rationally based on Realpolitik considerations to further state interests, not on domestic issues. By the end of the 19th century, the *Rankeian Primat der Aussenpolitik* was increasingly challenged throughout Europe by the need of governments for domestic consensus—a development with far-reaching implications for the conduct of strategy at the national level within the basic ends-ways-means paradigm.[16]

During much of that century, as the social and ideological upheavals unleashed by the French Revolution developed, military leaders in Europe generally attempted to distance their armed forces from their people. Nowhere was this more evident than in the Prussian *cum* German military, where the leaders worked *hard* over the years to prevent the adulteration of their forces by liberal ideas. "The army is now our fatherland," General von Roon wrote to his wife during the 1848 revolutions, "for there alone have the unclean and violent elements who put everything into turmoil failed to penetrate."[17] The revolutions in industry and technology, however, rendered this ideal unattainable. To begin with, the so-called *Technisierung* of warfare meant the mass production of more complex weapons for ever-larger standing military forces. The key ingredients for these forces were the great population increases and the rise of nationalism as well as improved communications and governmental efficiency—the latter directed at general conscription of national manhood, which, thanks to progress in railroad development, could be brought to the battlefield in unlimited numbers.

At the same time, this increased interaction between the government/military and the people was also tied to other aspects of the impact of technology on the Clausewitzian trinity. Technological innovations in weaponry during this period, for example, were not always followed by an understanding of their implications, societal as well as military. Certainly, there was the inability on the part of all European powers to perceive the growing advantage of defensive over offensive weapons demonstrated in the Boer and Russo-Japanese Wars. That inability was tied in with a trend in Europe at the time to combine elan with a military focus on moral force, bloodshed, and decisive battles. The result was that the military leaders of France, Germany, and Russia all adopted offensive military doctrines in some form.[18]

The fact that these doctrines led to the self-defeating offensive strategies of World War I ultimately had to do with the transformation of civil-military relations within the Clausewitzian trinity in their countries. In France, as an example, the officer corps distrusted the trend by the leaders of the Third Republic toward shorter terms of military service, which it believed threatened the army's professional character and tradition. Adopting an offensive doctrine and elevating it to the highest level was a means to combat this trend, since there was general agreement that an army consisting primarily of reservists and short-term conscripts could only be used in the defense. "Reserves are so much eyewash," one French general wrote at the time, "and take in only, short-sighted mathematicians who equate the value of armies with the size of their effectives, without considering their moral value.[19] Although these were setbacks for those who shared this sentiment in the wake of the Dreyfus Affair and the consequent military reforms, it only required the harsher international climate after the Agadir crisis of 1911 for General Joffre and his young Turks to gain the ascendancy. Their philosophy was summed up by their leader, who explained that in planning for the next war he had "no preconceived idea other than a full determination to take the offensive with all my forces assembled."[20]

Under these circumstances, French offensive doctrine became increasingly unhinged from strategic reality as it responded to the more immediate demands of domestic and intragovernmental politics. The result was France's ill-conceived strategic lunge in 1914 toward its former possessions in the East, a lunge that almost provided sufficient margin of assistance for Germany's Schlieffen Plan, another result of military operational doctrine driving policy. In the end, only the miracle of the Marne prevented a victory for the Germans as rapid and complete as that of 1870.[21]

There were other equally significant results as the full brunt of technological change continued to litter the relationship between the elements of the Clausewitzian trinity in all the European powers. The larger, more complex armies resulted in the growing specialization and compartmentalization of the military—a trend that culminated in the emulation of the German General Staff system by most of the European powers. It is significant that Clausewitz had ignored Carnot, the "organizer of victory" for Napoleon, when considering military genius. Now with the increase in military branches as well as combat service and combat service support organizations, the age of the "military-organizational" genius had arrived. All this in turn affected the relationship in all countries between the military and the government. For the very increase in professional knowledge and skill caused by technology's advance in military affairs undermined the ability of political leaders to understand and control the military, just as technology was making that control more important than ever by extending strategy from the battlefield to the civilian rear, thus blurring the difference between combatant and noncombatant.[22]

At the same time, the military expansion in the peacetime preparation for war began to enlarge the economic dimensions of conflict beyond the simple financial support of Clausewitz's era. As Europe entered the 20th century, new areas of concern began to emerge, ranging from industrial capacity and the availability and distribution of raw materials to research and development of weapons and equipment. All this, in turn, increased the size and role of the European governments prior to World War I—with the result, as William James perceptively noted, that "the intensely sharp competitive preparation for war by the nation is the real war, permanently increasing, so that the battles are only a sort of public verification of mastery gained during the 'peace' intervals."[23]

Nevertheless, the full impact of the government's strategic role in terms of national instruments of power beyond that of the military was generally not perceived in Europe, despite some of the more salient lessons of the American Civil War. In that conflict, the South lost because its strategic means did not match its strategic ends and ways. Consequently, no amount of operational finesse on the part of the South's great captains could compensate for the superior industrial strength and manpower that the North could deploy. Ultimately, this meant for the North, as Michael Howard has pointed out, "that the operational skills of their adversaries were rendered almost irrelevant."[24] The Civil War also illustrated another aspect of the changes within the strategic paradigm: the growing importance of the national will of the people in achieving political as well as military strategic objectives. That social dimension of strategy on the part of the Union was what prevented the early Southern operational victories from being strategically decisive and what ultimately allowed the enormous industrial-logistical potential north of the Potomac to be realized.

THE REVOLUTIONS JOINED: THE AGE OF TOTAL WARS

Strategy changed irrevocably with the full confluence in World War I of the trends set in train by the Industrial and French revolutions. In particular, the technology in that war provided, as Hanson Baldwin has pointed out, "a preview of the Pandora's box of evils that the linkage of science with industry in the service of war was to mean."[25] How unexpected the results of that linkage could be was illustrated by a young British subaltern's report to his commanding general after one of the first British attacks in Flanders. "Sorry sir," he concluded. "We didn't know it would be like that. We'll do better next time."[26]

But of course there was no doing better next time, not by British and French commanders in Flanders, not by Austrian troops on the Drina and Galician fronts in 1914, and not by the Russian officers on the Gorlice-Tarnow line in 1915. The frustration at this turn of events was captured by Alexander Solzhenitsyn in his novel *August 1914*. "How disastrously the conditions of warfare had changed," he wrote, "making a commander as impotent as a rag doll! Where now was the battlefield ..., across which he could gallop over to a faltering commander and summon him to his side?"[27] It was this milieu that demonstrated the inadequacy of classical strategy to deal with the intricacies of modern warfare. Napoleon had defined that strategy as the "art of making use of time and space."[28] But the dimensions of these two variables had been stretched and rendered more complex by the interaction of technology, with the elements of the Clausewitz's trinity. And that very complexity, augmented by the lack of decisiveness at the tactical level, impeded the vertical continuum of war outlined in Clausewitz's definition of strategy as the use of engagements to achieve policy objectives. Only when the continuum was enlarged, as the Great War demonstrated, was it possible to restore warfighting coherence to modern combat. And that, in turn, required the classical concept of strategy, to be:

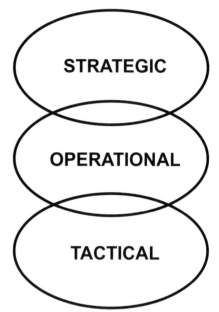

Figure 1-4. The Continuum of War.

> the level of war at which campaigns and major operations are planned, conducted and sustained to accomplish strategic objectives.... Activities at this level link tactics and strategy.... These activities imply a broader dimension of time or space than do tactics; they provide the means by which tactical successes are exploited to achieve strategic objectives.[29]

At the same time, the full impact of technology on the Clausewitzian trinity in each of the combatant states during World War I substituted the infinitely more complex concept of national strategy for that of policy. To begin with, the growing sophistication and quantity of arms and munitions, as well as the vast demands of equipment and supply made by the armies, involved the national resources of industry, science, and agriculture—variables with which the military leaders were not prepared to deal. To cope with these variables, governments were soon forced to transform the national lives of their states in order to provide the sinews of total war.

Looking back over fifty years later on the totality of this change in what Clausewitz had termed policy, Admiral Eccles defined the concept of national strategy that emerged in World War I as "the comprehensive direction of all the elements of national power to achieve the national objectives."[30] The U.S. Department of Defense (DoD) is more explicit, defining the new level of strategy that emerged at the national level after 1914 as the "art and science of developing and using the political, economic, and psychological powers of a nation, together with its armed forces during peace and war, to secure national objectives."[31]

National strategy, then, involves all the elements of national power. Those elements, in turn, can be conveniently broken down on a horizontal plane into the categories described in the DoD definition of national strategy: political, economic, psychological, and military (see Figure 1-5).

The linchpin in this horizontal design is the military instrument of power at the national strategic level—the apex, as we have seen emerging in World War 1, of the vertical continuum of war (see Figure 1-6).

Thus, the mix of ends, ways, and means at the national military strategic level will directly affect (and be affected by) the same paradigm operating at each level of the vertical continuum. Adding to the complexity is the interplay on the horizontal plane of national military strategy with the other strategies derived from the elements of national power, each operating within its own strategic paradigm and all contributing to the grand design of national strategy, as that strategy evolves within its own overall mix of ends, ways, and means. That this horizontal and vertical interplay has rendered the formulation and implementation of strategy at every level more difficult has become increasingly obvious. "Because these various elements of power cannot be precisely defined, compartmented, or divided," Admiral Eccles concluded about the "fog" of strategy, "it is normal to expect areas of ambiguity, overlap, and contention about authority among the various elements and members of any government."[32]

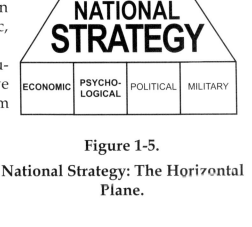

Figure 1-5.
National Strategy: The Horizontal Plane.

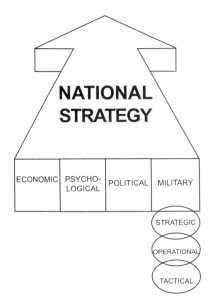

Figure 1-6.
National Strategy and the Vertical Continuum of War.

CONCLUSION

The United States is in an era in which the strategic landscape has changed and is continuing to change. Nevertheless, the core problems that make strategy so difficult for a global power remain essentially the same as they did for earlier powers ranging from Rome to Great Britain. To begin with, there are challenges to U.S. interests throughout the globe. In a constantly changing strategic environment, however, it is difficult in many cases to distinguish which of those interests are vital, not to mention the nature of the challenge or threat to them. In any case, there are never enough armed forces to reduce the risk everywhere; strategic priorities have to be established.

In addition, like the leaders of earlier great powers, U.S. governmental elites have to grapple with the paradox of preparing for war, even in peacetime, if they wish to maintain the peace. The dilemma in the paradox that makes strategy in any era so difficult is that to overdo such preparations may weaken the economic, psychological, and political elements of power in the long run. The solution is to so balance the total ends, ways, and means that the natural tension in national security affairs between domestic and foreign policy is kept to a minimum while still securing the nation's vital interests with a minimum of risk. This solution, as the leaders of the great global powers of the past would assuredly agree, is not easy to achieve. In an ever more interdependent world in which variables for the strategist within the ends-ways-means paradigm have increased exponentially, strategists are no nearer to a "Philosopher's Stone" than they ever were. Strategy remains the most difficult of all art.[33]

ENDNOTES - CHAPTER 1

1. Arthur F. Lykke, "Defining Military Strategy," *Military Review 69, No. 5,* May *1989,* pp. 2-8, and his testimony before the Senate Armed Services Committee, *National Security Strategy,* hearings before the Committee on Armed Services, United States Senate, One Hundredth Congress, First Session, Washington, DC: U.S. Government Printing Office (USGPO), 1987, pp. 140-145. See also *Sound Military Decision,* Newport, RI: Naval War College, 1942, pp. 32, 34, 164, 165; and Henry E. Eccles, *Military Power in a Free Society,* Newport, RI: Naval War College Press, 1979, p. 73.

2. John Shy, "Jomini," pp: 173-175, and Philip Crowl, "Mahan," p. 454, both in *Makers of Modern Strategy,* Peter Paret, ed., Princeton, NJ: Princeton University Press, 1986. See also Stephen M. Walt, "The Search for a Science of Strategy," *International Security,* Vol. 12, No. I, Summer 1987, pp. 144-145, and John I. Alger, *The Quest for Victory,* Westport, CT: Greenwood Press, *1982.* Admiral J. C. Wylie, *Military Strategy: A General Theory of Power Control,* Westport, CT: Greenwood Press, 1980, p. 20.

3. Wylie, *Military Strategy,* p. 10.

4. Martin van Creveld, "Eternal Clausewitz," in *Clausewitz and Modern Strategy,* Michael I. Handel, ed., London: Frank Cass, 1986, p. 41. "The formulation of strategy is the creative act of choosing a means, an end, a way to relate a means to an end." Carl H. Builder, *The Masks of War: American Military Styles in Strategy and Analysis,* Baltimore, MD: Johns Hopkins University Press, 1989, p. 50.

5. Original emphasis. Carl von Clausewitz, *Two Letters on Strategy,* Peter Paret and Daniel Moran, ed./trans., Carlisle, PA: U.S. Army War College, 1984, p. 9.

6. Carl von Clausewitz, *On War,* Michael Howard and Peter Paret, eds., Princeton, NJ: Princeton University Press, 1976, pp. 142-143.

7. Michael Howard, *Clausewitz,* New York: Oxford University Press, 1986, p. 16; Clausewitz, *On War,* pp. 127-132.

8. Clausewitz, *On War,* p. 111. "In the highest realms of strategy ... there is little or no difference between strategy, policy and statesmanship." *Ibid.,* p. 178. Winston Churchill relearned these lessons in World War I. "The distinction between politics and strategy," he wrote at that time, "diminishes as the point of view is raised. At the summit, true politics and strategy are one." Winston S. Churchill, *The World Crisis - 1911-1918, Part Two: 1915,* New York: Charles Scribner's Sons, 1929, p. 6.

9. Clausewitz, *On War,* p. 179.

10. *Ibid.,* p. 605.

11. *Ibid.,* pp. 592-593.

12. *Ibid.,* p. 89.

13. *Ibid.,* pp. 609-610.

14. *Ibid.,* p. 89.

15. Michael I. Handel, *War, Strategy and Intelligence,* London: Frank Cass, 1989, p. 63; Howard, *Clausewitz,* pp. 3-4; and van Creveld, "Eternal Clausewitz," p. 36.

16. Handel, *War,* p. 82. See also Dennis E. Showalter, "Total War for Limited Objectives: An Interpretation of German Grand Strategy," in *Grand Strategies in War and Peace,* Paul Kennedy, ed., New Haven, CT: Yale University Press, 1991, pp. 110-111.

17. Gordon A. Craig, *The Politics of the Prussian Army 1640-1945*, New York: Oxford University Press, 1956, p. 107; Michael Howard, "The Armed Forces as a Political Problem," in *Soldiers and Governments,* Michael Howard, ed., Westport, CT: Greenwood Press, 1978, p. 16.

18. Martin van Creveld, "Caesar's Ghost: Military History and the Wars of the Future," *The Washington Quarterly,* Winter 1980, p. 81. See also Michael Howard, "Men against Fire: The Doctrine of the Offensive in 1914," in *Makers of Modern Strategy,* p. 521; and Handel, *War,* pp. 21, 64-68.

19. Howard, "Armed Forces as a Political Problem," p. 17. See also Jack Snyder, "Civil Military Relations and the Cult of the Offensive, 1914-1984," *International Security,* Summer 1984, p. 109.

20. Theodore Ropp, *War in the Modern World,* New York: Collier Books, 1962, p. 229; Snyder, "Civil Military Relations," pp. 110-111, 130, 132-133.

21. The French military elite made a mirror image of their disdain for reservists in their estimates of German strength. The German General Staff made extensive use of German reservists, however, and instead of the 68 German divisions that had been expected in the implementation of French Plan XVII, there were 83. Howard, "Armed Forces as a Political Problem," p. 17. Joffre's failure to use French reservists more fully in 1914 proved to be, as Douglas Porch has pointed out, "like going to war without your trousers on." See Porch, "Arms and Alliances: French Grand Strategy and Policy in 1914 and 1940," in *Grand Strategies in War and Peace,* p. 142. See also Snyder, "Civil Military Relations," pp. 108, 133. It is true, of course, that had the French Army remained on the defensive instead of plunging into Alsace, it could have brought its full weight to bear on the German Army at the French frontier. Stephen Van Evera, "The Cult of the Offensive and the Origins of the First World War," *International Security,* Summer 1984, p. 89. It is also true, however, that the French offensive ultimately caused Moltke to weaken the right flank that was supposed to "brush the channel with its sleeve." Moreover, as Michael Howard has pointed out, the general concept behind Plan XVII—that France should take the strategic initiative rather than passively await the German offensive—did provide the flexibility that enabled General Joffre to recover rapidly from his opening reverses and redeploy his forces for the battle of the Marne. Howard, "Men against Fire," pp. 522-523.

22. Handel, *War,* pp. 60, 79. "The interchangeability between the statesman and the soldier," General Wavell stated later in summarizing these developments, passed forever ... in the last century. The Germans professionalized the trade of war, and modern inventions, by increasing its technicalities, have specialized it." Archibald Wavell, *Generals and Generalship,* London: Macmillan, 1941, pp. 33-34.

23. Handel, *War,* p. 58.

24. Michael Howard, "The Forgotten Dimensions of Strategy," *Foreign Affairs,* Summer 1979, p. 977. See also Gordon A. Craig, "Delbruck: The Military Historian," in *Makers of Modern Strategy,* p. 345.

25. Hanson W. Baldwin, *World War I: An Outline History*, New York: Harper & Row, 1962, p. 159.

26. Gordon A. Craig, War, *Politics and Diplomacy,* New York: Frederick A. Praeger, 1966, p. 197.

27. Alexander Solzhenitsyn, *August 1914,* New York: Bantam Books, 1974, pp. 330-331.

28. David G. Chandler, *The Campaigns of Napoleon,* New York: Macmillan, 1966, p. 161.

29. *Joint Chiefs of Staff (JCS) Pub 1-02, Department of Defense Dictionary of Military and Associated Terms,* Washington, DC: USGPO, December 1, 1989, p. 264.

30. Henry E. Eccles, *Military Power in a Free Society,* Newport, RI: Naval War College Press, 1979, p. 70.

31. *JCS Pub 1-02*, p. 244. This is what André Beaufre long ago termed total strategy: "the manner in which all-political, economic, diplomatic, and military-should be woven together." André Beaufre, *An Introduction to Strategy*, New York: Praeger, 1965, p. 30.

32. Eccles, *Military Power*, p. 70.

33. Kennedy, "Grand Strategy in War and Peace: Toward a Broader Definition," p. 7. During the Roman Republic, for example, Roman foreign policy was affected by the distrust and fear felt by the ruling patricians for the plebeians of Rome on the domestic front. Barr, *Consulting the Romans,* p. 6.

CHAPTER 2

A SURVEY OF THE THEORY OF STRATEGY

J. Boone Bartholomees, Jr.

A common language is both the product of and basis of any effective theory; people conversant in the theory habitually use words in the same way to mean the same thing. Such meanings may be unique to the theoretical context even if the word has other non-theoretical usages. Thus, the word "passion" used in a Christian context has an entirely different meaning than in secular usage. Similarly, doctrinal military terms, while hopefully used consistently by military individuals and organizations, may differ slightly (or even radically) in common usage. Strategy is such a word. Defining it is not as easy as one would think, and the definition is critical.

Part of the problem is that our understanding of strategy has changed over the years. The word has a military heritage, and classic theory considered it a purely wartime military activity—how generals employed their forces to win wars. In the classic usage, strategy was military maneuvers to get to a battlefield, and tactics took over once the forces were engaged. That purely military concept has given way to a more inclusive interpretation. The result is at least threefold: 1) Strategists generally insist that their art includes not only the traditional military element of power but also other elements of power like politics and economics. Most would also accept a peacetime as well as a wartime role for strategy. 2) With increased inclusiveness, the word "strategy" became available outside the military context and is now used in a variety of disciplines ranging from business to medicine and even sports. 3) As the concept mutated, the military had to invent another term—the U.S. settled on "operations" or "operational art"—to describe the high-level military art that had once been strategy.[1] All this, of course, affects any survey of strategy. Thus, this study acknowledges that strategy is now commonly used in non-military fields, and both the definition and overall theory must be compatible with such usage. Nevertheless, this discussion focuses on the national security arena and particularly on grand strategy and military strategy. In that context, we also follow the modern interpretation that strategy involves both military and non-military elements of power and has equal applicability for peace and war, although much of the existing theory we discuss deals exclusively with war.

Surprisingly for such a significant term, there is no consensus on the definition of strategy even in the national security arena. The military community has an approved definition, but it is not well known and is not accepted by non-military national security professionals. As a consequence, every writer must either develop his or her own definition or pick from the numerous extant alternatives. We begin by surveying some of those alternatives.

Clausewitz wrote, "Strategy is the use of the engagement for the purpose of the war. The strategist must therefore define an aim for the entire operational side of the war that will be in accordance with its purpose. In other words, he will draft the plan of the war, and the aim will determine the series of actions intended to achieve it: he will, in fact, shape the individual campaigns and, within these, decide on the individual engagements."[2] Because this is a classic definition, it is not satisfactory—it deals only with the military element and is at the operational level rather than the strategic. What Clausewitz described is really the development of a theater or campaign strategy. Historian Jay Luvaas used to say that because Clausewitz said something did not necessarily make it true, but did make it worth considering. In this case we can consider and then ignore Clausewitz.

The 19th-century Swiss soldier and theorist Antoine Henri Jomini had his own definition.

> Strategy is the art of making war upon the map, and comprehends the whole theater of war. Grand Tactics is the art of posting troops upon the battle-field according to the accidents of the ground, of bringing them into action, and the art of fighting upon the ground, in contradiction to planning upon a map. Its operations may extend over a field of ten or twelve miles in extent. Logistics comprises the means and arrangements which work out the plans of strategy and tactics. Strategy decides where to act; logistics brings the troops to this point; grand tactics decides the manner of execution and the employment of the troops.[3]

This again is military only and theater-specific.

Civil War-era soldier and author Henry Lee Scott had an interesting definition derived from the basic Jominian concept: "…the art of concerting a plan of campaign, combining a system of military operations determined by the end to be attained, the character of the enemy, the nature and resources of the country, and the means of attack and defence [sic]."[4] This actually has all the elements we look for and states them as a relationship that is more conceptually complex and satisfying than Jomini's. However, reflecting the classic paradigm, Scott still limited strategy to military endeavors and to theaters.

Military historian Basil H. Liddell Hart had another unique approach to the subject. Because he wrote as the concept of strategy was expanding to include more non-military aspects, his definition is more modern. Liddell Hart defined strategy as: "the art of distributing and applying military means to fulfill the ends of policy." Also: "Strategy depends for success, first and most, on a sound *calculation and coordination of the ends and the means*. The end must be proportioned to the total means, and the means used in gaining each intermediate end which contributes to the ultimate must be proportioned to the value and needs of that intermediate end—whether it be to gain an object of to fulfill a contributory purpose. An excess may be as harmful as a deficiency." Liddell Hart was talking specifically about military strategy, and he thought strategy was something akin to but different from the more expansive concept of grand strategy.

> As tactics is an application of strategy on a lower plane, so strategy is an application on a lower plane of 'grand strategy'….While practically synonymous with the policy which guides the conduct of war, as distinct from the more fundamental policy which should govern its objective, the term 'grand strategy' serves to bring out the sense of 'policy in execution.' For the role of grand strategy—higher strategy—is to coordinate all the resources of a nation, or a band of nations, towards the attainment of the political object of the war—the goal defined by fundamental policy.

Liddell Hart went on to say:

> Grand strategy should both calculate and develop the economic resources and man-power of nations in order to sustain the fighting services. Also the moral resources—for to foster the people's willing spirit is often as important as to possess the more concrete forms of power. Grand strategy, too, should regulate the distribution of power between the services, and between the services and industry. Moreover, fighting power is but one of the instruments of grand strategy—which should take account of and apply the power of financial pressure, of diplomatic pressure, of commercial pressure, and, not the least of ethical pressure, to weaken the opponent's will….Furthermore, while the horizon of strategy is bounded by the war, grand strategy looks beyond the war to the subsequent peace. It should not only combine the various instruments, but so regulate their use as to avoid damage to the future state of peace—for its security and prosperity. The sorry state of peace, for both sides, that has followed most wars can be traced to the fact that, unlike strategy, the realm of grand strategy is for the most part *terra incognita*—still awaiting exploration, and understanding.[5]

That is very close to modern doctrine, although the use of words is different. But Liddell Hart's entire exposition was really a means to get past all this uninteresting grand strategic stuff and on to his pet theory of the indirect approach—a technique of implementation that we will consider later.

Contemporary strategist Colin Gray has a more comprehensive definition. "By strategy I mean *the use that is made of force and the threat of force for the ends of policy* [emphasis in original]."[6] The problem with that definition is that Gray ties himself down when he links the definition of strategy to force—in actuality he is mixing definitions of war and strategy.

The U.S. military has an approved joint definition of strategy: "The art and science of developing and employing instruments of national power in a synchronized and integrated fashion to achieve theater, national, and/or multinational objectives." Unfortunately, that definition only recognizes strategy as a national security function, and although it is significantly better than earlier definitions, it remains fairly broad. The explanation in the Joint Encyclopedia goes a little further: "These strategies integrate national and military objectives (ends), national policies and military concepts (ways), and national resources and military forces and supplies (means)." That is more satisfactory, although still focused exclusively on national security issues, which is understandable considering the source. However, the Joint definition of national military strategy shows that the Joint community is divided or at least inconsistent on this subject. "National Military Strategy: The art and science of distributing and applying military power to attain national objectives in peace or war." That is a pure "how-to" definition—at best a correlation of objectives with methods with the emphasis on methods. There is no consideration of or recognition of the importance of developing means; there is also no consideration of developing military objectives to accomplish national objectives. The encyclopedia's further explanation of that term goes into the formal document of the National Military Strategy rather than the concept.[7]

The U.S. Army War College defines strategy in two ways: "Conceptually, we define strategy as the relationship among ends, ways, and means." Alternatively, "Strategic art, broadly defined, is therefore: The skillful formulation, coordination, and application of ends (objectives), ways (courses of action), and means (supporting resources) to promote and defend the national interests." The second definition is really closer to a definition of grand strategic art, but if one cut it off after "means," it would be essentially the same as the first definition.[8]

In my own view, strategy is simply a problem-solving process. It is a common and logical way to approach any problem—military, national security, personal, business, or any other category one might determine. Strategy asks three basic questions: What is it I want to do, what do I have or what can I reasonably get that might help me do what I want to do, and what is the best way to use what I have to do what I want to do? Thus, I agree with the War College that strategy is the considered relationship among ends, ways, and means. That sounds deceptively simple—even simplistic. Is it actually more than that relationship? Is there some deeper secret? I do not believe there is; however, the relationship is not as simple as it appears at first blush. First, a true strategy must consider all three components to be complete. For example, if one thinks about strategy as a relationship of variables (almost an equation but there is no equal sign), one can "solve" for different variables. Ends, which hopefully come from a different process and serve as the basis for strategy, will generally be given. If we assume a strategist wants to achieve those ends by specific ways, he can determine the necessary means by one of the traditional exercises of strategic art—force development. If a strategist knows both the ends to be achieved and means available, he can determine the possible ways. People, particularly military writers, often define strategy in exactly that way—as a relation between ends and means—essentially equating strategy with ways or at least converting strategy into an exercise of determining ways. That was the traditional approach of classic strategists, like Jomini and Liddell Hart, who unabashedly thought of strategy as ways.

That is also the typical short-term planning process that a theater commander might do. He cannot quickly change the means available, so he has to determine how to best use what is on hand to accomplish the mission.

Before we proceed, it is useful to address the issue of whether strategy is really necessary. It is certainly possible to conduct a war without a strategy. One can imagine very fierce combat divorced from any coherent (or even incoherent) plan for how that fighting would achieve the aims of the war—fighting for the sake of fighting. Alternatively, preemptive surrender is always an option for the state interested in avoiding strategic decisions; the only drawback is that preemptive surrender is incapable of achieving positive political objectives other than avoidance of conflict. Rational states, however, will always attempt to address their interests by relating ends with ways and means. Given the fact that they are fighting for some reason—that is, they have an end—there will be some (even if unconscious) design of how to use the available means to achieve it. Thus, while strategy may not technically be necessary, it is almost always present—even if poorly conceived and executed.

TESTS FOR STRATEGY

One can test a possible strategy by examining it for suitability, acceptability, and feasibility. Those three nouns test each of the three components of strategy. Suitability tests whether the proposed strategy achieves the desired end—if it does not, it is not a potential strategy. Acceptability tests ways. Does the proposed course of action or concept produce results without excessive expenditure of resources and within accepted modes of conduct? Feasibility tests means. Are the means at hand or reasonably available sufficient to execute the proposed concept? A strategy must meet or at least have a reasonable expectation of meeting all three tests to be valid, but there is no upper limit on the number of possible solutions. The art becomes the analysis necessary to select the best or most efficient or least risky.

Of the three tests, suitability and feasibility are fairly straightforward and require no further explication. Acceptability, however, has some complicating features. The morality and legality of strategies is an obvious case in point—morality and legality vary widely by nation, culture, and even individual. But those are not the only complicating features of acceptability. For example, Colin Gray talks about what he calls the social dimension of strategy "...strategy is made and executed by the institutions of particular societies in ways that express cultural preferences."[9] That is really an expression of the relation of the acceptability of a strategy to the Clausewitzian trinity. Beyond morality and legality, a truly acceptable strategy must fit the norms of the military, government, and people. Strategies that only meet the norms of one or two of the legs are possible if they are not in major conflict with deeply held norms of the other legs, but they must be achievable very quickly to avoid possibly disastrous conflict over acceptability.

The U.S. invasion of Panama in 1989 is an example of this phenomenon. It was an invasion of a sovereign foreign nation justified by fairly innocuous (certainly not vital) political issues. That was against the norms of all three legs of the American trinity; however, the government had convinced itself that action was necessary, and the military agreed or at least obeyed orders. The potential glitch was the response of the American people. Initial reaction was the predictable support for troops being deployed in harm's way. That support could have quickly turned into opposition had the operation not been extremely rapid and relatively casualty-free.

Even though one might occasionally get away with violating norms, one cannot safely violate deeply held norms even briefly. Thus, the U.S. has a norm against assassination (reinforced by a self-imposed presidential directive that adds a legal dimension). Our current mode of declaring contained elements of informational power. Since its major components were subsumed in other terms, social/psychological power fell into disuse.

In a war, the other elements of power (and the strategies developed for their employment) tend to support the military element; however, there is always a symbiotic relationship between the elements. Thus, diplomatic strategy may support military strategy, but military success may be an essential precursor for diplomatic success. Similarly, economic strategy may be designed to provide military means, but the military capture or loss of economic assets may directly influence the effectiveness of the economic strategy. Additionally, different types of warfare emphasize different elements of power. For example, in a civil war, the political element becomes especially important. It is for just this reason that the Washington community dealing with the War on Terrorism (WOT) has adopted a new model to think about power. Besides the traditional DIME elements, the counterterrorist community has added intelligence, legal or law enforcement, and financial to its list of elements of power—giving the acronym MIDLIFE or DIMEFIL. Those are useful tools to consider in the WOT, although the expanded categories of national power have not gained broad acceptance beyond the counterterrorism community.

STRATEGY AND THE TYPE OF WAR

Does (or should) one's strategy necessarily change based on the type of war he is fighting? If strategy is a function of ends, then it ought to change or be different as the political ends change. The alternative view, however, is that destroying the enemy's military force is always the best (to some theorists, the only legitimate) objective for the military regardless of political goals. This gets to what Clausewitz called the supreme judgment about a war—its nature. "The first, the supreme, the most far-reaching act of judgment that the statesman and commander have to make is to establish by that test the kind of war on which they are embarking; neither mistaking it for, nor trying to turn it into, something that is alien to its nature. This is the first of all strategic questions and the most comprehensive."[14] Based on the characteristics of the war, the military's objective may or may not have anything to do with destroying the enemy's military force. For example, one might have political goals that make avoiding battle at all costs, and instead maneuvering to seize specific locations, not only a viable but a desirable strategy. The strategist will only recognize this if he or she understands the kind of war that he or she is waging, recognizes when that changes, and adapts strategy accordingly.

The inclusion of potential changes in the nature of a war during its conduct raises another important question. If the nature of a war can change, then is not trying to shape that nature into a form that suits the strategist a legitimate strategic exercise? Is Clausewitz overlooking a useful strategic tool when he warns against trying to turn a war into something alien to its nature? Strategists should certainly try to control or influence the nature of a war as much as possible. The problem is when they do not recognize that their efforts have failed and persist in fighting the wrong kind of war. Thus, in the 1960's, the United States might legitimately have tried to turn the Vietnam war into a conventional international war between North and South Vietnam—that was the war the U.S. military was best prepared to win. However, when that effort failed, the strategists should have recognized that fact and adapted to the true nature of the war they were fighting. Unfortunately, that did not occur until it was too late to win that war; paradoxically, the nature of the war changed again in 1975, and the war became precisely the conventional international war the United States had initially wanted.

EXECUTING STRATEGY

Next we need to consider a few theories on potential ways to execute strategy. Knowing that strategy is a considered relation among ends, ways, and means is a necessary first step, but it does not help one actually do anything. Fortunately, hundreds of authors have given their thoughts on how to conduct strategy. Some are better than others. Most are "ways" determinations rather than comprehensive ends-ways-means analyses. Still, they are worth consideration. At a minimum, a competent strategist should be aware of each.

Sun Tzu.

The ancient Chinese philosopher Sun Tzu did not define strategy, but he offered pointers on its practice. At times, Sun Tzu can be so straightforward he is simplistic. For example, the statement, "Victory is the main object of war," is not especially informative. One can make all the tortuous interpretations one likes, but the statement is blunt and obvious in its intent. That is not to say it is trivial—in fact, it is well for anyone involved with war to remember that the object is to win—it is just wrong as an absolute. The object of war is not victory, but, as Liddell Hart says, "a better peace—even of only from your own point of view." One can strive so hard for victory that he destroys the subsequent peace. Liddell Hart again says, "A State which expends its strength to the point of exhaustion bankrupts its own policy, and future. If you concentrate exclusively on victory, with no thought for the after-effect, you may be too exhausted to profit by the peace, while it is almost certain that the peace will be a bad one, containing the germs of another war." Victory is certainly better than the alternative, but it cannot be the exclusive aim of war. I expound on that for two reasons. First, Sun Tzu should be treated like Jay Luvass recommended using Clausewitz—the fact that he said something makes it worthy of consideration. Second, the fact that Sun Tzu is both an ancient and an Asian author does not automatically mean he had all the answers or even addressed all the questions. There is a tendency to read volumes into fairly straightforward passages of Sun Tzu on the assumption that there must be something of deep significance behind each phrase of the book. In many (if not most) cases, the phrases actually mean exactly what they say. Sun Tzu was not saying that war is a political act when he said, "War is a matter of vital importance to the State"—reading the rest of the quote makes it quite apparent he was simply saying war is important and must be studied.[15] That does not need tortured interpretation to be significant.

It is commonplace to acknowledge that Sun Tzu advocated deception and winning without fighting. For example, he wrote, "For to win one hundred victories in one hundred battles is not the acme of skill. To subdue the enemy without fighting is the acme of skill." Sun Tzu has become the intellectual father of a school of warfare that advocates winning by maneuver or by psychologically dislocating the opponent. Although undesirable, the ancient Chinese soldier might not be as pleased about that paternity as his advocates believe. Sun Tzu expended lots of effort explaining how to maneuver and fight. In some respects, he is very like Jomini (of all people). For example, Sun Tzu advocated attacking portions of the enemy with your whole force: "If I am able to determine the enemy's dispositions while at the same time I conceal my own then I can concentrate and he must divide. And if I concentrate while he divides, I can use my entire strength to attack a fraction of his." Sun Tzu thought that the defense was the stronger form of warfare but that offensive action was necessary for victory. "Invincibility lies in the defence [sic]; the possibility of victory in the attack....One defends when his strength is inadequate; he attacks when it is abundant." He sometimes did incomplete analysis and thus provided advice that might be wrong, depending on the circumstances. For example, Sun Tzu said, "To be certain to take what you attack is to attack a place the enemy does not protect." It is easy to use that quote as an advocacy for Liddell Hart's indirect approach. That is, attack where the enemy does not expect. The problem is that there is almost always a reason why the enemy does not defend a place, and it usually has to do with the limited value of that place. However, Sun Tzu was not setting up Liddell Hart. The line after the original quote changes the meaning of the entire passage: "To be certain to hold what you defend is to defend a place the enemy does not attack."[16] We now have a statement on chance and uncertainty in war—that is, the only certain way to take a place is if the enemy is not there—not advice on the indirect approach. Nevertheless, Sun Tzu is known as the advocate of deception, surprise, intelligence, and maneuver to win without fighting. He is mandatory reading for the strategist.

Clausewitz.

Clausewitz is generally more useful for his philosophical musings on the nature of war than his "how-to" strategic advice. In that arena, much of what he preached was either commonplace or 19th century specific. The exceptions are three. First was his advocacy of seeking battle. This obviously sets him apart from Sun Tzu and many others, and Clausewitz is quite specific about his expectations of decisive battle. He wrote,

> ...the importance of the victory is chiefly determined by the vigor with which the immediate pursuit is carried out. In other words, pursuit makes up the second act of the victory and in many cases is more important than the first. Strategy at this point draws near to tactics in order to receive the completed assignment from it; and its first exercise of authority is to demand that the victory should really be complete.[17]

Next, Clausewitz originated the concept of attacking what he called the enemy's center of gravity. The center of gravity comes from the characteristics of the belligerents and is "the hub of all power and movement, on which everything depends. That is the point against which all our energies should be directed."[18] He offered several possibilities but decided that attacking the enemy's army was usually the best way to start a campaign—followed by seizing his capital and attacking his alliances. The concept, which the U.S. military adopted almost verbatim until the most recent doctrinal publications, has caused interminable debate both in the active force and the schoolhouses. Tactically the U.S. military has always identified and attacked vulnerabilities—now, some dead Prussian is telling us that strategically we should attack strengths (for whatever else one might believe, it is clear that a center of gravity is a strength, not a weakness). We thus see attempts to mix the two concepts and essentially do both—usually described as attacking strengths through vulnerabilities.

Clausewitz's final significant "how-to" idea is the concept of the culminating point. "There are strategic attacks that have led directly to peace, but these are the minority. Most of them only lead up to the point where their remaining strength is just enough to maintain a defense and wait for peace. Beyond that point the scale turns and the reaction follows with a small force that is usually much stronger than that of the original attack. This is what we mean by the culminating point of the attack."[19] Although Clausewitz only discusses culmination in terms of the attack (his later discussion of the culminating point of victory is a different concept), modern U.S. doctrine also identifies a culminating point for the defense—essentially a breaking point.

Jomini.

The Baron Antoine Jomini, a contemporary of Clausewitz with service in the French and Russian armies during the Napoleonic wars, also gave modern U.S. theory and doctrine several terms. He was much more specific in his "how-to" analysis than Clausewitz. Jomini believed war was a science and consequently one could discover, by careful study, rules about how it should be conducted. He offered the results of his study. Jomini is often criticized for being geometric; although such a depiction overlooks some aspects of his work, it is not totally unfair. Jomini was specific about how to plan a campaign. First, one selected the theater of war. Next, one determined the decisive points in the theater. Selection of bases and zones of operation followed. Then one designated the objective point. The line of operations was then the line from the base through the decisive points to the objective point. Thus, the great principle of war "which must be followed in all good combinations" was contained in four maxims:

1. To throw by strategic movements the mass of an army, successively, upon the decisive points of a theater of war, and also upon the communications of the enemy as much as possible without compromising one's own.

2. To maneuver to engage fractions of the hostile army with the bulk of one's forces.

3. On the battlefield, to throw the mass of the forces upon the decisive point, or upon that portion of the hostile line which is of first importance to overthrow.

4. To so arrange that these masses shall not only be thrown upon the decisive point, but that they shall engage at the proper time and with energy.[20]

Jomini's maxims remain good advice if not elevated to dogma, and his terms, such as "lines of operations," "decisive points," etc., form the basis of much of the language of modern operational art.

Liddell Hart.

B. H. Liddell Hart had his own approach to strategy, which has become famous as the indirect approach.

> Strategy has not to overcome resistance, except from nature. *Its purpose is to diminish the possibility of resistance*, and it seeks to fulfill this purpose by exploiting the elements of *movement* and *surprise*....Although strategy may aim more at exploiting movement than at exploiting surprise, or conversely, the two elements react on each other. Movement generates surprise, and surprise gives impetus to movement.[21]

> Just as the military means is only one of the means of grand strategy—one of the instruments in the surgeon's case—so battle is only one of the means to the end of strategy. If the conditions are suitable, it is usually the quickest in effect, but if the conditions are unfavorable it is folly to use it....His [a military strategist's] responsibility is to seek it [a military decision] under the most advantageous circumstances in order to produce the most profitable results. Hence *his true aim is not so much to seek battle as to seek a strategic situation so advantageous that if it does not of itself produce the decision, its continuation by a battle is sure to achieve this*. In other words, dislocation is the aim of strategy.[22]

The strategist produces dislocation physically by forcing the enemy to change front or by threatening his forces or lines of communication. Dislocation is also achieved psychologically in the enemy commander's mind as a result of the physical dislocation. "In studying the physical aspect we must never lose sight of the psychological, and only when both are combined is the strategy truly an indirect approach, calculated to dislocate the opponent's balance." Although Liddell Hart would be appalled at being compared with Clausewitz, this statement is similar to the Prussian's comment, "Military activity is never directed against material force alone; it is always aimed simultaneously at the moral forces which give it life, and the two cannot be separated."[23]

Liddell Hart and his indirect approach have won a wide following among strategists. However, the issue of direct versus indirect is actually a smoke screen. The indirect approach is a tactical concept elevated to the strategic level, and it loses some of its validity in the transition. Strategically, it is sometimes (if not often) advantageous to take a direct approach. This is particularly true in cases when the contending parties have disproportionate power—that is, when one side possesses overwhelming force. In such cases, the stronger side invariably benefits from direct action. The concept of the indirect approach is also a downright silly notion when we speak about simultaneous operations across the spectrum of conflict. Advocates will cry that I have missed the point. Liddell Hart seeks an indirect approach only because what he really wants is the mental dislocation it produces. I would counter that his real point was the avoidance of battle and winning without fighting. Surprise, which Liddell Hart acknowledges is how an indirect approach produces mental dislocation, is a tremendous advantage; however, designing strategies purely or even primarily to achieve surprise overlooks the rest of the equation—surprise to do what? Surprise for what purpose? If a strategist can accomplish his purpose in a direct manner, it might be more desirable than contending with the disadvantages inherent in achieving surprise. Nevertheless, the indirect approach is a recognized strategic tool that has tremendous utility if used intelligently.

Beaufre.

The French general and theoretician André Beaufre provided another way to think about strategy. He made significant contributions to deterrence theory, especially in his skepticism of the deterrent effect of conventional forces and his advocacy of an independent French nuclear force; however, his main contribution was in the realm of general strategy. Beaufre published an influential trilogy of short books in the mid-1960s: *An Introduction to Strategy, Deterrence and Strategy,* and *Strategy of Action*.[24] He was generally Clausewitzian in his acceptance both of the political and psychological natures of war and his characterization of war as a dialectic struggle between opposing wills. He was adamant that wars are not won by military means alone (destroying the enemy army) but only by the collapse of will.

Beaufre recognized the criticality of non-military elements of power—political, economic, etc. He also recognized that strategy was neither an exclusively wartime activity nor restricted to planning against an enemy—one might have strategies for relations with friends or allies as well. Beaufre is sometimes credited with expanding the concept of strategy beyond the purely military, although contemporaries were already doing that under the rubric of grand strategy—a term Beaufre disliked and replaced in his own writing with "total strategy." Total strategy defined at the highest national level how the war would be fought and coordinated the application of all the elements of power. Below total strategy was a level Beaufre called overall strategy, which allocated tasks and coordinated the activities for a single element of power (essentially national-level sub- or supporting strategies like a National Military Strategy or a National Economic Strategy). Below overall strategy was operational strategy, which corresponded fairly closely to the modern concept of operational art.[25]

All these strategic levels directed strategies that fell into "patterns," depending on the levels or resources available and the intensity of the interests at stake. The first pattern Beaufre called the direct threat; it occurred when the objective was only of moderate importance and the resources available were large. A threat of action was often sufficient to achieve the objective. If the objective was of moderate importance but resources were inadequate to back a direct threat, nations usually resorted to indirect pressure operationalized as political, diplomatic, or economic pressure. If freedom of action was restricted, resources limited, and objectives important, a third pattern resulted. That pattern was the use of successive actions employing both direct threat and indirect pressure—often with a limited use of military force. The fourth pattern was another possibility if freedom of action was great but the resources inadequate and the stakes high—*"protracted struggle, but at a low level of military activity* [emphasis in original]." If military resources were sufficient, a nation might try the fifth and final pattern: *"violent military conflict aimed a military victory* [emphasis in original]." Strategic analysis based on synthesizing both material and psychological data rather than habit or "the fashion of the moment" should dictate the selection of the pattern and the specific strategies.[26]

According to Beaufre, there were two general principles of strategy, which he borrowed from Foch: freedom of action and economy of force. There were also two distinct but vital components to any strategy—"1. *Selection of the decisive point* to be attacked (this depends on the enemy's vulnerable points). 2. *Selection of the preparatory maneuvers* which will enable the decisive points to be reached [italics in original]."[27] Beaufre then developed a list of nineteen components of maneuver: eight offensive—attack, threat, surprise, feint, deceive, thrust, wear down, follow-up; six defensive—on guard, parry, riposte (counterattack), disengage, retire, break-off; and five related to force posture—concentrate, disperse, economize, increase, and reduce. All of these aim at gaining, retaining, or depriving the enemy of freedom of action. Retaining the initiative was vital in every case.[28]

For Beaufre, total strategy might be executed in one of two modes: direct or indirect. All elements of power played in both modes, but the direct mode emphasized the military instrument. Indirect strategy, which he carefully distinguished from Liddell Hart's indirect approach, used primarily the non-military instruments to achieve political goals. Beaufre also developed a universal formula for strategy: $S=KF\psi t$. "S" represented strategy, "K" was any specific factor applicable to the case, "F" equated to material force, "ψ" represented psychological factors, and "t" was time. That formula is too general to be useful beyond illustrating the point that in direct strategy, F is the predominant factor while in indirect strategy ψ prevails.[29] Fortunately, that is all Beaufre really tried to do with his formula.

Another of Beaufre's major concepts was the strategy of action. This was a counterpart to deterrence. When deterring, the state wanted its opponent to refrain from doing something, while an action strategy aimed at causing someone to do something. The aim of one was negative and the other, positive. Other authors at the time and since have called this coercion, and Beaufre used that term, but he thought coercion too often implied use of military force and wanted action to include a broader range of options.[30] His broader interpretation and insistence on the high nature of total strategy actually pushed his strategic theory into potential collision or overlap with policy, which Beaufre had difficulty explaining away other than the different mindset of the practitioner of each (intuitive, philosophical, and creative for policy; pragmatic, rational, and policy subordinate for strategy).[31]

Beaufre's work is not well known in the United States. His books are not in modern reprint in English (a French reprint of one came out in 1998), are difficult to locate, and are not frequently consulted. He was innovative, but his ideas were not unique. His insistence on coining new language with which to discuss familiar topics probably worked against his long-term acceptance. Much of his thought has come to modern U.S. theory from, or at least through, other sources.

Luttwak.

Edward Luttwak, an economist and historian who has written extensively on strategic theory, talks about attrition and maneuver as the forms of strategy. For Luttwak, attrition is the application of superior firepower and material strength to eventually destroy the enemy's entire force unless he surrenders or retreats. The enemy is nothing more than a target array to be serviced by industrial methods. The opposite of attrition warfare is relational maneuver—"action related to the specifics of the objective." The goal of relational maneuver—instead of physically destroying the enemy, as in attrition—is to incapacitate his systems. Those systems might be the enemy's command and control or his fielded forces or even his doctrine or perhaps the spatial deployment of his force, as in the penetration of a linear position. In some cases relational maneuver might entail the attack of actual technical systems—Luttwak uses deception of radar rather than its destruction or jamming to illustrate the final category.[32]

> Instead of seeking out the enemy's concentration of strength, since that is where the targets are to be found in bulk, the starting point of relational maneuver is the avoidance of the enemy's strengths, followed by the application of some selective superiority against presumed enemy weaknesses, physical or psychological, technical or organizational.[33]

Luttwak recognizes that neither attrition nor relational maneuver are ever employed alone—there is always some mix of the two even if one or the other is decidedly dominant. Relational maneuver is more difficult to execute than attrition, although it can produce better results more quickly. Conversely, relational maneuver can fail completely if the force applied is too weak to do the task or it encounters unexpected resistance. Relational maneuver does not usually allow "free substitution of quantity for quality." There is always a basic quality floor beneath which one cannot safely pass. Only after that floor has been exceeded will quantity substitutions be possible.[34]

Luttwak also says that strategy is paradoxical.

> The large claim I advance here is that strategy does not merely entail this or that paradoxical proposition, contradictory and yet recognized as valid, but rather that *the entire realm of strategy is pervaded by a paradoxical logic of its own*, standing against the ordinary linear logic by which we live in all other spheres of life (except for warlike games, of course).

He believes paradoxical logic pervades the five levels (technical, tactical, operational, theater strategic, and grand strategic) and two dimensions (vertical across levels and horizontal in levels) of warfare.[35]

At the most basic level, Luttwak demonstrates both the presence and the desirability of choices in war that defy peacetime logic. His base example is the choice of an approach road to an objective. The alternatives are a wide, straight, well-surfaced road and a narrow, winding, poorly surfaced road. "Only in the conflictual realm of strategy would the choice arise at all, for it is only if combat is possible that the bad road can be good *precisely because it is bad* and may therefore be less strongly held or even left unguarded by the enemy." Thus, commanders make choices contrary to normal logic because they produce valuable advantages—advantages arising directly from the nature of war. Like Clausewitz, Luttwak believes the competitive aspect of war—that it is always a competition between active opponents—is one of the defining aspects of war. "On the contrary, the paradoxical preference for inconvenient times and directions, preparations visibly and deliberately incomplete, approaches seemly too dangerous, for combat at night and in bad weather, is a common aspect of tactical ingenuity—and for a reason that derives from the essential nature of war."[36] Commanders make paradoxical choices primarily to gain surprise and thus reduce the risk of combat.

> To have the advantage of an enemy who cannot react because he is surprised and unready, or at least who cannot react promptly and in full force, all sorts of paradoxical choices may be justified….Surprise can now be recognized for what it is: not merely one factor of advantage in warfare among many others, but rather the suspension, if only briefly, if only partially, of the entire predicament of strategy, even as the struggle continues. Without a reacting enemy, or rather according to the extent and degree that surprise is achieved, the conduct of war becomes mere administration.[37]

Gaining surprise, therefore, becomes one of the key objectives of strategy. In fact, whole schools of strategy (Luttwak refers specifically to Liddell Hart's indirect approach) have been founded on the principle of surprise. The problem is that paradoxical choices—those necessary to achieve surprise—are never free or even necessarily safe because every "paradoxical choice made for the sake of surprise must have its cost, manifest in some loss of strength that would otherwise be available." The choice itself may make execution more difficult (it is harder to fight at night); secrecy can inhibit preparations and is almost never total; deception may contain relatively cost-free elements (like false information leaked to the enemy) but as it becomes more sophisticated, complex, and convincing, it soaks up resources (units conducting feints are not available at the main point of contact). At the theoretical extreme, one could expend so much force gaining surprise that insufficient combat power remained for the real fight.[38]

> Obviously the paradoxical course of 'least expectation' must stop short of self-defeating extremes, but beyond that the decision is a matter of calculations neither safe nor precise. Although the loss of strength potentially available is certain, success in achieving surprise can only be hoped for; and although the cost can usually be tightly calculated, the benefit must remain a matter of speculation until the deed is done.[39]

All of this, of course, is complicated by friction, which Luttwak calls organizational risk. Also, acting paradoxically can become predictable. Thus, by 1982 in Lebanon, the Israelis had established such a reputation for paradoxical action that they were unable to achieve surprise until they broke their established paradigm and conducted the obvious frontal attack down the Bekka Valley. Luttwak recognizes that some situations call for straightforward, logical solutions. "If the enemy is so weakened that his forces are best treated as a passive array of targets that might as well be inanimate, the normal linear logic of industrial production, with all the derived criteria of productive efficiency, is fully valid, and the paradoxical logic of strategy is irrelevant."[40]

While he has some interesting and valid points, especially in the details, Luttwak's insistence on the paradoxical nature of war is too broad a generalization. There is much that is paradoxical in warfare; however, if war were completely paradoxical, as Luttwak asserts (his exceptions are too trivial to be significant), war would not yield to study. In fact, much of warfare—including its paradox—is very logical. In a sense, Luttwak's argument proves that proposition and refutes itself.

Van Creveld.

Martin Van Creveld's *The Transformation of War* is, according at least to the cover, "The most radical reinterpretation of armed conflict since Clausewitz." He represents a segment of modern scholars that believe Clausewitz no longer explains why, how, or by whom wars are fought. To Van Creveld, war is no longer a rational political act conducted among states—if it ever was. He points out that in 1991, warfare waged by non-state actors dominated conflict—rather than the organized, political, inter-state warfare between great powers that the international community seemed to expect (and Clausewitz seemed to predict). War is no longer fought by the entities we always assumed fought wars. The combatants in modern wars no longer fight for the reasons we always believed. Finally, they do not fight in the manner we always accepted as standard.[41]

Modern war takes many forms—the Clausewitzian trinitarian form of war being one of, but by no means the dominant one. For Van Creveld, Clausewitz does not apply in any case that does not involve exclusively state-on-state warfare. Since he sees a resurgence of "Low-Intensity Conflict," Van Creveld believes war will be dominated by non-state actors. "We are entering an era, not of peaceful economic competition between trading blocks, but of warfare between ethnic and religious groups." Current fielded military forces are irrelevant to the tasks they will likely face.

Should the states in question fail to recognize the changed reality, they will first become incapable of wielding appropriate force at all and eventually cease to exist as recognizable states.[42]

The nature of the participants dictates the nature of the reasons they fight. Because the participants are not states, they will not be fighting for state-like reasons. This follows logically from Van Creveld's assertion that politics applies only to states—not a more broadly defined interest in a more broadly defined community. Non-state actors fight wars for abstract concepts like justice or religion. Frequently, groups feel their existence is threatened and lash out violently in response. In any case, reasons are highly individualistic and do not yield easily to analysis—especially analysis based on the inappropriate model of the Clausewitzian universe.[43]

Finally, Van Creveld believes that Clausewitz did not understand how wars are fought—at least his assertion that they would tend naturally toward totality is wrong. He cites international law and convention, among other factors, as major inhibitors on the drift toward totality in state-on-state war. More significant is his critique of strategy. Like Luttwak, Van Creveld sees strategy as paradoxical. He believes pairs of paradoxes define strategy. If the object of war is to beat our opponent's force with our own, then we must design maneuvers to pit strength against weakness. Because war is competitive, our enemy is doing the same thing, and we must conceal or protect our weakness from the opponent's strength. Thus, the essence of strategy is ."..the ability to feint, deceive, and mislead." Eventually one can work so hard on concealing that he and his side may be deceived—where the distinction between feint and main effort is unclear. Van Creveld also discusses the paradox in time and space using the same argument as Luttwak that the shortest distance between two points may not be a straight line. Other paradoxes include those between concentration and dispersion (concentration is necessary to apply power, but concentration increases the chance of discovery) and between effectiveness and efficiency (the more economical, streamlined, or efficient a military organization becomes, the more vulnerable it is).[44]

Perhaps uniquely in the field of strategic theory, Martin Van Creveld has provided a critique of his own thesis. In a chapter of a book published in 2003, Van Creveld finds, not surprisingly, that on balance his earlier work, written in 1988-1989, holds up very well. The Gulf War was an aberration—the outcome of which was almost preordained. Otherwise, ."..the main thesis of *The Transformation of War*, namely that major armed conflict between major powers is on the way out, seems to have been borne out during the ten years since the book's publication." Conversely, non-trinitarian wars are on the rise and conventional forces do not seem able to bring them to satisfactory closure. ."..[T]he prediction that history is witnessing a major shift from trinitarian to non-trinitarian war seems to have fulfilled itself and is still fulfilling itself on an almost daily basis." He believes information warfare might be a wild card that could disrupt his predictions; however, on balance he sees information as advantageous to (or at least an equalizing factor for) non-state actors, and hence a confirmation of the trend toward non-trinitarianism. Thus, Van Creveld sticks with his criticism of Clausewitz and essentially every element of his original thesis.[45]

A Quranic Theory of War.

Pakistani Brigadier S. K. Malik, who was schooled in Western military thought, proposed a Muslim way of war in his book *The Quranic Concept of War*. First published in Pakistan in 1979 and republished in India thirteen years later, the book remains little known, and until recently, difficult to obtain in the west.[46] The book is heavy on theology, and a basic understanding of Islam—at least a reading of the Quran—helps immensely in understanding it. Malik says that the Quran gives a perfect and comprehensive understanding of every aspect of war and strategy. One of the basic premises is that as a divine religious work the Quran "does not interpret war in terms of narrow national interests but points towards the realization of universal peace and justice."[47] As between people, relations between nations should be peaceful; war can "only be waged for the sake of justice, truth, law and preservation of human society."[48] But Allah first granted the Muslims permission to wage war against oppressors and "later commanded them to fight...as a matter of religious obligation and duty."[49] The main cause of permissible war is delivery of the weak and persecuted from tyranny. This is to be done with "no semblance of any kind of adventurism, militarism, fanaticism, national interest, personal motives and economic compulsion."[50] The object of war is to set conditions of peace, justice and faith. This is accomplished by destroying oppressors.[51] The foundation for warfare is the fact that all wars must be waged for the cause of Allah. The Quran promises heavenly rewards for "those who fight for this noblest heavenly cause."[52] This basic fact makes Islamic armies psychologically and morally strong and thus grants immunity to psychological attacks.[53] Quranic war must be conducted ethically. While Muslims can "follow the law of Equality and Reciprocity," they are directed to show restraint.[54] Muslims are supposed to defeat the enemy and only after the destruction of the foe can prisoners be taken. Once taken, prisoners are to be treated well.[55]

In terms of strategy, Malik finds the Quran offers a unique approach for Muslims. The basis of this strategy is "*to prepare ourselves for war to the utmost in order to strike terror into the hearts of the enemies, known and unknown, while guarding ourselves from being terror-stricken by the enemy.*" [emphasis in original].[56] As Malik recognizes, the whole strategy is based on understanding war as a clash of wills. "In war, our main objective is the opponent's heart or soul, our main weapon of offence against this objective is the strength of our own souls, and to launch such an attack, we have to keep terror away from our own hearts." [emphasis in original][57] One wins war through spirited, complete and thorough preparation—thereby winning the war of wills before beginning the war of muscles. In peacetime, preparation becomes an expression of will. Preparation must be "to the utmost" in every respect and must include all the elements of power, not just the military.[58] States with few physical resources must rely more heavily on the spiritual dimension of war. Malik emphasizes that breaking the will of the enemy is not a means to an end as in Liddell Hart's concept, but the object of war. "It is the point where the means and the ends meet and merge. Terror is not a means of imposing decision upon the enemy; it is *the decision* [emphasis in original] we wish to impose upon him."[59] Muslim armies that practice the Quranic concept of war are totally immune to psychological attack.

It is unclear how well known or influential Malik's *Quranic Concept of War* is in the Muslim world. General Mohammad Zia-ul-Haq, who had overthrown the Pakistani government and was both President and Chief of Staff of the Army when Malik published his book, wrote a brief forward recommending and endorsing the book. Similarly, Allah Bukhsh K. Brohi, the Advocate-General of Pakistan, wrote a long Preface endorsing the most expansive concepts Malik found in the Quran. The publishers of the electronic version of the book claim it has been discovered on the bodies of dead jihadists in Afghanistan.[60] Malik's work certainly has aggressive elements that would appeal to Islamic terrorists.

MISCELLANEOUS ALTERNATIVES

There are also whole categories we can only classify as miscellaneous, alternative, possibly, strategic concepts:

Denial, Punishment, and Coercion.

These are proposed replacements for attrition, exhaustion, and annihilation. They actually describe the ends of strategy (or perhaps a limited set of ways) rather than a complete strategic concept. Their utility is limited and their acceptance as a group by the strategic community is minimal at best. Coercion, of course, is a recognized strategic concept on its own; it is just not commonly grouped with denial and punishment as a paradigm.

Jones.

Historian Archer Jones has a unique approach to strategy.

> The object for military strategy used herein is the depletion of the military force of an adversary. The definition of political-military strategy, a companion term, is the use of military force to attain political or related objectives directly, rather than by depleting an adversary's military force. Of course, military strategy usually endeavored to implement political or comparable objectives but sought to attain them indirectly, by depleting the hostile military force sufficiently to gain an ascendancy adequate to attain the war's political goals.[61]

Jones does not use attrition because of its association with a particular form of military strategy. Instead, he asserts that military force can achieve its objective of depleting the enemy through one of two methods. Combat strategies deplete the enemy by directly destroying his force in the field. Logistic strategies deprive the opponent of supplies, forces, weapons, recruits, or other resources. Either of these strategies can be executed in one of two ways. One can use "a transitory presence in hostile territory to make a destructive incursion," which Jones labels a raiding strategy, or one can conquer and permanently occupy significant segments of enemy territory, which he calls a persisting strategy. The two pairs—combat and logistics and raiding and persisting—define comprehensive strategy.[62]

> Jones then puts the factors into a matrix and uses them for all kinds of warfare—air, land, and sea. Air war, however, can really only be raiding because of the nature of the medium. This is a military only, ways only approach to strategy that works best as Jones applies it—in retrospect to analyze historical campaigns. The separation of a purely political strategy from military strategy based on whether or not the aim is depleting the enemy force is awkward to say the least. Jones has an interesting concept of "political attrition." This means that victory in battle raises morale and engenders optimism about winning in a reasonable time with acceptable casualties. Conversely, defeat in battle makes victory look less certain, farther away in time, and attainable only at high cost. He does not think that political attrition necessarily works in reverse—that is, you cannot store up good will during good times to tide you over during the bad times. (Although presumably you would start the bad times at a higher overall level of morale.) Elsewhere, Jones compares popular will to win with the classic economic supply and demand theory of elastic and inelastic demand.[63] That is a much less satisfying explanation. While perhaps of little use to practical strategists, Archer Jones' concepts are creative and not completely without merit. His ideas show up with increasing frequency in historical works.

Decapitation.

An attractive recent concept is a strategy we might characterize as decapitation, in which one targets specifically and selectively the enemy leader or at least a fairly limited set of upper-echelon leaders. This has most recently found expression in the expressed strategic objective of regime change, which tends to automatically focus on the enemy regime leadership regardless of the potential scope of the mission. Strategic treatises like the *Quadrennial Defense Review* and the *National Defense Strategy*, which use regime change as an evaluative factor, hint at a widening acceptance of the concept. A primary assumption, generally implied or asserted without proof, is that the current leader (perhaps aided by a small group of accomplices) is the whole cause of the international dispute. A corollary assumption is that eliminating the current evil leadership will result in its replacement by a regime willing to grant the concessions demanded by the opposing state or coalition.

There are several problems with this approach—most related to the validity of the assumptions. First, the assumption that the common people of a country are good and could not possibly support the policies of their evil ruler is (as a minimum) unproven in most cases and palpably false in many. Thus, decapitation will not solve the problem. In Clausewitzian terms, taking out the government does not automatically destroy or break the will of either the people or the military. Second, a potential follow-on regime can be either better than, about the same as, or worse than the current leadership. Hence, the odds of achieving one's policy objectives by decapitation are actually fairly poor. The U.S. experience in Iraq after successfully removing Saddam Hussein's regime demonstrate these caveats. The old saw about contending with the devil one knows may be worn, but that does not make it any less worthwhile advice, and while decapitation may work, it is neither easy nor a panacea.

Boyd.

U.S. Air Force Colonel John R. Boyd talks about the "OODA loop"—that is, the decision cycle of observation, orientation, decision, and action. The concept is derived from a fighter pilot in a dogfight. Like the pilot, a strategist wins by outthinking and outmaneuvering his opponent; by the time the opponent decides what to do and initiates action it is too late, since you have already anticipated and countered his move or made a countermove that makes his action meaningless. One accomplishes this by possessing sufficient agility to be able, both mentally and physically, to act a step or more ahead of the enemy. Thus, the successful strategist always works inside his enemy's decision cycle.[64] This theory describes a way, and really is a new and unnecessarily complicated rephrasing of the ancient concept of the initiative. Initiative is not critical or essential, and alone it is not decisive. Robert E. Lee had tactical, operational, and even strategic initiative at Gettysburg and lost tactically, operationally, and strategically. However, initiative is a tremendous advantage—if Boyd's paradigm makes it more clear or obvious to the strategist, it has provided a service. The caution is that one can think and act so swiftly and outpace the enemy so dramatically as to actually create friendly vulnerability. The OODA-loop concept predicts that the enemy will not be able to react effectively to an action; however, it does not postulate enemy paralysis and complete immobility. One can envision circumstances in which a confused enemy reacting to information or situations hours or days behind its opponent makes a devastatingly successful move that its opponent has long since discounted or thought negated.

Warden.

Another U.S. Air Force Colonel, John A. Warden III, translated his targeteering experience into a strategic theory, thus elevating the tactical process of allocating aircraft sorties to specific targets to a strategic theory. Warden views the enemy as a system of targets arrayed in five strategic rings; the innermost and most important is leadership. One can win by striking that inner ring so frequently and violently that the enemy is essentially paralyzed and never able to mount an effective defense. It is unnecessary to take on the outer and much more difficult target rings like the enemy's armed forces, although modern advances like stealth technology make simultaneous attack of the entire target array possible (instead of the traditional sequential attacks, in which one array had to be neutralized before proceeding to the next).[65] This is often considered an air power theory—and Warden used it to push the decisiveness of air power—but the conceptual approach has broader application. This concept's major drawback as a general theory of strategy is that it works best (if not exclusively) when one side has or can quickly gain total dominance of its opponent's airspace.

Underdog Strategies.

There are also a number of alternative strategies that seem to be intended specifically for, or at least, to be most appropriate for, weaker powers or underdogs:

Fabian.

Quintus Fabius Maximus Verrucosus was a Roman general during the Second Punic War. He advocated avoiding open battle, because he was convinced the Romans would lose, which they proceed to do when they abandoned his strategy. Thus, Fabian strategy is a strategy in which one side intentionally avoids large-scale battle for fear of the outcome. Victory depends on wearing down (attriting) one's opponent over time—usually by an unrelenting campaign of skirmishes between detachments. Somewhat akin to a Fabian strategy is a strategy of survival. In that case, however, the weaker power does not necessarily avoid battle. Instead, one reacts to his opponent's moves rather than make an effort to seize the initiative. The object is to survive rather than to win in the classic sense—hopefully, sheer survival achieves (or perhaps comprises) one's political aim. This is a favorite alternative strategy of modern critics for the Confederate States of America. Scorched-earth strategies are another variant of the basic Fabian strategy. The concept is to withdraw slowly before an enemy, while devastating the countryside over which he must advance so he cannot subsist his force on your terrain. Attrition will eventually halt the attack—it will reach what Clausewitz called a culminating point—and the retreating side can safely assume the offensive. This is actually the addition of a tactical technique to the basic Fabian strategy and not a major new school of strategy.

There is a whole subset of doctrine under the general heading of strategies for the weak that advocates guerrilla warfare, insurgency, and/or terrorism:

Lawrence.

T. E. (Thomas Edward) Lawrence was the first of the theorists of insurgency or revolutionary warfare. His *Seven Pillars of Wisdom*, originally published in 1926, recounted his experiences with Arab insurgent forces fighting the Turks in World War I.[66] The title—a reference to Proverbs that Lawrence carried over from an earlier incomplete book about seven Arab cities—is misleading, since Lawrence did not have seven theoretical pillars of guerrilla war. Lawrence's narrative explained the war in the desert by clearly defining the objective, carefully analyzing the Arab and Turkish forces, describing the execution of raids to maintain the initiative, and emphasizing the importance of intelligence, psychological warfare, and propaganda. The objective of the guerrilla was not the traditional objective of conventional forces—decisive battle. In fact, the guerrilla sought exactly the opposite—the longest possible defense.[67] Lawrence believed that successful guerrillas needed safe bases and the support of at least some of the populace—perhaps as little as 20 percent—although an insurgency might be successful with as little as two percent of the population in active support as long as the other 98 percent remained at least neutral. A technologically sophisticated enemy (so the guerrilla could attack his lines of communications) that was not strong enough to occupy the entire country was also advantageous. Tactically, the guerrilla relied on speed, endurance, logistic independence, and at least a minimal amount of weaponry. Lawrence compared guerrillas to a gas operating around a fixed enemy and talked about them as raiders versus regulars. Their operations were always offensive and conducted in precise fashion by the smallest possible forces. The news media was their friend and tool. Lawrence thought the Arabs were ideally suited for such warfare, and that "granted mobility, security, time, and doctrine" the guerrillas would win.[68] His theory got entangled in his flamboyant personality, so although he was a society darling, Lawrence had less impact on military circles.[69]

Mao.

Mao Zedong developed the most famous and influential theory of insurgency warfare. His concepts, designed initially for the Chinese fight against the Japanese in World War II, have been expanded and adapted by himself and others to become a general theory of revolutionary warfare. Mao emphasizes the political nature of war and the reliance of the army on the civilian population, especially the Chinese peasant population. He advocated a protracted war against the Japanese; victory would come in time through attrition. He believed the Chinese should avoid large battles except in the rare instances when they had the advantage. Guerrillas should normally operate dispersed across the countryside and concentrate only to attack. Because the Chinese had a regular army contending with the Japanese, Mao had to pay particular attention to how guerrilla and regular operations complemented each other. He postulated a progressive campaign that would move slowly and deliberately from a stage when the Chinese were on the strategic defensive through a period of strategic stalemate to the final stage when Chinese forces assumed the strategic offensive. The ratio of forces and their tactical activities in each stage reflected the strategic realities of the environment. Thus, guerrilla forces and tactics dominated the phase of the strategic defensive. During the strategic stalemate, mobile and guerrilla warfare would complement each other, and guerrilla and regular forces would reach approximate equilibrium (largely by guerrilla forces combining and training into progressively larger regular units). Mobile warfare conducted by regular units would dominate the period of strategic offensive. Although guerrilla units would never completely disappear, the regular forces would achieve the final victory.[70] Mao has had an enormous impact on the field of revolutionary warfare theory.

Guevara.

Ernesto "Che" Guevara de la Serna based his theory of revolutionary warfare on the Cuban model. He offered a definition of strategy that highlighted his variation of the basic guerrilla theme—especially his divergence from the Maoist emphasis on the political nature of the conflict and reliance on the people. Che wrote, "In guerrilla terminology, strategy means the analysis of the objectives we wish to attain. First, determine how the enemy will operate, his manpower, mobility, popular support, weapons, and leadership, Then, plan a strategy to best confront these factors, always keeping in mind that the final objective is to destroy the enemy army." To Che the major lessons of the Cuban Revolution were that guerrillas could defeat regular armies; that it was unnecessary to wait for all the political preconditions to be met before beginning the fight—the insurrection itself would produce them; and that the countryside was the arena for conflict in underdeveloped Latin America. Gradual progress through the Maoist stages of revolution was unnecessary—the guerrilla effort could not only establish the political preconditions of revolution but also win the war on its own. Parties, doctrine, theories, and even political causes were unimportant. The armed insurgency would eventually produce them all.[71] That was incredibly naive and even dangerous as an insurgent strategic concept, but Che became very well-known—if unsuccessful—pursuing it.

Terrorism.

Although there is no outstanding single theorist of terrorism, it is not a new strategic concept. Often used as a tactical part or preliminary stage of a larger campaign or insurgency, terrorism can, if fact, be a strategy, and sometimes even a goal in itself. Many ideological terrorists—perhaps the best examples are ecological terrorists—have no desire or intent to progress militarily beyond terrorism. Although political, most are not interested in overthrowing a government or seizing control of conventional political power. They simply want their espoused policies, ideologies, or political agendas adopted. Alternatively, anarchists, who traditionally have used terror, just want to destroy government without replacing it. They have no positive goal whatever.

The theory behind terrorism is fairly straightforward. A weak, usually non-governmental, actor uses violence, either random or carefully targeted and often directed against civilian targets, to produce terror. The aim is to make life so uncertain and miserable that the state against which the terror is directed concedes whatever political, social, economic, environmental, or theological point the terrorist pursues. The technique has not proven particularly effective as a stand-alone strategy in changing important policies in even marginally effective states. It is, however, comparatively cheap, easy to conceptualize and execute, requires minimal training, is relatively safe — since competent terrorist groups are extremely difficult to eradicate — and is demonstrably effective in gaining the terrorist publicity for himself and the cause.

Counter Underdog Strategies.

If there are strategies for the weak, the strong are sure to develop counter-strategies. Opponents generally fight a Fabian strategy by trying to exert enough pressure or threaten some critical location or capability to bring about the battle the Fabian strategist is trying to avoid. There is (and needs to be) no body of theoretical work on countering Fabian strategies. The same, however, cannot be said of countering insurgencies and terrorism.

Formal modern counterinsurgency theory developed as a result of the insurgencies that sprang up after World War II in the decolonizing world. It tended to be symmetric in the sense that it analyzed insurgencies and then attempted to beat them at their own game and in their chosen arena. Modern counterinsurgency theory tends to recognize the political nature of most insurgencies and approach them holistically rather than from a primarily military point of view. That is a fairly big break with traditional counterinsurgency techniques, that predominately concentrated on locating and destroying the guerrillas and often relied heavily on punishing the local population for guerrilla activity as the sole means of separating the guerrilla from his base of support. Discussion of some representative modern counterinsurgency theorists follows:

Callwell.

British Colonel Charles E. Callwell wrote *Small Wars — Their Principles and Practice* at the end of the 19th century. This was a guide for the conduct of colonial wars. Callwell distinguished three broad categories of small wars, which he defined as any war in which one side was not a regular army. His categories were: campaigns of conquest or annexation; campaigns to suppress insurgents; and campaigns to punish or overthrow dangerous enemies. Each was fundamentally different from any form of regular warfare. Small wars could take almost any shape — the most dangerous of which was guerrilla warfare. Callwell gave sound tactical advice about fighting a colonial or guerrilla enemy, but, from a theoretical or strategic point of view, his advice is of limited value. He recognized that colonial enemies could be skilled and dedicated warriors and recommended treating them as such — a refreshing change from standard colonial views. However, Callwell thought the small-wars experience was both exclusively military and unique to the colonies. He thus both did not develop the multi-disciplinary approach common to modern counterinsurgency strategy and did not recommend translating the colonial military lessons into lessons for the big wars of the European colonial powers. He thought the strategic aim of counterinsurgency was to fight, because the counterinsurgents had the tactical advantage but were at a strategic disadvantage. Callwell, while still touted today and worth a look for his tactical precepts, was a theoretical dead end for the strategist.[72]

Trinquier.

Roger Trinquier published *Modern Warfare: A French View of Counterinsurgency* in 1961. Trinquier served with the French paras in Indochina and Algeria. Those experiences shaped his views, and his theory heavily reflects French counterinsurgency practice in the 1950s. Trinquier argued that nuclear weapons were decreasing the significance of major traditional wars. The new form of war, which he called *modern warfare* (always in italics for emphasis), featured guerrilla war, insurgency, terrorism, and subversion. One of the major assumptions of modern war was that victory would not come from the clash of armies on battlefields, but from control of the support of the population.[73] Trinquier approached the study of counterinsurgency by examining how the goals and techniques of insurgents differed from traditional warfare. His conclusion was that traditional methods and organizations would not work in counterinsurgencies. Trinquier's concept of modern warfare advocated an interlocking system of political, economic, psychological, and military actions to undermine the insurgents' strategies, destroy their organization as a whole (not simply its military arm), and gain the support of the people.

Trinquier suggested three principles: separate the guerrilla from the population, occupy the zones the guerrilla previously used to deny him reentry, and coordinate actions over a wide enough area and long enough time to deny the guerrilla access to the population.[74] Following the successful technique of quadrillage used by the French in Algeria, Trinquier advocated a gridding system to divide up the country administratively and to facilitate sweeping and controlling the nation sequentially. Grids would be hierarchical from province to sector and so on down to block or even very large individual buildings in major urban areas. Leaders in every grid were responsible for everything from local defense to providing intelligence. Establishing and running the grids was largely a police function.[75] The army would then be basically reorganized in tiers to support the strategy. Grid units would provide strong points and patrols for local security; interval units would work in sectors to destroy the political and military structures of the enemy in their sector; and intervention units would be elite troops that sought out enemy refuges and destroyed major enemy units.[76] Trinquier was also a strong advocate of eliminating safe havens both inside and outside the national borders. He even recommended using modern war—in the form of clandestine guerrilla operations—against enemy bases in neighboring countries where conventional forces could not go without provoking international war.[77] Trinquier's basic approach—minus some of its more radical elements, like advocacy of harsh interrogation and radical reorganization of the military—is found in all modern counterinsurgency theory.

Galula.

David Galula wrote *Counterinsurgency Warfare: Theory and Practice* in 1964. He postulated a simple construct for counterinsurgencies that emphasized the political nature of the conflict, especially the relationship between the insurgent and his cause. His definition of "[i]nsurgency is the pursuit of the policy of a party, inside a country, by every means" was designed to emphasize that insurgencies could start before the use of force. Insurgencies are by their nature asymmetric because of the disparity of resources between the contenders. The counterinsurgent has all the tangible assets—military, police, finance, court systems, etc., while the insurgent's advantages are intangible—the ideological power of his cause. Insurgents base their strategies on powerful ideologies, while the counterinsurgent has to maintain order without undermining the government. The rules applicable to one side do not always fit the other. The logic of this asymmetric power relationship forced the insurgent to avoid military confrontation and instead move the contest to a new arena where his ideological power was effective—the population became the seat of war.

Politics becomes the instrument of war rather than force, and that remains true throughout the war. Politics takes longer to produce effects, so all insurgencies are protracted.[78]

The counterinsurgent warrior must begin by understanding the political-social-economic cause of his opponent. Large parts of the population must be able to identify with that cause. The cause must be unique in the sense that the counterinsurgent cannot co-opt it. The cause can change over time as the insurgency adapts. The power of the cause increases as the guerrilla gains strength and has success. Good causes attract large numbers of supporters and repel the minimum number of neutrals. An artificial or concocted cause makes the guerrilla work harder to sell his position, but an efficient propaganda machine can do that.[79]

Galula discussed several approaches to immunizing the population against the insurgent cause or message. Counterinsurgents must: continuously reassess the nature and scope of the problem with which they deal; address problems proactively; isolate the battlefield from external support; and work to increase support for the regime. They must be vigilant—they should not interpret a strategic pause by the insurgents as victory. Intelligence is critical. The counterinsurgent organization must have the authority to direct political, social, economic, and military efforts. The military cannot have a free hand—it must work within and be subordinate to the overall political campaign. Like Trinquier, Galula recommended a systematic division of the country and sequential search, clear, and hold operations. Counterinsurgent propaganda should focus on gaining and maintaining the neutrality of the population.[80] Galula is having a major influence on the development (or rediscovery) of U.S. counterinsurgency theory in 2006.

Kitson.

Frank Kitson wrote *Low Intensity Operations: Subversion, Insurgency, and Peacekeeping* in 1971. He added details to the basic structure of counterinsurgency theory already constructed by the French. Like the other theorists, Kitson recognized that counterinsurgency is a multidisciplinary job. He warned against abuses, but recommended that heavy force be used early to squash an insurgency while still in a manageable state. The military campaign must be coordinated with good psychological operations. Kitson conceptualized two kinds of intelligence—political and operational. Political intelligence is an ongoing process, while operational intelligence supports specific military operations. The military must be involved in the intelligence-gathering process (political as well as operational). Counterinsurgency forces must be attuned to the environment, able to optimize resources by phases of the campaign, and able to coordinate all the resources at their disposal.[81]

STRATEGIC ADVICE

There are also numerous advice books that give leaders and decisionmakers more or less specific advice about what to do or how to do it without necessarily offering a comprehensive strategic or theoretical paradigm. Examples include Niccolo Machiavelli's *The Art of War, The Discourses,* and *The Prince,* written to influence 16th-century Florentine leaders, and Frederick the Great's *Instructions for His Generals,* the title of which explains its intent. Alternatively, there are collections like *The Military Maxims of Napoleon* of military advice culled from the writings of great soldiers. As historian David Chandler noted in his introduction to a recent reprint of that work, 'The practical value of military maxims can be debatable....Consequently the collecting of his [Napoleon's] *obiter dicta* into any kind of military rule-book for future generations to apply is a process fraught with perils and pitfalls." In a more modern vein, Michele A. Flournoy, ed., *QDR 2001: Strategy-Driven Choices for America's Security* is essentially an advice book that presents a specific strategic solution without developing an overarching strategic theory.[82] Advice books are often beneficial; however, their generally narrow focus and frequent bumper sticker quality limit that utility.

DETERRENCE

During the Cold War the nuclear weapons field developed its own set of specific strategies based on deterrence theory. Deterrence theory itself is a useful strategic concept. Conversely, concepts like mutual assured destruction, counterforce or counter-value targeting, launch on warning, and first strike versus retaliation are terms of nuclear art that will retain some relevance as long as major nations maintain large nuclear stockpiles, but they no longer dominate the strategic debate as they once did. According to the Department of Defense, deterrence is "the prevention from action by fear of the consequences."[83] It is altogether different from compellence, in which one is attempting to make another party do something. Theoretically, one party can deter another either by threat of punishment or by denial. Threat of punishment implies performing an act that will evoke a response so undesirable that the actor decides against acting. Deterrence by denial seeks to avert an action by convincing the actor that he cannot achieve his purpose. In either case deterrence theory assumes rational decisionmakers with similar value systems. To be deterred, one must be convinced that his adversary possesses both the capability to punish or deny and the will to use that capability. Demonstrating the effectiveness of deterrence is difficult, since it involves proving the absence of something resulted from a specific cause; however, politicians and strategists generally agree that nuclear deterrence worked during the Cold War. It is not as clear that conventional deterrence works, although that concept has numerous advocates and is deeply embedded in modern joint doctrine.

Deterrence theory had many fathers, but some of the most prominent deserve mention. Albert Wohlstetter established his credentials when he wrote *The Delicate Balance of Terror* for RAND in 1958. Bernard Brodie wrote, among other things, *Strategy in the Missile Age* in 1959. Herman Kahn's *On Thermonuclear War* was groundbreaking in 1960. Thomas C. Schelling published *The Strategy of Conflict* in 1960 and *Arms and Influence* six years later; both remain classics.[84]

SEA POWER

Mahan.

There are also schools of single-service strategies devoted to sea power or air power. In the sea power arena the most famous strategic theorists are Alfred Thayer Mahan and Julian S. Corbett. American naval officer Mahan wrote several books and articles around the turn of the 20th century advocating sea power. Perhaps the most famous was *The Influence of Sea Power Upon History, 1660-1783*. Mahan developed a set of criteria that he believed facilitated sea power, but his major contribution was in the realm of the exercise of that capability through what he called "command of the sea." His study of history convinced Mahan that the powerful maritime nations had dominated history, and specifically, that England had parlayed its command of the sea into world dominance. At the grand strategic level Mahan believed that countries with the proper prerequisites should pursue sea power (and especially naval power) as the key to prosperity.

To Mahan, oceans were highways of commerce. Navies existed to protect friendly commerce and interrupt that of their enemies. The way to do both was to gain command of the sea.[85] For Mahan, the essence of naval strategy was to mass one's navy, seek out the enemy navy, and destroy it in a decisive naval battle. With the enemy's navy at the bottom of the ocean—that is, with command of the sea—your merchantmen were free to sail where they pleased while the enemy's merchantmen were either confined to port or subject to capture. Diversion of naval power to subsidiary tasks like commerce raiding (a favorite U.S. naval strategy in the early years of the republic) was a waste of resources, although in his later writing Mahan acknowledged some contribution from such tactics. The key to Mahanian naval warfare was thus the concentrated fleet of major combatants that would fight for and hopefully win command of the sea. Ideally, that fleet would have global reach, which required secure bases for refueling conveniently located worldwide. Although Mahan's theories actively supported his political agenda of navalism and imperialism, they contained enough pure and original thought to survive both the author and his age.

Corbett.

British author Julian S. Corbett had a different interpretation of naval warfare. A contemporary of Mahan, Corbett saw British success not so much as a result of dominance of the sea, as from its ability to effectively wield what we call today all the elements of national power. Corbett differentiated between maritime power and strategy and naval power and strategy. Maritime strategy encompassed all the aspects of sea power—military, commercial, political, etc. Naval strategy dealt specifically with the actions and maneuvers of the fleet. Like Mahan, Corbett saw oceans as highways of commerce and understood their importance. However, he emphasized not the uniqueness of sea power but its relationship with other elements of power. For Corbett, the importance of navies was not their ability to gain command of the sea but their ability to affect events on land. He believed that navies rarely won wars on their own—they often made it possible for armies to do so. The navy's role was thus to protect the homeland while isolating and facilitating the insertion of ground forces into the overseas objective area. Neither command of the sea nor decisive naval battle were necessarily required to accomplish either of those tasks. Although Corbett admitted that winning the decisive naval clash remained the supreme function of a fleet, he believed there were times when that was neither necessary nor desirable.[86] His theories most closely approximate current U.S. naval doctrine.

Jeune Ecolé.

Another school of sea power was the Jeune Ecolé, which was popular on the continent in the early 1880s. Its primary advocate was Admiral Théophile Aube of the French Navy. Unlike the theories of either Mahan or Corbett, which were intended for major naval powers, the Jeune Ecolé was a classic small-navy strategy. It was a way for land powers to fight sea powers. Advocates claimed that a nation did not have to command the sea to use it. In fact, modern technology made gaining command of the sea impossible. And one certainly did not have to have a large fleet of capital ships or win a big fleet battle. Rather than capital ships, one could rely on torpedo boats and cruisers (later versions would emphasize submarines). The naval strategist could either use those smaller vessels against the enemy's fleet in specific situations, such as countering an amphibious invasion, or more commonly against his commerce (to deny him the value of commanding the sea). Either use could be decisive without the expense of building and maintaining a large fleet or the dangers inherent in a major naval battle.[87] The Jeune Ecolé was an asymmetric naval strategy. It had a brief spurt of popularity and faded. Its advocates probably chuckled knowingly during World Wars I and II as submarines executed their pet theory without the benefit of a name other than "unrestricted submarine warfare." It is still available as an asymmetric approach to war at sea.

AIR POWER

Douhet.

The basis of classic air power theory—although paternity is debatable—is *The Command of the Air*, published first in 1921 by Italian general and author Giulio Douhet. Reacting to the horrors he had seen in the First World War, Douhet became an advocate of air power. He believed that the airplane could restore decisiveness to warfare that ground combat seemed incapable of achieving. It could fly over the ground battlefield to directly attack the enemy's will. Because of technical problems with detection and interception, stopping an air raid would be impossible. Big bombers carrying a mix of high explosive, incendiary, and poison gas weapons could target enemy cities. Civilian populations, which were the key to modern warfare, would be unable to stand such bombardment and would soon force their governments to surrender. Although civilian casualties might be high, this would be a more humane method of warfare than prolonged ground combat.

There were a few strategic dicta beyond that. First, a prerequisite for success was command of the air—a theory closely related to command of the sea. Command of the air granted one side the ability to fly where and when it desired while the enemy was unable to fly. Next, because the airplane was an offensive weapon, one gained command of the air by strategic bombardment—ideally catching the enemy's air force on the ground. Recognizing the technological limitations of his day, Douhet believed there was no need for anti-aircraft artillery or interceptors, since neither worked effectively. In fact, resources devoted to air defense or any type of auxiliary aircraft (anything that was not a large bomber) were wasted. The resource argument also featured shifting funding from the traditional land and sea services to the air service—a position not designed to win friends in the wider defense community. Like other airmen, Douhet believed that airplanes were best employed in an independent air force.[88]

Douhet captured the imagination of early airmen with his vision of decisiveness through command of the air. Generations of later air power enthusiasts continue to seek to fulfill his prophecy. Nuclear weapons were supposed to have fixed the technological shortfalls that prevented air power alone from winning World War II. That they were unusable made little difference. Precision guided munitions are the current mantra of the air power enthusiast—they have finally made decisive air attack possible. There may actually be something to the precision guided munitions claim; only time will tell. Douhet's assertion of the futility of air defense proved wrong when radar made locating aircraft possible and fighters became capable of catching and shooting down big bombers. Douhet's assertion of the fragility of civilian morale under air attack also proved false. Nevertheless, he still has a major influence on air power doctrine and is the father of all modern air power theory.

Other Air Power Theories.

Douhet may have been the father of air power theory, but others followed him quickly. Most of the later air power theorists worked on one or both of two primary issues that Douhet had first surfaced: the most efficient way to organize air power—a debate generally about an independent air force, or the proper mix of fighters, bombers, and ground-attack aircraft. The debate about separate air forces was important but not a true strategic issue. Conversely, the issue of proper mix of aircraft got directly to the issue of the proper role of air power. The early theorists presented a variety of views on the issue. William "Billy" Mitchell saw America's strategic problem as one of defense against sea-borne attack. A Douhet-like offensive air strategy was inappropriate. He also believed that aerial combat could provide effective defense against air attack. Thus, he developed a strategy based on a mix of fighters and bombers. In terms of both the necessity of command of the air and the potential strategic decisiveness of air power, Mitchell agreed completely with Douhet.[89]

Another early air power theorist was British Wing Commander John C. "Jack" Slessor. Slessor served a tour as an instructor at the Army Staff College at Camberley. His book *Air Power and Armies* is a collection of his lectures at the War College. Slessor was a believer in strategic bombing, but, perhaps because of his audience, he also emphasized the relationship between air power and ground operations. The first requirement was gaining command of the air. Next, air power could interdict the enemy's lines of communication. Using air power in direct support of committed troops (the flying artillery/close air support concept) was ineffective. Slessor did believe that both aspects of the air campaign could occur simultaneously—one did not need complete air superiority to begin interdiction. From the standpoint of the ground commander, supporting air power was most effective in facilitating a breakthrough, in the pursuit and in the defense.[90]

Slessor's advocacy of interdiction was not, however, the only way one might approach the air-ground support issue. German Chief of Air Staff during the interwar years Helmut Wilberg was a pioneer in direct air-ground support. He wrote some of and edited and approved all of Germany's immediate post-war studies on air force operations. Those studies concluded that strategic bombardment did not work, but that close air support did. Thus, it is not surprising that unlike either the British or the Americans, the Germans developed a tactical air force oriented on close support of ground forces. The opportunity for Germany to develop a strategic air force or doctrine occurred during the tenure of Walter Weaver as Chief of Air Staff between 1934 and 1936. Weaver was a bomber advocate of the Douhetian ilk. However, when he died in an airplane crash in 1936, the Luftwaffe canceled Weaver's pet four-engine bomber development program and slipped comfortably back into its ground support doctrine.

CONCLUSION

Which of these approaches to strategy is the best? What is the approved solution? The answer is simple—there is no best solution. All the above have utility for specific purposes but are lacking as generalizations on strategy. They tend to be: 1) war-oriented rather than general (i.e., military strategy rather than strategy in general); 2) too narrowly focused even within the wartime realm (that is, they address military-specific strategies rather than more general grand strategies, and in some cases represent single-service approaches); and 3) even in the military arena are too focused on one aspect of a multidimensional problem (i.e., they attempt to skip the basic ends-ways-means relationship and go straight to the solution). They are generally concerned with the how, while ignoring the what or why. The exceptions were the broad concepts like attrition, exhaustion, and annihilation and nuclear strategy that always aimed at deterrence and clearly linked ways with means to achieve that end.

So, why present all these strategic concepts if they do not work? Remember that although none of the paradigms works as a generalization, each has merit in specific circumstances. The strategist needs to be familiar with each so he can select the best approach or combination of approaches for the situation he faces. In that respect strategy is much like carpentry. Both are skills intended for solving problems. The carpenter uses a saw to cut, a hammer to drive, sandpaper to smooth, and myriad other tools depending on the need—there is a tool for every job. Similarly, the strategist needs to have a wide assortment of tools in his kit bag and be able to select the proper one for the task at hand. There is an old saying that if the only tool one has is a hammer, all problems look like a nail. That is as bad a solution in strategy as it is in carpentry.

ENDNOTES - CHAPTER 2

1. See, Hew Strachan, "The Lost Meaning of Strategy," *Survival,* Vol. 47, No. 3, Autumn 2005, pp. 33-54.

2. Carl von Clausewitz, *On War*, Michael Howard and Peter Paret, eds./trans., Princeton, NJ: Princeton University Press, 1976, p. 177.

3. Antoine Henri Baron de Jomini, *The Art of War*, G. H. Mendell and W. P. Craighill, trans., 1862, reprint, The West Point Military Library Series, Thomas E. Griess and Jay Luvass, eds., Westport, Connecticut: Greenwood Press, 1971, p. 62.

4. Henry Lee Scott, *Military Dictionary: Comprising Technical Definitions; Information on Raising and Keeping Troops; Actual Service, including Makeshifts and Improved Materiel; and Law, Government, Regulation, and Administration Relating to Land Forces,* 1861, reprint, The West Point Military Library series, Thomas E. Griess and Jay Luvass, eds., Westport, Connecticut: Greenwood Press, 1968, p. 574.

5. Basil H. Liddell Hart, *Strategy,* 2nd Edition, 1954, reprint, New York: Frederick A. Praeger, 1967, pp. 335-6.

6. Colin S. Gray, *Modern Strategy,* New York: Oxford University Press, 1999, p. 17.

7. United States Department of Defense, The Joint Staff, *Joint Publication 1-02, DOD Dictionary of Military and Associated Terms,* hereafter Joint Pub 1-02, available from *www.dtic.mil/doctrine/jel/new_pubs/jp1_02.pdf, 507, 357*; United States Department of Defense, The Joint Staff, *Joint Doctrine Encyclopedia,* pp. 731, 542, available from *www.dtic.mil/doctrine/joint_military_encyclopedia/htm.*

8. Robert H. Dorff, "A Primer in Strategy Development" in *U.S. Army War College Guide Strategy,* Joseph R. Cerami and James F. Holcomb, Jr., eds., Carlisle Barracks, PA: Strategic Studies Institute, 2001, p. 11; Richard A. Chilcoat, "Strategic Art: The New Discipline for 21st Century Strategists" in *U.S. Army War College Guide to Strategy,* Joseph R. Cerami and James F. Holcomb, Jr., eds., Carlisle Barracks, PA: Strategic Studies Institute, 2001, p. 205.

9. Gray, p. 28.

10. J. C. (Joseph Callwell) Wylie, *Military Strategy: A General Theory of Power Control,* New Brunswick, NJ: Rutgers University Press, 1967, reprint, Annapolis, MD: Naval Institute Press, 1989, pp. 22-27.

11. Russell F. Weigley, "Response to Brian McAllister Linn by Russell F. Weigley," *The Journal of Military History,* Vol. 66, No. 2, April 2002, p. 531.

12. Michael Howard, "Lessons of the Cold War," *Survival,* Vol. 36, No. 4, Winter 1994-5, p. 165.

13. Dorff, p. 12.

14. Clausewitz, pp. 88-9.

15. Sun Tzu, *The Art of War,* Samuel B. Griffith, trans., 1963, reprint, New York: Oxford University Press, 1973, pp. 73, 63; Liddell Hart, p. 366.

16. Sun Tzu, pp. 77, 98, 85, 96.

17. Clausewitz, p. 267.

18. *Ibid.,* pp. 595-6.

19. *Ibid.,* p. 528.

20. Jomini, pp. 61-3.

21. Liddell Hart, p. 337.

22. *Ibid.,* p. 339.

23. *Ibid.,* pp. 339-41; Clausewitz, p. 137.

24. André Beaufre, *An Introduction to Strategy, with Particular Reference to Problems of Defense, Politics, Economics, and Diplomacy in the Nuclear Age,* New York: Praeger, 1965; André Beaufre, *Deterrence and Strategy,* New York: F.A. Praeger, 1966; André Beaufre, *Strategy of Action,* London: Farber and Farber, 1967.

25. Beaufre, *An Introduction to Strategy*, pp. 30-1.

26. *Ibid.*, pp. 26-29.

27. *Ibid.*, pp. 34-5.

28. *Ibid.*, p. 36.

29. *Ibid.*, p. 129.

30. Beaufre, *Strategy of Action*, p. 28.

31. *Ibid.*, p. 132.

32. Luttwak, pp. 92-3.

33. *Ibid.*, p. 94.

34. *Ibid.*, pp. 94-5.

35. *Ibid.*, pp. 4, 87-91.

36. *Ibid.*, p. 7.

37. *Ibid.*, 8.

38. *Ibid.*, 9-10.

39. *Ibid.*, p. 10.

40. *Ibid.*, pp. 10-15, 17.

41. Martin van Creveld, *The Transformation of War*, New York: The Free Press, 1991, p. ix.

42. *Ibid.*, pp. 57, ix.

43. *Ibid.*, p. 125-156.

44. *Ibid.*, pp. 63-94, 119, 120-220.

45. Martin van Creveld, "The Transformation of War Revisited," in Robert J. Bunker, ed., *Non-State Threats and Future Wars*, London: Frank Cass, 2003, pp. 5, 7-14.

46. Small numbers of copies are generally available from online book dealers, but a PDF copy is now available from *wolfpangloss.files.wordpress.com/2008/02/malik-quranic-concept-of-war.pdf*.

47. S. K. Malik, *The Quranic Concept of War*, Delhi, India: Adam Publishers & Distrirbutors, 1992, p. 1.

48. *Ibid.*, p. 20.

49. *Ibid.*

50. *Ibid.*, p. 23.

51. *Ibid.*, p. 35.

52. *Ibid.*, p. 44.

53. *Ibid.*, pp. 44-5.

54. *Ibid.*, p. 47.

55. *Ibid.*, p. 48.

56. *Ibid.*, p. 58.

57. *Ibid.*

58. *Ibid.*, pp. 58-9.

59. *Ibid.*, p. 59.

60. Patrick Poole and Mark Hanna, "Publisher's Preface," in *The Quranic Concept of War*, p. 1.

61. Archer Jones, *Elements of Military Strategy: An Historical Approach*, Westport, CT: Praeger, 1996, p. xiii.

62. *Ibid.*, p. xiv.

63. Archer Jones, *Civil War Command and Strategy: The Process of Victory and Defeat*, New York: The Free Press, 1992, p. 35; Jones, *Elements of Military Strategy*, pp. 201-4.

64. Boyd never published his OODA loop theory. It is available in John R. Boyd, "A Discourse on Winning and Losing," unpublished paper, Air University document number MU43947, August 1987. The best summary is David S. Fadok, "John Boyd and John Warden: Airpower's Quest for Strategic Paralysis," in *The Paths of Heaven: The Evolution of Airpower Theory*, Maxwell AFB, Alabama: Air University Press, 1997, pp. 141-3.

65. John A. Warden III, "The Enemy as a System," *Airpower Journal*, Spring 1995, pp. 41-55.

66. T. E. (Thomas Edward) Lawrence, *Seven Pillars of Wisdom: A Triumph*, New York: George Doran Publishing Co., 1926, reprint, New York: Anchor Books, 1991.

67. *Ibid.*, pp. 104-5, 143-5; Robert B. Aspery, *War in the Shadows: The Guerrilla in History*, 2 Vols., New York: Doubleday & Co., Inc., 1975, p. 1:262-4.

68. T. E. (Thomas Edward) Lawrence, "Guerrilla Warfare" in *Encyclopedia Britannica*, 1957, Vol. 10, as quoted in Aspery, *War in the Shadows*, p. 1:269; Aspery, *War in the Shadows*, p. 1:263.

69. Peter Paret, ed., *Makers of Modern Strategy: from Machiavelli to the Nuclear Age*, Princeton, NJ: Princeton University Press, 1986, p. 831.

70. Mao Tse-Tung, *On Protracted War*, Peking, China: Foreign Language Press, 1960; *Mao Tse-Tung: An Anthology of His Writings*, Anne Fremantle, ed., New York: New American Library, 1972.

71. Ernesto "Che" Guevara de la Serna, *Che Guevara on Guerrilla Warfare*, "Introduction," by Maj. Harris-Clichy Peterson, USMCR, New York: Frederick A. Praeger, 1961, p. 10; Ernesto "Che" Guevara de la Serna, *Guerrilla Warfare*, New York: Monthly Review Press, 1961, p. 15.

72. Charles C. Callwell, *Small Wars – Their Principles and Practices*, 3rd Ed., London: His Majesty's Stationary Office, 1898, 1906; reprint, East Ardsley, England: EP Publishing Ltd. 1976, pp. 23, 25-33, 85-90, 125-148; Asprey, *War in the Shadows*, pp. 1:204-6.

73. Roger Trinquier, *Modern Warfare: A French View of Counterinsurgency*, Daniel Lee, trans., 1964, reprint, Westport, CT: Praeger International, 2006, pp. 5-6.

74. *Ibid.,* p. 54.

75. *Ibid.,* p. 37-8.

76. *Ibid.,* p. 72-3.

77. *Ibid.,* pp. 83-88.

78. David Galula, *Counterinsurgency Warfare: Theory and Practice*, New York: Frederick A. Praeger: 1964, pp. 6-10.

79. *Ibid.,* pp. 17-26.

80. *Ibid.,* pp. 74-79, 87-93, 96-106.

81. Frank Kitson, *Low Intensity Operations: Subversion, Insurgency, and Peacekeeping*, Harrisburg, PA: Stackpole Books, 1971, pp. 67-143.

82. Niccolò Machiavelli, *The Art of War*, Ellis Farnsworth, trans., New York: Da Capo Press, 1965; Niccolò Machiavelli, *The Discourses of Niccolò Machiavelli*, Leslie J. Walker, trans., Boston, MA: Routedge and Paul, 1975; Niccolò Machiavelli, *The Prince*, Luigi Ricci, trans., revised by E. R. P. Vincent, New York: New American Library, 1952; Frederick the Great, *Instructions for his Generals*, Thomas R. Phillips, trans., Harrisburg, PA: The Stackpole Company, 1960; The Military Maxims of Napoleon, George C. D. Aguilar, trans., with an "Introduction," by David G. Chandler, 1831, reprint, New York: Da Capo Press, 1995, p. 14; Michèle A. Flournoy, ed., *QDR 2001: Strategy-Driven Choices for America's Security*, Washington, DC: National Defense University Press, 2001.

83. See, for example, Bernard Brodie, *Strategy in the Missile Age*, 1959, reprint Princeton, NJ: Princeton University Press, 1971; Joint Pub 1-02, p. 156.

84. Albert Wohlstetter, *The Delicate Balance of Terror*, Santa Monica, CA: RAND, 1958; Brodie, *Strategy in the Missile Age*; Herman Kahn, *On Thermonuclear War*, Princeton, NJ: Princeton University Press, 1960; Thomas C. Schelling, *The Strategy of Conflict*, Cambridge, MA: Harvard University Press, 1960, and *Arms and Influence*, New Haven, CT: Yale University Press, 1966.

85. Alfred Thayer Mahan, *The Influence of Sea Power Upon History 1660-1783*, 1890, reprint Boston, MA: Little, Brown and Company, 1970, pp. 25, 26, 29-88.

86. Julian S. Corbett, *Some Principles of Maritime Strategy*, London: Longman, Green, 1911.

87. Theodore Ropp, *War in the Modern World*, 1959, reprint, New York: Collier Books, 1973, pp. 208-9.

88. Giulio Douhet, *The Command of the Air*, Sheila Fischer, trans., Rome, Italy: Rivista Aeronautica, 1958.

89. William Mitchell, *Winged Defense: The Development and Possibilities of Modern Air Power — Economic and Military*, New York: G. P. Putnam's Sons, 1925.

90. John C. Slessor, *Air Power and Armies*, Oxford, England: Oxford University Press, 1925.

CHAPTER 3

TOWARD A THEORY OF STRATEGY: ART LYKKE AND THE U.S. ARMY WAR COLLEGE STRATEGY MODEL

H. Richard Yarger

Gregory D. Foster argued in a *Washington Quarterly* article that there is no official or accepted general theory of strategy in the United States. In fact, he notes that, as a people, Americans seem to regard theorizing in general as a futile intellectual exercise. If one were to construct such a theory, Foster continues, it should incorporate those elements found in any complete theory: essential terminology and definitions; an explanation of the assumptions and premises underlying the theory; substantive propositions translated into testable hypothesis; and methods that can be used to test the hypotheses and modify the theory as appropriate.[1] Foster may have this theory thing right. There is little evidence that collectively as a nation there is any agreement on just what constitutes a theory of strategy. This is very unfortunate, because the pieces for a good theory of strategy have been laying around the U.S. Army War College for years--although sometimes hard to identify amongst all the intellectual clutter. Arthur F. Lykke, Jr.'s Army War College strategy model, with its ends, ways, and means, is the centerpiece of this theory.[2] The theory is quite simple, but it often appears unduly complex as a result of confusion over terminology and definitions and the underlying assumptions and premises.

One sees the term "strategy" misapplied often. There is a tendency to use it as a general term for a plan, concept, course of action, or "idea" of a direction in which to proceed. Such use is inappropriate. Strategy is the domain of the senior leader at the higher echelons of the state, the military, business corporations, or other institutions. Henry Eccles describes strategy as "...the comprehensive direction of power to control situations and areas in order to attain objectives."[3] His definition captures much of the essence of strategy. It is comprehensive, it provides direction, its purpose is control, and it is fundamentally concerned with the application of power.[4] Strategy, as used in the Army War College curriculum, focuses on the nation-state and the use of the elements of power to serve state interests. In this context, strategy is the employment of the instruments (elements) of power (political/diplomatic, economic, military, and informational) to achieve the political objectives of the state in cooperation or in competition with other actors pursuing their own objectives.[5]

The underlying assumption of strategy from a national perspective is that states and other competitive entities have interests that they will pursue to the best of their abilities. Interests are desired end states, such as survival, economic well-being, and enduring national values. The national elements of power are the resources used to promote or advance national interests. Strategy is the pursuit, protection, or advancement of these interests through the application of the instruments of power. Strategy is fundamentally a choice; it reflects a preference for a future state or condition. In doing so, strategy confronts adversaries, and some things simply remain beyond control or unforeseen.[6]

Strategy is all about *how* (way or concept) leadership will use the *power* (means or resources) available to the state to exercise control over sets of circumstances and geographic locations to achieve *objectives* (ends) that support state interests. Strategy provides direction for the coercive or persuasive use of this power to achieve specified objectives. This direction is by nature proactive. It seeks to control the environment as opposed to reacting to it. Strategy is not crisis management. It is its antithesis. Crisis management occurs when there is no strategy or the strategy fails. Thus, the first premise of a theory of strategy is that strategy is proactive and anticipatory.[7]

A second premise of a theory of strategy is that the strategist must know what is to be accomplished—that is, he must know the end state that he is trying to achieve. Only by analyzing and understanding the desired end state in the context of the internal and external environment can the strategist develop appropriate objectives leading to the desired end state.

A third premise of a theory of strategy is that the strategy must identify an appropriate balance among the objectives sought, the methods to pursue the objectives, and the resources available. In formulating a strategy, the ends, ways, and means are part of an inteagral whole, and if one is discussing a strategy at the national (grand) level with a national level end, the ways and means would similarly refer to national level concepts and resources. That is, ends, ways, and means must be consistent. Thus, a National Security Strategy end could be supported by concepts based on all the instruments of power and the associated resources. For the military element of power, the National Military Strategy would identify appropriate ends for the military to be accomplished through national military concepts with national military resources. In a similar manner a Theater or Regional Combatant Commander would have specific theater level objectives for which he would develop theater concepts and use resources allocated to his theater. In some cases these might include other than military instruments of power if those resources are available. The levels of strategy are distinct, but interrelated because of the hierarchical and comprehensive nature of strategy.

A fourth premise of strategy is that political purpose must dominate all strategy; hence, Clausewitz's famous dictum, "War is merely the continuation of policy by other means."[8] Political purpose is stated in policy. Policy is the expression of the desired end state sought by the government. In its finest form it is clear articulation of guidance for the employment of the instruments of power toward the attainment of one or more end states. In practice, policy tends to be much vaguer. Nonetheless policy dominates strategy by its articulation of the end state and its guidance. The analysis of the end state and guidance yields objectives leading to the desired end state. Objectives provide purpose, focus, and justification for the actions embodied in a strategy.[9] National strategy is concerned with a hierarchy of objectives that is determined by the political purpose of the state. Policy insures that strategy pursues appropriate aims.

A fifth premise is that strategy is hierarchical. Foster argues that true strategy is the purview of the leader and is a *"weltanschauung"* (world view) that represents both national consensus and comprehensive direction. In the cosmic scheme of things Foster may well be right, but reality requires more than a *"weltanschauung."* Political leadership ensures and maintains its control and influence through the hierarchical nature of state strategy. Strategy cascades from the national level down to the lower levels. Generally, strategy emerges at the top as a consequence of policy statements and a stated National Security Strategy (sometimes referred to as Grand Strategy). National Security Strategy lays out broad objectives and direction for the use of all the instruments of power. From this National Security Strategy the major activities and departments develop subordinate strategies. For the military, this is the National Military Strategy. In turn, the National Military Strategy leads to lower strategies appropriate to the various levels of war.

The U.S. Army War College (in consonance with Joint Pub 1-02) defines the levels of strategy within the state as:

- *National Security Strategy.* (also referred to as Grand Strategy and National Strategy). The art and science of developing, applying and coordinating the instruments of national power (diplomatic, economic, military, and informational) to achieve objectives that contribute to national security (Joint Pub 1-02).

- *National Military Strategy.* The art and science of distributing and applying military power to attain national objectives in peace and war (Joint Pub 1-02).

- *Theater Strategy.* The art and science of developing integrated strategic concepts and courses of action directed toward securing the objectives of national and alliance or coalition security policy and strategy by the use of force, threatened use of force, or operations not involving the use of force within a theater (Joint Pub 1-02).

The hierarchical nature of strategy facilitates span of control. It represents a logical means of delegating responsibility and authority among senior leadership. It also suggests that if strategy consists of objectives, concepts, and resources, each should be appropriate to the level of strategy and consistent with one another. Thus, strategy at the national military level should articulate military objectives at the national level and express the concepts and resources in terms appropriate to the national level for the specified objective.

At some level planning and action fall below the strategic threshold. Under the National Military Strategy, the Combatant Commanders develop Theater Strategy and subsequent campaign plans. At this juncture the line between strategy and planning merges with campaign planning that may be either at the theater strategic level or in the realm of Operational Art. Graphically the relationship between strategy and the levels of war appear as:[10]

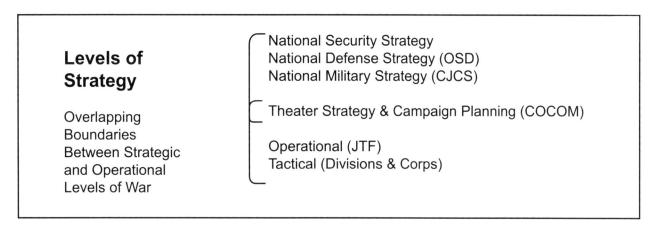

Figure 3-1. Strategic and Operational Art.

Strategy differs from operational art and tactics in functional, temporal, and geographic aspects. Functionally and temporally, tactics is the domain of battles—engagements of relative short duration. Operational art is the domain of the campaign, a series of battles occurring over a longer period of time. Strategy is the domain of war that encompasses the protracted level of conflict among nations, armed or unarmed. Tactics concerns itself with the parts or pieces, operational art with the combination of the pieces, and strategy with the combinations of combinations. Geographically, tactics is narrowly defined; operational level is broader and more regional in orientation; and, strategy is theater-wide, intercontinental, or global. It should also be noted that with the advances in transportation and communications, there has been a spatial and temporal convergence of strategy, operational art, and tactics. Increasingly, events at the tactical level have strategic consequences.[1]

A sixth premise is that strategy is comprehensive. That is to say, while the strategist may be devising a strategy from a particular perspective, he must consider the whole of the strategic environment in his analysis to arrive at a proper strategy to serve his purpose at his level. The strategist

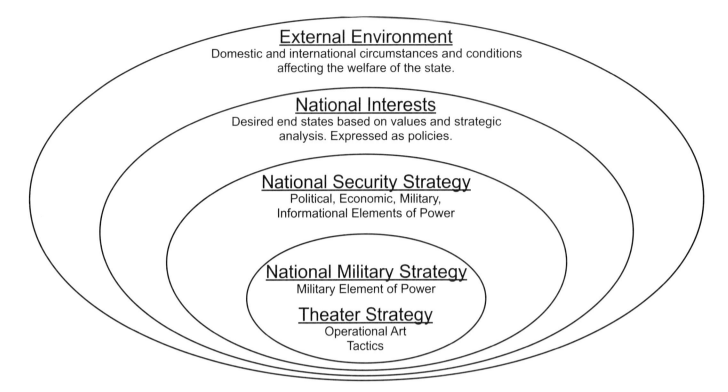

Figure 3-2. Comprehensiveness of Strategy.

is concerned with external and internal factors at all levels. On the other hand, in formulating a strategy, the strategist must also be cognizant that each aspect—objectives, concepts, and resources—has effects on the environment around him. Thus, the strategist must have a comprehensive knowledge of what else is happening and the potential first, second, third, etc., order effects of his own choices on the efforts of those above, below, and on his same level. The strategist's efforts must be fully integrated with the strategies or efforts of senior, coequal, and subordinate elements. Strategists must think holistically—that is, comprehensively. They must be cognizant of both the "big picture," their own institution's capabilities and resources, and the impact of their actions on the whole of the environment. Good strategy is never developed in isolation.

A seventh premise is that strategy is developed from a thorough analysis and knowledge of the strategic situation/environment. The purpose of this analysis is to highlight the internal and external factors that help define or may affect the specific objectives, concepts, and resources of strategy.

The last premise of a theory of strategy is that some risk is inherent to all strategy, and the best any strategy can offer is a favorable balance against failure. Failure can be either the failure to achieve one's own objectives and/or providing a significant advantage to one's adversaries.

Art Lykke gave coherent form to a theory of strategy with his articulation of the three-legged stool model of strategy, which illustrated that strategy = ends + ways + means and, if these were not in balance, the assumption of greater risk. In the Lykke proposition (model) the ends are "objectives," the ways are the "concepts" for accomplishing the objectives, and the means are the "resources" for supporting the con-

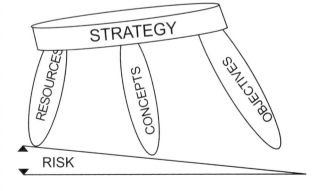

Figure 3-3. The Lykke Model.

cepts. The stool tilts if the three legs are not kept in balance. If any leg is too short, the risk is too great and the strategy falls over.[12]

It should be evident that the model poses three key questions for strategists. What is to be done? How is it to be done? What resources are required to do it in this manner? Lykke argues that if any leg of the stool is out of balance then one accepts a corresponding risk, unless one adjusts the legs. One might add resources, use a different concept, or change the objective. Or, one might decide to accept the risk. The theory is quite clear--a valid strategy must have an appropriate balance of objectives, concepts, and resources or its success is at greater risk.[13] Lykke's theory, like all good theory, does not necessarily provide a strategy. It is a paradigm that describes the questions to ask and the rules to follow. His strategic theory is supported by the underlying premises and assumptions above, and its practice is facilitated by the sharing of common definitions and formats.

Art Lykke wrestled with his proposition for many years and taught thousands of Army War College students to use his model properly through definition and illustration. These definitions and illustrations are important because they provide the common understanding by which strategists communicate. They include:

- *Ends (objectives)* explain "what" is to be accomplished. Ends are objectives that, if accomplished, create, or contribute to, the achievement of the desired end state at the level of strategy being analyzed and, ultimately, serve national interests. Ends are expressed with verbs (i.e., deter war, promote regional stability, destroy Iraqi armed forces).

- *Ways (strategic concepts/courses of action)* explain "how" the ends are to be accomplished by the employment of resources. The concept must be explicit enough to provide planning guidance to those who must implement and resource it. Since ways convey action they often have a verb, but ways are statements of "how," not "what" in relation to the objective of a strategy. Some confusion exists, because the concept for higher strategy often defines the objectives of the next lower level of strategy. A simple test for a way is to ask "in order to do what?" That should lead to the real objective. Some concepts are so accepted that their names have been given to specific strategies (containment, forward defense, assured destruction, and forward presence are illustrations). But note that in actual practice these strategies have specific objectives and forces associated with them, and the concept is better developed than the short title suggests.

- *Means (resources)* explain what specific resources are to be used in applying the concepts to accomplish the objectives and use no verb. Means can be tangible or intangible. Examples of tangible means include forces, people, equipment, money, and facilities. Intangible resources include things like "will," courage, or intellect.

- *Risk* explains the gap between what is to be achieved and the concepts and resources available to achieve the objective. Since there are never enough resources or a clever enough concept to assure 100 percent success in the competitive international environment, there is always some risk. The strategist seeks to minimize this risk through his development of the strategy—the balance of ends, ways, and means.

Ends, ways, and means often get confusing in the development or analysis of a specific strategy. The trick is to focus on the questions. Objectives will always answer the question of what one is trying to achieve. Concepts always explain "how" the resources will be used. Resources always explain what will be used to execute the concept. If the objective is "defend the United States (what?)"; "to develop, build, or establish a larger force" is a way (how?); and, "national manpower reserves, money, and training facilities" are examples of the means (resources to be used to support the "how"). The rule of thumb to apply here is that resources are usually physical and countable: Army, Air Force, Navy, units and armed forces of United States; personnel; dollars; facilities; equipment—trucks, planes, ships, etc.; and resources of organizations—Red Cross, NATO, etc. Means might also include such intangibles as "will, industrial capacity, intellect. etc.," but, state them as resources. Do not use means to describe concepts, and do not articulate resources as ways or concepts. In a very simplified manner, "diplomacy" is a *way* to promote regional stability (*objective*), but diplomats are the *means*. In the same manner, Clausewitz preferred "overthrow of the enemy's government" as the end, to fight a decisive battle as the way, and a larger army as the means. He saw the larger army as an appropriate resource to support his way—the decisive battle. To say "*use of* a larger army" infers a different concept for success and is an inappropriate statement of means (resources).

Over time thousands of students at the Army War College have tested Art Lykke's theory of strategy using the historical case study approach. His proposition is a common model for analyzing and evaluating the strategy of historical and current strategic level leadership. By using the theory to break a strategy into its component parts, Art Lykke argued that any strategy can be examined for suitability, feasibility, and acceptability, and, an assessment made of the proper balance among the component parts. In addition, his lecturing and presentations have led to the adoption of the basic model by a cohort of military and political strategists. This has, in turn, led to the proactive evaluation of strategy during development against the same standards of:

- Suitability—will its attainment accomplish the effect desired (relates to objective)?
- Feasibility—can the action be accomplished by the means available (relates to concept)?
- Acceptability—are the consequences of cost justified by the importance of the effect desired (relates to resources/concept)?[14]

Not only has the basic proposition been tested in historical case studies and practical application, it has also proven itself adaptable to explaining differing aspects of strategic thought. Art Lykke's argument that nations engage in two distinct types of military strategy concurrently—operational and force developmental—illustrates the theory's adaptability. Operational strategies are based on existing military capabilities. Force developmental strategies are based on future threats and objectives and are not limited by existing capabilities. In fact, the primary role of these strategies is to help determine and develop future capabilities.[15] Thus, the theory lends itself to both warfighters and force developers within the military.

Art Lykke's theory of strategy is an important contribution to strategic thought. In encouraging the strategist to use the term "strategy" correctly while applying the strategy model and its four parts—ends, ways, means and risk—he provided a viable theory of strategy. The assumptions and premises of this theory have proven valid for analyzing and developing strategy. Above all a valid strategy must find a balance among ends, ways, and means consistent with the risk the nation is willing to accept. Art Lykke's theory of strategy provides the basis for clearly articulating and objectively evaluating any strategy.

ENDNOTES - CHAPTER 3

1. Gregory D. Foster, "A Conceptual Foundation for a Theory of Strategy," *The Washington Quarterly*, Winter 1990, p. 43. Foster's analysis of the assumptions and premises of strategy is particularly thought provoking.

2. Arthur F. Lykke, Jr., "Toward an Understanding of Military Strategy," chap. in *Military Strategy: Theory and Application*, Carlisle Barracks, PA: U.S. Army War College, 1989, pp. 3-8. This document is the best written explanation of his ideas. Also used in this paper are the author's notes and recollections from Professor Lykke's lectures.

3. Henry E. Eccles, *Military Concepts and Philosophy,* New Brunswick, NJ: Rutgers University Press, 1965, p. 48.

4. Foster, p. 50.

5. David Jablonsky, *Why Is Strategy Difficult?*, Carlisle Barracks, PA: Strategic Studies Institute, U.S. Army War College, 1992, reprint, 1995. Professor Jablonsky's work, of which this is representative, gives the best explanation. He lists the elements of power as economic, psychological, political, and military. Socio-psychological is another term used as an instrument of power instead of psychological or informational. Note also that elements of power are more inclusive than instruments of power and include demographic/geographic elements. Dr. Jablonsky raised Art Lykke's proposition to the political level.

6. Foster, pp. 47-48.

7. *Ibid.*, p. 55.

8. Carl von Clausewitz, *On War*, Michael Howard and Peter Paret, eds./trans., Princeton, NJ: Princeton University Press, 1976, p. 87.

9. Foster, p. 50.

10. This chart is adapted from an older version commonly used to explain the overlapping. Abbreviations used: CJCS, Chairman, Joint Chiefs of Staff; COCOM, Combatant Commander; and, JTF, Joint Task Force.

11. Foster, p. 56.

12. Lykke, pp. 6-7.

13. *Ibid.*

14. Henry C. Eccles, "Strategy—The Theory and Application," *Naval War College Review,* Vol. 32, No. 3, May-June 1979, pp. 11-21.

15. Lykke, p. 4.

CHAPTER 4

THE STRATEGIC APPRAISAL: THE KEY TO EFFECTIVE STRATEGY

H. Richard Yarger

Strategy is best understood as the *art* and *science* of developing and using the political, economic, socio-psychological, and military powers of the state in accordance with policy guidance to create effects that protect or advance the state's interests in the strategic environment. The strategic environment is the realm in which the national leadership interacts with other states or actors and the possibilities of the future to advance the well-being of the state. It is inclusive, consisting of the facts, context, conditions, relationships, trends, issues, threats, opportunities, and interactions that influence the success of the state in relation to the physical world, other states and actors, chance, and the possible futures—all effects or other factors that potentially affect the well-being of the state and the way the state pursues its well-being. As a self-organizing complex system (a system of systems), the strategic environment is a dynamic environment that reacts to input but not necessarily in a direct cause-and-effect manner. Strategy is how the state exerts purposeful influence over this environment. Thus, strategy is a disciplined thought process that seeks to apply a degree of rationality and linearity to an environment that may or may not be either, so that effective planning can be accomplished. Strategy does this by identifying strategic ends (objectives), ways (concepts) and means (resources) that, when accomplished, lead to favorable effects in regard to the state's well-being.[1] It explains to planners what must be accomplished and establishes the boundaries of how it is to be accomplished and the resources to be made available. However, to formulate a proper strategy, the strategist must first determine the state's interests and the factors in the environment that potentially affect those interests. Only from such a strategic appraisal can the strategist derive the key strategic factors and determine the right calculation of ends, ways, and means.

The purpose of the strategic appraisal is to quantify and qualify what is known, believed to be known and unknown about the strategic environment in regard to a particular realm of strategy and identify *what is important* with regard to such strategy's formulation. It represents a rational, scientific approach to acquiring what Carl von Clausewitz referred to as *coup d'oeil*—the ability to see what is really important.[2] But while displayed below as a linear process to assist the reader's understanding of the concept, in reality the appraisal is always an iterative process wherein each new piece of information must be considered with reference to what is already known, and what is already known revalidated in light of the new information. In this process, the strategist determines pertinent desired end states (interests) that facilitate the well-being of the nation and evaluates the environment to determine what factors may preclude or assist realization of these interests. Based on his assessment of these factors, the strategist chooses key strategic factors on which to formulate ends, ways, and means that address or make use of these factors to create effects that favor the realization of the interests.

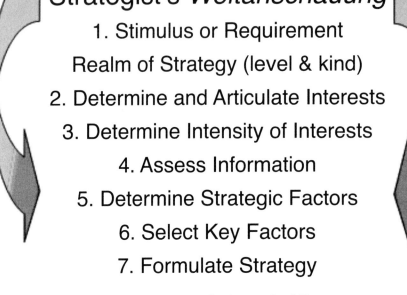

Figure 4-1. Strategic Appraisal Process.

Through constant study and analysis, the strategist maintains a holistic world view that gives meaning and context to his understanding of the strategic environment and the forces of continuity and change at work in it. Consequently, the strategist's *Weltanschauung* is both an objective view of the existing current environment and an anticipatory appreciation of the implications of continuities and change for his nation's future well-being. Appreciating that the strategic environment possesses the characteristics of a system of systems and exhibits some of the attributes of chaos theory, the strategist accepts that the future is not predictable but believes it can be influenced and shaped toward more favorable outcomes.[3] His *weltanschauung* makes the strategist sensitive to what national interests are and the threats, challenges, and opportunities in regard to them. However, a new, focused strategic appraisal is conducted when circumstances demand a new strategy or the review of an existing strategy is undertaken. Understanding the stimulus or the requirement for the strategy is the first step in the strategic appraisal. It not only provides the strategist's focus and motivation, but it will ultimately lend legitimacy, authority, and impetus to the appraisal and strategy formulation processes and the subsequent implementation of the strategy.

The levels and kinds of strategy fall in different realms. Realms reflect both the hierarchical nature of strategy and its comprehensiveness, thereby allowing the state's leadership to delegate responsibility for strategy at different levels and in different domains while maintaining control over a complex process. The strategic appraisal focuses on serving that realm of strategy undertaken—both the kind and level. For example, the term "Grand Strategy" encompasses both level and kind, implying an overarching strategy that integrates the use of all the state's power in service of all the state's interests. National strategies are at the national level, but they may apply to all elements of power and the associated departments and agencies as the National Security Strategy does, or they may focus on one element, as is the case with the National Military Strategy. Strategies may also have a regional focus, a force developmental focus, an organizational focus, and other foci as illustrated in Figure 4-2.

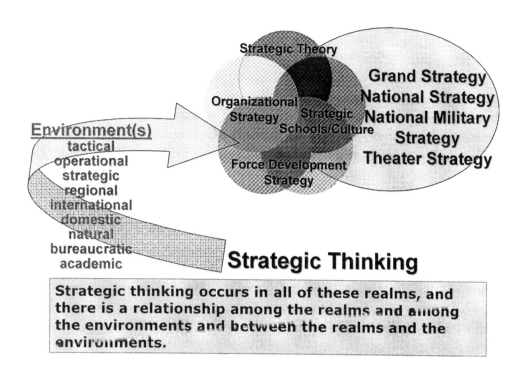

Figure 4-2. Realms of Strategy

Thinking about the kind and level of strategy helps develop specificity in the articulation of interests and better focuses the strategy with regard to the desired end states. It also clarifies and assigns responsibility, authority, and accountability. Nonetheless, the strategist at every level and in every domain must still maintain a holistic perspective.

Determining and articulating interests is the second step in the strategic appraisal process. The *DOD Dictionary of Military Terms* defines national security interests as: "The foundation for the development of valid national objectives that define U.S. goals or purposes. National security interests include preserving U.S. political identity, framework, and institutions; fostering economic well-being; and bolstering international order supporting the vital interests of the United States and its allies."[4] The nature of the strategic environment suggests a more generalized definition, such as the perceived needs and desires of a sovereign state in relation to other sovereign states, non-state actors, and chance and circumstances in an emerging strategic environment expressed as desired end states.[5] This broader definition encapsulates the dynamism of a strategic environment in which multiple actors, chance, and interaction play, and both external and internal components are recognized. Interests are expressed as general or particular desired end states or conditions. For example, "U.S. economic well-being" would be a generalized interest; while "international access to Middle Eastern oil" illustrates a more particular economic interest. While some interests may change over time, general interests such as free trade and defense of the homeland are persistent.

Interests are founded in national purpose. National purpose is essentially a summary of our enduring values, beliefs, and ethics as expressed by political leadership with regard to the present and the future they foresee. At the highest level, political leadership uses policy to identify state interests and provide guidance for subordinate policy and strategy. Such policy may appear as general as a vision statement that proclaims a desired future strategic environment, or as a more specific statement of guidance—with elements of ends, ways, and means. It is found in various documents, speeches, policy statements, and other pronouncements made on behalf of the government by various officials, or it may be provided by leadership as direct guidance for the development of specific strategy. Policy may be inferred as well as stated. It may be the result of a detailed strategic appraisal or arrived at intuitively. Regardless, state policy flows from the formal and informal political processes and the interpretation of the national purpose in the current and desired future strategic environments. Thus, national interests are the general or specific statements of the nation's desired end states within the strategic environment based on the policymakers' understanding of what best serves national well-being.

Interests may be expressed as physical or non-physical conditions. They may represent continuities or changes—things to be protected, things to be promoted, or things to be created. Ideally, interests flow logically from the policy formulation process, but the nature of the political and bureaucratic environments, particularly in a democracy, can make identifying and clearly articulating interests and their relative importance or intensity a difficult task. As stated above, in the real world policy appears in many formats, often is not clearly stated, and may not be comprehensive in its statement of interests and guidance for serving interests. Policy may also come from multiple and contradictory sources, such as the executive or legislative branches, and it may be emerging from the interagency process at the time a strategy is demanded. While strategy is subordinate to policy, the strategist must search out and clarify policy intentions and appropriately identify and articulate interests. In cases where policy intentions or interests statements conflict with the reality of the strategic environment and clarification is appropriate, the strategist provides appropriate recommendations to the approval authority.

Theorists have proposed various methodologies for determining interests and levels of intensity. Sometimes, presidential administrations impose their own methodologies to express categories of interests and their associate levels of intensity. In recent years, course material at the Senior Service Colleges, such as the U.S. Army War College, has focused on three that are termed core U.S. interests: physical security, promotion of values, and economic prosperity. In the Army War College process model these three interests lead directly to three grand strategic objectives: preserve American security, bolster American economic prosperity, and promote American values.[6] In a much earlier argument, Donald E. Nuechterlein referred to these "core" interests as categories and listed four: Defense of the Homeland, Economic Prosperity, Favorable World Order, and Promotion of Values. Nuechterlein suggested these four end states were so general in nature that their primary utility lay in considering them as categories to help organize thinking about interests, and that actual interests must be stated with more specificity to be of any use in strategy formulation. He also noted that such categorization is somewhat artificial, and interests tend to bleed over into other categories.[7] Nuechterlein was right in both regards. Specificity is critical to good strategy formulation. Specificity in interests lends clarity to policy's true intent and aids in the identification of the strategic factors important with regard to the interests. In addition, since in the strategic environment everything is interrelated, greater specificity helps define the nature and context of the interest and clarifies the level and kind of strategy appropriate for addressing an interest.

Interests as statements of desired end states do not imply intended actions or set objectives—policy guidance and strategy does that. Consequently, interests are stated without verbs or other action modifiers. As argued above, interests are expressed with an appropriate degree of specificity. For example, "access to oil" is an expression of a desired end state, but is very general. It could apply anywhere in the world. "Access to oil in the Middle East" is a regionally stated interest, focusing strategic efforts on a specific region; however, it still allows the use of various elements of power and a wide range of objectives and concepts. "Freedom of navigation in the Persian Gulf" as an expression of a specifically stated interest in the CENTCOM theater military strategy gives an even narrower focus to the desired end state and emphasizes the military instrument. Hence, statements of interests in strategies achieve specificity by word choice, directing the focus and narrowing the context. Expression of interests, like most things in strategy, remains a matter of choice, but the strategist should be aware of the fact he is making a choice and the potential implications of word selection—a matter worthy of deliberation and discussion! Therefore, strategists often achieve the right degree of specificity through an iterative process in which they articulate an interest and then restate it as they learn more about the implications of pursuing that interest.

Specificity in interests serves the multiple purposes of clarifying the intent of policy in different realms, focusing attention on the appropriate strategic factors, enabling better strategy formulation, and helping to identify responsibility, authority, and accountability. For example, a military strategy would logically, but not exclusively, focus on end states that could be accomplished through the application of the military element of power. Not exclusively so, because as Nuechterlein observed, interests tend to bleed over into other categories, and the military instrument may also facilitate accomplishment of diplomatic, economic, or informational focused interests. In a similar manner, other instruments of power may play crucial roles in support of military strategies.

Having determined and articulated the interests, the third step in the strategic appraisal is to determine the level of intensity of each interest. Different methodologies and models have also guided the determination and expression of levels of intensity. Both Nuechterlein and Army War College methodologies advocate applying levels of intensity to interests to indicate criticality and priority. Levels of intensity at the Army War College include: Vital, Important, and Peripheral.[8] Nuechterlein labeled the important level as "major" and argued for the existence of a fourth intensity—Survival—aimed at those threats or changes that challenged the very existence of the nation as we know it.[9] Dropped from most methodologies with the ending of the Cold War, Nuechterlein's Survival level deserves reconsideration in light of the increase of weapons of mass destruction (WMD) proliferation among nation-states and the potential access and use of WMD by terrorists. Various actors can pose an imminent, credible threat of massive destruction to the U.S. homeland if their demands are not met. In a period of globalization such as the world is currently experiencing, an imminent, credible threat of massive disruption to the transportation and informational systems that undergird national existence and a stable world order may also reach Survival intensity. Thus, interests must have both specificity relative to the realm of the strategy being formulated and a means to identify criticality and priority in order to provide focus in determining strategic factors and formulating strategy.

Levels of intensity indicate criticality and priority of interests with regard to the well-being of the state. They help the strategist understand the relative importance and urgency among interests, but do not imply that any should not be considered or addressed in some manner—all interests are worthy of some level of concern. Levels of intensity suggest relative importance and have temporal, resource, and risk-acceptance implications, but the decision to act or how to act with regard to them flows from the whole of the strategy formulation process—not the assignment of the intensity. Intensity levels are transitory in that they are subject to change based on the perception of urgency associated with them at any time. Intensity is dependent on the context of the strategic situation and the policy maker or strategist's interpretation of the context and the importance of the interest to national well-being. The definitions of the four intensity levels of Survival, Vital, Important, and Peripheral are provided in Figure 4-3.[10]

> **Levels of Intensity**
>
> **Survival** - If unfulfilled, will result in immediate massive destruction of one or more major aspects of the core national interests.
>
> **Vital** - If unfulfilled, will have immediate consequence for core national interests.
>
> **Important** - If unfulfilled, will result in damage that will eventually affect core national interests.
>
> **Peripheral** - If unfulfilled, will result in damage that is unlikely to affect core national interests.

Figure 4-3. Levels of Intensity.[11]

The fourth step in the strategic appraisal is to assess the information relative to the interests. In doing this the strategist casts a wide net. Information includes facts and data relating to any aspect of the strategic environment with regard to the interest(s), including: both tangible and intangible attributes and knowledge; assumptions; relationships; and interaction. The strategist considers all information from friendly, neutral, and adversarial perspectives, and from objective and subjective perspectives in each case. While his emphasis is logically on his realm of strategy, the strategist applies holistic thinking that looks both vertically and horizontally at other realms and across the environment. From this assessment the strategist identifies and evaluates the strategic factors that affect or potentially affect the interests—whether promoting, hindering, protecting, or threatening them. From this evaluation of the factors he selects the key strategic factors—the factors on which his strategy's ends, ways, and means are based.

The determination of the key strategic factors and the strategist's choices with regard to them is one of the most poorly understood aspects of strategy formulation. It represents a major shortcoming in theoretical consideration of a strategic mindset. Clausewitz's use of *coup d'oeil* describes this aspect. He argues "the concept merely refers to the quick recognition of a truth that the mind would ordinarily miss or would perceive only after long study and reflection."[12] It is the "inward eye" that leads to sound decisions in a timely manner. What Clausewitz is referring to is the ability to see what is really important in the strategic situation and to be able to devise a way to act with regard to it.[13] In strategy formulation "what is really important" are called strategic factors—the things that determine or influence the realization of the interest. Not all information or facts are strategic factors. Strategic factors have meaning relative to the expressed interests. From these the strategist will determine the key strategic factors on which the success of the strategy potentially rises or falls. The figure below outlines the distinctions between information, strategic factors, and key strategic factors.

Information	Facts and data relating to any aspect of the strategic environment with regard to the interest(s), including both tangible and intangible attributes and knowledge; assumptions; relationships; and interaction.
Strategic Factors	The things that can potentially contribute to or detract causally from the realization of the specified interests or other interests.
Key Strategic Factors	Factors the strategist determines are at the crux of interaction within the environment that can or must be used, influenced or countered to advance or protect the specified interests.

Figure 4-4. Strategic Factors.

Seeing what is really important flows from a thorough assessment of the realities and possibilities of the strategic environment—tempered by an understanding of its nature and strategic theory. Strategy in its essence is about creating a more "favorable future" for the state than might exist if left to chance or the actions of adversaries and others. It is proactive, but not predictive. Thus, in dealing with the unknowns and uncertainties of the future, the strategist forecasts from a knowledge and understanding of the systems of the strategic environment—what they are (facts and assumptions) and how they interact (observation, reason and assumptions) within the various dimensions of interaction. He considers these in terms of continuities and change—thinking in time streams to see how the present can be affected by change and how continuities of the past and changes today may play out in the future. From this assessment the strategist derives the strategic factors—the things that can potentially contribute to or detract causally from the realization of the interest. Factors may be tangible or intangible, representing any aspect of the environment. The existence of other states and actors, geography, culture, history, relationships, perspectives, perceptions, facts, and assumptions all represent potential factors that must be considered in the strategic appraisal. What the strategist understands they are, and what others believe them to be, are both important.

Having identified strategic factors, the strategist continues his assessment to determine which are the key strategic factors—those critical factors at the crux of interaction within the strategic environment, representing the potential critical points of tension between continuities and change in the system of systems where the strategist may choose to act or must act to realize the interest. In strategy formulation these critical strategic factors are the "keys" to developing an effective strategy, because using, influencing, and countering them is how the strategist creates strategic effects and advances or protects interests. The strategist seeks to change, leverage, or overcome these, in effect modifying or retaining the equilibrium in the strategic environment by setting objectives and developing concepts and marshaling resources to achieve the objectives. When successfully selected and achieved, the objectives create strategic effects that tip the balance in favor of the stated interests. The strategist's assessment of how to best do this is reflected in his calculation of the relationship of ends, ways, and means—the rationally stated output of strategic thought. The calculation and each of its components are based on the strategist's assessment of the relationship between the desired end state and various key factors. It is the appraisal of the strategic environment and selection of the key strategic factors that sets up the calculation.

Hence, the biggest conundrum confronting the strategist in strategy formulation is identifying the key strategic factors. By definition, the strategic environment is big, and there is a lot of information and VUCA in it—the conundrum is to determine what is really important in an overwhelming amount of information and possibilities. How do we determine strategic factors? How does the strategist achieve the focus that enables him to disregard the unimportant and not overlook something critical? Of the strategic factors, how does the strategist choose those that are key and should be addressed by strategy? How do key strategic factors lead to the rational expression of strategic thinking as ends, ways, and means? The thought processes to answer these questions are the heart of the strategic appraisal. Models and insights offered by theorists and practitioners provide guides to assist and discipline the appraisal process, but it starts with an open mind that seeks inclusive answers to broad questions. From there the strategist applies strategic thinking competencies to narrow the focus through a successive series of questions and answers that lead to the distillation of the key factors.

Postulating broad questions creates the mindset necessary to see what is important. What are the U.S. interests and levels of intensity are broad questions and are steps 2 and 3 in the appraisal process. Factors flow from analysis and synthesis of information relevant to the interests and their intensities. What do I know with regard to facts—actors, geography, culture, history, economics, relationships, perspectives, and perceptions, etc.? For example, who else has relevant interests, what are they and what is the level of intensity? What do I not know, what can I find out, and what must I assume? What presumptions are at work in my thinking or that of others? Where can change be introduced to favorable effect? What or what changes create unfavorable effect? These are all big questions, and to answer them the strategist draws on his *weltanschauung*, focused individual research and study, and the expertise of others.

Factors are defined as pertinent facts, trends, threats, conditions, or inferences that imply an effect on the realization of the interest. Thus, factors are not accumulations of information or statements of simple facts. And their scope exceeds that of "facts bearing on the problem" in the problem-solving staff study because they are concerned with what has occurred in the past, what might occur in the future, and multi-ordered effects of any changes. Factors are distinguished from information by the strategist's assessment of their potential causal relationship with the interest. While some may have a visible direct cause-and-effect relationship, many will be less obvious, and their importance lies in their second, third, or further multi-ordered implications with regard to the interest.

Consequently, factors are stated to show their bearing on the interest. For example, if the stated national interest is "a stable, peaceful China," the fact the Great Wall is 4,000 miles long is interesting, but it is only information and not a factor with regard to the interest, because the Wall no longer plays a part in China's internal stability or defense. It is also a fact that the population of China is in excess of 1.3 billion. One could argue that it is a strategic factor because the sheer magnitude of the numbers involved has implications for the stated interest. However, in and of itself, the fact is of little help to the strategist other than no strategy with regard to China could ignore the inferences of such a large population. As stated, the fact has no real context with regard to the interest. A population-related fact better expressed as a factor potentially affecting the stability interest is: "The Chinese government is struggling to sustain adequate job growth for tens of millions of workers laid off from state-owned enterprises, migrants, and new entrants to the work force."[14] This trend could potentially threaten domestic stability in China and has a causal relationship with the interest. If the strategist considered this a key strategic factor, his strategy with regard to China would establish objectives or pursue strategic concepts that mitigate this trend. *The National Security Strategy of the United States of America* (September 2002) sought to influence global peace and domestic stability in China and elsewhere by promoting prosperity and reducing poverty around the world with an objective to "Ignite a New Era of Global Economic Growth Through Free Markets and Free Trade." The strategy argued that market economies were better than "command-and-control" economies.[15] It helped encourage China toward a more viable economy and subsequent job creation.[16] Numerous other strategic factors influenced this national strategy, but the growth of the Chinese economy and its successful integration into the American-led global economy did promote a more "stable, peaceful China."

Determining strategic factors is difficult, and ultimately, like most aspects of strategy, the selection of key strategic factors is a matter of choice by the strategist. Sorting through the VUCA of the strategic environment in search of what is really important requires the strategist to approach the appraisal from multiple perspectives using his understanding of strategic theory and applying all the strategic thinking competencies. Such strategic thinking competencies act as lenses to assist the strategist with an evaluation of the strategic environment, reminding the strategist of the dimensions of the intellect that should be applied to seek and sort information and to recognize which factors are key.[17] The U.S. Army War College identifies five such competencies.

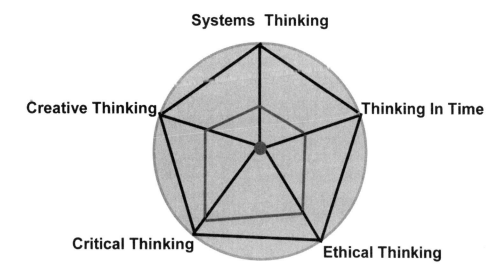

Figure 4-5. Strategic Thinking Competencies.[18]

Critical thinking processes are applicable to both problem solving and strategic thinking, suggesting a rational way to determine the interest and the related strategic factors. The major components of the process—clarify the concern, evaluate information, evaluate implications, and make decisions/use judgment—lead to an understanding of the facts and considerations relative to the interest and their implications. The assessment of points of view and the clarification of assumptions and inferences, as well as argument analysis and consideration of the impact of biases and traps, when applied to other actors and internally, clarify what is important in the strategic context internationally and domestically. By design, the critical thinking process seeks hard facts, forces consideration of the unknowns and the role of chance, and recognizes that the strategic environment consists of both physical and humanistic systems.[19] It is one thinking lens that has great application in the strategic appraisal process.

Richard E. Neustadt and Ernest R. May in *Thinking in Time: The Uses of History for Decision Makers* also place emphasis on determining all the factors and selecting the key factors as a basis for decision making. While their focus is on issue policy, and the terminology does not use the word "factor," their first step in asking for the identification of key elements that are known, unclear, and presumed is obviously focused on determining factors. One insightful approach that decisionmakers can use is to identify multiple past situations that appear analogous and list similarities and differences. Again, this process logically leads to identifying not only what is known and important in the current situation, but leverages history to get insights into potentially unrecognized factors and relationships among factors. Neustadt and May's concept of "thinking in time" connects discrete phenomena over time and is able to relate the connections to potential futures and choices for a desired future—hence this thinking process identifies factors that matter in a strategy seeking a more favorable future.[20] Thinking in time is a disciplined process that helps mitigate uncertainty, complexity, and ambiguity.

Other strategic thinking competencies also offer insights into how to think of and identify strategic factors. Systems thinking focuses on comprehending the whole, but the process identifies systems, interdependence among systems, individual aspects of particular systems with regard to their roles or functions within the whole, and the effects of any changes induced on the whole.[21] It is synthesis-centric, rather than using analysis—asking how things come together as opposed to breaking them apart and addressing them individually as a planner might. Creative thinking processes offer new and different ways of looking at information and relationships among data, actors, and events. They help strategists view information in new and creative ways.[22] Ethical thinking processes force the examination of moral factors.[23] From each perspective and process, the strategist acquires information and insights; the processes reveal what is important with regard to interests. The strategist seeks factors relative to his own state's interests, factors relative to his adversaries' interests, factors relative to others' interests, and factors relative to the physical world and chance—looking for what is important that must be addressed or affords an opportunity to serve the state's interests. By disciplining his thinking to consider the five different lenses, the strategist precludes blind spots and creates opportunities for looking at things differently—thereby increasing the probability of seeing what is important.

Structural analysis models can also assist in sorting what is important in the vast information available, and thus, lead to the identification of the key strategic factors. One simple structure to use is to look at the information from the perspective of the elements of power. Facts or trends that indicate or affect balance and relationships in power are potential strategic factors. Hence, focusing on the natural and social determinants of power of the various actors serves as a filter for sorting through the overwhelming volume of information to see what is important. The elements of power are listed below.

Natural Determinants	**Social Determinants**
• Geography	• Economic
• Population	• Military
• Natural Resources	• Political
	• Socio-Psychological

Such a filter works because there are casual and interdependence relationships among interests, power, and strategy that become apparent under disciplined consideration. Power is relative, dynamic, and contextual, and the examination and weighing of information with regard to power reveals relevant factors and suggests which are key.[24] Again, the strategist considers this from the multiple perspectives of self, adversaries, others, the physical world, and chance.

Since the strategic environment is a system of systems, and the people and other human entities depicted below are part of the interaction, an actor structural analysis is another way to filter information to see what is really important with regard to specific interests. Individual personalities and collective mentalities matter in the pursuit of interests. Here the strategist poses broad questions such as: who is affected by this interest and how; who else shares or opposes this interest and why; how will others act or react with regard to this interest and how and why; and what influences others' actions with regard to this interest and why? Answers to these questions reveal factors that must be considered.

Actor Structures

- Individual
- Leadership
- Groups
- Organizations
- Institutions
- Interagency/Bureaucracy
- Movements
- States
- International Business Organizations
- Private Organizations
- International Governmental Organizations
- Society/Culture

Since factors relate strategy to the interests and a proper focus of strategy is interaction, the dimensions of interaction in the strategic environment are another important information filter. In this construct, the strategist uses the dimensions as lenses to focus attention on what is important among the profusion of information. These dimensions are in play to a greater or lesser extent at all times. Colin S. Gray identifies some 17 strategic dimensions as depicted below, but acknowledges there may be many more. The strategist must consider factors derived from analysis using these dimensions both individually and holistically—that is each distinctly but at the same time in context with each other. Since particular dimensions play a greater role or are more critical at particular times in history, the strategist must be attuned to this potential and the fact that none of the dimensions can be ignored over time. A dimension of strategy approach is a valid methodology for identifying what is important with regard to an interest because it allows the question: "What is important relative to this interest in this dimension and how does it interact with the whole of the environment?"

Dimensions of Strategy[25]

- People
- Society
- Culture
- Politics
- Ethics
- Economics and Logistics
- Organization
- Administration
- Information and Intelligence
- Strategic Theory and Doctrine
- Technology
- Operations
- Command
- Geography
- Friction/chance/uncertainty
- Adversary
- Time

Different realms of strategy may suggest other constructs for discerning what is important in the vast array of information available to the strategist. Regardless, the appraisal process is similar. From his assessment and synthesis of the information, the strategist determines the relevant factors—facts, issues, assumptions, presumptions, threats and opportunities—that *act or interact to affect the interest*. These factors are written as simple factual statements in a manner that makes clear how they affect, and if they assist or hinder U.S. interests. From this broad understanding and list of factors, the strategist develops a refined list of key strategic factors by asking a new series of questions.

What can most likely detract from or preclude the realization of the interest? What best supports or can be leveraged to realize the interest? What does policy guidance allow or preclude? What assumptions are inherent to my understanding of the situation and realization of the interests? Can these assumptions be made factual? What changes in facts or assumptions would affect the realization of interests and how? What role does chance play—are there wild cards? These questions lead to the selection of the key strategic factors—the factors the strategy must account for or that the strategist thinks provides the key to successful pursuit of the interest.

The strategist is now poised to formulate a specific strategy. Using the strategic appraisal framework he has applied to strategic thinking competencies and various models to clarify interests and levels of intensity, the strategist has culled out strategic factors relevant to the realization of the interests from an overabundance of information, and he has further refined this broad list of factors into a more focused list of key strategic factors on which to base a strategy. However, the strategic appraisal framework has done much more than this. It has immersed the strategist in the strategic environment from the perspective of specific national interests. It has identified what is important relative to those interests, forced the strategist to distinguish between fact and assumption, and alerted him to the consequences of change. Thus, the framework focuses the strategy formulation process on the key strategic factors, suggesting where flexibility is needed and how strategy might be made adaptive. Further, it provides indicators for potential future issues and prepares the strategist for considering changes in strategy.

Once the strategic appraisal is complete, the strategist uses his understanding of the key strategic factors to influence the strategic environment favorably without inadvertently creating other unfavorable effects. These factors suggest suitable objectives, suggest or limit concepts, and identify appropriate resources. In addition, the key strategic factors both suggest and bound what is feasible, acceptable, and suitable in strategy formulation. The assessment of the factors also provides the basis for the consideration of risk in a strategy. Through his formulation of appropriate ends, ways, and means to leverage and account for these factors, the strategist creates favorable strategic effects leading to the realization of the interest. Which factors to act upon, what objectives to set to create favorable strategic effects, what concepts to use to achieve those objectives without adverse effects, and what resources to provide to implement the concepts are all choices made in strategy formulation from the knowledge gained in the strategic appraisal. To the extent this is done well, the strategist creates more favorable effects and brings the strategy closer to the realization of the interest.

The strategic appraisal framework serves to discipline the strategist's thought process and codify its output. Like all theory, it educates but does not dictate—the human mind must make the choices. Yet, through education, the appraisal framework leads to potentially better appraisals and a more careful consideration of what the interests are and the factors to be considered with regard to them. Through codification, it allows critical review and a shared understanding of how a strategy is expected to work. As such, the framework is a useful tool, but a healthy *weltanschauung* is essential to retain the proper perspective on the validity of a strategy and to recognize when and whether modification or a new strategy is necessary. Theory can aid the practice of strategic *coup d'oeil* and strategy formulation by offering a framework for identifying and considering the relevant factors, but the strategist's choice of what to do, how to do it, and the resources to be made available remain a creation of the active intellect.

ENDNOTES - CHAPTER 4

1. Arthur F. Lykke, Jr., "Toward an Understanding of Military Strategy," chap. in *Military Strategy: Theory and Application*, Carlisle, PA: U.S. Army War College, 1989, pp. 3-8.

2. Carl von Clausewitz, *On War*, Michael Howard and Peter Paret, ed./trans., Princeton, NJ: Princeton University Press, 1976, p. 102.

3. Harry R. Yarger, *Strategic Theory for the 21st Century: The Little Book on Big Strategy*, Carlisle, PA: Strategic Studies Institute, February 2006, pp. 17-29.

4. Joint Chiefs of Staff, Joint Staff, J-7, *Joint Publication 1-02, Department of Defense Dictionary of Military and Associated Terms*, Washington, DC: United States Joint Staff, April 12, 2002, amended through September 14, 2007, p. 360.

5. Donald E. Nuechterlein, *America Overcommitted: United States National Interests in the 1980s*, Lexington, KY: The University Press of Kentucky, 1984, p. 4. This is a modification of Nuechterlein's definition.

6. Department of National Security and Strategy, *Course Directive: National Security Policy and Strategy Academic Year 2007*, Carlisle, PA: U.S. Army War College, 2006, p. 106.

7. Nuechterlein, pp. 8-14.

8. *Course Directive: National Security Policy and Strategy Academic Year 2007*, pp. 106-108.

9. Nuechterlein, p. 10.

10. *Ibid.*, pp. 9-14, 17-28. Nuechterlein identifies vital interests with regard to various value and cost/risk factors, discussing eight of each. These are still useful, but not inclusive.

11. *Course Directive: National Security Policy and Strategy Academic Year 2007*, pp. 106-108.

12. Clausewitz, p. 102.

13. *Ibid.*

14. The Central Intelligence Agency, *The World Factbook*, available from *www.cia.gov/library/publications/the-world-factbook/print/ch.html*.

15. George W. Bush, *The National Security Strategy of the United States of America*, Washington, DC: The White House, September 2002, pp. 17-18.

16. George W. Bush, *The National Security Strategy of the United States of America*, Washington, DC: The White House, March 2006, p. 26. Here, the administration takes credit for success.

17. Richard M. Meinhart, "Leadership and Strategic Thinking," in *Strategic Thinking*, Carlisle, PA: U.S. Army War College, 2007, pp. 36-37.

18. *Ibid.*

19. Colonel Stephen J. Gerras, Ph.D., "Thinking Critically About Critical Thinking: A Fundamental Guide for Strategic Leaders," in *Strategic Thinking*, Carlisle, PA: U.S. Army War College, 2007, pp. 47-75.

20. Richard E. Neustadt and Ernest R. May, *Thinking in Time: The Use of History for Decision Makers*, New York: The Free Press, 1986, pp. 232-240, 252-256.

21. George E. Reed, "Systems Thinking and Senior Level Leadership," in *Strategic Thinking,* Carlisle, PA: U.S. Army War College, 2007, pp. 158-162.

22. Colonel Charles D. Allen, "Creative Thinking for Individuals and Teams," in *Strategic Thinking*, Carlisle, PA: U.S. Army War College, 2007, pp. 47-75.

23. Meinhart, p. 44.

24. David Jablonsky, "National Power," in *U.S. Army War College Guide to National Security Policy and Strategy*, 2nd Ed., J. Boone Bartholomees, Jr., ed., Carlisle, PA: Strategic Studies Institute, U.S. Army War College, June 2006, pp. 127-142.

25. Colin S. Gray, *Modern Strategy*, Oxford, UK: Oxford University Press, 1999, pp. 23-44.

CHAPTER 5

MANAGING STRATEGIC RISK

James F. Holcomb

In a tactical situation one is able to see at least half the problem with the naked eye, whereas in strategy everything has to be guessed at and presumed.[1]

Carl von Clausewitz

The hierarchical chart of the Army War College strategy formulation model at Appendix II shows a final block labeled "Risk Assessment." The implication of the diagram is that risk assessment is the final step in the strategy formulation process and is a discreet action. However, policy and strategy, properly arrived at, demand a continuous and thorough assessment and reassessment of risk throughout the total process.

Strategists and strategic theorists throughout history have grappled with the concept of risk and methodologies for its assessment. The motivation to eliminate uncertainty in policy and strategy development as well as execution is natural, if at times chimerical. There will always be uncertainty. It often will be unmeasurable. The very nature of war and conflict and the increasingly complex strategic environment ensures that this is so. Where then does this leave the aspiring student of strategy? Is risk assessment simply the "comfort level that senior planners experience as they assess key variables?"[2] It is this and more. The concept of risk assessment is worth examining in more detail to put some substance to the form.

DEFINING RISK

Defining risk is a relatively simple task. John Collins, in his primer on grand strategy, reduces it to its essentials: "Discrepancies between ends, which we have identified as interests and objectives, and means—available resources—create risks, which can rarely be quantified."[3] At its core, risk arises when ends and means are not in consonance. This is known as an "ends-means mismatch." Collins is on solid ground with this definition, the legacy of which springs from Clausewitz and his discussion of "the political object of war and the effort to be made."[4] B. H. Liddell Hart also focused on this basic truth: "Strategy depends for success, first and most, on a sound calculation and coordination of the end and the means….An excess may be as harmful as a deficiency."[5] Strategic risk then is the probability of failure in achieving a strategic objective at an acceptable cost. The concept is simple to articulate and easy to understand. But, as in war, the simplest things in strategy are the most difficult.

The first difficulty is with understanding what Clausewitz and others meant by "means" in the ends-means equation. Current use of the term generally accepts that means constitute resources; that is, personnel, treasure, equipment, political will, time, and so on. Clausewitz also intended a larger meaning that includes concepts or courses of action (what we term "ways") to achieve particular objectives; these coupled with resources constitute the means or "effort to be made."[6] It has become increasingly useful to separate these two components of Clausewitz's "means" for consideration in strategy formulation without confusing Clausewitz's original intent. Consequently, risk can be represented by a mismatch in ends and *ways or means*.

Art Lykke makes the case for this approach in presenting his well-taught model comprising three variables: ends (objectives), ways (concepts, options or courses of action for achieving them), and means (resources). Using a simple metaphor of a three legged stool, he points out that if the ends, ways and means (the legs of the stool) are not of equal length, then we are left with a stool (and a strategy) that is out of balance. Continuing the analogy, he defines this angle of imbalance as risk. The greater the mismatch between ends, ways and/or means, the greater the risk of achieving ones objectives.[7] This is a subtle but important addition to the simple ends-means equation. One can correctly and accurately identify the objective to be achieved and provide adequate resources to achieve it. However, if the "way" of achieving it is not in balance then there is an inherent risk of failure to achieve the strategic objective. For example, during the Cuban Missile Crisis the objective of the Kennedy administration was fairly straightforward: Get the missiles out of Cuba. The means available were adequate and deliverable. However, there were several different ways to achieve the objective. Graham Allison identifies six major categories of possible response: Do nothing, apply diplomatic pressure, secretly approach Castro, conduct an invasion, conduct air strikes, or blockade.[8] Risk was present in the debate over the strategy for Kosovo and the viability of the use of air power alone to achieve particular political objectives. It was present in the debate in the fall of 2009 over strategy for Afghanistan and whether to target al Qaeda in its sanctuaries or invest in a full-up counterinsurgency campaign. In the Lykke model of the stool, the balance varies depending on which option is chosen. The degree of lopsidedness or imbalance defines risk. Choosing the right policy option (or way) to achieve the strategic objective is therefore a critical consideration, even assuming a clear objective and adequate means. That is, an adequately resourced "way" that is inappropriate to the "end" would still create risk of failure to achieve the strategic objective.

Thus, the definition of risk is the degree to which strategic objectives, concepts, and resources are in or out of balance. Since strategy is a dynamic process, one must understand that all three elements are variable and subject to change over time and circumstance. The formulation of effective strategy for any endeavor is a constant quest to ensure balance among the variables. The definition applies to all aspects of strategy development, whether dealing with national security (grand) strategy, defense, military or theater strategies, business strategy, or even personal strategies.

WHY IS STRATEGIC RISK ASSESSMENT DIFFICULT?

The subtitle is borrowed from David Jablonsky's piece, "Why is Strategy Difficult?"[9] (See Chapter 1 in this volume). The very nature of war and conflict presupposes a relationship between thinking adversaries. This, in turn, ensures that a degree of ambiguity, uncertainty and yes, risk will exist in any developed strategy. Indeed, Clausewitz devotes the central theme of *On War* to this very premise; that is what distinguishes his work from his predecessors and ensures its continued relevance to the present day. Clausewitz was not the only one to recognize the subjective nature of war, but he was the first to mark that characteristic as preeminent. Throughout his work, there are allusions to "chance," "luck," "guesswork," "uncertainty," "probabilities," and so on. The search for hard truths is a frustrating one. This in itself is a lesson. The analogies and metaphors the Prussian philosopher provides to help understand the nature of war are not based on chess, but reflect "a duel on a larger scale," "a pair of wrestlers," "commerce," a "collision of living forces," or a "game of chance." Formulating strategy presupposes "an animate object that *reacts*," and moreover, reacts unpredictably. This equates to André Beufre's definition of strategy as the "art of the dialectic of two opposing wills using force to solve their dispute."[10] Just as one actor identifies objectives, develops concepts and allocates resources, so does the potential or actual adversary. The variables in the strategic equation have now doubled, further complicating the task.

Moreover, ambiguity and uncertainty *increase* as one climbs up the strategic ladder as moral factors gain primacy over material ones.[11] The problem is that these moral factors can only be guessed at. Clausewitz explicitly refers to this transition from certainty to uncertainty in strategic analysis:

> At this point, then, intellectual activity leaves the field of the exact sciences of logic and mathematics. It then becomes an art in the broadest meaning of the term—the faculty of using judgement to detect the most important and decisive elements in the vast array of facts and situations.[12]

The strategist now faces a prospect "that Newton himself would quail before the algebraic problems it could pose."[13] Risk assessment is difficult because strategy is difficult; strategy is difficult because war is the most complex of human undertakings and filled with unknowns. Liddell Hart concludes in this regard: "This complicates calculation, because no man can exactly calculate the capacity of human genius and stupidity, nor the incapacity of will."[14] It is the inherent nature of war itself that sets the student adrift in a strategic sea of uncertainty.

GENIUS AND UNCERTAINTY

Despite this uncertainty, there is comfort in the knowledge that others have navigated these waters before. The challenge is to somehow structure or frame the strategic problem to minimize the unknown or, more importantly, to account for it. The effective strategist strives for the "closest approximation of the truth," knowing that full knowledge is an impossibility.[15]

Clausewitz identifies two preeminent qualities in a successful strategist that bear consideration:

> If the mind is to emerge unscathed from this relentless struggle with the unforeseen, two qualities are indispensable: *first, an intellect that, even in the darkest hour, retains some glimmerings of the inner light which leads to truth; and second, the courage to follow this faint light wherever it may lead* (emphasis in the original).[16]

These are the elements that define what Clausewitz terms "genius." The aspiring strategist should not be misled or discouraged by the use of the term, however. Clausewitz does not refer to the result of good genetics, but to the development of a mind through study and experience. He is clear on this point as he continues his discussion: "It is the *average result* that indicates the presence of military genius."[17] In other words, "genius" as Clausewitz describes it is not solely the unique gift of a Napoleon or Gustavus or Hannibal. It is an achievable skill, and the "inner light" can be taught and learned.

Von Moltke the Elder took up the same theme several generations later:

> What is necessary is to discover the situation, such as it is, in spite of its being surrounded by the fog of the unknown; then to *appreciate soundly* what is seen, to *guess* what is not seen, to *take a decision quickly*, *finally to act with vigour*, without hesitation[18]

The message is that an education in strategic subjects—followed by continuous historical study to maintain mental suppleness combined with vicarious experience through exercise, and actual experience—all contribute to acquiring the skills necessary for finding the "closest approximation of the truth." Strategic ability is rarely born, more often learned, but eminently achievable.

Acknowledging the theoretical uncertainties inherent in war, conflict and policy, and strategy development is an important, if unsatisfying, step in understanding risk assessment. It allows a better framing of the strategic puzzle. It is simply a matter of knowing what is not known in order to make better use of what is known and, as von Moltke suggests, to guess what is not seen. Guessing well is an inherent part of the art of Grand Strategy.

THE ENDS—WAYS—MEANS CONUNDRUM IN RISK ASSESSMENT

The essence of the challenge of strategy in general and risk assessment in particular is the core problem of relating ends to ways and means. Compounding this basic conundrum is the fact that most often the ends will be abstract while the ways and means will be relatively well defined.[19] In addition, the real test of the master of strategic art is to translate obtuse, politically couched, objectives into specific actions. This is likely to become more of a challenge as the nature, scope, and direction of potential threats multiply. Articulating the political objective in the event of a Major Theater War with conventional forces is relatively easy; however, achieving significant clarity in political objectives in multiplying crises around the world, especially against unconventional threats or where vital U.S. interests are not at stake can be increasingly problematic. One analyst notes in a critique of the U.S. foreign policy process:

> Any ambiguity in the ends-means relationship, any loss in the value roots of policy, or any failure to maintain a firm commitment to the achievement of the national purpose cannot help but deprive a foreign policy of essential meaning and effectiveness.[20]

A second related potential pitfall facing the grand strategist is the "tail wagging the dog" phenomenon. In the absence of clear political objectives or policy guidance, the means can in fact "deflect the direction of ends."[21] Or, as Michael Howard notes, "the strategy adopted is always more likely to be dictated rather by the availability of means than by the nature of the ends."[22] This is the infamous "strategy is what gets funded" trap. What gets done becomes what one has the capability of doing. The ways and means can develop a momentum of their own and the result is strategy by default, usually at the risk of desired political outcomes. The von Schlieffen Plan and America's experience in Vietnam are two stark historic examples of this effect. Strategy with regard to Afghanistan from 2003 to mid-2009 could also fall into this category.

This problem has been ascribed to the "triumph of technique" in American foreign policy. One critic specifically blames the militarization of foreign affairs during the Cold War and an emphasis on quantitative assessments based solely on capabilities.[23] In such cases, Clausewitz's "ephemeral factors" are discounted, and "consideration of political subtleties tends to be shunted aside."[24] Ferdinand Foch, writing in 1903, complained of the same phenomenon but went further: "While the moral factors were depressed as *causes* [of war], they were also suppressed as *effects*." The unintended result is that strategy can become a function solely of material factors.[25] The dramatic changes of the last two decades and the growing complexities and dimensions of current and future world problems make simplistic, capabilities-based approaches dangerous at their worst, or potentially ineffective at best. Getting ends, ways and means right has always been hard; it is becoming harder.

DETERMINING RISK

The simple definition of risk as an imbalance in ends, ways and/or means is straightforward but clearly incomplete. How does one measure the *degree* of risk in any particular strategic endeavor? This is the heart of the dilemma.

Neuchterlein and National Interests.

Risk assessment is inherent to the entire strategy formulation process. Donald Neuchterlein addresses risk in his discussion on identifying national interests and their intensities, a fundamental prerequisite to policy and strategy development. He posits sixteen criteria for assessing a particular issue as a vital interest.[26] These are divided into value and cost/risk factors[*]:

Value Factors	Cost/Risk Factors
Proximity of the danger	Economic costs of hostilities
Nature of the threat	Estimated casualties
Economic stake	Risk of protracted conflict
Sentimental attachment	Risk of enlarged conflict
Type of government and human rights	Cost of defeat or stalemate
Effect on the balance of power	Cost of public opposition
National prestige at stake	Risk of UN opposition
Support of allies	Risk of congressional opposition

* Note there is no direct correlation between value factors and cost/risk factors; they are randomly listed.

Neuchterlein advocates using a simple valuation process by rating each factor high, medium or low or even assigning numerical scores to the factors. Likewise, for a particular issue, some factors may be more important than others and can be appropriately weighted or prioritized. The factor scores are then totaled. If the value totals of a particular issue are high compared to a low or medium cost/risk valuation, then the issue probably constitutes a vital interest. Neuchterlein does not claim a scientific basis for his methodology, only that:

> [i]t provides for systematic analysis of specific foreign policy issues; it should therefore lead to better judgments about levels of interest for the United States and its antagonists and, one would hope, to wiser policies than would otherwise be the case.[27]

Thus, the process provides a simple tool that assists in the discrimination of interests in relative terms. Having determined "vitalness," the policymaker/strategist is in a better position to articulate a balanced set of ends, ways, and means in the strategy formulation process by accounting for degrees of risk upfront.

Calculated Risk.

The noted naval theorist, Admiral J.C. Wylie, took a more rigorous approach to the problem in a tongue-in-cheek article published in 1953 entitled "The Calculation of Risk."[28] The impetus for the short article apparently arose from the 1953 budget hearings in which the Army representative answered difficult questions with the rejoinder, "Mr. Congressman, that is a calculated risk." Of course no one knew what a calculated risk was or how to calculate it, so Wylie decided to try.[29] Although intended facetiously, Wylie's little paper does merit consideration in its own right. Using a series of variables and equations, he describes various strategic characteristics.[30]

P = Profit if successful

Cn = Cost if not attempted

Cf = Cost of attempt that fails

Cs = Cost of attempt that succeeds

S = Probability of success

Wylie defines risk as **P/Cf**, or the potential profit divided by the cost of a failed attempt. As long as this is greater than 1, the enterprise (or strategy) is "encouraged"; likewise, if less than 1, "discouraged." These machinations result in general determining equations:

If P x S < Cf (1-S) then "no go"

If P x S > Cf (1-S) then "go"

These equations describe what is already known instinctively: If the payoff times the probability of success is greater than the cost of failure times the probability of failure, the result is a winning strategy.

Risk is further defined by an equation:

Cf/Cs < S/(1-S)

That is, the cost of a failed attempt over the cost of a successful attempt must be less than the probability of success divided by the probability of failure.

Having had his fun with the reader, Wylie further stipulates that "To insure success in its use, there is only one condition that must be met: the factors involved must never be expressed in arithmetic quantities. That would blunt the fine edge of judgment and obscure the true balance of intangibles." Wylie clearly subscribes to the Clausewitzian notions of uncertainty and unpredictability in war; he makes this clear in his important and short book, *Military Strategy: A General Theory of Power Control*. In it he further admonishes the reader to plan for a complete spectrum of strategies in order to have a "reserve" of strategies for the inevitable changes that will occur. Wylie also warns that "the player who plans for only one strategy runs a great risk simply because his opponent soon detects the single strategy—and counters it…planning for certitude is the greatest of all military mistakes…"[31] Wylie's reserve of strategies is essentially conceptual hedging for uncertainty with its inherent risk. This, to borrow from operational art, is planning for strategic branches and sequels or for potential developments requiring adjustments in ends, ways, or means as a particular strategy is implemented

Although Wylie's formulations were intended to ridicule early whiz kids, he actually produced a relatively sophisticated approach to a difficult concept. For example, an examination of a study prepared by the CIA to address risk assessment and management of threats to security uses an identical formulation.[32] Defining risk as the potential of damage or loss to an asset, the study assesses the level of risk as the impact of loss or damage to the asset and the likelihood (probability) that a specific vulnerability could be exploited by a particular threat.[33] The formulation is defensive in nature, since it is addressing security protection issues. Nevertheless, it equates exactly to

Wylie's **Cf (1-S)**, that is, the **Cost of Failure times the Probability of Failure**. Strategy and risk assessment are indeed eternal.[34]

Risk Management.

The process of risk assessment is dynamic in nature over time and circumstance. That is, the variables are in constant flux. Risk assessment is simply the constant effort to identify and correct imbalances among the key variables. The first ability of the strategist is to recognize when variables change. The second is to adjust the remaining variables to account for the "delta" or, as it has been defined, the risk. This is known as risk management. In simplest terms, the strategist has several clear options:[35]

Modify Ends. When the price to achieve a particular objective is too high or the ability to affect a "center of gravity" is limited, it may become necessary to reduce the overall objective to more realistic terms. Examples include the decision to forego a cross-channel attack in 1942 in favor of North Africa, or accepting a lesser objective than the unification of the Korean peninsula after the Chinese intervention. Afghanistan is another example. Is the objective to establish a viable and self-sustaining democracy in the country or simply to ensure Afghanistan does not become a sanctuary for terrorists? The answer to that question has immense implications for "ways" and "means."

Modify Means. An increase or reallocation of resources may affect the ability to implement a strategy and achieve the objective. This is, however, not simply a quantitative solution. A definition of resources includes unpredictable and changeable elements as well. For example, public support of a particular policy/strategy is a key consideration in a democracy and must be accounted for even if difficult to measure. Vietnam is a classic example of not adequately modifying means by calling up the reserves and generating sufficient public support for the effort. More recently, the early failure to recognize the nature of the insurgency in Iraq, resulting in insufficient forces to deal with it, also reflects this part of the problem. The "surge" modified the "means" available and enabled a successful counterinsurgency strategy. In Afghanistan, COMISAF's Initial Assessment clearly establishes this linkage as well: "A 'properly resourced' strategy provides the means deemed necessary to accomplish the mission with *appropriate and acceptable risk*" (emphasis in the original).[36] To emphasize this point, General McChrystal goes on to say:

> Failure to provide adequate resources also risks a longer conflict, greater casualties, higher overall costs, and ultimately, a critical loss of political support. Any of these risks, in turn, are likely to result in mission failure.[37]

Modify Ways. Assuming that the objective is sound and resources are adequate, there will likely be multiple ways to achieve the desired end state. Use of the various elements of national power (political, military, economic, informational) in differing combinations with varying emphases may enhance the ability to achieve the same overall objective. The Kosovo case serves as a good example of modifying ways during a conflict: Having endured extended bombing during the one-dimensional air operation, Milosevic still showed no intention of withdrawing from Kosovo. However, the combination of the deployment of Task Force Hawk and increasing information about planning for possible ground options by the Allied Command Europe Rapid Reaction Corps (ARRC) coupled with expanded targeting are thought to have contributed to Milosevic's decision to withdraw forces. The debate over how to implement strategy in Afghanistan also reflects this. Do we target al Qaeda in their sanctuaries or conduct a classic counterinsurgency in Afghanistan itself?

Reassess the Risk. Over time some of the going-in assumptions may be proven invalid. Additional information may become available or gaps in knowledge filled. The strategist needs to recognize the potential strategic effect of more or less information, recognizing that the 100% solution will always be elusive due to the "ephemeral factors." It is important to reemphasize that this process is dynamic and "at once abstract and rational, [and] must be capable of synthesizing both psychological and material data."[38] Indeed, one man's risk is another man's certitude and therefore grist for the continuously grinding strategic mill.

Five Patterns of Strategy for Risk Assessment and Management.

André Beaufre addresses the "ends-means" conundrum in his classic book *Introduction to Strategy*. His intent is to provide a series of models, what he calls patterns of strategy, to assist in the process of strategic thinking.[39] The models are intended to show how various and fundamentally differing strategies can spring from the dynamic relationship between ends, ways, and means. These five patterns are macro-descriptors, and it is clear to see that countless variations are possible.

Ends Moderate, Means Large. This is described as a strategy of "direct threat"; nuclear deterrence strategy is given as example of this pattern.

Ends Moderate, Means Limited. Consisting of a pattern of "indirect pressure," this pattern is useful when freedom of action is limited. It emphasizes political, diplomatic, and economic elements of power at the expense of direct military action. It models the basis of Soviet strategy during the Cold War; that is, avoiding direct military confrontation with the United States.

Ends Important, Ways Limited (Low Freedom of Action), Means Limited. This pattern constitutes a combination of "direct threat" and "indirect pressure" applied in successive actions and reflects the strategy of indirect approach as described by Liddell Hart. It is most appropriate to nations strong defensively but with limited resources.

Ends Important, Ways Unlimited (High Freedom of Action), Means Inadequate. This reflects a strategy of protracted war but at a low level of military intensity. It is the theoretical basis for Mao Tse-Tung's theory of protracted struggle.

Ends Important, Means Unlimited. This traditional pattern is characterized by "violent conflict aiming at military victory." Beaufre describes it as the classic strategy of the Napoleonic era with Clausewitz as its principle theorist.

With these five patterns of strategy as a basis, Collins addresses risk specifically with seven examples of how to balance the strategic equation:[40]

- Eliminate waste [modifying ways and/or means]
- Compress objectives [modifying ends]
- Adjust strategy [modifying ways]
- Augment assets [modifying means]
- Reduce ends and increase means [modifying ends and means]
- Bluff [adversary misinterprets your ends, ways, means]
- Give up on the objective [the ultimate modification of ends]

Intended as examples, achieving strategic balance and hence strategic effectiveness may require application of one, more, or other creative elements to induce change in the strategic equation.

Readiness And Risk.

There do exist detailed and rigorously institutionalized processes for measuring risk within the U.S. defense establishment. The roots of these processes spring from the era of McNamara and the introduction of systems analysis to defense planning. In general, these methodologies represent an attempt to account institutionally for the unknown and help to "guess well." For example, as part of the Joint Strategy Review Process, a number of products result "that inform the Chairman's advice development and directive activities."[41] One of these products is the Chairman's Risk Assessment (CRA), which fulfills one of the Chairman's Title 10 responsibilities.[42] This is an annual classified report from the Chairman through the Secretary of Defense to the Congress outlining "the nature and magnitude of strategic and military risk in executing the missions called for in the [National Military Strategy]."[43] The CRA also addresses mitigation efforts. This in turn is informed in part by the scenario driven *Joint Quarterly Readiness Review* (JQQR), part of the Chairman's Readiness System.[44] Bureaucratically and institutionally, at least in the Department of Defense, strategic risk is thus related closely to readiness. However, there is no similar system in place for assessing risk in national strategy or "whole government" approaches to strategic challenges. This again, ensures a larger measure of "art" versus "science" in the process at the highest levels of policy making and strategy formulation.

CONCLUSION

Assessing and managing strategic risk is an inherently inexact process. It encompasses a combination of inputs, both material and moral, that defy empirical resolution. Weighing these inputs, identifying possible outcomes, and planning for uncertainty should be done with the clear understanding that a complete solution is impossible to achieve but always striven for. Once a strategy is developed, the most important strategic skill and the true mark of strategic "genius" is accounting for potential change and recognizing actual change in a timely enough manner to adjust the strategic variables and thereby ensure a valid strategic equation oriented firmly on achieving the political objectives at hand. This is increasingly difficult to do in a dynamically changing strategic environment with myriad conventional and unconventional threats, challenges, actors, and unclear potential effects. This is why the development and execution of strategy is primarily an art and why the requirement for developing masters of that art is so essential. As Colin Gray notes, "In historical practice, uncertainty, chance and risk assuredly attend war and warfare, but they are simply conditions under which strategically educated leaders must labor."[45] Indeed, these chapters are intended to help the reader become "strategically educated." In the end though, the essential elements of strategic risk are unchanged through the ages and consist in the proper balancing of ends, ways, and means to achieve the desired strategic outcome. Understanding that fundamental relationship and "guessing well" through study, exercise, and experience will ensure that assessing and managing strategic risk rises above simply "the comfort level of strategic planners." A gastrointestinal assessment is not good enough. It never was.

ENDNOTES - CHAPTER 5

1. Carl von Clausewitz, *On War*, Michael Howard and Peter Paret, eds., Princeton, NJ: Princeton University Press, 1976, pp. 178-179.

2. Henry C. Bartlett, G. Paul Holman, Jr., and Timothy E. Somes, "The Art of Strategy and Force Planning," in *Strategy and Force Planning*, The Strategy and Force Planning Faculty, ed., U.S. Naval War College, Newport, RI: Naval War College Press, 1995, p. 20.

3. John M. Collins, *Grand Strategy: Principles and Practices*, Annapolis, MD: Naval Institute Press, 1973, p. 5.

4. Clausewitz, pp. 81, 92, 585.

5. B.H. Liddell Hart, *Strategy*, 2nd Ed., New York: Meridian, 1991, pp. 322-323. Liddell Hart sounds here very much like Clausewitz. See Clausewitz, *On War*, p. 177, "A prince or general can best demonstrate his genius by managing a campaign exactly to suit his objectives and resources, doing neither too much nor too little."

6. Clausewitz, pp. 92-95 for a discussion of "ways."

7. Arthur F. Lykke, "Defining Military Strategy," *Military Review,* Vol. 69, No. 5, May 1989, pp. 2-8.

8. Graham Allison and Philip Zelikow, *Essence of Decision: Explaining the Cuban Missile Crisis*, 2nd Ed., New York: Longman, 1999, pp. 111-120.

9. David Jablonsky, *Why is Strategy Difficult?* Carlisle, PA: Strategic Studies Institute, U.S. Army War College, June 1992.

10. André Beaufre, *An Introduction to Strategy*, New York: Praeger, 1965, p. 20.

11. Clausewitz, pp. 178, 586.

12. *Ibid.*, p. 585.

13. *Ibid.*, pp. 112, 586. Attributed to Napoleon, it is interesting that Clausewitz uses it in support of two different discussions: one on "Military Genius" and the other on the "Scale of the Objective" and the "Effort To Be Made."

14. Liddell Hart, p. 323.

15. *Ibid.*

16. Clausewitz, p. 102.

17. *Ibid.*, p. 103.

18. Von Moltke is quoted here in Ferdinand Foch, *The Principles of War*, New York: Holt, 1920, p. 17.

19. Roger S. Whitcomb, *The American Approach to Foreign Affairs: An Uncertain Tradition*, Westport, CT: Praeger, 2001, p. 71.

20. *Ibid.*

21. *Ibid.*

22. Michael Howard, "British Grand Strategy in World War I," in Paul Kennedy, ed., *Grand Strategies in War and Peace,* New Haven, CT: Yale University Press, 1991, p. 32.

23. Whitcomb, p. 72.

24. *Ibid.*

25. Foch, p. 3.

26. Donald E. Neuchterlein, *America Overcommitted: United States National Interests in the 1980s*, Lexington, KY: University Press of Kentucky, 1985, pp. 18-28. Note that there is no direct correlation between value and cost/risk factors; they are randomly listed.

27. *Ibid.*, p. 28.

28. J.C. Wylie, "The Calculation of Risk," *United States Naval Institute Proceedings*, July 1953, p. 725.

29. See the introduction by John B. Hattendorf in J.C. Wylie, *Military Strategy: A General Theory of Power Control*, Annapolis, MD: Naval Institute Press, 1989, p. xxvii.

30. I have modified the variables for greater ease of understanding.

31. Wylie, *Military Strategy*, pp. 71-72.

32. Center for CIA Security, *Analytical Risk Management*, December 1998.

33. *Ibid.*, p. 29.

34. A reference to Chapter 13, "Strategy Eternal," in Colin S. Gray, *Modern Strategy*, Oxford, UK: Oxford University Press, 1999.

35. Bartlett, Holman and Somes, p. 19.

36. General Stanley McChrystal, *COMISAF's Initial Assessment*, August 30, 2009, p. 2-20.

37. *Ibid.*, p. 2-21.

38. Beaufre, p. 29.

39. *Ibid.*, pp. 26-29.

40. Collins, pp. 6-7.

41. CJSCI 3100.01B, *Joint Strategic Planning System*, December 12, 2008, p. B-6.

42. *Ibid.*, p. A-1.

43. *Ibid.*, p. B-8.

44. CJSCI 3100.01D, *Chairman's Readiness System*, December 10, 2004, Current as of June 12, 2008, p. A-2.

45. Colin S. Gray, *After Iraq: The Search for a Sustainable National Security Strategy*, Carlisle, PA: Strategic Studies Institute, U.S. Army War College, January 2009, p. 22.

CHAPTER 6

CONTINUITY AND CHANGE IN WAR

J. Boone Bartholomees, Jr.

Continuity and change are part of war; professionals must be comfortable with both. Change in warfare is ubiquitous. Some changes are random, but some occur in cycles or patterns that make general estimates—not predictions—possible. By examining history, we can use those cycles and patterns to provide insights into the conduct of war in the future. Conversely, although change is an invariable feature of war, so is continuity—a fact that is often overlooked as people who generally believe they understand war try to anticipate or keep up with the latest change. In some respects, the more war changes, the more apparent the continuity becomes. By understanding the continuities, we may prepare ourselves for the predictable. The U.S. military establishment and defense pundits seem enamored with the concept of change. They often belittle advocates of continuity as conservative troglodytes bent on keeping warfare firmly within their comfort zone by denying or resisting change. That, of course, can be the case; however, it is also true that advocates of continuity may see as half-full the same glass that self-proclaimed change advocates see as half-empty. The difference is one of perception, interpretation, and emphasis. In either case, professionals should understand the role of change *and* continuity in war.

The very nature of war is the single most steadfast element of continuity. Broadly described (not defined), war is a violent interactive contest between at least two groups of thinking human opponents acting simultaneously and in ignorance (to varying degrees) of the plans, actions, intentions, and even motives or goals of their opponent. Each is trying to impose his will on the other, and each is free to use whatever ways or means he can imagine or muster, bounded only by the limits of his own cultural or ethical framework, those "rules" or traditions he is willing to accept, and the realities of science and production. This was true of the first war, and it is true today.

Specific elements of war's general nature are equally unchanging. War must involve violence. Conflict without violence—physical violence, not emotional violence, virtual violence, or even the threat of violence—is not war. Making somebody feel awful (emotional violence) may be grounds for divorce, but it is not war. Virtual violence refers to the assault of electrons on electrons—in common parlance, hacking, although that term downplays significantly both the sophistication of the potential assaults and the magnitude of the potential results. Some claim attacks on national computer systems that control air traffic, significant economic activity, power grids, or other vital functions are acts of war. That may be so—the decision is a policy issue, and can go either way—but the act itself is not war and becomes war only if somebody decides to employ physical violence in retaliation, prevention, or anticipation of a cyber attack. The day-to-day exchange of hacking assaults that goes on around the world among private individuals, corporations, and countries may be intense and high-stake, but it is not war, at least in part because it involves no physical violence. For example, many analysts portrayed the recent denial of service attacks on PayPal and credit card companies in support of Wikileaks as modern acts of civil disobedience—nobody characterized them as war or even acts of war. Similarly, removing the threat of force from consideration in a discussion of the nature of war goes against many conventional modern definitions/understandings of war. However, the threat of violence is a normal diplomatic tool—like war, it is a continuation of political intercourse with the addition of other means. Should, and only if, violence actually follows the threat does war exist. Threatening war with all its implications for deterrence and coercion is a valid use of military power, but not every use of military power is war. On a scale of potential political maneuvers, threats of force still fall within the realm of diplomacy; it is analogous to threatening to impose sanctions or an embargo—potentially useful, but completely different from actually carrying out the threat.

There are various words for forceful interaction without physical violence, the best of which is probably competition. Competition is a part of life and a normal condition for states; however, not all competition is war, and any definition of war that includes nonviolent forms of competition makes the concept of war indistinguishable from competition, and thus meaningless. The expressions "trade war" or "war on poverty" use a different and distinct definition of war that simply implies use of maximum effort to achieve an objective.[1] The fact that you are trying hard may technically allow you to use the word "war," but it does not fit the military or national security meaning of that word. Without physical violence, there is never true war. Conversely, the use of physical violence does not automatically turn something into a war, so the war on drugs and gang wars can both be very physically violent; however, society considers both to be criminal activities in which violence is illegitimate and unusual, not as real wars that feature legitimate violence. As one of its defining elements, physical violence is an unchanging part of war.

War has always been (and will continue to be) conducted by/between groups. This is significant for two reasons. The first is that groups provide a scale that is essential for war. Regardless of how violent, physical confrontations between individuals are fights, not wars. Even small groups involved in violent physical confrontations do not rise to the status of war—there is just some unstated threshold below which violent conflict exists but simply is not war. Some political scientists in an attempt to quantify war have tried to establish a number of casualties or casualties per year that characterizes a war.[2] This is largely an attempt to bound larger studies rather than actually define war; however, such attempts do point out that some scale is necessary to have a true war. To an extent, this relates to the second reason the participation of groups in war is significant. Groups provide the social and political legitimacy that elevates violence from murder to war. It is the sanction of recognized political groups that makes war an honorable undertaking rather than a criminal act. A cynic might say it gives ethical and/or legal cover, but legitimization is extremely important.

The groups that fight wars are often states, but that is not necessarily a prerequisite. Increasingly we see nonstate actors fighting true wars against states. States continue to have difficulty with that notion, and seldom recognize nonstate actors as legitimate wagers of war. This (along with psychological factors rooted in the above distinction between legal war and murder) is why terrorists see themselves as warriors fighting for a righteous cause, and governments see terrorists as common, if very dangerous, criminals. The rules of war—traditional and under international treaty law—apply imperfectly if at all to nonstates. State and nonstate actors tend to be so completely different in terms of goals, cultures, and means that there is an automatic asymmetry in virtually every aspect of their relationship. There are no established procedures for negotiating conflict termination with nonstate actors—an action that would acknowledge some of the characteristics of a state and thus grant more status than states are likely to accept. None of that, however, changes the fact that groups—state or nonstate—fight wars.

The Prussian theorist Carl von Clausewitz identified three elements of war that he considered "its dominant tendencies" and the basis of its nature. Today called the Clausewitzian trinity, these were "…composed of primordial violence, hatred, and enmity, which are to be regarded as a blind natural force; of the play of chance and probability within which the creative spirit is free to roam; and of its element of subordination, as an instrument of policy, which makes it subject to reason alone."[3] These natural tendencies (and thus much of the continuity in war) all reflect the basic fact that war is a distinctly human endeavor.

Modern research has disproven the assertion that only man fights intraspecies war;[4] however, man's wars are on completely different scales of size and intensity than, for example, the territorial battles of chimpanzees. Because man fights wars, human emotions are a necessary component of warfare. Thus, passion, greed, fear, courage, etc.—all immutable elements of war and reflections of its nature as a human enterprise and what Clausewitz referred to when he wrote about primordial violence, hatred, and enmity—dominate warfare and are major elements of continuity. This changes somewhat (at least in its manifestation) as man withdraws further and further from the face-to-face battlefield, a trend that has been going on for centuries as weapons ranges increase. The artilleryman firing at an unseen enemy thousands of yards away faces a lower probability of death and thus feels less passion and encounters fewer examples of courage and cowardice than the infantryman engaging at 100 meters or less. Today, when *Predator* pilots are on a completely different continent than their targets, the human element of direct personal danger that has always been a part of the nature of war may at last be changing. However, other than a few radical airpower theorists who are usually reluctant to say so openly, the author is unaware of any serious work that predicts a war completely without human contact in the near future. Even the doomsday massive nuclear exchange scenarios popular at the height of the Cold War had conventional air, ground, and sea combat occurring, especially in Europe and the North Atlantic; often such conventional fights served as the trigger for the nuclear exchange, which might be decisive but was not a singular event. If and when we do see a totally standoff, sterile war, I believe human emotions will still be involved—perhaps not to the degree experienced during direct combat, but certainly in the political arena, where ego, ambition, avarice, cowardice, and courage will continue to play their roles. Thus, human emotions will remain elements of war.

In his theory, Clausewitz gave what is really an expansion of the second element of the trinity—the play of chance and probability—when he identified fog and friction as part of the nature of war. These concepts, so often stated together that they have become almost inseparable in common military parlance, are, in fact, distinct elements. "Fog" is the notion that nothing in war is known for certain—or, in Clausewitz's words, "the general unreliability of all information." He likened the resulting uncertainty to viewing something at twilight, through a fog, or by moonlight. Although it is traditional (and supported by comments elsewhere in the text) to consider this a slam on intelligence, it is obvious he was really writing about both friendly and enemy information. One simply cannot know exactly what is happening. Reports are wrong, enemy (and friendly) movements are misinterpreted, or things happen unobserved. The result is that "whatever is hidden from full view in this feeble light has to be guessed at by talent, or simply left to chance."[5] Man has made concerted efforts over centuries to reduce or eliminate fog—binoculars, flares, searchlights, standardized report formats, night vision devices, the Global Positioning System, satellite imagery, Blue Force Tracker, etc., are all examples. Each helps somewhat, but many of the most promising create their own forms of uncertainty, often unrelated to the problem they address. For example, too much information can be as crippling to a commander as too little. Knowing the location and even direction of movement of a unit does not tell anything about its intent or mission. Moreover, ground commanders of the past did not need to worry about the power supply to their headquarters, the maintenance status of hundreds of items of electronics, or bandwidth restrictions.

"Friction" is the idea that things go wrong in war. It is sort of Murphy's Law on steroids—instead of anything that can (which implies some things cannot) go wrong, will go wrong, Clausewitz would say everything is likely to go wrong, or at least differently than planned. As a man of his time, Clausewitz liked to give examples or draw parallels to physics, so he compared this aspect of war to the natural friction of moving objects. However, again the concept is really friction on steroids, since in war no movement is required to produce friction—things can actually go wrong without anybody doing or trying to do anything. For example, the weather can change with significant consequences but totally outside the control of anybody, or a vehicle can break down for no apparent reason while sitting in the motor pool. Clausewitz, however, did relate much of the friction to human activity, and he gave the useful comparison to working in a resistant medium (like walking in water). He also wrote, "Moreover, every war is rich in unique episodes. Each is an uncharted sea, full of reefs." Each reef represents a potential disaster through which the commander must steer without sure knowledge of the placement or even presence of the reefs. It is possible to at least partially overcome friction, but only practice and experience tell the general what is possible and what is not in war.[6] Discipline, battle drills, standard operating procedures, and spare parts/maintenance float equipment are all common processes designed to reduce or mitigate friction. Each helps—none solves the problem.

Fog and friction are part of the larger continuity in war that Clausewitz called the play of chance and probability.[7] Because things are unknown, because things go wrong, and because commanders have different levels of ability, war is usually little better than an informed bet and frequently a gamble. A military genius may have better odds than a mere mortal, and the probability of success increases as numbers, technology, training, morale, etc., pile up disproportionately on one side or the other, but the outcome is still always unknown. The underdog always has a chance—Manuel Noriega's chance of being struck by lightning may have been better than his chances of defeating the U.S. invasion of Panama, but it still existed. This is an unchanging element of war.

Finally, and famously, Clausewitz pointed out the central function of politics in war. This is the third element of the trinity, and his assertion of the political nature of war has held up better than the limits critics have tried to place on his work (primarily, that it is state-centric and not applicable for times before the modern state or in cases in which one side is a nonstate actor). Politics is the very nature of war. Man in groups resolves issues through political processes—whether the primitive interpersonal relations of a tribe or the highly structured processes of the modern nation-state. War is one potential aspect of those political processes. Political intercourse continues after the outbreak of war, and political processes control the conduct of war. Clausewitz likened war to a form of expression during political discourse. The fact that one was fighting did not change the underlying politics—it was simply another form of expression. Clausewitz put it thus: "Its [war's] grammar, indeed, may be its own, but not its logic."[8] This is a constant and extremely significant part of war.

For centuries, man has tried to determine why wars are won and lost. Several authors have developed, and many armies have adopted lists of words or phrases—usually called Principles of War—that describe strategic or operational best practices.[9] These may serve as an element of continuity. Certainly, soldiers from earlier generations thought so. The German general and radical "young Turk" reformer of the 1920s, Joachim von Stülpnagel, wrote, "The great principles of war remain unaltered; only their implementation changes in accordance with the age."[10] Thus, mass was a valid principle of war during the Punic Wars, and it is still valid today even if the ways and means of achieving it have changed. In the distant past, one massed by physically gathering troops; today a commander can achieve a similar effect by massing fires while the troops/firing units remain dispersed (or operate from a different medium like air or sea) and simply project their power to the desired spot. In either case, the principle of mass does not require that units, systems, or troops be physically concentrated, but that the commander "[c]oncentrate the effects of combat power at the decisive place and time."[11] While one should not push this too far, there may be eternal truisms like the Principles of War about the conduct of war that we should recognize in an essay on continuity and change.

If the nature of war (the logic in Clausewitz' words) remains the same, it is equally obvious that the conduct of war (its grammar) changes. How one fights a war is never a static, predictable process. Strangely, some of the changes in war occur within the elements of continuity. For example, war as a political act is an element of continuity, but the expression of that political process — the question of why men fight wars, if you wish — is very dynamic. History has seen cases of conquest for purposes of loot or power, wars of religion, colonial wars, nationalistic wars, wars of liberation, ideological wars, and mercantile wars, or wars over economic issues. Those are just some of the major categories — within each are numerous nuanced gradations of purpose/intent. In general, changes in why men fight reflect societal changes in a few basic elements — political ideology or philosophy, economics, and religion are some of the most prominent — and the acceptable means of pursuing goals rising from those elements. Thus, things like the introduction of Laws of War — essentially prearranged legal limits on the conduct of war — and Just War criteria — morally acceptable values about the resort to and conduct of war reflected and codified in international treaties like the United Nations (UN) Charter — change both the legitimate reasons and ways in which men fight.

Other than the changes inside the areas of general continuity mentioned above, change in the conduct of war tends to occur in two major categories: first, how wars are fought (ways), and next, with what wars are fought (means). How wars are fought includes issues like who participates, using what doctrine, in what type of campaign, and under what strategic concept. Thus, war necessarily changes as the composition of the military forces fighting it change. There is a difference between a tribal force, a village or territorial militia, a regular army, a mercenary army, a guerrilla army, a terrorist network, and a super-empowered individual. Each has had its day, and each fought (or fights) its wars in a different manner. Compounding this issue is the match or mismatch in perception and style of different types of forces as they face off. Thus, a regular force facing a guerrilla force encounters difficulties it would not experience if it fought another regular army. All of that produces outcomes that may appear as changes in the general characteristics of war or as the characteristics of the specific war under consideration.

Doctrine is important and directly related to the type of force that is fighting the war. For example, the specific military theories about how regular forces should fight are very different from theories of how guerrilla forces should fight. The doctrine reflects the tools expected to be available and the most probable situations the force is likely to face. It is the military equivalent of tactical, or in some cases operational, best practices, and it does make a difference in how one fights wars. Doctrine changes to reflect changed circumstances. The ancient Greeks formed in very close order with shields overlapping and used the mass of their formation to achieve battlefield dominance.[12] The Romans deployed in a checkerboard formation with room between soldiers for them to use their individual skills.[13] The Byzantines faced a significant cavalry threat, so they formed their infantry in a huge hollow square to provide a place of refuge and a base of maneuver for their cavalry.[14] The story of the evolution of the infantry line as gunpowder weapons improved is familiar. In each case, the doctrine defines certain characteristics (some more significant than others) of war in its age, and as the doctrine changes, the characteristics of war change.

The issues of what type of campaign and using what strategic concept are important and directly related. One approach is to try to win by destroying the enemy's fielded forces in a single decisive battle (a strategy of annihilation). Alternatively, one might achieve the same goal by whittling down the enemy's army over time (a strategy of attrition). In either case, the underlying objective is to make the enemy powerless by removing his military capability. Other strategies try to break the will of the enemy government or people over time by raids, bombing, or other means (strategies of exhaustion or erosion). Each general strategic category has numerous potential sub-strategies, and innovative commanders constantly create more. For example, under the general category of exhaustion, there are myriad strategies of the weak that try to win by not losing, erode political support of the government, or achieve political goals some other way. Nonstate actors can opt for any of the above or supplement the list with other concepts that suit their situation and resources. Each of these strategic choices changes the character of the immediate war, and that character can change rapidly and dramatically when the sides independently make radically different individual choices.

When one considers changes in the means of war, technology immediately comes to mind. One of the primary characteristics that distinguishes man from other animals is the use of tools. It was only natural for early man to apply tools to warfare. Another characteristic of man is innovation—we strive to find easier, cheaper, faster, more efficient, and effective ways of doing things. Thus, the application of innovation to weapons technology was inevitable. The result has been a gradual improvement in weapons that has accelerated dramatically in the modern era, but has always been present. We might look longingly at simpler, less complicated days when war seemed to be easier, but if they actually ever existed, they are gone forever.

Change in weapons technology has not followed a straight line. In fact, only the 20th century and the first decade of the 21st century, have seen constant exponential improvement in military technology. We went thousands of years using the spear, bow, sling, sword, and shield as our primary weapons, with only slight variations in design. Yet within that constancy, one can see cycles of change. The offensive or the defensive dominated as different societies applied technology to suit their cultures or strategic circumstances. Castles and fortifications had their periods as the dominant aspect of warfare, only to eventually fall to siegecraft techniques or new technology (like gunpowder). Thus, the effect of technological change has not been uniform or constant. In a sense, while the technology changes in a predictable manner, its application has not necessarily followed suit—people seem to continuously "reinvent the wheel" and bring back tactics, techniques, and procedures familiar from earlier days. One of the proposals for restructuring the U.S. Army for future war looks strangely reminiscent of the Roman legion, and Renaissance writers like Niccolò Machiavelli openly tried to reinstitute the same antique formation out of nostalgia, if for no other reason.[15] Nevertheless, technological change is one of the most easily recognizable elements of change in war.

Within that change, however, there are elements of continuity. Military technology has characteristics—call them rules, if you like—that seem to remain constant over time, space, and culture:

1. Once introduced, if technology proves effective, it tends to linger despite the introduction of other, newer, perhaps better technology (giving a high-low mix problem). The spear is a good example: It was probably the first intentionally designed weapon, but people were still using it in World War II. The Polish cavalry was armed with lances (although this was against government policy, and the legend of them attacking German tanks with spears is wrong); the British home guard also carried spears in the bleakest days of the war when other weapons were unavailable.[16] Similarly, the modern bayonet, still in use by many armies, is the linear descendent of the spear, and as a distinct bit of technology has been around since the 17th century, although it long ago lost its true utility.

2. New technology often gains ascendancy on the battlefield, but that ascendancy is never permanent. The introduction of significant technology automatically initiates a search for some means to counter, negate, minimize, or mitigate its effectiveness. Although a technology may maintain the upper hand for centuries, people eventually arrive at countertechnological or doctrinal solutions that either nullify a technology completely or at least make it no longer independently decisive. Frequently, the counter is simple, cheap, and easier to proliferate than the technology it

counters. Thus, heavy cavalry lost its ascendancy during the Middle Ages to simple combinations of disciplined infantry and archers. The deployment of tanks in the anti-tank role, and the eventual invention of relatively cheap anti-tank missiles, removed the tank from the decisive role it had achieved early in World War II. Likewise, poison gas begot the gas mask; the high-walled castle fell victim to artillery; and field fortifications countered the battlefield effect of rapid-fire artillery on infantry. However, remember Rule 1—once introduced, technology lingers—so all those old technologies are still around and at least potentially effective on the field.

3. There have been relatively few truly revolutionary technological breakthroughs in warfare. Gunpowder, the internal combustion engine (the truck, tank, etc.), the airplane and submarine that added new dimensions to the battle space (although many historians look at them as applications of the engine), and the atomic bomb are really the only ones that have proven to be revolutionary, and the gunpowder revolution took long enough that it might be considered evolutionary. Advocates tout information technology as the next revolutionary advance in warfare, and it holds promise of fundamentally altering the way we fight. There is no denying it is an important and extremely significant advance. However, we have yet to see the true impact of information technology on the battlefield, and remember Rule 2—the counter for information technology may be cheap and effective.

4. Technology depends absolutely on doctrine. One can have the best technology in the world and still manage to lose by failing to use it to the best advantage. Thus, the Allies had more and arguably better tanks than the Germans during the blitz in Western Europe, but they employed them in a way that nullified their potential effectiveness. Moreover, doctrine alone may be decisive in a world of equal technology. The Romans were able to use disciplined infantry (a doctrinal solution) and technological flexibility to rule the world for centuries without a significant technological advantage over their numerous opponents. Doctrine allows blending of perhaps old or low technologies into new and very lethal systems. This is particularly true when the new system is especially difficult for existing military systems to counter. This phenomenon has recently acquired the grand title of asymmetry, but it is an ancient rather than a newly discovered aspect of war. One example of this at work is the invasion of Europe by the Huns under Attila in the mid-5th century. The nomadic steppe people combined their natural horsemanship with the compound bow—both military technologies known to Western civilization for millennia—to create an army so mobile and lethal that it was essentially invincible. The Huns (like other steppe nomads that plagued the West for centuries) had unmatched strategic mobility, so they appeared where least expected, and tactically European forces could not catch or pin them while being vulnerable to their archery.

5. Technology works best against opponents who, for whatever reason, cannot equal or counter it. To continue the Hun example, their European/Byzantine enemies serve as an excellent example here. Culturally, they were neither equestrians nor archers, and neither their infantry forces nor their cavalry could catch or hurt the Huns. The Byzantines bought them off and/or hired them as mercenaries until they could learn the necessary skills to face them on near equal terms.[17] Similarly, the Great Wall of China worked because the barbarians it was designed to stop had no effective way to breach such an impressive fortification. When the Mongols arrived outside the wall with Persian engineers, it fell instantly, and the Mongols established a long-term domination of China (Yuan dynasty, 1271-1368). After the Ming dynasty rebuilt and strengthened the wall, it took the Manchu (who established the Qing dynasty, 1644-1911) 2 years of effort to cross the wall, and they only succeeded when they were able to bribe a general to open the gates.[18] Similarly, Westerners opened Japan largely because Western technology was vastly superior to that of the samurai. Within a generation, the Japanese had adopted Western technology and placed themselves on at least an equal footing with the rest of the world.[19]

6. Mass sometimes beats even the best technology. In some cases, the counter to technology may be as simple as overwhelming it with numbers. Joseph Stalin is reputed to have said, "Quantity has a quality all its own," and he was right.[20] Thus, General George Custer had the better-equipped force at the Little Big Horn and lost decisively. Similarly, at Isandlwana (January 22, 1879) during the Anglo-Zulu War, about 12,000 Zulus armed with short spears overwhelmed about 1,200 British and colonial troops equipped with modern rifles.[21] That battle provides a good opportunity for a caution, however. Beginning the same day as Isandlwana and only a few miles away at Rorke's Drift, 139 British soldiers held off about 4,500 Zulus in the contrasting and perhaps intuitively normal case, in which superior technology was at least partly responsible for the defeat of a numerically hugely superior force.[22] Still, numbers can have a quality of their own.

7. Even in adequate numbers and with good doctrine, technology still has limits—especially terrain and weather. Thus, the German chief Arminius beat the Romans in the Teutoburger Wald (9 A.D.) despite Roman superiority in weapons, armor, and discipline, because he caught them in densely wooded terrain that nullified their advantages.[23] Similarly, the Scythians (descendants of another of those steppe tribes that gave Western armies fits), using their horse-mounted archers that had no chance against the Romans in hand-to-hand combat, massacred 35-40,000 legionnaires at Carrhae in 53 B.C. The Scythians were able to keep the Romans on an open plain where they could stand off and destroy the Romans with arrows without ever closing to hand-to-hand range.[24] The Mujahidin in Afghanistan in the 1980s and the North Vietnamese both beat vastly superior enemies by refusing to fight them on terms where their technological advantage might have been effective. The impressive victory in Operation DESERT STORM might have been different had the conflict occurred on terrain less perfectly suited for the coalition (and particularly North Atlantic Treaty Organization [NATO]-member) armies.

8. Technological advances have tended to expand the reach of armies (either by increasing their speed or range) or to increase the distance at which they can strike their opponent. Crossing the deadly zone—that is, closing with the enemy—has become more and more difficult. In ancient days, that zone was frequently no deeper than a man could reach with his sword or spear, and never deeper than the range of a sling or arrow. Crossing it was a matter of a quick rush, perhaps holding a shield overhead to provide some protection from arrows. Today, we talk about battle space, and the most sophisticated armies can identify, engage, and destroy opponents at strategic distances. Nevertheless, people still manage to cross the deadly zone. Yet, remember Rule 2. It is easy to imagine an enemy cloaked in the electromagnetic clutter of an urban area or other simple countermeasures effectively shrinking the deadly zone to the range of a sword—in other words, leveling the technological playing field to the most primitive common denominator.

Is it possible to predict the future balance between change and continuity in war? If so, we should be able to determine the nature and characteristics of future war. Apparently, many people believe that is possible, and they usually claim to have already done the hard intellectual work when they inform the world of their startling conclusions. Most such arguments are unconvincing. They tend to follow one of two general patterns. First is the group that predicts that the future will be a lot like today, only more so. Fourth Generation War (4GW) theory, which in some cases has already mutated to Fifth Generation War, is an excellent example.[25] After establishing a pattern of change based on questionable historical analysis, 4GW advocates analyzed war today and predicted that it was the next generation of change in war and, with slight improvements possible, represented the future of war. That may be; it is equally likely that their ideas are pure bunk. While war in the immediate future is almost certain to look like war today and war in the more distant future is almost certain to contain elements of 4GW war, it is almost equally certain that future war will not be exactly what the 4GW warriors think. The second general pattern of predicting the future of war hinges on technology. Prophets pick a technology or class of technologies they believe will dominate the future of war and dictate its characteristics. Perhaps the best historical example is the tank/armored forces advocates before World War II. More recently, the advocates of net-centric warfare made similar claims for information technology. Just like the 4GW warriors, both saw portions of their predictions come true, and both overestimated the long-term (or length of term) impact of the technology they advocated. Also, just like the 4GW warriors, technology determinists can take solace that Rule 1 still applies, and their technologies will still be present and perhaps play significant roles in future war. The caution remains that all the other rules apply as well, and those tend to moderate the long-term effect of technological solutions.

In sum, nobody knows the future, and it takes extreme arrogance to claim to do so. However, that is not a reason to ignore people who have invested time and energy in thinking about the future of war. They may be right, and almost certainly some (and perhaps much) of what they say is right. We do need to think hard about the future of war. Prudent people will study the arguments and analyze the evidence, develop their own conclusions, realize they will be wrong, but hope Michael Howard was right when he said that military institutions never get the doctrine right in peacetime, and that does not matter—if they just get it close enough.[26]

The key to warfare, and what students of the profession should dedicate themselves to studying, is understanding the relationship between technology, doctrine, the changing characteristics of warfare, and its immutable nature. We need to understand those historical relationships to approximate an understanding of warfare today and in the future. Clausewitz said, "The first, the supreme, the most far-reaching act of judgment that the statesman and commander have to make is to establish by that test [i.e., that it is an instrument of policy] the kind of war on which they are embarking; neither mistaking it for, nor trying to turn it into, something that is alien to its nature."[27] Warfare in every age has distinct characteristics. The offense or the defense may be dominant; a single technology or doctrine may have the upper hand; operations may be concentrated or dispersed; war may be the domain of small professional forces or the province of drafted mass armies or even of paramilitary groups that do not fit traditional definitions of armies; military forces may not even be engaged in traditional combat or may fight an enemy they never see. The characteristics of the war will dictate the best force, the best technology, and the best doctrine for the situation. The strategic leaders of tomorrow need to determine what those characteristics are—we do not have to get it exactly right, just get closer to understanding the true character and nature of modern war than our potential opponents. Simply accepting the latest strategic fad with a catchy name peddled by glib pundits—regardless of their scholarly qualifications or military rank—is no substitute for deep personal study, analysis, and reflection on these issues.

ENDNOTES - CHAPTER 6

1. Merriam-Webster's *Collegiate Dictionary*, 10th Ed., and their on-line dictionary both give the first definition of war as "a state of usually open and declared armed hostile conflict between states or nations." The second part of a second meaning is "a struggle or competition between opposing forces or for a particular end (a class ~) (a ~ against disease)." Available from *www.merriam-webster.com/netdict/war*.

2. See, for example, the brief summary of several systems of categorization described on pp. 1-2, available from *www.ploughshares.ca/libraries/monitor/mons09c.pdf*.

3. Carl von Clausewitz, *On War*, Michael Howard and Peter Paret, eds. and trans., Princeton, NJ: Princeton University Press, 1976, p. 89.

4. See, for example, "Wired for War: Killer Chimps Fuel Debate on How War Began," February 2005, available from *www.world-science.net/exclusives/050209_warfrm.htm*. Also see "Wired for War . . . Is It in Our Genes?" available from *www.telegraph.co.uk/science/science-news/3317461/Apes-of-war...-is-it-in-our-genes.html*.

5. Clausewitz, p. 140.

6. *Ibid.*, pp. 119-120.

7. *Ibid.*, p. 89.

8. *Ibid.*, p. 605.

9. See, for modern example, The Joint Staff, *Joint Publication 1, Doctrine for the Armed Forces of the United States*, Washington, DC: U.S. Department of Defense, May 2, 2007 (incorporating change 1 March 20, 2009), p. I-1g and Figure I-1.

10. Joachim von Stülpnagel, "Gedanken über den Krieg der Zukunft," 1924, quoted in Gil-li Vardi, "Joachim von Stülphagel's Military Thought and Planning," *War in History*, Vol. 17, Issue 2, April 2010, p. 199.

11. U.S. Department of the Army, *Field Manual 3-0, Operations*, Washington, DC: Headquarters U.S. Department of the Army, February 2008, Appendix A, p. A-2, available from *usacac.army.mil/cac2/fm3-0/FM_3-0_C1_(WEB)1.pdf*.

12. See Victor Davis Hanson, *The Western Way of War: Infantry Combat in Classical Greece,* Berkeley, CA: University of California Press, 1989, p. 2000.

13. See Graham Webster, *The Roman Imperial Army of the First and Second Centuries A.D.,* 3rd Ed., Norman, OK: University of Oklahoma Press, 1998.

14. See George T. Dennis, trans., *Three Byzantine Military Treatises*, Dumbarton Oaks Texts IX, Washington, DC: Dumbarton Oaks, 1985; or John Haldron, *The Byzantine Wars,* Gateshead, United Kingdom: The History Press, 2001, p. 2009.

15. Niccolò Machiavelli, *The Art of War*, New York: Da Capo Press, 1521, p. 1965.

16. Available from *www.historynet.com/polish-cavalry-charges-tanks.htm; www.avalanchepress.com/PolishCavalry.php; www.historylearningsite.co.uk/home_guard.htm*.

17. See Edward N. Luttwak, *The Grand Strategy of the Byzantine Empire,* Cambridge, MA: The Belknap Press of the Harvard University Press, 2009, pp. 17-48.

18. Available from *www.kinabaloo.com/great_wall.html*.

19. See *afe.easia.columbia.edu/japan/japanworkbook/modernhist/meiji.html*.

20. Traditionally attributed to Stalin, although difficult to verify. The Wikiquote entry on Stalin with the discussion on authenticity of quotes is actually the best on this issue. See *en.wikiquote.org/wiki/Talk:Joseph_Stalin*.

21. Available from *www.britishbattles.com/zulu-war/isandlwana.htm*.

22. Available from */www.britishbattles.com/zulu-war/rorkes-drift.htm*.

23. Available from *www.unrv.com/early-empire/teutoburg-forest.php*.

24. Available from *www.unrv.com/fall-republic/battle-of-carrhae.php*.

25. On 4GW, see the original article by William S. Lind *et al.*, "The Changing Face of War: Into the Fourth Generation," *Marine Corps Gazette*, October 1989, pp. 22-26. The best of the newer version is Thomas X. Hammes, *The Sling and The Stone: On War in the 21st Century*, St. Paul, MN: Zenith Press, 2004. For the concept of an emerging 5th generation of war, see Thomas X. Hammes, "Fourth Generation Warfare Evolves, Fifth Emerges," *Military Review*, Vol. 87, No. 3, May/June 2007, pp. 14-23.

26. Michael Howard, A. J. Wilson in the Chair, "Military Science in an Age of Peace," *The RUSI Journal*, Vol. 119, Issue 1, March 1974, p. 7, available from *dx.doi.org/10.1080/03071847409421160*.

27. Clausewitz, p. 88.

CHAPTER 7

A THEORY OF VICTORY

J. Boone Bartholomees, Jr.

The United States is developing a reputation much like Germany had in the 20th century of being tactically and operationally superb but strategically inept. Often stated as a tendency to win the war but lose the peace, this problem has a huge theoretical component that the national security community has only recently begun to address. In fact, the concept of victory is the biggest theoretical challenge facing security professionals today. We simply do not really understand what victory is and how it happens. Worse, we do not have the necessary intellectual framework to think about the problem.

Doesn't everyone instinctively understand winning and losing—or at least hasn't everyone been taught since early childhood to understand those concepts? While there is truth in that assertion, it is not completely accurate in the field of warfare. What people understand as winning comes from the context with which they are most familiar—games and sports. In sports, winning is scoring more points or going faster than the other guy, usually within some pre-established parameters like time or distance. Card games, board games, and even computer games are similar in that there are clearly established conditions for winning—even if there might be multiple sets of potential outcomes that satisfy those conditions or multiple strategies for achieving them. The problem is that the concept of winning in sports and games is completely inadequate for understanding victory in war. Whatever war is, it is neither a sport nor a game, and analogies to either of those activities always fall short. In terms of a theory of victory, the first place a sports/game analogy falls short is specifically that there are no established or even universally accepted rules or conditions for winning in war. One might counter that soldiers and statesmen know—perhaps instinctively or perhaps as a result of training and study—that defeating the enemy's army produces victory. That may often be so, although it demonstrably does not work in every case, but our knowledge and understanding stops there. How does beating the enemy's army produce victory, and what can one do when that does not work?

The problem is that the security profession lacks a basic theoretical construct within which to think about winning wars. Because of this lack of theory, mankind has fought wars for at least 5000 years without systematically understanding why they are won or lost. In a sense, victory or defeat has always been a matter of serendipity or luck or intuition or genius or sheer hard fighting rather than the result of a well-thought-out and understood intellectual exercise. Gallons of ink have been expended over the centuries on how to win wars, but that effort has largely been uninformed by even a rudimentary theory of victory. Many existing theories of war skip over what victory is and why one theoretically wins or loses, to directly address the seemingly more difficult issue of how one wins a war militarily. When theorists do address winning, it is usually in passing, as an assumption from which their analysis proceeds, or as a tangential excursion from their primary topic. Clausewitz is an exception to this broad assertion, but his musings on winning are scattered and incomplete. There is a school of thought that claims theory is not necessary for competent performance.[1] While that might explain how mankind has done without a theory of victory for so long, it does not negate the utility of theory. William C. Martel of the faculty of the Fletcher School at Tufts asserts that the theory of victory is and must be distinct from the theory of war.[2] Whether that is true or not, security professionals need to think systematically about winning. That is not to imply that military victory without luck or genius or hard fighting is either possible or desirable, or that existing theories of war are somehow wrong. They just might benefit from some supplemental thought specifically on winning and victory. Fortunately, the extant theoretical literature contains enough material that we can begin to construct a theory of victory.[3]

The author, unsurprisingly, is not alone in believing we need a theory of victory. In fact, the low-level debate that has been going on since at least the 1960s about both the meaning and possibility of victory has been substantially widened since the events of September 11, 2001. Theoretical discussions on victory and winning through the end of the Cold War tended to center around the possibility of victory in a nuclear exchange—could one really win such an exchange? Authors tended to assume both definition and understanding of victory. More recent scholarship has addressed the theory of winning more directly. The theorist Colin S. Gray wrote a monograph on the possibility of decisive victory that addresses the concept of winning, although his primary thrust is at the concept of decisiveness.[4] William Martel published a book on the theory of victory in 2007.[5] Martel acknowledges his is not a complete theory of victory, he calls it a pre-theory, but he offers an excellent start. I certainly cannot present a comprehensive theory of victory either, but I offer the following thoughts to continue the discussion and debate.

Webster's Dictionary tells us a theory is simply a plausible or generally acceptable body of principles used to explain a phenomenon. A theory should provide basic definitions, assumptions, and testable hypotheses. The first task, then, is to define winning or victory in war. To get at the definitions, we will explore some hypothesis on victory around the issues of what victory is, how victory works, who decides the winner, and based on what criteria. Finally, we will present some thoughts on how one wins a war. These will be at a theoretical level rather than the more common debate about attrition versus maneuver, direct versus indirect approaches, etc. Regrettably, this paper may pose more questions than hard, reliable answers. That reflects the nature of the topic and is perhaps inevitable at this stage of the discussion.

WHAT IS WINNING AND VICTORY?

Victory in war is at the most basic level an assessment, not a fact or condition. It is someone's opinion—or an amalgamation of opinions. In sports terms, to use one of those bad analogies I warned against, it is taking score at the end of a game, but it is done by a combination of fans, sportswriters, players, coaches, and league officials voting, each with an indeterminate degree of impact on the final result and each able to review and alter his vote at any time. Victory in war may or may not have anything to do with objective criteria like respective casualties, territory taken or lost, tons of bombs dropped, or facilities destroyed. In winning a war, those things matter—at least at some level and always in terms of their effect on perception—but what matters most is the ultimate perception of the situation, not the facts. And the perception will be of the effects, not the effort—there is no credit for trying hard. Different people, depending on their perspective, can legitimately differ in their assessment. Initial assessments of victory are often merely gut feelings, much like the Supreme Court's definition of pornography as something that depends on community values and you know when you see it. The assessment aspect complicates the issue of winning exponentially, since it introduces the uncontrolled variables of whose assessment counts, for how much, and based on what criteria. More on that later.

Related to this idea is the hypothesis that the results of war can actually be different for the opposing sides. Obviously, results from any direct interaction of two bodies will be closely related and interdependent. This is especially true of a contest between them, but because winning is an assessment, not a fact, the results of wars are independent for each side and may vary by participant. That is, the fact that one side won big does not necessarily mean its opponent lost big. It may not even mean that the other side lost at all, at least in terms of its own assessment.

Second, winning a war (as opposed to a battle or campaign) is a political condition. If war is a political act, victory at the highest levels must be defined in political terms. That is a fairly uncontroversial assertion today, but one with enormous implications. Misunderstanding or misapplying this simple concept is exactly why the United States gets criticized for winning the war but losing the peace, which is code for attaining decisive tactical and operational victories that do not produce similarly gratifying strategic results. The implication is that military victory (tactical or operational victory) without favorable political outcomes is sterile, and by any reasonable assessment that is true. But is knowing that victory is a political condition a sufficient understanding of winning? Actually, I believe it only serves to complicate or obscure the issue.

Next, and an aspect hinted at above—because it is a perception or assessment—victory or winning is heavily dependent on perspective. In a military sense, this translates into being sensitive to the level of war. It is possible to have a smashing tactical military victory that does not produce either operational or strategic results. Is that really a win? It certainly is from the point of view of the tactical commander—the view from the perspective of the operational or strategic commander might be quite different. It is this characteristic that allowed Saddam Hussein to claim victory after the First Gulf War. He suffered a huge tactical and operational loss, but his regime had survived (his strategic objective after the coalition intervened). The war was thus a strategic win for him—at least in his eyes and from his perspective. This again suggests the issue of who decides who wins and loses, which we will address later.

The characteristic of perspective allows us to think of victory in war as three tiered—tactical, operational, and strategic. Other authors have approached this categorization from different angles; for example, Martel calls his levels tactical, political-military, and grand strategic, and they do not correspond directly to the military levels.[6] While I believe coining language retards theoretical debate when accepted language exists, I do not believe Martel's categories can yet be considered widely accepted, and my terminology, based on common military usage, makes sense. The issue is not the names of the levels, but the recognition that winning differs conceptually, depending on the perspective of the action and assessor. The levels correspond to increasingly complex conceptual (if not physical) tasks.

Because winning tactically is a fairly straightforward and almost exclusively military activity, we best understand it and can generally assess it through reasonably quantifiable criteria. Measures of effectiveness like comparative casualty ratios, ground taken or lost, sorties flown, tonnage sunk, prisoners captured, etc., all count and can actually produce a reasonable estimate of victory or defeat that is likely to be widely accepted. Again, however, the assessment is based on outcomes, not effort. There are complications inherent in fighting with allies or coalition partners, and fog and friction, chance and uncertainty, mean the outcome is never guaranteed, but the measures of tactical success are well understood. Operational victory is similarly transparent at least in its purest form; the campaign succeeds or fails based on criteria that are usually well understood and quantifiable. However, strategic victory is a more complicated issue.

It is worth reemphasizing that the relationship on the subject of winning between the levels of war, although closely linked, is not linear. Tactical success does not necessarily lead to operational success, which likewise does not guarantee strategic victory. In fact, winning on one level may actually lead to or result from losing on another. In Algeria in the 1950s, the brutal methods the French used to achieve a tactical victory were decidedly (perhaps decisively) counterproductive strategically. The art of war and strategy is largely making successes at each level contribute positively to successes at the higher levels.

Which level is most important? It is tempting to respond that all are equally important, but that would be incorrect. What counts in the end is the strategic outcome. The story comes to mind of COL Harry Summers talking to a North Vietnamese officer about that war. Summers commented that the U.S. had won all the battles, and the North Vietnamese replied,"That may be so, but it is also irrelevant."[7] That is a vivid illustration of the point that strategy counts most. Tactical and/or operational successes may set the stage for strategic victory—that is, they may be facilitators, and they certainly are huge contributors in any case—but they are not necessarily sufficient by themselves to achieve victory. The prudent strategist, however, knows full well that his brilliant strategy will be incredibly more difficult and risky without tactical and operational success. There are few examples, like Nathanael Greene's Southern campaign in the American Revolution, where one can lose the battles and win the campaign and war.

Finally, as Colin Gray and William Martel both point out, victory occurs on a sliding scale—or actually multiple sliding scales. Victory and defeat, although polar opposites, are not binary. There are thousands of points along the scale that delineate degrees of success. And winning may or may not be decisive in the sense of settling the underlying political issues, again on a whole range of degrees. Martel actually uses four scales, although the one he calls "levels" is analogous to the levels of war categorization and his "change in status quo" scale is essentially a measure of decisiveness. The other two categories of "degree of mobilization for war" and "extent of post-conflict obligations" are interesting, but I am not convinced they really relate theoretically to victory as much as they relate practically to the strategist as a means test.[8] Gray uses two scales—one that might be called achievement, running from strategic advantage through strategic success to decisive victory, and a second scale called decisiveness that is a measure of how well the victory or defeat decides the issue at question.[9] This is a useful concept. In some sense the two are so closely related that decisiveness might be considered part of the definition of winning. It is, however, a separate and important concept, especially since the significant interaction is the effect between levels (not to discount the fact that one might win on one level and still not produce decisive results even at that level). So, one might win a great battlefield victory that does not decide anything either militarily in terms of the campaign or politically in terms of the war. Gray's achievement scale looks only at the positive end of the spectrum. However, just as one can succeed to varying degrees, one can fail to varying degrees. Thus, the achievement scale must be modified to add a negative component.

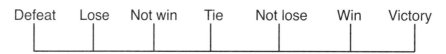

Figure 7-1. Scale of Success.

We hypothesize a scale of success that runs from defeat through losing, not winning, tying, not losing, and winning to victory with shades and gradations between each point (Figure 7-1). Victory is completely fulfilling while defeat is catastrophic, but the other possible results contain aspects of both winning and losing to at least some extent. Note that this model draws distinctions between winning and victory and losing and defeat. While the words are commonly used interchangeably, they offer a unique opportunity to distinguish important gradations that exist in the condition of success in war. The assertion here is that victory will be essentially total and probably final; that it will resolve the underlying political issues. However, it is certainly possible to succeed in a war without achieving everything one sought or resolving all the extant issues. Winning implies achieving success on the battlefield and in securing political goals, but not, for whatever reason, reaching total political success (i.e., victory). Thus, to win, one must accomplish one's immediate political goals, but not necessarily resolve all the underlying issues. Lesser levels of success reflect lesser degrees of battlefield achievement and/or lesser degrees of decisiveness in solving or resolving underlying issues. On the losing end, defeat is also a total concept. It implies failure to achieve battlefield success or to attain political goals and simultaneously not only not resolving underlying issues but actually exacerbating them. Thus, what we have is two components of success—or if you like, two measures of success—in war. They are portrayed here as the scales of achievement and decisiveness. These are related but independent variables.

Decisiveness reflects a wide range of potential outcomes. The decisiveness scale (Figure 7-2) shows potential outcomes varying from completely resolving the political issues at stake through various degrees of partial resolution, to no effect (or status quo) through degrees of worsened or deteriorated political conditions, to the final potential outcome that the war not only does not solve the problems for which it was fought, but actually exacerbates them. Decisiveness talks about the effect on the political issues.

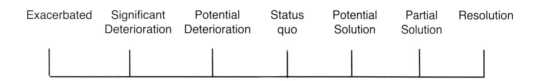

Figure 7-2. Scale of Decisiveness.

Achievement talks about how well one executes his strategy—in a sense, how well one did on the battlefield/campaign and in the immediate political realm. Achievement (Figure 7-3) can range from accomplishing nothing through increasing degrees of success until one is completely successful. The achievement scale is by far the primary scale in tactical and operational assessments of victory and is often confused with or used as synonymous with the success scale.

Figure 7-3. Scale of Achievement.

The two scales are closely related, particularly since at the operational and strategic levels the achievement scale considers political issues as well as military. The distinction is that one may accomplish one's political goals without necessarily resolving the political issues.

One might array the scales as axes and stack them by corresponding levels of war; however, I do not find that particularly useful or informative. All such manipulations really illustrate is that winning/victory requires separate definitions by level of war.

CHARACTERISTICS OF WINNING

How one defines the problem influences what you think you can or want to achieve, which influences what winning looks like. In a sense, this (a political job) is the most difficult task in initiating a war. It is a policy task—why are we fighting and what will winning look like? This is the concept we call defining the end state, which the U.S. military taught its political masters during the frustrating limited wars and peacekeeping of the 1980s and 90s. The problem is that end states change. What the modern military derisively refers to as mission creep is actually a legitimate political process of continual evaluation and assessment of possibilities and risks in a changing strategic environment. As an altered situation presents new strategic possibilities or challenges, a statesman would be negligent to ignore them. The effect of changing end states on winning is that every change in mission or end state alters acceptable strategic outcomes; that is, changes the conditions for victory. That changing end states should also cause the strategist to reevaluate ways and means is an important strategic problem that is not part of a theory of victory.

One author has postulated that winning is just achieving an outcome you like or at least prefer over other alternatives. The same author later writes, "*'Victory' is an all-purpose word used to describe imprecisely the concept of success in war* [italics in original]."[10] That has merit as far as it goes, but it is a fairly low bar, and I believe only a part of what winning really is. Achieving a preferred outcome or a success is perhaps the most basic element of conflict termination—theoretically one fights to achieve a favorable state of affairs or at least an outcome preferable to either the alternatives or a continuation of the war. It is not clear, however, how that equates to winning. It is fairly easy to postulate a desirable political and/or military condition that would be both better than losing yet less than victory—one example would be a tie or a stalemate. No widely accepted definition of victory considers a tie a win. As to victory being the concept of success in war, if we accept the sliding scale paradigm, success may just get one an outcome only slightly preferable to a tie—again not a condition most (including this paper) would accept as winning. Not losing is better than losing, but not equivalent to victory, just as not winning is better than losing, as long as it is not defeat.

However, it is clear that fighting will not stop unless the combatants see peace as more desirable than a continuation of conflict. In Clauswitzian terms, if the effort required exceeds the value of the political objective, the fighting must stop.[11] Achieving a desired or acceptable outcome may be a precondition for conflict termination, but the end of fighting does not necessarily signify victory. In fact, victory and conflict termination are two distinct and sometimes mutually antagonistic concepts. It is possible and sometimes desirable to terminate conflicts without producing a winner. Conversely, it is also possible to continue a war unnecessarily in hopes of achieving victory or avoiding defeat. To win, one must achieve at least to some extent one's immediate political goals. If avoiding fighting altogether or stopping it immediately once begun (the typical pacifist stance) is the political goal, then any outcome that stops the shooting is a win. However, few governments, and I contend few individuals, would seriously consider that victory. Simply stopping the shooting is not winning except perhaps in the domestic partisan political sense.

Conversely, winning a war almost certainly implies that a state of peace exists even if the existence of peace does not necessarily imply victory. If one thinks of peace as the normal state and war as an aberration, then peace should follow victory. That is, victory should bring the situation back to a sustainable steady state. If war is the normal state interrupted occasionally by periods of temporary peace, this may not be the case. However, Americans tend to view the world as normally at peace with occasional interruptions of war. Thus, an American definition of winning would be closely linked to peace and security. The immediate peace at the conclusion of a war is generally a period when combat ceases (a military condition), because one side collapses and either stops fighting or surrenders, or because one or both sides decide stopping is in their best interest. But none of that has anything to do with winning. One cannot discern from a postwar state of peace who won or lost the war. In fact, one can cite cases of decisive military wins that do not result in perfect peace—low-grade insurgencies often follow crushing military victories without altering the overall assessment of winning and losing. This is particularly true at the tactical and operational levels.

Winning is no different if your goal is positive or negative, that is, if you are trying to accomplish something or prevent something. The same is true for limited or total goals. It really makes no difference if the goal is something existential like continuing to exist as a nation or something less vital like "signaling." There is a difference, however, in the degree of difficulty. Total wars or wars for some concrete object like possession of territory are much more likely to be judged by concrete criteria—did you achieve or prevent the occupation of the territory; who was still standing at the end of a total war? There are also no absolute criteria that ensure victory. When President Bush announced the end of major combat operations after Operation IRAQI FREEDOM, he was proclaiming victory. He was (and remains) absolutely correct in his claim. At that moment and from an American perspective, the U.S. and its coalition partners stood victorious over a badly beaten Iraqi military. The coalition had achieved all the classic measures of a tactical and operational victory—destroyed the enemy military and occupied his capital and country. However, because there are no absolute criteria, and winning is not fixed or permanent, that victory slipped away as other political forces exerted themselves. Going back to the sports analogy, some of the voters changed their vote—or as the game reached the final innings, their votes suddenly became more significant. Perhaps it was a new game with new players and new rules. The point is that victory is an assessment, and assessments can change.

Can both sides win a war? If so, why fight? It would seem that reasonable men could discover the political solution that is likely to result from war without the unfortunate necessity of all the shooting and killing. That, however, has never been the case, and it is so because of both the nature of war and the nature of victory. War is a dynamic process. As it progresses the political objectives can change. Thus, the peace settlement upon which the assessment of victory and defeat will be made may have little relation to the initial political issues—although the most basic and loudly proclaimed are likely to get at least lip service in the final settlement. World War I is an excellent example of this phenomenon. The issues that provoked the war (at least the most immediate political issues) did not require four years of total war, so ends escalated as the effort expended escalated, and the final settlement had almost nothing to do with the original issues. Conversely, unexpectedly stiff resistance can force politicians to scale back on initial political objectives. The point is that it is impossible for all except the Monday morning quarterback to decipher the likely postwar political settlement. Additionally, if his political goals are very limited, such as demonstrating capability, showing resolve, or sending messages, the presumptive loser may be able to correctly claim he accomplished his objective and thus won. This is particularly true in cases of indecisive battlefield results, but it can occur after decisive tactical victories. The 1973 Arab-Israeli War provides an example. At the conclusion of hostilities, the Egyptians had crossed the Suez, still had forces on the eastern side, and had stood up to the Israelis. Politically, they could overlook the fact that when the ceasefire went into effect the Israelis were conducting a counterattack, had isolated one of the two attacking Egyptian armies, and were in position to complete its destruction. The Egyptians were in a difficult military situation, but President Sadat was able to negotiate and accept the Camp David peace accord precisely because he was able to persuasively (at least to the Egyptian people) claim victory in the war. Thus, one side can win big without the other side necessarily losing big—or even at all.

It is equally possible for neither side to win, unless one postulates an unwritten rule that a tie go to the underdog for not losing. The theorist Sir Basil H. Liddell Hart wrote, "Peace through stalemate, based on a coincident recognition by each side of the opponent's strength, is at least preferable to peace through common exhaustion—and has often provided a better foundation for lasting peace."[12] Liddell Hart was implying that no victory is sometimes a win. Does that mean that not losing can be the same as winning? Why not if that is the political goal? If one begins a war militarily in an underdog or even a hopeless military position—a not uncommon state of events historically—then isn't surviving that war a form of victory? While ethicists might question a decision to undertake a war without true hope of victory, politicians have frequently found it necessary. Of course, since aggressors seldom attack without a distinct advantage, examples of nations at extreme disadvantage when attacked abound. In such cases, the attacked party can hope for little more than survival. If it achieves that, isn't it a victory despite whatever battlefield success or failure it may have experienced? It has become fashionable to refer to this survival goal as regime survival when pursued by an unpopular government, as though there was something illegitimate or unsavory about regime survival, but isn't it really indistinguishable from national survival as the objective of total wars? Saddam Hussein claimed victory after the first Gulf War precisely because he had stood up to the world and survived.

Is there a temporal aspect to winning a war either in terms of achieving it or in terms of sustaining the assessment over time? Obviously winning takes some amount of time, and equally obviously, the amount of time and effort expended will influence assessments of the postwar political situation. A strategic victory must also have *some* temporal permanence—rational assessments of victory will never concede success to a condition that is only sustainable for a matter of weeks or months. However, because winning at the strategic level is an assessment of political results, it is subject to revision. Victory can be reevaluated either in terms of achievement or decisiveness, and is, therefore, not necessarily permanent. The degree of impermanence relates directly to the magnitude of the achievement and its decisiveness. World War I again provides an example. At the time, the outcome looked like an Anglo-French-American victory. Over time the degree of decisiveness has been reevaluated. Now the result is generally considered to be a military success that did not resolve and in some cases aggravated underlying issues. This *ex post facto* reevaluation of the decisiveness scale has so radically altered the assessment of victory that some authors talk about World Wars I and II as one long war.

Tactical and operational victories, because of their firmer basis of judgment, tend to remain fixed. Only very marginal victories at those levels are subject to reinterpretation. That is also true of significant, very decisive strategic wins. It is much more difficult to reevaluate a total victory that decisively settles the political issues involved than to reevaluate a situation somewhere lower on the sliding scales. For example, it is unlikely that anyone will ever seriously claim Germany or Japan won World War II. In each of those cases one can look at subsequent history and say the long-term outcome was overall beneficial for all the countries involved; however, that does not change the assessment of winning and losing. The degree of impermanence also relates to the degree of consensus on the assessment. Results that are universally accepted are difficult to change.

Does or should the cost affect victory? Of course it does. Liddell Hart pointed out that a victory is useless if it breaks the winner's economy or military or society.[13] Cost will certainly factor in to the equation about winning or losing. Costs, real and perceived, cannot help but be part of any postwar assessment. This goes back to the point that winning on one level of war can produce disastrous results on another. It is possible to win tactically at such an expense in men and materiel that it becomes a strategic defeat. The classic statement of this possibility was by King Pyrrhus of Epirus, who was alleged to have replied to congratulations on a bloody victory over the Romans in 279 B.C. that one more such victory would undo him.[14]

One final question for this section is, what does winning give you? We might say peace, but that is not certain. Liddell Hart asserts that, "The object of war is a better state of peace—if only from your own point of view," so perhaps winning is just a better peace.[15] I believe we can state with conviction that winning gives one the ability to dictate peace or at least the terms of the political settlement. That might translate into political gains or territorial acquisitions or a better sense of security. Theoretically, it should avoid, mollify, or negate future problems, but given human fallibility, that is not certain. In the purest sense, a total victory should give the winner anything he wants, but it may come down in reality to just the ability to influence, if not dictate, the solution to the political issues.

WHO DECIDES?

Because of the reasonably measurable victory conditions at the tactical and much of the operational levels, who decides who won or lost at those levels is not especially controversial. That is not true, however, at the strategic level, and the operational level also can get contentious as it merges with the strategic. If victory at the strategic level is an assessment of the postwar political conditions, then who does the assessment becomes a critical issue. Does the victor decide whether he won or lost? The vanquished? Both? Neither? What about a "disinterested" or uninvolved party? Can the decider be multiple people? If multiple people, must there be unanimity, a consensus, a majority, or a plurality? Of whom/what—public opinion, national opinion, world opinion? If the decider can be multiple, could one get several different (and equally valid) decisions? The issues here are endless, and that is just to decide who makes the assessment. There is a whole second set of issues around the question of what criteria should be used for the assessment. Is there an objective set of criteria? Are the criteria cultural? Are the criteria different for different kinds of war (total or limited)? Do the criteria vary over time? We must also keep in mind that everyone who makes an assessment uses his/her own scales and can place the degree of achievement and/or decisiveness wherever he or she wants.

Despite its complexity the question has a simple answer. Because we have defined this as an assessment of the postwar political condition, it is a political issue and everyone gets an opinion. Then the problem becomes not who decides but whose opinion matters, and that is a much more manageable issue. As a general rule, opinion counts based on the political clout of the opinion holder. For Americans the opinions that matter in order of priority are: 1) the American people; 2) American political and military elites (1 and 2 together might be thought of as American public opinion on military issues); 3) the opinion of our friends and allies; and, 4) world opinion—sort of everybody else. As the issue fades from the immediate political forum, the interested audience declines precipitously until eventually only historians will debate the issue. However, by then the base assessment of winning and losing will already have been established, and historical debates will be adjustments based on new evidence or consequences revealed by the passage of time.

Of course, the analogue of this process occurs in the enemy country or organization (if a non-state actor). Who decides in the enemy camp and how is a critical but very situationally dependent fact. It must be considered in the strategic estimate process, but this paper cannot attempt to speculate on how it might work.

Returning to our own side, how does one determine American public opinion? Usually the mass media and polling agencies sense and report public opinion. Is polling accurate for a war? Absolutely not, if "accurate" means that it reflects conditions on the ground; but it is generally accurate as a reflection of what the public believes. Is there ever a poll that asks, "Did we win such and such a war?" No, probably not. So, if the normal process does not function in this case, how do we determine who won and lost?

The determination results from the confluence of two other processes. First, political leaders try to convince the public. That is successful or not, based on the facts of the particular circumstances, the persuasiveness of the message, and the perceived legitimacy and veracity of the messenger. Credible politicians backed by convincing evidence of military achievement and political profit can proclaim victory and simply establish the fact. The second process is more like the pornography test—people just recognize victory when they see it. They make up their own minds using whatever evidence they have. This is a much more subjective process, which quickly escapes political control (or is controlled by atypical political forces). The consequence of this is that at the strategic level victory and defeat can be as much issues of public perception and even partisan politics as they are of battlefield achievement or diplomatic negotiations.

However, there is another key point to consider. Clausewitz said victory was tripartite. "If in conclusion we consider the total concept of a victory, we find it consists of three elements:

1. The enemy's greater loss of material strength.
2. His loss of morale.
3. His open admission of the above by giving up his intentions."[16]

This points out one significant fact about who decides—regardless of who makes the decision or on what criteria it is made, in order for it to stick, both sides have to acknowledge its correctness. Clausewitz was writing about tactical victory where his three points are usually apparent. At the strategic and even operational level the assessment is much more difficult and debatable. The admission of loss, however, is an important caveat for all levels, and at all levels it intertwines with the issue of who decides. This is particularly evident at the tactical level, but there are times when one side or the other for whatever reason—too dumb or too stubborn or too committed, even, to accept defeat—continues the fight. Usually, this leads to disaster, but occasionally the stubborn individual who refuses to accept defeat can actually snatch victory. Ulysses Grant at Shiloh is an example at the tactical level. Although he was and nearly driven off the field on the first day, Grant's refusal to admit defeat and his attack the next day produced a smashing tactical victory. Significantly, acceptance of defeat makes mute the issue of who decides who won—both sides acknowledge the outcome, and it is difficult for even the most radical reinterpretation to contest the decision.

Traditionally, governments indicate they are beaten by signing some form of peace accord or treaty, while armies acknowledge defeat by formally surrendering or perhaps agreeing to an armistice. Those are very important symbolic acts as an acknowledgement of victory and defeat—they are an integral and perhaps essential part of the political/social mythology of victory. They indicate to the other legs of the Clausewitzian trinity that the government and/or the army thinks itself beaten and that further resistance is futile. This is important even if parties not part of the process do not accept the verdict and try to continue the war. At a minimum, and disregarding for the moment all the impacts on legitimacy and logistics, formal governmental or military surrender will have a huge impact on the will of the remaining trinitarian elements. It is difficult for either the people or the military to continue fighting if the government has formally surrendered, and the government faces the huge challenge of recreating a military if its army has surrendered. Battleship Missouri-like ceremonies acknowledging victory and defeat are extremely important and significant. However, such ceremonies must be authentic to be useful. Contrived ceremonies for the sake of having a formal surrender do not convince the target audience. Unilaterally proclaiming victory from the deck of a U.S. aircraft carrier was better than conducting a trumped-up ceremony featuring "Bagdad Bob," but a formal surrender by Saddam Hussein or an acknowledged major subordinate legitimately representing the Iraqi government would have been better still.

The current thinking that there will not be such a ceremony at the conclusion of the War on Terrorism is probably correct; however, there should have been such a ceremony at the conclusion of the initial phases in both Afghanistan and Iraq. Especially in Iraq, the people needed to see and believe that the Saddam government was actually defeated. The difference in the War on Terrorism is that the enemy is a non-state actor. There are no internationally recognized procedures for accepting the surrender of non-state actors, and if there were, no state could take lightly legitimizing such an actor even by formally accepting its surrender. If non-state actors mirror/mimic in some ways the trinitarian characteristics of states, the impact of formal surrender might be similar, but the extent of such similarity is unclear. For example, it is not certain that the surrender of the leader of a non-state actor (who is presumably analogous to the government in a state sense) would have the same impact as the surrender of the head of a government. This is the reasoning behind warnings that the capture or death of Osama Bin Laden will not end the War on Terrorism.

So, what can we conclude about victory in warfare so far? It is an assessment of two variables—achievement and decisiveness—at three levels—tactical, operational, and strategic. At the tactical and in most cases the operational levels winning is a military condition, and the assessment rests on reasonably well understood military criteria. At the strategic level (and the portions of the operational that directly overlap the strategic), public opinion decides who wins and loses and to what extent, based on an assessment of the postwar political conditions. The military situation as the public understands or interprets it will, of course, play a huge role in the assessment, but the overriding criteria will be political. To be effective, a victory must be recognized and accepted by the opponent and sustainable over time. Thus, *strategic victory in war is a positive assessment of the postwar political situation in terms of achievement and decisiveness that is acknowledged, sustainable, and resolves underlying political issues.* Similarly, *Tactical victories are battlefield military outcomes that achieve their purpose and give one side a significant, acknowledged advantage over its opponent.* Substituting operational for tactical and eliminating battlefield in the above definition yields a satisfactory definition of operational victory.

HOW DOES ONE WIN?

Theoretically, how one wins a war is fairly straightforward—it is doing it that is difficult. Clausewitz pointed out that war is both a physical and moral struggle. His recipe for victory was simple: "If you want to overcome your enemy you must match your efforts against his power of resistance, which can be expressed as the product of two inseparable factors, viz. *the total means at his disposal* and *the strength of his will*." (italics in original)[17] One can express that as a mathematical formula:

$$R = M \times W$$

In the formula, **R** represents the power of resistance, **M** is the total means available, and **W** is the strength of will. Victory then, is achieved as **R** approaches zero; that is, as the power of resistance drops to an ineffective level. One can push **R** toward zero by reducing either **M** or **W** (or both). In some respects one might think of a strategy designed to attack the **M** aspect of the equation as a physical approach and a strategy designed to address the **W** aspect as psychological, although making such a distinction too starkly can be dangerous, since both elements will appear in any strategy. We will examine briefly both approaches.

The traditional concept of winning a war is based on reducing the enemy's means of resistance. This is generally done physically. Typically, it involves destroying or neutralizing the enemy's military or at least attriting it to the point of ineffectiveness. The underlying purpose is to remove the enemy's capability to resist so you can impose your will on him directly. The theorist of deterrence, Thomas Schelling, wrote about the use of military power to hurt. His point was that one function of militaries is to inflict pain on the enemy. Inflicting pain is easiest when the enemy cannot resist—that is, after you have beaten him in battle.[18] Thus, the real significance of the loss of one's army is that it leaves you vulnerable to whatever pain the enemy wants to inflict. That is why nations surrender when their armies are defeated. The trick has always been how one goes about destroying or attriting the enemy. Another physical approach attempts to avoid the issues of destruction or attrition through paralysis. The concept is that one paralyzes vital enemy systems, especially command and control, to make their resistance ineffective. Postulated by advocates of the indirect approach and some air power enthusiasts, the intent is to avoid hard fighting by maneuver or by precise attacks on specific targets.[19] However, the final mechanism for achieving victory is still placing the enemy is a situation in which your armed forces can directly impose their will. In every case, winning by reducing the enemy's physical means of resistance comes down to an evaluation of whether you can hit and hurt the enemy, the cost to do so, and the effectiveness of the resulting damage. The underlying theoretical rational is always that removing the enemy's ability to resist allows one to directly impose his will without the possibility of effective resistance.

Attacking psychologically to reduce the enemy's will to resist works somewhat differently. The intent of all action is not to place oneself in position to impose one's will but to cause the enemy to lose his will and quit. All strategies designed with this intent share two major issues. First, is whose will should one attack? If we accept Clausewitz's description of the forces interacting in war as the people, the government, and the military, then we can ascribe a will to each.[20] Whose will counts most? The French general and theorist André Beaufre wrote:

> Whom do we wish to convince? Ultimately it must be the enemy government but in some cases it may be easier to work on leading personalities (e.g. Chamberlain at Bad Godesberg or Munich), choosing arguments to which they are most susceptible. Alternatively it may be best to work directly on a certain section of public opinion which has some hold over the government or an influential Allied Government or through UNO [the United Nations].[21]

Regardless of the route he followed, Beaufre was focused ultimately on breaking the will of the enemy government. That is a very state-centric appreciation of a means of winning that deserves reconsideration in a world where non-state actors play increasingly significant roles, especially in war and warlike activities.

The recent rediscovery of counterinsurgency (COIN) theory provides other possibilities. COIN theory generally acknowledges the population as the objective — in terms of a theory of victory, it is the population that decides what victory is and who prevails. Winning hearts and minds is how one wins COIN because the people's will counts most. That is not the case in all wars.

The examples imply whose will matters most may be largely an issue of the type of war one is fighting. This goes back to Clausewitz's famous dictum about the first and greatest act of a commander and statesman being to understand the nature of the war in which he is about to engage.[22] In a total war, one probably has to break at least the government and the people's will. You may have to break all three, and certainly must to achieve a lasting settlement that is viewed as just. In limited wars for limited objectives, one may only have to break the will of the government — assuming sufficient governmental control — to prevent the people and/or the military from ignoring the government's decision and re-initiating the fight. As a caveat, there is no guarantee either that breaking the will of one of the trinitarian legs will produce victory or that both sides will be contesting over the same will. A second caveat is that the model may not fit non-state actors well.

The second issue in reducing the enemy's will is understanding how to break will. There is a classic approach that is highly physical. One physically seizes, perhaps preemptively, what he wants or what is important. That is, he directly imposes his will on the enemy. In its purest form, the idea is that the enemy will concede the political point (i.e., his will breaks) without further contest. This is the most easily understood concept and makes postwar assessment simple — you either have or don't have what you said you wanted. Execution is also theoretically simple. It involves directly taking or doing what you want. If the enemy's will persists, you are still presumably in a better position for the fight that follows than you were before the opening of the gambit. There is nothing wrong with this concept of winning, and it is a very useful approach when the desired end is suitable. It is, of course, both most useful and common when there is a significant disparity between opposing forces, since the enemy will presumably try to counter your move.

In other will-oriented approaches, physical effects are also important and are typically a primary method. Remember that Clausewitz said physical means and will were inseparable.[23] The distinction is in intent. The desired result of a psychological approach is the collapse of will rather than rendering the enemy incapable of resistance as in the physical approach. Some examples may help clarify. Early strategic air power theory as represented by the Italian theorist Gulio Douhet was based on the use of strategic bombing to directly attack the will of the enemy people and government. The bomber could fly over fielded forces and directly attack enemy cities. The intent was to break morale.[24] This theory, which is at the heart of all strategic bombing theory, has yet to work unambiguously. As with any attempt to produce psychological effect, the results are unpredictable. Similarly, John Warden's theory of directly attacking the will of the government or military (striking leadership) as manifested in spinoff concepts such as "Shock and Awe" should work theoretically—if you convince the government that you have an invincible capability to overwhelm it and the will to use that capability, the government should surrender—it just never has worked exactly like that.[25] The only proven way to break will is to convince the enemy that resistance is futile—the cost of resistance exceeds the potential gain. That is the real point of overwhelming force and related concepts. It may make the physical job easier, but is also an important element in the psychological equation of will.

The only method currently available to attack will directly is information operations; all the other options attack indirectly through some other aspect presumed to influence will. However, information operations are very blunt instruments whose impact is incredibly difficult to predict or target reliably. Second- and third-order effects are always present and may produce exactly the opposite of the intended result. Conversely, if victory is an assessment, information operations are strategically critical in deciding the winner. Our inability to come to grips intellectually, physically, or psychologically with this aspect of war in an age when control of information is impossible is a huge part of our current perceived inability to achieve positive strategic results.

What role do ethics play in winning? This is not the classic question of whether war is really a no-holds-barred fight to the finish, or whether there are or should be rules/ethical limitations. The ethical component of winning, if one exists, is limited to two aspects. The first, is how much weight, if any, the decider gives to the ethical conduct of the war. If the entity making the victory assessment uses ethics as a standard of measurement, ethics are significant in victory; if the decider ignores ethics in his analysis, ethics will play no role in victory. A second way ethics figure in the victory equation is that ethical (or unethical) conduct may have second- or third-order effects that influence durability. Thus, a war that initially looks like a victory may become something less as evidence of unethical conduct emerges. Like every other aspect of the victory assessment, the ethics standard does not necessarily apply equally to both sides, is a sliding scale rather than a binary ethical/non-ethical assessment, and considers or ignores acts/issues serendipitously. The American people expect ethical conduct of war and might very easily assess a war conducted in an unethical manner as a loss regardless of battlefield outcomes. That appears to be at least a portion of the attitude behind the resistance to the Iraq war, which rages as I write. Ethical considerations in the victory assessment are self-imposed and self-enforced, but they are real.

What is the bottom line? Victory in war is about breaking will. Eliminating means of resistance completely is impossible. Theoretically there will always be one enemy soldier armed with at least a knife who is willing to give his life to continue the fight. Destroying the enemy's means without breaking his will leaves you with a less capable but still hostile foe. Conversely, breaking the will to resist ends the war regardless of the enemy's remaining combat capability. The issue then becomes the much more practical one of how does one break an enemy's will? This is where we loop back on our argument. Will is a difficult concept to define—much less attack directly—so militaries invariable attack the enemy military as a means not to reduce his power of resistance to zero and win, but as a means to destroy his will. Concepts like classic strategic air power theory that attempts to bypass fielded forces to attack enemy will (either government or people) directly or John Warden's strategic rings that add to the classic approach the idea of striking command and control and other vital systems to make resistance ineffective are tempting, because theoretically they should work. They should not be ignored, but if one is looking for promising alternative approaches to victory, the field of information operations is the most fertile available. We just need to get out of the technological emphasis (or perhaps fixation) and approach it from the direction of understanding how one influences opinion, especially political will.

THE IMPLICATIONS FOR WAR

War is about winning. This is not a new concept. The general and theorist Raimondo Montecuccoli wrote in the 17th century: "War is an activity to inflict damage in every way; its aim is victory"—and the concept was already ancient by then.[26] Sun Tzu had expressed the same thought—"Victory is the main object in war"—a thousand years earlier.[27] Only an idiot would fight to lose—even fighting in an impossible cause is done in the hope of victory, if only by miracle. In *The Mouse that Roared* from the series of satirical books by Leonard Wibberley, made famous by the 1959 movie starring Peter Sellers in multiple roles, the fictional Duchy of Grand Fenwick fought to lose, but the goal was still to gain a better peace. The idea was to declare war on the U.S., lose quickly, and then graciously accept the flood of foreign aid that would surely flow to a defeated foe. The fact that the Duchy's military stumbled into military victory was fortuitous, but totally unplanned and unexpected. Fighting in a hopeless or losing cause is valiant and sometimes necessary, but difficult to justify morally. Politically, it is not difficult to justify, since one can always hope to achieve at least the survival objective. So, war is about winning.

However, the fact that war is about winning does not mean war is about victory. One can win a war, especially a limited war (a war that is consciously limited in either or all of ends, ways, or means), without achieving victory. Military force can legitimately be used to obtain goals short of the total victory where one's forces end up standing over a prostrate enemy with a bayonet at his throat dictating peace terms. It is also legitimate to use military force for immediate political advantage, even understanding that one may not resolve the underlying issues.

This points out that war is also about politics, and consequently in the final analysis, strategic victory must be a political state. It is a perception by the people that matter that one side did better overall in a war than the other. The judgment is based on results, not effort. At the strategic level the scale of assessment is political, although physical or military aspects like casualties influence considerations, and some acts (like the capture or loss of specific territory) may have a decisive impact on the assessment when that issue is the basis of the political dispute. Liddell Hart was correct when he asserted that the object of war is a better peace if only from our point of view. Attaining that object is a primary prerequisite for victory. That may translate in political terms into a fairly innocuous set of less-than-optimal conditions that are more acceptable than the alternative, but the public must assess their attainment as a positive achievement worth the cost. The assessment must be shared by the people that matter. In America that is the general public and the political elites. The enemy must also accept the assessment if we expect the condition to last for any reasonable amount of time.

Winning is different at different levels of war, and winning at some levels can produce unintended results and even losses at other levels. Because winning is an assessment and subject to interpretation, it is sensitive to perspective. Tactical conditions that look like winning may be counterproductive strategically. This is particularly true when the goal is overtly political, like winning the hearts and minds of the people.

War is a contest of wills conducted with physical means. This concept is absolutely critical to understanding the nature of war and the nature of victory. It leads directly to scales for weighing victory. One can assess any and every physical means employed against its probable outcome in terms of enemy and friendly will. If, despite how tactically effective it might be, the strategic result is likely to be minimal or unfavorable, its use must be very carefully considered. A great example is the 500-lb bomb in the counterinsurgency role. Five-hundred-pound bombs, regardless of how accurately targeted, inevitably produce collateral damage. In a COIN situation one might kill the targeted insurgents, perhaps in great numbers, but if the explosion also kills or injures bystanders (regardless of how innocent or complicit they might be) or even property, their use is inadvisable.

It is a characteristic of war that both sides try to dominate the opponent's will while protecting their own. The respective wills of the people, government, and military of both sides are potentially vulnerable. Protecting one's own will is as important as attacking that of the opponent. The military is responsible for its will—politicians are responsible for the wills of both the government and the people. While the will analysis works best for state-on-state contests, it is also applicable to wars with non-state actors. In their case, some of the components may be atrophied or combined in the same person or element, but because Clausewitz's initial concept of the trinity dealt with basic characteristics of war that he then ascribed to the legs of the trinity, each of the trinitarian elements is still represented by some entity, even in a non-state actor, where there may not be an identifiable people, military, or government. Targeting will in an enemy state is difficult enough; the same task against a non-state actor is extremely tough.

Because war is a contest of wills, and victory is an assessment made by peoples or governments, information is critical, and being clumsy or too scrupulous in that arena unnecessarily ties one's hands. Being inept at information operations can be strategically fatal regardless of the power of one's military, the skill of one's diplomats, or the size of the one's GDP.

Because war is about will and winning is an agreed-upon assessment, formal ceremonies to acknowledge victory and defeat are important traditional psychological tools and political/social symbols that should be sought whenever possible. However, sham ceremonies featuring insignificant functionaries do not accomplish the same objective and may in fact be counterproductive.

Have we answered (or even asked) all the relevant questions? Certainly not. There is much work remaining in this arena. I hope, however, that these thoughts can advance the discussion. If not, we may end the 21st century still bemoaning our inability to turn spectacular tactical victories into decisive strategic results.

ENDNOTES - CHAPTER 7

1. See, for example, Donald Schon, *The Reflective Practitioner: How Professionals Think in Action*, New York: Basic Books, 1983.

2. William C. Martel, *Victory in War: Foundations of Modern Military Policy*, New York: Cambridge University Press, 2007, p. 3.

3. Bradford Lee at the Naval War College has been working on a concept he calls a "theory of victory," which is very interesting; however, it is more a theory of winning specific contests against specific enemies in the terms we will develop in this paper.

4. Colin S. Gray, *Defining and Achieving Decisive Victory*, Carlisle, PA: Strategic Studies Institute, U.S. Army War College, 2002.

5. Martel.

6. *Ibid.*, pp. 94-5.

7. Harry G. Summers, Jr., *On Strategy: The Vietnam War in Context*, Carlisle, PA: Strategic Studies Institute, U.S. Army War College, 1981, fifth printing, 1989, p. 1.

8. Martel, pp. 94-5.

9. Gray, pp. 9-10; for Martel on sliding scales, see Figure 1 in Martel, pp. 4 and 95.

10. Martel, pp. 2, 87.

11. Carl von Clausewitz, *On War*, Michael Howard and Peter Paret eds., Princeton, NJ: Princeton University Press, 1989, p. 92.

12. Basil H. Liddell Hart, *Strategy*, New York: Frederick A. Praeger, 1954, reprint, 1967, p. 370.

13. *Ibid.*, pp. 366-370.

14. Plutarch, "Pyrrhus," John Dryden, trans., available from *classics.mit.edu/Plutarch/pyrrhus.html*.

15. Liddell Hart, *p.* 351.

16. Clausewitz, pp. 233-4.

17. *Ibid.*, p. 77.

18. Thomas C. Schelling, *Arms and Influence*, New Haven, CT: Yale University Press, 1966, pp. 4, 14.

19. Colonel John A. Warden III, "The Enemy as a System," *Air Power Journal*, Spring 1995, pp. 41-55.

20. Clausewitz, p. 89.

21. André Beaufre, *An Introduction to Strategy with Particular Reference to Problems of Defence, Politics, Economics and Diplomacy in the Nuclear Age*, R. H. Berry, trans., London, UK: Farber and Farber, 1965, p. 24.

22. Clausewitz, pp. 88-89.

23. *Ibid.*, p. 77.

24. David Jablonsky, ed., *Roots of Strategy, Book 4: 4 Military Classics*, Mechanicsburg, PA: Stackpole Books, 1999, pp. 270-1; Azar Gat, *A History of Military Thought: From the Enlightenment to the Cold War*, New York: Oxford University Press, 2001, pp. 577-81.

25. Warden, pp. 41-55.

26. Gat, p. 24.

27. Sun Tzu, *The Art of War*, Samuel B. Griffith, trans., New York: Oxford University Press, 1963, 1973, p. 73.

CHAPTER 8

TOWARD A STRATEGIC THEORY OF TERRORISM: DEFINING BOUNDARIES IN THE ONGOING SEARCH FOR SECURITY

Frank L. Jones

"More, more, more...to destroy whole cities, provinces, an entire country, the whole world, this would be the greatest happiness."[1] These words conclude Polish author Stanislaw Przybyszewski's novel of terrorism, *Satan's Kinder* (*Children of Satan*), as the protagonists delight in torching a nameless city. At the time of its publication in Berlin in 1897, this German-language novel was a popular work of fiction. Critics of the time, citing the limited technical means for carrying out such enormous devastation, dismissed the story as a mere fantasy or just another apocalyptic vision of the sort fashionable at the turn of the century.[2] Today, the subject of this story would be equally popular, but it has also become the topic of serious deliberation and debate by government officials, scholars, and citizens alike, because the ability and implied intent of terrorists to wreck mass destruction is no longer far-fetched.

Nonetheless, despite volumes of books, articles and studies of terrorism, there has been scant investment made in developing a theory of terrorism. Instead, scholars and practitioners devote their efforts to writing about the history of terrorism, examining a variety of terrorist movements, discussing the influence of political ideologies and religious belief on terrorists' motives, dissecting their operational environments, or analyzing the psychological makeup of terrorists. This has resulted in a broken-looking-glass approach to understanding terrorism, whereby each shard casts a portion of the image but not a complete likeness. As Richard Schultz points out, there has been intense study of terrorism, but the literature has been "primarily descriptive, prescriptive and very emotive in form."[3] This is still the case three decades after Schultz made that assertion, and such an approach continues to suggest why terrorism is often understood simply as a tactic.

This is an unfortunate state of affairs with serious repercussions, perhaps even disastrous results. It leads government officials to fixate on tactics, which, in turn, leads to the belief that there is a political, social, or economic antidote or vaccine—some combinatory "drug cocktail" that, if used, can eliminate terrorism. Tactics, as Carl von Clausewitz observed, are fighting techniques that can be addressed with prescriptive doctrine, that is, at a level where method and routine are useful and even essential. Strategy involves questions of broad purpose in which complexity, contingency and difficulty rule—doctrine is not only useless; it is unattainable.[4]

Therefore, this paper seeks to advance a strategic theory of terrorism as it relates to all orders of non-state actors by using an interdisciplinary approach that integrates social science and the theory of war and strategy. In essence, the proposed theory argues that terrorists make choices to attain a future state or condition. Those choices concern how (concept or way) they will use the coercive or persuasive power (resources or means) available to exercise control over circumstances or a population to achieve objectives (ends) in accordance with their policy. This calculated relationship among ends, ways, and means, which is a rational construct for strategy, forms the basis for this theoretical approach. Such a theoretical approach, like any theory, should specify essential terminology and definitions, explicate underlying assumptions and premises, present substantive propositions that can be translated into usable hypotheses, and lastly, provide or identify methods that can be used to test the hypotheses and modify the theory as appropriate. Ideally, this approach should also meet certain standards such as economy of language, applicability to the largest possible range of cases, and conformance to the facts.[5]

DEFINING TERRORISM

One of the reasons for a lack of focus on theoretical and conceptual issues, it is argued, stems from the definitional problems associated with the term "terrorism." Some scholars have become so discouraged by the lack of an accepted definition that they have abandoned any attempt to devise it. Walter Laqueur, a noted scholar of terrorism, contends, "A comprehensive definition of terrorism…does not exist nor will it be found in the foreseeable future."[6] However, sociologist Jack Gibbs suggested that it is impossible to pretend to study terrorism without some of form of definition; otherwise, discussion lapses into obscurantism. He also argues that one of the problems is definitional parsimony to the degree that oversimplification occurs: "… it is inconsistent to grant that human behavior is complex and then demand simple definitions of behavioral types."[7] As Martha Crenshaw remarked, clarity is often sacrificed for brevity.[8] In attempting to meet these challenges, Gibbs defines terrorism as "illegal violence or threatened violence directed against human or nonhuman objects" that has five characteristics: (1) the violence is undertaken to alter or maintain at least one putative norm in at least one population; (2) it has secret, furtive, and/or clandestine features so the participants can conceal their identity and location; (3) it is not undertaken to further the permanent defense of territory; (4) it is not conventional warfare, and because of the participants' concealed personal identity and concealment of their location, their threats, and/or their spatial mobility, the participants perceive themselves as less vulnerable to conventional military action; and, (5) this violence is perceived by the participants as contributing to the normative goal previously described by inducing fear of violence in persons (perhaps an indefinite category of them) other than the immediate target of the actual or threatened violence and/or by publicizing some cause.[9] This definition lacks one essential aspect, which one of the earliest definitions of terrorism found in the 1948 edition of the *Encyclopedia of Social Sciences,* provides. This text defines terrorism as a "method or a theory behind the method whereby an organized group or party seeks to achieve its avowed aims chiefly through the systematic use of violence."[10]

The value of joining these two definitions is not only that it seeks to explain a complex subject in the manner it deserves, that is, the complexity associated with human motivation, where the admixture of political motives, as an example, cannot be readily distinct from personal motives. It also has another valuable feature: it recognizes terrorism as a theory with violence as the essential feature. Violence—collective violence, to be precise—is the strategic concept, the way, used to advance a strategy consisting of a putative norm that the terrorists are attempting to alter and maintain using various tactics (e.g., bombing, assassination) in a strategic environment.

PREMISES

For the purposes of this paper, strategy is defined as a "synergy and symmetry of objectives, concepts and resources to increase the probability of policy success and the favorable consequences that follow from that success….Strategy accomplishes this by expressing its logic in rational, linear terms—ends, ways and means."[11] In taking such an approach, several premises are critical to framing a strategic theory of terrorism.

The first premise is that "political purpose dominates all strategy."[12] Political as defined herein is an enunciation of policy, an expression of the preferred end state, whether it is attainable or not. Ideally, this policy is clearly articulated by the terrorist leaders, as it represents guidance for the employment of means, the instruments of coercive or persuasive power, toward the achievement of aims. However, policy can change as the strategic environment or circumstances change—for example, limitations imposed by others on the means available to the terrorists.

A second premise is the primacy of the strategic environment, which has a number of dimensions.[13] Terrorist leaders strive to attain a thorough understanding of the strategic situation and knowledge of the strategic environment. The strategic environment is physical and metaphysical, domestic and international, requiring an understanding of cultures, beliefs, and worldviews of adversaries, allies (actual or potential), and neutralists. In implementing his strategy, the terrorist creates a security dilemma for other actors; he introduces change, and change upsets the status quo—the equilibrium of the strategic environment. The other actors are forced to do something.[14]

It is in the strategic environment that signaling occurs in order to have a psychological influence on politically behavior and attitudes.[15] The terrorist sends a signal that a target is vulnerable, that the perpetrators of violence exist, and that these perpetrators have the capability to strike numerous times. The signals are usually directed at three different audiences: the target or victims themselves, who may be killed and therefore can no longer be influenced; the group that identifies with the victim and therefore are affected by the implicit message that they are vulnerable as well; and all others, a "resonant mass." This group is composed of those who may react emotionally in a positive or negative manner—depending on which side they sympathize with in the conflict—as well as the government, the legitimate power, responsible for protecting the victims.[16]

The strategic environment should also be understood in terms of social geometry, which permits conspiratorial theories to flourish. David Black stresses, "Although a longstanding grievance usually underlies terrorism [and therefore justifies the resort to violence], the grievance alone does not explain the violence. It must have the right geometry—a particular location and direction in social space."[17] In other words, a condition of "social polarization" exists between society and the aggrieved. For the terrorist, society must be understood as having certain characteristics: it is sick and the illness cannot be cured, the state is violence itself and can be opposed only with violence, and the truth of the terrorist's espoused cause justifies any action that supports this stated objective.[18]

A third premise is that adaptation, that is, learning from experience, is required by all involved, and the key is who is adapting quicker—the terrorists or the government and its security forces. The terrorists and the governments with which they contend must recognize the magnitude of change required and strive for an improved fit between the organization and its external environment. The rate of change internal to the states, its leaders, institutions, and organizations must keep pace with the rate of change in the environment in order to cope with unfolding events and the terrorists' countermoves.[19] Thus, strategy is a "process, a constant adaptation to shifting conditions and circumstances in a world where chance, uncertainty, and ambiguity dominate."[20]

The fourth premise is that "strategy has a symbiotic relationship with time." Deciding when to execute the strategy is crucial to the terrorist leaders. If the historical timing is appropriate, then small actions can have large strategic effects. These effects can be cumulative and thus become part of the interplay between continuity and change. They also become part of the continuities of the strategic environment. If the timing is not propitious, then the results may be meager, require additional exertion, and cost more in terms of tangible and intangible resources. However, even in failure, the strategic effects become part of the framework of change and interaction in the strategic environment and thereby influence future actions.[21]

A fifth premise is that for terrorists efficiency is subordinate to effectiveness. This is not to suggest that efficiency is not valued, but that the purpose of the strategy is to attain strategic effect. If strategic objectives are achieved, they in turn generate or contribute to the generation of the strategic effects that favor the realization of the desired end state.[22] The strategic effect in terrorism is to create a sense of vulnerability and intimidation. It is "intended to create a state of fear that is acute and long-lasting enough to influence behavior."[23]

The sixth premise is that the terrorists' strategy seeks a proper balance among the objectives wanted, the methods used to pursue the objectives, and the resources available for the effects desired. In formulating the strategy, the ends, ways, and means are interconnected, working synergistically to accomplish the strategic effect.[24] Terrorist leaders must be understood as rational calculators.

The seventh and final premise is that terrorists understand the importance of strategic risk; recognize the inherent existence of uncertainty, chance, and nonlinearity in the strategic environment; and attempt to produce a favorable balance in the ends-ways-means calculation to overcome or at least ameliorate the impact. Nonetheless, the risk of failure remains.[25] Since action is imperative, terrorist leaders must take risks in order to maintain the organization. Action also serves to address internal factors such as solidifying shared values and objectives though a sense of belonging and unity, generating excitement, elevating social status, and acquiring interpersonal or material reward. It also promotes external objectives such as recruitment and material and popular support from sympathizers and constituencies. Therefore, the terrorist strategists and leaders must manage the friction between their need to preserve the organization (since action risks destruction by government forces) and the foot soldiers' demand for action. Inaction can breed internal power struggles and major disagreements on any number of subjects.[26]

To paraphrase Carl von Clausewitz, terrorism has a grammar of its own, changing from age to age and place to place, but its logic—the rationale for terrorism—remains durable. The violent act is designed to send a message to a wide audience, not just the immediate victim, generally, "to create, instill or perpetuate a perception of fear within that audience." Further, "no specific ideological, theological, or bases are assumed, since the intent is to create or foster a sense of fear beyond the immediate victim remains the principal *raison d'être* for the violent act or threat."[27] Thus, terror is the strategic effect and violence provides the strategic concept, which is why it must be discussed first.

THE STRATEGIC CONCEPT OF TERRORISM AND ITS MEANS

Violence is the principal way or strategic concept by which terrorists will achieve their espoused ends. The terrorist uses collective violence—that is, personal injury by a group, albeit a small one—as a form of protest, a quest for justice, and the purposeful expression of concrete and identifiable grievances, which are precipitated by any number of social, economic, [cultural], or political issues.[28]

Terrorism is also an organized form of violence that includes the concept of collective liability. Collective liability means that a group or members of the offender's group or social category are held accountable for the offender's conduct. The population of the offending government is answerable for the government's actions, the source of oppression, and impediment to the terrorists' ideal state. Thus, any member of this population, including women, children and the elderly, may be vulnerable to attack.[29] In the words of the French anarchist Emile Henry, "*Il n'y a pas d'innocents*,"[30] (There are no innocents); therefore, the violence is justified, since all are complicit.

Moreover, violence, as Martha Crenshaw notes, is the "primary method of action," and terrorists are individuals who have a bias for action—are "impatient for action."[31] This preference for violent action is made explicit to the victim of terror in the hope it will be coercive: "…the power to hurt is often communicated by some performance of it. Whether it is sheer terroristic violence to induce an irrational response, or cool premeditated violence to persuade somebody that you mean it and may do it again, it is not the pain and damage itself but its influence on somebody's behavior that matters."[32] This approach bypasses the Clausewitzian formula that resistance is a product of two variables—means and will.[33] The terrorist has no interest in reducing the adversary's means, because the terrorist is less powerful and less capable than the adversary is. The way must therefore focus almost exclusively on the will. The terrorist must determine "what an adversary treasures" and "what scares him;" while the adversary must comprehend what the terrorist wants in order to be compliant, to know how to avoid pain or loss. The threat of violence must be personalized so that the adversary's pain or loss is "so anguishing as to be unendurable" and makes surrender a relief.[34] It must also lead to political action on the part of the government.

There appear to be two factors that promote this aim of prompting governmental action. First, there is some evidence that if the terrorist tells the target how to find relief from the stress, there is less chance of inaction. Second, sporadic violence, as opposed to sustained relentless violence, appears to be more psychologically and socially effective by creating fear, anxiety, and a feeling of vulnerability as well as undermining society's networks of trust, solidarity, cooperation, and interdependence.[35] If emotional terror and social anomie occur, with each individual only concerned about his or her personal survival, then the state has failed, for this sense of insecurity signals the fact or at least provides the impression that the provision of security as a public good—the very purpose for the state—can no longer be guaranteed by the state.[36] The state becomes the locus of frustration, and people blame it for not protecting them. If, however, a certain level of violence can be tolerated psychologically, then the antidote to the violence lies in its management by the government with it offering prudent countermeasures to meet this objective.

Thus, for the terrorist, the threat of violence must combine with unpredictability in the mind of the potential victims. Violence becomes a form of "costly signaling." Terrorists employ costly signaling to signal their resolute and credible willingness to resort to violence, a costly action. The terrorists cannot afford to bluff or lie, since to do so would only undermine their claims of strength and capability to impose costs on those who oppose them.[37]

By inflicting pain (accomplishing the aim), the feeling of vulnerability is heightened and violence serves a purpose. Strangely, this purpose is not only one of coercion or destruction, but for the terrorist it can also be a redemptive act, symbolic in meaning. A terrorist act is a scene in a morality play within the theater of protest. The allusion to drama is strong: labeled by some social scientists as a form of symbolic action in a "complex performative field" and a "dramaturgical framework,"[38] or a "bloody drama played out before an audience."[39] As Georges Sorel notes, violence is a purifying act.[40] The terrorist is a moralist. A moral order must be returned to equilibrium.

The tactics of terrorism are simple. They are the visible and violent acts taken by the means or resources available, which include not only terrorist foot soldiers but also other resources such as finances, weapons, and other materiel. These tactics further the group's ends as well as provide inducements needed to recruit and maintain a membership. These acts consist of assassination, arson, bombings (including suicide bombings), armed robbery, and kidnapping for the purposes of extortion. They are used to destabilize society in three respects: political instability by killing government leaders and undermining the political process; social instability by disrupting various systems of exchange (social, economic) and by propagating such fear that distrust becomes normal and disorder results; and moral instability by provoking authorities to respond to these political and social threats with brutal actions that will delegitimate vital institutions in the society.[41]

DEFINING THE ENDS OF TERRORISM

The late Philip Windsor argued that terrorists' objectives are rooted in the "conditions of an historical legacy that have created a cause that can no longer be defined in terms of political compromise but instead must be redefined in terms of a moral claim."[42] "The agenda is dominated by long-standing historical legacies that have created a universe of moral problems." Thus, terrorists understand themselves to be "inheritors dispossessed by history." It is this historical grievance of being cheated of their "rightful" inheritance and their "quest for legitimacy in an as-yet only imagined proper order that lends them moral justification." This is an important distinction for the tendency on the part of those who seek to counter terrorism is that only two options are available. The first is that terrorism must be wiped out because it hampers civilized political discourse. The other is the belief that a dialogue with the terrorists is critical to co-opt them into the political process. Both of these avenues may prove sterile. The extermination of terrorists tends to breed more terrorists and thus confirms the moral claims of the terrorists, while co-optation can prove futile because moral claims cannot always be solved by political resolution.[43]

The objectives of terrorist organizations are often grandiose and visionary, calling for sweeping and uncompromising change in the allocation of power in society or contesting the legitimacy of political and social elites.[44] Yet, the commitment of terrorist organizations to a specific ideology is often weak or inconsistent;[45] it certainly is not homogenous. Ideas are often borrowed loosely from a number of theoretical sources to define ends that have ranged from Marxist-Leninism to a variety of religious doctrines. Instead, the ideology should be understood more broadly, "in the sense of being based on beliefs that comprise a systematic, comprehensive rejection of the present political world and the promise of future replacement."[46] In appealing to diverse audiences to support the terrorists or to at least cooperate and support them, the terrorists' ends are syncretist.

More dangerously, the vast majority of terrorists cannot articulate the political stages or tasks necessary to achieve their objectives but instead offer only an end state. Further, terrorism may be considered, according to Jeffrey Alexander, "*postpolitical*," that is, "it reflects the end of political possibility." If that becomes the case, then it is an experience of overwhelming political impotence expressed through "drawing blood." Its tactics "deliver maiming and death; they serve a strategy of inflicting humiliation, chaos, and reciprocal despair."[47] In other words, terror becomes an end unto itself. This has led one scholar to conclude that the "cause is not the cause." The cause, as articulated by the group's ideology, becomes the rationale for the violent acts the terrorists commit.[48]

TERROR AS AN END

In this respect, terrorism is a deliberate political choice by a political actor to use the power to hurt.[49] This power to hurt is not incidental to the use of force, but is an object itself. The power to hurt, as Thomas Schelling argued, is the capacity to "influence somebody's behavior, to coerce his decision or choice."[50] It is a coarse form of behavior modification in which both the afflicter and the victim know that pain can be imposed, even anticipated, and there is equally, the understanding that it might be avoided under certain conditions. However, as Windsor suggested, the terrorist has no patience with the complexities involved in political matters. This is not the protracted armed struggle of the people's army in the process of revolutionary war, as an example, where the people's army is built progressively during the course of the war. Where time, patience, or ingenuity is in short supply, the terrorist will slash through this Gordian knot. He reverts to brute force where destruction is the strategic end.[51]

This should not be surprising, because terrorism is a form of *social antimovement*, to use Michel Wieviorka's term. It is an "extreme, degenerate, and highly particularized variety of social antimovement."[52] Terrorist actors exhibit three defining principles of this phenomenon, principles that fuse or "feed on themselves." Terrorism "takes the form of a course of violence, which, possessed of a rationale all its own, propagates itself without its perpetrators having to verify their words or deeds with the people in whose name they claim to be acting."[53] Instead, the actor and the cause become indistinguishable. "In the most extreme of cases, and less often than one may think, he internalizes—sometimes to the point of nihilism and self-destruction—the inability of a social movement to assert itself." The enemy is objectified, a target to be assailed, a person to be eliminated, a system to be destroyed. Lastly, a radical disengagement occurs, a death struggle ensues, and attainment of a utopian state, a new order or a just society is dismissed. "The ends become confused with their means, with all sense of vision being reduced to plans for the destruction of all that stands in the way of the actor's subjectivity."[54] In other words, the desire for annihilation—self, opponent, and the state—comes to fore. In some cases, the oppressor's values are such an abomination that annihilation is the only course if the enemy will not convert to the terrorists' view. This is not the destruction of the politico-military power of the bourgeoisie or oligarchic state as part of the armed struggle of Marxist-Leninist theory. Terrorists are not interested in the eradication of their adversaries' military power. Instead, they are interested in radical change to structures or conditions through violent means or the threat of violence. The terrorist is committed to planning and strategy. "These plans and strategies presume a situation of total war" that advocates unlimited violence and a standard of action that, carried to its furthest extremes, can result in martyrdom and self-destruction. However, terrorism as an end unto itself is an anomaly and is not the usual manner in which terrorist organizations end.

Ultimately, terrorism is an exceedingly rational strategy, calculated in terms of costs and benefits with the terrorist relying on the accuracy of those calculations.[55] For the vast majority of terrorists, the strategic environment is reduced to a power struggle between opposing forces wherein the terrorist assumes an ethic of total resistance. In the system in which the terrorist lives and moves, "this ethic can only take a martial—and thereby planned and strategic—form."[56]

TERRORISM AND WAR

Terrorism operates in two dimensions simultaneously—as a theory of violence and as a strategy of violence perpetrated to achieve a putative end. Tying these two concepts together, which is the thrust of this essay, the strategic theory of terrorism is a theory of action—to paraphrase Bernard Brodie—with violence as the critical and defining element in both of these dimensions.[57] Thus, how should we understand the violence that terrorism uses, its "martial form"? The answer to this question is again hindered by the definitional debate highlighted previously, since scholars hold a legion of differing views describing what it is not rather than what it is, but largely distinguishing it from other forms of collective violence (e.g., lynching, rioting, and vigilantism).[58]

There are some problems with this categorization—of understanding terrorism as solely another variety of collective violence. These other types of collective violence are not modes of political behavior, nor do the people involved seek to challenge the authority of the state and to acquire political influence. Further, terrorist groups are not mobs, but organizations with "internally consistent values, beliefs, and images of the environment." They seek a logical means to advance a particular though not always clearly articulated ends using rational decision-making calculations to attain short-term and long-term objectives.[59] Colin Gray, however, offers a way out of the definitional wilderness by questioning whether terrorism is war.

Gray answers the question by referring to two theorists: Clausewitz and Hedley Bull. Clausewitz defined war as "an act of force to compel our enemy to do our will."[60] The political scientist Hedley Bull followed Clausewitz's line of reasoning and wrote, "war is organized violence carried on by political units against each other."[61] Thus, terrorism meets this definition, since terrorists apply this force, violence, for a political end. If it is not for this end, then it "may be sport, or crime, or banditry of a kind integral to local culture, but it is not war. War, its threat and actuality, is an instrument of policy."[62] As Colin Gray notes, "war has many dimensions beyond the political, but its eternal essence is captured by Clausewitz and Bull." From his perspective, the political context is principal, though he admits that it is far from the "sole, driver of the incidence and character of war."[63] In other words, Gray is willing to concede that terrorists use force to achieve ends that are political as well as social or religious in nature.

Some thinkers suggest that terrorism is a form of "new war," and that Clausewitz overlooks unconventional and so-called non-Trinitarian war, thereby arguing that Clausewitz and his remarkable trinity is not relevant.[64] These critics define the concept of the trinity as the commander and his army, the people and the government. In Gray's view, this is a serious misreading of Clausewitz and neglectful of the primary trinity, which still pertains. That primary trinity consists of passion (violence, hatred, and enmity), chance and probability, and subordination to reason, or policy.[65] In this context, policy can be understood as the decision to take an action and perform this act in a particular way, or it can be described as the activities and relationships that influence the formulation of policy. For Clausewitz, the formulation of policy was a matter of judgment and other qualities and could be undertaken by both states as well as non-states (he uses the example of the Tartar tribes). Thus, Clausewitz thought not only in terms of the nation-state model.[66]

Nonetheless, terrorism contains all three elements of both trinities with the primary trinity's relationship to terrorism being self-evident. In the secondary trinity, the titles are changed, but the functions remain the same: the strategist; the operational commander of terrorist groups consisting of foot soldiers and members of the support network who execute the missions or provide the financial and logistical support; and the broader populace, "which provides expressive and instrumental support for the terrorists or sympathy to their cause."[67]

Thus, terrorism fully meets the definitions set out by Clausewitz and Bull. It is a form of war, irregular war, similar to insurgency but having its own characteristics. Nonetheless, terrorism shares with insurgency and other forms of violent military conduct the capacity to generate a strategic effect. That effect can be produced upon the mind, the military or security forces of the opponent, or both, but, regardless, all have in common that they must have political consequences.[68] In truth, it matters not whether the character of the war has a regular or irregular feature—the qualifying adjectives are of no import. Clausewitz's general theory of war and strategy are equally valid to both. A general theory of war and strategy explains both regular and irregular [terrorism] warfare. While they are different forms of warfare, they are not different strategically.[69]

CONCLUSION

T. S. Eliot concluded his 1925 poem "The Hollow Men" with the words: "This is the way the world ends/Not with a bang, but a whimper." These are words worth remembering. Some scholars point to the apocalyptic cast of contemporary terrorism, particularly its religious variant, suggesting that this form of terrorism is unlike its predecessors in that the actors are irrational, self-destructive, and are marching willingly to martyrdom. Others point to the fact that religious terrorism represents a new "wave," or it is a "cosmic war," significantly different from political terrorism.[70] Nonetheless, the continuities terrorism manifests over the past centuries make one skeptical of any explanation that puts the emphasis on uniqueness.[71] Further, in classifying and giving prominence to terrorism in this form and with this ideology, theorists propagate a new stereotype of terrorism that is not conducive to thinking about terrorism as a rational, calculated strategic mode of thinking. This perspective perhaps underscores a strategy deficit, a failure to perceive war and politics as a unity in which war is fused with political considerations that include social and religious dimensions.[72] For how else should we interpret the notion of a caliphate but as a theocratic understanding of the notion of the state?

While terrorists' ideology, regardless of its stripe, offers a criticism of the existing political system and a prophecy of a perfectly just and harmonious society that will last the ages, it is imperative as well to understand the strategic challenge that terrorism represents. As Colin Gray reminds us, it would be imprudent to believe that terrorists are isolated from the world of strategy any more than that can be said of other practitioners of small wars and savage violence, even professional soldiers.[73]

ENDNOTES - CHAPTER 8

1. Quoted in Walter Laqueur, *The New Terrorism*, New York: Oxford University Press, 1999, p. 103.

2. *Ibid.*

3. Richard Schultz, "Conceptualizing Political Terrorism: A Typology," *Journal of International Affairs*, Vol. 32, No. 1, p. 7.

4. Jon Tetsuro Sumida, "The Relationship of History and Theory in *On War*: The Clausewitzian Ideal and Its Implications," *The Journal of Military History*, Vol. 65, April 2001, p. 336.

5. Gregory D. Foster, "A Conceptual Foundation for a Theory of Strategy," *The Washington Quarterly*, Vol. 13, No. 1, Winter 1990, p. 47; Roberta Senechal de la Roche, "Toward a Scientific Theory of Terrorism," *Sociological Theory*, Vol. 22, No. 1, March 2004, p. 3.

6. Walter Laqueur, *Terrorism*, London, U.K.: Weidenfeld and Nicolson, 1977, p. 5.

7. Jack P. Gibbs, "Conceptualization of Terrorism," *American Sociological Review*, Vol. 54, No. 3, June 1989, p. 329.

8. Martha Crenshaw Hutchinson, "The Concept of Revolutionary Terrorism," *The Journal of Conflict Resolution*, Vol. 16, No. 3, September 1972, p. 384.

9. Gibbs, p. 330.

10. Quoted in Hutchinson, p. 383.

11. Harry R. Yarger, *Strategic Theory for the 21st Century: The Little Book on Big Strategy*, Carlisle, PA: Strategic Studies Institute, U.S. Army War College, 2006, p. 1.

12. *Ibid.*, p. 6-7; Martha Crenshaw, "An Organizational Approach to the Analysis of Political Terrorism," *Orbis*, Fall 1985, p. 472.

13. Yarger, p. 7.

14. *Ibid.*, pp. 7-8.

15. Hutchinson, p. 385.

16. Charles Tilly, "Terror, Terrorism, Terrorists," *Sociological Theory*, Vol. 22, No. 1, March 2004, p. 9; H. Edward Price, Jr., "The Strategy and Tactics of Revolutionary Terrorism," *Comparative Studies on Society and History*, Vol. 19, No. 1, January 1977, p. 52; and T. P. Thornton, "Terror as a Weapon of Political Agitation," in H. Eckstein, ed., *Internal War*, New York: Free Press, 1964, pp. 78-79.

17. Donald Black, "The Geometry of Terrorism," *Sociological Theory*, Vol. 22, No. 1, March 2004, p. 18.

18. Arthur H. Garrison, "Defining Terrorism: Philosophy of the Bomb, Propaganda by Deed and Change Through Fear and Violence, *Criminal Justice Studies*, Vol 17, No. 3, September 2004, p. 260.

19. Amy Zegart, "An Empirical Analysis of Failed Intelligence Reforms Before September 11," *Political Science Quarterly*, Vol. 121, No. 1, Spring 2006, pp. 35-36, 39.

20. Williamson Murray and Mark Grimsley, "Introduction: On Strategy," *The Making of Strategy, Rulers, States, and War*, Cambridge, UK: Cambridge University Press, 1994, 1997, p. 1.

21. Yarger, pp. 13-14.

22. *Ibid.*, 14.

23. Alison M. Jagger, "What Is Terrorism, Why Is It Wrong, and Could It Ever Be Morally Permissible?" *Journal of Social Philosophy,* Vol. 26, No. 2, Summer 2005, p. 208.

24. Yarger, p. 14.

25. *Ibid.*, pp. 15-16.

26. Crenshaw, pp. 472-482; Randy Borum, *Psychology of Terrorism*, Tampa, FL: University of South Florida, 2004, pp. 24, 52-56.

27. Daniel S. Gressang IV, "Terrorism in the 21st Century: Reassessing the Emerging Threat," in Max Manwaring, ed., *Deterrence in the 21st Century*, Portland, OR: Frank Cass, 2001, p. 73.

28. Roberta Senechal de la Roche, "Collective Violence as Social Control," *Sociological Forum*, Vol. 11, No. 1, March 1996, pp. 97-98; Martha Crenshaw, "The Causes of Terrorism," *Comparative Politics,* Vol. 13, No. 4, July 1981, pp. 381-384.

29. de la Roche, p. 103.

30. Quoted in Garrison, p. 268.

31. Crenshaw, "An Organizational Approach to the Analysis of Political Terrorism," p. 466.

32. Thomas C. Schelling, *Arms and Influence*, New Haven, CT: Yale University Press, 1966, p. 3.

33. Carl von Clausewitz, *On War,* Michael Howard and Peter Paret, ed./trans., Princeton, NJ: Princeton University Press, 1984, p. 77.

34. Schelling, pp. 3-4.

35. Hutchinson, pp. 387-389.

36. Philip G. Cerny, "Terrorism and the New Security Dilemma," *Naval War College Review,* Vol. 58, No. 1, Winter 2005, p. 16.

37. Andrew H. Kydd and Barbara F. Walter, "The Strategies of Terrorism," *International Security,* Vol. 31, No. 1, Summer 2006, pp. 58, 78.

38. Jeffrey C. Alexander, "From the Depths of Despair: Performance, Counterperformance, and 'September 11,'" *Sociological Theory,* Vol. 22, No. 1, March 2004, pp. 88, 90.

39. Anthony Oberschall, "Explaining Terrorism: The Contribution of Collective Action Theory," *Sociological Theory* Vol. 22, No. 1, March 2004, p. 27.

40. H. Stuart Hughes, *Consciousness and Society: The Reorientation of Social Thought, 1890-1930,* New York, Vintage Books, 1958, p. 165.

41. Alexander, p. 89.

42. Philip Windsor, "Terrorism and International Order," in Mats Berdal, ed., *Studies in International Relations: Essays by Philip Windsor*, Portland, OR: Sussex Academic Press, 2002, p. x, 195.

43. *Ibid.*, p. 195.

44. Crenshaw, "An Organizational Approach to the Analysis of Political Terrorism," p. 466; Alexander, p. 89.

45. Crenshaw, "An Organizational Approach to the Analysis of Political Terrorism," p. 471.

46. *Ibid.*, 481.

47. Alexander, p. 89.

48. Borum, p. 24.

49. Martha Crenshaw, "Theories of Terrorism: Instrumental and Organizational Approaches," in David C. Rapoport, ed., *Inside Terrorist Organizations*, Portland, OR: Frank Cass, 2001, p. 13.

50. Schelling, p. 4.

51. Windsor, p. 193.

52. Michel Wieviorka, *The Making of Terrorism*, David Gordon White, trans., Chicago, IL: The University of Chicago Press, 1993, p. 9.

53. *Ibid.*, pp. 7-8

54. *Ibid.*, p. 8.

55. Hutchinson, p. 394.

56. Wieviorka, pp. 11-12.

57. Brodie's exact words are: "strategy is nothing if not pragmatic….Above, all, strategic theory is a theory for action." Quoted in Colin Gray, "What is War? A View from Strategic Studies," in Colin Gray, *Strategy and History: Essays on Theory and Practice,* New York: Routledge, 2006, p. 185.

58. de la Roche, p. 102.

59. Crenshaw, "The Causes of Terrorism," p. 379-386.

60. Clausewitz, p. 75.

61. Quoted in Gray, "What is War?," p. 185.

62. *Ibid.*, p. 185.

63. *Ibid.*, p. 187.

64. *Ibid.*, p. 186.

65. Gray, "What is War?," p. 187, and Colin S. Gray, *Irregular Enemies and the Essence of Strategy: Can the American Way of War Adapt?* Carlisle, PA: Strategic Studies Institute, U.S. Army War College, 2006.

66. Antulio J. Echevarria II, "Clausewitz and the Nature of the War on Terror," in Hew Strachan and Andreas Herberg-Rothe, eds., *Clausewitz in the Twenty-First Century*, Oxford, UK: Oxford University Press, 2007, pp. 196-230.

67. Borum, p. 54.

68. Gray, *Modern Strategy*, pp. 295-296.

69. Gray, *Irregular Enemies and the Essence of Strategy: Can the American Way of War Adapt?* pp. vi, 4-5.

70. See Mark Juergensmeyer, *Terror in the Mind of God: The Global Rise of Religious Violence*, Berkeley, CA: University of California Press, 2000; and David C. Rapoport, "The Four Waves of Modern Terrorism," in Audrey Kurth Cronin and James Ludes, eds., *Attacking Terrorism: Elements of a Grand Strategy*, Washington, DC: Georgetown University Press, 2004, pp. 46-73.

71. Oberschall, "Explaining Terrorism: The Contribution of Collective Action Theory," p. 27.

72. Gray, *Irregular Enemies and the Essence of Strategy: Can the American Way of War Adapt?* p. vi.

73. Bernard Crick, *In Defence of Politics*, 4th ed., Chicago, IL: The University of Chicago Press, 1992, pp. 34-35; Gray, *Modern Strategy*, p. 294.

CHAPTER 9

THUCYDIDES AND CONTEMPORARY STRATEGY

R. Craig Nation

A POSSESSION FOR ALL TIME

Nearly 2-and-a-half millennia have passed since the Greek historian Thucydides composed his famous history of the Peloponnesian War (432-404 B.C.E.).[1] Although well known among scholars, the text was not translated from the Greek original until 1478.[2] Contemporary interest in Thucydides dates to the European renaissance and emergence of the modern state system, whose dynamic of armed competition between contending sovereignties his work is often presumed to represent. Ever since, Thucydides has been a source of inspiration for policymakers as well as scholars. In our time no armed conflict anywhere in the world is fought to a conclusion without some attempt to use his work as a vehicle for interpretation.[3]

Thucydides's influence has been manifest in modern American strategic thought. In 1947 U.S. Secretary of State George Marshall turned to Thucydides to fathom the emerging Cold War: "I doubt seriously," he proposed, "whether a man can think with full wisdom and with deep conviction regarding certain of the basic issues today who has not at least reviewed in his mind the period of the Peloponnesian War and the fall of Athens."[4] A later U.S. Secretary of State and former general officer, Colin Powell, speaking upon his retirement as chairman of the Joint Chiefs of Staff in 1993, cited Thucydides to the effect that "of all manifestations of power, restraint impresses men most." Powell kept the passage posted at his desk for many years.[5] When Stanfield Turner set out to revamp instruction at the U.S. Naval War College in the 1970s, he made Thucydides the focal point of the curriculum. Today Carl von Clausewitz, Sun Tzu, and Thucydides are the only strategic theorists whose work predates the 20th century that are systematically studied at U.S. senior service schools.

In the past several decades, there has been an explosion of work devoted to Thucydides, no longer addressed primarily to an audience of classical scholars, but rather the larger community of security and strategic studies.[6] This attention rests on an appreciation of his work's multifaceted relevance. Leo Strauss represents Thucydides's text as a commentary upon war itself: "The Peloponnesian war is that singular event which reveals fully, in an unsurpassable manner, for all times, the nature of war."[7] Clifford Orwin sees it as a political primer: "Of all writers on politics, none stays closer than Thucydides to the world of citizen and statesman," whose work belongs "to students of political life of whatever time and place."[8] Richard Ned Lebow concentrates on Thucydides's contributions to international relations theory, as "the first writer to analyze the origin of war, the role of power in international relations, the relationship between domestic and foreign politics, the process by which civil and international orders unravel and what might be done to restore them."[9] Such commendations can be multiplied manyfold. Thucydides's *Peloponnesian War* is without question a seminal study of warfare and a "possession for all time" as the author aspired it to be.[10]

Why is this so? What does *The Peloponnesian War* have to teach us about the problems of war and strategy? It is in fact generally easier to assert the text's importance than to discern the character of its insights. Like any great work, its message is ambiguous and has been read in different ways depending on the prevailing *Zeitgeist*. In the early modern centuries, Thucydides was viewed as a guide to the primacy of power and *raison d'état* in the Westphalian state system. The young

Thomas Hobbes, who in 1624 authored one of the first English translations of *The Peloponnesian War*, provides an example. Hobbes's philosophical work, which considered the urge to power to be integral to human nature and emphasized the insecurity that results from an anarchic state of nature, was deeply influenced by his classical predecessor.[11] The realist tradition in international relations theory has consistently claimed Thucydides as a progenitor—Joseph Nye calls him "the founding father of Realism."[12] For Marshall, the war between Athens and Sparta became a prototype for the bipolar confrontation of the emerging Cold War, and the clash of values between democracy and totalitarianism that informed it. Others see the work as a humane reflection on the human condition whose overarching theme is "the suffering of war."[13] Powell, from the perspective of the victorious United States of the post-Cold War, found a cautionary tale about the limits of power. Today, Thucydides' work is being applied as a vehicle for understanding the logic of terrorism in the world after 9/11.[14] This is as it should be. Classic works of strategic literature cannot be read as users manuals. They offer illuminations rather than answers—their status as "timeless" works, in a sense demands, that it be so.

Policy and strategy, defined as the craft of statesmanship and the use of military force in the pursuit of political aims, are practical undertakings. Many U.S. commanders carried copies of Antoine Jomini's work onto the battlefields of the American Civil War—the Swiss theorist made a conscious attempt to provide maxims that could be applied to tactical and operational problems. Alexander the Great is reported to have slept on campaign with a version of *The Iliad* prepared by his tutor, Aristotle, at his bedside (as modern commanders might carry a Bible or Koran)—cultural inspiration may also serve as a foundation for waging war. It is difficult to imagine Thucydides in a knapsack on campaign; his insights are too complex to serve as guides on the tactical level, and his conclusions too elusive to provide cultural inspiration. His work has a different kind of merit, however, that is perhaps no less relevant and profound.

What Thucydides provides is strategic insight. He offers invaluable points of orientation for statecraft and supreme command in the domain of national policy, as well as searing judgments about the factors that lead states to victory or defeat in protracted strategic competition. His subject is the institution of war in all its dimensions, and his text illustrates that although we no longer fight with shields and stabbing spears, on the strategic level warfare has remained remarkably constant over time. Those who read Thucydides for the first time are usually struck by his work's astonishing current relevance—not so much as an agenda for action as a guide to understanding.[15] As a reflection on war intended to help us to come to terms with the larger strategic environment, *The Peloponnesian War* remains unsurpassed.

A WAR LIKE ALL OTHERS

Much of the current literature concerning the Peloponnesian War is focused on the conflict itself, considered as an event in space and time that can be understood empirically. Victor David Hanson's recent study, *A War Like No Other*, emphasizes the distinctiveness of the struggle, which he portrays as an armed conflict virtually unique in history in its scope and complexity.[16] This is potentially misleading. Almost everything that we know about the Peloponnesian War is based on what Thucydides tells us, and despite the best efforts of archeologists and classical scholars, that is not likely to change.

There is an ongoing debate about the accuracy of Thucydides's narrative, but it rests on distressingly few supplementary sources (essentially stone tablets containing state records and a very small number of fragmentary primary and secondary accounts). Basically, much of Thucydides's story must either be accepted on faith or rejected as improbable. Thucydides was in an excellent position to assemble an accurate record of events. His appreciation for the importance of the war gave him a strong motive to do so. And he went out of his way to demonstrate his objectivity, a trait for which his work has long been appreciated. David Hume, later echoed by Immanuel Kant, famously remarked that the first page of his text "was the commencement of real history," while even the skeptical George Cawkwell lauds his "monstrous passion for the truth."[17]

Up to the publication of Jacqueline de Romilly's seminal study of Athenian imperialism in 1947, the issue of chronology dominated Thucydides scholarship—when the work was composed, the stages of composition, and how much the author was in a position to know.[18] Today, scholars broadly accept that *The Peloponnesian War* was conceived and composed as a whole. Scholarship has shifted from issues of accuracy in narration toward an immanent reading of the text, viewed as an artful reconstruction used to convey the author's personal view of Greek political life.[19] This kind of research agenda may be exaggerated in its own right, but it is certainly true that Thucydides interprets as well as describes—his account is infused with the author's perspective. "Thucydides has imposed his will," notes the commentator Arnold Gomme, "as no other historian has ever done."[20] The Peloponnesian War was indeed a great armed conflict, but it was not the only one waged in classical antiquity. It may be perceived as a "war like no other" only because of the brilliance of Thucydides's rendition of events. And as a 19th-century commentator warns, Thucydides's masterly text can lead us to neglect the fact that "history does not consist of events in and of themselves, but rather in the impact that they have upon others."[21] For the purposes of strategic studies, as distinct from classical studies and historiography, it is Thucydides's *Peloponnesian War* that matters.

What do we know about Thucydides? Three vitae survive from the Byzantine period, but they are contradictory and sometimes clearly erroneous. Most of what we can assert derives from what Thucydides himself tells us in four brief references to his personal circumstances in *The Peloponnesian War*, and perhaps more importantly from what we can infer about the author from reading his text.[22]

Thucydides was born in the 5th century, around 460. He was therefore 29 years old and in the prime of life in 431 when the Peloponnesian War began, and 55 in 404 when it ended with Athens's defeat. The date of his death is not known with certainty, but probably occurred around 400-397. The author records his full name as Thucydides son of Olorus from the deme of Halimous. This indicates Thracian origin and possible familial ties to the powerful and conservative Philaidea clan, which included the Athenian statesman Miltiades (550-489) (the victor at Marathon in 490) and his son Cimon (510-450) (ostracized from Athens in 461). Thucydides was clearly of high social standing, and a man of means. At one point he mentions that his family possesses the Athenian concession for gold mining in all of Thrace. In 424 the citizens of Athens elected him to the post of general, one of only ten individuals to hold that post annually and therefore a leading figure in the state. In the same year, ordered to come to the relief of the commercial center of Amphipolis in Thrace with a small fleet of seven triremes (warships), he arrived too late to prevent the city's fall to the Spartan general, Brasidas. Returning to Athens, Thucydides was condemned as a sign of disfavor and exiled from the city for twenty years (a fairly common punishment in the era). For the remainder of the conflict he was therefore able to observe, from the perspective of a not entirely disinterested onlooker, the war swirling around him. During the war, when he may have spent much of his time on his Thracian estate, and after his return to Athens on the war's conclusion, he composed on a series of papyrus scrolls, what was in effect a contemporary history, recording in great detail the course of events from 431 to 411. Thucydides's history is left unfinished, and in fact breaks off abruptly in the midst of a paragraph.[23]

More important than the details of this modest biography is what it seems to indicate about the author's intellectual orientation. Thucydides's life ran parallel to the golden age of the classical Hellenic civilization. He lived to see the triumph of Athenian material civilization with the raising of the great temples on the Acropolis, the construction of the long walls linking Athens to the port of Piraeus, and the constant expansion of an Athenian maritime empire. He was contemporary with the political leader Pericles (495-429), the historian Herodotus (484-425), the sculptor Phidias (490-430), the philosophers Gorgias (483-375) and Socrates (469-399), and the dramatists Sophocles (497-406), Euripides (480-406), and Aristophanes (448-380).[24] Thucydides was therefore a participant in one of the greatest cultural flowerings in all of history, and present at the creation of what we call Western Civilization. He also lived to see the defeat and ruin of his native city, an event whose cultural as well as strategic importance he fully appreciated. Thucydides begins his history by remarking that its subject is "the war between the Peloponnesians and the Athenians…believing that it would be a great war, and more worthy of relation than any that had preceded it."[25] He makes no attempt to justify this focus, and in fact none is required. "War is the father and king of all," wrote the pre-Socratic philosopher Heraclitus (535-475), in a passage that is not incongruous for a civilization whose founding text was Homer's *Iliad*.[26] It was a valuation that Thucydides shared. The sentiment was echoed from the other side of the world by Thucydides's approximate contemporary Sun Tzu, for whom: "Warfare is the greatest affair of state, the basis of life and death, the way to survival or extinction. It must be thoroughly pondered and analyzed."[27] Thucydides's experience with hegemonic warfare led him to validate these conclusions, and to perceive war as the essential focus for all political life. The political, social, and cultural implications of the great war between the Athenians and the Peloponnesians are the real subject of his history.

One might surmise that as a young man Thucydides turned away from the oligarchic political preferences that would come naturally to someone of his social standing, and embraced the idealism of Periclean Athens. The tribute to the civic culture of democratic Athens that he transcribes in Pericles's funeral oration in Book Two of *The Peloponnesian War*, in which the Athenian leader honors the city's fallen soldiers by evoking the cause for which they offered their lives, is obviously sincere.[28] Thucydides also sees and describes in brutal detail the dark side of democratic governance, but his allegiance to Pericles as the embodiment of the ideal of an open society never wavers. In this sense his history takes on the contours of a tragedy—the account of the downfall, occasioned by its own hubris and tragic flaws, of a great civilization. W. Robert Connor notes a "recurring paradox" in Thucydides's history; "the intense emotional power of a work ostensibly so detached."[29] The paradox is only apparent. Thucydides's major themes, the harsh reality of warfare as a locus of political intercourse and the corruption of a civilized polity exposed to the pressures of total war, are passionately felt. It is the importance of these themes that leads him to insist on a dispassionate investigation of the questions of causation and responsibility. "The absence of romance in my history," he writes, "will, I fear, detract somewhat from its interest; but if it be judged useful by those inquirers who desire an exact knowledge of the past as an aid to the understanding of the future…I shall be content."[30] Thucydides's *Peloponnesian War* is important not primarily for what makes it unique, but for what it shares in common with and reveals about the nature of other hegemonic conflicts. It is a war like all others that poses themes of universal and enduring importance.

THE PELOPONNESIAN WAR

The war that Thucydides recounts certainly merits his judgment that in scope and importance it was "much greater than the wars which preceded it."[31] This is due to its length and extent, but also because of the cultural stakes. Thucydides begins his narrative with an account of the evolution of Hellenic civilization itself (known to modern students as the *Archaeology*), which demonstrates the development from the 7th to 5th centuries of a classic Greek civilization around the political unit of the city-state (*polis*). City-states were engaged in constant feuding over agricultural land at the margin of their territories, waging a "Greek way of war" with armed citizens' militias deployed as heavy infantry (hoplites) fighting in close formation (the phalanx) in a strategic context heavily constrained by myth and ritual.[32] This relatively harmonious system, whose value system Homer depicted in his epics, was soon to be swept away—first by external shocks and then by war waged between its leading polities.

The Greek world drew together to repel the Persians in the *Persian Wars* (490-479)—as recounted in the *Histories* of Herodotus, culminating with the famous battles of Marathon (490), Salamis (480) and Plataea (479).[33] What followed might be compared, with due allowance for changed circumstances, to the emergence of the Cold War after 1945, when disparate allies forced together to resist a common threat fell out when the threat was removed.[34] Athens and Sparta, the leading Greek powers, allies in the struggle against the Persians but possessed of radically different institutions and aspirations, were soon engaged in a struggle for dominion. Thucydides devotes a large section of his text (the *Pentecontaetia*, or "50 years") to describe the rise of a revisionist Athens, bent upon replacing Sparta as the leading power in Hellas, in the decades following the Persian War.

Thucydides's analysis of the causes of war has a strong cultural dimension. The author repeatedly refers to the differences in style, attitude, and values that divide the major belligerents. Sparta represents a distinctive variant of the oligarchic tyranny, with an agricultural economy based on the labor of a massive population of enslaved helots, and defense provided by professional warriors or Spartiates organized in elite infantry units famed for their courage and discipline. Sparta's force as a land power is justly famed—no other power in the Greek world is presumed to be capable of standing before it. Sparta also heads a loose alliance based on bilateral agreements with like-minded allies known as the Peloponnesian League. As an agrarian based oligarchy committed to traditional values and an unchallengeable land power with a status-quo geopolitical orientation, Sparta may be said to represent a conservative force in Greek life. By way of contrast, Thucydides portrays Athens as dynamic and innovative. Though like all Greek city-states its economy rests on slave labor, Athens is groundbreaking in developing democratic institutions and offers a considerable degree of empowerment to its free citizens. Its international position rests on sea power, commerce, and an empire of subject states (city-states in the Aegean, Thrace, and Asia Minor) that originally ally with Athens to resist the Persians and are organized under Athenian leadership in the Delian League in 478. Athens is culturally innovative, economically dynamic, and strategically expansive. After the construction of the long walls linking Athens to Piraeus in 450, it is also virtually invulnerable. Periclean Athens is bent on extending its power, and brash and assertive in its dealings with others.

When the city-state of Megara withdrew from the Spartan alliance and joined with Athens in 460, a First Peloponnesian War that pitted Athens and Sparta against one another as primary belligerents ensued. The war ended in 446 with a compromise known as the Thirty Years Peace, including a pledge to submit future differences to binding arbitration. Between 433 and 431, however, a series of events on the periphery of the Greek world drove the two antagonists to war once again. Thucydides's *Peloponnesian War* was waged from 431-404, over a span of 27 years. For purposes of simplification (the distinction is not made by Thucydides) historians generally divide the war into three phases: the *Archidamian War* from 431-421, named for the Spartan King Archidamus, who ironically opposed a resort to arms and sought to contain hostilities once in progress; the *Peace of Nicias* from 421-412, named for the Athenian general Nicias who negotiated the truce in 421 and went on to meet a tragic fate as commander of the doomed Athenian expeditionary force on Sicily; and the *Ionian War* from 412-404, beginning with an Athenian revival but concluding with her final defeat.

The Archidamian War unfolded as a stalemate between Spartan land power and Athenian sea power. Each side was capable of hurting its opponent, but not overthrowing it. A turning point came when Athens established a base on the Peloponnesus at the isolated outpost of Pylos, capturing several hundred elite Spartiate warriors and threatening to inspire a helot revolt. The Peace of Nicias was the result, but it did not strike deep roots. By this point the war had taken on a momentum of its own, with allies and local commanders refusing to respect ceasefires, and a war party on each side committed to pursue the conflict *jusqu'au bout*. Thucydides goes to some length to argue that the Peace of Nicias, which he calls a "treacherous armistice," does not divide the Peloponnesian War into two distinct parts, but rather represents an integral part of an extended conflict with a consistent strategic logic.[35]

In 416, with rivalry between the two parties unabated, Athens, led by the flamboyant, ambitious, and unprincipled young Alcibiades, launched a great armada with the intention of shifting the balance of power decisively by conquering the island of Sicily.[36] The destruction of its expeditionary force at Syracuse weakened Athens substantially, but not decisively. An oligarchy overthrew the Athenian democracy in 411, but democratic forces quickly regained political control of the city. Athens eventually recouped its strength and launched a military comeback, carrying the war into the Aegean and the Hellespont. The Ionian War was essentially a naval contest waged in these regions, with the Athenian fleet successful at the outset but unable to force the issue to decisive conclusion. In the end, it was the intervention in the Spartan cause of the former common enemy Persia that turned the tide. In 405, at the Battle of Aegonspotami, the Spartan admiral Lysander caught the Athenian fleet drawn up on shore and destroyed it. In 404, with its real center of gravity eliminated, Athens surrendered. The Spartan army occupied the Acropolis, tore down the long walls, and imposed an oligarchic tyranny under a kind of junta known to history as the Thirty Tyrants. As a competitive polity in the eastern Mediterranean, Athens's authority would eventually be restored, but its Golden Age, inspired by the ideals of Pericles, would not return. Thucydides's account of the war ends at the year 411, but it is clear throughout the narrative that he is aware of its eventual outcome, and that this awareness importantly shapes the way in which he structures his text and develops its themes.

THUCYDIDES AND GRAND STRATEGY

Even in brief outline, the Peloponnesian War presents the observer with an extraordinarily wide variety of strategic gambits, military adventures, and political ploys. Thucydides's history includes detailed descriptions of major fleet actions, pitched battles, sieges, unconventional operations, plague, revolution, atrocity and massacre, political confrontations, instances of decisive leadership, and, in fact, virtually every kind of circumstance that shapes the outcome of major wars. The story is engrossing, but as already argued, it is not unique. What is it that makes Thucydides's account the "classical and canonical work of Western culture" that it is universally considered to be?[37]

Part of the answer lies in the controlled emotion with which Thucydides infuses an account of a war that he firmly believes to be an unprecedented tragedy. Part lies in the author's methodological contributions. Thucydides sets out to chronicle a war, not to craft a general theory of warfare. But he clearly states the conviction that because human nature remains essentially the same, by examining the past we can identify recurrent patterns in social and political intercourse, learn from them, and on that basis develop strategies for more effective action in the future. The author's magisterial detachment, refusal to accept conventional explanations at face value, and unapologetic rationalism are nothing short of remarkable. Moses Finley calls Thucydides "the most careful and in the best sense the most skeptical historian the ancient world ever produced."[38] In this regard his work provides a solid foundation for modern historiography and the discipline of political science. Most importantly, perhaps, *The Peloponnesian War* is timeless because it develops an appreciation of warfare in a larger strategic context and poses classic problems in strategic analysis in a particularly lucid way. We can illustrate the way in which this occurs with three examples: Thucydides's reflections on the causes of war, the strategic level of warfare, and ethical and moral concerns.

The Origins of War: Identifying the causes and nature of war is a basic challenge that arguably has become more difficult in an era when declarations of war have become things of the past, when the state of war has lost much of its formal legal status, and when the United States finds itself engaged in an open-ended "war on terrorism and radical extremism" that may last for generations. Thucydides's account of the origins of the Peloponnesian War offers an interesting case study for working through these problems.

Thucydides devotes a great amount of attention to discussing the causes of the Peloponnesian War and makes a fundamental distinction, which he is sometimes said to have invented, between the immediate or short-term sources of the conflict and underlying or structural causes.[39] Simon Hornblower describes this aspect of his work as "a conscious, secular theory of causation in terms of deep and superficial political causes."[40] Perhaps the most famous sentence in Thucydides's history is the comment that however one might adjudicate immediate causes, ultimately "the growth of the power of Athens, and the alarm which this inspired in Sparta, made war inevitable."[41] The pessimistic fatalism that seems to be reflected here, the view of political life as an endless striving for power and dominion, has found great resonance in the realist camp of international relations theory. Hans Morgenthau quotes Thucydides to the effect that: "Of the gods we know, and of men we believe, that it is a necessary law of their nature that they rule whenever they can."[42] Athens's ambition, opines Raymond Aron, condemns it to brutality: "The servitudes of power are inescapable."[43]

In fact, Thucydides does not make any effort to develop a systematic theory of causation. He describes the origins of the Peloponnesian War in considerable detail, but leaves the reader to draw conclusions concerning the relative weight of the various factors on which he touches. Thucydides mentions Sparta's fear of growing Athenian power on several occasions.[44] Clearly, the security dilemma occasioned by the rise of a great power challenger, competitive bipolarity, and an impending power transition are powerful structural factors that contribute to systemic instability and increase the likelihood of war.[45] Much the larger part of Thucydides's description, however, is devoted to immediate causes. One set of variables that he discusses concern economic motivation. The Spartans emphasized the Megarian Decrees, which imposed a commercial embargo on Athens's rival, Megara, as a primary cause of war. In response, Pericles enjoined Athens to enforce the decrees rigorously. The origin of the war in an obscure dispute over a small settlement on the margin of the Greek world is not unrelated to the fact that the settlement in question is strategically poised along the trade route leading to Italy. Thucydides does not offer a reductionist explanation that locates the roots of war in an Athenian imperialism driven by the merchants of the Piraeus, but he is not insensitive to the weight of economic factors.[46]

Thucydides also probes the diplomatic interaction leading up to the war. Neither of the belligerents necessarily seeks to provoke war, but all become caught up in a maze of misperceptions, ambiguous communication, erroneous calculations, and policies of bluff and bluster. As in the July Crisis of 1914, there is a sense in which the Peloponnesian War becomes a "war by accident" as a result of the failure of diplomacy. Domestic politics and policy processes, including the critical role of charismatic leadership, also have their place. The Spartan decision for war results from the crude *va-t'en-guerre* rhetoric of the ephor Stenelaides, who declaims that he does "not pretend to understand" the long speeches of the Athenians, but nonetheless urges a "vote for war, as honor demands."[47] Pericles's personal authority and powers of persuasion are critical factors that turn Athens away from a policy of compromise that it might otherwise have preferred.

Thucydides's account does not resolve the issue of the relative importance of structural and immediate causes, nor does it seek to do so. What the text demonstrates is multiple causality.[48] Structural explanations alone do not suffice—the choice for war is an ambiguous action that is conditioned by numerous variables, "a confluence of causes at multiple levels of analysis."[49] While the calculus of power may be a necessary context for a decision for war, it must be filtered through a screen of perception and misperception, threshed out in the domestic policy process, refined by diplomatic interaction, and implemented in practice. Nothing is fixed and inalterable. Wars are seldom clear cut, war aims and strategic calculations are subject to change, and the precise combination of factors that may have motivated a choice for war at one point in time will alter as the dynamic of conflict unfolds.

The Strategic Level of Warfare.

Thucydides's depiction of warfare is nearly unparalleled in its intensity and power. There is no more sophisticated rendering of the complementary roles of land and sea power, the burden of command, the consequences of defeat, the impact of political faction on strategic choice, or the role of chance and circumstance in effecting strategic outcomes. Despite the best efforts of responsible leaders, momentous events continue to turn on the unpredictable and unexpected—an eclipse of the moon and bolt of thunder, cloud cover during a night attack, unidentified terrain features, or the personal foibles of leaders under stress. *The Peloponnesian War* is one of the greatest books ever written about the theme of war itself. But Thucydides does not just depict the face of battle. He places warfare in a grand strategic context where a multiplicity of factors must be explored to account for the difference between victory and defeat. Thucydides's appreciation for the strategic level of warfare is one of the most important, and neglected, dimensions of his work.

Thucydides depicts grand strategy as *comprehensive*. In great wars, everything matters and nothing is superfluous. In *The Peloponnesian War,* this includes such elements as: the *domestic political environment* (Sparta is chronically concerned with the possibility of a helot revolt, there is a constant struggle between oligarchic and democratic factions within individual city-states with serious strategic implications); *economic necessity* (control of commercial routes, access to strategic raw materials); *pride and reputation* (alliance defection becomes unacceptable because the hegemonic power will lose face); *military innovation* (the enhanced role of light infantry, including archers, slingers, and Thracian *peltasts,* as the war proceeds, the new Corinthian ramming tactics that wreck havoc with the Athenian fleet in the Great Harbor of Syracuse); *geostrategy* (control of maritime choke points and lines of communication); *alliance stability* (much of Spartan strategy consists of attacking the integrity of the Athenian alliance system); and *decisive battle* (the encounters at Delium, Mantinea, or Syracuse, where strategic outcomes hinge on a single day's fighting). Thucydides makes no attempt to identify a unique hub of power and movement capable of serving as a Clausewitzian Center of Gravity (even if his narrative provides plenty of material for making such an assessment retrospectively). What he depicts is an extraordinarily complex strategic environment in which victory can be a consequence of many things, some of which are virtually impossible to predict.

In addition to being comprehensive, Thucydides's strategic environment is *dynamic*. At the outset of the Peloponnesian War, the two major belligerents have clearly outlined strategies for waging and winning the war. Sparta's intention is to invade Attica and force the Athenians to confront their army in order to prevent the ravaging of their lands and homes. Presumably the Spartans will defeat the Athenians in a major battle between opposing hoplite armies, leaving Sparta in a position to dictate the terms of peace. Athens, led by Pericles, intends to withdraw its population from exposed rural regions and concentrate it inside the city walls, refuse battle, subsist by importing vital commodities via sea, avoid adventures, and use naval power to raid and harass the Peloponnesus. Eventually, the Athenians presume, Spartan resolve will flag, and Athens will be in a position to impose an advantageous peace.[50] Each set of assumptions proves misguided, and what follows is an extraordinary set of strategic innovations.

Athenian resolve is weakened by the great plague that strikes the overcrowded city in the second year of the war—a completely unforeseen event with great strategic consequences.[51] The most prominent victim of the plague is Pericles himself. After his passing, Athens, led by the demagogue Cleon, becomes more aggressive, establishing the base at Pylos and using it as a means for placing pressure on its enemy. Sparta, inspired by the generalship of Brasidas, counters by attacking the Athenian alliance in Boeotia and Chalcidice. Both sides make partial gains but come no closer to ultimate victory. The Peace of Nicias represents an attempt to impose a strategic pause, but it does not address the underlying sources of hostility and fails to break the momentum of confrontation. Enduring resentment allows the talented adventurer Alcibiades to up the ante by creating an alliance with Argos, Mantinea, and Elis to challenge Spartan control of the Peloponnesus. He succeeds in provoking a decisive battle at Mantinea in 418, in which the Spartans are compelled "to stake their all upon the issue of a single day," but in the end it is Sparta that prevails.[52] Alcibiades's next gambit is the Sicilian Expedition, a strategic disaster but not yet a decisive defeat. Athens recovers from the setback, and it is only when Sparta enters into a closer association with the Great King of Persia, builds a battle fleet, and finds a ruthless commander in the person of Lysander that it is able to win decisively at Aegospotami in 405.

This brief overview calls attention to a great diversity of strategic initiatives. Thucydides's history demonstrates that in protracted conflicts strategy must be flexible and adaptive. Security, of course, is grounded in a capacity for self-defense. The author has composed the history of a war, and his image of strategy is firmly tied to "the part which is played by force, or the threat of force, in the international system."[53] Strategy, the domain of force, is not a synonym for policy. But the clear implication of Thucydides's study is that on the level of grand strategy all instruments of national power must be leveraged in conjunction with military means in pursuit of national goals. Events and local circumstances as they unfold and develop will determine what "mix" of factors will be most relevant at any given point in the conflict.

Ethical and Moral Context.

Thucydides's *History* is notable for its lack of illusion. War, he remarks, is a "rough master that brings most men's characters to a level with their fortunes."[54] The strategic environment that he depicts is filled with instrumental logic, cynicism, abuse of power, and brutal massacre.[55] It is a Hobbesian universe where the struggle of all against all is often the essence of strategic interaction, and the limits of morality are defined by *Staatsraison*. Hugo Grotius used the remark of Thucydides's Athenian emissary, Euphemius, to the effect that "for a king or a free city nothing is wrong that is to their advantage" as a foil for his effort to assert a law of nations.[56] Finley argued that "nothing so marks Thucydides' work as the sense of living in a world where moral sensitiveness and inherited tradition were…a luxury, and the very survival of states hung on the skillful use of power and power alone."[57] The discourse of power that drives interstate relations leads inexorably toward the harsh doctrine of might makes right, as imparted by the Athenians to the Melians: "You know as well as we do that right, as the world goes, is only in question between equals in power, while the strong do what they can and the weak suffer what they must."[58]

In a recent attempt to update realist theory, John Mearsheimer describes the above passage as "Thucydides' famous dictum," but it is no such thing.[59] The Melian Dialogue, in which Athens lays down the law to the representatives of the would-be neutral power of Melos, is perhaps not quite so clear in its implications as might appear at first glance. The Athenian representatives speak the words during their negotiations with the Melians; they do not necessarily express the opinions of the author. The views of the Athenians are far from being self-evident, and in fact they belie the larger spirit of Thucydides's work as a whole. In *The Peloponnesian War* breaches of the moral order are punished, and pride comes before the fall. Sparta comes to believe that its early military misfortunes are the consequence of its unethical breaching of the Thirty Years Peace. Pericles's glowing funeral oration is followed immediately by the terrifying description of the great plague. The doctrine of naked power defended at Melos is the prelude to Athens's descent into the heart of darkness in Sicily. The blustering and violent Cleon comes to no good end. The unbridled ambition of Alcibiades leads him, and the policy he represents, to ruin.

These contrapositions are not accidental. Thucydides is not a moralist—he rejects the gods, strives for neutrality in his explanation, and does not preach. Nonetheless, his work forcefully poses the moral and ethical dilemmas of protracted strategic rivalry. Alternatives to the realist interpretation of Thucydides emphasize the compassion and austere humanity with which he contemplates the disasters of his time.[60] The Melian Dialogue, often read out of context as a set piece and touted as a foundation for political realism, can also be viewed as a depiction of the moral decline of Athens that leads inexorably to her defeat.[61] Viewed through this lens, the Athenian discourse at Melos is not prudent but pathological, and the crass exercise of overwhelming force that it embraces is intended to provoke revulsion rather than encourage emulation. The dialogue is in fact unique in Thucydides' text. Among the forty discourses cited verbatim it is the only one constructed as a real dialogue—a conversation between two parties with a theatrical structure and dramatic denouement. This gives it a unique intensity and centrality in the text that is clearly intended. In the dialogue, it is the Athenians who are dogmatic and inflexible and the Melians who argue instrumentally. The Melians see the big picture, calculate the odds of defiance on a cost-risk basis (even if their calculations are faulty), and attempt to point out that by striking at the vulnerable without constraint Athens will place its long-term interests at stake. And the Melians are right. Athens's harsh conduct reflects an overweening pride that eventually leads to disaster. Its policies and attitude offend allies, alienate neutrals, create new enemies, and encourage rivals to redouble resistance.

In *The Peloponnesian War*, power without principle does not prevail. Thucydides does not portray interest and justice as antithetical; they are rather "inextricably connected and mutually constitutive."[62] Thucydides does not shy from the carnage of war, but he also does not glory in it, as some "blood and guts" realists suggest.[63] His gripping narration places the reader on the ground alongside leaders, soldiers, and citizens caught up in the midst of calculated violence and coping as best they can, but he laments the "general deterioration of character throughout the Greek world" that protracted war promotes.[64] War is indeed a violent teacher, and as such, in the words of Leo Strauss, "it teaches man not only to act violently but also about violence and therefore about the truth."[65] *The Peloponnesian War* is in large part a cautionary tale about the use and abuse of power with the implicit moral warning "to use it wisely or lose it woefully."[66] For much of the war and despite many setbacks, Athens sustains its great power status, but in the end it abandons the high ground of legitimate authority and is lost. In a harsh world, administering force effectively demands rigorous professionalism, including a strong sense of purpose and adherence to an elevated moral code.[67] Successful strategy, one may conclude, must be developed within a sound and stable ethical context.

CONCLUSION

The real subject of Thucydides's history is the decline and fall of a political civilization under the strains of hegemonic warfare. Thucydides built the narrative on careful observation and detailed accounting, but the story line inexorably directs the reader's attention to the big picture, the grand strategic environment within which the decisions are made that lead to victory and defeat. What are the dynamics that cause great power war? Can they be contained, and if so, how? What kinds of policies are most conducive to the pursuit of victory? How can the various instruments of national power be combined in a coherent grand strategy? How should strategy be sustained or adapted in the course of protracted armed conflicts? What are the attributes of effective strategic leadership? How can power be linked to purpose, and justice to interest, in a balanced national strategy that sustains legitimate authority? These are the kind of questions that emerge from a careful reading of *The Peloponnesian War*. Thucydides does not reach the end of this history, and his text does not include a formal summary or conclusion, but he clearly intended it as a guide to statecraft and a plea for caution and moderation that is as relevant in our time as on the day it was written.

ENDNOTES - CHAPTER 9

1. There are several excellent modern English translations. Rex Warner's version, completed in 1954, appears in Thucydides, *The Peloponnesian War*, Harmondsworth: Penguin, 1986. The Richard Crawley translation, originally published in 1874 and rendered in eloquent Victorian prose, appears in Richard B. Strassler, ed., *The Landmark Thucydides: A Comprehensive Guide to the Peloponnesian War*, New York: The Free Press, 1996. The Strassler compilation, with extensive reader aides including maps and explanatory notes, is an invaluable tool. Henceforth, all dates cited will be B.C.E. unless otherwise noted.

2. The first English translation, by Thomas Nicolls, dates to 1550.

3. This is a long-standing tradition. See Gilbert Murray, *Our Great War and the Great War of the Ancient Greeks*, New York: Thomas Seltzer, 1920, for parallels with the First World War, or Carlos Alonso Zaldívar, "Tucídides, en Kosovo," *El Pais*, May 17, 1999, for applications to the war in Kosovo during 1999.

4. Marshall made this remark in a public address at Princeton University on Washington's Birthday in February 1947. The articulation of the Truman Doctrine was several weeks away.

5. See George F. Will, "Powell's Intrusion," *The Washington Post*, November 25, 2001, p. B07.

6. The publication of *The Landmark Thucydides* in 1996 was both a reflection of and contribution to swelling interest. Some subsequent works—the list is long—include George Cawkwell, *Thucydides and the Peloponnesian War*, London: Routledge, 1997, a sophisticated introduction; Gregory Crane, *Thucydides and the Ancient Simplicity: The Limits of Political Realism*, Berkeley, CA: University of California Press, 1998; Simon Hornblower, *Thucydides*, Baltimore, MD: The Johns Hopkins University Press, 2000; Philip De Souza, *The Peloponnesian War, 431-404 B.C.*, New York: Routledge, 2002, a detailed general history; Donald Kagan, *The Peloponnesian War*, New York: Viking, 2003, a one-volume summation of Kagan's earlier four-volume history; Richard New Lebow, *The Tragic Vision of Politics: Ethics, Interests and Orders*, Cambridge, UK: Cambridge University Press, 2003; John F. Lazenby, *The Peloponnesian War: A Military History*, New York: Routledge, 2004; the eloquent introduction by Perez Zagorin, *Thucydides: An Introduction for the Common Reader*, Princeton, NJ: Princeton University Press, 2005; and Victor Davis Hanson, *A War Like No Other: How the Athenians and Spartans Fought the Peloponnesian War*, New York: Random House, 2005, a series of essays that attempt to demonstrate the human dimension of the conflict.

7. Leo Strauss, *The City and Man*, Chicago, IL: Rand McNally & Co., 1964, p. 155.

8. Clifford Orwin, *The Humanity of Thucydides*, Princeton, NJ: Princeton University Press, 1994, pp. 3-4.

9. Lebow, *The Tragic Vision of Politics*, p. 26.

10. Strassler, *The Landmark Thucydides*, 1.22.4.

11. David Grene, ed., *The Peloponnesian War: The Complete Hobbes Translation*, Chicago, IL: University of Chicago Press, 1959. Hobbes's work contains some technical errors in translation.

12. Joseph S. Nye, Jr., "Neorealism and Neoliberalism," *World Politics*, Vol. 40, 1988, p. 235.

13. W. Robert Connor, *Thucydides*, Princeton, NJ: Princeton University Press, 1984, p. 32.

14. Hanson, *A War Like No Other*, pp. 89-122.

15. The conclusion is based upon student reactions in a seminar conducted by the author at the U.S. Army War College for the past eight years that was devoted to reading and discussing *The Peloponnesian War*.

16. Hanson, *A War Like No Other*.

17. Cited in Connor, *Thucydides*, p. 20, and from Cawkwell, *Thucydides and the Peloponnesian War*, p. 9. In the early-19th century, Thomas Macauley could declare Thucydides "the greatest historian who ever lived." Thomas Babington Macauley, *The Letters of Thomas Babinton Macauley*, Thomas Pinney, ed., 6 Vols., Cambridge, UK: Cambridge University Press, 1976, Vol. 3, p. 138.

18. Eduard Schwartz, *Das Geschichtswerk des Thucydides*, 3rd Ed., Hildesheim: Georg Olms Verlagsbuchhandlung, 1960; and Finley, *Thucydides*, outline, respectively, the "stages of composition" and "unitarian" approaches to the Thucydides Question. See also Jacqueline de Romilly, *Thucydides and Athenian Imperialism*, Oxford, UK: Basil Blackwell, 1963

19. Richard Ned Lebow, "Thucydides the Constructivist," *American Political Science Review*, Vol. 95, No. 3, September 2001, pp. 547-560.

20. Arnold W. Gomme, ed., *A Historical Commentary on Thucydides*, 5 Vols., Vols. 4 and 5, co-edited with Anthony Andrewes and K.W. Dover, Oxford, UK: The Clarendon Press, 1945-1981, Vol. 1, p. 29.

21. Schwartz, *Das Geschichtswerk des Thucydides*, p. 19.

22. A survey of what we know of Thucydides's life appears in John H. Finley, Jr., *Thucydides*, Ann Arbor, MI: University of Michigan Press, 1967, pp. 1-35.

23. The history of the Peloponnesian War from 411 to its conclusion in 404 is taken up, in a conscious attempt to complete Thucydides's account, by Xenophon in his *Hellenica*. See the Rex Warner translation in *Xenophon: A History of My Time*, Harmondsworth, UK: Penguin Books, 1979.

24. G.W.T. Patrick translation from Heraclitus, *Fragments*.

25. Strassler, *The Landmark Thucydides*, 1.1.

26. G.W.T. Patrick translation from Heraclitus, *Fragments*.

27. Sun-tzu, *The Art of War*, Ralph D. Sawyer, trans., Boulder, CO: Westview Press, 1994, p. 167.

28. Strassler, *The Landmark Thucydides*, 2.35-2.46.

29. Connor, *Thucydides*, p. 6.

30. Strassler, *The Landmark Thucydides*, 1.22.4.

31. *Ibid.*, 1.21.2.

32. Victor Davis Hanson, *The Western Way of War: Infantry Battle in Classical Greece*, Berkeley, CA: University of California Press, 2000.

33. Herodotus, *The Histories*, London: Penguin Books, 2003.

34. Donald Kagan, *The Outbreak of the Peloponnesian War*, Ithaca, NY: Cornell University Press, 1969, p. 41, specifically compares the Delian League to the Cold War's North Atlantic Treaty Organization (NATO).

35. Strassler, *The Landmark Thucydides*, 5.26.

36. Steven Forde, *The Ambition to Rule: Alcibiades and the Politics of Imperialism in Thucydides*, Ithaca, NY: Cornell University Press, 1989, sees Alcibiades as the apotheosis of Athenian individualism and self-aggrandizement. His rise to prominence is not accidental—he embodies both the dynamism and self-destructive egoism of the polity he represents.

37. Zagorin, *Thucydides*, p. 8.

38. M. I. Finley, *The World of Odysseus*, New York: The Viking Press, 1965, p. 34.

39. Kagan, *The Outbreak of the Peloponnesian War*, p. 345, makes the assertion that Thucydides "invents" the distinction between immediate and underlying causes of war.

40. Hornblower, *Thucydides*, p. 191.

41. Strassler, *The Landmark Thucydides*, 1.23.6.

42. Hans J. Morgenthau, *Politics Among Nations: The Struggle for Power and Peace*, 5th Ed., New York: Alfred A. Knopf, 1978, p. 38. The passage is cited from the Melian Dialogue, Strassler, *The Landmark Thucydides*, 5.105.2.

43. Raymond Aron, *Peace and War: A Theory of International Relations*, New York: Doubleday & Company, Inc., 1966, p. 137.

44. When the Spartan Assembly voted in 432 that Athens has violated the Thirty Years Peace, Thucydides remarks that the decision was made because "they feared the growth of the power of the Athenians, seeing most of Hellas already subject to them." At the conclusion of the *Pentecontaetia*, he notes that Sparta has concluded that "the growth of the Athenian power could no longer be ignored" and "that they could endure it no longer." Strassler, *The Landmark Thucydides*, 1.88 and 1.118.2.

45. See the classic study by Geoffrey Blainey, *The Causes of War*, New York: The Free Press, 1973.

46. In his popular history of the Sicilian Expedition, Peter Green places particular emphasis upon Athens's economic motivation: "The constant foreign aggression, the search for *Lebensraum*, the high-handed treatment of the subject-allies—all these things had as their aim the securing of desperately needed raw materials." Peter Green, *Armada from Athens*, Garden City, NY: Doubleday & Company, Inc., 1970, p. 46.

47. Strassler, *The Landmark Thucydides*, 1.86.

48. Crane, *Thucydides and the Ancient Simplicity*, p. 37, suggests that Thucydides's famous reference to the growth of Athenian power as the "real cause" of the war can be adapted to multiple causation with a more refined translation. The best rendering of the passage, he suggests, refers to the "truest cause," that is, one among many.

49. Lebow, *The Tragic Vision of Politics,* p. 112.

50. The German military historian Hans Delbrück interpreted Periclean strategy as a prototype for what he called strategies of "attrition." Hans Delbrück, *Die Strategie des Perikles: erläutet durch die Strategie Friedrich des Grossen mit einem Anhang über Thucydides und Kleon,* Berlin, Germany: Reimer, 1890.

51. Thucydides' description of the plague is justly famed. See Strassler, *The Landmark Thucydides,* 2.47-2.54.

52. Strassler, *The Landmark Thucydides ,* 6.16.6.

53. Cited from "The Strategic Approach to International Relations," in Michael Howard, *The Causes of Wars,* 2nd Ed., Cambridge, MA: Harvard University Press, 1984, p. 36. See also Hew Strachen, "The Lost Meaning of Strategy," *Survival,* Vol. 47, No. 3, Autumn 2005.

54. Strassler, *The Landmark Thucydides,* 3.82.2.

55. Hanson, *A War Like No Other,* pp. 89-121.

56. Hugo Grotius, *The Law of War and Peace,* Roslyn, NY: Walter J. Black, Inc., 1949, p. 3. This passage is rendered in Strassler, *The Landmark Thucydides,* 6.85, as "for tyrants and imperial cities nothing is unreasonable if expedient."

57. Finley, *Thucydides,* p. 29.

58. Strassler, *The Landmark Thucydides,* 5.89.

59. John J. Mearsheimer, *The Tragedy of Great Power Politics,* New York: W. W. Norton & Company, 2001, p. 163.

60. See in particular Strauss, *City and Man;* Lebow, *The Tragic Vision of Politics;* Orwin, *The Humanity of Thucydides;* and Thomas L. Pangle and Peter J. Ahrensdorf, *Justice Among Nations: On the Moral Basis of Power and Peace,* Lawrence, KS: University Press of Kansas, 1999, pp. 13-32.

61. Finley, *Thucydides,* pp. 208-212; and Peter J. Euben, *The Tragedy of Political Theory: The Road Not Taken,* Princeton, NJ: Princeton University Press, 1990, pp. 178, 197-198.

62. Lebow, *The Tragic Vision of Politics,* p. 166.

63. See Michael W. Doyle, *Ways of War and Peace,* New York: Norton, 1997, pp. 49-92.

64. Strassler, *The Landmark Thucydides,* 3.82-85.

65. Strauss, *The City and Man,* p. 162.

66. Cawkwell, *Thucydides and the Peloponnesian War,* p. 19.

67. Note the uncompromising statement of this premise in the Antistrophe of Euripides's *Andromache,* composed during the Peloponnesian War: "It is better not to have a victory that sullies reputation than to overthrow justice by force and win hatred. Such gain brings men delight at first but in time it withers in their hands and voices of reproach beset their house. This is the way of life I approve, this the one I wish to make my own, to wield no power in my home or my city that transgresses justice." Euripides, *Andromache,* lines 779-784.

CHAPTER 10

EASTERN STRATEGIC TRADITIONS: UN-AMERICAN WAYS OF WAR

Glenn K. Cunningham

Western military studies are often dominated by the writings of Carl von Clausewitz, the Prussian theorist and author of the epic *On War*, and Antoine Henri de Jomini, his contemporaneous Swiss counterpart and prolific author of several works on military art, including *The Art of War*.[1] Clausewitz is remembered and often cited for his clear pronouncements on the political nature of strategy and the importance of a holistic, systems-based approach to understanding the nature of warfare as an instrument of policy. In comparison, Jomini's precise, geometric concepts are essential to modern American approaches to operational art, which owes its terminology largely to his writings. In many ways (even if a grand simplification), development of American political-military strategy is based on Clausewitz, while American military operational planning has been based on Jomini.

Close examination reveals that Clausewitz and Jomini share many assumptions and precepts, as one might expect from two similarly talented analysts who emerged from the Napoleonic campaigns of 1792-1815. They shared a conviction that war is more art than science, and also that the role of the commander is of paramount importance in exercising military art and science to bring order to the otherwise chaotic business of warfare and extended campaigning. Modern Western military doctrine and practice have absorbed these thinkers' insights and concepts; their impact on modern Western military strategy has been monumental, by any measurement.

That acknowledged, non-Western cultures have had their own theorists, and these approaches to military strategy have ardent followings of their own. Significantly, China, India, and Japan each have a robust military tradition that, in part at least, reflects the thinking of a particular military theorist. In fact, the writings of these venerable civilizations predate those of Clausewitz and Jomini by centuries. Given the global nature of modern warfare, 21st-century military commanders would be well advised to familiarize themselves with these writings in this age of coalition warfare, where potential coalition partners and possible adversaries may be grounded in strategic thinking derived from major non-Western military theorists.

This is no small undertaking. From Chinese history, Sun Tzu's *The Art of War* is a collection of aphorisms and maxims, disjointed in presentation and only loosely connected in thematic chapters. The text was allegedly compiled in the 5th century B.C., and it has been edited, amended, and revised by commentators and subsequent theorists—some of whom are identifiable and others unknown.[2] Indian Kautilya's *The Arthashastra*, variously credited as written from 321-150 B.C., is another ancient military text that is daunting in its scope and range of subject matter. It includes a good deal of prescriptive tabular material on such nonmilitary topics as civil punishments, tax rates, and even seed preparation for crop planting.[3] A more recent addition was Japanese Miyamoto Musashi's *The Book of Five Rings*, which seems to be an extended allegory, more poetry than prose. Musashi's work can be dated accurately to 1645.[4]

These theorists, especially Sun Tzu and Kautilya, are so removed from the 21st century and so mythical in reputation that their very existence is moot. Even Musashi, a person whom one can date with reasonable precision, is a figure whose martial exploits are clouded in legend. It is not the purpose of this chapter to debate their actual historicity or determine the accuracy of the attribution of the works credited to them. For our purpose, we accept their authorship, era, and attributed works, if only out of a useful sense of tradition.

Accepting that as a premise, these ancient strategists present contemporary strategists and planners a cultural lens through which to view strategic thought and campaign design. When aspects of cultures are applied to strategic issues, the refraction that occurs in that culture is, by nature, an accretion of almost imperceptible and invariably local influences. Cultural mores, norms, and folkways begin with the family and the infancy of any member of a society. It is questionable whether an outsider can ever fully appreciate the full depth and scope of a different culture unless that person has been shaped in that same crucible.[5] Conversely, strategic thinking is, by its nature, cross-cultural and universal in its intent. Principles of war generally come from the integration of locally generated culture and the universal purposes of strategy. These principles are difficult to codify even in a stable, homogeneous culture, much less across diverse ones.[6] However, as culture reflects the approaches a people use to solve problems, attempting to grasp the cultural context of another society's actions, whether adversary or ally, is essential to designing the actions that one may take in his or her own context. Any number of proposed solutions may differ, but the problems may well be shared. The American way of war may have to be exercised in a distinctly un-American context.

A LOOK BACK AT CHINA: SUN TZU

Little is known about Sun Tzu as a historical person. This is not surprising, since he was most likely born in the late Eastern Zhou Dynasty when the Zhou kings had become nominal figureheads, and China fragmented into over a hundred feudal states governed by competing warlords. Records from that period are understandably sparse. He may be entirely mythical. He is variously attributed as a citizen of the states of Wu and of Ch'i. However, enough details exist to ascertain that *The Art of War* probably was generated during the Warring States period in China (c. 403-221 B.C.), most likely by Sun Tzu or perhaps a knowledgeable general like him.[7]

Sun Tzu acted as a general and strategist at the beginning of the Iron Age in China. Myriad small states had amalgamated into seven major powers and about 15 smaller states on which these great states preyed. Despotism, unsettled social conditions, and constant warfare were commonplace; thus, the supply of people making up the agricultural, artisan, and military bases was of paramount importance. Despite the continual conflict, trade and society generally flourished, and major powers possessed the resources to field huge armies of well over 100,000 men.[8] The sustainment of such forces over long campaigns required great attention to procurement, logistics, and mobility. Sustained warfare was a costly matter, and military operations were constrained by the manpower, logistical, and fiscal limitations inherent in maneuvering forces at such a scale. Talented individuals could advance and thrive through military service. By Sun Tzu's time, military service was an established profession, and great attention was paid to arming, disciplining, and sustaining a core element of well-drilled, obedient, and organized formations. As Samuel B. Griffith points out:

> A Chinese army of the Warring States in battle array was an impressive spectacle as its ranks stood firm and scores of lavishly embroidered flags and banners whipped in the wind. These, decorated with figures of tigers, birds, dragons, snakes, phoenixes, and tortoises, marked the command post of the commander-in-chief behind the center and those of the assistant generals who commanded the wings. Constant maneuvering distracted the enemy and provided opportunity for *ch'i* [irregular or unorthodox] operations against his deep flanks and rear.[9]

The structure of *The Art of War* conforms to this military context. The text is condensed and fragmented, a collection of aphorisms rather than a descriptive narrative. Such an abstract and concise presentation would be improbable outside of a long-established tradition of military art and science based on extensive battle experience. Understandably, Sun Tzu was writing to an audience already well schooled in basic military leadership, functions, and procedures.[10]

In the social and military conditions of the Warring States, any state that risked all in a total effort at supremacy over a neighbor faced potential disaster at the hands of a heretofore uninvolved kingdom. That neighboring state might seize the opportunity created by the unbalancing of power to conquer both belligerents. Under these circumstances, intrigue, deception, diplomacy, and other forms of political skullduggery played an important, even crucial, role in sustaining national power and husbanding military resources. In such an environment, we find Sun Tzu's opening comment fully appropriate in describing the context and intent of his work: "War is a matter of vital importance to the state; the province of life or death; the road to survival or ruin. It is mandatory that it be thoroughly studied."[11]

Sun Tzu's philosophical Taoist approach to military operations must be viewed in the context of the Warring States period. Warfare threatened the existence of every warring state and imposed heavy burdens on the populations of both attacker and defender. Still, the ultimate goal of every potentate was to become a hegemon of "All-under-Heaven." Thus, Sun Tzu's main concepts in *The Art of War* evolve from this extant sociocultural condition, recalling that a robust and healthy population of farmers and artisans was essential to the survival of the state. Manpower could not be risked arbitrarily, or the ultimate goal of hegemony would be unattainable. Moreover, to destroy unconditionally a neighboring state left nothing of value to justify the military action. Hence, Sun Tzu placed prime emphasis on diplomacy and informational uses of power. To him, the highest form of military art was to conquer a neighboring state without recourse to the full panoply of military actions: "Generally in war the best policy is to take a state intact; to ruin it is inferior to this. . . . For to win one hundred victories in one hundred battles is not the acme of skill. To subdue the enemy without fighting is the acme of skill."[12]

Sun Tzu's world was one of restrained, limited warfare. Pitched, decisive engagements were to be avoided at all costs and undertaken only when no other recourse was feasible. No commander should embark on military action without thorough intelligence gathering, detailed analysis of one's own and one's enemy's capabilities and resources, and precise planning: "Know the enemy and know yourself; in a hundred battles you will never be in peril."[13] Deception, maneuver, and manipulation were a commander's principle tools: "Now war is based on deception. Move when it is advantageous and create changes in the situation by dispersal and concentration of forces."[14]

In general, Sun Tzu's conceptual approach was one of indirect, even circuitous, lines of operation: "Nothing is more difficult than maneuver. What is difficult about maneuver is to make the devious route the most direct and to turn misfortune to advantage."[15] Sun Tzu encouraged maneuver and indirect methods of action, exploiting intelligence, resource depletion, and deception. He urged the avoidance of battle until the commander determined that conditions were auspicious. That said, while Sun Tzu's maxims of war were terse—usually rather accessible and easy to grasp, and cover a range of diplomatic, informational, military, and economic factors—his statements are sometimes rather tenuously linked. *The Art of War* is not really a holistic, connected treatise. It is easy to read into Sun Tzu's writings one's own predilections.[16] It is also easy to follow his advice selectively. Hence, Sun Tzu's maxims are often quoted in isolation and not used in a sophisticated, cohesive way when applied to strategy development and campaign design.

Are Sun Tzu's principles the basis for effective military strategy? Yes and no—the principles are not a sure recipe for success, but may be applied in specific military contexts. Samuel B. Griffith served in China prior to World War II, during Mao Zedong's long, ultimately successful, campaigns against Chiang Kai-shek. Griffith, who translated *The Art of War*, observed that both Mao and his army commander, Chu Teh, were steeped in Sun Tzu's writings. Griffith surmised that many of Mao's own writings are paraphrases or elaborations of Sun Tzu. Indeed, in several writings, Mao cited Sun Tzu directly:

> When Sun Wu Tzu said in discussing military science, 'Know the enemy and know yourself, and you can fight a hundred battles with no danger of defeat,' he was referring to the two sides in a battle.... But our comrades often look at problems one-sidedly, and so they often run into snags.[17]

Griffith described Sun Tzu's influence on Mao positively:

> Mao apparently observed that Sun Tzu's precepts are readily adaptable to the conduct of war of either the hot or cold variety, and although it was many years before he had the opportunity to apply them against foreign 'imperialists,' he had not long to wait for a chance to use them with startling effect against Chiang Kai-shek in a hot one.[18]

Elsewhere, Sun Tzu's precepts have not been adapted so successfully. During World War II, Japanese strategists relied heavily on Sun Tzu's teachings in developing complex, dispersed campaigns that often did not serve them well. Throughout the war, particularly in crucial naval campaigns, the Japanese could not forego a bias toward complex plans involving multiple, widely divided formations. This pervasive preference for intricacy had at its heart the teachings of ancient oriental masters of military art, especially Sun Tzu. Throughout the 1920s and 1930s, the Japanese navy conducted exercises that stressed separate naval columns converging over wide distances, operations intended as elaborate traps for adversaries. The strategic foundation of victory, according to Japanese planners, lay in Sun Tzu's emphasis on deception and indirect maneuver.[19]

Such emphasis was especially apparent during the battle for Leyte Gulf, posited by some historians as the last chance the Japanese had to stop the American advance across the Pacific theater by thwarting the invasion of the Philippines. The Japanese *Sho Ichi Go* (or Operation TO CONQUER I) plan called for two dispersed naval squadrons to converge on the Leyte assault beaches, while a carrier task force operated to the north to deceive the Americans as to Japanese intentions and lure forces away from the Philippines. Air coverage for the Japanese fleet would not come from the carriers but from land-based aircraft scattered in dispersed airfields throughout the Philippines and other islands. *Sho Ichi Go* was feasible, but crucially depended on the Japanese capacity for coordination and precise timing and the assumption that the lure of the northern carrier fleet would work.[20] However, the inability of these air and naval fleets to mutually support each other when faced with the powerful combined American fleets greatly contributed to the destruction of Japanese ships and aircraft. This battle all but eliminated Japanese naval power for the remainder of the war.

A LOOK BACK AT INDIA: KAUTILYA

Chandragupta Maurya was the first leader to unify most of the Indian subcontinent in a single empire. Chandragupta turned back Alexander the Great's successors, defeated the Nanda kings, and established effective imperial rule. Kautilya, or Chanakya as he is sometimes known, was the architect of Chandragupta's rise from obscurity to empire. *The Arthashastra* (*The Science of Politics*) is Kautilya's comprehensive record of actions and advice on governing a vast empire, to include military strategy.[21]

Like Sun Tzu's writings, understanding the intent of *The Arthashastra* largely depends on grasping the context of the actions on which the writing was based. Kautilya faced a more unstructured, dynamic set of conditions than did Sun Tzu. At the death of Mahapadma Nanda in about 362 B.C., the just-formed Nanda Empire that stretched across the north of India had fallen into instability, occasioning a rapid succession of rulers and tetrarchs. After Alexander the Great died his empire fragmented into Greek-Persian satrapies, which controlled territories as far as the Indus River. The remainder of the subcontinent was a patchwork of small feuding states and ungoverned lands.

In this state of disruption and decay, Kautilya singly envisioned a great, united nation, such as he had seen among the Greeks under Alexander.[22] Kautilya's initial attempt to implement this vision through the last of the Nanda kings, Dhana Nanda, however, was embarrassingly rebuffed. Incensed and vengeful, Kautilya vowed to destroy the Nanda Empire, using Chandragupta Maurya, an ambitious young prince from the western border region, as his primary weapon. In 305 B.C., Seleucus I Nicator surrendered much occupied territory as far as the Indus River to Chandragupta, who then turned his attentions eastward, conquering the corroding Nanda Empire.

The Arthashastra, then, was a compilation of Kautilya's memoirs on how he accomplished this epic feat as well as advice to Chandragupta on how to consolidate and maintain his power. Kautilya accepted as a starting point that insecurity and instability are the dominant characteristics of the Indian environment.[23] *The Arthashastra* was the embodiment of ruthless realism, based on bold, pitiless action. Its reliance on duplicity was not artful subterfuge, but deliberate deception and bloody assassination. The ultimate aim remained conquest, pure and simple.[24] As Max Weber noted about *The Arthashastra*, "Compared to it, Machiavelli's *The Prince* is harmless."[25]

With the fundamental aim of national strategy established as conquest, Kautilya determined that all elements of power be directed at that end. In Kautilya's cynical and suspicious mind, the *vijigishu* (king in search of fresh conquests) faced a challenging world of anarchy, fierce self-interest on the part of absolutely everyone, and deadly, immediate risk at home and abroad. Thus, for the *vijigishu* to survive, much less succeed, he must use every means at his disposal to gain and cement power. In such a context, a ruler must promote the welfare of the people, as the people are the source of his wealth, and wealth makes it possible to finance more conquests. Conquest, in turn, enlarges his domains and brings more subjects under his control, and the cycle can be repeated until there is nothing left to conquer.[26] Only then can real peace be obtained.

Statecraft was a key factor in the march of conquest. Kautilya framed the *vijigishu's* problem as a *mandala*, a finely patterned ring of concentric circles. The *vijigishu* himself was at the center. Next to him was likely to be an enemy plotting his destruction. Next to that enemy was that enemy's enemy, and the enemy of one's enemy is a friend. Of course, once the extant enemy was disposed of, the problem was reframed because the former ally became a probable enemy. In this ever-threatening situation, peace was preferable to war only insofar as it bought time to recover from a weak position. It was a temporary expedient, and conquest should resume as soon as it is practical, whether by open warfare, preemptive surprise strikes, or secret sabotage.[27] Such an aggressive foreign policy was always justified. After all, stated Kautilya, "Any king whose kingdom shares a common border with the conqueror is an antagonist."[28] This assumption is Clausewitzian strategy turned on its head—instead of all warfare being an instrument of policy, all policy is a means to prosecute war.

Nothing, then, was beneath a potentate's attention. Internal administration of the kingdom was as important as foreign relations, since the resources to conduct conquest must first be controlled and developed. Hence, *The Arthashastra* covered subjects as diverse as how to manage forests (forests harbor elephants, and elephants are useful for war), how Indian society functioned, income from crown property, types and purposes of marriages, how to plan a campaign, and how to treat a subjugated population. *The Arthashastra* is one of the earliest and most complete treatments of holistic strategic-level leadership in existence. It is also one of the most single-minded works of its kind. Every resource, every element of national power, every waking moment of a ruler's days, should be spent with one intent: hegemonic conquest.

The question arises: Does *The Arthashastra* represent current 21st-century thinking of leaders on the Indian subcontinent? Some authors believe Kautilya's counsel resonates even today with Indian national leaders, as it did for Chandragupta. They hold that the common understanding of Indian culture as nonviolent and peace loving is a Western myth. Military historian Robert Leckie reminded us that the form of nonviolent civil disobedience practiced by Mahatma Gandhi against the British and Portuguese in the mid-20th century that became the archetypical image of Indian action is largely misinterpreted.

> When Gandhian nonviolence was employed for the 'passive invasion' of Goa, that is, an offensive march by unarmed people, the applauding pacifists did not seem to understand that they were cheering another form of coercion. 'Passive resistance' may be nonviolent, but so are other successful forms of coercion such as excommunication, ostracism or economic boycott.[29]

In Kautilyan terms, Gandhi skillfully employed his strengths (popular support) against an enemy weakness (Western ethical compunctions). It was an asymmetric approach to conquest, which Kautilya would have both understood and approved of and that fits into contemporary pragmatic Indian culture.[30]

The cursory nod that modern Indian politics gives to nonviolence as a culture does not replace a long and bloody history of warfare, riots, and strife. Nomadic Indian ascetics, known as *sadhus*, were as likely to be predatory as holy—not begging for food, but commandeering it, including actual robbery and plunder.[31] Indian politics and culture, whether Hindu or Muslim, continue to take on an ethic of suspicion, preparation for conflict, and violent action when necessary.[32] Indeed, the late-20th-century Indian policy of nonalignment was directly Kautilyan—a means of enhancing security by a low-risk strategy of playing one superpower off against another until India could gain sufficient strength to protect its own security. India's current negotiating strategies on nuclear deterrence, weapons procurement, and international trade issues reflect both Kautilyan trends and India's 21st-century self-perception of its role as an emerging world power.[33] While *The Arthashastra* is no magical tome that offers a full explanation of Indian culture, it sets forth traditions and background that offer helpful insights into Indian strategic policies and actions even today.

A LOOK BACK AT JAPAN: MUSASHI

In contrast to Sun Tzu's aphoristic approach to strategic planning and to Kautilya's broad, whole-of-monarchy nesting of all elements of national power, Miyamoto Musashi's "two swords" approach presented in *Go Rin No Sho*, or *The Book of Five Rings*, is directly operational and focused rather pointedly on direct approaches to combat operations. Of the three theorists, he most closely reflects Clausewitz's emphasis on center of gravity.

Musashi was born into a minor samurai family in 1545. This period was one of great change following centuries of civil unrest and warfare. After the death of Emperor Toyotomi Hideyoshi in 1598, Tokugawa Ieyasu established pervasive autocratic rule as shogun of Japan. Musashi participated in the great battle of Sekigahara in 1600 that established Ieyasu as shogun and dwarfed any contemporary military action in Europe. This epic battle involved an estimated 60,000 matchlocks, at a time when only 3,000 such firearms existed in the entire French army.[34] The resulting shogunate endured, dominating all aspects of Japanese society until the arrival of Commodore Matthew Perry in Japan in 1853.

In 1643, after a legendary life in which he fought over 60 duels without a defeat, Musashi retired to a cave on Kyushu Island. He completed *The Book of Five Rings* shortly before his death there in 1645. Compared to the writings of Sun Tzu and Kautilya, *The Book of Five Rings* is far less accessible. It was, foremost, not so much a book of strategy as guidance on how to think strategically. Secondly, it took the form of a broadly conceived allegory. Musashi wrote as if he were crafting a fencing manual, but his broad conceptual intent was to create a strategic treatise. Musashi stated this openly, "The principles of strategy are written down here in terms of single combat, but you must think broadly so that you attain an understanding for ten-thousand-a-side battles."[35] That frank statement of intent, however, does not make the allegory itself any less enigmatic. Lastly, *The Book of Five Rings* became widely available in English in 1974, making Musashi a relative newcomer to Western students of strategic art.[36]

The decisive battle of Sekigahara must have made a lasting impression on Musashi, as this culminating battle not only secured military victory, but also ushered in a prolonged period of national security and relative peace. Musashi's strategic advice hence emphasized directness and thoroughness. In contrast to Sun Tzu, he advocated no flourishes or deceptive maneuvering, teaching instead that success depends on clear focus on the objective of defeating the enemy:

> The primary thing when you take a sword in your hands is your intention to cut the enemy, whatever the means. Whenever you parry, hit, spring, strike, or touch the enemy's cutting sword, you must cut the enemy in the same movement. It is essential to attain this. If you think only of hitting, springing, striking, or touching the enemy, you will not be able actually to cut him. More than anything, you must be thinking of carrying your movement through to cutting him. You must thoroughly research this.[37]

Musashi based his approach to strategy on intense, focused attention on clear objectives. Whatever stance one takes, or whatever strategic ends, ways, and means one considers, Musashi advocated an objective-driven, no-nonsense attitude: "Think only of cutting."[38]

Like Kautilya, Musashi was committed to a holistic approach to military strategy. In his fencing allegory, he portrayed this as the proper use of two swords. The samurai of Musashi's time carried two swords, a long sword generally wielded only outdoors and a shorter companion sword carried at all times. Musashi called his approach *Ichi Ryu Ni To*, or *One School, Two Swords*. By this, he did not mean always fighting with both swords at the same time (he gave no such advice in *The Book of Five Rings*), but rather using all resources at one's disposal. "This is a truth: when you sacrifice your life, you must make fullest use of your weaponry."[39] He elaborated: "According to this Ichi school, you can win with a long weapon, and yet you can also win with a short weapon. In short, the Way of the Ichi school is the spirit of winning, whatever the weapon and whatever its size."[40]

Musashi then pointed out the importance of a holistic mindset after explaining how to best employ various weapons. What he advocated strategically, however, was judicious balancing of ends, ways, and means when choosing a course of action. He pointed out, "In large scale strategy, the superior man will manage many subordinates dexterously, bear himself correctly, govern the country and foster the people, thus preserving the ruler's discipline."[41] However, no real strategist should ever lose sight of his ultimate objective, which is to win, advance oneself, and gain honor.[42]

Musashi's writings stand in sharp contrast to Sun Tzu's penchant for adroit maneuver. The Chinese theorist advocated skillful battlefield gymnastics, but his later Japanese counterpart saw deception and maneuver as a far-less-efficient means to the end than a single-minded, powerful thrust at the heart. "Do nothing which is of no use," he cautioned.[43] Once defeated, an enemy must not be offered respite, but crushed. "If we crush lightly, he may recover. . . . The primary thing is to not let him recover his position even a little."[44]

Musashi's exploits and writings became foundational to a tradition of samurai honor called *bushido,* which is deeply ingrained in Japanese culture and finds expression there today across Japanese society. It is ironic, however, that the Japanese theorist's strategic concepts were largely discarded by his own nation in World War II. Instead, they were demonstrated more powerfully in use *against* his nation by the bellicose American advocate of unrestrained strategic bombing, Curtis LeMay.[45] In his view, the entire strategic effort of the Pacific theater was aimed at bringing the Japanese home islands in range of repeated pummeling by one weapons system—the long-range, high-altitude B-29 bomber. LeMay never faltered from his conviction that strategic bombing, resulting in destruction of Japan's industrial capacity, was the key to American success against the Japanese. Like a Japanese samurai of the 17th century, LeMay deeply believed that death was secondary to achievement of this objective, even if he and all his aircrews were lost in the effort.[46]

To achieve his ends, LeMay used a strategy similar to Musashi's "two swords" approach, employing every means at his disposal and repeatedly altering flight patterns and bomb loads to maximize destruction of Japan's major cities. From March to August 1945, LeMay's XXIst Bomber Command struck repeatedly at Japan's major urban areas with incendiary bombs, producing catastrophic destruction—culminating with the flattening of Hiroshima and Nagasaki by atomic bombs on August 6 and 9, 1945. Frankly put, LeMay's strategy was so effective that by August 1945 he was running out of targets.[47] Even embittered Americans of the occupying forces were often shocked by the extent of destruction that LeMay's unrelenting strategic bombing campaign had caused.[48] LeMay's focus on what Musashi had earlier called "cutting" and "crushing" made it clear that unless they unconditionally surrendered, the Japanese people faced not defeat, but complete annihilation. While it is extremely unlikely that LeMay had ever read Musashi's text, his actions in World War II were remarkably in consonance with that Japanese warrior's understanding of strategy.

A LOOK AHEAD AT AMERICA IN THE 21ST CENTURY

It is perhaps too easy to equate familiarity with these ancient writers with discipleship and authority. It is a quick-thought exercise to link Chandragupta's rise with Kautilya's advice, but it is a far longer stretch to tie Napoleon's operational art to Sun Tzu's maxims, and Curtis LeMay undoubtedly never read *The Book of Five Rings*. The terse, bulletized methodology of the non-Western writings makes them too prone to reinterpretation and misapplication by modern strategists and planners, who often advocate their own convictions by reference (often somewhat forced) to these military philosophers.[49] Still, there are recognizable influences, and even a cursory grasp of the key essential orientation of these sages can have some bearing on the way later great captains put in practice their own approaches to warfare.

These three Eastern military philosophers represent variant forms of thought, bounded by culture and appearing in differing historical contexts. In contrast to Clausewitz and Jomini, whose strategic thinking came into being in a single period in a specific theater (and was even dominated by a single commander in the person of Napoleon), conceptualizations of military art from ancient China and India and shogun-era Japan present both distinct contrasts as well as interesting convergences. However, the disparity in their writings makes them hard to link together in a coherent way.

Of course, one could claim the same about Clausewitz and Jomini. However, at least these two theorists are acknowledged as authorities with a tradition of inclusion in Western military thought. In practice, one suspects that while Sun Tzu, Kautilya, and Musashi may appear on many recommended reading lists, American strategists seldom actually read them and, even more rarely, seriously study them. Perhaps unfortunately, it is mainly among practitioners from their own cultures that these writers are likely to develop a following. Cultural patterns make Western military educations predisposed to follow the precepts of Clausewitz and Jomini, as those theorists align best with our history. It is a good bet, however, that professional military education in other cultures will rely on local traditions and history. An Indian general may have studied Kautilya to a greater degree than he has Jomini, and a Japanese officer may be more steeped in Sun Tzu and Musashi than his Western counterpart.

As a global power, the United States has its own military traditions and arguably a uniquely American way of war, and those approaches may be more useful in the 21st century than attempting to implement the doctrines of foreign strategists who have been dead for over a millennium. However, the global interconnectivity of the 21st century makes it certain that Americans will interact with other cultures, whether as allies, adversaries, or perhaps over time, both. Each culture will have developed along far different historical paths, and close study of the foundation documents of these other cultures can prove useful, if not vital, to U.S. warfighting efforts. Aside from a few familiar quotations from Sun Tzu, these Eastern military philosophers are largely unheralded outside of their own cultures. They are not incorporated into U.S. professional military education or ongoing adaptive strategic planning, whether for deliberate contingency planning or emergent crisis response.

This unfamiliarity is unfortunately shortsighted, and quite possibly strategically dangerous. Cross-cultural understanding is always difficult to reach and often takes both time and serious effort to gain. Indeed, one may never progress beyond a modicum of cross-cultural awareness and never progress to comprehension with any degree of real depth. Given that difficulty, decades may be necessary to inculcate an understanding of Eastern thinking into future American strategic decisionmakers. In developing future strategies and plans, the current state of world affairs need not remain constant. Quite possibly, given the globalized nature of human endeavor in the 21st century, it *cannot* remain constant. Prudent preparedness suggests that more attention to non-Western cultural traditions in military strategy is a way of mitigating the risks of such uncertainty.

Warfare remains a function largely of the human mind and heart. Students of military art would do well to consider the import of these three ancient theorists when framing their own operational problems—and designing approaches to solve them—within a cultural context that may be alien to them. That perspective is one that all three of these strategic thinkers—along with Clausewitz and Jomini, no doubt—would espouse.

ENDNOTES - CHAPTER 10

1. Carl von Clausewitz, *On War*, Michael Howard and Peter Paret, eds. and trans., Princeton, NJ: Princeton University Press, 1976; Antoine Henri de Jomini, *The Art of War*, U.S. Military Academy, trans., London, UK: Greenhill Books, 1992.

2. Sun Tzu, *The Art of War*, Samuel B. Griffith, trans., London, UK: Oxford University Press, 1963.

3. Kautilya, *The Arthashastra*, L. N. Rangarajan, ed. and trans., New Delhi, India: Penguin Books, 1987.

4. Miyamoto Musashi, *The Book of Five Rings*, Victor Harris, trans., Woodstock, NY: Overlook Press, 1974.

5. Fons Trompenaars and Charles Hampden-Turner, *Riding the Waves of Culture: Understanding Diversity in Global Business*, 2nd Ed., New York: McGraw-Hill, pp. 1-11.

6. Benjamin R. Maitre, "Echoes and Origins of an American Way of War," *Comparative Strategy*, Vol. 27, No. 3, May/June 2008, pp. 249-251.

7. Ralph D. Sawyer, *The Seven Military Classics of Ancient China*, New York: Basic Books, 2007, pp. 150–151.

8. *Ibid.*, pp. 11-13.

9. Griffith in Sun Tzu, *The Art of War*, p. 37.

10. Sawyer, p. 150.

11. *Ibid.*, p. 63.

12. Sun Tzu, p. 77.

13. *Ibid.*, p. 84.

14. *Ibid.*, p. 106.

15. *Ibid.*, p. 102.

16. J. Boone Bartholomees, "Sun Tzu and the Art of Modern Warfare," *Parameters*, Vol. 32, No. 3, Autumn 2002, pp. 146-148. (A review of *Sun Tzu and the Art of Modern Warfare* by Mark McNeilly, New York, NY: Oxford University Press, 2001).

17. Mao Tse-Tung [Zedong], "On Contradiction," in *Selected Readings from the Works of Mao Tse-Tung*, Honolulu, HI: University Press of the Pacific, 2001, p. 101.

18. Griffith in Sun Tzu, *The Art of War*, p. 46.

19. Jonathan B. Parshall and Anthony P. Tully, *Shattered Sword: the Untold Story of the Battle of Midway*, Washington, DC: Potomac Books, 2005, pp. 408-409.

20. Thomas J, Cutler, *The Battle of Leyte Gulf: The Greatest Naval Battle in History*, New York: Pocket Books, 1994, pp. 74-77, 81.

21. Roger Boesche, "Kautilya's Arthashastra on War and Diplomacy in Ancient India," *Journal of Military History*, Vol. 67, No. 1, January 2003, pp. 9-37.

22. Kautilya, p. 17.

23. Lalit Kumar Das, "Culture as the Designer," *Design Issues*, Vol. 21, No. 4, Autumn 2005, pp. 41-53.

24. Rashed Uz Zamam, "Kautilya: The Indian Strategic Thinker and Indian Strategic Culture," *Comparative Strategy*, Vol. 25, No. 3, January-March 2009, pp. 66-88.

25. Max Weber, "Politics as a Vocation," in W. G. Runciman, ed., and Eric Matthews, trans., *Weber: Selections in Translation*, Cambridge, UK: Cambridge University Press, 1978, p. 220.

26. Uz Raman, p. 235.

27. *Ibid.*, pp. 236-238.

28. Kautilya, p. 555.

29. Robert Leckie, *Warfare*, New York, NY: Harper & Row, 1970, p. xiii.

30. Arthur L. Basham, *The Wonder That Was India*, New York: Taplinger Publishers, 1968, pp. 55-56.

31. Nirad C. Chaudhuri, *Hinduism*, New York: Oxford University Press, 1979, pp. 142-143.

32. Sudhir Kakar, *The Colors of Violence: Cultural Identities, Religion, and Conflict*, Chicago, IL: University of Chicago Press, 1996.

33. Amrita Narlikar, "Peculiar Chauvanism or Strategic Calculation? Explaining the Negotiating Strategy of a Rising India," *International Affairs*, Vol. 82, No. 11, January 2006, pp. 59-76.

34. Mark Borthwick, *Pacific Century: The Emergence of Modern Pacific Asia*, 4th Ed., Boulder, CO: Westview Press, 1998, pp. 58-61.

35. Musashi, p. 53.

36. *Ibid.*

37. *Ibid.*, p. 59.

38. *Ibid.*, p. 56.

39. *Ibid.*, p. 45.

40. *Ibid.*, p. 46.

41. *Ibid.*, p. 49.

42. Benjamin R. Maitre, "Echoes and Origins of an American Way of War," *Comparative Strategy*, Vol. 27, No. 3, May/June 2008, pp. 248-266.

43. Musashi, p. 49.

44. *Ibid.*, p. 80.

45. Thomas M. Coffey, *Iron Eagle: The Turbulent Life of General Curtis LeMay*, New York: Random House, 1986.

46. Williamson Murray and Allan R. Millett, *A War to Be Won*, Cambridge, MA: Belknap Press, 2000, pp. 506-508, 523.

47. Robin Cross, *The Bombers: The Illustrated Story of Offensive Strategy and Tactics in the Twentieth Century*, New York: Macmillan & Co., 1987, p. 181.

48. Ferron A. Olson, "Forgiveness at Wakayama," *Ensign*, Vol. 41, No. 12, December 2011, pp. 56-57.

49. Bartholomees, p. 148.

Part II:
Instruments and Elements of Power

CHAPTER 11

NATIONAL POWER

R. Craig Nation

Power is an essential concept in international theory, but also an essentially contested and chronically ambiguous one.[1] The word itself, derived from the Old French *pouvoir* (to be able) connotes capacity. As a concept power can be usefully defined as the capacity to impose a desired outcome in the face of resistance. In the words of Robert Dahl: "A has power over B to the extent that he can get B to do something that B would not otherwise do."[2] This makes power both a dispositional concept and a function of coercive behavior—the purposeful exercise of capacity in order to arrive at a determined end in a context of conflict or goal incompatibility. Power can also be defined more broadly, as the ability to shape the operational environment in such a way as to encourage certain kinds of behavior and discourage or place beyond the pale various alternatives. The scope of what is considered legitimate behavior is thereby reduced—what does not happen is as important as what does. In this framework, power implies securing compliance by leveraging influence and authority.[3] Desired outcomes can be imposed coercively (power to), but also assured by the consensually grounded institutionalization of authority and a corresponding code of values (power over).[4]

Much of the formal literature addressing the concept of power focuses on social systems and domestic political order, in which the institutionalization of authority is placed front and center. Writing in this context, Hannah Arendt anchors the concept of power to popular will: "All political institutions are manifestations and materializations of power; they petrify and decay as soon as the living power of the people ceases to uphold them."[5] Thomas Hobbes's famous evocation of mankind's "perpetual and restless desire for power after power, that ceaseth only in death" describes a proclivity to dominate others grounded in human nature that must be constrained by the power of the state, presumably sanctioned by some kind of hypothetical social contract.[6] On the level of domestic governance, coercive capacity and legitimate authority combine to allow the effective application of political power as an alternative to the unregulated struggle of all against all.

On the international level, different priorities prevail. The classic realist vision of international order rests on the assertion that the modern state system (the so-called Westphalian state system) is defined first of all by the *absence* of any effective supranational authority. It is an anarchic, self-help system in which sovereign states must act without recourse to institutions of world governance to confront "the conflicts of interests that inevitably arise among similar units in a condition of anarchy."[7] Morgenthau accepts Hobbes's tragic vision of the human conditions. He quotes Thucydides's Athenians address to the Melians to the effect that: "Of the gods we know, and of men we believe, that it is a necessary law of their nature that they rule wherever they can."[8] The domestic analogy does not apply—international law and associated norms of state behavior will be ignored when vital interests are at stake, or at best evoked hypocritically as rhetorical justification for the pursuit of selfish goals. No international civil society of sovereign states is possible. In the words of Hobbes's great contemporary Baruch de Spinoza, in interstate competition the strong are bound to "devour" the weak.[9] Power, unmitigated by systemic constraint, becomes the currency of relations between states and the driving force of statecraft, famously capsulated by Morgenthau as "interest defined as power."[10] The strategic image of statecraft that came to dominate both the theory and practice of international relations in the post-World War II era makes the pursuit of power its most basic premise. Speaking on behalf of the realist camp, Donald Kagan defines power austerely as "the capacity to bring about desired ends," and asserts that "in the world in which we all live, it is essential, and the struggle for it is inevitable."[11]

STRUCTURAL MODELS OF POWER

Power is the measure of a relationship. It has no objective stature in and of itself and can be manifested in many ways. It is not a fungible commodity. The combination of power resources required to accomplish Task A, can be completely different from the combination required to address Task B. Physical strength, for example, will be a useful facilitator for positive outcomes in some contingencies (a wrestling match) but altogether irrelevant in others (a chess contest). Morgenthau defines power as "man's control over the minds and actions of other men" and "a psychological relation between those who exercise it and those over whom it is exercised,"[12] thus adding a subjective dimension to the calculus of power grounded in personal and cultural considerations. National power is also a dynamic concept, whose components have changed considerably through the modern centuries and which continues to evolve.

Modern policy analysis has been predisposed to emphasize the primacy of national security as a motive for state behavior and the essential role of military power as the guarantor of national survival and state interests. There is no doubt that in the modern centuries military power has been the most important arbiter in relations between states. But superior military capacity has never been a sufficient condition for achieving successful outcomes in international competition. Military strength is only one dimension of what are sometimes referred to as *hard power* assets: the capacity to coerce, including both the threat of and resort to armed force; economic pressure including fiscal and commercial sanctions; subversive techniques; and, various other forms of intimidation. Moreover, the capacity of states to develop and sustain military capacity rests on a more complex combination of power attributes, including economic, organizational and motivational assets.

Military power has always been employed as one of several tools of statecraft. Edward Gullick notes that in the age of the classic European balance of power, the calculus of power rested on the diverse mechanisms of alliance, coalition, and compensation, with resort to arms or warfare as a popular but also last resort.[13] Immanuel Wallerstein describes the constituents of power in the early modern European state system complexly as: (1) *mercantilism*, implying the use of state capacity to promote economic strength; (2) *military power*; (3) *public finance*; (4) *effective bureaucracy*; and, (5) the *hegemonic bloc,* defined as the capacity of dominate social groups to impose their own vision of national priorities.[14] The 19th-century Concert of Europe used consultation between the great powers to prevent systemic conflict on the scale of the Napoleonic era, relying on a series of "rules of the game" defined by Paul Schroeder as "compensation; indemnities; alliances as instruments for accruing power and capability; *raison d'état*; honour and prestige; Europe as a family of states; and finally, the principle or goal of balance of power itself."[15] Among the classic realists, Morgenthau's emphasis on the subtleties of diplomacy and Raymond Aron's identification of prudence as the foundation for statecraft make clear that their image of the role of force in interstate relations is a nuanced one.[16]

During the Cold War, confronting what was consensually identified as the real and present danger of aggressive Soviet power, the United States and its allies made the quest for security their most important national priority. This demanded the cultivation of military power as a balance to the considerable Soviet arsenal. The Cold War was a militarized interstate rivalry, but it was also something more. Military containment was accompanied by a successful diplomacy of alliance, the purposeful use of economic power, and, critically, the moral force provided by the example of the open society and Free World when contrasted with Soviet totalitarianism. In the end it was the non-material dimensions of power that were decisive. The vulgar realist image of military power as all important has never been reflected in sophisticated political theory or real world state practice.

Beginning with the publication of Robert Keohane and Joseph Nye's *Power and Interdependence* in 1977, there has been an ongoing effort by international relations scholars to develop a more nuanced view of the concept of power in international relations that breaks with some of the core assumptions of the realist paradigm. In the interdependent world of the late-20th century, Keohane and Nye argued, the relative importance of military power as an instrument of statecraft is in decline. Survival remains the primordial national goal, and force is still the ultimate guarantor of security. But in a more interdependent world, relationships of mutual dependence bind countries more closely together, and "in most of them force is irrelevant or unimportant as an instrument of policy."[17] In his subsequent work, Nye has championed the concept of *soft power*, including cultural and ideological assets, transformational diplomacy, information strategies, the power of example, and the like—as an alternative that leverages the power of attraction in place of the coercive strategies of traditional statecraft.[18]

Many analysts have developed variations on this theme. Alvin Toffler's *Powershift* identifies three main sources of power, defined as violence, wealth, and knowledge. The role of violence is exclusively punitive and negative, wealth can be used both to punish and reward, but only the leveraging of knowledge has the potential to be transformational under 21st-century conditions—for Toffler the knowledge sector will be the key to national power looking into the future.[19] In her *States and Markets,* Susan Strange develops a "structural model of power" with four sectors: productive, fiscal, military, and informational. Strange asks how the United States has been able to expand its global influence despite the relative contraction of its productive and fiscal sectors. She finds the answer, in part, in military dominance, but also, and perhaps more importantly, in the attraction of America's open society and "way of life," the unparalleled prestige of U.S. institutions of higher education, cutting-edge scientific and technological innovation, the status of the English language as the *lingua franca* of international communication, effective public diplomacy, and, in general, the capacity to mobilize cultural power in service of U.S. interests.[20] The United States has embraced this kind of more complex image of national power, and a series of formal policy documents have introduced contrasting models of power intended to convey the conclusion that viewed comprehensively national power has multiple and overlapping sources. These models are expressed by the increasingly ambitious acronyms DIME (Diplomatic, Informational, Military, and Economic power); DIMEFIL (Diplomatic, Information, Military, Economic, Financial, Intelligence, and Law Enforcement); and MIDLIFE (Military, Intelligence, Diplomacy, Legal, Information, Financial, and Economic power).[21]

The nuances of any one of these models and the degree of appropriateness of this or that particular term being attached to the power equation are less important than what the models share in common. That includes the conclusion that in the globalized world of the 21st-century, conventional military power has indeed lost at least some of its salience as the *ultima ratio* of statecraft. Global interdependence and the democratic peace dynamic have arguably made conventional armed conflict between great powers less likely.[22] Nuclear weapons have made all-out war between nuclear armed states virtually unthinkable. International Law places formal constraints on the institution of war that can and do impact on states' prerogative to opt for a resort to force.[23] Economic competition, on the other hand, has become more important as a driver of international competition. Analysts like Edward Luttwak have coined the notion of "geo-economics" to characterize a world order in which competition between nations will be based more on economic rivalry than an older vision of geopolitics built on contention by force.[24] Power has become more diffused, and a more diverse palette of instruments of power is required to pursue national interests effectively.

THE FOUNDATIONS OF NATIONAL POWER

National power is constituted on a number of distinct levels: (1) physical resources and attributes (latent power); (2) the effectiveness of national institutions in mobilizing, sustaining, and applying the instruments of power (applied power); and (3) the structural context (facilitators or constraints on the application of power derived from the international environment). The ultimate measure of effective national power should be outcomes or performance. Measuring outcomes, however, depends on the strategic setting—the ends toward which national power is being directed, or "power over whom, and with respect to what?"[25]

Latent Power.

The physical attributes of national power include human resources (population), agricultural potential and the endowment of strategic resources, productive capacity, and geostrategic characteristics.

From the military revolution of the early-modern centuries to the present, powerful states have required a population base sufficient to raise and sustain strategically competitive mass armies. Large populations also contribute to greater productive power and a larger gross domestic product (GDP), a basic measure of economic strength. Indeed, it is virtually impossible to imagine a state rising into the ranks of the great world powers without a significant population base. The United States' ability to attract and assimilate large immigrant populations, and to sustain demographic growth, has been a meaningful source of national power. Demographic decline in the European Union (EU) and Russian Federation threaten their capacity to function as great powers in the long term. But large impoverished populations can also place constraints on development and the mobilization of strategic power. Contemporary China presents the example of a rising power that is committed to what some consider a draconian policy of limiting population growth. Size matters, but there is no direct correlation between the size of a country's population and its underlying national strength.

Agricultural potential and the endowment of strategic raw materials can also be critical facilitators of national power. All things being equal, nations with the capacity to feed themselves have a strategic advantage over competitors who are dependent on imports. Historically, its great agricultural potential has been a significant source of U.S. strength. Strategic raw materials can also provide a foundation for economic and military power. Oil-rich states such as Saudi Arabia carry weight beyond their inherent capacity specifically because of the degree to which they control access to a vital strategic resource. The dramatic revival of the Russian Federation over the past decade, driven by a tenfold increase in the price of oil and natural gas on world markets between 1998 and 2008, is a clear example of how a raw material endowment can be translated into strategic power. Conversely, dependence on foreign sources of supply for vital resources can place states at a competitive disadvantage unless compensated for by special diplomatic or commercial arrangements. Like other potential pillars of national power, however, control of vital raw materials does not translate directly into strategic leverage. A raw material endowment can also be squandered due to lack of technological expertise, corruption and disreputable political direction, or insufficient social discipline—the modern world offers many examples. The nature of strategic resources also changes over time in tandem with technological development. Salt and ship timbers were once considered to be strategic raw materials on a par with hydrocarbon reserves today. In the near future environmental pressures may make access to fresh water resources a vital national interest as well—with considerable implications for the global balance of power.

Industrial capacity was once considered to be the bedrock of national power. It was the foundation of Britain's preeminence as a European great power and global empire all through the 19th century. The stage was set for the First World War by the power transition implicit in the relative decline of France as an industrial power and the rise of Germany as the continent's leading center of industrial production. The United States assumed the mantle of leadership in the productive sector at the same time that it was supplanting the United Kingdom as the leading world power, and its stature as the "arsenal of democracy" was a key to victory in the 20th century's most destructive industrial war.[26] In the wake of the Second World War, the idea of European unification came to life as the European Coal and Steel Community in an effort to promote functional cooperation in key productive sectors as a basis for a lasting peace. Today, however, development has become associated with the rise of post-industrial economies based on the service sector, in which informational assets have become more important than productive power. The extent to which the nature of power itself remains contested is revealed by continuing controversy over whether this trend is salutary and should be encouraged. There is no lack of voices to argue that in allowing its industrial capacity to degrade, the United States, is sacrificing a vital pillar of national power, and to call for a state-directed "industrial policy" to revive domestic production.[27]

A state's geostrategic situation can also either facilitate or retard its ability to mobilize national power. Access to the world's oceans, serviceable harbors, and control over maritime choke points and strategic lines of communication are essential to maritime capacity. Even in the space age, the United States continues to derive benefit from the extent to which it is shielded from strategic threats by the great oceans that flank it east and west, and the absence of predatory neighbors in North America. Russia's strategic situation in the heartland of the Eurasian land mass has always been a source of national strength, but the lack of naturally defensible frontiers has also left it exposed to a series of catastrophic invasions. Strategic exposure can also contribute to state power by reinforcing national will and the commitment to survive—the case of Israel is an excellent illustration. Cultural geography also matters. Ethnic, linguistic, and confessional diversity can be culturally enriching, but also create strategic vulnerabilities. The relative homogeneity of American culture, extended over a vast continental expanse, is commonly and correctly cited as an important source of unity and national strength (which some see as endangered by uncontrolled immigration and increasing cultural diversity). China's powerful and integral cultural legacy, combined with overwhelming Han dominance on the Chinese mainland, is also a facilitator of national power. On the other hand, the Soviet federation fractured along ethnic fault lines and collapsed despite its immense military potential. Europe's rich linguistic and cultural diversity places barriers in the way of efforts to create a more united Europe capable of functioning as a strategic actor in world affairs under the aegis of the EU.

Applied Power.

Resources are the raw material of national power. They must be translated into applied power to be relevant to the pursuit of national goals. The degree of efficiency that states bring to the task of converting latent power into applied power is determined by political, social, and organizational interactions. The stability and effectiveness of governing institutions, economic performance, aptitude for innovation, educational standards, social structure, organizational proficiency, and reputation are more difficult to quantify than the resource endowment, but arguably no less important as foundations for national policy.

Military strength is the classic foundation of national power. It can be quantified rather handily using national defense budgets and militarily related expenditures as a comparative measure. Currently the U.S. defense budget represents 46 percent of global military spending—larger than the next 168 countries combined and approximately ten times greater than the nearest competitors (China, Japan, Russia, France, and the United Kingdom, each with between 4 and 5 percent of the global total).[28] At 3.7 percent of GDP, the U.S. budget represents a lesser military burden than that borne by some other states (in Saudi Arabia, for example, defense spending represents over 10 percent of GDP), but globally the U.S. quantitative advantage is overwhelming.[29]

Unfortunately, bean counting has never been a reliable measure of real military capacity. From the campaigns of Alexander the Great to the present, history provides many examples of smaller but more highly motivated, effectively led, and technically proficient armed forces defeating larger rivals. Militaries are social institutions whose performance rests upon a number of criteria outside the control of the uniformed services—including societal levels of educational achievement and standards of physical conditioning, technological capacity, social disciple and motivation, and strategic leadership. Effectiveness will also be a function of the kinds of tasks that military organizations are called on to perform. Traditionally, the U.S. Armed Forces have been configured to engage in conventional and nuclear warfare with major peer competitors. At present and for the foreseeable future the need to counter various kinds of asymmetric threats will arguably require a very different configuration of forces and new approaches to strategic competition. High levels of military spending that exceed the capacity of the national economy can undermine national power in the long run—the fate of the Soviet Union, armed to the teeth but collapsed of its own weight without a shot fired in anger, is a salutary example.

Globalization, understood as a process of enhanced international interdependence and space/time compression driven by technological change, has changed the nature of economic power. GDP and GDP per capita remain valid measures of overall economic strength. The World Bank's categorization of low-, middle-, and high-income countries (representing 60 percent, 25 percent, and 15 percent of the world population, respectively) provides a fair global index of relative economic power.[30] The United States continues to lead the global economy in terms of overall GDP and remains the world's largest national market and most powerful national economy. But raw numbers can also obscure important variables. Is economic performance based on extractive industry, declining manufacturing sectors, or advanced, technologically driven sectors? Are growth models sustainable in the face of resource, environmental, and competitive constraints? Is growth balanced and equitable? In fact, the pressures of globalization seem to have provoked an increase in inequality even in the best performing national economies, a trend with unsettling political implications—societal and class division can undermine national purpose and reduce a state's capacity to leverage national power.[31] In the new world economy, the familiar distinction between domestic and global markets has been obscured if not obliterated. Economic volatility has increased, and the challenge of leadership has become more acute. Market power will be built on different kinds of assets than in the past—efficiency and productivity, educational attainment and the quality of human capital, the ability to adapt, technological creativity, environmental sensitivity, and social stability, among them.[32] Education is critical, and the purposeful developmental of the tertiary educational sector has become a conscious strategy for some emerging states. China now produces more than twice as many university graduates as the United States, which was for many years the world leader. The nineteen countries associated with UNESCO's World Educational Indicators Project (Argentina, Brazil, Chile, China, Egypt, India, Indonesia, Jamaica, Jordan, Malaysia, Paraguay, Peru, Philippines, Russian Federation, Sri Lanka, Thailand, Tunisia, Uruguay, and Zimbabwe) graduate more students from university than the 30 Organization for Economic Co-operation and Development (OECD) countries combined, and devote 53 percent of GDP to support tertiary education, compared with 40 percent in the OECD.[33] Such trends could culminate in significant shifts in the global balance of power. In the future, qualitative factors may have as much or more to say about overall economic performance than many traditional quantitative indicators.

The strength of governing institutions and effectiveness of the policy process can also enhance or inhibit the application of national power. Different kinds of governments can accomplish these tasks in various ways. Authoritarian regimes usually lack popular legitimacy, but can be adept at imposing coherent national strategies and pursuing them consistently over time. But authoritarian leaders can also become isolated by in-groups of sycophantic courtiers and denied the kind of realistic appraisals that are required for intelligent strategic choices—as seems to have been the case, for example, with Iraq's Saddam Hussein. Democratic polities must construct policy by consensus building and persuasion, and vet it through a complex decisionmaking process, with a certain degree of incoherence an almost inevitable result. It is usually more difficult for democratic states to build and sustain a national consensus on strategic options and to shift course rapidly in the face of changed international circumstances. Nonetheless, a state with respected and legitimate institutions grounded in popular consensus, and capable of mobilizing its population to accept sacrifices in the face of real threats to national well being, will be inherently stronger, often in subtle ways, than an authoritarian polity imposed and sustained by force.

The policy process itself can become an independent variable. Improved strategic education and professional development for civil servants working in the national security sector, better coordination between government agencies, and more adept management can arguably lead toward more effective strategic choices. Coordinating the varied instruments of national power, including diplomatic, intelligence, informational, and legal tools, demands professional insight and an efficient decisionmaking environment within which ideas can be exchanged freely and alternative courses of action considered on their merits.

The ability to apply power effectively also depends on social cohesion and the degree to which a country is regarded as an honorable and trustworthy member of the community of nations. National values, political stability, an active and engaged citizenry and dynamic civil society, and international reputation can all be meaningful sources of national power. If states are convinced that the ideals and priorities of a potential rival are sincere and worthy of respect, they are more likely to opt for policies of accommodation that acknowledge mutual interests. This is the case along a continuum stretching from bilateral relations to systemic competition. Hegemonic powers cannot sustain their position on the basis of coercive strategies alone—they must construct a framework of authority and system of values to which subordinate states accord voluntary acquiescence—the "power over" accorded by non-material sources of national power. Dysfunctional or rogue states that fail to cultivate this kind of cohesion or flout the normative context within which interstate relations are conducted will inevitably pay a price.

In the classic statement of the philosophy that might makes right, Thucydides's Athenians tell their Melian interlocutors that "right, as the world goes, is only in question between equals in power, while the strong do what they can and the weak suffer what they must."[34] Moses Finley remarks that "nothing so marks Thucydides' work as the sense of living in a world where moral sensitiveness and the inherited tradition were…a luxury, and that the very survival of states hung on the skillful use of power and power alone."[35] And yet the Athenian polity that Thucydides so admires was ultimately destroyed by a war in the course of which it gradually abandoned the values and progressive spirit that originally had made it great. The Pope may have no divisions (to paraphrase Joseph Stalin), but moral force and reputation are critical enablers of national power that states ignore at their peril. Faith and morale, remarks Niall Ferguson, are "perhaps as important a component of power as material resources."[36]

International Context.

National power is contextual and relational in the sense that it can only be measured in the context of a particular pattern of interstate relations and against the capacities of other national and non-state actors. The constantly evolving nature of threats to national well-being must also be taken into account. These are dynamic variables—the power equation in international relations is never stable, and the substance of national power is constantly changing. What are the most salient characteristics of the current international system, and the most significant trends working to transform it? How is systemic transformation affecting the structure of threats against which states are required to maneuver? These kinds of dynamic factors, embedded in the mechanisms of international society, will affect the ways in which national power is configured, conceptualized, and realized.

Globalization pushes toward the diminution of *de facto* state sovereignty. The diffusion of technology has made the effort to maintain an effective non-proliferation regime appear increasingly quixotic. As access to weapons of mass destruction becomes more widespread, including potentially to terrorist and extremist organizations, even the most comprehensively armed states will find themselves increasingly exposed. The phenomenon of global migration has strained the ability of states to maintain physical control over their borders, once considered the most basic attribute of sovereignty. The revolution in information technology has shattered the state's monopoly over certain kinds of information, and created new and powerful channels of communication across borders. It has also enabled the global market, which can now react to economic stimuli with a speed and flexibility that states cannot rival or control. A variety of non-state actors (multinational corporations; non-governmental organizations [NGO], such as Amnesty International or Oxfam International; multilateral forums, such as the International Monetary Fund [IMF], the North Atlantic Treaty Organization, [NATO], or the Shanghai Cooperation Organization [SCO]; regional economic associations, such as the EU or the Association of Southeast Asian Nations [ASEAN]) now rival states in an effort to "set the agenda" and impose priorities in world politics. Some argue that the most critical challenges confronting the international community—the proliferation of weapons of mass destruction and effects; environmental disintegration; impoverishment and economic marginalization; the threat of pandemic disease; trans-boundary crime, including drug and human trafficking; terrorism; low intensity conflict, sometimes extending to the level of genocidal violence produced by dysfunctional regional orders and failing states; traditional mass casualty events; and, cyberterrorism—can no longer be confronted by nation-states acting in isolation. Global threats that transcend the capacity of individual states, no matter how powerful, have become more important.[37] What is needed, champions of a pluralist image of international relations will argue, is more effective instruments of global governance that look beyond the anarchic and archaic character of the Westphalian state system.[38]

The case for the decline of the state can easily be overstated. States are no doubt more subject to transnational forces than they were in the past, but they remain the building blocks of international society and by far the most significant repositories of the kind of power resources that will have to be mobilized to confront new global challenges. States are the only effective guarantors of popular empowerment and basic social security, and there is no one to replace them. International cooperation is still overwhelmingly generated on the interstate level, whether bilaterally in the legal and normative framework of international regimes, or in international organizations. Nor have traditional threats to national well-being altogether disappeared. The United States, as the world's predominant power, confronts the emergence of potential new peer competitors in the EU and the rising economic challengers of the so-called BRIC group (Brazil, Russia, India, and China). Regional security complexes are still preoccupied by competitive interaction between states and the very traditional threat of armed aggression. The effort to increase national power, and the security dilemmas to which that effort gives rise, remains a driver of international political competition. But the dynamic of enhanced sensitivity and vulnerability born of globalization cannot be ignored, and the way that we understand national power must be adjusted to take it into account.

THE CHANGING NATURE OF POWER

How does globalization impact on the configuration of national power? On the international level, power has become more diffused, and states are no longer its unique proprietor. The leverage available to various kinds of non-state actors and their ability to shape and affect the power of states has become more significant. In discrete areas such as human rights and international humanitarian law, environmental policy, and humanitarian assistance, NGOs have been successful in imposing frameworks for international action that on some level states are obliged to respect. The Ottawa Treaty and Kyoto Protocol are only two examples. The diffusion of information through the worldwide net and a proliferation of "virtual networks" tying people together across borders in what some have called a nascent "international civil society" have eroded states' capacity to dominate the dissemination of ideas and sustain control through compliance.

The nature of national security, the fundamental challenge of traditional statecraft, is also changing. The physical attributes of national power, including territory, population, and resources, remain salient. But in an age of increased international interconnectedness and interdependence the Westphalian premise of territoriality has lost some of its force—control over terrain is no longer the kind of driver in international political competition that it once was. Even the largest and inherently most powerful states confront new and unfamiliar kinds of vulnerabilities for which the traditional instruments of national security policy are not always well suited.

Conventional military power has lost at least some of its centrality. Traditional conceptions of the role of military power emphasize the forceful defense of borders and the containment of threats to national integrity posed by "Napoleonic neighbors" and armed adversaries. But traditional military priorities are less well adapted to confront the new threat structure emerging in an age of "sacred terror" and new kinds of existential concerns. The security problem has become more complex and multidimensional. In his seminal *People, States and War*, first published in 1983, Barry Buzan spoke of military, political, economic, societal, and ecological security as diverse facets of a broader security equation.[39] The so-called Copenhagen School has explored the "securitization" of non-military challenges, with particular emphasis on societal security and identity issues.[40] Other analysts argue for a deepening of the security agenda in a Kantian sense, with the referent for security displaced from the sovereign state to the autonomous human subject. In its 1994 *Human Development Report*, the United Nations Development Programme introduced the concept of *human security* manifested in seven issue areas (economic, food, health, environmental, personal, community, and political) and six threats (unchecked population growth, disparities in economic opportunity, migration pressures, environmental degradation, drug trafficking, and international terrorism).[41] Such arguments take us some distance away from the traditional priorities of defense policy, but they point to emerging vulnerabilities that may become increasingly relevant to the calculus of national power under 21st-century conditions.

It is still possible to draw up an approximate index of national power using quantitative measures such as population, territory, resource base, GDP, defense spending, average educational attainment, per capita expenditure on research and development, and the like. A recent study sponsored by the National Security Research Division of the RAND Corporation uses a basket of such metrics to calculate that the U.S. holds about 20 percent of total global power, compared with 14 percent each for the EU and China, and 9 percent for India.[42] This is an interesting exercise that may have some relevance as a rough measure of overall capacity. It does not effectively address what is ultimately the most basic issue of shaping outcomes by translating latent power into applied power and using it judiciously to promote national interests. This remains the domain of strategy and the art of statecraft, where the instruments of national power must be applied in a dynamic and uncertain international environment and in a context of mutual vulnerabilities that demands careful calculation, prudence, and a healthy dose of strategic restraint.

ENDNOTES - CHAPTER 11

1. For the notion of "essentially contested concepts," which "inevitably involve endless disputes about their proper uses," see W. B. Gallie, "Essentially Contested Concepts," *Proceedings of the Aristotelian Society,* Vol. 56, 1955-56, pp. 167-198.

2. R. A. Dahl, "The Concept of Power," *Behavioral Science,* No. 2, 1957, pp. 201-215.

3. P. Bachrach and M. S. Baratz, *Power and Poverty: Theory and Practice,* Oxford, UK: Oxford University Press, 1970.

4. These categories correspond to the "two dimensions" of power defined in the seminal work of Steven Lukes, *Power: A Radical View,* Houndsmills, Basingstoke, UK: Palgrave Macmillan, 2005, pp. 14-29. Lukes goes on to elaborate a "three dimensional" image of power built on the Gramscian notion of hegemony.

5. Hannah Arendt, *On Violence*, New York: Allen Lane, 1970, p. 41.

6. Thomas Hobbes, *Leviathan*, Harmondsworth, UK: Penguin Books, 1968, p. 161.

7. Kenneth Waltz, *Man, the State and War*, New York: Columbia University Press, 1959, p. 238.

8. Hans J. Morgenthau, *Politics Among Nations: The Struggle for Power and Peace,* 5th Ed., New York: Alfred A. Knopf, 1978, p. 38.

9. See Ian Clark, *Reform and Resistance in the International Order,* Cambridge, UK: Cambridge University Press, 1980, pp. 55-77.

10. Morgenthau, pp. 5-6.

11. Donald Kagan, *On the Origins of War and the Preservation of Peace,* New York: Doubleday, 1995, p. 7.

12. Morgenthau, p. 30.

13. Edward Vose Gullick, *Europe's Classical Balance of Power: A Case History of the Theory and Practice of One of the Great Concepts of European Statecraft,* Westport, CT: Greenwood Press, 1982, p. 39.

14. Immanuel Wallerstein, *The Modern World System II: Mercantilism and the Consolidation of the European World Economy, 1600-1750,* New York: Academic Press, 1980, pp. 113-114.

15. Paul W. Schroeder, *The Transformation of European Politics, 1763-1848,* Oxford, UK: Clarendon Press, 1994, p. 6.

16. Raymond Aron, *Peace and War: A Theory of International Relations,* New York: Doubleday & Company, Inc., 1966, pp. 591-600.

17. Robert O. Keohane and Joseph S. Nye, *Power and Interdependence: World Politics in Transition,* Boston, MA: Little, Brown and Company, 1977, p. 27.

18. Joseph S. Nye, Jr., *Soft Power: The Means to Success in World Politics,* New York: Public Affairs, 2004.

19. Alvin Toffler, *Powershift: Knowledge, Wealth, and Violence at the Edge of the 21st Century,* New York: Bantam Books, 1990.

20. Susan Strange, *States and Markets,* 2nd Ed., London: Pinter Publishers, 1994.

21. For these designations, see, The White House, *National Strategy for Combating Terrorism,* Washington, DC, U.S. Government Printing Office, September 2006; Chairman of the Joint Chiefs of Staff, *National Military Strategic Plan for the War on Terrorism,* Washington, DC: The Pentagon, February 1, 2006; and Homeland Security Council, *National Strategy for Homeland Security,* Washington, DC: U.S. Government Printing Office, October 2007.

22. John M. Owen, "Give Democratic Peace a Chance: How Liberalism Produces Democratic Peace," *International Security,* Vol. 19, No. 2, Autumn 1994, pp. 87-125.

23. Ingrid Detter, *The Law of War,* 2nd Ed., Cambridge, UK: Cambridge University Press, 2000, pp. 62-81.

24. Edward Luttwak, *The Endangered American Dream: How to Stop the United States from Becoming a Third World Country,* New York: Simon & Schuster, 1993.

25. David Jablonsky, "National Power," in J. Boone Bartholomees, ed., *U.S. Army War College Guide to National Security Policy and Strategy,* 2nd Ed., Carlisle, PA: U.S. Army War College, June 2006, p. 127.

26. R. J. Overy, *Why the Allies Won,* New York: W. W. Norton, 1996.

27. Dani Rodrik, John F. Kennedy School of Government, Harvard University, "Industrial Policies for the 21st Century," September 2004, available from *ksghome.harvard.edu/~drodrik/UNIDOSep.pdf.*

28. Statistics from Chapter Eight, "Military Expenditures," *SIPRI Yearbook 2007: Armaments, Disarmament, and International Security,* Stockholm, Sweden: Stockholm International Peace Research Institute, 2007.

29. *Ibid.*

30. *World Development Indicators, 2007,* Washington, DC: The World Bank, 2007.

31. *World Economic Outlook: Globalization and Inequality,* Washington, DC: International Monetary Fund, October 2007.

32. Thomas L. Friedman, *The World is Flat: A Short History of the 21st Century,* New York: Farrar, Straus and Giroux, 2005.

33. UNESCO Global Education Digest 2007, available from *www.uis.unesco.org/ev.*

34. Cited from Richard B. Strassler, ed., *The Landmark Thucydides: A Comprehensive Guide to the Peloponnesian War,* New York: The Free Press, 1996, p. 5: 89.

35. Moses I. Finley, *The World of Odysseus,* New York: The Viking Press, 1965, p. 29.

36. Niall Ferguson, "What Is Power?" *Hoover Digest,* No. 2, 2003.

37. See, for example, Joseph S. Nye, *The Paradox of American Power: Why the World's Only Superpower Can't Go It Alone,* Oxford, UK: Oxford University Press, 2002.

38. James P. Muldoon, Jr., *The Architecture of Global Governance: An Introduction to the Study of International Organizations,* Boulder, CO: Westview Press, 2004.

39. Barry Buzan, *People, States, and Fear: The National Security Problem in International Relations,* Chapel Hill, NC: University of North Carolina Press, 1983.

40. Ole Waever, "Securitization and Desecuritization," in Ronnie Lipschutz, ed., *On Security,* New York: Columbia University Press, 1995, pp. 45-86.

41. United Nations Development Programme, *Human Development Report 1994,* Oxford: Oxford University Press, 1994. See also the subsequent Commission on Human Security, *Human Security Now,* New York: United Nations, 2003.

42. Gregory F. Treverton and Seth G. Jones, *Measuring National Power,* Santa Monica, CA: RAND, 2005. The study sees the relative U.S. power position in decline, and demotes the U.S. from "hegemonic" status in the first post-Cold War decade to the status of "preponderant" power in the first decade of the 21st century.

CHAPTER 12

STRATEGIC COMMUNICATION: WIELDING THE INFORMATION ELEMENT OF POWER

Dennis M. Murphy

It is generally accepted in the U.S. Government today that information is an element of national power along with diplomatic, military, and economic power, and that information is woven through the other elements, since their activities will have an informational impact.[1] Interestingly, however, one needs to go back to the Ronald Reagan administration to find the most succinct and pointed mention of information as an element of power in formal government documents.[2]

Subsequent national security documents allude to different aspects of information but without a specific strategy or definition. Given this dearth of official documentation, Drs. Dan Kuehl and Bob Neilson proffered the following definition of the information element: "Use of information content and technology as strategic instruments to shape fundamental political, economic, military, and cultural forces on a long-term basis to affect the global behavior of governments, supra-governmental organizations, and societies to support national security."[3] Information as power is wielded in an increasingly complex environment consisting of physical, informational, and cognitive dimensions. This chapter will focus on strategic communication and how the U.S. Government wields power in the cognitive dimension of the information environment. Specifically, it will consider how information is used to engage, inform, educate, persuade, and influence perceptions and attitudes of key audiences in order to ultimately change behavior.

Before addressing strategic communication as a U.S. Government process, it is important to consider the complex environment in which that process occurs. Consequently, the information environment is initially covered in some detail, including a description of "new media" capabilities and their impact. Information as power is both colored and informed in the psyche of Americans through the historical lens of "propaganda," and so it is also addressed in this section. With this foundational knowledge established, strategic communication is then considered from historical and current perspectives. Finally, recognizing both challenges and opportunities, a way-ahead is offered for future U.S. Government efforts to wield information effectively as power.

THE CHALLENGES OF TODAY'S INFORMATION ENVIRONMENT

The current information environment has leveled the playing field for not only nation-states but non-state actors, multinational corporations, and even individuals to affect strategic outcomes with minimal information infrastructure and little capital expenditure. Anyone with a camera cell phone and personal digital device with Internet capability understands this. On the other hand, the U.S. military has increasingly leveraged advances in information infrastructure and technology to gain advantages on the modern battlefield. One example from Operation IRAQI FREEDOM is the significant increase in situational awareness from network-centric operations that enabled coalition forces to swiftly defeat Iraqi forces in major combat operations.[4] Another includes the more prevalent use of visual information to record operations in order to proactively tell an accurate story, or as forensic evidence to refute enemy "disinformation" effectively.

Even a cursory look at advances in technology confirms what most people recognize as a result of their daily routine. The ability to access, collect, and transmit information is clearly decentralized to the lowest level (the individual). The technology is increasingly smaller, faster, and cheaper. Consequently, the ability to control and verify information is much more limited than in the recent past—nor will it get any easier:

In 1965, the physical chemist Gordon Moore, co-founder of Intel, predicted that the number of transistors on an integrated chip would double every 18 months. Moore predicted that this trend would continue for the foreseeable future. Moore and most other experts expect Moore's Law to remain valid for at least another 2 decades.[5]

So, if you wish to control (as nation-states, bureaucracies, and militaries tend to wish), the future may appear bleak, since not only is the ability to access, collect, and transmit information decentralized; the capacity to do so continues to increase exponentially. These challenges are readily apparent in the examination of many current information capabilities collectively referred to as "new media."

The Internet.

The Internet is the obvious start point for any discussion of the impact of today's new media. It is important to note that the World Wide Web is essentially ungoverned, providing obvious freedoms and cautions. The Web gives the individual a voice, often an anonymous voice, and a potentially vast audience. Websites are easily established, dismantled, and reestablished, making them valuable to extremist movements. Terrorists routinely use the Internet for propaganda, recruiting, training, cybercrime, and fund raising.[6] The United States has actively responded. In September 2011, President Barack Obama established the Center for Strategic Counterterrorism Communications, which, in part, "challenges and counters extremist messages online in Arabic and Urdu, including through original video content."[7] The Department of State's (DoS) broader policy guidance was articulated in a speech on Internet freedom by Secretary of State Hillary Clinton in January 2010. That policy explicitly addresses "three fundamental elements: the human rights of free speech, press, and assembly in cyberspace; open markets for digital goods and services to foster innovation, investment, and economic opportunity; and the freedom to connect—promoting access to connection technologies around the world."[8]

Web logs (blogs) are an example of the power that the Internet provides to individuals along with the dilemma it poses for nation-states. Of the over 150 million blogs in the world as of this writing, most have little effect on the conduct of nation-states or their militaries; but those that gain a following in the national security arena can have a huge impact. President George W. Bush cited Iraqi bloggers to point to progress being made in Iraq,[9] having apparently learned both the importance and value of blogs in 2004 when investigative bloggers cleared his name after an infamous CBS airing that questioned his military service.[10]

Social media sites such as Facebook and Twitter have also skyrocketed in popularity in recent years. The U.S. Department of Defense (DoD) has established a policy to allow broad use of social media by military members, recognizing the importance of educating and informing through the dialogue that these media offer. Senior military officers, policymakers, and their organizations and staffs actively engage in these forums, both to inform proactively as well as to counter enemy disinformation immediately. One cannot ignore the value of social media to the political activism that enabled such significant events as the so-called "Arab Spring." While perhaps not the cause for revolt and uprisings, social media certainly provides a means for like-minded individuals to communicate instantaneously and organize more rapidly than ever before.[11] The flip side of these opportunities is the challenge of maintaining operations security in the open, unconstrained environment of the World Wide Web, as well as the ability of authoritarian governments to spy on and manipulate their own people by monitoring and surreptitiously engaging social media forums.[12]

Video use and dissemination has skyrocketed as the capabilities of the Internet have increased. The YouTube phenomenon's power and access are evidenced by its purchase for $1.6 billion by

Google only 20 months after its founding. Like blogs, YouTube serves a variety of purposes to include entertainment. But, also like blogs, YouTube can empower individuals to achieve strategic political and military effects where easy upload of their videos (without editorial oversight) allows access to a nearly unlimited audience. Thus, the use of the improvised explosive device (IED) by insurgents shifts from a military tactical weapon to a strategic information weapon when the IED detonator is accompanied by a videographer. Again, like blogs, the U.S. military has recognized the importance of competing in the video medium, using near-real-time streaming video to show ongoing images of U.S. operations in Afghanistan.[13]

While websites, social media, and video proliferate in today's Internet ("Web 2.0"), the technology of "Web 3.0" (and the "semantic Web") is rapidly increasing in popularity. Web 3.0 is generally about being inside a three-dimensional (3D) virtual world that is low-cost and emotive. This is the "metaverse," or virtual universe, of applications like Second Life and others. These metaverses are attractive as opportunities to socialize where there is no need to compete and can be exploited as tools for learning. Multinational corporations are already planning and executing business plans in the 3D Internet world.[14] But, like the other internet based applications, Web 3.0 provides opportunities for darker undertakings. The virtual universes show signs of providing training grounds for terrorist organizations and anonymous locations for criminal money laundering.[15]

Mobile Technologies.

The Internet clearly is part of the new media phenomenon, but the Internet has not penetrated large areas of the world, especially in the poorest areas of underdeveloped countries. The cell phone, however, as a means of mobile technology, is increasingly available worldwide and deserves discussion as a potentially powerful capability to affect national security and military issues—arguably even more so than the internet.

There are numerous examples of cell phone Short Message Service (SMS text) messaging shaping political campaigns by mobilizing and revolutionizing politics. As previously discussed, it also is used both to call people to popular protests as well as by governments to provide information or misinformation in order to quell such protests. Combine this with the viral nature of social networking sites, and the impact can be significant. Text messaging is the medium of choice in overseas countries. It bypasses mass media and mobilizes an already persuaded populace as a means of lightweight engagement. Cell phones contain the technology to text, provide news, video, sound, voice, radio, and Internet. The number of mobile subscriptions worldwide was scheduled to pass 5 billion in 2010. Recognizing the power of mobile technology, the Obama administration released the President's Cairo speech to the Muslim world in 13 languages over text message.[16] Like any other new media capability, cell phone technology provides opportunities and challenges. Many young Iranians are turning to cell phones as a means for political protest . . . an opportunity that can be exploited.[17] On the other hand, criminals and terrorists can use cell phones to quickly organize an operation, execute it, and disperse using phone cards to provide cover from being traced. On an international scale, the challenge is often in the same laws that provide individual protections in democratic societies. Witness court battles in the United States regarding eavesdropping on foreign conversations without a court order when those conversations may be routed through a U.S. cell phone service provider.[18]

Mainstream Media in the Age of New Media.

Mainstream media certainly takes advantage of technological advances in order to remain competitive. Marvin Kalb in the Harvard Report on the Israeli-Hezbollah War of 2006 (the "Second Lebanon War") notes that:

> To do their jobs, journalists employed both the camera and the computer and with the help of portable satellite dishes and video phones 'streamed' or broadcast their reports . . ., as they covered the movement of troops and the rocketing of villages—often, (unintentionally, one assumes) revealing sensitive information to the enemy. Once upon a time, such information was the stuff of military intelligence acquired with considerable effort and risk; now it has become the stuff of everyday journalism. The camera and the computer have become weapons of war.[19]

This real-time reporting from the field has obvious impacts on the warfighter, but competition with new media for the first and fastest story also means that today's mainstream media is not your parents' mainstream media. Because of the plethora of information available today, newspapers, which once competed for knowledge as a scarce resource, today compete for a new scarce resource: the reader's (or listener's, in the case of broadcast media) attention.[20] Perhaps that is why increasing numbers of young adults turn to Jon Stewart's "The Daily Show" for their news.[21] It should come as no great shock then that "good news" stories about military operations do not appear with regularity in mainstream print and broadcast journalism.[22] Good news does not sell . . . because it does not grab the reader's (or viewer's) attention.

Of course, in an environment where the speed of breaking news means viewership and thus advertising dollars, accuracy is sometimes sacrificed as well. In a strange twist, mainstream media now turns increasingly to bloggers for their stories, and the most respected bloggers require multiple sources to verify accuracy.[23] Consequently, the distinction between new and mainstream media sources becomes blurred, leaving it to the reader, already bombarded with information, to distinguish fact from fiction (or, perhaps more accurately, "spin" from context).

Propaganda and American Attitudes toward Information as Power.

Until recently, propaganda was described by the U.S. Government as "any form of communication in support of national objectives designed to influence the opinions, emotions, attitudes, or behavior of any group in order to benefit the sponsor, either directly or indirectly."[24] Certainly propaganda has been used from time immemorial as a tool in warfare. But it is only since the U.S. experience of World War I that this rather innocuously defined term has become pejorative in our national psyche. That historical context included not only the obvious abhorrence of Adolf Hitler and Joseph Stalin's propaganda machines, but also an introspective reflection of the way the United States used information as power in both World Wars. The resulting perspective may likely be the reason that information as an element of power remained mostly absent from recent official government strategy documents until the May 2007 publication of a National Strategy for Public Diplomacy and Strategic Communication, well over 6 years after September 11, 2001 (9/11). That is not to say that the U.S. Government does not recognize the value and importance of information to wield power—but it appears that the term "propaganda" keeps getting in the way.[25]

In 2005, the Lincoln Group, a government contractor, paid Iraqi newspapers to print unattributed pro-U.S. stories in an effort to win the war of ideas and counter negative images of the U.S.-led coalition. Their actions were immediately and loudly condemned as propaganda by the mainstream U.S. press, members of Congress, and other government leaders for being contrary to the democratic ideals of a free press.[26] The subsequent Pentagon investigation, however, found that no laws had been broken or policies ignored. But even prior to this, the DoD showed both its need to use information as power and its squeamishness toward accusations of propaganda use. The Pentagon established the Office of Strategic Influence (OSI) within weeks of 9/11. Its stated purpose was simple: to flood targeted areas with information. It did not take long for the mainstream media to pick up on the office and complain that disinformation was being planted abroad and would leak back to the U.S. public. These claims of propaganda were all it took to doom OSI, which was shut down soon thereafter, even though subsequent investigations proved that the information they provided was, in all cases, truthful.[27] In a similar vein, a 2011 Pentagon investigation concluded that there were no inappropriate actions on the part of the DoD in establishing a program to inform military broadcast analysts. The investigation was prompted by *New York Times* articles questioning the program as "an improper campaign of news media manipulation."[28]

This conundrum, in which the United States must fight using propaganda but faces internal criticism and backlash whenever it does, produces an information environment that favors an adversary bent on exploiting it with his own strategic propaganda. Propaganda is the weapon of the insurgent franchised cell. In a broad sense, terrorist organizations have learned the lessons of propaganda well. Hezbollah integrated an aggressive strategic propaganda effort into all phases of its 2006 conflict with Israel. "Made in the USA" signs sprung up on Lebanese rubble immediately after the war, courtesy of an advertising firm hired by the insurgents. There was no doubt who the intended audience was, since the banners were in English only.[29]

It is in this challenging environment of both new media capabilities and a cautionary American attitude toward propaganda that the United States finds itself attempting to compete and win. Given these challenges, it may become increasingly difficult to gain and maintain information superiority or even information dominance; however, the U.S. Government should be expected to manage that environment effectively. It does that through the use of strategic communication.

STRATEGIC COMMUNICATION: AN OVERVIEW

The executive branch of the U.S. Government has the responsibility to develop and sustain an information strategy that ensures that strategic communication occurs consistent with and in support of policy development and implementation. This strategy should guide and direct information activities across the geostrategic environment. Effective strategic communication supports the national security strategy by identifying and responding to strategic threats and opportunities with information-related activities. It is focused U.S. Government efforts to understand and engage key audiences to create, strengthen, or preserve conditions favorable for the advancement of U.S. Government interests, policies, and objectives through the use of coordinated programs, plans, themes, messages, and products synchronized with the actions of all instruments of national power,[30] whose primary supporting capabilities are Public Affairs, Military Information Operations, and Public Diplomacy.

Public Affairs within the DoD is defined as "those public information, command information, and community relations activities directed toward both the external and internal publics with interest in the Department. . . ."[31] The definition of public affairs in the DoS more broadly discusses providing information on the goals, policies, and activities of the U.S. Government. While the DoS sees a role for public affairs with both domestic and international audiences, the thrust of its effort is to inform the domestic audience.[32]

Information Operations (IO) are "the integrated employment, during military operations, of information-related capabilities in concert with other lines of operation to influence, disrupt, corrupt, or usurp the decisionmaking of adversaries and potential adversaries while protecting our own."[33] The DoD recognizes that the primary IO capability in support of strategic communication is military information support operations (formerly called psychological operations).[34]

Public diplomacy is primarily practiced by the DoS. It is defined as "those overt international public information activities of the United States Government designed to promote United States foreign policy objectives by seeking to understand, inform, and influence foreign audiences and opinion makers, and by broadening the dialogue between American citizens and institutions and their counterparts abroad."[35]

International broadcasting services are cited as a strategic communication means in some definitions. The Broadcasting Board of Governors (BBG) includes all U.S. civilian international broadcasting. This includes Voice of America (VOA), Radio Free Europe/Radio Liberty, Radio Free Asia, Radio and TV Marti, and the Middle East Broadcasting Networks (Radio Sawa and Alhurra Television). VOA increasingly uses the Internet, mobile devices, social media, and other digital platforms.[36]

Unfortunately, this list limits the perceived means available to *communications* (emphasis intentionally added) based activities and so reinforces the lexicon of the term (strategic "communication") itself. Therein lies a rub with current interpretations of strategic communication by many leaders. Considering strategic communication as a menu of self-limiting communications capabilities will significantly lessen its impact. Instead, interpretation of the definition itself must serve as the basis of understanding by practitioners who plan and implement it.

Strategists use a model of "ends, ways, and means" to describe all aspects of a national or military strategy. Strategy is about how (the way) leaders will use the capabilities (means) available to achieve objectives (ends).[37] Understanding and engaging key audiences is meant to change perceptions, attitudes, and ultimately behaviors to help achieve military (and, in turn, policy) objectives. Thus, parsing the definition, it is apparent that strategic communication is a "way" to achieve an information effect on the cognitive dimension of the information environment (the required "end").[38] Strategic communication employs multiple "means," and these means should be restricted only by the requirement to achieve the desired information effect on the intended audience.

Messages are certainly sent by verbal and visual communications means, but they are also sent by actions. (Note that the definition specifically includes "actions.") In fact, senior officials point out that strategic communication is "80% actions and 20% words."[39] Specifically, how policies are implemented and supporting military operations are conducted affect the information environment by impacting perceptions and attitudes. Examples include use of U.S. Navy hospital ships in regional engagement and Pakistani earthquake relief efforts in permissive environments.[40] But operations in hostile environments like Afghanistan also provide opportunities to positively shape the information environment. This clarification and expanded understanding of the definition is critical in order to fully exploit strategic communication to support U.S. Government policy and military operations. Fully integrated actions, images, and words are necessary. Key to success is an organizational culture that values, understands, and thus considers strategic communication means as important capabilities to be integrated within established development and planning processes. Strategic communication must be considered at the beginning of the planning process and not as a reactive crisis response when something goes wrong.

THE HISTORY OF STRATEGIC COMMUNICATION

While "strategic communication" is a fairly new term in the U.S. Government lexicon, the concept, theory, and practice behind it is not. Winfield Scott recognized the importance of strategic communication at the theater level at Veracruz, Mexico, in 1847. Realizing the influence of the Catholic Church on Mexican society, Scott attended Mass with his staff at the Veracruz Cathedral to display the respect of U.S. forces. He further ordered U.S. Soldiers to salute Mexican priests in the streets. Each of these measures was "part of a calculated campaign to win the friendship of the Mexicans."[41]

The more recent history of national strategic communication shows concerted efforts to portray the U.S. story positively in order to persuade and influence. The Committee on Public Information (CPI) (1917), also known as the Creel Committee after its chief newspaperman, George Creel, sought to rally U.S. public opinion behind World War I on behalf of the Woodrow Wilson administration.

The committee's focus was the domestic audience, as such, the committee used public speakers, advertising, pamphlets, periodicals, and the burgeoning American motion picture industry.

The CPI's domestic efforts during the war met with high success: Draft registration—the first since the tumultuous call-up of the Civil War—occurred peacefully, bond drives were oversubscribed, and the American population was generally behind the war effort. CPI operations in foreign capitals enabled Wilson to relate his war ideals and aims to the world audience. Indeed, Wilson was taken aback by this effective dissemination of his peace aims and the world's reaction to it. He remarked to George Creel in December 1918, "I am wondering whether you have not unconsciously spun a net for me from which there is no escape."[42]

The post-war appraisal of the CPI was darker. George Creel compiled his official report on the Committee's activities in June 1919 and soon after authored his public account, *How We Advertised America*, in 1920. But at home and overseas, the reality of the peace lagged behind Wilsonian aspirations. The Allies forged a treaty that many Americans and others believed unfair and incomplete. Americans also started to reflect on an ugly side to the war enthusiasm in the United States. Germans and German culture had been vilified; sauerkraut had become liberty cabbage, hamburger was Salisbury steak, but, more seriously, teaching the German language and subject matter in schools became viewed as disloyal, and authorities banned it in some states. There were incidents of physical attacks and even lynchings of suspected German sympathizers and war dissenters. The attorney general enlisted volunteer "loyalty enforcers" who carried official-looking badges and who were encouraged to report which of their neighbors who spoke out against the war.[43]

World War II saw the establishment of The Office of War Information (OWI), which focused both domestically and overseas, with broadcasts sent in German to Nazi Germany. The VOA began its first broadcast with the statement, "Here speaks a voice from America. Every day at this time we will bring you the news of the war. The news may be good. The news may be bad. We shall tell you the truth."

There were several significant differences between the the OWI and its CPI predecessor of 23 years earlier. Some of these were by design, but others reflected the style of the President. Franklin Roosevelt was highly adept at communicating to the public, doing so directly over radio via his addresses and "Fireside Chats." In 1941, 60 million radio receivers reached 90 percent of the U.S. population in their homes.[44] Roosevelt was, however, not entirely comfortable with a formal propaganda apparatus, and the leadership of the OWI, unlike Creel, did not have direct access to the President. Unlike Wilson, Roosevelt, preferring to be ambiguous regarding policy guidance, provided little political cover for the OWI in its skirmishes with the Congress.

Operating in the absence of such policy guidance the OWI staff, particularly in the Foreign Branch, sometimes got out ahead of stated government pronouncements, or it responded with what its members thought American policy should be. Some OWI techniques came under very pointed criticism. The use of pseudonyms by some OWI authors in their articles was denounced by prominent newspapermen, such as Arthur Krock of *The New York Times*. *The New York World Telegram* said the practice "smells of dishonesty."[45] President Harry Truman disbanded the OWI in 1945.

The Smith-Mundt Act (1948) (formally, "The U.S. Information and Educational Exchange Act" [Public Law 402; 80th Congress]), established a statutory information agency for the first time during a period of peace, with a mission to "promote a better understanding of the United States in other countries and to increase mutual understanding" between Americans and foreigners. The act also forbade the Voice of America to transmit to an American audience (based on the experiences of the World Wars). It is worth noting that Smith-Mundt is often cited today as the basis to limit the use of government information activities, since they may result in propagandizing the

American public. This, of course, is complicated by the inevitable "blowback" or "bleedover" of foreign influence activities based on the global information environment, as previously described.[46]

The United States Information Agency (USIA) (1953) was established by President Dwight Eisenhower as authorized by the Smith-Mundt Act. USIA encompassed all the information programs including VOA (its largest element), that were previously in the DoS, except for the educational exchange programs that remained at State. The USIA Director reported to the President through the National Security Council and received complete, day-to-day guidance on U.S. foreign policy from the Secretary of State.

A 1998 State Department reorganization occurred in response to calls by some to reduce the size of the U.S. foreign affairs establishment. (This is considered the State Department's "peace dividend" following the Cold War.) The act folded the USIA into the DoS. It pulled the Broadcasting Board of Governors out of the USIA and made it a separate organization. The USIA slots were distributed throughout the State Department, and its mission was given to the Bureau of International Information Programs.

CURRENT STRATEGIC COMMUNICATION PROCESSES

The demise of the USIA is often regarded (in retrospect) as diluting the ability of the United States to effectively promulgate a national communication strategy, coordinate and integrate strategic themes and messages, and support public diplomacy efforts worldwide.[47] Additionally, organizations and processes have experienced great flux in recent years. Strategic communication efforts under the George W. Bush administration provided mixed results. While some interagency committees and offices were ineffective or became dormant, there was some notable progress under Ambassador Karen Hughes (who assumed duties as the Under Secretary of State for Public Diplomacy and Public Affairs in the early fall of 2005 and departed in late 2007). The Under Secretary helps ensure that public diplomacy (described as engaging, informing, and influencing key international audiences) is practiced in harmony with public affairs (outreach to Americans) and traditional diplomacy to advance U.S. interests and security and to provide the moral basis for U.S. leadership in the world.[48] Ambassador Hughes provided specific guidance to public affairs officers at embassies throughout the world that either cut short or eliminated the bureaucratic clearances needed to speak to the international press. She established a rapid-response unit in the DoS to monitor and respond to world and domestic events. She reinvigorated a once-dormant Strategic Communication Policy Coordinating Committee and established communication plans for key pilot countries. She established processes to disseminate coordinated U.S. themes and messages laterally and horizontally in the government. Finally, and perhaps most importantly, a long awaited *National Strategy for Public Diplomacy and Strategic Communication* was published under her leadership in May 2007.

The Obama administration's efforts to advance strategic communication appear to be reaching a steady state as of this writing. While the national strategy developed under the previous administration is no longer an active document, President Obama has issued a "National Framework for Strategic Communication" in response to a congressional requirement. While not a strategy per se, this document provides the first U.S. Government definition of strategic communication and outlines the organizations and processes to implement it at the national level. A Global Engagement and Strategic Communication Interagency Policy Committee was initially active but has recently become dormant—with a shift of focus on very specific and localized grass-roots efforts to combat violent extremism overseas. In light of this shift, a Center for Strategic Counterterrorism Communication (CSCC) was formally codified by Presidential Executive Order to:

coordinate, orient, and inform Government-wide public communications activities directed at audiences abroad and targeted against violent extremists and terrorist organizations, especially al-Qa'ida and its affiliates and adherents, with the goal of using communication tools to reduce radicalization by terrorists and extremist violence and terrorism that threaten the interests and national security of the United States.[49]

The CSCC replaces the operational level Global Strategic Engagement Center at the DoS.

Judith McHale was sworn in as Under Secretary of State for Public Diplomacy and Public Affairs on May 26, 2009. McHale published her own strategic framework for public diplomacy entitled "Strengthening U.S. Engagement with the World." That document calls for the linkage of public diplomacy efforts to foreign policy objectives. It directs the redistribution of funding based on national priorities and the assignment of Deputy Assistant Secretaries of State for Public Diplomacy in each of the regional bureaus, among other initiatives. Under Secretary McHale resigned her position to return to the private sector in July 2011. Assistant Secretary Ann Stock assumed the authorities of the Under Secretary for Public Diplomacy and Public Affairs on July 8, 2011. She had previously led the Bureau of Educational and Cultural Affairs in McHale's office. (As of this writing Tara Sonenshine has been nominated, but not yet confirmed, to succeed McHale.)

The DoD has responded to the challenges posed by the current information environment, but also with mixed results. The 2006 *Quadrennial Defense Review* (QDR) conducted a spin-off study on strategic communication that resulted in a roadmap addressing planning, resources, and coordination.[50] Actions to achieve roadmap milestones are no longer formally monitored. However, in response to the same congressional directive that produced the "National Framework for Strategic Communication," the DoD produced a "Report on Strategic Communication" in December 2009. The report significantly noted that "Emergent thinking is coalescing around the notion that strategic communication should be viewed as a process, rather than as a set of capabilities, organizations, or discrete activities."[51] Still enduring are "Principles of Strategic Communication" published by the office of the Assistant Secretary of Defense (Public Affairs) in 2008.[52]

The Joint Staff has moved forward with a first draft of strategic communication doctrine. As of this writing, however, it appears that the progress of that document will be delayed until a Department of Defense Instruction (DoDI) is completed, thus providing a policy basis for the subordinate doctrinal manual. This DoDI is still in an embryonic stage.

THE WAY AHEAD

The current information environment, the American attitude toward propaganda, bureaucratic processes that are—by their very nature—cumbersome and slow, all combine to make effective strategic communication difficult indeed, but not impossible. Along with the challenges are opportunities. Overcoming the challenges while exploiting the opportunities, however, requires procedural and cultural change and the leadership necessary to force that change.

Procedurally, the United States must approach strategic communication as an integral part of policy development. To do otherwise will doom the United States to always remain on the defensive in an effort to gain trust and credibility—and that certainly has not worked well to date. Incorporation of such a plan in the policy development process allows for both cautions to policy developers regarding potentially negative foreign reactions and the proactive ability to explain the policy with messages to all audiences. On the other hand, understand that poor policy will not be salvaged by any messages or themes that attempt to explain it. ("You can put a lot of lipstick on a pig, but it's still a pig."[53])

Failure to react quickly and accurately to adversary propaganda cedes the international information environment to the enemy. "Quickly" here is often measured in minutes, not hours, days, or weeks. The reality of instant communications means that individuals on the ground at the lowest tactical levels must be empowered to respond to enemy propaganda to the best of their ability. This requires a cultural change on the part of both individual "messengers" and their leaders. Training and education can provide the baseline competencies to equip American officials (be they Soldiers, diplomats, or others) to respond appropriately to propaganda. But the driving force in allowing the freedom to do so will come from leaders who are willing to delegate the authority to communicate publicly. This comes with an understanding that "information fratricide" may occur, but also with an acceptance that to do otherwise takes the United States out of the information fight. A culture of information empowerment to the lowest levels must be inculcated among U.S. Government officials, with clear guidance provided to subordinates, risk mitigation procedures established and, perhaps most importantly, acceptance that this will not be a zero-defect undertaking.

Winning hearts, minds, trust, and credibility, in the end, requires a local approach. Consider a major U.S. metropolitan area. Neighborhoods take on their own personalities driven by socioeconomic factors and ethnic and racial identity, among other considerations. Value sets are different among the diversity of communities that make up the melting pot that is a large U.S. city. It should not be difficult, then, to understand how it is nearly impossible to influence perceptions among audiences in a foreign nation with a "one size fits all" set of messages and actions. Long-term U.S. presence and engagement on the ground in foreign nations allows for a deep understanding of cultural differences within communities. These cultural underpinnings, combined with the hard work of relationship building, allow for effective tailoring of messages and successful identification of key influencers. Engagement is the key, whether it is by U.S. soldiers in their area of operations,[54] diplomats in Provincial Reconstruction Teams, U.S. Agency for International Development (USAID) workers, or Nongovernmental Organizations. Where no U.S. presence exists, efforts must include recruiting key influencers for U.S. exchange programs such that they will tell the story for the nation upon their return home.

The National Framework for Strategic Communication notes that "every action that the United States Government takes sends a message." The U.S. hospital ship *Mercy* completed a 5-month humanitarian mission to South and Southeast Asia, resulting in improved public opinion of the United States in those predominately Muslim nations where the missions took place. Similar increases in favorability ratings occurred following the U.S. response to the Indonesian tsunami and Pakistani earthquake.[55] These low-cost, high-visibility efforts pay significant dividends in improving the image of the United States. Leaders need to understand that strategic communication is more than programs, themes, and messages; it is, perhaps most importantly, actions as well.

Countering the inherent national aversion to the inflammatory term "propaganda" again lies in both process and culture driven by leadership. A U.S. Government organization paying to have articles printed (under Iraqi pseudonyms) in Iraqi newspapers, regardless of whether it is ultimately found to be legal, is simply asking for trouble in today's information environment. Supporting the government of Iraq to tell its own story is a better way to go. Leading from the rear in the information environment still gets the message told while avoiding direct confrontations with democratic ideals. On the other hand, an "Office of Strategic Influence" had the potential to provide focus, resources, and potentially significant results; but a few misguided articles in the mainstream press were all it took to bring about its quick demise. So, ultimately countering American angst over perceptions of propaganda requires strong national leadership. National leaders must admit that the United States actually *does* want to (truthfully) influence foreign audiences. To do anything less abrogates the information environment to our adversaries. Attempts to influence foreign audiences, however, will almost certainly produce some bleed over to American audiences. That must be accepted and, with knowledge of forethought, preparations must be made to both educate the media proactively regarding information efforts and to respond to any potential media backlash. The recent initiatives to incorporate strategic communication into the policy development process as previously described are encouraging in this regard.

CONCLUSION

The National Framework for Strategic Communication appears to be a step in the right direction to allow the United States to compete in the information environment and proactively tell its story. Defeating an enemy whose center of gravity is extremist ideology requires nothing less than an all-out effort in this regard. But changing perceptions, attitudes, and ultimately behavior is a generational endeavor. It remains to be seen whether processes can be adopted that endure beyond political cycles, and whether national leadership can step forward to lead a charge to change the current culture of reticence to apply information as power while competing in an increasingly challenging information environment. Only then can the information battlefield be leveled and the battle of ideas won.

ENDNOTES - CHAPTER 12

1. Emergent North Atlantic Treaty Organization (NATO) doctrine on Information Operations cites Diplomatic, Military, and Economic activities as "Instruments of Power." It further states that Information, while not an instrument of power, forms a foundation, since all activity has an informational backdrop. See *Allied Joint Pamphlet (AJP)-4, Allied Joint Logistic Doctrine*, Brussels, Belgium: NATO, December 2003.

2. Ronald Reagan, *National Security Decision Directive 130*, Washington, DC: The White House, March 6, 1984, available from *www.fas.org/irp/offdocs/nsdd/nsdd-130.htm*.

3. Daniel T. Kuehl and Robert E. Neilson, "Evolutionary Change in Revolutionary Times: A Case for a New National Security Education Program," *National Security Strategy Quarterly*, Autumn 1999, p. 40.

4. Jeffrey L. Groh and Dennis M. Murphy, "Landpower and Network Centric Operations: How Information in Today's Battlespace Can be Exploited," *NECWORKS Journal*, Issue 1, March 2006.

5. Kevin J. Cogan and Raymond G. Delucio, "Network Centric Warfare Case Study, Vol. II," Carlisle, PA: U.S. Army War College, 2006, p. 4.

6. Catherine A. Theohary and John Rollins, "Terrorist Use of the Internet: Information Operations in Cyberspace," *Congressional Research Service Report*, March 8, 2011, pp. 3-4.

7. "The Center for Strategic Counterterrorism Communications," *Information Operations Primer*, Carlisle, PA: U.S. Army War College, November 2011, p. 103.

8. U.S. Department of State, "21st Century Statecraft," available from *www.state.gov/statecraft/overview/index.htm*.

9. Sheryl Gay Stolberg, "Troop Rise Aids Iraqis, Bush Says, Citing Bloggers," *New York Times*, March 29, 2007, p. 17.

10. James B. Kinniburgh and Dorothy Denning, "Blogs and Military Information Strategy," *IOSphere*, Summer 2006, p. 5.

11. For interestingly different perspectives on the impact of social media on political movements, see Robert Cohen, "Revolutionary Arab Geeks," *New York Times*, January 27, 2011; and Malcolm Gladwell, "Small Change: Why the Revolution Will Not be Tweeted," *The New Yorker*, October 4, 2010.

12. Evgeny Morozov, *The Net Delusion*, New York: Public Affairs, 2011, p. xiv.

13. "After Deadly Kabul Siege, NATO Takes on Taliban . . . on Twitter," *ABC News*, available from *abcnews.go.com/Blotter/kabul-siege-nato-takes-taliban-twitter/story?id=14518138*.

14. The author attended a conference on "New Media" sponsored by the Open Source Center at the Meridian House in Washington, DC, in April 2007. The referenced comments reflect panelists' presentations. IBM already has a presence in Second Life with over 7,000 associates meeting and conducting business there. The conference was held under Chatham House rules allowing free and open dialogue while ensuring the anonymity of speakers.

15. Natalie O'Brien, "Virtual Terrorists," *The Australian*, July 31, 2007, available from *www.theaustraliannews.com.au/story/0.25197.22161037-28737.00.html*.

16. Anand Giridharadas, "Where a Cell Phone is Still Cutting Edge," *New York Times*, April 9, 2010, available from *www.nytimes.com/2010/04/11/weekinreview/11giridharadas.html?ref=weekinreview*.

17. John Moody, "A 'Celler's' Market for Information in Iran," *FoxNews*, June 14, 2007, available from *www.foxnews.com/story/0,2933,282456,00.html*.

18. Richard Willing, "Growing Cell Phone Use a Problem for Spy Agencies," *USA Today*, August 2, 2007, p. 2.

19. Marvin Kalb and Carol Saivetz, "The Israeli-Hezbollah War of 2006: The Media as a Weapon in Asymmetrical Conflict," Research Working Papers Series, Cambridge, MA: John F. Kennedy School of Government, February 2007, p. 4.

20. Phillip Meyer, "The Proper Role of the News Media in a Democratic Society," *Media, Profit, and Politics*, Kent, OH: The Kent State University Press, 2003, p. 12.

21. "Americans Spending More Time Following the News," *The Pew Research Center for the People and the Press*, September 12, 2010, p. 66.

22. J. D. Johannes, "How Al Qaeda is Winning Even as it is Losing," *TCS Daily*, July 11, 2007. The author provides a statistical analysis using "gross rating points" to convey that 65 percent of coverage of the Iraq war is pessimistic.

23. Roxie Merritt, Director of Internal Communications and New Media, Armed Forces Information Service, interview with the author, February 22, 2007.

24. Apropos to the discussion above, the DoD recently changed the definition of propaganda from that shown in this article to "any form of adversary communication, especially of a biased or misleading nature, designed to influence the opinions, emotions, attitudes, or behavior of any group in order to benefit the sponsor, either directly or indirectly." See *DOD Dictionary of Military Terms*, Washington, DC: Department of Defense, November 15, 2011, available from *www.dtic.mil/doctrine/dod_dictionary*.

25. Interestingly, the U.S. Government avoids using the term "propaganda" in any of its official publications, short of the DoD definition. Instead, the terms "military information support operations (formerly psychological operations)," "information operations," "public diplomacy" and "strategic communication" are found, apparently as an ironic twist to change American perceptions favorably toward the use of information to influence foreign audiences.

26. Lynne Duke, "The Word at War; Propaganda? Nah, Here's the Scoop, Say the Guys Who Planted Stories in Iraqi Papers," *The Washington Post*, March 26, 2001, p. D1.

27. David E. Kaplan, "How Rocket Scientists Got Into the Hearts and Minds Game," *U.S. News and World Report*, April 25, 2005, pp. 30-31.

28. David Barstow, "Pentagon Finds No Fault in Ties to TV Analysts," *New York Times*, December 24, 2011, available from *www.nytimes.com/2011/12/25/us/pentagon-finds-no-fault-in-its-ties-to-tv-analysts.html?pagewanted=all*.

29. Kevin Peraino, "Winning Hearts and Minds," *Newsweek International,* October 2, 2006.

30. Various definitions of strategic communication exist. The one shown here is taken from the *DoD Dictionary of Military Terms.*

31. *Ibid.*

32. U.S. Department of State, available from *www.state.gov/r/pa/.*

33. *DoD Dictionary of Military Terms.*

34. *Quadrennial Defense Review (QDR) Strategic Communications (SC) Execution Roadmap,* Washington, DC: Department of Defense, 2006, p. 2.

35. *DoD Dictionary of Military Terms.*

36. *Information Operations Primer,* p. 12.

37. Harry R. Yarger, "Toward a Theory of Strategy: Art Lykke and the Army War College Strategy Model," J. Boone Bartholomees, ed., *U.S. Army War College Guide to National Strategy and Policy,* 4th Ed., Carlisle, PA: Strategic Studies Institute, U.S. Army War College, June 2006, p. 107.

38. Chairman of the Joint Chiefs of Staff, *Joint Publication (JP) 3-13, Information Operations,* February 13, 2006, p. I-1. This publication indicates that the information environment consists of three interrelated dimensions: physical, informational, and cognitive.

39. The author has attended numerous briefings by the Deputy Assistant Secretary of Defense for Joint Communication (DASD, JC) and his staff, where this has been stated. Note: The DASD, JC is responsible for the DoD Strategic Communication Roadmap.

40. Anju S. Bawa, "U.S. Aid Ship Cures Public Opinion," *Washington Times,* November 17, 2006, p. 15.

41. John S. D. Eisenhower, *Agent of Destiny: The Life and Times of General Winfield Scott,* New York: The Free Press, 1997, pp. 245-246.

42. Margaret McMillan, *Paris 1919: Six Months That Changed the World,* New York: Random House, 2002, p. 15.

43. David M. Kennedy, *Over Here: The First World War and American Society*, New York, Oxford University Press: 1980, p. 81.

44. Allan Winkler, *The Politics of Propaganda: The Office of War Information, 1942-1945,* New Haven, CT: Yale University Press, 1978, p. 60.

45. *Ibid.,* p. 97.

46. The Smith-Mundt Act is still in effect to include the requirement not to "target" U.S. audiences. The current information environment—with ubiquitous, worldwide media outlets, satellite communications, and real-time reporting—makes it difficult to target foreign audiences without exposing U.S. audiences to the message. This is a fact not envisioned in 1948 when the act became effective, and one that continues to cause friction between the military and media.

47. David E. Kaplan, "Hearts, Minds, and Dollars," *U.S. News and World Report,* April 25, 2005, pp. 25, 27.

48. U.S. Department of State, "Senior Officials: Under Secretary for Public Diplomacy and Public Affairs—Karen Hughes," *U.S. Department of State Homepage,* available from *www.state.gov/misc/19232.htm.*

49. Executive Order 13584, *Federal Register*, Vol. 76, No. 179, September 15, 2011, available from *www.carlisle.army.mil/dime/documents/Executive%20Order%2013584.pdf*.

50. *QDR Strategic Communication Execution Roadmap*, p. 3.

51. Robert Gates, "Department of Defense Report on Strategic Communication," Washington, DC: December 2009, p. 1.

52. Robert T. Hastings, "Principles of Strategic Communication," memorandum for Secretaries of the Military Departments *et al.*, Washington, DC, August 15, 2008.

53. Torie Clark, *Lipstick on a Pig*, New York: Free Press, 2006, p. 1. Clark was the chief spokesperson for the Pentagon during the first George W. Bush administration. The quote is the title of the first chapter of her book.

54. An excellent overview of the effectiveness of a local military approach can be found in an article written by Colonel Ralph Baker, U.S. Army, on his application of information operations as a brigade commander in Baghdad, Iraq. The article appears in the May-June 2006 issue of *Military Review*.

55. Bawa, p. 15.

CHAPTER 13

DIPLOMACY AS AN INSTRUMENT OF NATIONAL POWER

Reed J. Fendrick

A diplomat is an honest man sent abroad to lie for his country.

Apocryphal

The patriotic art of lying for one's country.

Ambrose Bierce[1]

The media and intellectual elites, the State Department (as an institution), and the Foreign Service (as a culture) clearly favor the process, politeness, and accommodation position.

Newt Gingrich[2]

Ordinary Americans have often been uncomfortable about the art and practice of diplomacy. Frequently, they associate diplomacy and American diplomats either with elitist, pseudo-aristocratic bowing and scraping before supercilious foreigners whose aim is to impinge on our sovereignty and partake of our largesse; or as naïve country bumpkins whose gullibility allows them to forsake key American goals and objectives; or as ruthless, cynical practitioners of Bismarckian *realpolitiek* whose aims and practices fall far short of our Founders' noble aspirations; or as liberal, one-worldists whose collective ideology is far from the American mainstream and who seek to undermine the political aims of elected administrations. These stereotypes go back to our country's origins and have been reinforced by such traumatic events as Wilson's perceived failure at Versailles, the Yalta Conference near the end of World War II, Henry Kissinger's role as architect of the opening to China, and the failure to obtain a UN Security Council resolution endorsing the use of force in Iraq.

Is any of this true? True or not, does it matter? What is diplomacy supposed to do? Does the U.S. wield diplomacy effectively? Can democracy and diplomacy function harmoniously? How does diplomacy fit in with the protection and furtherance of national security?

First, diplomacy is one instrument among many that a government utilizes in its pursuit of the national interest. Among others are: military power, actual or potential; economic power; intelligence-gathering and operations; cultural and information or "soft power"; relative degrees of national unity; and probably others. Diplomacy never functions in isolation from the other instruments of power but may at times be emphasized as the situation warrants. In its simplest, most original form, diplomacy is the official means by which one state formally relates to other states. Although ambassadors have existed since antiquity representing one sovereign to another, the earliest diplomats often functioned more as de facto hostages to ensure peace or compliance with some agreement than in the modern understanding of an ambassador's role. Since nation-states were more or less legitimized by the Treaty of Westphalia in 1648, a whole series of codes and protocols have been established to create a framework for the practice of diplomacy. These include such seeming anomalies (and irritants to common citizens) as diplomatic immunity; creation of embassies; establishing and breaking diplomatic relations; sending and receiving diplomatic notes, demarches, non-papers and other forms of communication; holding international conferences; and many other means of inter-state communication and relations.

Diplomats are agents of the State. In theory, they act on instruction. Until the advent of modern communications, their instructions necessarily had to be general; they required a nearly innate understanding of the national interest of the country they represented. Both because of the non-democratic nature of nearly all States before the American and French Revolutions, and the need for confidentiality to protect state secrets and national security, diplomatic exchanges and even treaties or agreements were often undertaken in secret or with quiet discretion. When Woodrow Wilson's Fourteen Points called for "open covenants openly arrived at" (a reference to Allied agreements for post-World War I division of spoils from the Central Powers that appeared to make a mockery of claims the War was meant to make the "world safe for democracy"), he was publicly challenging the entire edifice of traditional diplomacy that had, however, begun to be modified with the rise of the mass media and popular participation in the 19th century. Increasingly, mounting scrutiny from democratic media and academics and ever-increasing intrusive clandestine intelligence-gathering make formal secret agreements less and less palatable.

One prism through which to view diplomacy is to think of it as an element on the spectrum of national security devices. In the "normal" course of events, most nations most of the time while competing for influence, markets, relative perceived power, and other markers of strength, relate to one another the way competitors do in seeking market-share — not as gangs fighting over turf. In other words, the assumption is that peaceful approaches, use of agreements and treaties, and normal intercourse will prevail. In this scenario, diplomacy provides the lubricant for acceptable relations, seeks to remove irritants, and strives for mutual understanding. However, even in the relations between traditionally peaceful entities — in the semi-Hobbesian universe of contemporary international relations — diplomacy holds in its quiver, the potential threat of force. In the cases where rivalry becomes equated with threats to vital national interests (a determination that is difficult to define objectively, but that governments make drawing on their specific cultural, historical, and political traditions and bringing to bear whatever institutions or individuals wield predominant influence on this subject), diplomacy becomes an adjunct to overt or masked displays or use of armed force. In this situation, diplomacy becomes the main instrument to build coalitions, influence publics and elites in other countries of the justice of the cause, and works closely with the military establishment to make available critical spaces in non-national territory for the possible deployment of armed force (i.e. aircraft overflight rights, port visits, shipment of men and materiel). Finally, if armed conflict does erupt, diplomacy continues during that period (albeit with a lower emphasis) focusing on post-war planning, cost and burden-sharing, and international organization endorsement (or at least non-condemnation) of the military actions.

Diplomacy fundamentally consists of a constant assessment of other countries' power potential, perceived vital interests, and relationships with other states, in an attempt to maximize one's own country's freedom of action with the ultimate purpose of ensuring the achievement of the nation's vital interests — the core of which is survival. Diplomacy traditionally and currently utilizes a variety of practices or maneuvers to obtain the protection or furtherance of national goals or interests. Essentially all these practices are elements of diplomatic strategy that seek advantage for the state short of war (although war always remains the ultimate recourse). From the realist perspective, all strategies, while perhaps amoral in themselves, have as the ultimate goal the moral aim of the survival of the state and its core values. Thus, leaders must take account of the particular circumstance of the place of their state in the international order to determine what would be an effective strategy and tactics or maneuvers to enable its success. Thus, from the British and French perspective in 1938, the decision to appease Germany over the Sudetenland may have been a misperception of the relative power of each state but was not, *a priori*, an invalid tactic. The constant politically charged accusation of "Munich" or "Yalta" in quite different circumstances is meaningless. Sometimes appeasement is good or unavoidable. In the case of Nazi Germany, in hindsight, it was a bad tactic, because Hitler could not be appeased, and the Allies simply postponed the inevitable clash to a moment when they yielded military advantage to Hitler. Détente (especially the series of arms control and human rights agreements) as practiced by Nixon and Kissinger was an effort to reach accommodation with the Soviet Union at a time when it appeared a balance of power in nuclear weapons had been struck and neither side could expect to gain a decisive advantage. The effort by President George H.W. Bush to create a coalition in the First Gulf War was not so much to increase U.S. military advantage over Iraq as it was to demonstrate—especially in the Arab and Islamic worlds—the broad support to repel Iraqi aggression in Kuwait. In the recent Gulf War, the relative absence of a significant coalition was largely a function of the Administration's desire to not be constrained in tactics, operations (targeting), and strategy in the way it believed NATO operations in Kosovo had been hampered.

DIPLOMATIC INSTRUMENTS

The main instrument of diplomacy is negotiation, whether in a formal or informal setting. In a sense all diplomacy is a constant adjustment of relations among states pursued simultaneously through multiple, overlapping dialogues: bilateral, multilateral (e.g., United Nations); special conferences; and other venues. The goal is usually, but not always, to reach an agreement that could range from those containing significant enforcement mechanisms for implementation (e.g., the Non-Proliferation Treaty) to hortatory proclamations such as the Kellogg-Briand Pact, which purported to outlaw war. One of the special advantages diplomats as a profession may have is that they should possess significant knowledge of the personalities and national cultural styles of their interlocutors. Since much diplomatic maneuvering by states consists of bluffs and feints as well as subtle signals either of accommodation or willingness to risk war, a capable diplomat can discern and characterize the meaning of a given action. Misinterpretation, ignorance, lack of knowledge, or arrogance can lead to unforeseeable consequences (e.g., ignoring India's warning during the Korean War that China would intervene if U.S. forces approached the Yalu River).

Diplomatic relations among countries have long followed a common set of practices. The necessity to maintain contact as a means to facilitate dialogue between states leads to diplomatic recognition that can be of the state but not the government (e.g., North Korea by the United States) or of the government as well. Normally, such recognition is not a moral stamp of approval but a reflection that a regime controls the preponderance of national territory, and that it is in the interest of the other country to have formal channels of communication. Breaking relations can be a prelude to war; more often it is a mark of extreme disapproval. But if the regime survives, non-recognition can be a cause of great inconvenience, since maintaining a dialogue usually involves talking either through third parties or in multilateral institutions. There are also anomalous situations, such as is currently the case with Cuba, where the United States maintains a large Interests Section under the technical protection of the Swiss embassy in order to pursue business with the Castro regime without compromising its disapproval. Sometimes a decision is made to withdraw the ambassador, temporarily or for longer periods, to deliver a significant rebuke for some policy or action of the host government. The downside to such an action is that dialogue between the states may become more rigid and is certainly conducted at a lower level of authority. In normal practice, the ambassador heads an embassy that is usually divided into numerous sections, each specializing in a particular subject area. The number of persons granted diplomatic status, which, under the Vienna Convention imparts immunity to certain host government laws, is negotiated between the two states.

An American embassy is normally organized in the following manner: at the apex is the Ambassador, appointed by the President as his personal representative and confirmed by the U.S. Senate. The Ambassador may be a career Foreign Service Officer from the Department of State or may be chosen form other agencies or the private sector. The Ambassador's alter ego is the Deputy Chief of Mission (DCM), who serves under the Ambassador to ensure the timely, efficient, and correct carrying-out of instructions and to ensure good management practices in the Embassy (i.e., avoidance of waste, fraud and mismanagement). There are usually several functional State Department Sections (i.e. Political, Economic, Consular, and Administrative) that handle the reporting, management and protection of U.S. citizens and issuance of visas to foreign nationals. Many Embassies also maintain a Defense Attaché Office with representatives from one or more of the armed services; a Defense Cooperation Office that manages foreign military sales and transfers; a Foreign Commercial Service that promotes U.S. exports; a Foreign Agricultural Service that does the same for agricultural commodities; a Legal Attaché (normally FBI) that liaises with host-country police authorities; Drug Enforcement Agency that does the same on narcotics issues; and a representative from Customs, possibly the Immigration and Naturalization Service. Depending on the country, many other Federal agencies may be represented. Similarly, the receiving country may have similar sections in its Embassy in Washington.

How, in the real, contemporary world, does modern American diplomacy work? With or without the publication of the National Security Strategy, which is an explicit annual overview of an Administration's top priorities often together with a general roadmap on how to achieve the objectives, the Department of State—usually in conjunction and coordination with the other foreign affairs agencies under the auspices of the National Security Council—will send telegraphic (or sometimes e-mail or telephone) instructions to an Embassy in a given country or international organization. It might be a request for information on a matter that has risen to the attention of at least the Country Director in a regional or functional bureau of the Department of State (perhaps due to media attention, pressure from a lobbyist, or a request from a member of Congress). Or the department could instruct the Ambassador to raise with the host country a matter of concern such as the arrest of an American citizen, a report of human rights abuse by a military unit, allegations of unfair commercial practices harmful to an American firm, sale of military weapons, a request for port visit of a U.S. warship, surveillance of a suspected terrorist, or many other possible items. In what becomes a continuous conversation, the appropriate section in the embassy (Political, Economic, Consular, Defense Attaché, Commercial Service, or others) would be tasked to take the necessary action. Sometimes the Embassy itself reports on a matter and offers a recommendation. In rare cases where immediate action is vital, the Embassy might report what it did and implicitly request endorsement of the action. Often, in parallel fashion, especially on important issues, the Department would convoke the Ambassador or an appropriate official from the relevant Embassy in Washington or its Mission to the United Nations to make similar points. Because embassies and foreign ministries are organized on highly hierarchical principles, it is often possible to adjust the tone and content of the message to a particular rank, thus making clear the relative importance of the message. Depending on response, the message's content, deliverer and recipient can be ratcheted up or down accordingly.

DIPLOMATIC ROLES

What are the principal roles of a diplomat? First, he is an agent of his government ordered to carry out instructions from authorized superiors. In the American case, there is often a vigorous internal debate throughout the foreign affairs agencies of the government on a given policy, as well as on the tactics of its proposed execution, a dialogue in which both Department of State and embassies continuously engage. However, once a decision is made, the action is carried out.

Whatever an individual diplomat's private feelings on a given issue may be, he is duty-bound to carry out the instructions. If the diplomat's conscience does not so allow, he may request a transfer to another assignment or region or offer to resign. In effect, the diplomat in this role functions as a lawyer, with the U.S. Government as his client. Just as a lawyer's ethical responsibility is to make the most vigorous possible advocacy for the client regardless of the lawyer's personal opinions of the client's innocence, so is a diplomat in public or in conversation with foreign interlocutors expected to make the best possible presentation on behalf of his government.

The diplomat is also an information-gatherer and analyst. Although not expected to compete in real-time with the media organizations such as CNN or *The New York Times* on basic facts, due to his presumed experience and familiarity with a country, its culture, institutions, and key personalities, the diplomat should be able to bring added value by analyzing and putting in context what to harried Washington senior leaders can seem like isolated, meaningless events. So, for the diplomat to be well-informed, he ideally should speak, read and understand the local language, extract from the mass media key nuggets of important information, develop a string of well-informed contacts covering a wide spectrum, and attend major events such as political party congresses. As a message-drafter, the diplomatic drafter needs to be succinct, clear, and pungent enough to both hold busy readers' attention and to answer the "so-what" question. The analysis needs to be substantiated by fact and interpretation, each clearly labeled as such. While never writing with the intent to provoke, when necessary, the drafter may have to call attention respectfully but clearly to actual or potential situations that may be unpleasant or resented by policymakers. At the same time, national leaders must be careful not to shoot the messenger even if they disagree with the analysis or recommendations. Sometimes, this requires courage from the drafter and restraint from the recipient. It is always the policymakers' prerogative to choose other courses. But retaliation against unwanted advice or analysis can lead to self-censorship and ultimate harm to the national interest through failure to assess events realistically.

In Washington, the middle-level diplomat is not as concerned with interpreting events in a foreign country as with assisting in defining his agency's position on a given issue (usually a whole host of them), while interacting with other elements of the foreign affairs agencies in order to glean their positions to support their own agency's position better.

A diplomat is also a negotiator. Depending on the issue, a diplomat may have more or less freedom to adjust from basic instructions, tactics and goals. In order for a negotiation to succeed, which may not always be desirable or the preferred outcome, the astute diplomat will have a good general understanding of his counterpart's baseline requirement, some sense of the national cultural manner of negotiating, and a willingness to bargain—but not to bargain away essential or vital objectives. This propensity for negotiation, also an inherent part of a lawyer's toolkit, is what sometimes infuriates ideological or idealistic individuals, since they believe it immoral to negotiate with either blatantly evil states or leaders or they believe it puts the U.S. in a position of appearing to make compromises on what can be construed as vital interests. Unless there is no longer a need to negotiate at all because of acknowledged overwhelming power of one country, or because diplomacy has yielded to open war, such compromises are an inherent property of having to deal with a Hobbesian world of sovereign states. Even criminal prosecutors make plea-bargains with criminals to achieve a balance of justice, resource use, and the likelihood of conviction on the most serious charges.

In a slightly different key, a diplomat facilitates and maintains dialogue with his counterparts, hopefully with a view to arriving at complementary assessments of threats, benefits, and actions to take to maximize their respective national interests. If the dialogue goes far enough, it can lead to commitments usually expressed in the form of treaties or agreements. They can range from reciprocal reduction of tariffs to willingness to go to war on behalf of another country.

Diplomats also act as spokespersons and sounding boards for the country. A good diplomat will be effective in public and private gatherings at furthering his country's interests and refuting criticism of it by couching his advocacy in a manner best suited to the culture where he is stationed. Because of the ubiquity of media outlets, a good diplomat learns how to access the host country media, key decisionmakers, and most relevant institutions (parliament, military, chambers of commerce, labor union federations etc.), and gets his point across over the blare of "white noise" emanating in the modern media.

At the more senior level, diplomats serve as counselors to national leaders, few of whom are regional or global experts. While diplomats rarely have the final say in the most solemn decision a nation can make—the decision to go to war—they can serve to make clear the potential costs as well as benefits of such acts and the likely prospects of coalitions in favor of (or opposed to) their country. While certainly not pacifists, diplomats are temperamentally and professionally inclined to seek non-violent solutions partly because that is what they do, and partly because they frequently can foresee second- and third-order consequences that can lead to a worse situation than the status quo ante bellum. It is at this juncture that politicians and the media sometimes confuse reporting and analysis that may be at odds with national leadership goals with disloyalty. It is not a desire for the status quo, let alone a preference for dealing with dictators, that may drive diplomats as some have charged. Rather it is a realization that in the absence of comprehensive universally acknowledged supremacy, negotiation with other regimes, no matter how unpalatable, may be necessary. The obvious classic quote is that of Winston Churchill, who, despite being before and after World War II an adamant anti-Communist, said upon Hitler's attack on the Soviet Union in 1941, "If Hitler invaded hell, I would make at least a favorable reference to the devil in the House of Commons."[3]

CONCLUSION

To sum up, diplomacy is a mechanism—one among many—used in furtherance of the national interest and in protection of the national security. While styles of diplomacy may differ by national cultures, personal idiosyncrasies, and historical memories, they all have a common purpose. As long as there are states, and they hold differing assessments of their national interests, there will be diplomacy. While technology is making certain traditional means of conducting diplomacy obsolete, the core functions of diplomacy will remain. In the past, airplanes and telegraphs made clipper ships and quill pen instructions obsolete. New information technology is already making reporting far more focused on analysis than on simple news-gathering, which is done better by CNN, and e-mail and cell phones are replacing cabled instructions. Such advances occasionally produce serious suggestions to eliminate some or many embassies, but only because of a perceived more efficient manner of performing their functions. Diplomacy is still a vital element of national power.

ENDNOTES - CHAPTER 13

1. Ambrose Bierce, *The Devil's Dictionary*, Sioux Falls, SD: NuVision Publications, LLC, 1906, available from *www.alcyone.com/max/lit/devils/d.html*.

2. Newt Gingrich, "Rogue State Department," *Foreign Policy*, July-August 2003, available from *www.foreignpolicy.com/story/story.php?storyID=13742&PHPSESSID=7580b0d87d9d1e0995f9bc68fbeab56d*.

3. Winston Churchill, *The Grand Alliance*, New York: Houghton Mifflin Company, 1950, p. 370.

CHAPTER 14

THEORY AND PRACTICE OF MODERN DIPLOMACY: ORIGINS AND DEVELOPMENT TO 1914

Louis J. Nigro, Jr.

Diplomacy, broadly defined as the peaceful dialogue and interaction between political units, is as old as civilization itself. The first known peace treaty was signed about 2300 BC between a king of Ebla, in what is today Syria, and the king of Assyria. The Amarna tablets record the diplomatic correspondence between Egypt and Syrian rulers more than 1,400 years ago, while *Genesis* 14 talks of Abram's "treaty of alliance" with Amorite kings. From the 8th to the 3rd century BC, China was divided among several "warring states" that conducted diplomacy as well as made war on each other in order to survive and succeed, as Sun Tzu's writings indicate. Other early civilizations offer similar examples of diplomatic activity.

This chapter, concerning the development of modern diplomacy from its origins in 15th-century Europe until the 20th century, seeks to accomplish five things. First, the chapter describes the origins of the modern state in Renaissance Italy and shows how that new type of political organization developed a new kind of diplomacy that met its needs. Second, it examines the role of Florentine political thinker Niccolò Machiavelli in providing a theoretical basis for the new state and for the new diplomacy used to accomplish its goals. The chapter stresses that Machiavelli gave directions to rulers of the new states—whether monarchies, principalities, or republics—on how to be successful in an international system characterized by constant interaction among geographically sovereign units for power, influence, and security. Third, the chapter describes the parallel development of the modern sovereign, or Westphalian, state and the modern diplomacy that serves it. Fourth, it looks at the application of modern diplomacy to the classic European age of grand strategy and the balance of power from 1648 to the First World War. Finally, the chapter provides additional background and supporting information for the other essays in this volume that deal with the characteristics of the state, the nature of the international system, and the role of diplomacy as an element of national power in the contemporary world.

FROM MEDIEVAL TO MODERN

Europe created modern diplomacy because Europe created the modern, geographically sovereign state—the so-called Westphalian state—after the Peace of Westphalia in 1648. The new form of international actor that has characterized the modern international system required a new kind of diplomacy, matched to its needs and consonant with its nature.

The modern, geographically sovereign state (or, nation-state) began to emerge in Europe during the 16th century as the old structures of European international order began to break down. The international order that Europe had inherited from the Middle Ages was composed of structures of power that were different from the nation-states that compose our contemporary international system. There were structures that existed above and beyond today's nation-state, structures that we can call *supra-statal* and structures existing below and within today's nation-state that we can call *infra-statal*.

The chief supra-statal institutions were the Papacy and the Holy Roman Empire, both rooted in the spiritual domain and both reflecting the glory of the ancient Roman Empire. Both Popes and Emperors claimed to be the heirs of Rome. Popes and Emperors claimed wide and broad powers over other rulers and over the subjects of other rulers, which gave them legal, religious, financial, and other authorities. The primary infra-statal institutions were a bewildering (to us, not to contemporaries) assortment of thousands of autonomous jurisdictions, starting from "national" kingdoms like England, France, and Aragon, and continuing down a long hierarchical chain of political organizations through principalities, duchies, free counties, bishoprics, free cities, commercial alliances (like the Hanseatic League), baronies, petty lordships of all types and sizes, to corporate bodies like guilds, military orders, and religious orders. All of them exercised what we would call political power in various ways. The jurisdictions, rights, powers, and responsibilities of both the supra-statal and the infra-statal institutions often conflicted and overlapped.

Together these supra-national and infra-national institutions made up what contemporaries called Christendom. Christendom's institutions drew their strength and legitimacy from feudal traditional practices that mixed public office and public functions with private property and hereditary rights; from religious and spiritual sanctions; and from social and cultural habits a thousand years in the making. Political order in Christendom was characterized by interlocking networks of rights and responsibilities fragmented into many small, autonomous parts. The focus of political authority was personal, feudal, and local. The idea that political rule was strictly linked to control of territory rather than to other sources of authority was largely absent, so that rulers were not geographically sovereign in the sense of exerting supreme and monopolistic authority over and within a given territory and population. Christendom as a political system appears to us to have been ambiguous, complicated, messy, and illogical, but it worked as long as people believed in it.

The medieval order of Christendom started to break down under pressure from rising political units that drew their strength and legitimacy from new territorial and demographic realities; that were sanctioned more by the possession and use of practical power than by religion and tradition; and that were evolving behind borders that were more definite and more restrictive than the old porous, overlapping medieval political units. The growth of vernacular languages and the concomitant beginnings of national consciousness aided the process of the development of the new political units, which would eventually become the legally equal, sovereign states. This would intensify into the process of state formation at the expense of both the old supra-national institutions and the old infra-national institutions.

THE ITALIAN RENAISSANCE ORIGINS OF MODERN DIPLOMACY: 1450-1500.

Italy was the birthplace of the Renaissance and also of the first prototypes of the modern, geographically sovereign state. The reason for this was Renaissance Italy's vanguard status in most areas of European endeavor—art, literature, science, jurisprudence, philosophy, economics, and finance—but also in political development. Jacob Burckhardt's classic 1860 interpretive essay, *The Civilization of the Renaissance in Italy,* had as its central theme the problem of politics and of political anthropology. Burckhardt believed that it was the unique political environment of Renaissance Italy that led to the development of the Renaissance mind with its more liberated ideas, ideals, morals and attitudes. The two overarching organizing institutions of the pre-Renaissance West, of what people thought of, not as Europe, but as Christendom—the universal Papacy and the universalistic Holy Roman Empire—had been effectively absent from Italy and had therefore exerted little or no influence in Italian political life for over a century and a half. That absence, Burckhardt wrote, "left Italy in a political condition which differed essentially from that of other countries of the West" and explained why "in them we detect for the first time the modern political spirit of Europe."[1]

The Italian Microcosm.

Because the foundations of the medieval international order crumbled in Italy around 1300, the Italians began to create a new political institution to fill the void left by that collapse. This new institution was called in Italian the *stato*, transforming a word that until then had been used to describe the legal classes into which people fell within a political unit. Now *stato*—and all its cognates, such as *state* in English, *état* in French, *estado* in Spanish, *Staat* in German, and so on—would become the term used to describe the basic political unit of the new international order. The Italian microcosm was an anarchic political space. The new states that the Italians evolved to fill that space were the prototypes of the future Westphalian state. They were, in contemporary eyes, illegitimate, existing outside the medieval and feudal hierarchies of political authority. They had to create their own legitimacy by defending their existence. They were, therefore, warlike and aggressive. They were geographically discrete—separate and distinct from other states or any other authorities and were nearly "sovereign" in the modern sense of the term, jealously guarding a monopoly of political authority within their borders and recognizing no other authority higher than themselves.

The power vacuum created by the absence of higher authority in Renaissance Italy resulted in the growth of several Italian city-states into territorial states that absorbed smaller and weaker neighbors. This Darwinian process of political consolidation by conquest resulted eventually in the creation of a miniature state system in Italy, an enclosed political space with five "great" powers contending among themselves for hegemony and influence over smaller, weaker city-states. By 1450, the five principal territorial states of Florence, Venice, Milan, Naples, and the Papal State (based on Rome) dominated the Italian peninsula. As they maneuvered against one another for power and advantage, making and breaking alliances among themselves, the Italian peninsula came to constitute an enclosed system of interacting states—a state system—that was a microcosm of the European state system to follow. In 1454, a series of wars to resist Milanese hegemonic aggression resulted in the general Peace of Lodi. In 1455, most of the five powers and other smaller ones signed a mutual security agreement, the Italic League, which guaranteed the existence of signatory states and called for common action against outsiders. These arrangements led to nearly fifty years of peace on the peninsula. Managing the peace was largely the work of Lorenzo "the Magnificent," the Medici ruler of Florence who believed that maintaining a balance among the five powers was better policy than trying to eliminate enemies. This was the first conscious balance of power policy in a post-medieval state system.

The State as a Work of Art.

The 15th-century Italian states were prototypes of the modern state in the sense that they interacted as equals with the other states of their microcosmic systems and in the way they interacted with the other powers and lesser political units of Italy. The new territorial states existed because of the absence in Italy of the great, overarching, hierarchy-anchoring, legitimacy-conferring institutions of Papacy and Empire. As such, the new, legitimacy-challenged Italian states had to struggle to survive, and they knew it. The Italian state was "a new fact appearing in history—the state as the outcome of reflection and calculation, the state as a work of art," according to Burckardt.[2] The Italian states, lacking the luxury of traditional legitimacy, were on their own. To survive, they adopted an approach to statecraft that responded more to necessity than to the traditional approach that enjoined Christian moral standards on rulers and the diplomats that served them. They acted if not in an *immoral* way then at least in an *amoral* way, according to the medieval canons of princely comportment. The end—the survival of the state—justified the means—whatever efforts the state was capable of—regardless of the established standards of international conduct. This is the argument that makes *raison d'état* (reason of state) the ultimate justification for action by states vis-à-vis other states.

As the Italian states became more self-conscious of their circumstances, they began to recognize that the medieval way of diplomacy was no longer adequate to their needs. Medieval diplomacy was based on the occasional dispatch and receipt of very prestigious but often untrained individuals as envoys on specific, short-term missions. Occasionally, diplomats were as much hostages as negotiators. The diplomat usually viewed himself as serving as an emissary for the higher needs of Christendom, not the political ruler who sent or received him. But the new Italian territorial states needed diplomatic institutions and mechanisms more effective, more durable, and more permanent than the old medieval ones. They needed both continuous dialogue with their neighbors and continuous intelligence regarding their neighbors' designs. The Renaissance ruler needed a mechanism to gather and report intelligence and to sustain diplomatic dialogue. They invented therefore the key institution of modern diplomacy—the resident ambassador endowed with diplomatic immunity—to conduct the relations between the five states of the system continuously and seamlessly. During the second half of the 15th century, all five of the major Italian states and many smaller ones established permanent accredited diplomatic missions headed by ambassadors in each of the five major capitals.[3]

In summary, the Italian Renaissance produced the basic elements of the future European state system. It created the geographically sovereign international actor called the "state." It posited an anarchical international environment in which states struggled ceaselessly for power, and rulers deployed statecraft, diplomacy, and military force according to calculations, not of right or wrong, but of political expediency. The Italian Renaissance developed the notion of *raison d'état*; that what was good for the state was the right thing to do, because in politics the end justified the means. It created the mechanism for continuous, sustained diplomacy to manage the state's engagement with the world. Finally, Renaissance Italy developed the idea of the balance of power as a goal of the state system.

At the end of the 15th century, the days of the Italian microcosm of an enclosed and protected peninsular state system were numbered. The world beyond the Alps, with political units much more militarily powerful than the Italian states, began to influence Italian affairs. In 1494, the French invaded successfully, drawing other non-Italian powers, especially Spain and the revived Holy Roman Empire, into a struggle for control of the peninsula that made Italy a battle field for sixty years. The Italian microcosm was destroyed, but not before its transalpine destroyers adopted the diplomatic methods and diplomatic institutions that the Italian states had developed and deployed to meet the needs of their prototypical modern state system. The Italian Renaissance way of diplomacy became the basis of the European way of diplomacy for the future.[4]

MACHIAVELLI AND THE THEORY OF MODERN DIPLOMACY

Concepts like the amorality of politics, the ends justify the means, and *raison d'état* are usually labeled "Machiavellian," referring to the ideas of the Florentine statesman, diplomat, and political thinker Niccolò Machiavelli (1465-1527). His works have come to epitomize the difference between the pre-modern, medieval international system, and the modern, geographically sovereign one that first appeared in the Italian state system of the 15th century.

Machiavelli received a typical Italian Renaissance education based on the ancient Greek and Roman classics. That was the essence of the Renaissance, which means rebirth—the Italians and others believed that they were presiding over a rebirth of learning, art, and philosophy based on the recovery of ancient examples of those pursuits. The Renaissance was obsessed with ancient Greek and Roman culture, as the Reformation would latter be obsessed with ancient Jewish and Christian culture. Renaissance humanism was a preference for those areas of ancient Greek and Roman culture that were oriented toward empowering human beings in this world rather than preparing them for another, better world. The Renaissance humanist curriculum stressed rhetoric, history, and ethics, because these were tools men could use to pursue secular, and especially political, economic, and social objectives.

Machiavelli put those tools to work as a bureaucrat in the government of the Florentine Republic. From 1498 to 1512, he worked in the equivalents of its war and foreign ministries and went on many diplomatic missions to the other courts of Italy and those of France and the Empire. He was a participant in the political and diplomatic life of Italy in the last years of the existence of the Italian microcosm as well as the first years of the spread of the new state structure and the new diplomacy to the rest of Europe. In 1512, the republic he served underwent a revolution and the autocratic Medici family returned to power. Machiavelli was forced into exile in a hamlet near Florence. There he wrote his principal works, especially *The Prince*, *The Discourses*, and *The Art of War*, all classics of political realism. *The Prince* gives advice to monarchical regimes, especially to princes newly raised to power, on how to retain and extend their power and influence. *The Discourses* does much the same thing for republican regimes. *The Art of War* analyzes the military element of national power in terms of its relationship to the political and social bases of the state.

Machiavelli's contribution to political thought was instantly, inevitably, and lastingly controversial. Most of his readership was confined to *The Prince*, a short, enigmatic, epigrammatic, and elusive work that lent itself to misinterpretation. (Machiavelli's other more straightforward works, including *The Art of War* and *The Discourses*, were less often read.) In *The Prince*, Machiavelli gave practical advice to an Italian prince trying to create a new state. His advice was blunt: In order to be successful the new prince had to use every tool available to him, including violence, deceit, treachery, and dissimulation. The desired end was to increase his own and his state's power. The means were politically expedient actions, without reference to justice or traditional morality. The standard of a ruler's conduct was *raison d'état*, not Christian ethics.

Contemporaries and later writers interpreted *The Prince* as the bible of the doctrine of political expediency that justified immoral conduct if it produced the desired result; elevated power over principle; and that denied that Christian morality applied to politics. He was accused of justifying any means to accomplish political goals, especially the retention of and extension of state power. He was denounced for advising rulers to use cunning, duplicity, and bad faith to enhance their own power and undermine their enemies. Criticism of Machiavelli's ideas developed into a genre of writing on political theory, as thinker after thinker wrote an "anti-Machiavelli" attack on his doctrines. Shakespeare called him "the murderous Machiavel." The Catholic Church condemned all Machiavelli's writings and placed them on its Index of Prohibited Books. Later, Machiavelli was praised for the very same doctrines, now seen as *Realpolitik*—the "politics of reality" or "power politics"—based on practical and material factors rather than theoretical or ethical objectives. Proponents hailed *The Prince* as an attempt to "liberate" politics from morality and ethical concerns and to see politics "as it really is." Louis XIV called *The Prince* his "favorite nightcap;" Napoleon annotated his copy of the book heavily; Benito Mussolini extolled it as a "handbook for statesmen;" and Adolf Hitler said he kept a copy of it by his bedside.[5]

Machiavelli's Message.

Machiavelli's ideas went much further and deeper than such readers of *The Prince* realized. In fact, when one takes into account his ideas as expressed in his more substantial political works, Machiavelli emerges as the first and still the preeminent theorist of the new geographically sovereign state. He was also the first theorist of the new diplomacy that the new states required in order to survive and prosper. Machiavelli's political theory is a reflection of the rise of the state system in Italy and the new diplomacy that kept them running. As such, his ideas both descriptive and prescriptive. Machiavelli's political theory constitutes the "user's manual" for rulers and servants of the new state—statesmen, diplomats, and military leaders alike—in the new international environment. Machiavelli's political theories instruct those who ruled the new state and directed its engagement with the world how to succeed at statecraft under the new conditions.

Machiavelli's world view is a primer for the realist theory of international affairs. In all his major works, Machiavelli assumed a Westphalian international order long before the Peace of Westphalia gave its name to such an order—one composed of geographically sovereign states with durable boundaries, equal in legal standing and legitimacy, in which the ruler monopolized the lawful use of force. Machiavelli assumed an anarchic international order, with no higher court of justice or authority than the state itself in defending and advancing its interests. He assumed that recourse to war will be frequent and that the new state must be organized for war to be successful. And he assumed that the state's engagement with the world would be constant; the state must also be organized for continuous, professional diplomacy, in order to be successful. If we read Machiavelli broadly—not just *The Prince*, but *The Discourses* and *The Art of War* as well—with these assumptions in mind, we take away a coherent theoretical structure that reflects the Italian microcosm's political realities that were already on their way to becoming the future international political realities of Europe as a whole.

Machiavelli's lessons for statecraft, war, and diplomacy were generally valid for monarchies and republics. Rulers were responsible for the good of their state, for its survival and stability—in a word, for its security. Rulers were judged by their success in defending and advancing the interests of the state, not by any other standards, moral or political. The more legitimate the government, that is, the more recognized its use of state power by constitutions, laws, tradition, custom, and religious sanction, the stronger it would be, and the less the ruler would need recourse to extreme measures. The less legitimate the government, the more likely its ruler would need to use extreme measures to enforce the government's rule. Republics and monarchies could possess strong legitimacy. But republics were by virtue of their representative nature stronger and more stable than monarchies. Republics owed their strength and stability to their ability to mobilize the loyalty and power of the people better than monarchies, because the will of the people lent powerful reinforcement and legitimacy to any state that represented their interests rather than those of the monarch. Well-constituted republics were internally stable and externally strong because they were better able to promote and exploit the economic prosperity, military potential, and patriotism of their people. But the rulers of a republic had the same responsibility for the security of the state as monarchs, and they were judged by the same standard—reason of state. Machiavelli advocated a return to ancient Roman republican values, especially the replacement of decadent Christian religious values with a Roman-style "civic religion" that worshiped service to the state as the highest value, in order to reform the Italian states of his day and prepare them for success in the anarchic international order in which he lived.

One of Machiavelli's key legacies was the concept that the state's primary role was external, to deal with other states through diplomacy and war—the primacy of external policy. Another was that all states, including republics, needed a strong executive power in their constitutions to facilitate action against external threats. The state that Machiavelli designed in his major works would be able to fulfill its mission of active and successful participation in an anarchic international system. That state could contend with other sovereign states for power, influence, and security and would justify its actions by their success according to the measure of reason of state.[6]

THE SPREAD OF MODERN DIPLOMACY TO EUROPE: 1500-1650

The French King Louis XI led his army into Italy, took and occupied cities from the border to Naples, and then successfully retreated despite suffering tactical defeat by Italian forces. This revealed the stark power differential between the small Italian states and their European counterparts, especially the strong monarchies of France and Spain. Italy became a battleground for foreign powers for the next sixty years. The invasions of Italy helped spread the Renaissance to all of Europe, including the new Italian political institutions. The idea of the new state with its exclusive territorial basis and its concentration of power in the ruler's hands was attractive to Western European rulers. And the European rulers had one thing that the Italian Renaissance new states lacked—legitimacy. Their rule, whether over kingdoms, principalities, duchies or other jurisdictions, was sanctioned and supported by the soft power of legitimacy based on religion, tradition, or custom. When these rulers adopted the ways of the Italians in concentrating power within defined territorial limits, they became more and more powerful at the expense of the old medieval system. Diffused authority and fragmented rights and responsibilities among nobility and church, cities and social orders, and all the other atomized institutions that claimed a share of political power on traditional and feudal grounds could not withstand the new state system.

The northern rulers also adopted the diplomacy that the Italians had developed to serve their new states. More and more, diplomacy was restricted to political units that had pretensions to sovereignty—a monopoly of legitimate force within the borders of the territory they controlled. The Italian system of permanent, resident ambassadors, duly accredited and endowed with diplomatic immunity, rapidly became the standard for Europe. The resident ambassadorial system gave rulers ways to influence other states by representing policies and views to other rulers, by providing timely and accurate political intelligence back to the capital, and by concerting actions with allied and friendly governments; the system soon became the norm throughout Europe.

The Reformation.

The invasions of Italy and the spread of the Renaissance Italian state system to the rest of Europe in the early-16th century coincided with the beginnings of the Protestant Reformation. The Reformation had great influence on the development of the modern state system and modern diplomacy because it discredited the two great supra-statal political institutions of Christendom, the Papacy and the Empire. The Reformation radically reduced those institutions' ability to influence the international system, and at the same time greatly strengthened the power of the rulers of the new states. The Reformation strengthened the hand of Protestant rulers by transferring to them the effective leadership of the reformed churches. The Reformation therefore intersected with the rise of territorial states in ways that powerfully accelerated the process of state formation that the Renaissance had begun. The Reformation harnessed the immense power of religion to the *raison d'être* of the state and added religious differences to the already long menu of reasons for states to conflict with other states. In the short run, the expansion and development of diplomacy suffered as states of different religions downgraded or interrupted normal diplomatic relations for a time. In the long run, however, the development of diplomacy resumed its previous trajectory, keeping pace with the development of state power and self-awareness, as well as with the extension of a state system that required continuous and consequential diplomatic activity in order to function effectively.

The Reformation led to a long series of religious struggles, first in Germany and Central Europe, and later in France, the Low Countries, and elsewhere. It led, too, to the Catholic Counter-Reformation, which reorganized the Church in Catholic lands as the Reformation reorganized the churches in Protestant lands. In both Catholic and Protestant Europe, however, the religious breakdown of the unity of Christendom resulted in a tremendous source of political influence for the new states—religious uniformity under the control of the state and its ruler became the norm. Everywhere, the sanction of guardian of the faith was added to the secular ruler's authority, vastly increasing the concentration of his power. This fact was recognized in international law and practice by the Peace of Augsburg of 1555 between the Catholic Emperor Charles V and the rebellious Protestant states of his Empire. The question of which religion people would be allowed to practice—in this case, either Catholicism or Lutheranism—was to be decided by the local ruler. This arrangement was expressed as the principle of *cujus regio, ejus religio*—the ruler's religion is the religion of the ruler's people. At the state level, no toleration of religious minorities was foreseen. At the macro level, the result was greater toleration for religious diversity in the international system of sovereign states.

Balance-of-Power Diplomacy and the Wars of Religion.

As the modern state system developed, its characteristic dynamics developed as well. In an anarchic system, hegemonic threats appeared as one state grew stronger than others. The system began to respond to hegemonic threats through the mechanism of the balance of power, in which coalitions developed to resist, restrain, and reduce the would-be hegemon's power and influence to manageable proportions. This happened even during the wars of religion. The attempts of Habsburg Emperor (and King of Spain) Charles V to restore and extend the power of the Holy Roman Empire from the 1530s until his abdication in 1556 led to the formation of coalitions against him on both religious and purely political grounds (although the distinction was losing its edge). This was the last serious attempt by a Holy Roman Emperor to achieve European hegemony and Christian unity, another indication that the modern state was succeeding in crowding out pre-modern political forms. The development of the major European states into absolute monarchies was another. The balance of power mechanism was extended beyond Europe, when France signed a treaty with the Turkish Sultan in 1536 to bring the Ottoman Empire into play diplomatically in its resistance to Charles's hegemonic effort.

Habsburg dynasts made two more attempts to assert hegemony over Europe using religion as a justification. Charles V's son, King Philip II (1556-1598) of Spain, tried to leverage the power of his realm and its wealthy overseas empire to achieve European hegemony, but met the opposition of coalitions that linked his Dutch and Belgian Protestant subjects with England and France. Between 1618 and 1648, the Habsburg rulers of Spain and the Empire again grasped for hegemony, trying to exploit the Counter-Reformation's partial successes to impose a Habsburg-controlled order on Europe once again. The Thirty Years War that prevented that from happening was the result of the resistance of a wide coalition of German Protestant states backed by Catholic France and Lutheran Sweden. The leading anti-hegemonic statesman of the first half of the 17th century was France's Cardinal Richelieu, who knitted together the anti-Habsburg coalition that won the Thirty Years War by blocking the Spanish and Austrian branches of that family's bid for mastery of the continent.

THE ABSOLUTE MONARCHIES AND BALANCE-OF-POWER DIPLOMACY: 1650-1815.

The Westphalia settlement of 1648 ended the period of religious wars and ushered in one in which the Great Powers engaged in episodic struggles to extend their power and influence in order to achieve hegemony for themselves, or to prevent the achievement of hegemony by others. The settlement itself is generally considered to have established definitively the sovereign state as the basic international actor and to have christened the European state system as one composed of distinct and juridically equal, sovereign states. These Westphalian sovereign states monopolized the legitimate use of force within well-defined borders and struggled for power in an anarchical international environment. The reality was not quite so advanced, but the idea of the modern Westphalian state would gradually become accepted as the norm. A constant search for equilibrium governed the system through diplomacy that sought to restore the balance of power among competing states. The universalist idea was no longer seriously considered outside the Papal Apartments in the Vatican.

Adam Watson describes how the period from Westphalia to Vienna contributed to the development of modern diplomacy. First, there was the propagation of the concept of the professional career diplomat, who cultivated specific skills that ensured effective performance of his duties. Second, there arose the idea that these professional diplomats belonged to informal but useful groups of accredited diplomats at various courts of Europe who shared a common outlook and common goals. These groups included a common need to protect their status and privileges; mutual advantage in exchanging information and evaluations, especially among representatives of allied and friendly states; and reciprocal advantage in maintaining good working relations, even as their governments quarreled. The diplomatic corps had taken shape and would become permanent, although its members came and went. Third, diplomatic congresses began to play an increasingly important role in ending and regulating conflict, and began to be seen not as isolated events, but as "climaxes in dialogue."[7]

Diplomacy was becoming continuous and general, as war was becoming occasional and limited to certain principals, while some neutrals normally stood aside. Negotiation was increasingly regarded as valuable in and of itself, as Cardinal Richelieu stated in his *Political Testament*. Richelieu also sought to remain in constant diplomatic contact with the enemies of France, including during war, in order to be better placed to influence their policies even as their respective armies fought. Fourth, diplomacy was increasingly conceived of as the management mechanism for the balance of power, which ensured the continued existence of all international actors by adjusting and readjusting the alignment of states to compensate for changes in the level of power of individual states. Diplomacy was needed to negotiate these adjustments. Finally, institutions to manage the conduct of diplomacy in capitals coalesced into regular ministries of foreign affairs, as a "logical complement of resident envoys."[8]

The balance of power could ensure the survival of most states, but it could not preserve the peace entirely. First, France under Louis XIV (1640-1715) threatened to become the European hegemon, especially by unifying France and Spain into one grand-dynastic empire that would include Spain's far-flung international holdings. This brought coalitions led by the Netherlands, the Holy Roman Empire, and Britain into play to deny French ambitions. Such coalitions fought the French and their allies four times between 1667 and 1713, exhausting France and Spain. The last of these wars, the War of the Spanish Succession—Queen Anne's War in America (1702-1713)—was very nearly a world war, because it involved operations and alliances with local rulers on several continents.

Through the rest of the 18th century, French attempts to reassert itself and English efforts to prevent France from dominating Europe while extending its own colonial and commercial empire were played out in a series of wars based on shifting alliances—the War of the Polish Succession (1733-1738); the War of the Austrian Succession, or King George's War in America (1740-1748); the Seven Years War (1756-1763), called the French and Indian War in America (1754-1763); and the War of the American Revolution (1775-1783). The war in America became a Great Power struggle, as skillful diplomacy and astute use of intelligence by the colonists intersected with the French desire for revenge on Britain. That produced an American-Franco-Spanish alliance that fought the British militarily, and a pro-American, Russian-led League of Armed Neutrality served to isolate Britain diplomatically and economically.

The French Revolution and the Napoleonic period brought a renewed French drive for continental hegemony as well as British resolve to prevent it, involving coalitions on both sides. Napoleon, in fact, realized albeit briefly (1807-1811) the general European hegemony about which Charles

V and Louis XIV had dreamed. In Europe in 1811, only Britain was outside the French orbit. The French Empire was surrounded by satellite states and allies of dubious loyalty but unwilling to oppose Napoleon's dictates openly. Napoleon's political overreach in Spain and military defeat in Russia in 1812 revived British efforts to create an anti-French coalition. British diplomacy was ultimately successful in exploiting the state system's inherent unwillingness to tolerate an aggressive hegemon by constructing and maintaining a Grand Coalition of all the other Great Powers to defeat Napoleon and finally to impose regime change on the French.

BALANCE-OF-POWER DIPLOMACY AND EUROPEAN EQUILIBRIUM: 1815-1914

The post-Napoleonic settlement began an unprecedented period of comity in the European state system. After the Congress of Vienna that codified the post-Napoleonic settlement, no general wars lasting more than a few months or involving all of the Great Powers were fought for nearly a century. The statesmen and diplomats gathered at Vienna were intent on restoring the 18th-century balance of power in the European state system as the best way of ensuring peace. The territorial changes they made and the institutional initiatives they took were successful in providing the basis for a durable peace among the Great Powers for nearly a hundred years. No shock to the international system as great as that produced by the French Revolution and the Napoleonic Hegemony has yet been followed by such a sustained period of peace.

Sir Harold Nicolson described the chief characteristics of the diplomacy of the period from Vienna to the First World War, when grand strategy was implemented on the basis of the balance of power, first in Europe and then in the rest of the world, as the European powers spread their influence internationally. First, diplomacy was Eurocentric. Europe was regarded as the most important area of the world and the other continents of secondary importance. Second, diplomacy was Great-Power-centric. The smaller and weaker powers were drawn into the orbits of one of the Great Powers in order to play their supporting roles in the unending maneuver to maintain, restore, or overthrow the existing balance of power. Third, the Great Powers possessed a "common responsibility for the conduct of the Small Powers and the preservation of peace between them." This implied a right of intervention by the Great Powers in crises and conflicts involving the smaller and weaker powers. Fourth, there was the establishment in every European country of a "professional diplomatic service on a more or less identical model." These professional diplomats developed a kind of corporate identity based on a common belief, notwithstanding the policies of their various governments, "that the purpose of diplomacy was the preservation of peace." Finally, diplomacy was conducted on "the rule that sound negotiation must be continuous and confidential."[9]

From 1815 to 1848, Britain followed its successful wartime diplomatic leadership with an ambitious attempt at peacetime coalition diplomacy. The British aimed to create a system of collective security based on dynastic legitimacy and participation in periodic international congresses to regulate the balance of power diplomatically. British foreign secretary Lord Castlereagh was the architect and inspiration both of the anti-Napoleonic coalitions and of the post-war settlement. Charles de Talleyrand, who served in leading political and diplomatic roles for every French government from the Old Regime before 1789 to Napoleon's Empire, deserted Napoleon to lead the French diplomatic effort to preserve key territorial gains since 1789 and win a seat at the table of European Congress diplomacy after 1815, thereby rescuing and restoring France's Great Power status. In 1818, the victorious powers—Britain, Austria, Russia, and Prussia—welcomed the same France they had defeated into a quintuple alliance that would exert a kind of collective supervision over the European state system. Five-power congresses authorized French intervention in Spain and Austrian interventions in Italy to put down revolutions there in the 1820s. The collective security arrangements of the Congress System did not last long, but the idea of a less institutionalized but still effective Concert of Europe, with the Great Powers acting as a kind of continental directorate, ensured general peace among themselves while permitting minor adjustments to the prevailing order for 30 years. Austrian Prince Clemens von Metternich, called "the coachman of Europe," guided the concert system on the continent through the second quarter of the century, successfully pursuing peace and stability through the Concert of Europe and the conservative Holy Alliance of Russia, Austria, and Prussia to defend dynastic legitimacy against the threat from the most dangerous non-state actors, the nascent national movements. Even so, the system peacefully absorbed the effects of revolutions in France, Belgium and Poland in 1830.

During the period 1848-1871, the wave of nationalistic political and social revolutions that swept over Europe in 1848-1849 strongly challenged the system, and the gradual breakup of the Ottoman Empire in Europe, which led to the Crimean War of 1856, further taxed it. The processes of Italian and then German national unification were severe tests for the state system and deeply affected the balance of power, but even these events involved short, limited wars that were not allowed to become general European conflicts. The forces of nationalism were managed without recourse to general war. Italy was united under the Kingdom of Piedmont-Savoy through the diplomatic virtuosity of Prime Minister Camillo di Cavour, who joined the Franco-British alliance against Russia in the Crimean War (1854-56). This gained him the British diplomatic support and French military assistance he needed to defeat the Austrians (1859) who ruled northern Italy and to begin the unification process completed by his successors in 1870. Prussian Chancellor Otto von Bismarck united Germany by isolating France diplomatically, while constructing an anti-French coalition among the smaller German states to defeat France in 1870 and proclaim the creation of the German Empire in 1871 with the Prussian king as Kaiser. Lord Palmerston put British naval and financial might to work to influence the balance of power on the continent to London's advantage. The American Civil War did not tempt the European powers, especially Britain and France, to serious intervention, either militarily or diplomatically. U.S. diplomacy, aimed at keeping the Europeans out of the issue, bested Confederate diplomacy—which sought European intervention and eventual recognition of the Confederacy as a legitimate, sovereign state. Even under the difficult conditions created by a rising tide of nationalism and political and social revolutionary sentiments, the European powers managed to regulate their state system without recourse to general war or war between certain powers for more than a few months.

During the years 1871-1914, European diplomacy was concentrated on the peaceful management of two intense contests among the European powers, the competition for the remnants of the dissolving Ottoman Empire, especially in Europe, and the competition for colonial expansion in Africa and Asia. Bismarck's political foresight and diplomatic skill were demonstrated in both spheres; the first was when he assembled the Powers in Berlin in 1878 to craft a general settlement to the Russo-Turkish War of 1877-78 that involved multiple changes of boundaries and prevented war from spreading. Bismarck called them together again in 1885 to submit a number of African colonial disputes to general arbitration and international decision. The United States under Theodore Roosevelt played a leading diplomatic role in ending the Russo-Japanese War of 1904-05 through mediation at Portsmouth, New Hampshire.

The 19th century produced advances in diplomatic institutions in response to developments in military affairs, economic expansion, nationalist ambitions, and the rise of public opinion. From the 1830s, military attachés were added to embassy staffs, reflecting the growing complexity of the military element of national power. Soon after, commercial attachés made a similar appearance in the diplomatic world, reflecting the growing importance of the economic element of national power. Governments also began to engage in cultural diplomacy by supporting missionaries they saw as spreading their languages and cultures as well as faith, and by promoting cultural associations like the French *Alliance Française* and the Italian *Società Dante Alighieri* to encourage familiarity with and respect for their respective languages and cultures. Finally, Governments started to exploit the possibilities of influencing foreign public opinion, usually by trying to influence the popular press to report and comment favorably on their policies and actions.[10]

The ability of the European powers to continue to manage their diplomatic relations without recourse to general war ended in the cataclysm of 1914-1918. Historians would later see the First World War, and especially the inability of the powers to reach a durable settlement after it in Paris in 1919, as the end of the European state system and the beginning of the global state system of the 20th and 21st centuries. Diplomacy would, nevertheless, continue as a crucial element of power.[11]

ENDNOTES - CHAPTER 14

1. Jacob Burckhardt, *The Civilization of the Renaissance in Italy*, Oxford: Paaidon, 1944, p. 2. A long struggle for pre-eminence between the Popes of Rome and the Holy Roman Emperors resulted in the defeat of the German emperors and their expulsion from the Italian peninsula from 1250-1275. The Popes had called on French arms to do so and soon thereafter fell under French influence. From 1307-1378, most Popes were French and resided in Avignon in Southern France rather than Rome. That period of "Babylonian Captivity" in France was followed by nearly 50 years of deep division in the Church government, the Great Schism, when two or three different popes, each one of them considering the others "antipopes," were elected by different factions and residing in different places inside and outside Italy, contended for the papal authority. The schism was only fully healed when Pope Martin V won general recognition as the only legitimate Pope and returned to reside regularly in Rome in 1420.

2. Burckhardt, p. 2.

3. Several Italian states had long experience with intelligence systems based on agents resident in foreign capitals. The Papacy had clerical envoys in every Christian court, and the repository of their reports in the Cancelleria palace in Rome was the prototype for the foreign ministries of later times; some governments still refer to foreign ministers as chancellors. The Venetian Republic also had its commercial agents all over Europe and the Middle East who were tasked with providing topical information to the city's rulers. In the 15th century, the Medici family that ruled Florence started to require the managers of the foreign branches of the family banking house to submit similar reports.

4. A superb introduction to Renaissance diplomatic history, theory, and practice is Garrett Mattingly's *Renaissance Diplomacy*, London: Jonathan Cape, 1955. The same author's *Catherine of Aragon*, London: Jonathan Cape, 1955, captures the political transformation of medieval Christendom into pre-modern Europe during the 16th century.

5. Good introductions to Machiavelli and his influence on political theory and practice are J. R. Hale, *Machiavelli and Renaissance Italy*, New York: Collier, 1960; Maurizio Viroli, *Machiavelli's Smile: A Biography*, New York: Farrar, Strauss and Giroux, 2000; Bernard Crick, Introduction to Niccolò Machiavelli,*The Discourses*, London: Penguin, 1970, pp. 13-69; and Torbjörn L. Knutsen, *A History of International Relations Theory: An Introduction*, Manchester, UK: Manchester University Press, 1992, pp. 25-40.

6. Machiavelli was a major influence on Clausewitz, who read the Italian's main works and admired his approach to war and politics: "No book on earth is more necessary to the statesman than Machiavelli's; those who affect disgust at his principles are idealistic dilettantes . . . The twenty-first chapter of Machiavelli's *Prince* is the basic code for all diplomacy – and woe to those that fail to heed it!" Carl von Clausewitz, *Historical and Political Writings*, Peter Paret and Daniel Moran, eds./trans., Princeton, NJ: Princeton University Press, 1992, pp. 268-269.

7. Adam Watson, *Diplomacy: The Dialogue Between States,* New York: McGraw-Hill, 1983, p. 103. Adam Watson served in the British Diplomatic Service from 1937 to 1974, including as ambassador in West Africa and to Cuba. He later taught at the University of Virginia. He is the author of many books on history, diplomacy, and international relations, including *The Evolution of International Society: A Comparative Historical Analysis*, London and New York:

Routledge, 1992; and *The War of the Goldsmith's Daughter*, London: Chatto and Windus, 1964. He is considered one of the leading figures in the English school of international relations theory.

8. Watson, p. 107.

9. Harold Nicolson, *The Evolution of Diplomacy*, Oxford, UK, and New York: Oxford University Press, 1966, pp. 100-105. Sir Harold Nicolson was a distinguished British diplomat and historian. From 1909-1929, he represented the British government in various parts of the world. He was an active participant in the Paris Peace Conference of 1919, which he described in the study *Peacemaking, 1919*, Boston, MA: Houghton Mifflin, 1933. He served in the House of Commons from 1935 to 1945 and was knighted in 1953. See also his *Diplomacy*, Oxford, UK, and New York: Oxford University Press, 3rd Ed., 1963; and *The Congress of Vienna: A Study in Allied Unity, 1812-1822*, New York: Viking, 1964.

10. M. S. Anderson, *The Rise of Modern Diplomacy, 1450-1919*, New York: Longman, 1993, pp. 128-141.

11. Besides the references cited elsewhere, I consulted the following in preparing this essay: G. R. Berridge, Maurice Keens-Soper, and T. G. Otte, *Diplomatic Theory from Machiavelli to Kissinger*, New York: Palgrave, 2001; Keith Hamilton and Richard Langhorne, *The Practice of Diplomacy: Its Evolution, Theory, and Administration*, London and New York: Routledge, 1995; David Jablonsky, *Paradigm Lost? Transitions and the Search for a New World Order*, Carlisle, PA: Strategic Studies Institute, U.S. Army War College, 1993; Henry A. Kissinger, *Diplomacy*, New York: Simon and Schuster, 1994; Paul W. Schroeder, *The Transformation of European Politics, 1763-1848*, Oxford, UK: Oxford University Press, 1994; and A. J. P. Taylor, *The Struggle for Mastery in Europe, 1848-1918*, Oxford, UK: Oxford University Press, 1954. I recommend them for further study.

CHAPTER 15

ECONOMIC DIPLOMACY: VIEWS OF A PRACTITIONER

Constance Phlipot

The urgency prevailing in Europe as the common currency comes under threat of collapse makes brutally clear the linkage between economics and national security. Polish Foreign Minister Radislaw Sikorski could not have been more direct when he stated to an audience of the German intellectual elite that the Eurozone crisis poses a greater threat to Poland than terrorism or the Taliban.[1] Coming from the diplomat of a country that has faced invasion, occupation, and even national extinction over the course of the past few centuries, these are indeed strong words. As European Union (EU) leaders engaged in endless diplomacy to save the EURO know, economics is at the heart of a nation's ability to project power. The U.S. power to lead has been challenged by the costs of funding the recovery from the earlier (2008-09) financial crisis. Our liberal, market-based economic strategy has come under question as a model for other countries and is under greater scrutiny in our own country. In an internationally integrated economy, economic strength is not only the enabler of national power, but also the objective for the use of other instruments of power. A very important time and labor-consuming task of a nation's foreign policy is advancing its economic agenda. In the terms of our national security strategy studies, economics is a way, means, and end of strategy.

The British economist and diplomat, Nicholas Bayne, one of the leading writers on the subject, defines economic diplomacy as the "method by which states conduct their external economic relations. It embraces how they make decisions domestically, how they negotiate internationally, and how the two processes interact."[2] The intent of this chapter is to explain why nations undertake these international efforts and how they do it. As we will see, the lines between foreign and domestic policy are more blurred in the economic arena than in other policy issues. Likewise, the actors are more diverse than in traditional diplomacy, frequently representing domestic interests in and outside the government. Drawing on some 30 years experience as a practitioner of economic diplomacy, the author focuses on real-life examples of how the United States attempted to influence economic relations with other countries to our own benefit. Finally, the chapter will look at some of the issues that make the craft truly part of the "dismal profession," and why its practice is not likely to get any easier.

What does a country try to achieve by engaging in economic diplomacy? Clearly, for a country as large and well endowed as the United States, enhancing economic prosperity is a task first directed to the home front. Sound monetary and fiscal policies are essential for a strong, growing economy for which no clever foreign policy can substitute. That said, trade and financial integration makes even the U.S. economy depend highly on developments outside its borders. However, that raises a second question: Why does commercial activity between mostly private companies require the intervention of diplomats? International trade and financial flows, like their domestic equivalents, require a host of regulations, rules, and agreements to proceed smoothly. Domestically, negotiation of the rules among different industries, states, and other government entities can be complicated. Played across national borders, the complexity increases logarithmically. Enter the pinstripers to get everyone to agree. The stakes are high. Whereas domestically, the ultimate compromise among economic actors will be in accord with federal law, internationally the most adept or powerful nation will win. And who makes the rules, rules.

Shaping the rules and institutions is the most effective, albeit difficult, means to advance a nation's economic goals. In the aftermath of World War II, the United States was able to control the design of the economic and financial institutions governing trade and financial flows so that they served U.S. interests by institutionalizing free market principles. As the only large economy left standing after the devastation of the world war, the ability of the United States to control and shape developments was unparalleled and unlikely to be achieved again by the U.S. or any other power. Though our relative weight in the global economy has diminished, we still play a significant role in developing international regulations to stop practices we consider unfair for U.S. business, e.g., anti-bribery conventions and efforts to untie assistance from commercial interests.

Simply put, the objective of economic policy is to define the playing field so that we can pursue our economic interests as easily as possible. Broadly defined, those interests are:

1. Access to markets for our exports and for raw materials. As intellectual property is one of our most valuable exports, pursuing this interest includes promoting measures to protect intellectual property rights (IPR);
2. Maintenance of orderly international financial systems that are not vulnerable to use by criminal and terrorist elements; and,
3. Promotion of market economics worldwide.

THE PLAYERS

The cast of players in economic diplomacy comprises an interagency process that is every bit as competitive and contentious as that of the national security strategy, but is not limited to governmental entities. The lead government agency for developing and coordinating U.S. trade policy and conducting international trade and trade-related investment negotiations is the Office of the United States Trade Representative (USTR). A Cabinet-level position, reporting directly to the President, the USTR was established in 1963 as the Office of the Special Trade Representative with limited powers.[3] The Trade Act of 1974 expanded its legal responsibilities, which were institutionalized in the 1979 governmental reorganization that centralized U.S. Government (USG) trade policymaking and negotiating functions.

Encompassed in USTR's trade responsibilities is trade in services, including financial, investment issues, and intellectual property rights. The latter is one of the agency's top priorities. Legislation in the 1974 Trade Act, referred to as Special 301, requires the administration to assess annually each country's record on protecting intellectual property rights. The U.S. Department of State (DoS) does much of the gathering and compiling of relevant information, with heavy input from American industry. (The pharmaceutical, motion picture, and software industries are the most actively involved.) Countries found guilty of insufficiently protecting IPR (in some cases, governments are suspected of direct involvement in piracy) are put on a priority or priority-watch list. The most egregious violators are subject to sanctions and, when relevant, suspension of assistance.

Whereas USTR as a rule eschews political considerations in trade policy decisionmaking, a key role of the DoS is to balance U.S. foreign political and economic interests. In a series of speeches on economic statecraft in the second half of 2011, Secretary Hillary Clinton highlighted the linkage between foreign and economic relations and the need for the DoS to improve its capacity to promote U.S. economic interests.[4] This is a key theme of the first *Quadrennial Diplomacy and Development Review* (QDDR), issued by the DoS in 2010.[5] In line with recommendations of the QDDR, in October 2011 the Department announced the creation of the new post of Under Secretary for Economic Growth, Energy, and the Environment to enhance the Department's effectiveness on global issues. At the time of creation of the new post, the official holding the position of Under Secretary for Economic, Energy, and Agricultural Affairs, up to now the most senior economic official in the Department, would serve in this new role. Secretary Clinton also announced that the Department would establish a chief economist to advise the Secretary and the Under Secretary. In addition, the QDDR called for the creation of a new Bureau for Energy Resources to complement the existing Bureau for Economic, Energy, and Business Affairs (EEB). Both bureaus have heads at the Assistant Secretary of State level.

The conflict between economic and foreign policy interests often manifests itself in discussions between the EEB and the regional geographic bureaus. Traditionally, the geographic bureaus were more powerful and foreign policy trumped economics, but over time, the Department leadership has come to understand the importance of economic interests. Ambassadors are formally charged by the President with promoting U.S. businesses. The Ambassador in all but the smallest or poorest country spends a considerable portion of his/her time meeting with and advising U.S. companies and advocating for their interests at the highest levels of the host country. The usually close relationship between the U.S. Embassy and the American Chamber of Commerce or its equivalent is an example of the nexus of public and private interests that characterizes economic diplomacy. Few economic agencies other than the United States Agency for International Development (USAID) and the Foreign Commercial Service (FCS) of the U.S. Department of Commerce post employees abroad. Therefore, DoS economic officers work closely with other agencies in Washington to advance their interests in the field. The FCS has representatives at U.S. embassies and missions in 80 countries. In smaller posts, DoS personnel perform FCS functions.

The International Trade Administration in the U.S. Department of Commerce (USDoC) promotes American exports and investments and, together with USTR, monitors adherence to fair trade practices. The International Trade Commission supports the latter objective by determining whether U.S. industry has been injured by imports subsidized or sold at below market prices by exporting countries. The Department's Bureau of Industry and Security administers and enforces exports regulations, including issuance of licenses for export of controlled items (other than weapons). The U.S. Department of Agriculture (USDA) performs a similar function for agricultural producers. Through its Foreign Agricultural Service (FAS), the USDA posts officers overseas at selected regional missions.

A key U.S. Department of the Treasury mission is protecting the stability of the international financial system and protecting U.S. financial interests. The department is the liaison between the USG and international financial institutions, but voting decisions on loans to specific countries are made at the interagency level. Treasury also administers and enforces economic trade sanctions and is responsible for combating money laundering and criminal and terrorist financial flows.

The U.S. Department of Energy's (DoE) Office of Policy and International Affairs is staffed with regional and subject experts who advise on national and international energy policies. In Washington, the DoE can be a significant force in interagency policy discussions. Its overseas presence is limited; Moscow, Russia, is one of the few capitals where the DoE maintains an office. However, frequently through its national labs, the DoE implements energy conservation and nuclear security projects in transitioning and developing countries.

Several other smaller agencies support U.S. international economic objectives by supplying services that the private sector is unable or unwilling to provide. The Trade and Development Agency (TDA) provides technical assistance, training, visits, and feasibility studies for U.S. companies seeking export-generating investment projects in developing and middle-income countries. The Overseas Private Insurance Corporation (OPIC) provides financing through loans and loan guarantees for investment projects, maintains investment funds, and insures against political risk. The Export-Import Bank (EXIM) assists in financing the export of U.S. goods and services, in cases when credit and country risks make the private sector unwilling to provide credit at market rates for U.S. exports.

Though its mission is to promote development, USAID as the principal implementer of U.S. foreign assistance is vital to pursuing the U.S. interest of expanding market economies. As part of the assistance reform of the last administration, USAID activities came more directly within the authority of the DoS; the Director of Foreign Assistance at the DoS is dual-hatted as the USAID administrator. In part, the reforms are intended to further the collaborative process among DoS, Embassy teams, and USAID Washington and field missions in developing assistance strategies for countries and regions.

Beyond these traditional players, regulatory agencies in our country and our trading partners heavily influence our export potential, attractiveness as an investment recipient, and our position in international trade negotiations. As a negotiation stance, we seek to lessen the impact of safety, labor, and environmental standards on our competitiveness. One means of doing that is persuading countries to adapt standards that we consider valid—not permitting exceptions—or persuading them to adopt common standards through bilateral or multilateral agreements. For years, the U.S. and EU governments, together with business, have been working on enhancing transparency of regulations on both sides of the Atlantic Ocean. One of the more well-known cases in which we have not been successful in narrowing the gap pertains to genetically modified organisms (GMOs) about which the European concerns are not (in the U.S. view) consistent with available scientific information. If a country believes regulations or standards purposely inhibit trade and therefore constitute a nontariff barrier, the complaining country can bring a case to the World Trade Organization (WTO).

Business groups play bit parts in traditional diplomacy; in economic diplomacy, they have a starring role. At the end of the day, economics in a free market is about private business. Business frequently drives the agenda by providing the bulk of relevant information, as noted in the description of Special 301. Industry support or lack thereof is critical in the passage of free trade agreements. At times, business also takes an enlightened view in working with government to pursue common interests, such as providing training in developing countries on intellectual property or customs protection. Given the huge volume of mutual trade and investment, cooperation among EU and U.S. firms is critical to improving economic relationships. In recognition of the powerful force of international business, in 1995 the late Secretary of Commerce Ron Brown proposed the Trans-Atlantic Business Dialogue (TABD) to bring public and civil society together to strengthen EU-U.S. commercial relations.[6] The fledgling Extractive Industries Transparency Initiative (EITI) is an innovative form of cooperation among governments, business, and nongovernmental organizations (NGOs), which have decided that greater transparency in countries receiving income from extractive industries is to the advantage of all of them.[7]

NGOs often push against business interests—sometimes successfully. Despite the abundance of unexploited hydrocarbon resources, U.S. nongovernmental opponents to the Burmese (Myanmar) regime persuaded many American companies to abandon their economic interests and were instrumental in getting a congressional ban on investment in the country in 1997.

Congress's role in economic diplomacy surpasses that of other players. The U.S. Constitution gives Congress primary power over trade policy. Technically, the President can negotiate and enter into trade agreements by virtue of his power to run foreign policy. However, as he cannot impose duties unless Congress delegates that authority, the agreements would not be enforceable if not approved by Congress. Between 1974-94 and 2002-07, Congress granted the President "trade promotion authority," previously referred to as "fast track authority." Under this authority, Congress agreed to consider legislation to implement nontariff trade agreements quickly with no amendments and limited debate. The latest authority expired July 1, 2007, and has not been renewed.

Congress can also pass restrictions on trade, such as the infamous Jackson-Vanik Amendment, which denied the Soviet Union and Warsaw Pact countries Most-Favored Nation (MFN) tariff treatment if they restricted Jewish emigration. (Under MFN, a country's exports receive the same tariff treatment as any other country with MFN status.) The Soviet Union is gone and emigration restrictions eliminated, but Jackson-Vanik is still on the books except for Armenia, Georgia, Kyrgyzstan, Ukraine, and the countries of Eastern Europe that have been "graduated" from the law. Although the law is essentially a formality, as it allows for a waiver on national security grounds, grounds that are always invoked, the Russians consider it a very annoying and humiliating formality. In a different but similar case and signaling increased interest in foreign economic relations, in October 2011, Congress passed a bill on misaligned exchange rates around the world, including in China.

In our political system, Congress is also the conduit of U.S. business complaints about trade policy or the practices of individual countries. As discussed more completely below, the presence of chicken farmers in most congressional districts amplified concern over Russian poultry import bans. Similarly, large American companies are strategically dispersed across congressional districts to magnify their impact. Congress also serves as a voice for nonbusiness interests that have an impact on international trade. Labor unions are a vocal example of groups that exercise influence on the process directly. Environmental concerns also make their way into trade legislation and agreements through Congress.

Epistemic communities—virtual communities of experts across national borders—can have a powerful influence on international economic (and other) policies. In this concept, groups of experts define issues and push policies that differ from, or are ahead of, those of their national governments. Climate change is a striking example of when scientists irrespective of their nationality were able to set the agenda by virtue of their expertise rather than their power base.[8]

INSTRUMENTS

The architecture of economic diplomacy is not unlike that of other forms of diplomacy. Bilateral and international agreements provide the struts for the institutions and arrangements. Diplomats labor in these structures, employing the tools of soft power to influence and cajole other actors into accepting their countries' views. The range of acronyms and organizations in the economic realm is bountiful and often highly technical: from the International Telecommunications Union (ITU), the International Labor Organization (ILO) to the World Intellectual Property Organization (WIPO) and conventions on the allocation of radio air waves or the provisions of the law of the sea. The role of the diplomat is frequently that of a go-between with the technical experts and the host government bureaucrats. Although it is safe to say that no new major international organizations are likely to be created, tinkering or even comprehensive reform of many is continuously underway. Diplomats are always busy in delegations or in capitals convincing governments of the rightness of their governments' approaches to proposed changes. A perennial and vital concern is to influence the choice of leadership in these organizations. Missions employ the full scope of public diplomacy techniques to influence governments and publics. High-ranking government officials write editorials and deliver speeches; notable experts in the field are invited to speak and conduct roundtables with host country counterparts; decisionmakers are sent on USG-funded International Visitor Programs (IVP) trips for on-site exposure to the U.S. experience with the issue. The DoS, together with USTR and the USDA, used these devices in a full court press to influence skeptical European and Asian audiences about the goodness of U.S. biotechnology.

Coalition building is a key element in the economic diplomacy tool kit. Coalitions can be comprised of like-minded countries, such as the so-called Cairns group of 17 agricultural exporting countries (excluding the United States) that advocated freer trade in agricultural goods. Government and private sector cooperation is a growing phenomenon as governments realize they have neither the power nor the resources to accomplish their objectives. The American Chamber of Commerce (AMCHAM) is a force multiplier for USG efforts to convince governments to adopt economic policies amenable to the United States. Representing potential future investment, the AMCHAM can be a more persuasive voice than the government. Moreover, it can bring more resources to the table for hosting conferences or visits.

USG resources, while never as abundant as desired, can also help achieve outcomes. The contribution of the above-mentioned EXIM, TDA, and OPIC, while not sufficient alone to convince a government to accept an American investment or buy an American export, can provide the tipping point. In the broader goal of promoting market economies, the technical assistance agencies such as the TDA provide can be critical. For example, in Azerbaijan, the TDA used assistance funds to advise the Azeri government on the transparent and sound operation of a stabilization fund. Much of the assistance funding for the former Soviet Union was directed at creating the foundation for a stable market economy. This assistance included advice on its negotiations for joining the WTO. Similarly, the EU assisted the Eastern Europe and the Baltic States in their bids to comply with EU membership requirements.

Multilateral trade agreements can be the most powerful of all instruments to liberalize trade, due to the scope and number of countries and volume of trade involved. The first such negotiations were launched in the mid-1940s, resulting in the General Agreement on Trade and Tariffs (GATT) signed by 23 countries. Subsequent rounds focused on further tariff reductions until the Kennedy Round in the mid-1960s, which took on anti-dumping and development issues. The Tokyo Round (1973-78) went further into nontariff barriers and reform of the trading system. Uruguay (1986-94) was a major breakthrough—with the agreement to turn the GATT into an international organization, the WTO. This round was the first to approach the prickly issue of agricultural subsidies, allowed under the GATT, by establishing a timetable for liberalization of agricultural trade. Uruguay also tackled trade in services, such as banking, telecommunications, tourism, and professional services, producing the General Agreement on Trade in Services (GATS). The fate of the now-stalled Doha Round, launched in 2001, illustrates the problems of reaching agreement when the low-hanging fruit has long ago been picked. The most contentious issue in Doha is agriculture—with the developing world lined up against developing, potential agricultural exporting countries.

Regional trade agreements (RTA), involving two or more countries, not necessarily geographically adjacent, are an increasingly common method for countries to achieve both economic and political objectives. The WTO reports that as of November 15, 2011, it had received notifications for 505 RTAs and that approximately 313 are already in force. Of these, 90 percent are free trade agreements or partial scope agreements; the rest are the more comprehensive customs unions (with common tariffs for nonmembers). The United States has 20 free trade agreements. Congress approved the last three (Colombia, Korea, and Panama) in October 2011, several years after negotiations were completed. RTAs can augment and complement multilateral agreements by including agreement on complex regulations and in areas other than trade that would be too difficult to negotiate in a larger group. However, as the WTO literature points out, RTAs are discriminatory by their nature and can cause trade distortions. Their growing number leads to overlaps in membership and the potential for inconsistencies.

RTAs often have as much political as economic impact, especially for the larger partner like the EU or the United States, which can use the agreements to signal its interest in a closer political or security relationship. The EU concludes free trade agreements with potential new members as a first step in the accession process, in part to keep the candidate country interested in market reforms and the onerous accession negotiations. Similarly, the United States has concluded some 44 Trade and Investment Framework Agreements (TIFA), with individual countries or regions that are mechanisms for dialogue and consultations on trade and investment issues. Depending on the depth of our economic engagement with the partner country, these can be useful in resolving problems or simply a means to bolster the bilateral relationship. The 40 Bilateral Investment Treaties (BITs) designed to protect U.S. private investment and promote market oriented development are serious documents that can help substitute for strong investment laws in the recipient countries. They also promote high expectations in the smaller partner country as a sign of U.S. intent to invest in that country.

Encouraging and protecting U.S. investment is as important as securing access to export markets, although its benefits are not always as readily obvious. The DoS estimates that in 2006, Foreign Direct Investment directly or indirectly contributed 9.93 percent of U.S. gross domestic product (GDP) ($1.25 trillion) through in-bound investment, export-generation, and investor earnings.[9] The United States works through a number of multilateral fora to promote nondiscriminatory, open, and transparent investment practices. These fora include the Organization for Economic Cooperation and Development (OECD) Freedom of Investment project, the G-8 Heiligendamm process, the United Nations (UN) Conference on Trade and Development (UNCTAD), and the Asia-Pacific Economic Cooperation forum (APEC).

The OECD, headquartered in Paris, whose 34-country membership comprises major market-oriented countries, is an important forum for the United States to pursue measures to eliminate obstacles to our overseas trade and investment objectives. Discussions of common problems frequently develop into agreements, conventions, or recommendations to which members and nonmembers can accede. One of the most significant initiatives of recent years is the Convention on Combating Bribery. Other conventions regard protection of foreign property and untying commercial interests for foreign assistance. The latest round of OECD expansion, however, brought to light debate over the goals of the organization. Would the organization's effectiveness be enhanced by expanding membership to encompass a larger share of the world's economy by including countries less committed to market and democratic principles, or would that decrease effectiveness by reducing decisionmaking to the lowest common denominator? The organization took a cautious step in the direction of greater inclusiveness, but the debate is still open.

Until the Eurozone crisis brought monetary and fiscal policies to the forefront of international diplomacy, financial diplomacy was not as well developed as trade and investment. Central bankers, whose independence from the political process and penchant for secrecy make financial diplomacy much less visible than trade diplomacy, are the chief practitioners of financial diplomacy. Due to its near-hegemonic position in financial markets in the second half of the 20th century, the United States tended to go its own way in financial policies. In the 1980s, the Europeans pleaded with the United States to ease its high interest rates, which were diverting European funds from needed European investment. The United States ignored these pleas for cooperation, but changed course by the mid-decade when the high dollar was choking U.S. trade competitiveness. The Europeans agreed in the Plaza Accords to intervene in currency markets to gradually devalue the U.S. dollar and raise the yen and mark.

That said, the high degree of global financial integration requires closer cooperation among monetary policymakers, as has been made clear by the flurry of international activity aimed at containing and resolving the current crisis. Domestic policy actions, such as altering exchange rates or expanding the money supply, have an impact on exchange rates and thus influence foreign markets and the value of overseas foreign currency holdings. Furthermore, financial sector reform cannot be effective unless coordinated among developed economies. The Federal Reserve and its

Central Bank counterparts consult in the Bank for International Settlements (BIS), the Basel Committee on Banking Supervision (BCBS), the International Monetary Fund (IMF), OECD, as well as Asian Pacific Economic Cooperation (APEC) Finance Ministers' Process, G-7/G-8, and the G-20.[10] In 1999, G-7 Central Bankers, Finance ministers and financial regulators, along with monetary authorities from Australia, Hong Kong, Netherlands, Singapore, and the European Central Bank, convened the Financial Stability Forum in the wake of the 1997-98 Asian financial crisis.

The scope of the 2008-09 crisis, however, called into question the adequacy of the existing international financial coordinating mechanisms. The IMF was called on to play a larger role in resolving the international credit crunch. The G-20 summit in April 2009 pledged to triple the IMF's lending capacity; the IMF will be issuing its own bonds, denominated in special drawing rights that could potentially become an alternative to the dollar for reserve holdings.[11] However, the IMF does not have the financial capacity to bail out a larger developed economy such as Italy's if it were to fail in the current EURO crisis. More fundamentally, emerging economies are demanding a greater voice in the running of the IMF. Voting rights are now disproportionately held by the United States and Europe. The fact that the G-20, rather than the G-7, was the convening authority for the high-level discussions underscores that the action is moving toward the larger, emerging markets.

ECONOMIC DIPLOMACY IN ACTION: FROM CHICKEN LEGS TO MONEY LAUNDERING

A few examples drawn from the author's personal experience will help illustrate the interplay of domestic and foreign policy interests and the use of various instruments. These cases are not groundbreaking in the annals of economic diplomacy, but as bilateral activities they typify the day-to-day work of economic diplomacy. We will first look at the U.S. relationship to two WTO accession cases, those of Russia and Latvia. Both countries emerged from communism as newly independent countries, albeit Russia picked up the somewhat diminished mantle of the former Soviet Union. The accession bids of Russia and Latvia were also part of the overarching goal of normalization and making Europe whole and free. However, there the similarity stops; while their accession bids were made at roughly the same time, Latvia has been a WTO member for 12 years (February 1999), while Russia did not complete negotiations until November 2011. It is important to note that while the United States is a key player in a country's accession, the process involves all WTO members, though some might choose not to participate actively. Candidate countries are bound to meet certain specific treaty requirements that begin with an exhaustive description of their trading and investment regimes. Additionally, the candidates must conclude a market access agreement with each WTO member who exercises that right.

Russia applied for membership in the WTO (then still the GATT) in 1993 and began the formal accession process the following year. Latvia submitted its official communiqué to the WTO in December 1993. In comparing the two accessions, the issue was largely the degree of political and economic interest for each side. For the Latvians, WTO accession was of paramount political and economic interest in its own right and as a necessary first step for the equally great prize of EU membership. As a very small, open-trading country with scant resources, Latvia had to have guaranteed access to other markets. (Some former republics of the Soviet Union were also motivated to complete WTO accession before the Russian Federation in order to preclude Russia from blocking their accession on political grounds.) The importance of the goal ensured unity of effort, which was able to overcome ingrained resistance to free trade among old thinkers in some parts of industry and agriculture. The United States was solidly behind Latvia in its quest and provided technical assistance for meeting accession obligations. The strength of political will, however, did not mean that Latvia was not obliged to fulfill all the treaty requirements. Given that Latvia had been fully integrated economically into the Soviet system, the scope and depth of reform necessary to meet the requirements of a fully functioning market economy were enormous.

Despite the unanimity of U.S. views toward Latvian accession, a complication arose that put the United States and the EU at loggerheads involving a perennial transatlantic dispute over broadcast media policy. The EU's broadcast directive required members to reserve, whenever possible, more than half of their television (TV) transmission time for European works ("broadcasting quotas"). The United States opposes this directive in principle, because it limits choice for consumers and restricts the ability of U.S. producers to sell programs to EU TV stations. Additionally, in this case, the United States maintained that the EU was demanding that Latvia fulfill an EU requirement before it was an EU member, in contradiction to WTO agreements. Obviously, given the small size of the Latvian market, the issue was not about U.S. economic interests in Latvia, but about setting a precedent for a larger issue of great concern to the U.S. motion picture industry. The dispute delayed Latvian accession, but was eventually resolved through compromise.

In contrast, the 17 years of the Russian WTO accession process was a prolonged series of ups and downs. Initially, in the glow of the collapse of the Soviet Union and the ascendancy to power of economic reformers in Russia, the political will and economic interests were abundant in both the United States and Russia. Over time, Russian commitment to reform and openness slipped as old protectionist sentiments re-emerged. Unlike tiny Latvia, Russia is under the illusion that its market is large enough to sustain its own industry. The United States provided technical advisers for Russian accession, but the Russians did not trust them and eventually rejected the assistance. While Russian accession has been a stated U.S. foreign policy goal, economic/business as well as political interests have not always been strong enough to overcome the technical and other issues that have continued to emerge in the negotiations. Nonetheless, the United States and Russia did conclude market access negotiations in November 2006. If invited to join the WTO at the 8th WTO Ministerial, December 15-17, 2011, as expected, Russia will have until June 15, 2012, to ratify its accession package and will become a member 30 days later.

The case of "Bush legs" serves both as an example of the kind of problems that economic diplomats face with transitioning countries as well as the political dimensions that outwardly trivial trade issues can assume. U.S.-produced chicken legs were introduced to the Russian market as food aid during the early 1990s, thus acquiring the nickname of the 41st President. Cheap and nutritious, the drumsticks became a popular food among the Russian masses. However, as the Russian poultry industry began to recover, opposition to the cheap American product grew, even after the legs were being sold in Russia on commercial terms. The Russians turned to a traditional Soviet-era tool of harassment—sanitary inspection—to deal with the unwanted competition. Although absurd to anyone who has visited a Russian outdoor market, the Russian agriculture ministry insisted that American producers did not meet Russian sanitary standards. The United States attempted to counter these accusations by arranging meetings of experts and visits by Russian phytosanitary officials to American chicken-processing facilities. The issue rose to the very highest levels in the bilateral relationship. The United States achieved small and temporary victories, but the force of corruption and vested interests on the Russian side have precluded a definitive solution to this day. Russia absorbs 29.2 percent of American broiler exports, with leg quarters making up most of that figure.[12] Moreover, poultry is exported from nearly every U.S. state—all of which have very concerned congressional representatives. Consequently, Congress lost any interest in overturning the hated Jackson-Vanik Amendment on Jewish emigration from the former Soviet Union. The political loss for the Russians far exceeded the short-term increase in domestic poultry sales.

U.S. intervention in the case of the criminally caused collapse of Latvia's major bank illustrates the simultaneous pursuit of two of the objectives of economic diplomacy: promoting the development of market economies and fighting international economic crime. Latvians awoke one spring day in 2005 to learn that the bank that had been paying fantastic interest rates was "empty." Economists predicted the bank's collapse would cause the Latvian GDP to drop by several percentage points—a sharp blow to a struggling country eager to join the EU, the North Atlantic Treaty Organization (NATO), and the WTO. The banking system had developed very rapidly in Latvia after the collapse of communism with a huge number of banks for the size of the economy. Many of those banks were "pocket banks," which functioned principally as the financial arm of an economic enterprise. Baltija, however, was a large bank that sought out both commercial and consumer business. The lack of good laws and regulatory institutions, and the country's apparent stability, made Latvian banks attractive as a place to park and launder ill-gotten gains for business people further to the East. The owner of Baltija, a chess champion with known ties to organized crime, took the game a step further with an elaborate series of false loans and fictitious companies.

The Latvian government was eager for U.S. assistance in resolving the crisis. The Embassy responded with a two-track approach that reflected our dual concerns. On the development side, USAID bolstered its financially related technical assistance by providing experts to shore up the regulatory and bank supervisory system. To deal with the financial crime aspect, the Embassy requested Federal Bureau of Investigation (FBI) assistance to help the Latvians sort through the complicated web of criminal financial transactions. The FBI invited law enforcement experts from Latvia and several nearby countries in which Baltija had been involved, including Russia, to participate in the investigation. The FBI was not able to get deeply involved in the investigation because there was no direct U.S. connection, but the hands-on training and contacts with U.S. law enforcement were very useful. Moreover, the wake-up call of the bank's failure gave the U.S. diplomats the opening to talk to the Latvian government about the necessity of drafting tough anti-money laundering legislation. The Latvian Central Bank and Finance Ministry were very receptive to the message and reversed their earlier reluctance to impose restrictions on money flows. The United States was able to increase its persuasiveness with technical assistance on drafting and implementing the legislation. By moving quickly and combining the tools of economic diplomacy, the United States was able to advance its economic agenda and strengthen its political relationship with Latvia. Timely action on the Latvian side also prevented the bank collapse from spilling over into the rest of the economy and limited the impact on its GDP to only one percent of lost growth.

ECONOMIC DIPLOMACY IN A GLOBAL ECONOMY

While economic diplomacy shares much in common with traditional political diplomacy, many peculiarities of economics complicate the work of the economic diplomat. The most significant difference is that foreign relations are still largely in the domain of governments, but economic relations are formed by the interactions of the (largely) private sectors. Governments negotiate the international operating rules and regulations; how those rules are interpreted or whether they are followed in the real economy is beyond the scope of government officials. Another complication in economic diplomacy is the tension between economic and political priorities. An economic desire to exploit a potential market calls for bringing out all the tools available to the USG for trade promotion, but the country's record on human rights violations, trafficking in persons, support to terrorists, or neglect of democratic norms creates a dilemma for policymakers. As much as promoting economic prosperity, these are a part of U.S. national interests, and are often embodied in U.S. law. Conversely, policymakers are often hesitant to address violations of our economic and business interests if the potential damage to the bilateral relationship might have serious consequences for national security. The debate extends to use of foreign assistance and the promotion of democratic vice economic reform. One school of thought maintains that assistance on economic reform – generally better received by the host government than democratic reform - is more effective and can eventually lead to democratic development. The other side argues that economic assistance props up the undemocratic governments at the expense of limited resources for the support of democratic reform.

Two global trends that heavily influence the conduct of foreign relations—globalization and the "rise of the rest"—are largely economic phenomena and therefore profoundly change the nature of economic diplomacy. The real internationalization of companies and production poses some serious dilemmas for trade officials seeking to promote U.S. business. Should one lobby on behalf of a U.S.-based company if the production takes places outside of the United States? Should the United States lobby for a foreign company whose production is largely in the United States? What about a company that is not U.S.-based, but in which Americans are the majority stockholders? Ten years ago, the author found herself in the odd position of joining with an Austrian diplomat to lobby their host governments on behalf of a formerly U.S.-owned company, now owned by an Austrian conglomerate, that was trying to sell massive turbines manufactured in Pennsylvania. For large exports, production can take place in many countries. For years, the USG has supported Boeing in its rivalry with the European Airbus, although, in fact, American companies located in the United States make major Airbus components such as engines.

When Western countries and companies operating with a Western business ethos dominated the global economy, negotiating consensus on international rules was much easier than today. The shift of economic weight to countries without such a business tradition makes coming to an agreement much more difficult. This issue came into play during the OECD's recent enlargement exercise. Is it better to bring the new economic leaders into the rule-making process, rather than exclude them, at the risk of diluting consensus? While these developments make the job more difficult, they also underscore the increased importance of economic diplomacy. The rise of non-likeminded stakeholders calls for a greater need for global rules and regulations. More skillful economic diplomats are needed to find and build areas of consensus. Furthermore, as the nature of conflict has become more regional and sub-national, and more likely to be caused or exacerbated by economic hardship and disparity, attention to economic tools is more important. The wars in Iraq and Afghanistan demonstrate that building infrastructure, developing open markets, and securing transparent contracts are critical to ending conflict.

The financial crises of the past 3 to 4 years —and more importantly—their global nature, has made clear the importance of economics to national security. As we have seen, there are a host of tools and resources that practitioners of the craft of economic diplomacy use to promote a country's economic interests. Current global trends are likely to increase the role of economics in our conduct of foreign relations at the same time those same trends make wielding the economic instrument increasingly difficult.

ENDNOTES - CHAPTER 15

1. Radek Sikorski, "Poland and the Future of the EU," speech delivered in Berlin, Germany, November 28, 2011, available from *www.111.msz.gov.pl*.

2. Nicholas Bayne, "Financial Diplomacy and the Credit Crunch: The Rise of Central Banks," *Journal of International Affairs*, Fall 2008, Vol. 62, Issue 1, p. 1.

3. Available from *www.ustr.gov/about-us/history*.

4. Hillary Rodham Clinton, "Remarks at the 2011 U.S. Global Leadership Coalition," delivered in Washington, DC, July 12, 2011, available at *www.state.gov/secretary/rm/2011/07/168061.htm*; "Remarks on Principles for Prosperity in the Asia-Pacific," delivered in Hong Kong, July 25, 2011, available from *www.state.gov/secretary/rm/2011/07/169012.htm*; "Remarks at the Asia Pacific Economic Cooperation Women and the Economy Summit," delivered in San Francisco, September 16, 2011, available from *www.state.gov/secretary/rm/2011/09/172605.htm*; "Economic Statecraft," delivered in New York City, October 14, 2011, available from *www.state.gov/secretary/rm/2011/10/175552.htm*.

5. "Leading Through Civilian Power," *The First Quadrennial Diplomacy and Development Review* (QDDR), 2010, available from *www.state.gov/qddr*.

6. Available from *www.tabd.com*.

7. Available from *www.eiti.org*.

8. Stephen Woolcock, "State and Non-State Actors," in Nicholas Bayne and Stephen Woolcock, eds., *The New Economic Diplomacy*, Burlington, VA: Ashgate Publishing Company, 2003, pp. 61-62.

9. The Department of State, "Open Investment and American Jobs Fact Sheet," Washington, DC: Bureau of Economic, Energy and Business Affairs, October 6, 2009.

10. The Group of Seven (G7), now the G8, is a club of advanced industrialized states that meets annually to discuss important economic, financial, and political issues. The first summit, held in Rambouillet in 1975, was attended by the G5 (France, Germany, Japan, the United States, and the UK) and Italy. Canada and the European Community joined in 1976 and 1977 respectively. From 1991 on, Russian Presidents attended select G7 meetings. Full Russian participation at the 1998 Birmingham Summit marked the birth of the G8. See *www.answers.com/topic/g7-g8*. The G-20 is a group of finance ministers and central bank governors from 20 major economies—19 countries plus the EU. Their economies account for more that 80 percent of the global GNP, 80 percent of world trade, and two-thirds of the world population.

11. Special Drawing Rights (SDR). The SDR is an international reserve asset, created by the IMF in 1969 to supplement the existing official reserves of member countries. SDRs are allocated to member countries in proportion to their IMF quotas. The SDR also serves as the unit of account of the IMF and some other international organizations. Its value is based on a basket of key international currencies.

12. John T. Barone, "Russia threatens U.S. pork and poultry trade," *Nation's Restaurant News*, October 13, 2008 Vol. 42, Issue 40, p. 30.

CHAPTER 16

ECONOMICS:
A KEY ELEMENT OF NATIONAL POWER

Clayton K. S. Chun

Modern conflict, from conventional warfare to diplomatic disputes, has increasingly involved economics in some form. Nations use economic tools to pursue objectives, seek economic resources as national goals, or are affected by economic events that influence their national security. Both state and non-state actors use economic power to wage war and to influence events regionally or globally. Economic considerations range from simple access to resources like water or raw materials through transforming resources into finished products or services to providing financial resources. The ability to gather, transform, and use resources is a key component of national security. Many human activities, including those involving national security, can be either severely limited or dramatically enhanced by economic factors. Military operations and other national security actions frequently depend on the results of economic capability. Without the capacity to produce, finance, or support key national security activities, a nation would have a limited ability to protect its domestic and international interests.

Economic power has spread widely and gained importance in recent years. Globalization, the reliance on economics, and the diffusion of economic power from a few industrial states to many developing ones has radically changed the world. Global economic success has also conferred power on a large group of sovereign governments and even corporations. The threat or actual action by a government, organization, or cartel can create enormous economic impact. Markets are extremely sensitive to news that would affect potential financial or economic activity. Oil prices can rise rapidly if tensions increase in the Persian Gulf or if a natural disaster occurs. Single events with little obvious international significance could ignite a sell-off by investors in overseas and domestic stock markets. Global communications can spread panic and exacerbate the condition.

The changing environment has altered the emphasis on national elements of power so that military power is not necessarily the primary coercive tool in international relations, and economic power has gained increased importance. During the age of total war that spanned World Wars I and II, military power was the coin of the realm in foreign affairs. Economic power played a role in those wars, but the fight for national survival overrode the impact of domestic and international macroeconomic stability or growth. Economics served primarily as a provider of resources to the military element of power. In an era of increased consumer demand, technological growth, changes in society, and the evolving nature of conflict, the importance of economic considerations rose. During the Cold War, national survival was still at stake, but even then economic considerations became just as important as nuclear parity with the Soviet Union. President Dwight D. Eisenhower warned of military expenditures impeding future economic growth—the net result of which would degrade security for the nation. The Kennedy administration raised questions regarding how much defense spending was sufficient to ensure national security. The United States engaged the Soviet Union in a nuclear arms race while it fought a war in Vietnam, but Washington tempered its strategy to constrain defense spending. Nuclear sufficiency became acceptable, rather than superiority with the associated costly numbers of intercontinental ballistic missiles, strategic bombers, and submarines. "Guns versus butter" questions also arose as the challenges of an undeclared Cold War against Moscow pitted social spending against defense resources.

Today, economic issues play a pivotal role in conflict. Advanced technology, contractors on the battlefield, volunteer militaries (which tend to be more expensive than conscript armies), reconstruction of battle-ravaged nations, and other considerations make war and conflict expensive. Countries do not have inexhaustible resources to conduct long wars even if there is a direct and desperate threat to national survival. Questions of national treasury, consumer demand, labor constraints, finance, and other economic considerations can sway public sentiment against a conflict. If one nation wages war or takes other actions to isolate another state, investors around the world become nervous. Stock and commodity markets could affect financial conditions and create unforeseen reactions. These reactions may create adverse conditions that could force a change in strategy by the nation trying to influence a rival's behavior.

As economic issues affect national security capabilities and activities, so might efforts that involve national security create global economic impacts. War or political disruption in an oil-producing region will initiate tremors in the international energy sector. Although a nation might not be directly affected by the initial problem, the populace can suffer from increased prices from petroleum products, which could result in greater unemployment, inflation, credit issues, and foreign exchange problems. Demands for added military expenditures could translate to increased taxes that discourage consumer spending and business investment or reductions in other governmental activities that can directly shape the economic landscape. Competition for limited resources to meet national security policy objectives could also hamper private or other governmental activities. Nations can increase borrowing, raise taxes, spend surpluses, confiscate resources, or monetize debt. All of these options have unique economic effects on a nation.

Economics is an element of national power. Normally, one of a nation's key national interests is maintaining a viable economy to ensure a certain standard of living for its citizenry. States can use economic power to deter, compel, coerce, fight, and even rebuild a former opponent to meet a particular need. Economics becomes a vital component of the ends, ways, and means of security. Perhaps uniquely among the traditional elements of national power, economics might be any of the three aspects of strategy—the objective of a nation's strategy might be economic; economics might provide the means to achieve the end; or a nation might pursue its ends, using economics as the primary way to exert power. Whether economics is a way or a means to achieve a national interest or if it is a cause or motivation to take an action, national leaders must play attention to this increasingly significant security factor.

ECONOMICS AS AN OBJECTIVE OR AN END TO A NATIONAL INTEREST

States and non-state actors have historically fought over economic issues. Wars about open access to resources, trade routes, competition, profit, and other economic issues are common in military and diplomatic history. A keen competition for resources among governments, individuals, corporations, and other actors has created a complex web of economic dependencies and rivalries that was not as important in the past. Similarly, economic conditions can create an environment that fosters demands for change that could create a civil war, a fight for access to markets or resources, or other forms of economic competition. Countries with weak or failing economies may resort to actions that they might not have considered had their economies been stronger.

One specific area that deserves a brief discussion is oil as a cause or objective of war. Reliable access to oil at reasonable rates is a vital national security interest for every developed and many of the more-developing nations. Governments or international organizations that control oil production or pricing can effectively disrupt global economic conditions—whether purposefully or accidentally. A monopoly or oligopoly that controls a strategic asset, capability, or raw material has great potential to disrupt economies and create political instability, although few commodities have the same potential impact as oil. Major perceived or actual disruptions in the oil market are serious events that easily can trigger hostile responses from concerned governments. Today, oil is the best example of a resource that is both scarce and vital; however, other resources like water are also likely sources of conflict. We can expect economic issues—particularly access to raw materials and resources—to remain one of the significant objectives of international relations and causes of conflict.

ECONOMICS AS WAYS OR MEANS TO ACHIEVE A NATIONAL INTEREST

Differentiating whether economics is being used as the ways or means of strategy or policy-making can be difficult. The distinction is often in the eye of the beholder. Fortunately, making a fine distinction between ways and means is not necessary for the purposes of this article. Thus, we will discuss the two together—fully recognizing they are distinctly different functions in the strategy and policy process.

One prerequisite for maintaining long-term government activities is a strong and vibrant economy. The economy serves as the source of government revenue. In the short term, assuming a nation has a relatively resilient economy, a government can spend money fairly freely without serious consequences. However, that is not true in the long term. Government actions like high taxes, irresponsible borrowing, or spending surpluses under a failing or substandard economy will ultimately create political and economic conditions that will create significant future problems. In a national emergency, a government can take a number of actions to raise vital capital. During World War II, the U.S. Government spent massive amounts of funds to fight the war. Despite lingering effects from the global 1929 depression, the Treasury Department started to raise revenues for military and foreign aid expenditures before the U.S. entry into the war. Congress passed two key tax increases in 1940 and 1941 on individual and corporate taxes. Tax rates and the requirements on who must file income taxes expanded to fund the war. Simultaneously, War and Navy Department demands for weapons and personnel injected a fiscal stimulus into the economy that allowed some of the sustained tax increases. In 1940, Washington collected about $5.4 billion from individual and corporate taxpayers; by 1945, collections rose to $46.5 billion.[1] Although the government could set price controls on products, limit military pay due to conscription, and appeal to the public and corporations to make financial sacrifices, the efforts could make only limited reductions in expenditures. The Treasury Department recouped some of the government expenditures through increased taxation, but that too was insufficient to fund the war. War Department expenditures skyrocketed from $695 million in 1940 to $50.1 billion by 1945. World War II costs amounted to more than $90 billion for 1945. Tax revenues alone could not sustain the war effort.

The U.S. Government could raise custom duties on imported goods, but during World War II the market for consumer imports was small. Most of the imported goods and raw materials went to the war effort; raising prices on those was counterproductive.

Another major way to pay for military and other national security-related expenditures was through public debt. During the Great Depression, Washington used a number of public works projects to employ people who had lost their jobs. By 1940, the public debt was about $3.7 billion; it ballooned to $53.9 billion at the end of the war. The federal government conducted a series of massive bond drives to fund World War II. The public was encouraged to lend excess cash to the government. Repayment would be made later with interest, so bond sales placed the burden of war expenditures on future taxpayers, unlike raising taxes during the conflict. Additionally, the government reissued bonds that reached maturity rather than paying them off. These policies would limit future discretionary government spending, but the war took precedence. During the Vietnam War, the Johnson administration was initially unwilling to raise taxes to pay for military operations in Southeast Asia and to support new domestic social programs. Raising taxes to fight an unpopular war would be difficult. Instead, the Federal Reserve System used its ability to sell Treasury securities to finance government debt—an action it had not taken since 1951. The Federal Reserve System acquiesced to the Johnson administration to fund the war through massive bond sales.[2] Inflation, a general rise in prices, rose greatly, and Johnson was forced to raise taxes temporarily with a 10 percent surcharge on income taxes. He later repealed investment tax credits, revoked certain tax-exempt claims among organizations, and widened the eligibility of workers who had to pay taxes.

Countries could monetize their government budget deficits. The government could simply print or coin more money for its expenditures. Unless the money is not backed by some standard, like gold, this action only cheapens its currency and may produce undesirable effects like inflation. These negative impacts can be severely injurious to an economy. In many respects, one could argue the selling of Treasury securities acts to monetize government deficits.

Related to deficit spending is supporting another nation's debt. Global open trading of official government securities allows a state to use its economic power to assist a friend by underwriting his debt. Buying another nation's securities can transfer resources to that nation immediately. Additionally, the aid provided must be repaid, which eliminates some of the stigma of a grant or aid and often makes the strategy more politically palatable at home. The only "cost" to the securities purchaser is the upfront expense and time to recover repayment. However, the purchaser also bears a risk of default if the government seller of the securities falls, losses a war, or suffers some other catastrophic collapse. Short of such drastic events that make repayment impossible, the risk of default may be manageable. Debtor countries may not be able to make payments on schedule, but they generally attempt to repay debt in the long run. Reneging on debt repayment might provide short-term benefits to a debtor nation strapped for cash, but default devastates future credibility in the security market. Conversely, if a sovereign power purchases securities, it acquires some influence, at least theoretically, over the debtor country. The power resides in the lender's ability to demand or withhold demands for repayment or to hold or sell the securities on the international market. Threats to sell the debtor nation's securities could weaken its currency, cause a drop in the value of the securities, or drain resources from the government depending on the conditions of the bond. However, exercising the power inherent in holding the debt of another nation is not a costless tactic. As the lending country starts to sell, the price of the securities will begin to fall. The amount of the decline will vary with the magnitude and timing of the sales. At some point, the sell-off becomes economically counterproductive, as the value the seller receives falls below what he paid for the securities. In the case of a massive sell-off, the targeted country could actually benefit, since it can repurchase its debt at discounted prices—assuming it can generate the necessary funds to purchase the securities.

Economic intervention in or withdrawal from the economy of a foreign nation—as opposed to supporting its debt—can have tremendous impact on the financial well-being of a region or country. Governments do not usually participate directly in the economy of another nation. However, direct participation in the economy of another nation through private companies is widespread. Depending on the business and political climate of firm's home state, such participation may provide some degree of power for that home state. Regardless of the degree of external governmental control, decisions by private firms and multinational corporations to invest or do business in a country can influence national policies. Such decisions are independent and can be contrary to a host nation's interests. In an age of globalized financial markets, almost any corporation, organization, or individual can transfer capital into a country or take it out. This transfer generally can occur by using national or international stock, bond, commodity markets, or through direct investment into business ventures. Rapid inflow of capital can provide a needed boost to growth, while rapid outflow can sink a nation into recession.

Governments can use their economic power through other means. For example, rather than lending money by bond purchases, they can provide direct support to another nation through a variety of programs that essentially provide money or services. Foreign aid, loan guarantees, technical aid and services, and other assistance can provide a number of flexible tools to support national interests. The State Department distributes foreign aid in support of national policy objectives that include sustaining and strengthening key allies. Another use of the economic tool is to fight one of the major causes of global strife today, failed states. The United States Agency for International Development (USAID) provides help to nations to fight poverty. Poor economic health frequently breeds political conflict and potential civil war in a state. Economically poor regions often become breeding grounds for terrorists. USAID promotes economic development through humanitarian relief, food and commodity aid, training, construction, technical support, small-enterprise or micro-loans, credit guarantees, human health aid, and fostering economic growth to a market economy. This aid can strengthen fragile states, support transformational development, support geostrategic interests, address global and regional issues, and provide humanitarian relief.[3] Along with diplomatic and military capability, development aid gives national leaders another tool to help prevent conditions that could lead to civil and eventually military unrest.

The transfer of wealth from developed to developing countries that sell raw materials or manufacture low-cost products can create economic problems. Governments worried about the outflow of capital, goods, services, industries, and jobs might erect barriers to restrict or stop trade. Such actions rarely go unchallenged, and a counter-tariff barrier or legal challenge is a likely response. Conversely, governments willing to accept what are hopefully temporary trade imbalances for potential future benefits may allow the transfer of wealth and even industries and jobs to continue. Such is the political and economic theory behind the whole free trade movement—the North Atlantic Free Trade Agreement (NAFTA) being a visible example. Transfer of key technologies, processes, equipment, or skills can also enable foreign governments and private firms—granting in some cases access to capabilities that would have taken years and many resources to acquire independently.

Economic power normally involves the trade of finished goods or raw materials. Few countries can claim to produce all of the goods and services that their citizens use. Many nations require energy imports to subsist. Conversely, nations that may have oil, natural gas, or other energy sources might need food imports or other foreign services like skilled labor. Nations can work within international trade agreements, or they may take unilateral action to expand or restrict trade. A country might try to limit trade to hurt a rival. A government may impose import or export quotas, limit certain business activities, set requirements for strict "quality" standards for imports, designate excessive administrative requirements to import the items, enact tariffs or taxes on selective foreign goods, subsidize domestic competition to make the imports appear more expensive, dump or sell large quantities of goods at a much lower price than a foreign opponent to destroy competition, enact laws to force citizens to purchase only domestic products, or other measures. A major concern about enacting such measures is retaliation by the injured state, other nations, and organizations such as the World Trade Organization. Trade imbalances and currency fluctuations can also have adverse impact on domestic and global markets.

Economic power could also prevent or limit actions taken by a rival. Suppose a country requires a scarce raw material. If an adversary has sufficient funds, influence, or credit, it could purchase and withhold that raw material from its foe. The nation could also coerce sellers to prevent the sale of that raw material to the opponent. States could put pressure indirectly on an opponent's allies to force a nation to take certain actions. After the 1973 Yom Kippur War, Arab oil-producing countries refused to sell oil to the United States and other nations that supported Israel. This embargo boosted oil prices and shifted international power from the developed nations to ones that relied primarily on oil extraction. Political and economic power was redistributed when these actions were combined with the nationalization of private, foreign-owned petroleum companies in these oil-exporting nations.[4] Although in most cases, expropriating foreign assets endangers future investment or business, oil is different. Oil is the lifeblood of the world economy. Oil companies risk future confiscation of infrastructure, equipment, and capital to get this vital raw material.

The classic uses of economic power as coercive tools are embargoes, blockades, and sanctions. All of these are aggressive, hostile actions intended to restrict the target's economic access to the global economy. While often the first tool thought of, none of these are without disadvantage. Blockade, for example, is an act of war—not even considering the legal and practical necessity to make it effective by positioning naval forces to enforce the declaration. Sanctions work best when they are multilateral, massive, immediate, and used to achieve relatively minor policy changes from countries that value world opinion. Economic sanctions work poorly as a tool to coerce significant policy shifts, and they work best when used against countries where the common people, who are most immediately and directly affected by any sanction, have some political power. The imposing countries always suffer some economic cost, since cutting off trade to a nation means you lose the value of that trade as well as the target. Also, there are usually nations that for political or economic reasons are willing to trade with sanctioned nations; they reap a benefit while undermining the effectiveness of the sanction.

THE PRIVATE SECTOR AS A STRATEGIC TOOL

Although not generally controlled by governments, disregarding currency manipulations designed to offset them, commercial balance of payments are another form of debt that can have foreign policy implications. The United States has been a major recipient of surplus foreign savings that has allowed the nation to purchase imports and pay for its current account deficit. From 1999 to 2006, foreign sources have lent America $4.4 trillion, about 85 percent of foreign surplus savings.[5] Fears of a pending financial disaster could cause lenders to pull capital out of the market and further exacerbate the situation. Unfortunately, globalized communications can now spread fears among global investors almost instantaneously. The result is that economic issues that might have been localized events only decades ago can now turn into global issues. Additionally, since private investors may act contrary to government desires, governmental and even international efforts to stem economic crises may be ineffective. Some nations fear excessive foreign investment, due to a perceived influence or concern over precipitous withdrawal; others accept the risk and welcome foreign investment as a reasonably available source of funds. Although some nations find these actions helpful, critics argue that this capability can also be used to stifle competition, protect national interests, or create "geopolitical troublemaking."[6] Foreign funds do provide a needed economic boost, but they can also disappear quickly should confidence fail.

Multinational corporations and firms typically have the resources and ability to get access to once-closed markets. Governments might offer subsidies or grant special benefits to attract business to their country. Once established, the multinational corporation could exert a powerful influence on the government, since its affairs affect the nation's economy. Similarly, in highly contested markets, a multinational corporation could offer restricted technologies, move production of key subcomponents, offer bribes, expand production beyond the initial plan, or provide other incentives to gain access to the market. Companies can lobby their home country's government (assuming it favors the move into the other nation's market) for help lifting trade restrictions or access to technology or for influencing the host nation's foreign policy.

ECONOMICS AS A SOURCE OF OTHER INSTRUMENTS OF POWER

In the most basic sense, economic power is an entity's ability to acquire, produce, and use raw materials, goods, and services. A nation cannot engage in conflict over an extended period without an adjustment to its economy. In many cases, countries must devote goods or services to prepare for or fight a war or even to conduct other activities that affect the national interest. Humanitarian aid, defense expenditures, diplomacy, alliance membership, and other vital actions depend on a country's ability to raise and spend tax revenues, borrow funds, use surpluses, or finance these measures. Economic power allows players to conduct actions by providing the personnel, equipment, operating materials, infrastructure, and short- or long-term sustainment of that capability. Governments purchase commodities and equipment like a business, obtain labor (military, government civilian, and contractor), maintain physical infrastructure, conduct research and development, and in some cases also produce unique goods and services peculiar to national security. The government funds these capabilities by extracting resources from the public and businesses that must sacrifice their own economic well-being. Within the government, the competition for resources is very tough, especially in times when the domestic economy has a downturn that may limit funding of large or new initiatives. Skeptical lawmakers and the executive branch that must choose between these requirements and other programs of national interest must be convinced that military or diplomatic programs are the best use of scarce resources.

Resource decisions mold the creation of force structure to include investments in weapons, recruitment and retention of military and civilian personnel, decisions to fund military or nonmilitary government programs, and a host of other concerns that affect national security policy. Further, economic conditions—once the exclusive concern of financial institutions, investors, and businesses—now affect military decisions that range from recruitment to government borrowing that directly influences a power's ability to provide military capability. Arms sales, transfers of key military technologies or technologies related to weapons of mass destruction, contracting for goods and services by individuals and firms, and other economic activities can influence the national security environment.

Nations that have sufficient resources can upgrade their military forces with more and better capabilities. Military forces that lack personnel or equipment could rely on contracted services or purchase advanced weaponry from other nations. If the state has limited forces, it can change the composition of its military forces by hiring specialized services that would have taken years to develop or that they only need for a limited time. Contractors on the battlefield are not new phenomena. The U.S. Government has used contractors in several wars. Other nations have hired military pilots and aircraft, logistics, and combat forces to expand and enhance their limited capabilities. Today, governments can lease satellite communications, photographic imagery, multispectral analysis, and navigational systems that were once the province of superpowers that had exclusive use of space systems. Individuals, firms, and governments can use these functions—for a price. This capability can change a balance of power at critical times during a conflict.

Economic success empowers nations with new capital, technology, raw materials, and influence. This can be translated into military power and allow a formerly impoverished nation to complicate another state's security. For example, after the end of the Cold War the Russian Federation could not compete economically with free nations. A culture of economic inefficiency based on state-owned enterprises and centrally planned economies destroyed entrepreneurship, investment, and innovation. The Russian economy was barely alive. Russia turned to raw materials exploitation to include natural gas and oil. Demand for energy has expanded, and with problems in the Middle East, oil prices have risen greatly. Russia's real Gross Domestic Product (GDP), a measure of the country's total value of consumption, government, investment, and foreign trade, rose 64 percent from 2000 to 2008. In comparison, the real GDP of the United States increased by 18 percent over the same period. Oil profits have allowed the Russian government to finance a larger military budget, which has given Moscow the ability to build a new intercontinental ballistic missile, aircraft, and other weapons to revitalize its national security and foreign policies. Other countries, like Iran and Venezuela, also fuel their defense and security programs by oil sales. Nations building advanced technology consumer goods like information systems could use similar technologies to improve their military forces.

While national leaders consider and adapt economics as an element of national power, these same leaders are also affected by economic events that may limit their policies options. Economic considerations can have very influential impacts on the conduct of military operations and diplomatic actions. Globalization has allowed nations to conduct business with allies, former enemies, and potential rivals. New relationships between citizens and governments that highlight cost reductions, profits, and long-range business activities can impact national security measures in a host of ways.

Government expenditures, borrowing, taxes, and other direct financial effects on a nation's public, financial markets, and business can skew short-term consumption and longer-term investment. The challenges government faces in the economic realm are not limited to these direct effects. A wider scope of national economic health is involved. The ability to pay for national security or the influence of foreign policies on business may strongly shape operations. Conversely, certain international events that affect a country's economic health may heighten support for aggressive national security policies. For example, policies that advocate the use of naval forces to arrest criminals or stop piracy would be hailed by a number of individuals from international shippers, insurers, consumers of goods transiting the area, and producers of exported and imported goods and raw materials.

Current economic conditions also have a large impact on military operations. Inflation contributes to reduced purchasing power by a government. This includes activities from purchasing fuel, paying for contracted work, demands for greater pay for military and civilian workers, and other acquisition activities. Similarly, a recession—a sustained downturn in economic activities—reduces tax revenues and encourages moves by politicians to stimulate the economy or support the unemployed or struggling citizens. These policies can significantly reduce the amount of defense spending for a nation. However, some of these conditions might provide relief to the government. Unemployment may ease recruitment and retention problems in the military. Increased competition for fewer government contracts might reduce the cost of operations. Tools to fight economic problems may also create unforeseen issues. A central bank could raise or lower interest rates. These actions can affect the availability of investors to purchase government debt and the cost of borrowing for contractors to build the latest fighter aircraft.

Economic crises can, if left unchecked, create an environment that leads to political upheaval and disintegration. A victorious British and French Allied delegation demanded economic reparations from Imperial Germany at Versailles after World War I. That move was partly a punishment and partly a way to repair the financial and economic problems caused in France and Britain during the war. A defeated Germany now faced the loss of Alsace-Lorraine, coal mining rights in the Saar for 15 years, territory in eastern Germany, and the payment of financial reparations. The German government was willing to pay damages to civilians and civilian property due to the war. Britain and France wanted Germany to admit guilt for the war and pay damages for the entire cost of the conflict, to include their loans from the United States. There was no fixed sum for the war debt during the surrender negotiations, and Germany was unable to start payment immediately. Instead, the Allies demanded that payments of $5 billion per year be made until 1921. The Allies would later issue a final accounting of war costs, and Germany would pay the remainder for another 30 years.[7] These demands limited Germany's ability to rebuild and ensured that Berlin was incapable of becoming a military threat to France. In 1929, the global depression created great, universal economic hardship. Unemployment increased, and governments tried a series of moves to fix problems within their borders. Most of these moves failed, since many of the actions were uncoordinated and sometimes inappropriate in the global context of the depression. Germany was hit hard with reparations, the Great Depression, unemployment, and hyperinflation that made its currency worthless. German citizens demanded a change in government to fix economic problems; a democratically appointed Adolf Hitler replaced the Weimar Republic.

OTHER ECONOMIC SECURITY CONSIDERATIONS

Expanding trade can provide several benefits to nations. It can create better efficiencies in production by seeking the lowest-cost, most-effective producers. This situation could lead to greater economic growth and improved standards of living around the world. However, not all nations find an economic niche that allows economic growth. Cheaper outsourced services and imported goods may destroy domestic industries. Large numbers of unemployed workers could create domestic problems for a government. Further, reliance on foreign imports could impoverish the state and complicate its financial and credit situation. If nations rely on foreign goods, then any problem that hinders trade could cause issues globally. A natural disaster, potential conflict, trade dispute, or other problem could restrict the flow of needed products.

Modern economic crises have had greater impact on nations than they might have in the past. Global investment and business have tied disparate business partners to global ventures as diverse as manufacturing computers and call center services. What used to threaten domestic economies can now become the basis for a worldwide economic crisis. In mid-1997, the Thai currency, the baht, collapsed due to a number of reasons to include overvaluation of the baht, poor financial systems, overextended credit, and a construction and real estate "bubble." Banks, financial institutions, investors, and citizens started to panic and pull their money out of Thailand. They demanded payment in American dollars. Riots ensued in Bangkok and throughout Thailand. The World Bank and the International Monetary Fund took action. The Thai government almost collapsed. Investors lost millions of dollars, and the panic spread to South Korea and then throughout Asia. The contagion jumped as far as Latin America and Russia. Today, a quick glance at any copy of a financial newspaper will reveal issues from oil production problems, credit concerns, or other local problems that have the potential to create another global crisis and instability in almost any region of the world.

Government financial or policy changes actions can also shape the domestic markets in the short and long terms in ways that can affect a state's health and security. The attacks on New York, Washington, and the plane crash in Pennsylvania on September 11, 2001, shook global financial markets. Investors and firms were concerned about global market panic. The terrorist attacks on New York were partly intended to target Wall Street, which meant there were global financial implications. Immediately, the Federal Reserve and the Treasury Department stepped in to assure financial markets. Some of their actions included expanded bank borrowing opportunities to increase consumption among firms and individuals, ensuring the bond market that adequate Treasury securities were available for trading to compensate for bond trading offices that had been destroyed, and injecting funds into the economy by purchasing Treasury securities through open market operations.[8] These steps served to settle domestic and global markets and ensured that a catastrophic failure of the United States economy with the attendant effects on the global economy did not occur.

Today, the United States faces economic problems from a global recession. Financial issues caused by massive mortgage and banking problems created a credit crisis that spread worldwide. Unemployment, failed businesses from the automobile industry to small firms, government bailouts, huge private and public debt, and falling consumer confidence have affected societies, governments, and individuals. These problems have created questions about the future of international trade agreements, credit, funding federal discretionary programs, and the dollar's value relative to other currencies. A solution to the government deficit by some is a reduction in the defense budget, foreign aid, and other areas that influence directly on several national security capabilities.

Similarly, a government could take a number of domestic economic actions to settle cyclic downturns and uncontrolled growth. Injection of funds into an economy like tax rate reductions, increased aid from extended unemployment benefits, entitlement and other income supplements, tax rebates, greater federal programs aimed at expanding employment, and other programs could provide stimuli to help turn a struggling economy toward recovery. Federal programs that target certain industries could provide areas of new growth or repair damaged ones. Investment in energy programs, advanced technology, and other programs could in time provide solutions to some key economic problems. Although expensive, these programs could head off massive unemployment and social disruption that may create political issues and unrest. Legislation to reduce prices, like petroleum and other limited products, is an oft-mentioned option. Price and wage controls normally do not work. These are temporary measures that lapse and leave the underlying reasons for the crisis unresolved.

War and conflict has always been an expensive proposition. Spending national treasure to fight for sovereignty or survival is normally an unquestioned policy choice. Debate about participating in smaller, limited wars that do not involve a vital national interest is another matter. Limited budgets create competition among government agencies, the public, and other interested parties that can result in bitter debates between guns and butter priorities. A public accustomed to receiving generous social, health, or income redistribution programs would object to greater demands to spend on national defense, foreign aid, or other activities that absorb discretionary funds that might otherwise be added to social spending. National leaders might be forced to curtail or end funding for a conflict. In extreme situations, such considerations may radically affect foreign policy.

Defense spending in the United States is the largest single expense for national security purposes. Budgetary pressure has mounted to reduce defense spending to pursue other types of federal programs. During the height of the Cold War, defense spending consumed approximately 6 percent of the nation's GDP. In 2000, the amount of defense spending had fallen to 2.1 percent of GDP. After September 11, 2001, the defense budget increased greatly to fund operations in Iraq, Afghanistan, and homeland defense. The defense budget's share of GDP more than doubled to 4.7 percent. In 2007, Washington spent $622 billion on defense that included $173 billion for operations in Iraq and Afghanistan.[9] The Congressional Budget Office estimates that defense spending will approach $671 billion for 2008. Defense spending is not without limits. Concerns about acquiring new and replacement equipment, increased military and civilian pay and benefits for existing and expanded forces, and operating costs may cause major adjustments to future defense budgets. Funding these budgets will force tough prioritization decisions.

National leaders can take several paths. If all government programs are fully funded, leaders must find new sources of federal revenue. Increased taxes are an obvious source of resources, but may come at the expense of future economic growth, since individual and business investment and consumption may react negatively to tax increases. Borrowing the funds may damage future business investment due to interest rate hikes to attract capital to purchase securities. Large federal budget deficits can strangle the economy by siphoning investment funds from individuals and firms. Additionally, corporations compete for the same investment funds, so the interest rates they pay will rise. In 2000, the federal debt amounted to $5.6 trillion; by 2008 the estimated debt is poised to jump to $9.5 trillion.[10] These debt levels may slowly squeeze out discretionary funding like defense, and limit federal spending to mandatory expenditures. Non-discretionary spending like interest payments and pensions is mandated by law and must be funded. The popularity of health, welfare, and other programs makes drastic social program cuts politically infeasible. The most likely scenario is that no federal program will receive all of its requested funding.

ECONOMICS AND FUTURE NATIONAL SECURITY ISSUES

There are only a few nations that can possibly pose a military challenge to the United States in a conventional conflict. There are fewer still that possess nuclear weapons with the appropriate delivery systems to threaten major American cities. In the future, security conflict among nations may change from predominately military contests to ones primarily featuring other elements of national power. That option is also open to non-state actors. While there has always been economic competition, the conscious, planned, coercive use of economic power as the main tool to achieve national security objectives has been largely uncommon in American history. Moving to the use of non-military instruments of power to accomplish national security goals will take greater integration, coordination, planning, vision, time, and patience.

Using economics as an element of power will require consideration of a host of issues and unintended effects. National leaders will find numerous challenges from domestic and international camps that will complicate and constrain policy options. In the past, the American public has been largely spared from sustained, large-scale military actions inside the national borders. That may not be the case with economic conflicts. If the nation uses a trade sanction to force another country to change its behavior, it may be targeted with its own set of counter-sanctions. Suppose that Washington applies trade restrictions against a country. That country could seize assets of American-owned firms, organize a boycott of American-made goods and services, ban the sale of critical raw materials, or undertake other retaliatory acts. That does not even consider the opportunity cost of lost potential trade with the target country. Many or most American citizens could suffer from higher prices, less choice, unemployment, or other economic disruption. The resulting political pressure could influence national decisionmaking.

National security issues involving economics will only expand in the future. Global economic growth has introduced new powerhouses like China and India that complicate American national security and foreign policy decisions. Economic tools, once the province of a few developed countries, are now available to many developing and smaller powers. If these states can cause economic disruption, they can influence the behavior not only of regional rivals but of nations around the world. Small states, non-state actors, or even super-empowered individuals who have the economic ability to turn a local action into a global one must be expected to use that power to their advantage. In the past, such actors might have constrained their foreign policy, due to a lack of military power or in the case of non-state and individual actors been incapable of exerting effective influence. Today, economic power or leverage could allow those entities to become more proactive and willing to flex their muscles in the belief their economic power will deter an opponent's military power. Conflict by pocketbook could spread from a localized disagreement to a global one. Globalized markets and the dependence of nations on one another have made them vulnerable to many new threats; economic ones will find a greater place on the world stage in the future.

ENDNOTES - CHAPTER 16

1. U.S. Department of Commerce, *Statistical Abstract of the United States, 1946,* Washington, DC: U.S. Department of Commerce, 1946, p. 312.

2. Paul Poast, *The Economics of War*, New York: McGraw-Hill, 2006, p. 33.

3. U.S. Agency for International Development, *USAID Primer: What We Do and How We Do It*, Washington, DC: U.S. Agency for International Development, January 2006, p. 3.

4. Daniel Yergin and Joseph Stanislaw, *The Commanding Heights: The Battle for the World Economy,* New York: Touchstone, 2002, p. 71.

5. Matthew Higgins and Thomas Klitgaard, "Financial Globalization and the U.S. Current Account Deficit," *Current Issues in Economics and Finance*, Vol. 13, No. 11, December 2007.

6. "The Invasion of the Sovereign-wealth Funds," *The Economist*, January 18, 2008, p. 11.

7. Donald Kagan, *On the Origins of War and the Preservation of Peace,* New York: Anchor Books, 1996, p. 288.

8. James J. McAndrews and Simon M. Potter, "Liquidity Effects of the Events of September 11, 2001," *Economic Policy Review,* November 2002, p. 69.

9. Congressional Budget Office, *Long-Term Implications of Current Defense Plans: Summary Update for Fiscal Year 2008*, Washington, DC: Congressional Budget Office, December 2007, pp. 2-3.

10. Council of Economic Advisers, *Economic Indicators*, Washington, DC: Government Printing Office, December 2007, p. 32.

CHAPTER 17

MILITARY POWER AND THE USE OF FORCE[1]

John F. Troxell

> Force without wisdom falls of its own weight.
>
> Horace

International politics is a struggle for power. Power, in the international arena, is used to protect a nation's interests by influencing potential competitors or partners. The most important instrument of power available to a nation-state is military power. "In international politics in particular," according to Hans Morgenthau, "armed strength as a threat or a potentiality is the most important material factor making for the political power of a nation."[2] The other elements of power are certainly important and can contribute to the furtherance of national interests; however, as long as states continue to exist in a condition of anarchy, military power will continue to play a crucial role in international politics. As Kenneth Waltz aptly put it, "In politics force is said to be the ultima ratio. In international politics force serves, not only as the ultima ratio, but indeed as the first and constant one."[3]

The current world situation once again focuses the international community's attention on the role of military power, due in part to the absolute and relative dominance of the world's sole superpower, the United States. According to recent figures, U.S. defense expenditures account for 39 percent of the world's total spending on defense. The United States spends more than eight times the combined defense budgets of China and Russia, and more than 25 times the combined defense spending of the remaining six "rogue nations" (Cuba, Iran, Libya, Sudan, Syria, and North Korea). These comparisons do not reflect the defense contributions of the closest U.S. allies, nor do they include the impact of the Pentagon's fiscal 2005 budget request of $400 billion—a cumulative increase of 24 percent over the past three years.[4] The resultant gap in military capabilities is huge, and may even be greater than that reflected in a comparison of defense budgets, due to the technological lead and the high-quality professional Armed Forces of the United States. Recent conventional operations in Kosovo, Afghanistan, and Iraq, only confirm this dominance.

As important as military power is to the functioning of the international system, it is a very expensive and dangerous tool of statecraft—one, as Robert Art recently pointed out, that should not be exercised without a great deal of wisdom:

> Using military power correctly does not ensure that a state will protect all of its interests, but using it incorrectly would put a great burden on these other instruments and could make it impossible for a state to achieve its goals. Decisions about whether and how to use military power may therefore be the most fateful a state makes.[5]

Art's caution is clearly evident in the emerging security environment of the 21st century. Despite undisputed U.S. military supremacy, the United States and its allies sense a greater vulnerability to their basic freedoms and way of life than at any time since the height of the nuclear standoff with the Soviet Union. Military supremacy has yet to find an answer to the combined threats of proliferation of weapons of mass destruction and international terrorism. Failed states and rogue states continue to present security concerns and the resultant demand for military forces to contain conflicts and rebuild nations. The United States faces two strategic challenges—one of ends and the other of means. The most prominent declinist of the last decade, Paul Kennedy, argued that great powers succumb to "imperial overstretch" because their global interests and obligations outpace their ability to defend them all simultaneously. James Fallows recently echoed this concern in claiming that "America is over-extended" because the U.S. has so many troops tied down in so many places that we can no longer respond to emerging crises. Beyond the concern with over-ambitious ends, Fallows also claims that the United States is in danger of actually breaking the military instrument of power through overuse and thus returning to the days of the post-Vietnam "Hollow Army."[6]

The purpose of this chapter is to examine the role of military power in the international arena in an effort to address challenges, highlighted above, associated with its use. There are two major parts to this discussion. The first concerns the political purposes of military power, and the second concerns the actual use of military force. The use of force discussion will include a brief consideration of employment options (the Range of Military Operations), a presentation of various guidelines for the use of force, and a look at the issue of legitimacy.

POLITICAL PURPOSES OF MILITARY POWER

Despite all of the changes that have occurred in world politics since the end of the Cold War, there is, in many respects, an underlying continuity with earlier eras. The recent conflicts in Bosnia, Kosovo, Afghanistan, Iraq, and mass-casualty terrorism are evidence that the use of military power as an instrument of political purpose remains as relevant today as in the past. Clausewitz's famous dictum continues to ring true, "that war [the application of military power] should never be thought of as something autonomous but always as an instrument of policy," and that "war is simply a continuation of political intercourse, with the addition of other means." While still serving as the Chairman of the Joint Chiefs of Staff, Colin Powell analyzed the military successes that the United States had experienced through most of the 1990s. The principal reason for these achievements, he concluded, "is that in every instance we have matched the use of military force to our political objectives."[7]

From a modern day American perspective, the U.S. Constitution establishes the political context in which military power is applied and the framework for civilian authority over the Armed Forces. An earlier version of the capstone publication for the U.S. Armed Forces, *Joint Publication (JP) 1, Joint Warfare of the Armed Forces of the United States*, which addressed the employment of the U.S. military as an instrument of national power, was very explicit on this point: "Under the Constitution's framework, American military power operates for and under conditions determined by the people through their elected representatives. This political context establishes the objectives and the limits of legitimate military action in peace, crisis, and conflict in the United States and abroad."[8]

Military power can be matched to several different categories of broadly defined political objectives. The traditional categories that were developed and articulated during the Cold War, in the context of the U.S./USSR nuclear rivalry, included deterrence, compellence, and defense.[9] Since the threat of large-scale nuclear war between competing nation-states has largely receded, it seems more appropriate to focus on the political purposes behind the use of conventional forces. In this context the categories can be modified, as shown in Figure 17-1.

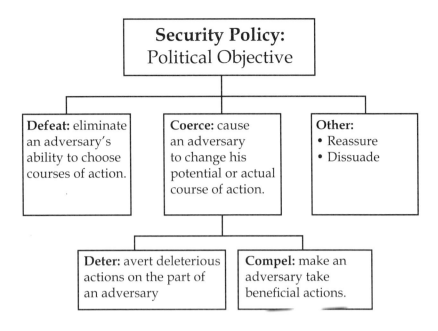

Figure 17-1: Components of Security Policy.[10]

Defeat.

Military power can be used in its purest sense to defeat an adversary physically. United States military doctrine clearly articulates this objective as the fundamental purpose of military power—to fight and win the nation's wars. Although recognizing other, potential non-combat objectives, U.S. doctrine argues that "success in combat in defense of national sovereignty, territorial integrity, societal values, and national interests is the essential goal and measure of the profession of arms in American society."[11] Thomas Schelling, in the classic *Arms and Influence*, used the phrase "brute force," and referred to a country's ability—assuming it had enough military power—to forcibly seize, disarm or disable, or repel, deny, and defend against an opponent.[12] Schelling's discussion clearly recognizes both offensive and defensive uses of force. Robert Art, on the other hand, focuses on the defensive use of force as the deployment of military power to either ward off an attack or to minimize damage if the country is actually attacked. Despite this focus, Art also argues that a state can use its forces to strike first if it believes that an attack is imminent or inevitable. This leads to the distinction between a preemptive attack—in response to an imminent threat, and a preventive attack – in response to an inevitable attack. A preventive attack can be undertaken if a state believes that others will attack it when the balance of forces shift in their favor, or perhaps after key military capabilities are developed. In the case of either preemptive or preventive actions, Art concludes that "it is better to strike first than to be struck first," and supports the maxim that "the best defense is a good offense." The defeat aspect of military force seeks to eliminate the adversary's ability or opportunity to do anything other than what is demanded of it.[13]

Coercion.

Because of the high cost and uncertainty associated with combat operations, a nation's primary strategic objective is usually an attempt to cause an adversary to accede to one's demands short of war or actual combat operations. As such, most states attempt to achieve their goals through coercion. Successful coercion is not warfighting, but is the use of threatened force—including the limited use of actual force to back up that threat—to induce an adversary to behave differently than it otherwise would. Coercion relies on the threat of future military force to influence an adversary's decisionmaking.[14] As opposed to brute force, coercion is the "threat of damage, or of more damage to come, that can make someone yield or comply."[15] From this perspective, it is withheld violence that can influence an adversary's choice. It is this perception of withheld consequences that causes a nation to acquiesce to a coercer's demands. Those consequences can take the broad form of anticipated punishment in response to an action, or anticipated denial or failure of an opponent's chosen course of action. Punitive coercion seeks to influence an opponent through fear, and coercion by denial, through hopelessness. Finally, just as it is important to recognize the dynamic nature of the strategy formulation process, strategists should also view coercion as a dynamic, two (or more) player contest. Each side acts, not only based on anticipation of the other side's moves, but also based on other changes in the security environment. The adversary can react to alter the perceived costs and benefits and certainly has a vote in assessing the credibility of the coercer's threat.[16] Coercion has two subcategories: deterrence and compellence.

Deterrence.

Deterrence, in its broadest sense, means persuading an opponent *not to initiate* a specific action because the perceived benefits do not justify the estimated costs and risks. Deterrence can be based on punishment, which involves a threat to destroy what the adversary values, or on denial, which requires convincing an opponent that he will not achieve his goals on the battlefield. In either case, the adversary is assumed to be willing and able to engage in well-informed cost-benefit calculations and respond rationally on the basis of those calculations. An irrational (or ill-informed) opponent who will accept destruction or disproportionate loss may not be deterrable.[17] Deterrence theory became almost synonymous with strategy during the Cold War, as both superpowers sought to ensure their survival through mutual threats of massive nuclear retaliation.[18] Nevertheless, there are certain important distinctions concerning the term:[19]

- General (strategic) or immediate (tactical) deterrence—the former refers to a diffuse deterrent effect deriving from one's capabilities and reputation; the later to efforts to discourage specific behavior in times of crises. An example of tactical deterrence was the evidently successful threat conveyed to Saddam Hussein during the first Gulf War to dissuade Iraq from using WMD against coalition forces. An unsuccessful example was the U.S.-UAE tanker exercise that failed to dissuade Iraq from invading Kuwait.

- Extended and central deterrence (the former alludes to endeavors to extend deterrent coverage over friends and allies; the latter to the deterrence of attack upon one's homeland). Examples continue to abound concerning extended deterrence—one particularly difficult issue concerns the U.S. security guarantees extended to Taiwan.

There are two challenges to the future deterrent posture of U.S. forces. The first is the ongoing issue of trying to evaluate the effectiveness of a deterrent policy. The willingness of a legislative body to allocate resources to various elements of military power is normally contingent on recognition of beneficial results. Henry Kissinger aptly describes the problem:

> Since deterrence can only be tested negatively, by events that do not take place, and since it is never possible to demonstrate why something has not occurred, it became especially difficult to assess whether existing policy was the best possible policy or a just barely effective one. Perhaps deterrence was unnecessary because it was impossible to prove whether the adversary ever intended to attack in the first place.[20]

The second challenge deals with the changing nature of the threat. During the Cold War deterrence was based on a known enemy operating from a known location and under the assumed direction of a rational leader. The emergence of rogue states and transnational terrorist networks that could gain access to weapons of mass destruction has created what Colin Gray defines as the current crisis of deterrence. These new actors do not necessarily share the long-standing and highly developed theory of deterrence that emerged from the Cold War, and the cost-benefit calculus that underpins deterrence may be clouded by cultural differences and varying attitudes toward risk. In fact, as Gray observes, "…some of the more implacable of our contemporary adversaries appear to be undeterrable. Not only are their motivations apparently unreachable by the standard kind of menaces, but they lack fixed physical assets for us to threaten."[21] The current U.S. *National Security Strategy* is in full accord with these views: "Traditional concepts of deterrence will not work against a terrorist enemy whose avowed tactics are wanton destruction and the targeting of innocents; whose so-called soldiers seek martyrdom in death and whose most potent protection is statelessness."[22]

Compellence.

Compellence is the use of military power to change an adversary's behavior. It attempts to reverse an action that has already occurred or to otherwise overturn the status quo. Examples include evicting an aggressor from territory it has just conquered or convincing a proliferating state to abandon its nuclear weapons program. According to Thomas Schelling, who initially coined the term, "Compellence…usually involves initiating action that can cease, or become harmless, only if the opponent responds."[23] Physical force is often employed to harm another state until the latter abides by the coercer's demands. It is important to recognize the difference between compellence and deterrence. The distinction, according to Robert Art, "is one between the active and passive use of force. The success of a deterrent threat is measured by its not having been used. The success of a compellent action is measured by how closely and quickly the adversary conforms to one's stipulated wishes."[24]

Compellence may be easier to demonstrate than deterrence, because of the observable change in behavior; but it tends to be harder to achieve. It is usually easier to make a potential aggressor decide not to attack in the first place than to cause the same aggressor to call off the attack once it is underway. A state that is deterred from taking a particular action can always claim that it never intended to act in such a way, and thus publicly ignore the deterrent threat. However, if a state succumbs to compellent actions, it is much harder to change behavior without an associated loss of prestige and possible national humiliation. Consequently, compellent threats should be accompanied by a complementary set of concessions or face-saving measures to make it politically acceptable for a state to comply. Success can also be driven by the perceived or actual imbalance of interests at stake. As the American experience in Vietnam demonstrated, compellence tends to fail when the issue is of vital importance to the adversary but possibly only represents an important or peripheral interest to the coercing state.[25]

In the post-Cold War era, three broad conditions have emerged that facilitate the effective use of military threats. These relationships are expressed in Figure 17-2. Together, the credibility of the threat and the degree of difficulty of the demands shape the targeted leader's evaluation of the likely cost of complying or of not complying with U.S. demands. If the threat is perceived to be wholly incredible, the anticipated cost of noncompliance will be low. The balance between the cost of compliance and the cost of defiance represents the potency of the threat. In the post-Cold War period, despite overwhelming U.S. military supremacy, it has been extremely difficult for the United States to achieve its objectives without actually conducting sustained military operations.

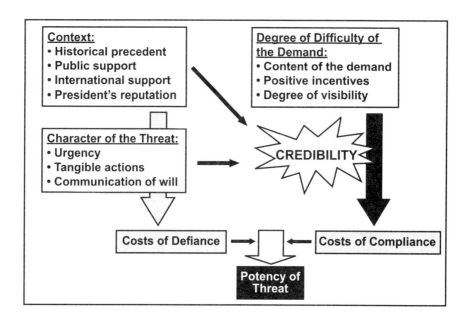

Figure 17-2. Evaluations of Compellent Threats.[26]

A principal reason for this difficulty is the existence of a generation of political leaders throughout the world whose basic perception of U.S. military power and political will is one of weakness. They enter any situation with a fundamental belief that the United States can be defeated or driven away.[27]

Echoing Colin Gray's crisis of deterrence, perhaps there is a similar crisis of compellence. According to Blechman and Wittes:

> American presidents have been reluctant to step as close to the plate as had been required to achieve U.S. objectives in many post-Cold War conflicts. They have made threats only reluctantly and usually have not made as clear or potent a threat as was called for by the situation. They have understood the need to act in the situation but have been unwilling or perceived themselves as being unable to lead the American people into the potential sacrifice necessary to secure the proper goal. As a result, they have attempted to satisfice, taking some action but not the most effective possible action to challenge the foreign leader threatening U.S. interests. They have sought to curtail the extent and potential cost of the confrontation by avoiding the most serious type of threat and therefore the most costly type of war if the threat were challenged.[28]

This conclusion was written prior to the tragic events of 9/11 and the subsequent operations in Afghanistan and Iraq. Time will tell if Americans will sustain their support for two very challenging and increasingly costly nation-building projects.

Reassurance.

Finally, there are two other political objectives listed on Figure 17-1. The first of these is reassurance, a term that began as a key element of U.S. nuclear strategy. In particular, reassurance was closely associated with the notion of extended deterrence in that its objective was to extend security guarantees to friends and allies. As a consequence, reassurance played a crucial role in the Cold War if for no other reason that the concept helped to prevent the proliferation of nuclear weapons to states like Germany and Japan. In a similar manner, the current U.S. defense policy includes, as its first objective, the goal of assuring friends and allies. This assurance is gained through the forward presence of U.S. forces and ensures allies and friends that the United States will honor its security commitments and continue to be a reliable security partner. In addition to the stationing of large numbers of U.S. military personnel overseas, the political objective of reassurance/assurance is achieved through numerous security cooperation activities and agreements. Security cooperation serves U.S. national interests by advancing U.S. values and beliefs, promoting regional stability, and improving cooperation among allies, partners and friends.[29] From this perspective, security is this country's most influential public-sector export. "We are the only nation on earth," one analyst observes, "capable of exporting security in a sustained fashion, and we have a very good track record of doing it."[30] A primary consequence of a more secure environment is the promotion of global economic growth. With this focus on both security and economic interests, the ultimate purpose of U.S. military engagement, according to some analysts, is to maintain international order, thereby allowing the American people to continue to reap the benefits of globalization.[31]

Dissuasion.

The final political objective is dissuasion, sometimes presented as the ultimate purpose of both defense and deterrence—that is, persuading others not to take actions harmful to oneself. The notion here, however, is more in keeping with that of the *National Security Strategy*, which describes building U.S. military forces strong enough "to dissuade potential adversaries from pursuing a military build-up in hopes of surpassing, or equaling the power of the United States."[32] The QDR elaborates on this objective: "Well targeted strategy and policy can therefore dissuade other countries from initiating future military competitions. The United States can exert such influence through the conduct of research and development, test, and demonstration programs. It can do so by maintaining or enhancing advantages in key areas of military capability."[33] The goal is clearly to maintain, if not grow, the tremendous capability gap that U.S. military forces enjoy over virtually all other militaries. The origin of this objective dates back to the formerly discredited draft 1992 Defense Planning Guidance. When initially leaked to the press, this document included a call to preserve American global military supremacy, to discourage others from challenging our leadership, and to maintain a military dominance capable of "deterring potential competitors from even aspiring to a larger regional of global role."[34] More recently, Secretary of Defense, Donald Rumsfeld has been equally explicit: "Just as the existence of the U.S. Navy dissuades others from investing in competing navies—because it would cost them a fortune and would not provide them a margin of military advantage—we must develop new assets, the mere possession of which discourages adversaries from competing."[35]

The concept, however, need not be so rough edged; dissuasion can also apply to countries that are not full-fledged adversaries, but those with which the U.S. has a mixed relationship—mutual suspicions and common incentives to avoid violence. The term goes to the heart of the new geo-strategic era. "In short, dissuasion aims at urging potential geopolitical rivals not to become real rivals, by making clear that any sustained malevolent conduct will be checkmated by the United States. It involves military pressure applied with a velvet glove, not crude threats of war and destruction."[36] The key relationship for U.S. dissuasion is that with China, in terms of preventing the People's Republic from developing assertive and menacing geo-political policies. Colin Gray is much more sanguine about this policy's prospects, noting, "we should expect state-centric enemies to attempt to organize to resist the American hegemony, and in particular to work hard in search of strategic means and methods that might negate much of our dissuasive strength."[37]

In all this, it is important to recognize that military power alone is not sufficient to conduct a successful foreign policy. Military power must be properly integrated with the other elements of statecraft—political, economic, diplomatic, and informational. Even for the greatest of nations, as Joseph Nye argues, military power is always in short supply and consequently must be rationed among competing goals: "The paradox of American power is that world politics is changing in a way that makes it impossible for the strongest world power since Rome to achieve some of its most crucial international goals alone."[38]

RANGE OF MILITARY OPERATIONS

The broad political purposes for the use of military power clearly encompass many different employment options for military force. These operations vary in size, purpose, and combat intensity in what the Joint Staff calls the "Range of Military Operations (ROMO)" that extends from military engagement, security cooperation, and deterrence activities to crisis response and limited contingency operations and, if necessary, major operations and campaigns (Figure 17-3).[39] The dividing lines between various categories of military operations have become much less distinct over the years.

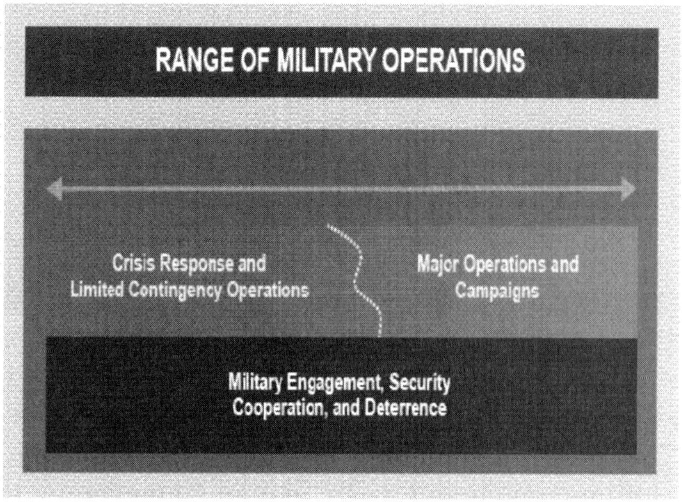

Source: Joint Publication 1 Doctrine for the Ariel Forces of the United States, May 4, 2007, p. 1-16

Figure 17-3. Range of Military Operations.

Major operations and campaigns generally involve large-scale combat, placing the United States in a wartime state. Crisis response and limited contingency operations can be a small-scale, limited duration operation not involving combat or a significant part of an extended duration major operation involving combat. The level of complexity, duration, and resources depends on the circumstances. These operations may include humanitarian assistance, civil support, noncombatant evacuation, peace operations, strikes, raids or recovery operations.

Peace operations can be considered as either peace enforcement or peacekeeping operations. Peace enforcement operations are also referred to as Chapter VII operations, referring to Chapter VII of the UN Charter, which addresses enforcement actions "with respect to threats to the peace, breaches of the peace, and acts of aggression." A closely related category is peacemaking, which assumes that one of the protagonists opposes the status quo. These operations take place in a non-consensual environment. Peacekeeping is often referred to as a Chapter VI operation under the UN Charter, which addresses "pacific settlement of disputes." Peacekeepers are impartial and relatively passive, called upon to monitor or verify troop withdrawals, separation of forces, or to provide security during elections. These operations take place in a consensual environment.

Using military forces for military engagement, security cooperation, and deterrence represent ongoing operations that shape the environment and maintain cooperative relations with other nations. In general these missions are below the threshold of armed conflict and are designed to build trust and confidence, develop partner capacity and, in the case of deterrence, to present a credible threat of counteraction.

In any event, all of these different classifications of military operations can be viewed as fulfilling one of the three principal political purposes: defensive, compellent or deterrent. For example, the political goal of humanitarian interventions and peacekeeping operations is to save lives; this is defense of parties under attack. The political goal of nation-assistance is to construct a viable government; this can be viewed as compelling armed groups or other elements of the society to obey the new central government. As a final example, the political goal of any collective security arrangement is to prevent aggression; which is deterrence.[40]

There is one important type of military operation that is not explicitly cited in the "Range of Military Operations" chart—covert action. These actions are a specialty of the U.S. Special Operations Forces (SOF) community, which is currently enjoying an unprecedented prominence within the U.S. military. Covert action is defined by U.S. law as activity meant "to influence political, economic or military conditions abroad, where it is intended that the role of the United States Government will not be apparent or acknowledged."[41] According to the U.S. Special Operations Command (USSOCOM) posture statement, "SOF are specifically organized, trained, and equipped to conduct covert, clandestine, or discreet counterterrorism missions in hostile, denied, or politically sensitive environments."[42] The current definition of covert operations was adopted as part of the effort to fill gaps in oversight that led to the Iran-Contra scandal. According to the law, covert actions must first be authorized by a written presidential finding, and the House and Senate intelligence committees must be notified before the operation has begun.[43]

In the past, SOF missions were viewed as "traditional military activities" in support of ongoing or anticipated military campaigns and were thus not subject to the covert action oversights just mentioned. However, in the ongoing, and broadly defined campaign against global terrorism—a campaign in which the Special Operations Command directly plans and executes its own missions—there is some concern that this type of use of force will be completely removed from congressional oversight. On the one hand, the U.S. government should be able to use every tool available in the fight against terrorism. However, such broad-brush authority, combined with an increasing propensity to use SOF in covert operations in support of an aggressive preemption strategy, may lead to abuse and risks to U.S. foreign policy.[44]

One final point concerning the current nature of military operations is the increasingly cluttered battlefield from the standpoint of other coalition partners, interagency elements, and even non-governmental organizations. The Joint Staff describes the nature of these operations as *unified action*. The concept of unified action highlights the synergistic application of all of the instruments of national and multinational power and includes the actions of nonmilitary organizations as well as military forces.[45]

GUIDELINES FOR THE USE OF FORCE

> War cannot be divorced from political life; whenever this occurs in our thinking about war, the many links that connect the two elements are destroyed and we are left with something pointless and devoid of sense.
>
> Clausewitz

> If not in the interests of the state, do not act. If you cannot succeed, do not use troops.
>
> Sun Tzu

> Madeleine Albright asked me in frustration, "What's the point of having this superb military that you're always talking about if we can't use it?" I thought I would have an aneurysm.
>
> Colin Powell[46]

These quotations emphasize the importance of linking political objectives to the use of military force. One of the best ways to ensure this is to use military force only in support of the national interest and when success is assured. The difficulty with such a straightforward prescription is reconciling the various degrees of interests, to include valid concerns about furthering important national and international values. In addition, the resort to war or conflict always unleashes the forces of chance and friction—creating in one analyst's description, "a fearful lottery."[47] Creating the conditions for success, let alone guaranteeing success, is much easier said than done. Decisions concerning the use of force are the most important that any nation can make. Given that the post-Cold War experience supports the necessity of resorting to force and the threats of force, but also emphasizes the risks of doing so, national security decisionmakers are left with a critical issue in the theory and practice of foreign policy: under what conditions and how can military force and threats of force be used effectively to accomplish different types of policy objectives. In the final analysis, political leaders should come up with convincing answers to these questions before sending soldiers in harm's way.[48]

Debates in the United States about appropriate guidelines for the use of force normally revolve around the Weinberger Doctrine – which is habitually viewed as an outgrowth of the lessons from the Vietnam War.[49] However, the origins of the current debate actually go back to the Korean War. Two schools of strategic thought developed from an assessment of that limited and inconclusive war. The first was the never-again, or all-or-nothing school, which advocated that either the United States should do everything necessary to win a decisive military victory or it should not intervene at all.[50] At the other extreme was the limited-war school. Proponents of this view held that the United States could expect to become involved in regional conflicts demanding intervention in support of less-than-vital interests. Colin Powell, although normally associated with the all-or-nothing school, has argued that all wars are limited; either by territory on which they are fought, the means used, or the objectives for which they are fought.[51]

Secretary of Defense Casper Weinberger articulated his six criteria for the use of force in response to two major issues—the lessons of the Vietnam War and an ongoing policy debate in the Reagan administration about the appropriate response to terrorism. Both issues are clearly relevant as the debate on the use of force enters the 21st century. Lessons from Vietnam included the recognition that military victory does not always result in political victory and that sustaining public and political support throughout a prolonged war can be difficult. Both of these issues continue to resonate in the debate about U.S. operations in Iraq. Senator Kennedy, for instance, recently charged that "Iraq has developed into a quagmire," and has become George Bush's Vietnam.[52]

Concerning terrorism, when the Weinberger Doctrine was unveiled in 1984, the national security elites were in a heated debate about this issue, particularly as it related to the failure of U.S. policy in Lebanon. Weinberger was reluctant to commit troops to such an indeterminate and chaotic situation. Secretary of State George Shultz, on the other hand, argued that the Weinberger Doctrine counseled inaction bordering on paralysis, and that "diplomacy could work these problems most effectively when force—of the threat of force—was a credible part of the equation." The *Wall Street Journal* referred to "Mr. Shultz's sensible anti-terrorist policy of 'active-prevention, pre-emption and retaliation.'"[53] Shultz was on the losing end of this debate in the 1980s, but 20 years later his approach seems to have carried the day, at least in the Bush administration. Figure 17-4 shows the Weinberger Doctrine and several more recent versions of guidelines for the use of force.

Guidelines for the Use of Force

Weinberger Doctrine (November 28, 1984)	Powell (Fall, 1992)	Perry (Clinton NSS) (April 1995 / NSS '99)	Rumsfeld (Nov 2002)
	• No fixed set of rules • Relevant questions • Evaluate the circumstances	• Political: interests • Military: success • Ethical	

WHEN
- Weinberger: 1. Vital interests at stake; 3. Clearly defined political and military objectives; 5. Public support; 6. Last resort
- Powell: Unambiguous military objective; Last resort
- Perry:
  1. Vital interests
     - overwhelming force
     - unilateral (if necessary)
  2. Important interests
     - ability to succeed
     - cost/risk assessment
     - last resort
     - limited options
  3. Humanitarian interests
     - catastrophic
     - urgent need
     - unique resources
     - minimal risk
     - end state
  • Clear mission
  • Public support
- Rumsfeld — Questions for the use:
  1. Necessary?
     - national interest
  2. Doable?
     - clear goals
     - military capabilities
     - clear Cmd structure
  3. Is it worth it?
     - public support
     - worldwide consequences

HOW
- Weinberger: 2. Commitment to victory (sufficient force); 4. Continuous reassessment
- Powell: Will the force be successful?; • Costs & risks; • Decisive means (overwhelming force); End state consequences (exit strategy)
- Perry: • Multilateral; • Opportunity cost on the force (OPTEMPO); • Exit strategy
- Rumsfeld — Guidelines for how:
  • Action – offensive
  • Don't restrict options
     - no arbitrary deadlines
  • Use all elements of power
     - military last choice
  • Brutally honest
     - don't promise what can't be delivered

Figure 17-4. Guidelines for the Use of Force.[54]

When to use force is the first critical question. The linkage of such use in support of vital national interests harkens back to the Napoleonic notion of fighting wars for grand purposes. Samuel Huntington defined national interest as a public good of concern to all or most Americans; and a vital national interest as one that Americans are willing to expend blood and treasure to defend. The 2000 *National Security Strategy* defined vital interests as those directly connected to the survival, safety, and vitality of the nation. There are two problems with this very straightforward proposition. The first is the difficulty in determining what those vital interests are. The domestic consensus that supported U.S. foreign policy during the Cold War has been shattered, resulting in a lack of agreement on the nature and importance of U.S. national interests.[55] The recent focus on commercial and ethnic interests exacerbates the lack of widespread agreement on national interests. "The institutions and capabilities created to serve a grand national purpose in the Cold War," according to Huntington, "are now being suborned and redirected to serve narrow subnational, transnational, and even nonnational purpose."[56] Conversely, the attacks of 9/11 have undoubtedly contributed to a recognition of grand purposes and vital national interests, at least as associated with the War on Terrorism.

The second concern is that states often use force in support of secondary and even tertiary interests. They do this either to protect vital interests, or to support important national values. Secretary of Defense William J. Perry supported the selective use of force and thus distinguished between three categories of interests—vital, important, and humanitarian. He argued that different uses of limited force, and not necessarily applied in an overwhelming manner, were appropriate to protect these interests in the pursuit of limited objectives.[57] Perry's Chairman of the Joint Chiefs, General Shalikashvili, also desired more flexibility in the use of force. He reportedly claimed that he did not have the right to put a sign on his door saying, "I'm sorry—we only do the big ones." The United States has clearly continued to use force in support of non-vital interests or important national values. And wars waged in the name of values invariably turn out to be more controversial than wars waged for interests.[58]

Weinberger borrows heavily from Clausewitz for his third, and relatively uncontroversial, criterion: the importance of having clearly established objectives. According to Clausewitz, "No one starts a war…without first being clear in his own mind what he intends to achieve by that war and how he intends to conduct it."[59] This criterion is common across all of the sets of guidelines. Recognizing the need for clear objectives, however, does not necessarily remove all debate on the issue. The objectives chosen, just as the articulation of the national interests at stake, may not reflect broad agreement.

There are two other points worth considering on this criterion. First, once a war begins, chance, friction, and uncertainty take effect and original political objectives and force requirements, as Michael Handel has observed, can change:

> Weinberger's assumptions are more correct for military interventions/operations that can be carried out swiftly and decisively,…than they are for prolonged interventions and wars. The problem, of course, is that it is often very difficult to tell in advance which interventions will be short and decisive, and which will be costly and long.[60]

The second point is that it is always difficult to determine in advance if a certain compellent or deterrent action will have the desired effect, or result in an unanticipated counterreaction by an adversary. As Richard Haass so aptly puts it, "It is as simple—and as basic—as the difference between winning a battle and winning a war. It only takes one party to initiate hostilities, but it takes everyone involved to bring hostilities to an end."[61]

The next two criteria—public support and last resort—are also common across all of the sets of guidelines. The need to maintain public and political support is common sense but not completely without debate, and certainly not without potentially great difficulty in execution. In the original argument over the Weinberger doctrine, Secretary Shultz took issue with the need for public support prior to initiating action. In his view, the duties of leadership could require action before the mobilization of public support.

> My view is that democratically elected and accountable individuals have been placed in positions where they can and must make decisions to defend our national security. The risk and burden of leadership is that those decisions will receive, or not receive, the support of the people on their merits. The democratic process will deal with leaders who fail to measure up to the standards imposed by the American people….[62]

There is a great deal of historical validity to the "rally-around-the-flag" and "support-the-troops" effect. That approach can be particularly effective for short and decisive campaigns. In prolonged wars, however, the difficulty does not lie so much in obtaining initial public and political support as it does in sustaining it for the duration.[63] Leaders must lead and mobilize public support. That can most easily be done by appeals to moral values or national interests. In any event:

> the inertia of the governed can not be disentangled from the indifference of the government. American leaders have both a circular and a deliberate relationship to public opinion. It is circular because their constituencies are rarely if ever aroused by foreign crises, even genocidal ones, in the absence of political leadership, and yet at the same time U.S. officials continually cite the absence of public support as grounds for inaction.[64]

"Last resort" is an important component of the just war theory of *jus ad bellum*, or just resort in going to war. Americans have traditionally been very reluctant to resort to force unless they have been directly attacked. There is always a strong desire to give diplomacy a chance, or obtain sufficient results through the application of economic sanctions or other pressures. Time is also needed to mobilize domestic and international support. However, it may not always be wise to delay military action. Once again, George Shultz challenged this point, "The idea that force should be used 'only as a last resort' means that, by the time of use, force is the only resort and likely a much more costly one than if used earlier."[65] General Wesley Clark, in his examination of the Kosovo campaign, concluded that the key lesson must be that "nations and alliances should move early to deal with crises while they are still ambiguous and can be dealt with more easily, for delay raises both the costs and the risks. Early action is the objective to which statesmen and military leaders should aspire."[66] All of this has direct relevance for the threat of catastrophic terrorism. Countering undeterrable terrorist organizations armed with weapons of mass destruction places the other instruments of statecraft at a huge disadvantage. "To consider force as a last resort is appropriate when trying to settle inter-state conflict," according to Ivo Daalder, "but when it comes to…preventing the proliferation of weapons of mass destruction, or defeating terrorism waiting too long to employ force can both enhance the cost and reduce the effectiveness of its use."[67]

The last two items on Weinberger's list concern how force should be used. The first of these addresses the importance of committing sufficient forces to accomplish the objectives. The goal is to avoid a long, drawn-out gradual employment of force that may not accomplish the objectives in a swift and decisive manner. This is the essence of the Vietnam Syndrome. The U.S. military wants to avoid a half-hearted approach that results in higher casualties, a prolonged war, and a decision to quit before the mission is accomplished. One significant deterrent to U.S. action in Bosnia was the estimated steep cost of intervening in terms of troops required. For instance, the Joint Staff estimated in 1992 that it would take 50,000 U.S. ground troops to secure the Sarajevo Airport for humanitarian relief operations. The airlift was eventually conducted under the watchful care of only 1,000 Canadian and French forces.[68]

On the other hand, it is normally better to go into a hostile environment with too much rather than too little force. General Powell used the phrase "decisive force"; he indicated that decisive means and results are always preferred, and that if force is used "we should not be equivocal: we should win and win decisively."[69] Decisive means eventually evolved into overwhelming force, and related concepts, such as shock and awe. The controversy about U.S. end strength in Iraq, in both the initial combat phase and the subsequent stabilization and reconstruction phase, will only contribute to renewed military reluctance to undertake operations with less than overwhelming or decisive force. General Wesley Clark has argued in this regard that Operation IRAQI FREEDOM took "unnecessary risk because it skimped on the forces made available to the commanders," during the combat phase, and he claimed the existence of excessive risk during the post-combat phase. "The result was a U.S. force at the operation's end that was incapable of providing security, stopping the looting and sabotage, or establishing a credible presence throughout the country."[70] The all-or-nothing versus limited objective (limited war) debate continues.

Michael Handel refers to the final item, the need for continuous reassessment, as the escape clause. Circumstances may change, or the enemy may respond in an unexpected manner, all necessitating a reassessment of objectives (ends), concepts (ways), and forces (means). That criterion also implies that if the costs become too high or if the objectives do not justify a greater commitment of resources, it may be prudent to terminate the conflict.[71]

Figure 17-4 clearly shows that several of the Weinberger guidelines have evolved and been modified over the years. One of the most important and far-reaching evolutions is the expansion of applicable interests categories and the recognition that limited options for the use of force may be appropriate in the pursuit of less-than-vital interests. Another is the inclusion of the concern about multilateral or international support. That guideline was added in the Clinton administration's national security strategies and reflected a growing interest in ensuring multilateral responses to security issues. Multilateralism obviously included deliberations and support from NATO, but also recognized an enhanced role for the United Nations. America's alliances were one of the keystones of Clinton's selective engagement strategy, and the administration saw the UN as an important actor in the new world order. Having partners when it comes to using force also contributes to gaining and sustaining public support. As Charles Krauthammer argued at the close of the Gulf War, "Americans insist on the multilateral pretense. A large segment of American opinion doubts the legitimacy of unilateral American action, but accepts action taken under the rubric of the 'world community.'" He went on to say that the ultimate problem with "multilateralism is that if you take it seriously you gratuitously forfeit American freedom of action."[72]

Finally, in terms of the evolution of the Weinberger guidelines, there is the inclusion of end state and exit strategy concerns. The desire to establish an exit strategy is principally associated with interventions that do not involve vital interests. If vital interests are at stake, national security experts generally assume that politicians will apply overwhelming force, unilaterally if necessary, until the conflict is resolved. For interventions in support of important or humanitarian issues, there is much more of a premium placed on quickly reaching an agreed-upon end state, getting U.S. forces out, and reconstituting them for the next "big one." Some analysts have argued that this criteria should be expanded to include specific termination conditions, paths to success, and milestones along those paths. Rumsfeld's guidelines, however, seem to challenge this point by specifically cautioning against arbitrary deadlines. He is supported in this view by Richard Haass, who argues that it is important to "avoid a specific end point or certain date for ending the commitment regardless of local developments. Artificial boundaries on a U.S. intervention run the risk of emboldening adversaries, who need only to wait until the deadline has passed, and unnerving allies."[73] End states can also be very ambiguous and constrained, since they rarely include unconditional surrender, regime change, or destruction of the war-making capability of the other side.[74]

Michael Handel's analysis of the Weinberger Doctrine concluded that it represented a utilitarian, realistic yardstick not much concerned with moral and ethical questions, although it does in fact provide useful insights for moral and ethical decisions about the use of force.[75] The proliferation of intrastate conflicts in the post-Cold War world, and the growing threat posed by nonstate actors, will continue to place pressure on decisionmakers to decide when and how to use force. Figure 17-5 represents a score card of sorts to portray a subjective assessment of the application of the Weinberger Doctrine to recent U.S. military operations.

LEGITIMACY

One of the main tenets of the Weinberger Doctrine was the need to garner public and congressional support—"some reasonable assurance we will have the support of the American people and their elected representatives in Congress."[76] Public support represents the will of the people, and as Harry Summers concluded, the failure to invoke that national will was one of the principal strategic failures of the Vietnam War, producing a strategic vulnerability that the North Vietnamese were able to exploit.[77] Public support and national will are both a reflection of the legitimacy with which the use of force is viewed. Legitimacy is fostered and sustained through many channels, including the steadfast application of Weinberger Doctrine-like guidelines, Congressional resolutions and legislation, presidential leadership, and actions of the international community. Legitimacy is thus grounded in both domestic processes and international or multilateral organizations and processes.

Weinberger Doctrine from Vietnam to Iraq

Criterion	Vietnam	Grenada	Lebanon	Panama	Persian Gulf War	Somalia	Haiti (1994)	Bosnia	Kosovo	Iraq (2003)
1. Vital interests at stake	NO	NO	NO	NO	YES	YES	NO	NO	NO	YES
2. Commitment to victory	NO	YES	NO	YES	YES	NO	YES – for regime change NO – nation bldg	NO	NO	YES – for regime change ? – nation bldg
3. Clearly defined pol/mil objectives	NO	YES	NO	YES	YES	YES then NO	NO	?	YES – short term ? – long term	YES
4. Continuous reassessment	YES	YES	YES	YES	YES	YES	YES	YES	YES	YES
5. Public support (mobilized by the gov't)	NO	NO	NO	NO	YES	YES (at first)	YES	YES (?)	YES	YES
6. Last resort	NO	NO	NO	NO	NO	NO	YES	NO	NO	YES/NO
Success or Failure	FAILURE	SUCCESS	FAILURE	SUCCESS	SUCCESS	FAILURE	FAILURE	?	?	?

Figure 17-5. Weinberger Doctrine from Vietnam to Iraq.[78]

The President and the Congress.

Constitutional provisions represent the foundation of legitimacy in the United States. Under the Constitution, the President and Congress share the war powers. The President is commander in chief (Article II, Section 2), but Congress has the power to declare war and raise and support the armed forces (Article I, Section 8). Congress, however, has declared war only on five occasions, the last being World War II. Despite having considerable constitutional authority over decisions about the use of force, Congress has largely deferred to the President as commander in chief, in general recognition that this role makes him responsible for leading the armed forces and gives him the power to repel attacks against the United States. Consequently, the executive branch has executed most military interventions.[79]

In an effort to regain some control over decisions on the use of force, and as a backlash to the Vietnam War, Congress passed the War Powers Resolution (WPR) over President Nixon's veto in 1973. The purpose of the War Powers Resolution was to ensure that Congress and the President share in making decisions about the use of force. Compliance becomes an issue when the President introduces forces abroad in situations that might be construed as hostilities or imminent hostilities. The law included a broad set of triggers for executive consultations and explanations of the rationale for, and the scope and duration of, military operations. If Congress does not grant authorization in a certain period, the law does not permit the action to continue. Presidents have never acknowledged the constitutionality of the War Powers Resolution; however, they have made modest efforts to comply with its reporting requirements, submitting 104 reports to Congress concerning troop deployments abroad.[80] Some deployments were not reported because of the brevity of the operation or the perceived lack of hostilities or imminent hostilities. Most of the reports submitted to Congress are done "consistent with the War Powers Resolution," and not in "compliance" with the WPR.

Despite this record on reporting, a longer-term issue concerns the degree to which Congress is actually participating in the decisions to employ force. The WPR requires the President to consult with Congress prior to introducing U.S. forces into hostilities and to continue consultations as long as the armed forces remain. The conclusion of one Congressional Research study is that there has been very little executive consultation with Congress, "when consultation is defined to mean seeking advice prior to a decision to introduce troops."[81] It is certainly in the country's best interest to garner congressional support, and thus the two branches of government need to work out useful political processes that debate, inform, and support the country's engagement in conflict. From this perspective, a major purpose behind the WPR was not necessarily to constrain the President, but to force the Congress to meet its obligations to share in decisions on the use of force. This would compel members to face within a predictable period and under specified procedures the fundamental question regarding military action by the United States: Does the Congress endorse or oppose the commitment of American blood and treasure to a particular mission?"[82] The question is appropriate for Congress. As confirmed by Secretary Weinberger, U.S. military personnel want to know that it has the backing of the public—a commitment affirmed through a constitutional political process.[83]

The WPR played an important role in the Persian Gulf War of 1991. In response to the Iraqi invasion of Kuwait in 1990, President Bush notified Congress that he had deployed forces to the region. Although he had not consulted with Congress before acting, both Houses later adopted resolutions supporting the deployment. Throughout the fall of 1990, there was intense debate within Congress concerning the use of force. Urged by congressional leaders, President Bush later asked for a resolution supporting the use of all necessary means to implement the UN decrees on Iraq. On January 12, 1991, both Houses, by narrow margins, approved a joint resolution authorizing the use of force pursuant to UN resolution 678, which had been passed on November 29, 1990.[84]

In the crisis in Bosnia, on the other hand, the United States participated without congressional authorization in humanitarian airlifts into Sarajevo, naval monitoring and sanctions, and aerial enforcement of no-fly zones and safe havens. In late 1995, after President Clinton committed over 20,000 combat troops as part of the NATO-led peacekeeping force, Congress considered several bills and resolutions authorizing this deployment, but failed to reach a consensus. In 1999, President Clinton ordered U.S. military forces to participate in the NATO-led military operation in Kosovo, without specific authorization from the Congress. This was a state of affairs that one analyst has termed "virtual consent," in which the public is consulted but the formal institutions of democracy are bypassed: "The decay of institutional checks and balances on the war-making power of the executive has received almost no attention in the debate over the Kosovo conflict. This suggests that citizens no longer even care whether their elected politicians exercise their constitutional responsibilities. We have allowed ourselves to accept virtual consent in the most important political matter of all: war and peace."[85]

The catastrophic events of 9/11 initially created a united sense of purpose between the executive and Congress. Only three days after the terrorist attacks, Congress passed a Joint Resolution authorizing the President "to use all necessary and appropriate force against those nations, organizations, or persons he determines planned, authorized, committed, or aided the terrorist attacks." Three weeks later, "consistent with the War Powers Resolution," President Bush reported to Congress the use of force against Afghanistan.[86] In a similar manner, Congress passed the Joint Resolution, "Authorization for the Use of Military Force Against Iraq," in October 2002. This resolution authorized the President to use the armed forces of the United States "as he determines to be necessary and appropriate," to defend the United States against the threat posed by Iraq and to enforce all relevant UN Security Council Resolutions regarding Iraq. The President, in turn, dutifully reported to the Congress on March 21, 2003, "consistent with the War Powers Resolution" and pursuant to his authority as commander in chief, that he had "directed U.S. Armed Forces operating with other coalition forces, to commence operations on March 19, 2003, against Iraq."[87]

The political storm gathering around the 9/11 Commission and the ongoing struggle in Iraq will constitute a severe test of the nation's willingness to support a prolonged and deadly conflict. The legitimacy of these actions will largely be dependent on the President's ability to mobilize public opinion, and the willingness of Congress to continue to provide support. According to Alton Frye, "unless there is continuing consultation in good faith between Congress and the Executive, the unity that marks the beginning of the campaign against terrorism could degenerate into the profound disunity that scarred American politics thirty years ago."[88] But the harsh reality is that Congress rallies around victory and piles on in defeat. Success matters more than procedure in the politics of making war.[89]

The United Nations.

The founding of the United Nations substantially narrowed the legitimacy of the use of force by individual nation-states. The UN Charter indicates in its Preamble that the UN is established "to save succeeding generations from the scourge of war," and its substantive provisions obligate the member states to "settle their international disputes by peaceful means" (Article 2(3)) and to "refrain…from the threat of use of force against the territorial integrity or political independence of any state…." (Article 2(4)). In place of the traditional right of states to resort to force, the charter creates a system of collective security in which the Security Council is authorized to "determine the existence of any threat to the peace" and to "decide what measures shall be taken…to maintain international peace and security" (Article 39).[90]

The UN security apparatus, created in 1945, was a hybrid, combining a universal quality with a great power concert. The system did not work well during the Cold War because the UN was kept on the sidelines by U.S.-Soviet bipolar rivalry. With few exceptions, UN involvement in use of force decisions began in the 1990s. The evolving nature of global threats, however, has caused a reexamination of the collective security apparatus. UN Secretary General Kofi Annan helped set the stage for this process: "The United Nations Charter declares that 'armed force shall not be used, save in the common interest.' But what is the common interest? Who shall define it? Who shall defend it? Under whose authority?"[91]

Article 51 of the UN Charter recognizes the inherent right of self-defense: "Nothing in the present Charter shall impair the inherent right of individual or collective self-defense if an armed attack occurs against a member of the United Nations, until the Security Council has taken measures necessary to maintain international peace and security." Some authorities interpret Article 51 to permit anticipatory self-defense in response to an imminent attack. Such an interpretation allows action, either unilaterally or collectively, in self-defense, or preemptively based on an interpretation of imminent threat. The threat of catastrophic terrorism argues for a requirement to establish intelligible and transparent criteria of imminent threat that could provide for legitimate unilateral, coalition of the willing, or, hopefully, UN Security Council action.[92] Even Kofi Annan has suggested that UN members should consider developing "criteria for an early authorization of coercive measures to address certain types of threats—for instance, terrorists groups armed with weapons of mass destruction."[93] Article 106 of the charter can be interpreted to allow coalitions of states to take action to maintain international peace and security pending UN Security Council action. This article was originally added to accommodate regional alliances such as the RIO Pact and NATO. By modifying certain aspects of the charter to include Article 106, a better understanding may be developed for the legitimate requirements for multilateral response to threats outside the confines of the Security Council.

Based on the use of force in the last decade, some analysts have argued that the UN Security Council must be reformed: enlarged to become more representative, and restructured to replace the veto system. One rationale for the elimination of the veto power of the permanent five is based on the need for legitimacy:

> All modern military operations need international legitimacy if they are going to succeed. Consequently, the great powers, especially America, face a difficult choice: they can either maintain the veto, and embark on unsanctioned military adventures with their partners only to see these fail because of lack of international approval; or they can surrender veto power in return for the increased likelihood of securing majority approval for the use of military power.[94]

As this argument relates to the debate in the UN about Iraq, France, or any other country on the Security Council, should be in a position to adopt and support a particular view, but it should not be in a position to block pursuit of a vital interest and put at risk the entire UN enterprise. "What do you do if, at the end of the day, the Security Council refuses to back you?" asks Charles Krauthammer, "Do you allow yourself to be dictated to on issues of vital national—and international security?"[95] Thomas Friedman answered the question, "The French and others know that…their refusal to present Saddam with a threat only guarantees U.S. unilateralism and undermines the very UN structure that is the best vehicle for their managing of U.S. power."[96]

This debate also touches on the concept of multilateralism. Americans define multilateralism as a policy that actively seeks to gain the support of allies. As such, Security Council authorization is a means to an end—gaining more allies—not an end in itself. The Europeans, on the other hand, view multilateralism much more narrowly as a legitimate sanction from a duly constituted international body—the Security Council. Despite the fact that the United States enjoyed the support of dozens of nations for the war in Iraq, and is supported by 33 troop-contributing coalition partners as I write, many critics continue to charge that the United States is acting unilaterally. The current debate "over multilateralism and legitimacy is thus not only about the principles of law, or even about the supreme authority of the UN; it is also about the transatlantic struggle for influence. It is Europe's response to the unipolar predicament."[97] In any event, it is clear that any new arrangements to exercise collective security need to be developed and given legitimacy by the international community.

CONCLUSION

War between nation-states endures because human interests, values, and commitments are often irreconcilable. In addition, because of the existence of a much more insidious kind of violence—catastrophic terrorism—military power remains the ultimate defender of common human values, and the ultimate arbiter of human disagreements:

> The efficacy of force endures. For in anarchy, force and politics are connected. By itself, military power guarantees neither survival nor prosperity. But it is almost always the essential ingredient for both. Because resort to force is the ultimate card of all states, the seriousness of a state's intentions is conveyed fundamentally by its having a credible military posture. Without it, a state's diplomacy generally lacks effectiveness.[98]

Strategists must be able to answer the classic charge from Clausewitz, "No one starts a war…without first being clear in his own mind what he intends to achieve by that war and how he intends to conduct it." The political objectives for the use of force must be continually reassessed in light of the changing nature of warfare and the proliferation of nontraditional threats. Likewise, remembering the caution raised by President George H.W. Bush that there can be no single or simple set of fixed rules for the use of force, the prudent strategist needs to keep in mind relevant questions and issues he should evaluate in each particular circumstance that might require military force. Finally, democracies have the unique challenge of dealing with the elusive and malleable concept of legitimacy. "Discovering where legitimacy lies," according to Robert Kagan, "at any given moment in history is an art, not a science reducible to the reading of international legal documents."[99] Still, there are immutable principles, such as that of Horace, who cautioned that "force without wisdom falls of its own weight." Today, more than ever, the key question concerning the use of force is not whether it is lawful, but whether it is wise.[100]

ENDNOTES - CHAPTER 17

1. The author would like to acknowledge the grateful assistance of Dr. Charles Krupnick and Dr. David Jablonsky in reviewing and making valuable suggestions for this chapter.

2. Han J. Morgenthau, *Politics Among Nations*, 5th Ed., New York: Alfred A. Knopf, 1973, p. 29.

3. Anarchy refers to the absence of government, but should not be confused with chaos. International politics exhibits a great deal of order, regularity, and cooperation, but also includes much coercion, unpredictability, and bloodshed. Robert J. Art, *A Grand Strategy for America*, Ithaca, NY: Cornell University Press, 2003, p. 4. Kenneth Waltz is quoted in Robert J. Art, "The Fungibility of Force," in Robert J. Art and Kenneth N. Waltz, eds., *The Use of Force: Military Power and International Politics*, 5th Ed., New York: Rowman & Littlefield Publishers, Inc., 1999, pp. 5-6.

4. *The Military Balance: 2003-2004*, London: The International Institute for Strategic Studies, 2003. Also refer to Anup Shah, "High Military Expenditures in Some Places," available from *www.globalissues.org/Geopolitics/ArmsTrade/Spending.asp*.

5. Art, "The Fungibility of Force," p. 4.

6. Paul Kennedy, *The Rise and Fall of the Great Powers*, New York: Vintage Books, 1989, p. 515. Kennedy posits two challenges for the longevity of every major power: "whether, in the military/strategical realm, it can preserve a reasonable balance between the nation's perceived defense requirements and the means it possesses to maintain those commitments; and whether, it can preserve the technological and economic bases of power," p. 514. His basic declinist argument is that if a "nation overextends itself geographically and strategically" and chooses "to devote a large proportion of its total income to 'protection,' leaving less for 'productive investment,' it is likely to find its economic output slowing down, with dire implications for its long-term capacity to maintain both its citizens' consumption demands and its international position," p. 539. The United States was able to harness the economic vitality of the information age and thus avoid the predictions of decline at the end of the 20th century. Perhaps it will not be as fortunate in this new century. James Fallows, "The Hollow Army," *The Atlantic Monthly*, March 2004.

7. John Baylis and James J. Wirtz, "Introduction," in John Baylis, James Wirtz, Eliot Cohen, and Colin Gray, eds. *Strategy in the Contemporary World: An Introduction to Strategic Studies*, Oxford, UK: Oxford University Press, 2002, p. 12; Carl Von Clausewitz, *On War*, Michael Howard and Peter Paret, eds./trans., Princeton, NJ: Princeton University Press, 1976, pp. 88, 605. As famous as this dictum is, it is not fully accepted without some debate. Colin Gray goes into some depth about this issue in his book, *Modern Strategy*. He goes so far as to say, "Although Clausewitz was more wise than foolish in this dictum, the wisdom in the formula is hostage to the folly." He concludes his initial review of this topic by stating that "the idea of force as an agent of political purpose is generally persuasive," but should be viewed as the product of not only political purpose, but also of an ongoing political process. Colin S. Gray, *Modern Strategy*, Oxford, UK: Oxford University Press, 1999, p. 30, and Chapter 2, "Strategy, Politics, Ethics," pp. 48-74; Colin L. Powell, "US Forces: Challenges Ahead," *Foreign Affairs*, Vol. 71, No. 5, Winter, 1992/93, p. 39. General Powell contrasted the success of military operations in the 1990s with the failed mission to Lebanon in 1983. Concerning Lebanon, he stated that we, "inserted those proud warriors into the middle of a five-faction civil war complete with terrorists, hostage-takers,

and a dozen spies in every camp." Perhaps the successes of the 1990s resulted from simpler problems or an avoidance of the very complex—a prescription that the West may not be able to follow in the new century.

8. *Joint Publication (JP) 1, Joint Warfare of the Armed Forces of the United States,* Washington, DC: The Joint Staff, November 14, 2000, p. I-4.

9. Robert J. Art, "To What Ends Military Power?," *International Security,* Vol. 4, No. 4, Spring 1980, pp. 3-35.

10. Figure is a modified version from David E. Johnson, Karl P. Mueller, and William H. Taft, V, *Conventional Coercion Across the Spectrum of Operations: The Utility of U.S. Military Forces in the Emerging Security Environment,* Santa Monica, CA: Rand, 2002, p. 9. Several noted analysts, including Art and Gray, are more inclined to classify compellence as the sole coercive component. Colin Gray, in *Maintaining Effective Deterrence,* Carlisle, PA: Strategic Studies Institute, U.S. Army War College, August 2003, p. 13, refers to compellence as coercion or coercive diplomacy. But he later recognizes that deterrence is "executed as a coercive strategy intended to control unfriendly behavior," p. 17. Thomas Schelling, who coined the term "compellence," also concluded that, "'Coercion'...includes 'deterrent' as well as 'compellent' intentions." *Arms and Influence,* New Haven: Yale University Press, 1966, p. 71.

11. JP 1, p. III-1.

12. Schelling, pp. 1-2.

13. Art, "To What Ends Military Power," pp. 5-6. Richard Haass includes preventive attacks and punitive attacks, along with deterrence and compellence, as the principle uses of military power. See Richard N. Haass, *Intervention: The Use of American Military Force in the Post-Cold War World,* Washington, DC: The Carnegie Endowment for International Peace, 1994, pp. 50-56. For another interesting discussion of preventive war and preemption as strategic choices, refer to Richard K. Betts, *Surprise Attack,* Washington, DC: The Brookings Institution, 1982, pp. 141-149.

14. Daniel Byman and Matthew Waxman, *Confronting Iraq: U.S. Policy and the Use of Force Since the Gulf War,* Santa Monica, CA: Rand, 2000, p. 6.

15. Schelling, p. 3.

16. Johnson et al., pp. 15-17; Byman and Waxman, pp. 8-9.

17. John J. Mearsheimer, *Conventional Deterrence,* Ithaca, NY: Cornell University Press, 1983, p. 14; Amos A. Jordan, William J. Taylor, Jr., and Michael J. Mazar, *American National Security,* Baltimore, MD: The John Hopkins University Press, 1999, p. 38. A fundamental debate concerning U.S. grand strategy involves the continued deterrability of U.S. opponents. Failed and rogue states may not be viewed as rational, particularly from a Western perspective. Nevertheless, as David Jablonsky argues, even crazy states can be deterred: "...a state may behave rationally in an instrumental sense of effectively achieving its ends or goals which in themselves may be 'crazy.'" He emphasizes that there must be at least a modicum of instrumental rationality on the part of a nation to be deterred. David Jablonsky, *Strategic Rationality is not Enough: Hitler and the Concept of Crazy States,* Carlisle, PA: Strategic Studies Institute, U.S. Army War College, 1991. Unfortunately, the current list of opponents includes highly lethal non-state organizations, such as the al Qaeda terrorist network. As Paul Davis and Brian Jenkins argue, this class of terrorist, driven by extremely strong, messianic, religious views, lacks instrumental rationality, and therefore cannot be deterred and must be eradicated. Paul K. Davis and Brian Michael Jenkins, *Deterrence & Influence in Counterterrorism,* Santa Monica, CA: Rand, 2002.

18. Henry Kissinger, *Diplomacy,* New York: Simon & Schuster, 1994, p. 608. There is a vast literature on the evolution of nuclear strategy during the Cold War. One source for a systematic and comprehensive treatment of the major themes of nuclear strategy is Lawrence Freedman, *The Evolution of Nuclear Strategy,* New York: St. Martin's Press, 1983. Despite using the word "evolution" in the title, he claims that it is somewhat misleading. In the introduction he mentions the cyclical character of the debates and states that "much of what is offered today as a profound and new insight was said yesterday; and usually in a more concise and literate manner." The utility of military power during the Cold War, particularly concerning great power competition, was constrained by the logic of nuclear deterrence. As Bernard Brodie declared, "Thus far the chief purpose of our military establishment has been to win wars. From now on its chief purpose must be to avert them." Bernard Brodie, "Implications for Military Policy," in *The Absolute Weapon: Atomic Power and World Order,* San Diego, CA: Harcourt Brace, 1946, p. 76.

19. Gray, *Maintaining Effective Deterrence*, p. 13. See also Johnson et al., pp. 10-12; Haass, pp. 50-51; Philip Bobbitt, *The Shield of Achilles: War, Peace, and the Course of History*, New York: Alfred A. Knopf, 2002, pp. 14-15, 328-329. Bobbitt makes the argument that extended deterrence has driven U.S. nuclear strategy, not central deterrence. Concerning a more contemporary issue—missile defense—Bobbitt reiterates the ongoing importance of extended deterrence: "Extended deterrence is the single most effective instrument the United States has to prevent major-state proliferation because it permits these states to develop their economies without diverting vast resources to the nuclear arms competition, and yet remain relatively safe from nuclear attack." Although the United States has vastly reduced and restructured its nuclear force posture, nuclear deterrence retains its relevancy even after the end of the Cold War.

20. Kissinger, p. 608.

21. Gray, *Maintaining Effective Deterrence*, p. vii. See also William T. Johnsen, *The Future Roles of U.S. Military Power and their Implications*, Carlisle, PA: Strategic Studies Institute, U.S. Army War College, April 17, 1997, p. 7; and Bobbitt, p. 12. Colin Gray points out that the current concern is not about irrational leaders—those leaders who cannot connect means purposefully with ends. "The problem is not the irrational adversary, instead it is the perfectly rational foe who seeks purposefully, and rationally, to achieve goals that appear wholly unreasonable to us." He goes on to argue that he believes al Qaeda is deterrable. "Al Qaeda has many would-be martyrs in its ranks, but the organization is most careful of the lives of its key officers, and it functions strategically. It can be deterred by the fact and expectation of strategic failure," Gray, *Maintaining Effective Deterrence*, pp. vii, viii, 21-22. He also recommends several practical measures to enhance the role of deterrence under the current circumstances and recognizes the synergy achieved through combining elements of both deterrent and defensive, preventive-preemptive postures. "A little prevention-preemption would do wonders for the subsequent effectiveness of deterrence in the minds of those whose motives were primarily worldly and pragmatic." *Ibid.*, pp. v, 29. Gray's bottom line is that deterrence, though diminished in significance, remains absolutely essential as an element of U.S. grand strategy.

22. *The National Security Strategy of the United States of America*, Washington, DC: The White House, September 2002, p. 15. Also, see John Lewis Gaddis, *Surprise, Security, and the American Experience*, Cambridge, MA: Harvard University Press, 2004, pp. 69-70.

23. Byman and Waxman, p. 6; See also, Art, *Grand Strategy*, 5; Schelling, 72.

24. Art, "To What Ends Military Power?," p. 8. See also, Schelling, pp. 69-91. Byman and Waxman argue that it is often difficult to distinguish between compellence and deterrence. "Classifying cases as compellence as opposed to deterrence is always speculative to some degree, given the inherent opacity of enemy intentions. And, ultimately, general deterrence and compellence are codependent, as success or failure in coercion affects the coercing power's general reputation to some degree and thus its overall ability to deter," p. 7.

25. Art, "To What Ends Military Power?," pp. 8-10; and Haass, pp. 53-54.

26. A slightly modified version of a chart found in, Barry M. Blechman and Tamara Cofman Wittes, "Defining Moment: The Threat and Use of Force in American Foreign Policy," *Political Science Quarterly*, Vol. 114, No. 1, Spring 1999, p. 7.

27. *Ibid.*, pp. 5-11. This point was explicitly expressed by Mohamed Farad Aideed to Ambassador Oakley concerning the disastrous U.S. involvement in Somalia: "We have studied Vietnam and Lebanon and know how to get rid of Americans, by killing them so public opinion will put an end to things."

28. *Ibid.*, p. 27.

29. Bobbitt, p. 14; *The Quadrennial Defense Review Report*, Washington, DC: The Department of Defense, September 30, 2001, p. 11. For a good discussion of the benefits of forward presence, see Art, *A Grand Strategy for America*, pp. 139-145; Johnsen., p. 11.

30. Thomas P.M. Barnett, "The Pentagon's New Map," *Esquire*, March 2003, p. 228.

31. Andrew Bacevich, *American Empire: The Realities & Consequences of U.S. Diplomacy*, Cambridge, MA: Harvard University Press, 2002, p. 128. Bacevich argues that the United States has been pursuing a grand strategy of "open-

ness" since the days of Woodrow Wilson. This strategy seeks economic expansion and aims to foster an open and integrated international order, thereby perpetuating the undisputed primacy of the world's sole remaining super power.

32. *National Security Strategy*, 2002, p. 30.

33. *QDR*, 2001, p. 12.

34. Barton Gellman, "Keeping the U.S. First: Pentagon Would Preclude a Rival Superpower," *The Washington Post*, March 11, 1992, p. 1. The principal author of the document was then Under Secretary of Defense for Policy, Paul Wolfowitz. When the draft DPG was leaked it was roundly criticized and, consequently, dramatically toned down in the final version. It seems that the Secretary meant what he said 10 years ago, in that it is now an accepted tenet of the U.S. defense strategy.

35. Donald H. Rumsfeld, "Transforming the Military," *Foreign Affairs*, Vol. 81, No. 3, May/June 2002, p. 27. He goes on to cite several specific examples: deployment of effective missile defenses to dissuade ballistic missile programs; hardening U.S. space systems to dissuade the development of killer satellites; and new earth-penetrating weapons that would make deep-underground facilities obsolete as hiding places for terrorists or WMD capabilities.

36. Richard Kugler, "Dissuasion as a Strategic Concept," *Strategic Forum*, Institute for National Strategic Studies, NDU, No. 196, December 2002, pp. 1-2.

37. Gray, *Maintaining Effective Deterrence*, p. 14.

38. Joseph S. Nye, Jr., "U.S. Power and Strategy After Iraq," *Foreign Affairs*, Vol. 82, No. 4, July/August 2003, p. 72.

39. This list is taken from JP 1, *Doctrine for the Armed Forces of the United States*, May 14, 2007, pp. I-15 – I-17; and Haass, pp. 51-65.

40. Art, *A Grand Strategy for America*, pp. 5-6.

41. Jennifer D. Kibbe, "The Rise of the Shadow Warriors," *Foreign Affairs*, Vol. 83, No. 2, March/April 2004, p. 104. Covert actions are distinct from clandestine missions. The term "clandestine" refers to the secrecy of the operation itself; "covert" refers to the secrecy of its sponsor.

42. United States Special Operations Command, *Posture Statement 2003-2004*, p. 36.

43. Kibbe, p. 105. The definition and oversight requirements were contained in the Intelligence Authorization Act for fiscal year 1991.

44. Donald Rumsfeld, *2003 Secretary of Defense Annual Report to the President and the Congress*, Washington, DC: The Pentagon, 2003, p. 2. This report highlights the historic change in the charter of the USSOCOM, from supporting missions of the other regional combatant commanders, to planning and executing its own missions in the global War on Terrorism. Kibbe, p. 109.

45. *Joint Publication (JP) 3-0, Doctrine for Joint Operations*, September 10, 2001, pp. II-3-II-4.

46. Clausewitz, *On War*, p. 605; Sun Tzu, *The Art of War*, Samuel B. Griffith, trans., New York: Oxford University Press, 1963, p. 142; and Colin Powell, *My American Journey*, New York: Ballantine Books, 1995.

47. Michael Ignatieff, *Virtual War: Kosovo and Beyond*, New York: Picador USA, 2000, p. 179.

48. The discussion in this section is related to the discussion on just war theory, as presented in Chapter 3, "Ethical Issues in War: An Overview," by Martin L. Cook, in *U.S. Army War College Guide to National Security Policy and Strategy*, J. Boone Bartholomees, Jr., ed., Carlisle, PA: Strategic Studies Institute, U.S. Army War College, 2006. This section will focus on political and military considerations, as opposed to the international legal framework associated with just war theory. However, it should be clear that many of the issues overlap.

49. Michael I. Handel, *Masters of War: Classical Strategic Thought*, 3rd Ed., London: Frank Cass, 2001, pp. 10-11.

50. Edward Luttwark refers to this as "Napoleonic" warfare—wars fought for grand purposes, implying the decisive employment of large forces. Edward N. Luttwark, "Toward Post-Heroic Warfare: The Obsolescence of Total War," *Foreign Affairs*, Vol. 74, No. 3, May/June 1995, pp. 113-114.

51. Alexander L. George, "The Role of Force in Diplomacy: Continuing Dilemma for U.S. Foreign Policy," talk at CSIS Security Strategy Symposium, June 25, 1998, available from *www.pbs.org/wgbh/pages/frontline/shows/military/force/article.html*; Colin Powell, "U.S. Forces: Challenges Ahead," *Foreign Affairs*, Vol. 71, No. 5, Winter 1992/93, p. 36. Also see, Les Aspin, "The Use and Usefulness of Military Forces in the Post-Cold War, Post-Soviet World," from an address to the Jewish Institute for National Security Affairs, Washington, DC, September 21, 1992, excerpted in Haass, pp. 183-190.

52. Handel, p. 10; Evan Thomas, "The Vietnam Question," *Newsweek*, April 19, 2004.

53. George P. Shultz, *Turmoil and Triumph: My Years as Secretary of State*, New York: Charles Scribner's Sons, 1993, p. 650.

54. The Weinberger doctrine was first presented in a speech before the National Press Club, November 28, 1984. It's rendition for the figure is from Handel, pp. 310-311. The criteria are numbered in accordance with the sequence in which they were originally presented. However, that sequence is broken on the chart to help categorize criteria as either addressing the "when" or "how" of using force. Colin Powell's list is taken from Aspen, as excerpted in Haass, pp. 184-185. The best first person account is from Powell's *Foreign Affairs* article which was previously cited. Secretary William Perry's list is from "The Ethical Use of Military Force," the Forrestal Lecture, Foreign Affairs Conference, U.S. Naval Academy, Annapolis, MD, April 18, 1995. These points were largely incorporated in all subsequent National Security Strategies issued by the Clinton Administration. The final set, from Secretary Donald Rumsfeld, is taken from his remarks before the *Fortune* Magazine Global Forum, November 11, 2002.

55. Samuel Huntington, "The Erosion of American National Interests," *Foreign Affairs*, Vol. 76, No. 5, September/October 1997, p. 35. Huntington goes on to state that "national interests usually combine security and material concerns, on the one hand, and moral and ethical concerns, on the other." *A National Security Strategy for A Global Age*, Washington, DC: The White House, December 2000, p. 4; George, p. 3.

56. Huntington, p. 37.

57. Handel, p. 312; Bobbitt, p. 298. Perry was initially responding to the ongoing debate about committing U.S. forces to help solve the crisis in Bosnia. The National Security Advisor for Bush, 41, Brent Scowcroft, clearly reflected the opposite view that helped keep U.S. forces out of Bosnia for years. "We could never satisfy ourselves that the amount of involvement we thought it would take was justified in terms of U.S. interests involved… We were heavily national interest oriented… If it [war] stayed in Bosnia, it might be horrible, but it did not affect us." Quoted in Samantha Power, "*A Problem From Hell*": *America and the Age of Genocide*, New York: New Republic Book, 2002, p. 288.

58. David Halberstam, *War in a Time of Peace: Bush, Clinton, and the Generals*, New York: Scribner, 2001, pp. 390-391; Ignatieff, p. 72.

59. Clausewitz, p. 579.

60. Handel, p. 316.

61. Haass, p. 74.

62. Shultz, p. 650.

63. Handel, p. 318.

64. Power, p. 509. Public support can be very fickle, based on the latest news from the battlefield, and is particularly problematic in prolonged and costly military operations. Handel, p. 319.

65. Haass, pp. 88-89; Shultz, p. 650.

66. Wesley K. Clark, *Waging Modern War: Bosnia, Kosovo and the Future of Combat*, New York: Public Affairs, 2001, p. 423.

67. Ivo H. Daalder, "The Use of Force in a Changing World – U.S. and European Perspectives," Washington, DC: The Brookings Institution, November 25, 2002, p. 12.

68. Handel, p. 314; Power, p. 283. Another example cited is the claim, once again in 1992, by LTG Barry McCaffrey, to Congress, that 400,000 troops would be needed to enforce a ceasefire. Scowcroft conceded that the military's analysis was probably inflated.

69. Powell, "U.S. Forces: Challenges Ahead," p. 40.

70. Wesley K. Clark, *Winning Modern Wars: Iraq, Terrorism, and the American Empire,* New York: Public Affairs, 2003, pp. 86-87. Clark went on to conclude that the "ensuing disorder vitiated some of the boost in U.S. credibility won on the battlefield, and it opened the door for deeper and more organized resistance during the following weeks."

71. Handel, p. 317.

72. Quoted in Harry G. Summers, Jr., *On Strategy II: A Critical Analysis of the Gulf War*, New York: Dell Publishing, 1992, p. 252.

73. Haass, pp. 76-77.

74. Ignatieff, p. 208. As an example of an ambiguous end state, he cites the military technical agreement that concluded the conflict between NATO and Serbia. It specified the terms and timing of Serbian withdrawal and the entry of NATO troops, but left entirely undefined the juridical status of the territory over which the war was fought.

75. Handel, p. 324.

76. Handel, p. 311.

77. Summers, *On Strategy*, p. 43.

78. This chart has been modified from one that appears in Handel, p. 326. Handel's chart did not include Haiti, 1994, and Iraq, 2003. Handel had also included a column for Central America, which has been omitted. As mentioned in the body of the chapter, these ratings should be viewed as subject to open debate and discussion. In fact a useful exercise would be to determine your own ratings for particular interventions. As one example of the subjectiveness of these ratings, concerning Kosovo, Handel concluded that the public supported the operation. Ignatieff, on the other hand, stated that "the public did not sign up to 78 days' worth of bombing, and had they been asked, most would have said no," p. 183

79. Roger H. Davidson and Walter J. Oleszek, *Congress and Its Members*, 9th Ed., Washington DC: Congressional Quarterly, Inc., 2004, p. 439.

80. Richard F. Grimmett, "War Powers Resolution: Presidential Compliance," *Issue Brief for Congress*, Washington, DC: Congressional Research Service, updated March 24, 2003, CRS; Robert B. Zoellick, "Congress and the Making of US Foreign Policy," *Survival*, Vol. 41, No. 4, Winter 1999-2000, p. 33; Grimmett. Of the 104 reports, Ford submitted 4; Carter, 1; Reagan, 14; George H.W. Bush, 7; Clinton, 60; and George W. Bush, 18; p. CRS-11.

81. *Ibid.,* p. CRS-13.

82. Alton Frye, "Applying the War Powers Resolution to the War on Terrorism," testimony before the Senate Judiciary Committee, April 17, 2002.

83. Zoellick, p. 34.

84. George Bush and Brent Scowcroft, *A World Transformed*, New York: Vintage Books, 1998, p. 446. For a superb discussion of the intricacies of gaining both domestic and international support for the use of force, refer to pp. 355-449. Concerning this debate, Brent Scowcroft had this to say: "We were confident that the Constitution was on our side when it came to the president's discretion to use force if necessary: If we sought congressional involvement, it would not be authority we were after, but support," p. 398, and President Bush added; "…even had Congress not passed the resolutions I would have acted and ordered our troops into combat. I know it would have caused an outcry, but it was the right thing to do. I was comfortable in my own mind that I had the constitutional authority," p. 446.

85. Grimmett, pp. CRS-3 – CRS-4; Ignatieff, pp. 180-181.

86. Davidson and Oleszek, p. 440.

87. "Congressional Joint Resolution to Authorize Use of Force Against Iraq," *Washington Post*, October 11, 2002, p. A12; Grimmett, p. CRS-12.

88. Frye, testimony before the Senate Judiciary Committee.

89. John Lindsay, cited in Zoellick, p. 34.

90. David M. Ackerman, "International Law and the Preemptive Use of force Against Iraq," *CRS Report for Congress*, Washington, DC: Congressional Research Service, updated march 17, 2003, p. CRS-3.

91. Kofi Annan, "The Legitimacy to Intervene," *Financial Times,* December 31, 1999, available from *www.globalpolicy.org/secgen/interven.htm.*

92. John Burroughs et al., "The United Nations Charter and the Use of Force Against Iraq," October 2, 2002, p. 2; Robert S. Litwak, "The New Calculus of Pre-emption," *Survival*, Vol. 44, No. 4, Winter 2003/04, p. 73.

93. Quoted in Robert Kagan, "America's Crisis of Legitimacy," *Foreign Affairs*, Vol. 83, No. 2, March/April 2004, p. 81.

94. Ignatieff, p. 182.

95. Charles Krauthammer, "The Unipolar Moment Revisited," *The National Interest*, Number 70, Winter 2002/03, p. 17.

96. Thomas Friedman, "Present At…What?" *New York Times,* February 12, 2003.

97. Kagan, pp. 82-83.

98. Art, "To What Ends Military Power?" p. 35; The United States Commission on National Security/21st Century, *New World Coming: American Security in the 21st Century*, September 15, 1999, pp. 3-5.

99. Kagan, p. 77.

100. Michael J. Glennon, "Why the Security Council Failed," *Foreign Affairs*, Vol. 82, No. 3, May/June 2003, p. 16.

III.

Strategic Issues and Considerations

CHAPTER 18

APPLYING CLAUSEWITZ AND SYSTEMS THINKING TO DESIGN

Glenn K. Cunningham
Charles D. Allen

Strategic campaign planners and statesmen often begin their analyses by assuming a linear cause-and-effect relationship, similar to a move-countermove exchange in chess. Although such linear formulations may sometimes be a useful starting point, they can also be disastrously misleading. Systems thinking, however, provides an alternative that compensates for the limits of linear reasoning in military design. This chapter considers the implications of systems thinking as a theory and applies the implications of systems complexity specifically to military operational design. The perspectives of Carl von Clausewitz, the Prussian military theorist, inform current doctrine on design, and the Clausewitzian concept of center of gravity provides an essential tool for commanders to employ in designing campaigns.

For centuries, the basic approach of science relied on linear logic and a belief that the best method for understanding any phenomenon was to break that phenomenon into parts that could be studied independently. Doing so was thought to simplify a problem, thereby making it more manageable for the scientist. The approach assumed the whole was simply equal to the sum of its parts. The logic of this linear thinking and its associated mechanical metaphors transferred outside of the natural sciences and applied to many other disciplines.

Beginning in the 1950s, pioneers of the systems paradigm questioned whether this mechanistic approach was the best method for gaining knowledge of the natural and social worlds. Some of these theorists were concerned that the expansion of knowledge was so great that it resulted in excessive specialization, which prevented scientists from communicating across disciplines, so that physicists, biologists, and sociologists were isolated from one another. The advocates of a systems approach wanted to create a general theory that could identify the existence of laws that might apply to similar structures in different fields. Underlying this emerging view was recognition that the whole was *not* merely the sum of its parts, but rather, something synergistically more. Consequently, a new approach organized around the concept of *systems* took root. Ludwig von Bertalanffy, one of systems theory's early proponents, saw the purpose of systems theory as "an important means in the process of developing new branches of knowledge into exact science, i.e., a system of mathematical laws."[1] Such a conception of systems theory implied a promise of greater certainty with increased ability to predict than the earlier mechanistic approach.

The dynamic behavior of closed systems is quite different from that of open systems in that the former allow greater certainty and prediction. Closed systems consist of limited variables and often impermeable boundaries between elements and so typically act in a predictable, mechanistic way. For example, a person knows what the response of a thermostat will be when one adjusts the temperature up or down. In contrast, a more open system, like a social-political system, does not respond to some stimulus, say, a stock market fluctuation, in a predictable pattern. The unpredictability of open systems stems in part from the fact that many more variables are at work than in closed systems, boundaries between elements are permeable, and linkages are often both tenuous and connected in unforeseeable ways. Ironically, initial systems thinking sought greater certainty and control to facilitate prediction and enhance interdisciplinary communication. However, when the concepts were applied to more open systems like organizations or societies, the expected outcomes did not materialize and instead resulted in both unanticipated and unintended consequences.

SYSTEMS THINKING AND ORGANIZATIONAL DESIGN

When thinking of an organization, one tends to look at its structure as a wiring diagram that depicts departments and functions in the form of a bureaucracy—hierarchical and well-defined. Military organizations in particular have long been considered illustrative of such structure and processes. Gareth Morgan conceptualized organizations as functioning like a machine.[2] The machine metaphor views organizations as closed systems with inputs, internal processes, and outcomes. Each part of the organization fits together by design so the smoother and more standardized the operation, the more efficient is its production. The scientific management concepts of Frederick Taylor supported the view of organizations as closed systems.[3] Taylor sought to reduce all production to component processes, define key activities, minimize variations, and then manage the performance of workers with precision. This scientific approach assumed direct cause-and-effect relationships in what happened on factory shop floors. The role of leaders in general and strategic leaders in particular was to remove any fluctuation in the external environment to allow for the predictability of both inputs and outputs. As such, strategic leaders designed internal systems that demanded maximum efficiency from workers, acquired resources for production, and either captured or developed demand for the product in the market. In other words, strategic leaders were the only "thinkers" in the organization—most other direct-level roles in such a system were intended to only be "doers."

As one would expect, this machine metaphor, while potentially effective in a stable, predictable environment, had some drawbacks. The emergence of larger and more complex organizations led to the discipline of systems analysis and the rise of Operations Research and Systems Analysis (ORSA). ORSA practitioners sought to identify all key parameters of closed production systems by observation, measurement, and analysis. Analysts then developed mathematical models and simulations to determine the optimal design of systems and processes. This ORSA approach attained prominence in military circles with the "whiz kids" of Secretary of Defense Robert McNamara in the 1960s. In the 1980s, the emphasis on systems analysis led to systems engineering, with the focus on design and control.[4] Army officers will remember the emergence of Battlefield Operating Systems (BOS) and System of Systems Analysis (SOSA) as the Army tried to quantify combat operations in the era of Air-Land Battle. The methodology for systems analysis was to observe potentially critical events, collect data to reveal trends, establish causal relationships, and then seek to design systems with control mechanisms to attain optimal performance. Attempts to quantify large-scale combat operations to reduce the fog and friction of war through BOS and SOSA led to a false sense of certainty challenged by contemporary 21st-century experience in operations in Iraq and Afghanistan.

The focus on the scientific reductionism of processes by managers resulted in them doing things right (that is, following established procedures) within well-defined structures. However, as the complexity of globalization and the interconnectivity of near-instantaneous communications and data processing increased, this approach proved less and less efficacious. Organization theorist and systems thinking pioneer Russell Ackoff presented another perspective of organizations as human enterprises with people as integral components, and organizations as part of open systems.[5] His approach to systems thinking challenged the purely scientific approach by examining social, cultural, and psychological aspects of people in organizations. Ackoff offered that systems thinking was required by leaders to determine what were the "right" things to do for organizations. This holistic view of organizations coincided with the acceptance that an organization was more than the sum of its parts. As part of an open system, there are organizational interactions with the external environment that are beyond the control of management, as well as internal feedback mechanisms that indirectly influence operations in unforeseen ways. The desire to have an organization that acts like a well-oiled machine with clock-like precision does not mirror the reality of most organizations. As we talk about organizations in the context of systems thinking, the terms "dynamic," "nonlinear," "second-" and "third-order effects," and "unintended consequences" are used to describe actions in organizations. There are other intangibles that defy quantification—affective factors, motivation, cohesion, organizational climate and culture, and leadership—that either support or detract from organizational performance.

Peter Senge introduced and captured in his book *The Fifth Discipline* the treatment of an organization as an entity that actually "learns."[6] He noted that something was missing in our understanding of organizations as systems when:

- Over 75 percent of re-engineering efforts fail to achieve targeted improvements in performance.
- Many initiatives to reduce cost in one part of a system result in increased cost elsewhere.
- The vast majority of restructuring efforts fail to achieve intended synergies and generate unintended consequences.
- Large-scale projects tend to overrun schedule, budget, or both.
- Metrics result in more reports and administrative burdens but shed little light on the levers that can be pulled to meet targets.

Senge offered a view of organizations as social activities that perform best when all members are able to contribute to achieving their goals. While some have called this empowerment, systems thinking is the critical competency in an organization that develops the synergy of the other four disciplines.[7] Systems thinking provides a framework for understanding and explaining organizational processes and how they perform over time. The use of system-thinking models helps members understand complex problems and develops shared team understanding while suggesting ways to leverage the problems and identify and test solutions—all processes that support learning organizations.

Senge's insights apply to the Department of Defense (DoD) and its armed services, which are undeniably large, stratified organizations composed of systems within systems. A review of any DoD organizational chart will illustrate the functions and assignment of responsibilities to provide a product or service in the pursuit of national defense. The Army Organizational Life Cycle Model (AOLCM) depicts the linkage of systems for acquiring, developing, employing, and then retiring resources (see Figure 18-1). A vivid example of the AOLCM in action is personnel—the Army recruits, trains, and educates people, then assigns them to perform missions until they are eventually released from service. Some may naively believe that such a personnel system is a simple linear process, but in truth, it is inherently convoluted and complex. A typical U.S. Army War College student, after 18 or more years of service and over a decade at war, demonstrates a career characterized by four or five promotions, three or four deployments, 10 to 12 jobs at five or six different locations, four or five formal educational opportunities, and eight to 10 moves for the Soldier and family. Moreover, the personnel system is interdependent with systems for compensation, promotion, health care, and family support. The personnel system is also influenced by operational concepts that seek to determine the types of people needed to man weapons systems and equipment to fight according to Army doctrine. There are series of interactions that have second- and third-order effects as well as unintended consequences. Hence, any decision on military personnel should consider its relation to other functions. The linkage of systems for acquiring, developing, employing, and then retiring resources is inherently complex, interconnected, and self-adapting.[8]

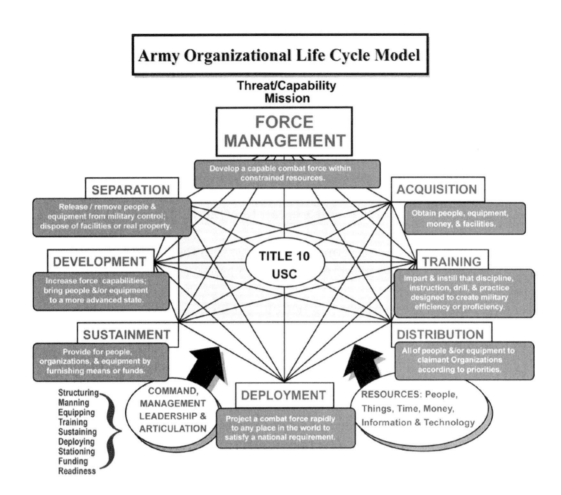

Figure 18-1. The Army Organizational Life Cycle Model.

The U.S. Army realizes that simple linear depictions do not reflect actual cause-and-effect relations; thus, the Army looks for intervening variables and interactions between the variables. Interconnectedness and unintended consequences abound in the most mundane decisions in large and complex organizations, and the U.S. Army and operational commands are not immune from this reality. This reality will become more pressing when budget reductions force a rethinking of the capabilities required of the DoD and the Services, and how they will organize, man, train, equip, and fight in an era of persistent tension. The uncertain and ambiguous future requires effective application of systems-thinking principles.

The machine metaphor used to characterize organizational design is more troublesome when applied to open political and social systems. Thus, the impact of interactions, associated negative feedback, and unintended consequences is central to the security dilemma underlying dynamic processes in international relations. The dilemma stems from the fact that states often seek to maximize their power by increasing the resources devoted to their security. By doing so, states are able to threaten others who are likely to respond with efforts to neutralize or counterbalance the effort of the first state. The result is that no state is more secure than when the process began, and the first state was unable to maximize its power as intended. Similarly, the balance of power illustrates the negative feedback found in international politics. States may respond to threats by balancing against any state that might threaten their security, so that any move that could bring a state great competitive advantage can be expected to generate opposition from others. For example, one can look at the North Korean attack on South Korea in 1950 as reflecting such a response. That attack was sanctioned by both the Union of Soviet Socialist Republics (USSR) and the People's Republic of China (PRC) on the assumption that the North Korean advance would strengthen their position in Northeast Asia against the United States and Japan. However, the attack had the opposite effect because it led the United States to triple its defense budget, conclude defense treaties around the globe, and transform the North Atlantic Treaty Organization (NATO) into a functioning military command.[9]

U.S. contemporary experiences in Afghanistan and Iraq served to reinforce the necessity to understand system complexities and dynamics. It is clear that policymakers did not appreciate the multiple components of Iraqi society nor the interrelationship between Afghanistan and Pakistan at the outset of operations. As the linkages became clearer and the underlying assumptions were invalidated, senior national security and defense policymakers were forced to reevaluate goals and eventually adjust strategies. Such was the case in 2006 for Iraq and 2009 in Afghanistan, which resulted in the surge and the refinement of military objectives. Challenges persist for military leaders to develop effective strategies in an uncertain future of persistent tension and fiscal constraints. Developing operational capabilities will require rethinking the systemic complexities associated with institutional systems and processes.

SYSTEMS COMPLEXITY IN MILITARY OPERATIONS

What, then, are the aspects of a systems approach that are most helpful for military leaders in strategic thinking and design? Systems thinking applied to the kinds of open systems with which commanders and staff planners deal provides a caution against the hazards of simple linear cause-and-effect reasoning. A starting point for appreciating differences between systems thinking and linear thinking lies with the definition of *system*. A system is a set of units (or elements) interconnected in such a way that change in some elements produce changes in other parts of the system. In addition, the changes induced in other elements will not necessarily be proportional to the initial change. The aphorism, "the straw that broke the camel's back," nicely captures this disproportion between inputs and outcomes. Initially inputs and outcomes seem at balance. One straw, or even several straws, appear to cause the camel no discomfort. However, eventually the addition of a single straw, no different from the others, causes our unfortunate beast to crumble—a seemingly disproportionate outcome, given our earlier experience with camel loading. Similarly, in the realm of economics, the "law of diminishing returns" suggests that at a particular inflection point returns will decrease despite increased input, again demonstrating an example of the disproportion between inputs and outcomes. In addition, the system as a whole exhibits properties or behaviors different from its individual parts. Following from the definition of system, interactions and interconnections within and outside the system must affect strategic thinkers contemplating military design.

Any theater of war presents a complex array of intermixed physical, geographical, psychological, social, political, and economic factors such that experts have long recognized that military operations must be approached from a systems perspective.[10] That said, the 21st century, with the globalized and digitally enhanced nature of human enterprises of all sorts, presents particularly compounding structural and interactive complexities. Commanders must approach operations as a holistic system of subsystems—a process complicated even more by adaptive interventions on the part of the many actors who are involved, whether supportive, neutral, or adversarial. Such complex adaptive systems "exhibit coherence under change, via conditional action and anticipation, and they do so without central direction."[11] This coherence makes it difficult for a single actor, such as a commander, to compel outcomes effectively.

Historically, military operations are among the most complex of human activities. They take place in and across a range of decisive actions, yet this continuum is prone to overlap, indistinct transitions, varying magnitudes, and contemporaneous actions.[12] Across this field, threats are neither stable nor monolithic, and violence can range widely from infrequent criminal attacks during otherwise peaceful periods to the ongoing, full-scale hostilities of general war. Operational themes include but are probably not limited to peacetime military engagement, limited interventions, peace operations, irregular warfare, and major combat operations. These thematic descriptions may not occur in sequence or in isolation but may well surface simultaneously as a mixture of activities increasingly termed hybrid warfare.[13]

The electronic information age allows great advances in military affairs, because collaboration and information sharing can proceed simultaneously at multiple levels. The same electronic advances underlie precision guided munitions that increase the lethality of attack. Digital communications systems synergistically network command elements at longer ranges with greater numbers of synchronized participants, enhancing mission command. Nevertheless, the 21st-century operational environment continues to pose problems that can be variously well-structured, medium-structured, or ill-structured, thus defying easy discernment and presenting no uniform, definitive way of formulating solutions.[14] Hence, traditional requirements for effective leadership remain in effect alongside state-of-the-art technology—in particular, disciplined critical thinking, relevant experience, and insightful judgment are more important in decisionmaking and problem solving than ever. That is, the commander must add value to the process of understanding the operational environment or risk being overwhelmed by systems complexity—and be defeated by an adversary who can, despite systems complexity, design approaches to problem solving faster than the commander can.

Accordingly, an operational or strategic commander cannot focus on purely military matters in his operational environment and ignore other subsystem or related system elements. Certainly potential adversaries realize this, as it is clear that U.S. military power is overwhelming. If an enemy cannot hope to prevail militarily, that foe is likely to choose other battlespace. Instead of a military-to-military confrontation, modern warfare is likely to require the application of all elements of national power (diplomatic, informational, military, and economic) against adversary systems (political, military, economic, social, informational, and infrastructure).[15]

CLAUSEWITZ AS A SYSTEMS THINKER

The great Prussian theorist of war, Carl von Clausewitz, posited two ways out of systems-generated conundrums. The first was to recognize that just as all things in war are complex and cause friction, not all things are of equal importance or equal difficulty. Tactical tasks are relatively self-contained, and logistical concerns are restricted along certain channels of action by the limitations of time and space. However, as the functions to be performed become increasingly intellectual, the more the commander's cognition and experience becomes of paramount importance.[16] Secondly, Clausewitz postulated that a senior commander should remain adaptable and not be bound by doctrine, but guided by principles that are "intended to provide a thinking man with a frame of reference for the movements he has been trained to carry out, rather than to serve as a guide that, at the moment of action, lays down precisely the path he must take."[17]

Thus, Clausewitz focused on the central role of the commander in design—framing the strategic or operational problem to be addressed by military planning. Clausewitz's position on this matter is echoed in contemporary calls for emphasizing the role of the commander in operational design. Design highlights critical actions toward which a commander should direct personal efforts: understanding the strategic goals to be achieved, comprehending the operational context, framing the nature of the problem, and considering operational approaches to solving that problem.[18] The first two actions describe the nature of both extant factors and discover the conditions that must be altered to change those factors favorably. The third clarifies the nature of the problems to be faced, and the fourth sets the stage for the development of courses of action that will enable the achievement of the desired end states that resolve those problems.

Design as a creative thinking methodology is not new, but rather reemphasizes an approach to systems thinking that postulates that the commander must appreciate the operational environment facing him/her and must further be able to assess the relative qualities and values of systemic operational factors. Only by thus framing the nature of the problems confronting the organization can a commander visualize a concept of operations and describe to others a mission narrative about how to effectively bring about change.[19] Primary tools used to initiate and guide this process, which perforce must be undertaken in some detail by the commander's staff, are the initial commander's intent, the commander's planning guidance, and the commander's critical information requirements.[20]

On the modern battlefield, the commander cannot be a passive approval authority for the insights, initiative, and industry of others. The commander must be an integral and additive part of the process and make a personal, positive contribution to mission success through all aspects of design, planning, and execution. Indeed, the commander may well be the only person with the requisite experience, long-range time horizon, judgment, and intuition who is in a position to make those additive contributions to staff inputs and estimates. Field Marshall Sir William Slim described this unalterable responsibility:

> I suppose I have published dozens of operations instructions and orders, and I have never written one myself because I have always had excellent staff officers who could do it. But, there is one part of an order that I have always made a point of writing myself. That is the object [that is, the commander's intent]. I do recommend it to you, gentlemen, that when long orders are being written for complicated operations, you take up your pen yourself and write the object in your own words so that object goes down to everybody.[21]

The commander's responsibility to understand strategic guidance, visualize a design concept, and communicate it succinctly and thoroughly to his/her subordinate planners and commanders cannot be delegated, but are, in fact, fundamental elements of strategic senior leadership. The commander's personal role in design is perhaps his/her most essential contribution to campaign success.[22] As Clausewitz pointed out:

> If we pursue the demands that war makes upon those who practice it, we come to a region dominated by the powers of intellect. War is the realm of uncertainty; three quarters of the factors on which action in war is based are wrapped in a fog of greater or lesser uncertainty. A sensitive and discriminating judgment is called for; a skilled intelligence to scent out the truth.[23]

That discrimination and judgment, that skilled intelligence, is something only a seasoned, discerning commander can provide.

CENTER OF GRAVITY DETERMINATIONS IN SYSTEMS THINKING AND DESIGN

In the joint doctrinal context, design is directly applicable to operational art. Design involves the formation and use of a conceptual and contextual framework as the foundation for understanding the situation and the problem relative to implementing strategic direction. Design reduces system complexity and ambiguity to enable campaign planning, joint operations order development, and subsequent execution of the campaign.[24] Thus, design inherently requires a systems perspective at its forefront.

However, it is the nature of complicated systems to defy rational analysis and linear thought. As Clausewitz pointed out, there is no quick and easy process that will eliminate friction and dissipate the fog, enabling the commander to crystallize an appropriate course of action in an operational environment comprised of numerous interrelated subsystems. The resultant systems interaction of complexity, indistinctness, internal dynamics, and human cognitive limitations place heavy demands on planners and make the commander's decisionmaking imprecise and risk-prone.[25] Hence, a common tendency is to pursue imprecise and vague objectives that are often in actuality multiple objectives. This poses problems for design and planning, because the pursuit of such multiple ends with limited means and restricted ways implies that many factors must be simultaneously counterbalanced and many criteria satisfied at once—thus increasing risk.[26] Hence, one of the most important determinations facing a commander and his/her staff in design is the identification of the centers of gravity.

The Clausewitzian concept of center of gravity is a useful construct in design. It provides a means by which commanders and planners can frame the complicated interlocking systems making up the operational environment, set priorities, and coordinate and synchronize efforts across the range of warfighting functions. Clausewitz described this concept thusly:

> One must keep the dominant characteristics of both belligerents in mind. Out of these characteristics a certain center of gravity develops, the hub of all power and movement, on which everything depends. That is the point against which all our energies should be directed. Small things always depend on great ones, unimportant on important, accidentals on essentials. This must guide our approach. . . . [Only] by constantly seeking out the center of his power, by daring all to win all, will one really defeat the enemy.[27]

Clausewitz's concept of center of gravity has generated much discussion, but for the purposes of this treatment, it is sufficient to clarify its importance and relevance to systems thinking and design. The selection of a center of gravity serves to solidify the commander's understanding of the operational environment and provides insights about the system, its constituent elements, and where and how operations should be executed. It is key to the design elements of framing the operational environment, framing the nature of the problem, and considering

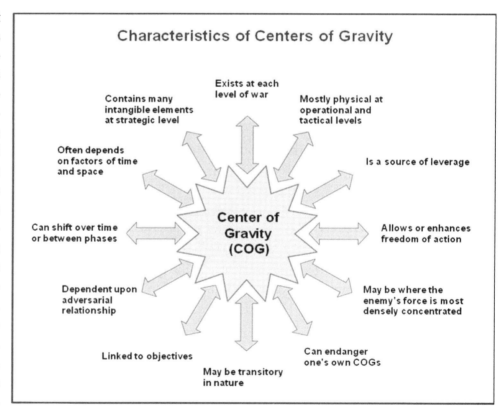

Figure 18-2. Characteristics of Centers of Gravity.

operational approaches. A center of gravity is "a source of power that provides moral or physical strength, freedom of action, and will to act."[28] JP 5-0 suggests characteristics of centers of gravity (see Figure 18-2), emphasizing that centers of gravity may be transitory, shift over time or between operational phases, and may be largely intangible at the strategic level. That is, a center of gravity is a design tool, not a magic talisman. There may be more than one, but for design and planning purposes it would be wise to limit proliferation, since that dilutes both focus in design and concentration of effort in both planning and operations. Thus, the determination of a center of gravity is a key output of design in terms of understanding the operational environment. In theory, as operational art attempts to generate the right conditions to neutralize or destroy a center of gravity, it links lines of operations and effort to a center of gravity producing the most direct path to mission accomplishment. However, as with most attempts to influence or alter elements in a system, this is not an empirical, mathematically precise process. Design, as a general methodology for framing the situation and the nature of the problem confronting a commander, facilitates such operational art.[29] Note the repeated references to inconstancy and mutability intimated by the characteristics presented, indicative of this concept as part of a systems approach to campaign design. Thus, for a variety of reasons, center of gravity determinations may change over the course of a campaign.[30]

Under such a methodology, a center of gravity constitutes that part of the operational environment against which planning and operations will be pressed. It may not be a specific node or a particular relational link, but rather may consist of a judiciously identified and deliberately selected limited set of nodes and related links (see Figure 18-3). Hence, the uncovering of a center of gravity is applicable to framing both the environment and the problem and in delineating an operational approach. Note that strategic and operational centers of gravity may differ and that a center of gravity may include more than one specific key node or link. It also may cross boundaries between conceptual domains of analysis.[31]

In this systems context, it becomes less imperative that a center of gravity be precisely, absolutely, and irrevocably correct. While assuredly it cannot be arbitrarily or capriciously determined, it is far more important that it be

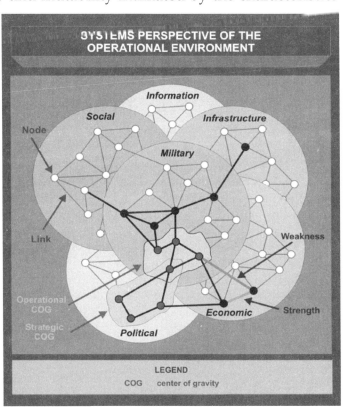

Figure 18-3. Determining Center of Gravity in a Systems Perspective of the Operational Environment.

reasonable and credible than that it be exactly, immutably right. A center of gravity is a construct— a mental model on which to predicate analysis and planning. Continued situational awareness and the unfolding of events as a campaign progresses will allow reframing of the appropriateness of the center of gravity. This lack of certainty is no impediment to resolute action; rather, it is simply the nature of warfighting as a systems activity requiring insightfulness, strength, and adaptability on the part of commanders and planners alike. As Clausewitz suggested, "Four elements make up the climate of war: danger, exertion, uncertainty, and chance. If we consider them together, it becomes evident how much fortitude of mind and character are needed to make progress in these impeding elements with safety and success."[32] Center of gravity selection is no more certain. That said, without the identification of a reasonable center of gravity as the foundation of design, there is no place to enter the system and begin credible planning.

Understanding the operational environment as a complex, interrelated system is central to operational art. The design process set forth in current doctrine accepts the systemic nature of warfighting and seeks to impose a consistent, rational model on the system to mitigate uncertainty and facilitate further analysis and planning on the part of commanders and staffs. Design cannot eradicate friction and the fog of war, but it can enable resolute and insightful commanders to frame the nature of the campaign and impose their will in the context of unruly and ever-changing operational environments. As Clausewitz recognized, a systems approach to design can enhance a commander's appreciation for the operational environment in which he or she must attain objectives and accomplish missions, and so achieve political and military end states that truly matter in national security and international affairs.

ENDNOTES - CHAPTER 18

1. Ludwig von Bertalanffy, "An Outline of General System Theory," *British Journal for the Philosophy of Science*, Vol. 1, 1950, pp. 134-165.

2. Gareth Morgan, *Images of Organizations*, Thousand Oaks, CA: Sage Publishing, 2006.

3. Frederick. W. Taylor, *The Principles of Scientific Management,* New York: Enna, 2008. Original work published in 1911.

4. The U.S. Army emphasized the ORSA approach in the 1980s with a separate Military Occupational Specialty (MOS) identifier, 49A for officers, and the United States Military Academy established Systems Engineering as an academic major in 1988.

5. Russell L. Ackoff, "Towards a *System* of *Systems* Concepts," *Management Science,* Vol. 17, No. 11, July 1971, pp. 661-671, *Business Source Complete, EBSCOhost.*

6. Peter Senge, *The Fifth Discipline: The Art and Practice of the Learning Organization*, New York: Doubleday/Currency, 1990.

7. The four other disciplines are shared vision, mental models, personal mastery, and team learning. See Senge, pp. 12-13.

8. Harold W. Lord, ed., *How the Army Runs: A Senior Leader Reference Handbook 2011-2012*, Carlisle, PA: Department of Command, Leadership, and Management, U.S. Army War College, 2011, p. 7.

9. Janeen Klinger, in Charles D. Allen, G. K. Cunningham, and Janeen Klinger, eds., "Strategic Thinking for Strategic Leaders" [Unpublished manuscript], Carlisle, PA: U.S. Army War College, 2009.

10. *Joint Publication (JP) 5-0, Joint Operation Planning,* Washington, DC: U.S. Joint Chiefs of Staff, August 11, 2011, pp. III-9-III-10.

11. John J. Holland, *Hidden Order: How Adaptation Builds Complexity*, Reading, MA: Addison-Wesley, 1995, p. 55.

12. *Army Doctrinal Publication (ADP) 3-0, Unified Land Operations,* Washington, DC: U.S. Department of the Army, October, 2011, pp. 2-4.

13. James N. Mattis and Frank Hoffman, "Future Warfare: The Rise of Hybrid Wars," *United States Naval Institute Proceedings,* Vol. 131, No. 11, November 1, 2005, pp. 18–19.

14. *U.S. Army Training and Doctrine Command, Pamphlet 525-5-500, Commander's Appreciation and Campaign Design,* Fort Monroe, VA: U.S. Department of the Army, January 28, 2008, pp. 5–11.

15. JP 5-0, pp. IV-4-IV-5.

16. Carl von Clausewitz, *On War*, Michael Howard and Peter Paret, eds. and trans., Princeton, NJ: Princeton University Press, 1976, p. 140.

17. *Ibid.*, p. 141.

18. *Field Manual (FM) 5-0, The Operations Process,* Washington, DC: U.S. Department of the Army, March, 2010, pp. 3-7-3-8; JP 5-0, p. III-7.

19. FM 5-0, p. 3-12.

20. JP 5-0.

21. Sir William Slim, "Higher Command in War," *Military Review,* Vol. 70, No. 5, May 1990, pp. 10–21. (His remarks to the U.S. Army Command and General Staff College, Fort Leavenworth, KS, April 1952.)

22. FM 5-0, p. 3-6.

23. Clausewitz, p. 101.

24. JP 5-0.

25. Dietrich Dörner, *The Logic of Failure: Recognizing and Avoiding Error in Complex Situations*, Reading, MA: Addison-Wesley, 1996, p. 37; Herbert A. Simon, *Administrative Behavior: A Study of Decision Making Processes in Administrative Organizations*, 4th Ed., New York: Free Press, 1997, p. 92, originally published in 1945.

26. Simon, p. 51.

27. Clausewitz, pp. 595–596.

28. JP 5-0, p. III-22.

29. *Ibid.*, p. II-5.

30. *Ibid.*, p. III-23.

31. *Joint Publication (JP) 2-01.3, Joint Intelligence Preparation of the Battlefield*, Washington, DC: U.S. Joint Chiefs of Staff, June 161, 2009, p. II-66.

32. Clausewitz, p. 104.

CHAPTER 19

INTELLIGENCE AS A TOOL OF STRATEGY

John Aclin

The story is told of two Pentagon strategists who decided to relax one weekend by going for a flight in a hot air balloon. After traveling above the clouds for a time, they realized they had lost their bearings. Dropping below the clouds, they found themselves over an open field and spotted a man hiking nearby. They drew close enough for him to hear and called out, "Can you tell us where we are?"

The man looked at them blankly for a moment, then responded, "You're in a hot air balloon."

One strategist looked at the other and muttered, "Just our luck—we had to find an intelligence analyst."

The other asked, "How did you know he was an intelligence analyst?"

The first strategist replied, "Because his answer was prompt, accurate, and of no use whatsoever!"

Unfortunately, while the anecdote may be apocryphal, the sentiment is all too common. Many strategists fault the intelligence community for failing to provide information and analysis relevant to the issues with which they are dealing. Why does this situation exist, and what can be done to improve it?

The failure of intelligence to support strategy properly stems from several sources. For various reasons, intelligence analysts may not have insight on the challenges faced by or the perspective of the strategists. The information delivered may have limited relevance to the actual problems confronting those developing or implementing the strategy. At times, the information may be relevant and timely, but the strategists may deem it unconvincing or unhelpful. If the strategists are unfamiliar with the limitations and capabilities of intelligence, they may not understand how to interpret the information provided.

While there is no perfect solution to these challenges, if the intelligence analyst becomes part of the strategy team, the information he provides will be more relevant to the problems under consideration, and the strategists will better understand how to use what has been given to them. The question then becomes, how is intelligence—and the intelligence analyst—best integrated into the strategy team?

DEFINING INTELLIGENCE

One of the challenges in discussing the role of intelligence in strategy formulation is finding a useful definition of the term "intelligence." How is it different from information? Like many other basic terms associated with national security, definitions of intelligence abound, shaped by the experience or perspective of the individual giving the definition.

No less an authority than Sherman Kent—considered by many as the father of strategic intelligence in America – pointed out that intelligence is simultaneously knowledge, an activity, and an organization.[1] Focusing on the informational aspect of intelligence in the preface of his book, *Strategic Intelligence*, Kent stated, "Intelligence, as I am writing of it, is the knowledge that our highly placed civilians and military men must have to safeguard the national welfare."[2]

Kent raises an important point. Intelligence is knowledge, not just facts or data. Intelligence activities collect data they process into information that can be used by intelligence analysts. Intelligence analysts must assess the validity and import of the new information and use it, in conjunction with background data, to develop intelligence products that describe the strategic environment and provide estimates of the future.

Vernon Walters, a former Deputy Director of Central Intelligence, offered a slightly more detailed definition of intelligence. "Intelligence is information, not always available in the public domain, relating to the strength, resources, capabilities, and intentions of a foreign country that can affect our lives and the safety of our people."[3] This definition is helpful, because it brings out the idea that intelligence is related to information that is not generally available. However, Walters' exclusion of non-state actors makes his definition somewhat dated. Also, he only addressed the informational aspects of intelligence; the very fact that the needed information is not readily available shapes intelligence as an activity to gather that same information.

Perhaps the CIA's journal *Studies in Intelligence* offered the best definition in 1958 when a CIA operations officer using the pseudonym R.A. Random proposed the following:

> Intelligence is the official, secret collection and processing of information on foreign countries to aid in formulating and implementing foreign policy, and the conduct of covert activities abroad to facilitate the implementation of foreign policy.[4]

Although still focused on foreign states and foreign policy, the advantage of this definition is that it highlights the fact that intelligence involves official (i.e. government) activities to gather information that other groups are attempting to conceal or prevent the United States from obtaining. While foreign policy and strategy are not synonymous, the two terms could be interchanged in the definition above without harming the meaning. The collection, analysis, and dissemination of secret information to strategists provides them a key tool needed to develop sound courses of action by identifying the critical strengths and vulnerabilities of other players, important trends and factors driving the strategic situation, and projections of reactions to proposed courses of action.

This last definition also addresses the use of covert activities in support of foreign policy, bringing forward the concept that intelligence is more than an informer of strategy. It may also serve as a means for carrying out a strategy. Both these roles of intelligence—as an source of information used in the development of strategies and as a tool to be used in implementing those strategies—work best if intelligence is fully integrated in the strategy team.

VIEWS ON UTILITY OF INTELLIGENCE

Intelligence is first and foremost an enabler of strategy. It not only provides a baseline of information on which to build plans, but also projects potential reactions by others—both adversaries and neutrals—to those plans, helping strategists evaluate the feasibility of proposed courses of action. Additionally, since strategy is by definition proactive, intelligence helps strategists identify both opportunities and threats to national security so they can develop appropriate plans.

This concept of intelligence as a predictive enabler of strategy is hardly new. The ancient Chinese philosopher Sun Tzu saw intelligence as a fundamental tool of the strategist, stating, "Know the enemy and know yourself; in a hundred battles you will never be in peril."[5] Speaking specifically about the use of espionage, Sun Tzu opined, "Now the reason the enlightened prince and the wise general conquer the enemy…is foreknowledge."[6] He went on to clarify the source of this foreknowledge, writing, "It must be obtained from men who know about the enemy situation."[7] Sun Tzu took a holistic view of intelligence, focusing on the need to understand the adversary—its values, capabilities, objectives, and vulnerabilities.

Of course, others see intelligence more from the perspective of our two balloonists. Carl von Clausewitz viewed intelligence as an impediment to sound strategy—unreliable, contradictory, often false, and usually uncertain. In *On War*, he stated that the "difficulty of *accurate recognition* constitutes one of the most serious sources of friction in war."(Italics in the original).[8] However, Clausewitz was addressing intelligence at the tactical or operational level—information pertinent to battlefield operations – and not intelligence at the strategic level. Nonetheless, while many current strategists might be more generous, they often see intelligence as often uncertain, equivocal, and "of no use whatsoever."

Part of the mission of the strategist is to use intelligence in such a way that it serves as an aid and not a hindrance to the development of sound plans. The best way to achieve this is by integrating the intelligence function in the strategy team.

INTELLIGENCE AS A TEAM PLAYER

There are generally two schools of thought on the proper relationship between strategists and intelligence officers. The "distance" school holds that in order to avoid tainting the analytic process, intelligence analysts should be kept separate from the policy/strategy community. The "proximity" school believes that close coordination between analysts and strategists is necessary to ensure the assessments are relevant to the questions at hand.

Traditionally, the U.S. Intelligence Community has preferred to maintain the separation of intelligence from policy/strategy development, answering questions when requested by the strategy community and providing alerts to opportunities and threats whenever they are detected. By maintaining their distance, the thinking goes, analysts are sheltered from undue pressure and can form their assessments independently. Analysis that is uncorrupted by outside influences best serves strategists.

Unfortunately, while this philosophy may protect the objectivity of the intelligence community, Sherman Kent highlights the inherent problem. He stated that when strategists are "formulating something new in our foreign policy they often come to intelligence and ask for background. (They should do this more than they actually do.)"[9] By waiting until asked, the intelligence community risks never being consulted at all. If this happens, the intelligence community can rapidly become disconnected from strategy development. More frequently, when asked, the analysts do not understand the context or background behind the question. Their responses may be prompt, accurate, and irrelevant. Consequently, the strategist will have an incomplete or possibly even erroneous understanding of the operational environment.

The alternative view is to integrate the analysts in the strategy team—what former CIA Deputy Director for Intelligence John McLaughlin termed "bridging the divide." McLaughlin and others suggest analysts should be embedded within policy shops and planning staffs to understand not only their immediate intelligence requirements, but also how the strategists view and use intelligence in their work. Without this insight, the intelligence analysts may write products without any clear connection to the needs or perspectives of the consumers, with the result that it is often off the mark or, worse yet, appears uninformed.[10]

Regular interaction between strategists and intelligence analysts provides several benefits. First, by understanding the priorities and challenges strategists face, analysts can work to ensure ongoing analytic and collection efforts focus on the policy issues currently being addressed. Perhaps more importantly, if analysts sit in on deliberations over various courses of action, they are more likely to bring up relevant information on the spot, informing the debate and helping the strategist think through choices and possible outcomes. Such exchanges of information allow the strategist to not only assess what the analyst knows and thinks, but to understand the underlying assumptions and degree of uncertainty in the judgment. An appreciation of the limitations of the intelligence judgments helps the strategist develop proposals that acknowledge and take into account the uncertainty. Fog is inevitable in strategic planning. If intelligence cannot always penetrate the fog, it can aid in at least defining the breadth and depth of the fog.

Integrating intelligence analysts in the strategy team does entail some risks. While analysts should seek to influence strategy deliberations by providing relevant information on the issues at hand, they cannot advocate for a policy. Analysts may offer informed opinions if asked, but generally need to restrict themselves to the identification of opportunities or estimates of likely reactions to a proposed course of action. If intelligence analysts begin to support a particular policy option, their assessments may become biased, depriving their work of the objectivity that is at the heart of intelligence analysis. They may fall victim to confirmation bias, seeking out data that conforms to their preconceived ideas and ignoring information that does not match the preferred policy option. While these risks exist even when the analysts are not integrated in the strategy team, the potential for analytic bias increases when the intelligence officers are involved in policy discussions.

The relationship between analysts and strategists is not reciprocal. While analysts cannot advocate for a specific policy, strategists may always form their own judgments on the intelligence provided them. Mark Lowenthal, former Assistant Director of Central Intelligence (DCI) for Analysis, likened the relationship between analysts and policymakers to a semipermeable membrane that allows flow in one direction but not the other; analysts cannot recommend policy, but policymakers may always be their own intelligence analysts.[11] In the end, the strategist can—and should—integrate intelligence with other sources of information to develop a holistic judgment of proposed courses of action. Intelligence is a critical piece in this judgment, but only one piece.

WELCOME TO THE TEAM

Integrating intelligence analysts in the strategy team takes time; because intelligence analysis is a subjective art, not a precise science, the strategist has to develop a sense of trust in the judgment of the analyst. Conversely, the analyst needs to develop a sense of how to best provide information to the strategists—what formats and approaches are most useful or persuasive for the individuals being supported. A good place to start building a relationship is for the strategist to establish the level and area of expertise of the analyst. If the strategist is going to place any reliance on the judgment of the analyst, the strategist must be comfortable that the analyst has sufficient background and training to render useful and reliable assessments.

Intelligence analysts embody two separate kinds of expertise—topical and tradecraft. Topical expertise comes from the study of a particular issue or region. Analysts may derive their topical expertise from formal schooling, life experiences, or a combination of both. Topical expertise provides the analyst with the background and knowledge needed to assess the substance of an issue under investigation. Expertise in tradecraft generally comes from experience and some analytic training courses. It provides the analyst with the tools to be able to gather the right kinds of information, critically assess sources and data, and provide well-grounded and properly qualified judgments. Good tradecraft aids analysts in clarifying assumptions and properly couching levels of uncertainty. Analysts need to possess both types of expertise to provide insightful and well-supported estimates and projections to the strategy team.

As with any profession, intelligence analysts have greatly varying levels and areas of expertise. Some have a narrow focus and deep knowledge on a particular subject, while others will have held multiple assignments on widely varying topics—building their tradecraft but lacking depth in any one area. Only in the rarest of instances will the strategy team find the analyst assigned to assist them has precisely the expertise needed to help them delve into the exact problem with which they are wrestling. However, the analyst is able to tap into the knowledge and experience of other analysts in the greater intelligence community.

Most commonly, the analyst will research and bring in relevant finished intelligence reports that address a question at hand. The analyst can also send out ad hoc questions to solicit the views from experts around the intelligence community. Collection requirements can be developed to fill identified information gaps. The analyst can arrange for intelligence experts to brief the team or work with them on a particular problem. The intelligence officers assigned to the team serve as much as a liaison to the greater intelligence community as they do as intelligence experts in their own right.

Rarely will an intelligence organization or a military command have the luxury of being able to assign an analyst full-time to a strategy team. In almost all instances analysts will work with the strategy team on a part-time basis, having other responsibilities to fulfill as briefers, writers, managers, and so forth. Both analysts and the strategy team must be committed to the relationship or it will become overwhelmed by other priorities. Strategic leaders must insist on the full participation of intelligence in the strategy formulation process. Better participation can be fostered, for example, by requiring an analyst's review of any policy recommendations to ensure the operational environment properly reflects the intelligence information available. Similarly, by having regularly scheduled sessions to discuss the status of projects and problems the team is facing, analysts can offer relevant information in a timely manner or can develop new collection requirements to fill intelligence gaps identified by the team.

When outside analysts are brought in to brief the strategy team or provide expert assistance on an issue under consideration, the strategist should establish the bona fides of the analysts in much the same way and for the same reasons as discussed for the embedded analyst. Knowing the background and depth of experience of the analysts will help the strategists understand exactly how much weight they should place in the judgments of the intelligence analyst. Are the analysts offering first-hand judgments based on their own expertise, or is their assessment based more on their interaction with other experts and finished analysis done elsewhere? This sort of critical weighing of the analyst is especially important when the nature of the exchange is more ad hoc and interactive. When an analyst has to provide judgments "on the fly," rather than rely on prepared products, the strategist needs to be comfortable with the analyst's background. In the end, the strategist must believe he or she can use the judgments of the analyst as a basis for developing strategies. Therefore, trust and confidence are crucial.

This development of trust becomes all the more critical when the analysts are providing information or estimates that do not conform to the conventional wisdom or otherwise are contrary to the preferences or preconceived ideas of the strategists. In such cases, even a well-grounded and soundly reasoned analysis may not be persuasive. The willingness of the strategists to accept contrary or inconvenient analyses will rely at least as much on their assessment of the credibility of the analyst as it will on the analysis itself. Henry Kissinger is reported to have once said with regard to an intelligence warning, "You warned me—but you didn't convince me."[12] The facts are important, but so is the messenger. Therefore, strategists should take time to become comfortable with the messengers.

WORKING WITH INTELLIGENCE ASSESSMENTS—EMBRACING UNCERTAINTY

By definition, strategy deals with the future. Unfortunately, no amount of art or effort can pierce the veil of time and provide a clear vision of the future. This does not mean that strategists cannot know anything about the future—but they must deal with assumptions about how that future is likely to play out. And since the entire purpose of strategy is to influence the future, the activities of the strategist will affect and alter that outcome. The job of the strategist—and the particular role of intelligence in the development of strategy—is to assess the outlines of the uncertainty and develop plans to deal with it. As Colin Gray put it, "The challenge is to cope with uncertainty, not try to diminish it."[13]

Given the impossibility of knowing the future, Gray recommends "the path of prudence is to cover all major possibilities as well as possible, without becoming overcommitted to one particular category of danger."[14] Intelligence can help define the most likely scenarios—those strategic trends for which the strategist must develop approaches. To a lesser degree, intelligence can also assist in anticipating low-probability/high-impact challenges—those "game changing" events that alter the strategic landscape. An intelligence analyst can help bound the problem, aid the strategist in thinking through the potential results of proposed courses of action on the identified threats or opportunities, and develop collection requirements to allow earlier detection on which way the situation is trending. Intelligence can provide insight, and to a degree can bound the uncertainty, but does not eliminate it. The strategist must develop an approach that copes with this uncertainty.

Obviously, the best intelligence is to have insight into the plans of adversaries, allies, and other actors in the system, but this is both rare and unreliable. It is rare because other groups protect their plans carefully. It is unreliable because plans do not tell what *will* happen, only what another actor *intends* to do. Just as the strategist's plans don't survive contact with reality, neither do the enemy's. Competition for resources, fog, friction, and incompetence all affect reality. Implementation of a strategy affects the strategic environment, causing the adversary to react, often in ways he had not previously planned. But plans can give insight into the objectives, concerns, vulnerabilities, and mindset of key actors. They can shed light on opportunities that the strategists can exploit.

Effective strategies must take into account a wide range of possibilities, addressing the most likely future while providing the flexibility to adapt to unexpected changes or trends. Intelligence can help provide earlier warning that the future is veering off from the anticipated path.

Strategy is about balancing ends, ways, and means and assessing the risks involved in a proposed course of action. Therefore, strategists must acknowledge the vulnerabilities of a recommended approach. Strategists should ask the intelligence analysts, "What would I expect to see if the opponent were going to attack my vulnerability? Is there any evidence to suggest the adversary is taking this course?" Intellectual engagement early in the strategy formulation process allows the intelligence analyst to develop collection requirements to reveal if the adversary is taking steps that would hamper or counter the intended course of action. Although by no mean infallible, proactive planning of intelligence collection can provide early warning that the strategy may need adjustment to account for the adversary's reactions.

High-impact, low-probability events are one of the most difficult areas for strategists to take into account. No country has the resources to prepare completely for every possible event that, though unlikely, could have devastating impact on a society.[15] Strategists make an assumption whenever they characterize scenarios as "low probability." Such a characterization means there is little or no information to suggest the events are expected or foreseeable. Strategists can use intelligence to challenge and monitor the validity of such assumption. What intelligence would change the assessment? Is there sound information the event is not happening, or has the analyst assumed the absence of information means there is no activity? A good axiom in the intelligence community is "The absence of intelligence is not the same as intelligence of absence." Of course, taken to an extreme, the strategist runs the risk of putting too much effort into fighting phantoms. The strategist does not have to plan for every possibility, but does have to recognize the risk inherent in the assumption that a specific possibility is unlikely.

Former Deputy Secretary of Defense Paul Wolfowitz used the Iraqi invasion of Kuwait as an example of the role of intelligence in anticipating low-probability/high-impact events. While the conventional wisdom held that Saddam Hussein would not make any moves toward his neighbors in the late 1980s, the intelligence community did provide data documenting Saddam's aggressive tendencies. Wolfowitz did not fault intelligence for failing to predict the invasion when Iraq first moved troops to the Kuwaiti border—Saddam had not yet made the decision to invade—but argued that too little attention was paid to what might have been done to deter Hussein from acting aggressively. He stated, "Analysis, in this instance, would have usefully pointed to the fact that events were not going in the direction we had expected or hoped for."[16] Insightful, fact-based intelligence assessments are a critical key in assessing and adjusting strategies, for challenging assumptions and seeing if they are still valid as events unfold.

Good use of intelligence while developing, implementing, and adjusting strategies can be the difference between having an effective plan and being strategically surprised. As Gray noted, strategist must cope with uncertainty. Intelligence cannot eliminate surprise or risk, but can certainly reduce both.

THREE QUESTIONS

Even if the intelligence analysts are fully integrated in the strategy team, understanding and focusing on the specific goals and information requirements of the team, not every intelligence product will automatically fulfill the needs of the policymaker. However, there are three key questions that the strategist can ask of intelligence that will increase the relevance of the information provided.

What Does It Mean?

Many intelligence analysts deal primarily in tactical, current, or basic intelligence. This is the realm of concrete data—orders of battle, economic reports, current events reporting. The focus is on facts—who, what, where, when. While this information is important—even vital—for strategists, it is only a starting point. This type of information forms part of the library from which strategists can draw data for planning. And because most strategists have risen from the ranks of tactical operators, it is this type of information with which they are most familiar and comfortable.

However, strategists require far more from intelligence than just the facts. Intelligence analysis should provide a strategic context—a sense of how the information or events being reported fit into the bigger picture. Ideally, every analytic intelligence product would include this sense of "so what?" However, we do not live in an ideal world; many intelligence products provide the facts of a matter, but fail to put them in context. The strategic consumer of intelligence must often ask the all-too obvious question, "Why do I care? What does it mean?"

If the intelligence analysts are excluded from the strategy team, such a question is usually muttered in an office, the intelligence is set aside as irrelevant, and the process does not improve. The strategists either assume the intelligence community cannot provide the context for the analysis or they do not know to whom the question should be directed. However, if intelligence is fully integrated in the strategy process, the strategist can ask these questions directly to the analysts. Occasionally, the intelligence officer may have the answer at hand; more often, if he or she is not the author or expert on the topic, they may have to go back to the originator to get further background.

The response to this question will not only better inform the strategist on the relevance of the information, but will also shed light on the limitations of the data. In some cases, the analysts know about an activity and report on it factually, but they may be unsure of its import or intent. They know *something* is going on, but not what it really means. The fact that the intelligence analysts don't know the import of an event may be sufficient for the strategist to take this unknown into account.

What Will Happen Next?

Ideally, strategists need a glimpse into the future. Strategy is much simpler when one knows for sure what will happen. Unfortunately, certainty of events is the realm of history, not strategy (and most historians would argue that point.) Intelligence deals in the world of estimates and projections, not predictions. Predictions describe what *will* happen. There is an element of inevitability or certainty in predictions. The intelligence community is not in the business of providing predictions.

Obviously, the future is never truly predictable. Not only is the human mind incapable of unfailing foresight, but the very nature of strategy affects the future, making accurate predictions impossible. Strategy is anticipatory. By carrying out a strategy, a nation will impact the course of events, changing what might have been into what that country hopes is a more beneficial future. This is the whole point of having a strategy. Similarly, the other actors in a strategic system interact with the system, either carrying out their own strategies or reacting to the strategies of others. Every action changes the environment. It is in this uncertain and, to a degree, unpredictable realm that intelligence can shed some light to guide the development of strategy.

Estimates describe the intelligence community's best understanding of what *is* happening and where such trends will *most likely* lead. Projections are the futuristic element of estimates; they deal with likely scenarios and the factors that make a particular outcome most probable. Projections are the extrapolation of existing trends and their interrelationships, leading to an estimate of a future situation.

Understanding the distinction between predictions and projections is critical if strategists are to make proper use of intelligence. Expecting too much from estimates results in frustration. Misunderstanding the limitations of projections can lead to flawed strategies, based on a belief the future is more certain than it really is. Appreciating the uncertainty in a projection helps the strategist assess the risk in a proposed course of action. The most common mistake, however, is for the strategist not to understand what data led to an assessment. By knowing the assumptions and key trends underpinning a projection, strategists gain insight into warning signs that suggest the future is no longer following the projected track. Even more importantly, knowing the key influences and trends helps strategists identify individuals, groups, or issues that are critical nodes or vulnerabilities for either changing or sustaining the strategic situation.

Projections cannot predict the future, but they can reduce the risk of strategic surprise. While an adversary can frequently achieve tactical surprise, the efforts required for strategic shifts are more difficult to hide. While the attack on Pearl Harbor came as a shock to the United States (a tactical surprise), there were ample signs—understood by many in Washington—that relations with Japan were approaching a breaking point (strategic warning). For strategists, intelligence projections aid in thinking through possible courses of action and their potential impact on the underlying trends driving those projections.

What Can I Do About It?

By far the most controversial question a strategist can ask of intelligence is, "What can I do about this situation?" If properly engaged, intelligence analysts can provide insights into centers of gravity and potential opportunities that a sound strategy must consider. However, opportunity analysis can easily cross the line into actually advocating a policy option. Exactly where this line lies and how to provide proper policy support is at the heart of the debate over whether to integrate intelligence analysts in the strategy team.

Intelligence can identify vulnerabilities, political agendas, or internal fissures in a foreign government that the strategist can use to further strategic ends. Knowing which ministers have the ear of a head of state can be the key to successful negotiations. Understanding what an adversary most values or fears can shape informational, diplomatic, or military aims. Assessments of this type are termed opportunity analysis—an identification of areas in which the system of interest is open to change. Good opportunity analysis can reveal to the strategist avenues of approach not previously considered.[17] However, while the analysts can identify potential vulnerabilities, they should avoid advocating specific *ways* to take advantage of these opportunities, lest their analysis become politicized.

Intelligence becomes politicized when the assessments are no longer objectively reached, but rather are predetermined or biased to reach a specific judgment. Analysts may begin to deliberately slant their judgments to support the party line, either because they have bought into the perspective of the strategists or out of a desire to be seen as a team player. Some analysts may believe that they will be excluded from discussions over options if they bring in unwelcome analysis. Somewhat less extreme but more likely, the analysts may subconsciously begin seeking data that supports the preferred judgment—a practice labeled as confirmation bias or cherry-picking. While these risks are real, they can be mitigated through proper analytic tradecraft—and by the strategists establishing a proper relationship, neither asking too much, nor too little, of opportunity analysis.

Striking the proper balance between politicizing intelligence or irrelevance is a delicate matter.[18] The strategist should push the intelligence analysts to identify opportunities in a situation or the vulnerabilities of an adversary. Although analysts are often reticent to put such ideas in their written products, they often have real insights regarding the priorities, concerns, and perspectives of foreign entities. By engaging in a dialogue with the analysts, strategists can investigate various scenarios and solicit the analysts' views on likely reactions. Analysts can identify opportunities and centers of gravity. Put another way, intelligence can identify "levers" that the strategist can pull. Good analysis can project the likely outcome if one of these levers is used. However, it is the realm of the strategist to decide which levers to pull in what sequence. Intelligence analysts will have crossed the line into politicization if they take part in the debate to decide which options are best.

Ultimately, it is incumbent on both strategists and intelligence analysts to maintain an appropriate relationship—close enough for the analysts to understand the information requirements of the strategists and provide timely, relevant analysis, yet distant enough to avoid losing objectivity. Analysts should neither advocate specific strategies, nor should they feel compelled to provide data to support the preferences of the strategists. Good intelligence estimates should help the strategist think through choices without attempting to recommend a particular course of action. The difference between opportunity identification and the politicization of intelligence is not a fine, clear line. It is a gray zone in which professionals—both analysts and strategists—must operate. The intelligence analyst should be viewed as a resource and advisor to the strategy team, almost as a consultant—valued but not part of the decisionmaking team. As John McLaughlin put it, intelligence needs to be "timely, digestible, and informed about the policy context while stopping short of pandering to or prescribing the policy."[19]

In the end, intelligence cannot eliminate risk from the development and implementation of strategy. But the answers to the three questions posed above may very well serve to reduce the amount of risk inherent in any forward-leaning endeavor. Through the discussion fostered by these questions, intelligence should provide greater insight into the key trends and variables, the relevance of each factor, the relationships between them, the motives of other actors in the system, and the opportunities and risks available to the strategist.

CRITICALLY ASSESSING INTELLIGENCE PRODUCTS

Access to intelligence analysts does not remove the requirement for strategists to use good, critical thinking throughout the strategy-formulation process. As Powell's three questions illustrate, analysts need to be challenged for the basis of their judgments. It is not sufficient for an analyst to have a view on the likely reaction of an adversary to a proposed course of action; the analyst owes the strategist the factual basis for this judgment. How sure is the information? Are there alternative views?

The breadth of the United States intelligence community is both a blessing and a curse for strategists. On the positive side, the strategist can potentially solicit and receive multiple perspectives on a key issue. Particularly in the political-military sphere, the Central Intelligence Agency (CIA), Defense Intelligence Agency (DIA), State Department's Bureau of Intelligence and Research (INR), and possibly the regional Joint Intelligence Operations Center may all have views on the matter. Various centers may have differing assessments of a situation. In the past, one agency might have access to privileged information not shared with other groups, though after September 11th this problem has been significantly reduced. Based on the institutional biases of the organization or the experiences and preferences of the leading analysts, two organizations using the same data can still arrive at very different conclusions. This diversity of perspectives can guard the strategist

---

Interaction with the Analysts – the "Powell Rules"

Former Secretary of State Colin Powell also had three questions that he used during his military career to probe the intelligence given to him. These questions deal with critical thinking, separating facts from assumptions and giving the strategist a firmer base of information on which to build a strategy. Powell's troika are simple but powerful tools. What do you know? What do you not know? What do you think? And he insisted the analysts be clear in differentiating between what they knew and what they thought.

What do you know? This deceivingly simple question can often uncover assumptions and leaps of logic. Embedded in this question is the corollary—how do you know it? What are your sources? Are they reliable? At the heart of the Iraqi WMD controversy was reliance on limited sources of questionable reliability. Based on the Silberman-Robb (WMD) Commission report, the Director of National Intelligence established standards to improve the documentation of sources, giving analysts—especially those who are incorporating finished intelligence from other analysts or agencies—better insight into the original sources of information. Probing carefully on the facts—not judgments—behind intelligence analysis is a critical strategic leader skill.

What do you not know? Strategists have to deal with a world of uncertainty. Good intelligence can narrow the information gaps, thereby reducing uncertainty. However, all too often strategists fail to inquire into the gaps in the intelligence. Unsurprisingly, intelligence analysts often do not offer up this information without being asked, especially if the communications are in writing. Not infrequently, analysts may not even have systematically thought through what critical information is missing. In some cases, analysts have inserted an assumption, but regarded it as a fact. Often adversary intentions and interests—critical assumptions—become regarded as facts, unquestioned by both analysts and strategists.

Clearly identifying the gaps in the intelligence allows the strategists to systematically think through the implications of the gaps. At a minimum, a strategy has to acknowledge risk when using an assumption in place of a fact. In some cases, the strategy will need to be broadened to account for the potentiality that events will unfold very differently than forecast due to critical gaps in the intelligence. Explicitly identifying gaps reduces—though it can never eliminate—the probability of surprise. Knowing what you do not know allows the strategist to place bounds on the likely outcomes and build strategies that accommodate this uncertainty.

What do you think? Secretary Powell's third question underlies the first two questions posed. The heart of intelligence is analysis. While collection of data is crucial, until that information is sifted through, organized, assessed, and analyzed, it is of limited use to the strategists. Intelligence analysts are more than reporters; their assessments of the data—its significance, salience, opportunities, threats, and validity—are important inputs for strategists. While some level of assessment should be integral to any good intelligence product, regular dialogue between the strategists and the intelligence analysts will usually yield far better results, as the analysts become

Figure 19-1. Interaction with the Analysts.[20]

against being blindsided. Independent analysis from multiple agencies helps avoid the trap of group-think, although analytic coordination across the intelligence community still makes false consensus possible. On the negative side, the diversity of views may leave the strategist no way to reconcile multiple analyses. The analysts assigned to the strategy team can help the strategists understand the basis for the differing views, although the analysts may have strong biases toward one particular assessment. Even if the analyst's position is supportive of the preferred strategic option, to avoid being surprised, the strategist should ask for alternative views from other agencies.

When developing a course of action that relies heavily on an intelligence judgment, strategists should inquire what information might change the overall judgment. Often a critical analytic judgment is based on an assumption or marginal data. In the absence of hard information, analysts must make some assumptions in order to provide projections or assessments. By probing for the most critical assumptions, the strategists can gauge how much uncertainty their courses of action must take into account. For example, in 1990, while analysts could see Iraqi forces massing on the border of Kuwait, there was a presumption that this was a show of force. For a number of good reasons, they did not believe Saddam Hussein would risk a major conflict by actually invading.[21] While analysts at the time could have justified their judgment, they would have admitted their views were based on presumed Iraqi priorities, not on actual data. Such an admission might have reduced the surprise when Saddam crossed the border.

INTELLIGENCE AS A TOOL FOR IMPLEMENTING STRATEGY

While intelligence is most commonly thought of as an enabler of strategy, it also can serve as an instrument of strategy. The National Military Strategic Plan for the War on Terrorism cited intelligence along with financial and legal instruments as tools of national power, alongside the more commonly listed diplomatic, informational, military, and economic instruments of national power. Although this expanded list of elements of power has not gained broad acceptance, intelligence has long been a tool used to attain strategic ends. While space limitations preclude a complete discussion on the ways and means of intelligence as a tool for executing a strategy, some key considerations on the strategic use of intelligence are covered below.

Intelligence Sharing.

While the War on Terror has highlighted the importance of intelligence sharing between countries, the United States has had foreign liaison arrangements since at least the early-20th century.[22] Such sharing of information can benefit both nations. For the United States, providing data to another country on activities and actors within its borders can lead to that country acting either unilaterally or in conjunction with the United States to neutralize the threat. Conversely, in many regions, an ally or friendly country will have better access to local intelligence sources than the U.S. For allies who regard terrorism or WMD proliferation as a common threat, there is motivation to share and act on intelligence data. Sharing is particularly critical when the threats are transnational, since one country may see only part of the network. Leveraging the capabilities and expertise of the intelligence services of other countries can potentially expand the information available to American analysts at a relatively low cost in terms of resources expended.

The strategist can use sharing of intelligence as a tool to forge closer relationships between the United States and other nations. The kind and utility of the information provided may signal a level of trust and confidence in the partner, fostering cooperation in other spheres. Bilateral agreements are most commonly used for intelligence sharing. Multilateral agreements, whether through established organizations such as NATO or ad hoc coalitions, provide broader access to the information provided, with attendant greater counterintelligence concerns. In many situations, intelligence-sharing arrangements can become a blend of multilateral and bilateral arrangements. In such scenarios, there is a significant risk of some partners balking when they discover or at least suspect that they are not receiving the same information as another coalition partner. Strategists must think through ahead of time how to handle the disparities in intelligence-sharing arrangements.

As with every strategic tool, there are risks and potential liabilities associated with sharing intelligence. Since good intelligence relies on the secrecy of both the data and the methods used to collect it, sharing information risks exposing methods and losing sources. The standards for internally sharing and protecting information vary widely between nations, and we must often establish special procedures to protect American interests. The counterintelligence risk may be higher in other countries. Third countries may deliberately target American information provided to a partner nation. If the third country is a traditional ally of the partner nation, the counterintelligence risk can be very high indeed.

The inverse of the counterintelligence risk to information provided to a partner are the risks involved in the intelligence provided *by* a partner. Without direct access to the sources of information—something that most intelligence services are loath to give—the American intelligence community has limited ability to validate the information provided. The partner service may unwittingly pass on fabricated information. Alternatively, the partner may provide information—possibly fabricated, but usually true—whose primary purpose is more to influence U.S. perceptions and evaluations than to inform. And there is always a risk of circular reporting; multiple reports coming from several different sources that, if traced back through the reporting chain, actually originate from a single source. Such circular reporting can mislead intelligence analysts into placing greater credence in a report than the actual sourcing warrants.

Intelligence cooperation is often asymmetric in the sense that nations have different capabilities, and their capabilities bound what they can provide in a cooperative context. Given differing strengths and weaknesses, the United States might offer technical assistance or intelligence training in return for access to information the partner country collects and analyzes. Allies may also represent resources for translation of dialects in which the American intelligence community lacks translators. Foreign governments may even be willing to undertake some intelligence operations in coordination with or on behalf of the United States.

Intelligence as Information.

One reason intelligence often is not seen as an instrument of national power in its own right is because the distinction between the intelligence tool and the informational element of national power is at best unclear and in many regards artificial. Intelligence *is* information—albeit government-gathered, secret information. Some aspects of the employment of intelligence information are identical to the uses of other information sources. We leave to other authors the proper use of information in diplomatic, influence, or psychological operations; however, a few unique aspects of intelligence as information are worth covering here.

First, as noted earlier, intelligence sharing can be used to convey a message of trust and confidence to other nations. Which information is provided to which allies on what topics constitutes a strategic communications decision that ought be integrated with the overall engagement strategy.

Governments can also use the public disclosure of intelligence assessments to shape domestic and international opinion in support of a strategic objective. The administration of Tony Blair in Great Britain, for example, published a 55-page intelligence report on Iraqi WMD as part of a campaign to bolster support for its efforts to put pressure on the Saddam regime.[23] The Bush administration similarly used the unclassified key judgments of several National Security Estimates to justify policy decisions.

The use of intelligence in the public arena is a tool that strategists must use sparingly and judiciously. Every public disclosure, even if unclassified, provides adversaries with a better understanding of the strengths and limitations of U.S. intelligence capabilities. Also, if an intelligence assessment is being specifically crafted for public release, there potentially will be greater pressure placed on the analysts to make the estimates support the desired policy. Individual phrases will be carefully scrutinized not just by the intelligence leaders, but by the policy community. The risk of politicization of the intelligence rises quickly when the assessments become part of the public debate on a strategy. While this risk can be managed through good tradecraft, strategists must carefully monitor themselves to ensure they do not become part of the problem.

Thanks to the voluminous information publicly available on intelligence methods—and even more, perhaps due to Hollywood's portrayal of intelligence capabilities—many adversaries and intelligence targets have views on the threats and risks U.S. intelligence poses to their operations. Adroit disclosure of intelligence priorities and capabilities—including perhaps misinformation—can be used to constrain an adversary. If a terrorist network, for example, believes any use of the Internet can be monitored, then one communication channel may be closed to them, complicating operational planning. The decision to disclose such information needs to be carefully weighed, since a capability, once revealed, is generally lost forever. As a rule, any decision to disclose intelligence capabilities rests with the Director of National Intelligence. Like every tool of strategy, the strategist must find the best possible balance between risks and gains.

Covert Action.

The topic of covert action is far too diverse and complex to attempt to cover here. Suffice to say that strategists need to be aware of the strengths and limitations of this particular use of intelligence services as part an overall strategy. Covert operations were used very successfully in the Cold War to support friendly governments and fend off Communist influences.

By definition, covert operations mask the involvement of the U.S. government in the activity. However, in a democracy it is difficult, if not impossible, to keep government involvement hidden. While an activity may still provide plausible deniability, the role of the government in an action may become an accepted fact, shaping both domestic and international views on the strategy. When considering covert action, the strategist must take into account the implications to the overall strategy when, not if, the covert action becomes public knowledge.

WHAT'S A STRATEGIST TO DO?

Strategists deal with the future—a future that is volatile, uncertain, complex, and ambiguous. The purpose of strategy is to influence that future to serve one's national interests better. Intelligence cannot remove all the uncertainty, but can provide a solid grounding in the present and bound the likely directions of future events.

Good intelligence is vital for defining the strategic environment. Intelligence can identify opportunities and estimate the likely reactions and outcomes of different approaches. The strategist must combine these insights with other considerations of resources (means) and methods (ways) in the specific strategic context to find the best possible balance of risks to achieve the desired ends. Intelligence will not tell the strategist what to do, but, if used properly, it can illuminate the issues and aid in finding the best path.

These benefits, however, are unlikely to accrue if the intelligence analysts are kept out of the strategy-development process. If strategists ask questions for which the analysts do not know the context, the answers they get will often be like those provided to our balloonists. After receiving a few irrelevant or unhelpful responses, most strategists will stop engaging with the intelligence analysts at all. But if the analysts work regularly with the strategists, understand their needs and perspectives, and provide regular inputs to the policy deliberations, they can provide timely and insightful information—resulting in better-informed, and hopefully more successful, strategic decisions.

ENDNOTES - CHAPTER 19

1. Sherman Kent, *Strategic Intelligence for American World Policy*, Princeton, NJ: Princeton University Press, 1949, Kent used this breakdown of definitions to organize his seminal work, *Strategic Intelligence.*

2. *Ibid.,* p. vii.

3. Vernon Walters, *Silent Missions*, Garden City, NY: Doubleday, 1978, p. 621.

4. R. A. Random, "Intelligence as a Science," *Studies in Intelligence,* Spring 1958, p. 76, quoted in Michael Warner, "Wanted: A Definition of 'Intelligence': Understanding Our Craft," *Studies in Intelligence,* Vol. 46, No. 3, 2002, available from *www.cia.gov/library/center-for-the-study-of-intelligence/csi-publications/csi-studies/studies/vol46no3/article02.html.*

5. Sun Tzu, *The Art of War*, Samuel B. Griffith, trans., New York: Oxford University Press, 1963, p. 84.

6. *Ibid.,* p. 144.

7. *Ibid., p.* 145.

8. Carl von Clausewitz, *On War*, trans. Michael Howard and Peter Paret, Princeton, NJ: Princeton University Press, 1976), 117.

9. Kent, p. 151.

10. John McLaughlin, "Serving the National Policymaker," in *Analyzing Intelligence: Origins, Obstacles, and Innovations*, Roger Z. George and James B. Bruce, eds., Washington, DC: Georgetown University Press, 2008, p. 74. See also Roger George, "The Art of Strategy and Intelligence" in the same volume for a very clear description of the many ways the strategist benefits from a close interaction with intelligence analysts.

11. Mark M. Lowenthal, *Intelligence: From Secrets to Policy*, 4th Ed., Washington, DC: CQ Press, 2009, p. 5.

12. Roger George, "The Art of Strategy and Intelligence" in *Analyzing Intelligence*, George and Bruce, eds., p. 113.

13. Colin Gray, "The 21st Century Security Environment and the Future of War," *Parameters,* Vol. 38, No. 4, Winter 2008, p. 15.

14. *Ibid.,* p. 16.

15. For example, the acquisition of and plans to employ weapons of mass destruction by a terrorist group is currently thought to be unlikely. While some resources are devoted to preventing this from happening, the balance of resources would be radically different were intelligence gathered that made this event more likely.

16. Jack Davis, "Paul Wolfowitz on Intelligence Policy-Relations," *Studies in Intelligence,* Vol. 39, No. 5, 1996, available from *www.cia.gov/library/center-for-the-study-of-intelligence/csi-publications/csi-studies/studies/_96unclass/_davis.htm.*

17. Lowenthal provides a succinct review of the benefits of opportunity analysis, as well as why this type of analysis is so difficult and rare. Lowenthal, *Intelligence: From Secrets to Policy*, p. 134. See also Martin Petersen, "What We Should Demand from Intelligence," in *Intelligence and the National Security Strategist: Enduring Issues and Challenges*, Roger Z. George and Robert D. Kline, eds., Washington, DC: National Defense University Press, 2004.

18. Gregory Trevorton explored this issue at length, describing the benefits and pitfalls of a closer relationship between analysts and policymakers. Gregory Treverton, "Intelligence Analysis: Between 'Politicization' and Irrelevance," in *Analyzing Intelligence,* George and Bruce, eds.

19. McLaughlin, p. 74.

20. Powell's questions have become so well known in the intelligence community they have become axioms used for training new analysts. The former Secretary of State offered a fuller version of his questions in remarks made to the Senate Governmental Affair Committee on September13, 2004. "Tell me what you know. Tell me what you don't know. And then, based on what you really know and what you really don't know, tell me what you think is most likely to happen. And there's an extension of that rule with my intelligence officers: I will hold you accountable for what you tell me is a fact; and I will hold you accountable for what you tell me is not going to happen because you have the facts on that, or you don't know what's going to happen, or you know what your body of ignorance is and you told me what that is," available from *www.fas.org/irp/congress/2004_hr/091304powell.html.*

21. Davis, "Paul Wolfowitz on Intelligence Policy-Relations."

22. Derek Reveron, "Old Allies, New Friends: Intelligence-Sharing in the War on Terror," *Orbis,* Vol. 50, No. 3, Summer 2006, p. 454.

23. Christopher Andrews, "Intelligence, International Relations, and 'Under-theorisation,'" *Intelligence and National Security,* Vol. 19, No. 2, 2004, p. 171.

CHAPTER 20

THE AIRPLANE AND WARFARE: THEORY AND HISTORY

Tami Davis Biddle

As we evaluate any military instrument, we must ask ourselves, "How can it contribute to the achievement of a political aim, either in peacetime or in war?" What leverage does the instrument offer those who employ it? What are its primary strengths? Primary limitations? How does it interact with other instruments of power, both military and nonmilitary? Can it be used independently? What are the advantages and risks of doing so?

This chapter will combine a basic historical narrative with excerpts from primary source literature, the latter articulating the views of some of the most prominent air power theorists in order to encourage thinking about the questions listed above. The role that airplanes should play in war (and which service should own them) developed into one of the most contentious and sustained military debates of the 20th century. Echoes of the struggle still exist, although the movement toward jointness has had a moderating effect. As you read, ask yourselves why the different theorists held particular views. What influenced their thinking? (Technology, culture, bureaucratic contests for resources?) What underlying assumptions did they make? How did these assumptions hold up in the test of actual warfare?

THE EARLY YEARS

The *idea* of aerial warfare long predated the physical manifestation of airplanes. For centuries before the Wright brothers' first flight, humans had tried to imagine all the future roles that "aircraft" might play—not the least in war. Prior to World War I, the use of aircraft in war was very limited, and planning in this new realm was necessarily speculative. During World War I, aircraft underwent a revolutionary transformation, driven by the intensely competitive demands of the war. In 1914, warplanes were primitive machines held together by wire and twine. By 1918, large, sophisticated four-engine bombers had been developed and used. The arrival of these new instruments had major institutional and organizational ramifications for all modern military services.

The prewar expectations of individual observers tended to influence their interpretations of wartime experience. Since the interpretation of data and evidence is heavily conditioned by what people *expect* to see, their observations—rather than being wholly objective—are colored by social, cultural, and political influences, by their life experiences, and by the bureaucratic positions they hold.

Prior to the outbreak of World War I, civilian writers generally held higher expectations for air warfare than military planners did. The latter were more conservative, expecting an airplane's main contribution to be in improved reconnaissance. But a minority—officers who came to hold formative roles in the development of air power and thus came to hold an institutional stake in the future of air warfare—emerged from the war with strong convictions and bold claims about the revolutionary impact of the airplane on war.

During World War I, airplanes had proved their worth in a variety of realms. Indeed, nearly every modern mission of aircraft (as developed through the 20th century) received at least a rudimentary trial between 1914 and 1918. As many had expected, airplanes proved to be extraordinary reconnaissance tools, revolutionizing the way that intelligence would be gathered and battle space would be monitored. Indeed, the obvious value of air space created an instant need for instruments that could both seek it out (over enemy territory) and preserve it (over one's own territory). This led directly to the rise of fighter aircraft—and to their rapid, ongoing modification during the course of the war.

The relatively primitive state of communications technology in 1914 meant that air-ground and air-air contact was limited, but it improved generally over the course of the war and enhanced the battlefield role of the airplane. The tactics for the employment of aircraft were worked out just as ground combat tactics were worked out: through intensive trial and error. By the end of the war, a fairly sophisticated body of doctrine existed for the battlefield uses of aircraft.[1]

The record of long-range ("strategic") bombardment during the war was more mixed. The hardware and tools needed to make it a viable proposition—including engines, airframes, navigation methods, and bomb development—were very primitive at the outset of the war. By 1917, the Germans had twin and four-engine bombers capable of waging attacks on Britain, but these were limited in number. The British were then developing a large bomber to be used over Berlin in 1919, but the war ended before it could be brought into service. The Italians also developed a large bomber during the course of the war.

While attacking bombers usually could get to their targets (especially in the early phases of an air campaign before adequate air defenses could be brought to bear), it was difficult for them to bomb accurately and thus achieve serious levels of destruction. Also, the limited numbers of bombers put a low ceiling on the damage that could be achieved through air attacks. Improving defenses around valuable targets would make it increasingly difficult for attackers to reach those targets unscathed. All this meant that it was hard to produce any systematic reduction of the enemy war economy. However, by 1917-18, some rather impressive *plans* were worked out, in particular by the British, for long-range bombing. One planner in particular, Lord Tiverton, produced sophisticated targeting plans while he worked for the Royal Naval Air Service and later on the staff of the newly independent Royal Air Force.[2] He stressed sustained attacks on key targets in the German war economy, including munitions, chemicals, and the steel industry. Perhaps this kind of campaign might have been carried out if the war had continued into 1919. American observers liked the work of Tiverton; indeed, they incorporated it into the first American air plan for what they termed "strategical" bombing, compiled by Lieutenant Colonel Edgar S. Gorrell in 1917 but never implemented.[3]

The impact of World War I bombing on civilian morale was difficult to interpret, and observers tended to draw from it what they expected to see or what was institutionally congenial. Because the long-range attacks were neither heavy nor sustained, they did not compel civilians to pressure their governments to sue for peace. What they did do, however—especially in the case of Britain—was to embolden civilians to demand better air defenses, and to call for retaliation against their attackers. Aerial attacks that provoked no governmental response (either air defense or retaliation) made many civilians indignant. Nervous about civilian morale under air attack, many elites assumed that these public demands were fueled by panic and terror, but a close look at the primary sources indicates, instead, that they were fueled by anger. For their part, the Germans were disappointed with the impact of their own long-range bombing. While they knew their effort had been limited in resources and scale, they realized, too, that they had not been able to undermine the British war economy seriously or reduce the British will to fight.

However, the very fact that long-range bombing had been a marginal effort compared to the vast clashes of ground forces meant that the wartime experience was not the end of the story, but only the beginning. To the emerging air power advocates, the experience suggested trends for the future—trends that could be extrapolated and fleshed out through a bit of imagination and visioning. At the end of the war, interpretations of the value of independent air operations varied widely.[4] The analysis of actual wartime experience was limited, and it lacked rigor.

During the interwar years, those making bold claims for air power gained degrees of legitimacy for a variety of reasons. The war had indicated that technological advancement could take place in a highly telescoped way. Many observers thus concluded that the technological development of air power would be fast and relentless—and that the capabilities of bombers would outstrip the capabilities of fighters. In a related way, they systematically downplayed the prospects for ground-based defenses. Many assumed that some of the most daunting weapons of the war (including chemicals and gas) would see intensified and expanded use in any future war. While these observers viewed such expansion as regrettable, they also believed it would have the effect of shortening wars—because wars would become so terrible and unendurable. Air advocates argued this in reaction to the trench stalemate of World War I—a catastrophe that politicians were eager to avoid repeating. Air power, its advocates argued, would restore the impact of offensive operations to the battlefield, and would offer the prospect of directly undermining the enemy's all-important "will to fight." Finally, air advocates argued that all modern states would embrace airplanes as essential tools of war and deterrence, insisting that those which failed to do so would put themselves at an enormous disadvantage in the ongoing competition among nations.

GIULIO DOUHET

Giulio Douhet was born into a military family and became an artillery officer. By 1909, Douhet had begun thinking seriously about air power, and, prior to the start of World War I, he commanded the Italian Army's aviation section. During the war, he recommended breaking the land war stalemate with Austria by using a 500-plane bomber force. Because his proposal also contained a strong critique of Italian military leaders, he was court-martialed. However, he was recalled to service in 1918 to head the Italian Central Aeronautical Bureau.[5] His 1921 book, *The Command of the Air*, painted a graphic vision of societal collapse in the face of air attack. Indeed, it was the futurist drama he conveyed rather than the analytical rigor of his ideas that gave Douhet a lasting place in the canon of air warfare.[6] A poet, painter, playwright, and amateur novelist, Douhet brought to bear on his work "the intense modernist fascination with the latest advances in science and technology . . . prevalent in prewar Italian protofascist *avant-garde* culture."[7] Both British and American airmen had developed indigenous theories of air warfare before Douhet published his book, but *Command of the Air* was cited widely (especially after it was widely translated) and used to support apocalyptic visions of air warfare. Douhet's vision stressed the offensive; indeed, he referred to aircraft as the offensive weapon "par excellence." Though Douhet believed that technology had given the defensive a permanent pride of place in ground warfare, he argued just the opposite with respect to air war. He believed that the vastness of the sky made defense against the airplane virtually impossible: The defender's inability to know the exact position and timing of air attack gave the attacker a tremendous edge. Douhet also largely dismissed the potential of ground defenses. As historian Phillip Meilinger has noted, "Douhet sarcastically concluded that ground fire might down some aircraft, much like muskets shot in the air might occasionally hit a swallow, but it was not a serious deterrent to air attack."[8]

Douhet noted several target categories of primary significance: industry, transport, infrastructure, communication, seats of government, and the will of the people. Douhet emphasized the latter in particular, since he argued that wars in the future would see no distinction between combatants and noncombatants, and that urban targeting would do the most to collapse enemy will. While he admitted that a strong and wealthy nation might opt to build both tactical and strategic air forces, he believed that the utility of the latter vastly outweighed the former.[9]

Much of the power of Douhet's vision came from his linkage of airplanes and chemical warfare. Gas weapons had evoked a sense of dread in the public mind that was felt throughout Europe.

Douhet asked his readers, "How could a country go on living and working under this constant threat, oppressed by the nightmare of imminent destruction and death?" He was impressed by the possibilities of attack against those of "least moral resistance" such as factory workers.[10] His vision was one of technological determinism: "The brutal but inescapable conclusion we must draw is this: in the face of the technical developments of aviation today, in case of war the strongest army we can deploy . . . and the strongest navy we can dispose . . . will provide no effective defense against determined efforts . . . to bomb our cities."[11]

However, Douhet's perspective was narrow, and he saw only the evidence that supported his view. As historian Michael Sherry has pointed out, Douhet's idea of the future rested on crude extrapolation, and like many other interwar prophets of air power, he failed to see how it "might evolve unpredictably, strengthening the defense as well as the offense, creating its own futile charges and bloody stalemates."[12]

SIR HUGH TRENCHARD

Hugh Montague Trenchard served as a field commander for the British Army's Royal Flying Corps during World War I. He would ultimately become known as the "Father of the Royal Air Force," although this was ironic, since he initially had little interest in the creation of a separate service. The establishment of an independent air service in Britain came about because of public demands for better air defense and retaliation following German air attacks on Britain (beginning in 1915 with Zeppelin raids and escalating to bomber raids by 1917). Trenchard was called on to be the first head of a long-range bombardment force (the "Independent Force") in 1918. He accepted the task reluctantly. Since he had relatively few airplanes, he had little ability to implement any kind of systematic bombardment of the German war economy. It was clear to him, though, that the British public expected to see results from the retaliatory raids. Able to produce little sustained destruction of German targets, he argued expediently that the *psychological* effect of bombardment was much greater than the physical effect.[13]

Trenchard was appointed the first post-World War I Chief of the Royal Air Force (RAF), where he was responsible for the future of the new service. Placed in this position, he became a convert to and defender of independent air power. After the war, the British Army and the Royal Navy sought to regain control of their air arms. In order to head this off, Trenchard—who had a particularly strong rivalry with the Navy—worked to make the newly independent RAF relevant to British defense policy. He argued that "air control" over British colonial possessions would enable a cheaper administration of Britain's vast empire. Moreover, he argued that long-range bombardment would be a key feature of all future warfare.

Trenchard proved to be a particularly effective bureaucratic infighter, resurrecting his wartime arguments about the psychological or "moral" (pronounced "morale") effect of air war, and claiming that an attacking air force would be in a position to undermine an enemy's will to fight by placing pressure directly on the enemy population. Attacks on enemy "vital centers" would cause the enemy population to call for better air defenses (as the British had done in World War I). The heavier and more persistent these offensive attacks, the more the enemy would be driven on the defensive by popular cries for protection. The enemy's increasing defensive effort would soak up resources and would place the enemy state on a slippery slope from which it could not recover. Many of Trenchard's ideas were articulated in the memorandum he wrote for the Chiefs of Staff Sub-Committee (May 1928) on *"The War Object of an Air Force."* Quotations from that text follow below (original spelling used).

I would state definitely that in the view of the Air Staff the object to be sought by air action will be to paralyse from the very outset the enemy's productive centres of munitions of war of every sort and to stop all communication and transportation.

Air power can . . . pass over the enemy navies and armies, and penetrate the air defenses and attack directly the centres of production, transportation and communication from which the enemy war effort is maintained.

It will from time to time certainly be found advantageous to turn to the attack of an enemy air base, but such attacks will not be the main operation. For his main operation, each belligerent will set out to attack directly those objectives which he considers most vital to the enemy. Each will penetrate the defenses of the other to a certain degree. The stronger side, by developing the more powerful offensive, will provoke in his weaker enemy increasingly insistent calls for the protective employment of aircraft. In this way he will throw the enemy on to the defensive and it will be in this manner that air superiority will be obtained, and not by direct destruction of air forces.

What is illegitimate . . . is the indiscriminate bombing of a city for the sole purpose of terrorising the civilian population. It is an entirely different matter to terrorise munition workers (men and women) into absenting themselves from work or stevedores into abandoning the loading of a ship with munitions through fear of air attack upon the factory or dock concerned. . . . [A]ir attacks will be directed against any objectives which will contribute effectively towards the destruction of the enemy's means of resistance and the lowering of his determination to fight.

We shall attack the vital centres of transportation and seriously impede these arms and munitions reaching the battlefield and, therefore, more successfully assist the Army in its direct attack on the enemy's Army. We shall attack the communications without which the national effort cannot be co-ordinated and directed.

The moral effect of such attacks is very great. Even in the last war ten years ago, before any of the heavier bombers had really been employed to any extent, the moral effect of such sporadic raids as were then practicable was considerable. With the greater numbers of aircraft, the larger carrying capacity and range, and the heavier bombs available today, the effect would seriously impede the work of the enemy's Navy, Army, and Air Forces. . . . Once a raid has been experienced false alarms are incessant and a state of panic remains in which work comes to a standstill.

There can be no question, whatever views we may hold in regard to it, that this form of warfare will be used. . . . Whatever we may wish or hope . . . there is not the slightest doubt that in the next war both sides will send their aircraft out without scruple to bomb those objectives which they consider to be most suitable.[14]

BILLY MITCHELL

William L. "Billy" Mitchell, son of a wealthy Wisconsin Senator, enlisted as a private in the U.S. Army during the Spanish American War and later gained a commission. He served successfully in the Signal Corps and began taking flying lessons at the age of 38. Mitchell went to France in 1917 (as a lieutenant colonel), and helped pave the way for an American air contribution to the war. A tireless and flamboyant leader, he rose quickly to Brigadier General, commanding all American air units in France. He led nearly 1,500 aircraft in the 1918 battle of St. Mihiel. Despite his rapid rise, though, Mitchell alienated many with his aggressive style and tendency toward self-righteousness.

On his return from the war, Mitchell continued to be controversial. He feuded with his own service, and his air attacks on stationary battleships in 1921 and 1923 placed him in the midst of a passionate fight with the Navy. His harsh criticism of the crash of the Navy dirigible *Shenandoah* (he argued there had been "an almost treasonable administration of the national defense") led to his court-martial and ouster from the Army.[15] He devoted the rest of his career to making a public case for air power. More an advocate than a theorist or systematic thinker, Mitchell nonetheless was tireless in his quest for air force service autonomy, for aerial resources, and for "air-mindedness" among the American public.

Below are direct quotations from Mitchell's 1925 book, *Winged Defense: The Development and Possibilities of Modern Air Power – Economic and Military*:

> The air-going people actually form a separate class. They are more different from landsmen than are landsmen from seamen. At the present time, the air-going people in the national services are not accorded the position nor the rank to which the importance of their duties entitles them.

> The world stands on the threshold of the 'aeronautical era.' During this epoch the destinies of all people will be controlled through the air.

> The air force has ceased to remain a mere auxiliary service for the purpose of assisting an army or navy in the execution of its task. . . . The air force fights in three dimensions –on the level, from up above, and from underneath. . . . [To date] the only defenses against aircraft are other aircraft which will contest the supremacy of the air by air battles. Great contests for air control will be the rule in the future. Once supremacy of the air has been established, airplanes can fly over a hostile country at will.

> How can a hostile air force be forced to fight, it may be asked, if they do not desire to leave the ground? The air strategist answers: 'By finding a location of such importance to the enemy that he must defend it against a bombardment attack by airplanes.'

> As air power can hit at a distance, after it controls the air and vanquishes the opposing air power it will be able to fly anywhere over the hostile country. The menace will be so great that either a state will hesitate to go to war, or, having engaged in war, will make the contest much sharper, more decisive, and more quickly finished. This will result in a diminished loss of life and treasure and will thus be a distinct benefit to civilization. Air forces will attack centers of production of all kinds, means of transportation, agricultural areas, ports and shipping; not so much the people themselves. . . . Today to make war we must have great metal and chemical factories that have to stay in one place, take months to build, and, if destroyed, cannot be replaced in the usual length of a modern war.

> The role of armies and their way of making war will remain much the same in the future as it has in the past, if air power does not entirely prevent them from operating. Navies, however, are able to control only the areas of water outside of the cruising radius of aircraft. These areas are constantly diminishing with the increasing flying powers of aircraft. It will be impossible for them to bombard or blockade a coast as they used to, or to ascend the rivers, bays, or estuaries of a country adequately provided with air power.

> Each year the leading countries of the world are recognizing the value of air power more and more. . . . People who are unused to or unfamiliar with air work are incapable of visioning what air power should be, of training the men necessary for work in the air, or of devising the equipment that they should have.

> It was proved in the European war [WWI] that the only effective defense against aerial attack is to whip the enemy's air forces in air battles. In other words, seizing the initiative, forcing the enemy to the

defensive in his own territory, attacking his most important ground positions, menacing his airplanes on the ground, in the hangars, on the airdromes and in the factories so that he will be forced to take the air and defend them. . . . The whole arrangement of ground protection against aircraft, sound ranging, searchlights and guns cannot stand up under intelligent air attack and is incapable of serious effect on airplanes. The only defense against aircraft is by hitting the enemy first, just as far away from home as possible. The idea of defending the country against air attack by machine guns or anti-aircraft cannons from the ground is absolutely incapable of being carried out.[16]

THE INTERWAR ERA AND WORLD WAR II

Douhet, Trenchard, and Mitchell were all influenced by the circumstances in which they found themselves. While there were some differences in their views, there were many commonalities as well. Many of their assumptions would prove to be flawed. For instance, their central assumption about the inherently offensive nature of air power and the ability of an attacking force to always "get through" relied on a selective interpretation of the evidence from World War I. In fact, in many instances during World War I, aerial defenses (especially fighters) had been effective in preventing other airplanes from gaining access to airspace. In *Winged Defense*, Mitchell explained how he had conducted air defense in World War I, but he then largely dismissed it as misplaced effort. He convinced himself of the validity of his position by arguing that airplanes would only grow more capable in the future (they would fly faster, higher)—and would thus be harder to defend against. He was also impressed by the sheer vastness of the sky. This physical fact, he believed, would give a permanent advantage to the attacker.

In the 1920s, bombers did tend to develop more quickly than fighters. However, the momentum began to shift in the 1930s as fighter development began to catch up. Moreover, the advent of radar changed the air defense equation very significantly.[17] Air defense later took many forms and proved much more robust than the early theorists had predicted. During World War II, the Germans in particular would develop highly effective flak guns that could reach and destroy bombers flying at high altitude, and disrupt the flight paths of many others. (Flak is an acronym from the German word for air defense guns: Fliegerabwehrkanonen.) In terms of passive defense, the Germans built decoy factories and towns; they lit decoy fires to divert British nighttime bombers to incorrect locations.[18] They also managed to disperse a great deal of their industry and to place some of it underground.

The role that a nation's air force played going into World War II varied with that nation's history, experience, and geopolitical situation. Nearly all industrialized nations took an interest in air power and long-range bombardment. However, not all nations developed the latter. Under Trenchard and his successors, the RAF developed and espoused a doctrine for strategic bombing, but did not back it up with rigorous analysis of how to carry out such bombing effectively. The French, the leading aviation power in World War I, never entirely recovered from the devastating effects of that war. Economic and political problems, as well as overall war-weariness, kept France from regaining any semblance of the position she had held up to 1917-18. Russia, wracked by civil war and then devastated by the paranoid politics of Josef Stalin, recovered only just in time to save herself (with Allied help) from Adolf Hitler. The Russians would develop highly capable air power in the course of World War II, but it remained tied closely to the Red Army. Although the Versailles agreement had prevented Germany from having an interwar air force, the Germans continued to take an interest in aviation and in long-range bombing (and retained very active glider clubs!). The development of advanced, long-range bombers lagged in Germany for a variety of reasons under Hitler.[19] Nevertheless, the Luftwaffe did develop highly effective methods of coordinating tactical aviation and maneuver warfare on the ground. Indeed, this cooperation was the heart of what the West termed "Blitzkrieg" early in World War II.

The Americans, despite taking an interest in the antics and aggressive salesmanship of Billy Mitchell, did not feel the need to create an independent air service before World War II. The United States was largely defensive in its military posture, and those serving officers who wrote about air warfare had to do so within careful boundaries. Nonetheless, the organization that was first called the U.S. Army Air Service, then the Air Corps, and later the Army Air Forces, did gain increasing levels of autonomy during the interwar years. Ideas about bombing an enemy war economy—developed by Britain's Tiverton and his colleagues and incorporated into World War I planning by the American, Lieutenant Colonel Edgar S. Gorrell—were preserved in the documents and lectures of the Air Service and Air Corps School system. In 1926 another unsung hero of air power, William C. Sherman, put forward an early but articulate version of what would become, in the 1930s, the "industrial fabric" theory of bombing heralded by the Air Corps Tactical School. Sherman, an instructor of air tactics at Fort Leavenworth, was mindful about the moral and ethical ramifications of bombing city centers, and he was, in any event, most interested in finding and hitting an enemy's specific industrial sites. He wrote:

> Industry consists . . . of a complex system of interlocking factories, each of which makes only its allotted part of the whole. . . . Accordingly, in the majority of industries it is necessary to destroy certain elements of the industry only, in order to cripple the whole. . . . On the declaration of war, these key plants should be made the object of a systematic bombardment . . . until they have been sufficiently crippled."[20]

Despite the fleshing out of a reasonably specific bombardment doctrine, the development of the B-17 bomber, and the helpful addition of Sperry and Norden bombsights, the interwar Air Corps was officially prevented from thinking in terms of offensive action. Even as Hitler made his aims increasingly clear in the 1930s, the American people expressed no desire to be pulled into another European war. By the late-1930s, however, President Franklin Roosevelt began to increase military budgets, giving special attention to the Air Corps. Perhaps it should be no surprise that both Britain and the United States had been drawn toward air power. Armies are expensive, and can be politically and socially disruptive. Britain and the United States, both blessed with geographical good fortune, had eschewed large standing armies in favor of seapower. They followed a similar pattern with respect to airplanes and airpower as these became available. Their desire to substitute technology for manpower was only reinforced by the distasteful memories of World War I's trench battles.

In the late-1930s, the British realized there was a considerable discrepancy between their bomber doctrine and their capacity for carrying it out. They tried to close the gap prior to the start of the war, but did not make great progress. The Battle of France revealed that neither the French nor the British had paid nearly enough attention to air-ground cooperation on the battlefield. While Trenchard and his colleagues had given rhetorical prominence to long-range bombing, they had not—happily—neglected air defense. This enabled the British to prevail in their quest to maintain control over their own air space during the Battle of Britain in the summer of 1940. Luftwaffe commander Hermann Goering, boastful about the capabilities of his force, was embarrassed by the Luftwaffe's failure and by the British retaliatory attacks against Berlin that he had argued were impossible. However, the Germans, like the British, constructed formidable defenses centered on radar, and this had the effect of greatly disrupting British plans for their own air offensive. The British discovered early in the war that they could not bomb in daylight without prohibitive losses, and they thus shifted to nighttime attacks. The RAF knew that such raids would suffer from inaccuracy, but they did not fully appreciate the degradation until the summer of 1941, when a thorough photo-reconnaissance analysis revealed that only about one in five bombers was getting within five miles of its target. In February 1942, the British formalized what had become obvious: Since cities were the only targets that Bomber Command could reliably find and hit at that time,

Bomber Command would attack German cities, particularly those areas with dense populations of workers.[21]

Later in the year, Churchill invited the Americans to join the nighttime bombing effort, but they declined. They were convinced that by flying in groups of high-altitude, self-defending bombers, they could prevent high attrition and find their way to specific industrial targets.[22] This proved to be overly optimistic. The Americans suffered high attrition, particularly in late-1943, when they began to attack targets regularly deep in German territory. The losses prompted the Americans to change course as well, but they changed tactics rather than targets. By bringing large numbers of long-range fighters equipped with droppable, self-sealing fuel tanks into the European theater, they were able to provoke extensive and important aerial battles of attrition. (Some of this echoed Douhet and Mitchell's assertion that battles for air supremacy would be necessary and vital.) This American offensive began to overwhelm the Germans' ability to train pilots quickly enough, provoking a downward spiral from which the Germans ultimately could not recover.[23]

In Europe, the Americans tried in a general way to limit themselves to industrial targets. However, this quest was imperfect. The weather in northern Europe was so poor that the Americans frequently had to bomb "blind" rather than with a bombsight. This meant that much of the time, American accuracy was no better than British accuracy. (Indeed, because the British bombed on instruments so much of the time, they became very good at it.) During poor weather in the winter of 1944-45, 42 percent of U.S. 8th Air Force bombs fell more than five miles from the target.[24] Similarly, cloud cover and jet stream winds prevented successful "precision" bombing in the Pacific theater. In 1945, the Americans abandoned this effort and turned to low-level incendiary attacks on Japanese cities. Over 60 such attacks were waged—the most devastating on March 9-10, 1945, when over 100,000 Japanese died in a single attack on Tokyo. These incendiary attacks continued right up until the Japanese surrender—some taking place in between and after the two atomic attacks.[25]

What all air forces discovered in World War II was that long-range bombardment is much more difficult and demanding to prosecute than the interwar theorists had predicted. Air defense methods proved to be formidable, and it was by no means the case that "the bomber would always get through." In addition, finding and hitting targets reliably—especially in challenging weather conditions—was anything but a simple process.

Both the RAF and the U.S. Army Air Force (USAAF) were learning institutions, and they were able to continue to prosecute their offensives even as they adapted to the very demanding conditions that they had failed to anticipate. The British improved their navigation, bomb aiming, and the overall sophistication of their tactics throughout the war; by 1944, they were able to hit specific targets under the right conditions. Likewise, the insistent American determination to defeat the Luftwaffe proved to be deeply consequential. The attainment of air superiority over Europe made the D-day Landings a feasible operation, kept the bombing offensives alive, hastened the progress of Anglo-American armies eastward, and opened the skies to more devastating bombardment than had been possible earlier in the war.

Civilian populations proved to be much less fragile and much more robust than the interwar theorists had predicted. British civilians during the Blitz and German civilians during the long years of Anglo-American air attacks found ways to adjust to life under fire. Indeed, British experts discovered, much to their surprise, that many of their expectations turned out to be exactly wrong. Rather than the nervousness and psychosis they expected to see, British psychologists and doctors saw rates of suicide and drunkenness fall; they saw bombed populations pull together, overcoming previous class differences.[26] In addition, the effect of local, immediate coercion (the Gestapo in Germany) could trump the effect of more distant coercive mechanisms, such as enemy bombers.

Finally, culture could play a role, too. The strong commitment to the Emperor, who held religious status in Japanese society, made it difficult for Japanese civilians to turn their anger or desperation toward the existing government.

Because the strategic bombing of World War II did not have the early and profound impact that the interwar theorists had predicted, many postwar analysts concluded that it had failed to live up to its promise and had contributed only marginally to victory. However, these harsh critiques deserve carefully scrutiny. In any analysis, the first issue to consider is whether a different expenditure of resources would have been likely or even possible. Neither Britain nor the United States was comfortable with large standing armies (since they were not continental powers, they had no overriding need for such armies). They both had bitter memories of World War I and were anxious not to repeat that experience. They were both technologically advanced and proud of their industrial heritage and capabilities. It is unrealistic to expect that they would have eschewed the promise of air power (alongside sea power) in favor of a strategy that relied principally on armies and tactical aviation.

The second issue is the actual performance of aircraft in the war in both long-range and tactical applications. Even if bombing in Europe was imprecise and highly imperfect, it still served to place a ceiling on the expansion of the German war economy. Moreover, this effect was crucial at certain moments in the war. Bomber Command's 1943 campaign against the Ruhr for instance, prevented German munitions czar Albert Speer from carrying out a vast expansion of German munitions production in that year—an expansion that would have greatly benefited the Germans on the Eastern Front.[27] Heavy American attacks on the Luftwaffe cleared the way for the Normandy invasion. Pre-invasion bombardment by heavy bombers greatly disrupted the French transport network and kept the Germans from being able to wage optimal maneuver warfare in the post D-day European Theater. Subsequent air attacks (both British and American) on the German transport net and synthetic oil industry went a long way toward shutting down the German war economy, which depended on coal delivered by rail, making it impossible for Luftwaffe planes to fly or Wehrmacht tanks to run. The firebombing of Japan remains highly controversial and heavily debated among World War II historians. The naval victories and sea blockade of Japan were devastating to the Japanese people because they cut off their food source and their ability to keep the American enemy at bay. The two atomic attacks, because they were so devastating and technologically unusual, probably gave Hirohito an opportunity to surrender without losing face. For the Japanese Army, though, the convincing blow was the entry of the Soviet Union into the war, on August 8th (after the Hiroshima attack and before the Nagasaki attack).[28]

Tactical aviation was an incredibly powerful asset to the Allied cause once the Anglo-Americans had relearned how to do if effectively. Indeed, the military utility of tactical aviation *cannot be overstated*. Talented aviators like Arthur Tedder and Maori Coningham of Britain, and Pete Quesada of the United States, raised tactical airpower to a high art; they leveraged an Anglo-American asset in a way that gave immense advantages to their national fighting forces. (In the United States, we often forget that we take tactical air supremacy entirely for granted.)

Unfortunately, the interwar theorists' assumption that air war would be too terrible to be endured for long did not prove to be the case. The moral ramifications of long-range bombardment in both the European and Far Eastern theaters cannot be sidestepped. Anglo-American wartime decisions had immense consequences for enemy civilians. As we critique those decisions, though, we must look carefully at the possible alternatives and their likely ramifications: What would the outcomes and costs have been if there had been no long-range bombing used in the war? What would they have been if the bombing had been waged in a far-more-restricted way? Once they discovered that "precision" bombing of industrial targets was frequently impossible, should the Anglo-Americans have reconfigured their war effort?

The debates over air power that began with Douhet, Trenchard, and Mitchell were not resolved during World War II. Indeed, in many respects they intensified. Many analysts accused air forces of overselling their wares and falling short on their promises. Air advocates fought back by pointing to the many wartime contributions of air power. General Henry "Hap" Arnold, who commanded the USAAF during the war, was one of its most outspoken proponents and defenders. He not only put his service in a good position to achieve independence by 1947, but he also envisioned a future filled with many more tools of aerial warfare, including long-range missiles. Another passionate advocate of this era was Alexander de Seversky, a Russian who became a U.S. citizen in the 1920s and, in the 1930s, started the Seversky Aircraft Corporation. In his 1942 book, *Victory Through Air Power*, he wrote: "The most significant single fact about the war now in progress is the emergence of aviation as the paramount and decisive factor in warmaking.... All experts agree that air power will play an ever more decisive part in determining the power balance among the nations of the earth." With regard to future aviation, he argued: "We must not merely outbuild any potential enemy or combination of enemies—that is the lesser half of the job for a machine-age nation like the United States. We must out-think and out-plan them, in a spirit of creative audacity."[29]

THE COLD WAR

After World War II, bomber aircraft became the centerpiece of the American nuclear deterrent. The possession of such a strike force enabled the Americans to hold enemy assets at risk from a long distance. While the USAAF would have won its autonomy after the war anyway, the nuclear mission underscored the legitimacy of that autonomy, and brought considerable resources to the newly created Strategic Air Command (SAC). SAC started to become a highly professional and capable force in the late-1940s. Under the fiscally conservative Dwight Eisenhower administration, SAC offered the United States a reasonably inexpensive way of balancing against the large army maintained by the postwar Soviet Union. From the 1950s to the 1980s, the U.S. Air Force (USAF) was a SAC-dominated institution; its focus was geared toward maintaining a robust deterrent force that would head off a nuclear conflict between the superpowers. (SAC's motto was "Peace is our Profession.")

The two Asian wars fought by the Americans during the Cold War, in Korea and Vietnam, were frustrating for practitioners of long-range bombardment. Early restrictions on long-range bombing tended to erode as the wars dragged on and became increasingly costly. Incendiary attacks on Pyongyang, Korea, in early-January 1951, burned out 35 percent of the city. Training for atomic missions went forward, but authorities withheld permission for actual use of A-bombs.[30] The wider use of bombers, however, did not translate into discernable progress toward victory, and as time passed, American B-29s became increasingly vulnerable to North Korean air defenses.[31] The USAF was frustrated by the politics of the limited war, which ensured that enemy supply sources outside of North Korea (in China and Russia) remained permanently off the target lists, and that, therefore, the industrial fabric theory would remain a poor fit with the reality of the situation. General Curtis LeMay would later say about the war, "We never did hit a strategic target."[32] In 1952, further attacks on Pyongyang, on smaller towns and cities, and on North Korean hydroelectric plants failed to break the war's stalemate. The bombardment campaign culminated in 1953 with the breaching of dikes that led to the flooding of portions of the rice crop. That the armistice followed shortly thereafter was interpreted by some to mean that this final form of aerial coercion had worked. However, it is hard to know for sure, since many other factors (including, importantly, the death of Josef Stalin), were bearing in significant ways on the peace process. As in World War II, skillful use of tactical aviation was an irreplaceable asset to the Americans. Once the Korean War ended, the USAF reverted to its priority focus: the SAC deterrent and preparation for possible war with the Soviet Union.

When President Lyndon Johnson and his advisors dramatically increased the U.S. commitment to South Vietnam in 1964-65, they hoped that air power might facilitate a relatively quick and painless campaign that would not divert too many resources from the broader national agenda, including Johnson's "Great Society" program. They hoped that air strikes would demonstrate U.S. resolve, convince North Vietnam that supporting the insurgency in the South would be too costly, bolster morale in the South, erode the morale of Viet Cong cadres, and generally intimidate the leadership of the insurgency, thereby convincing them that they could not win.[33] In April 1964, the Joint Chiefs had compiled a list of 94 bombing targets in North Vietnam. The Air Force wished to attack these targets immediately and heavily, to impose psychological shock as well as physical damage. However, the administration instead chose a more graduated approach, which would punish (by reprisal) acts of terror committed by the Viet Cong and hold enemy targets of value at risk. After Viet Cong guerillas struck a U.S. Special Forces camp at Pleiku in February of 1965, American policymakers implemented Operation ROLLING THUNDER, an aerial interdiction campaign that would run for 4 years and involve increasing pressure on the enemy. In August 1965, Secretary of Defense Robert McNamara rejected a Joint Chiefs of Staff (JCS) recommendation for attacks on North Vietnam's strategic oil facilities and electric power plants. The Hanoi government began to disperse the nation's limited industry and to erect passive and active air defenses; supplies and workers from the Soviet Union and China aided their efforts. In light of this, the JCS called for an expanded bombing program late in 1965. The Johnson administration did, in fact, expand the air campaign in 1966 and 1967: In June 1966, North Vietnam's oil storage facilities were bombed for the first time; in May 1967, Hanoi's main power station was attacked.[34]

Unsurprisingly, the Air Force chafed at the early restrictions. However, while it is true that the destruction of all major targets was not completed until 1967, vice the Air Force's preferred date of 1965, the civilian intervention may not have been as consequential as critics claim. The JCS list grew from 94 targets to 242 targets shortly after Operation ROLLING THUNDER began, and the latter number changed little through the rest of the campaign. In 1965, 158 of these targets were destroyed (nearly all of them military targets below the 20th parallel); in 1966, 22 more were destroyed. The President released nearly all the remaining targets for attack in 1967, and by December, almost all of North Vietnam's industrial war capacity had been destroyed. During the course of the war the USAF dropped some 6,162,000 tons of bombs—more tonnage than had been dropped by the Allied powers in all of World War II.[35]

However, the insurgents required few supplies, and they could often move what they needed through territory that was off limits to the bombers. They could fight the war at their own pace, backing off when their losses became costly, and recommencing when they had recovered. The slow pace—and the inability of the Americans to either drain the enemy's will or to build an effective government in the South—eroded American public support for the war. Structural factors (including the economy and geography of Vietnam) and the nature of the war itself helped insulate the North Vietnamese and Viet Cong against the effects of interdiction and coercive air power. Finally, even if an earlier all-out air assault had convinced the North Vietnamese to stop supporting the Viet Cong insurgency, this is no guarantee that the Viet Cong would not have continued the war on their own and at their own pace.[36]

Operation LINEBACKER, an air campaign designed to halt Hanoi's 1972 spring ground offensive, largely achieved its purpose and appeared to put a settlement in reach. But North Vietnamese negotiators stalled late in the day, prompting Operation LINEBACKER II, an 11-day campaign (December 18 to December 29, 1972) to bring enemy negotiators back to the table to sign a final accord. Operation LINEBACKER II concentrated on military assets in and around Hanoi. On the 29th, communist leaders indicated willingness to resume serious negotiations. This outcome reflected the impact of both LINEBACKER campaigns, which were—by that point in the war—oriented to fundamentally different circumstances and goals than the ROLLING THUNDER campaign had been.[37] Many observers later argued that a LINEBACKER-style campaign executed at the outset would have concluded the war promptly. Writing in the June 1975 edition of *Air Force Magazine*, General T. R. Milton, USAF (Ret.) argued that Operation LINEBACKER II was "an object lesson in how the war might have been won, and won long ago, if only there had not been such political inhibition."[38] However, this perspective overlooked the crucial differences between 1965 and 1972. The success of the LINEBACKER I campaign was facilitated by the fact that Hanoi had shifted to a conventional war strategy that was far more vulnerable to the effects of strategic air power than the earlier guerilla war had been. Moreover, when Operation LINEBACKER II commenced, the Hanoi leadership had already achieved most of its political goals and was prepared to sign an accord that would put its ultimate aims in easy grasp. As one wry American diplomat observed, "We bombed them into accepting our concessions." The more important lesson, perhaps, is simply that all military campaigns take place in a political context that will impose important constraints—constraints outside the control of military planners. For a variety of reasons, including proportionality, the Johnson administration was not prepared to wage an all-out air assault in 1965.

AFTER THE COLD WAR

The first war of the post-Cold War era was very different in nature from the two limited wars fought by the Americans during the Cold War.[39] The Persian Gulf War of 1991 saw the implementation of an air campaign that bore the imprimatur of Colonel John A. Warden, USAF. The air campaign in the Kuwaiti theater of operations had three primary objectives: suppression of Iraqi air defenses, preparation of the battlefield for coalition ground attack, and support of the ground attack.[40] The strategic air campaign over Iraq was designed to support the war aim by directly pressuring Saddam's regime on a number of levels. Warden, who had been in charge of the Deputy Directorate for Warfighting Concepts in the Air Staff Directorate of Plans, was a primary intellectual influence on the strategic air campaign. In 1988, Warden had circulated a paper in the Air Staff that posited a targeting theory based on five principal categories, envisioned as five concentric rings (like the rings in a bull's eye) that increase in value as they approach the center. The focal point—his designated "center of gravity"—was the enemy leadership. Just outside of that, in the position of second priority, were the enemy state's energy sources, advanced research facilities, and key war-supporting industries. Beyond that, in the third ring, was enemy infrastructure, such as transportation systems. The fourth ring was comprised of the enemy's population, and the fifth ring designated the enemy's fielded military forces. Warden's ideas, which he promulgated effectively and energetically, brought back to the surface some heated service debates over the primacy of independent air operations.[41]

Warden's book, *The Air Campaign* (begun when he was a student at the National Defense University), argued that air power allows for strikes against the full spectrum of enemy capabilities, with leadership first and foremost. The Five Ring model was an extension of the operational concepts he had first explored in his book. Warden would become the theorist associated with coercion through decapitation. In an essay published in 1992 called "Employing Air Power in the 21st Century," he wrote:

> The command structure . . . is the only element of the enemy . . . that can make concessions. In fact, wars through history have been fought to change (or change the mind of) the command structure—to overthrow the prince literally or figuratively or to induce the command structure to make concessions. . . . In modern times, however, it has become more difficult—but not impossible—to capture or kill the command element. At the same time, command communications have been more important than ever,

and these are vulnerable to attack. When command communications suffer extreme damage . . . the leadership has great difficulty in directing war efforts. In the case of an unpopular regime, the lack of communications not only inhibits the bolstering of national morale but also facilitates rebellion on the part of dissident elements.[42]

Only days after Saddam's invasion of Kuwait, Lieutenant General Charles A. Horner went to the theater to receive incoming American air forces. The plan that Warden and his staff developed, called INSTANT THUNDER, focused on strategic air attacks on Iraqi centers of gravity; it was designed to pit American strengths against Iraqi weaknesses while minimizing U.S. casualties, collateral damage, and civilian deaths. INSTANT THUNDER won theater commander General Norman Schwarzkopf's endorsement, and Warden went to Riyadh, Saudi Arabia, to brief Horner. Uneasy with the plan's failure to consider fully the offensive capabilities of the Iraqi army, Horner modified it, changed its name, and appropriated several members of Warden's staff to comprise a secret "Central Air Forces Special Planning Group," nicknamed the "Black Hole."

Even though the aircraft coming into the theater comprised the vast majority of the USAF's precision-delivery capability at the time, the force was not ideally suited to the task Warden had set for it. Technological evolution throughout the Vietnam War had yielded some promising results in highly precise, guided-bomb technology, but the Air Force had been leisurely in acquiring it.[43] Still, the USAF had the capacity to employ air-delivered, precision-guided munitions with hard-target-penetrating capability, and this would become a centerpiece of its war effort. A dramatic new delivery system in the U.S. arsenal was the F-117A *Stealth* fighter, introduced to the public in late-1988.

The Black Hole planners, led by Lieutenant Colonel David Deptula, updated the air war plan right through the opening hours of the war on January 17, 1991; they emphasized simultaneous attacks on target sets that would have overlapping and linking effects. Rather than attacking targets in sequenced priority order, Coalition air forces were able to carry out simultaneous counter-air, interdiction, close air support, and strategic missions into Iraq. By mid-February, Coalition bombers had struck the Iraqi Ministry of Defense, the Baghdad Conference Center, TV and press buildings, and the Military Intelligence Headquarters. As the month went on, strategic attacks targeted airfields, nuclear and chemical sites, communication facilities, and mobile Scud missile launchers.

Attacks on Iraqi communication targets had a corrosive effect on the speed and efficiency with which Saddam could conduct his war. However, fiber-optic nets were more redundant and elusive than the Black Hole had anticipated. The precise military and political impact of raids on leadership targets—the focus of Warden's theory—has been difficult to discern. As historian Richard Davis concluded, "little solid data is available to connect the bombing of leadership or command and control facilities with specific consequences."[44] In other words, it was not clear precisely how communications paralysis would translate into concessions and/or surrender.[45]

The strikes on Iraqi oil produced the collapse of refinery capacity by the end of the war. However, the short duration of the war meant Iraq was able to rely on stored supplies for military operations. Pressure on the Iraqi population due to strikes on the electrical grid and other fuel sources may have contributed to the postwar uprisings by the Kurds and the Shi'ites, but did not lead to a weakening of the Sunni commitment to Saddam's regime.[46] The strength of the Iraqi internal security forces, of course, mitigated the political pressure of air attacks.

The 5 months between the invasion of Kuwait and the commencement of Operation DESERT STORM gave Saddam time to further disperse and hide his weapons of mass destruction (WMD) capability—a set of resources already dispersed in reaction to the Israeli strike in 1981. The targets proved to be elusive, and postwar inspections revealed that the target planners (who had operated with limited and outdated intelligence) had missed many facilities.

The Coalition achieved its main aims, including the withdrawal of all Iraqi forces from Kuwait, the right of the United Nations (UN) to install peacekeepers on the border, and the right to inspect and eliminate any WMD in Iraq. The speed and apparent ease of the victory prompted many commentators to proclaim that a "revolution in military affairs" (RMA) had occurred, based on the sophisticated technology employed by American forces. Indeed, the one-sided outcome had resulted from the *interaction* of American proficiency and Iraqi incompetence. Poor skills and training ensured that the enemy's modern military toolkit and operational proficiency punished Iraqi armies disproportionately.[47]

Warden continued to refine his ideas after the war. He followed in the tradition of the early theorists in a number of ways. Like Mitchell and Douhet, he placed a high emphasis on winning command of the air. One of Warden's protégés, Lieutenant Colonel (later Lieutenant General) David Deptula, would help to preserve and elevate many of Warden's ideas in the Air Force. In particular, Deptula highlighted the idea of parallel warfare (reflecting a principle of electrical circuit design) that "was based on achieving specific effects, not absolute destruction of target lists." Parallel warfare facilitates simultaneous attacks on leadership targets, key essentials (oil and electricity), communications, and fielded military forces. Deptula argued that it "exploits three dimensions—time, space, and levels of war—to achieve rapid dominance." He saw parallel warfare as part of the post-Gulf War RMA that could offer alternatives to the attrition and annihilation strategies of older-style warfare. The specific effects that Deptula highlighted were the new objects of war, achievable through "effects based operations." In introducing this concept, Deptula drew parallels between it and the work of theorists at the Air Corps Tactical School in the 1930s: "Effects-based operations takes [their] ideas one step further, aiming not just to impede the means of the enemy to conduct war or the will of the people to continue war, but the very ability of the enemy to control its vital functions."[48]

BY AIR POWER ALONE?

In 1999, the North Atlantic Treaty Organization (NATO) went to war in an air-only operation, trying to halt Serbian mistreatment of the population in the province of Kosovo. Ethnic Serbs formed a small part (about 10 percent) of the population of the province, which consisted mainly of Albanian Muslims. The failure to bring the opposed parties together at the Rambouillet Conference in early-1999 led to a NATO decision to try to coerce the Serbian President, Solbodan Milosevic, and the Serbs into accepting terms. The Bill Clinton administration expected Milosevic to cave in under air strikes in a few days. In actuality, he encouraged his forces to run amok in Kosovo and compounded the problem. Muslims poured out of the province and into refugee camps in neighboring states. Air strikes, waged from high altitude to minimize the risk to NATO pilots, could not halt events on the ground, and the strikes seemed only to unify the defiant Serbs behind Milosevic. NATO was cautious in all regards, and there was considerable anxiety about whether the alliance would hang together. President Clinton, who could hardly escape recent memories of the American public's ambivalence about Bosnia, would not agree to the use of ground troops. In May, an increasingly alarmed NATO took advantage of improving weather to intensify the bombing—attacking rail lines and bridges in Kosovo and Serbia and striking the electrical net inside Serbia. Significantly, NATO began to discuss the use of ground troops. This put the Russians—old allies of the Serbs—in a particularly awkward situation, since they had no intention of ending up in a shooting war with NATO. Pressure from the Russians surely helped convince Milosevic that he had to accept defeat. The bombing ceased in June, and the United States and NATO sent a force of 60,000 troops (Kosovo Force, or KFOR) into Kosovo. Milosevic, who in the meantime had been indicted as a war criminal by the International Criminal Tribunal, was ousted from power in the autumn of 2000.[49]

The air war over Kosovo rekindled the debate about whether airplanes can coerce successfully enough to win wars on their own. Clearly, air strikes had not been able to halt the ethnic cleansing; indeed, they hastened it. However, the relationship between the intensification of NATO strikes in May and the acceptance of terms by Milosevic in June suggested that the strikes on Serbia proper had a role in the outcome. The war was brought to a conclusion before any ground forces were introduced, and thus it was hard to take this victory away from the air forces. RAND analyst Benjamin Lambeth stated appropriately, "We may never know for sure what mix of pressures and inducements ultimately led Milosevic to admit defeat."[50] But, his admission seemed to represent a victory for those who believed that air power could have an independent coercive role in war.

Any historical outcome is driven by a particular interweaving of events and perceptions of events, and those seeking to explain historical events must identify the contributing elements and arrange them into a structure that is logically coherent and robust relative to other possible explanations. However, fitting together the puzzle pieces is a complex process that tends to develop slowly as additional bits of evidence come to light and as the perspectives of all the key actors are brought to bear on the story. The very fact that NATO managed to sustain a 78-day campaign that—Milosevic believed—might have continued indefinitely, must have convinced the Serb leader that his opponents were committed to the cause. As another RAND analyst, Stephen Hosmer, has pointed out, Milosevic and others in his circle seemed to fear that there might be no limit to the level of destruction NATO might be willing to impose; indeed NATO, led by the United States and Britain, might continue escalating to the point of "carpet bombing" Serbia.[51] As much tension, political wrangling, and inefficiency as there was in NATO, the members of the alliance held together in a campaign that grew more intense over time. Clear evidence that NATO was preparing to authorize the use of ground troops was an unmistakable sign of this continued commitment. Not only did it spur the Russians to pressure Milosevic into accepting terms, but it also signaled to the Serb leader that his political and personal fortunes were more at risk from a continuation of the war than from a cessation of it. (A direct clash between NATO and Serbian ground troops would have been a nightmare for the Russians on multiple levels.) In addition, the way the campaign played out revealed that Milosevic had miscalculated on virtually every important strategic issue of the war.[52]

THE RECENT DECADE

Although the decade of the 1990s was tumultuous, the first decade of the new millennium would prove to be even more so. The U.S. Air Force had important roles to play in the wars fought in both Afghanistan and Iraq and in the stabilization efforts that have followed those wars.

U.S. Air Force Basic Doctrine dated November 17, 2003, echoed elements of Warden and Deptula:

> The US Air Force provides the Nation a unique capability to project national influence anywhere in the world on very short notice. Air and space forces, through their inherent speed, range, and flexibility, can respond to national requirements by delivering precise military power to create effects where and when needed.

> The 'American way of war' has long been described as warfare based on either a strategy of annihilation or of attrition and focused on engaging the enemy in close combat to achieve a decisive battle. Air and space power, if properly focused, offers our national leadership alternatives to the annihilation and attrition options. It is possible to directly affect adversary sources of strength and will to fight by creating shock and destroying enemy cohesion without close combat. While such attacks may not totally eliminate the need to directly engage the adversary's fielded military forces, they can shape those en-

gagements so they occur at the time and place of our choosing under conditions more likely to lead to decisive outcomes with minimized risk to friendly forces. The aggressive use of air and space power can also reduce the size of forces needed for conflict termination, risking fewer American lives.

Strategic attack is defined as offensive action conducted by command authorities aimed at generating effects that most directly achieve our national security objectives by affecting the adversary's leadership, conflict-sustaining resources, and strategy. . . . As a concept, strategic attack builds on the idea that it is possible to directly affect an adversary's sources of strength and will to fight without first having to engage and defeat their military forces.

Even though strategic attack best describes the airman's overall vision for striking the enemy, counterair is the pivotal prerequisite for success. Counterair consists of operations to attain and maintain a desired degree of air superiority by the destruction, degradation, or disruption of enemy forces.[53]

The wars in Afghanistan and Iraq, while resting very heavily on the efforts of the U.S. Army and Marines, have nonetheless seen air power applied in a range of ways. Extensive air operations were a major part of the offensive against the Taliban in 2001-02. During the brief major combat phase of the Iraq War in 2003, air power was able to continue to press the offensive when weather conditions halted the ground troops; air assets continued to provide crucial support to ground troops even as the nature of the war shifted. Sometimes, doctrinal differences between services, and lack of joint exercises, complicated the wartime integration of ground and air, but all parties revealed a commitment to adaptation and real-time learning.[54] The experience of warfighting in the first decade of the 21st century underscored the importance of educating officers to hold a "jointness" mindset and orientation. Combined arms warfare is never as effective as when powerful instruments work together in ways that leverage their synergistic capabilities.

In counterinsurgency operations, the use of air strikes independent of ground operations can be tricky and, indeed, at times, counterproductive. A misguided bomb that kills civilians can quickly upset efforts to win hearts and minds, undermining the strategic purpose of the campaign. Insurgent forces that often control the pace of the war can use cover and concealment to avoid air strikes much of the time. In addition, these forces may intermingle with civilians in urban areas or use human shields to protect themselves from the superior air power wielded by their opponents. All of these factors put very real constraints on the use of air power. They do not, however, rule out the use of air power in counterinsurgency campaigns. Moreover, inter- and intra-theater transport of personnel and equipment is always a critical mission.

If used carefully and sparingly, independent air strikes can be invaluable in reaching high-value targets. Moreover, with the precision capabilities now available—particularly through unmanned aerial vehicles—such strikes can target particular individuals who may be instrumental in the planning and implementing of terrorist activity. However, caution, care, and intentionality are warranted. As Major Jason Brown wrote in 2007:

When operational-level commanders can 'watch' insurgents in real time by means of ISR [intelligence, surveillance, and reconnaissance] feeds, they tend to fall back to the tactical level, thus reinforcing the 'we must do something now' mentality. This reactive approach can quickly devolve into a game of 'whack a mole,' which can cause commanders to neglect other important lines of operation and lose focus on the strategic end state.

To avoid this, Brown insists that "commanders and planners must integrate the use of airpower for dynamic targeting into the operational design of a counterinsurgency campaign."[55] In addition, allied air forces can offer invaluable assistance to newly developing indigenous air forces opposing insurgents. Well into the foreseeable future, the USAF is very likely to continue its role in advising, training, and equipping partner air forces.[56]

The decision by NATO in early-2011 to support the rebel forces opposing Libyan dictator Colonel Moammar Gaddafi highlighted the political appeal of reaching for the air power instrument to solve political problems. However, it has also raised to the surface many of the issues and complications associated with the strictly independent use of air power in conflict. Even though Gaddafi was wielding state power, his forces were adopting many of the tactics associated with insurgents. He manipulated the pace of the war to erode the will of his enemies; he used cover and concealment to take his forces out of the reach of superior air power; and he resorted to co-mingling in cities and using human shields to deter NATO air strikes. As defense analyst Stephen Biddle wrote in a *Washington Post* editorial, "Locals with existential stakes often prove more stubborn than distant Americans expect, and even high-tech firepower has serious limitations against low-tech but determined enemies who control the people on the ground through close-up violence." He added, "Especially when the multilateral action is based on protecting civilians, rather than defeating one side, a dictator willing to mix ruthless fighters with innocent noncombatants poses serious challenges to limited applications of precision air power. The result could easily be a drawn-out, grinding stalemate."[57]

Leaders of the contemporary USAF are well aware of the range of missions they may be called upon to fulfill in the future. They will work hard to continue to oversee a service that possesses not only a wide-ranging skill set, but also detailed operational knowledge in any given skill. In addition to working with service partners and international partners to leverage strengths and create synergies, the USAF will continue to develop capabilities in realms where it leads the world, including aerospace and intelligence technologies. Intelligence, which is central to effective targeting, always will be a core element of air power. And intelligence partnered with precision capability will give the USAF the ability to take on difficult, high-priority missions (some of which may develop on short notice, and/or in crisis situations). Ever since Operation DESERT STORM, the USAF has fully realized the power and potency of genuine precision capability. The Service now sees this capability as central to its identity, its culture, and its future effectiveness.[58]

As we look to the future, any discussion of air power theory must include the themes that have run through this survey. Under what circumstances and in what ways are airplanes effective tools for achieving political aims? What limits the independent coercive effect of air power? What enhances it? How have service rivalries affected the debate over the use of air power? Do these still afflict nations possessing air forces? Has the ideal of "jointness" gained traction? What roles should air forces prepare to perform in the future?

ENDNOTES - CHAPTER 20

1. See Tami Davis Biddle, "Learning in Real Time: The Development and Implementation of Air Power in the First World War," in J. S. Cox and Peter Gray, eds., *Air Power History: Turning Points from Kitty Hawk to Kosovo*, London, UK: Frank Cass, 2002, pp. 3-20.

2. The Royal Air Force became a separate military institution in Great Britain in April 1918.

3. On Tiverton, see George K. Williams, "The Shank of the Drill: Americans and Strategical Aviation in the Great War," *Journal of Strategic Studies*, Vol. 19, No. 3, September 1996, pp. 381-431.

4. Tami Davis Biddle, *Rhetoric and Reality in Air Warfare*, Princeton, NJ: Princeton University Press, 2002, pp. 69-110.

5. Editor's introduction to Giulio Douhet, *The Command of the Air*, Washington, DC: Office of Air Force History, 1983, reprint of the edition published in New York in 1942 by Coward-McCann, pp. xii-xiii.

6. For some overviews of Douhet in English from this period, see: "The Air Doctrine of General Douhet," *The Royal Air Force Quarterly*, Vol. IV, No. 2, April 1933, pp. 164-167; "General Giulio Douhet--An Italian Apostle of Air Power" and "Air Warfare--The Principles of Air Warfare by General Giulio Douhet," in *The Royal Air Force Quarterly*, Vol. VII, No. 2, April 1936, pp. 148-151, 152-168. Also see Azar Gat, "Futurism, Proto-fascist Italian Culture and the Sources of Douhetism," *War and Society*, Vol. 15, No. 1, May 1997, pp. 31-51.

7. Gat, p. 39.

8. Phillip Meilinger, "Guilio Douhet and the Origins of Air Power Theory," in *The Paths of Heaven: The Evolution of Air Power Theory*, Maxwell Air Force Base, AL: Air University Press, 1997, pp. 9-10.

9. See Meilinger, pp. 12-13.

10. He asserted that "when the working personnel of a factory sees one of its machine shops destroyed, even with a minimum loss of life, it quickly breaks up and the plant ceases to function." See Douhet, *The Command of the Air*, pp. 22-23.

11. *Ibid.*, p. 10.

12. Michael S. Sherry, *The Rise of American Air Power*, New Haven, CT: Yale University Press, 1987, p. 27.

13. For Trenchard's personal history and the details of his ideas, see Biddle, *Rhetoric and Reality in Air Warfare*, pp. 26-29.

14. The memorandum is dated May 2, 1928. It has been reprinted in Sir Charles Webster and Noble Frankland's official history of the British air campaign in World War II, *The Strategic Air Offensive Against Germany*, Vol. IV, London, UK: HMSO, 1961, p. 75. It has also been reprinted in Gerard Chaliand, *The Art of War in World History*, Berkeley, CA: University of California Press, 1994, pp. 905-910.

15. See Phillip Meilinger, *Air Men and Air Power Theory*, Maxwell Air Force Base, AL: Air University Press, 1997, pp. 7-9; Mark Clodfelter, "Molding Air Power Convictions: Development and Legacy of William Mitchell's Strategic Thought," in Phillip Meilinger, ed., *The Paths of Heaven: The Evolution of Air Power Theory*, Maxwell Air Force Base, AL: Air University Press, 1997, pp. 79-114.

16. William Mitchell, *Winged Defense: The Development and Possibilities of Modern Air Power – Economic and Military*, New York: G. P. Putnam's Sons, 1925. Portions have been reprinted in David Jablonsky, ed., *Roots of Strategy*, Book 4, Mechanicsburg, PA: Stackpole Books, 1999, pp. 409-533.

17. Biddle, *Rhetoric and Reality*, pp. 125, 164-170.

18. Edward Westermann, *FLAK: German Anti-Aircraft Defenses, 1914-1945*, Lawrence, KS: University Press of Kansas, 2005.

19. For insights, see Richard Overy, *Why the Allies Won*, New York: Norton, 1997 (especially pp. 101-131). On German air power generally, see Peter Fritzsche, *A Nation of Flyers*, Cambridge, MA: Harvard University Press, 1994; also see James Corum, *The Luftwaffe: Creating the Operational Air War, 1918-1940*. Lawrence, KS: University of Kansas Press, 1999.

20. William C. Sherman, *Air Warfare*, New York: The Ronald Press, 1926, p. 218.

21. Sir Charles Webster and Noble Frankland, *The Strategic Air Offensive Against Germany, 1939-1945*, Vols. I-IV, London, UK: HMSO, 1961. On the photo-reconnaissance study, see Vol. IV, Appendix 13, pp. 205-213. For the February Directive, pp. 143-147 (Appendix 8, p. xxii).

22. Webster and Frankland, Vol. I, pp. 353-363.

23. Stephen McFarland, *America's Pursuit of Precision Bombing, 1910-1945,* Tuscaloosa, AL: University of Alabama Press, 2008.

24. Biddle, *Rhetoric and Reality*, p. 243.

25. On the air campaign in Japan, see generally, Conrad Crane, *Bombs, Cities, and Civilians,* Lawrence, KS: University of Kansas Press, 1993; and Michael S. Sherry, *The Rise of American Air Power,* New Haven, CT: Yale University Press, 1987.

26. See, for example, "War, Drunkenness, and Suicide," *Nature*, Vol. 146, July 1940; Dr. Felix Brown, "Psychiatric Air Raid Casualties," *The Lancet*, May 31, 1941.

27. For a recent, authoritative assessment, see Adam Tooze, *The Wages of Destruction: The Making and Breaking of the Nazi Economy,* London, UK: Penguin, 2006.

28. For an interesting discussion of war termination in the Far East, see Robert Pape, *Bombing to Win*, Ithaca, NY: Cornell University Press, 1996, pp. 129-136.

29. De Seversky, quoted in Chaliand, pp. 962-964.

30. On air power in Korea, see Conrad Crane, *American Air Power in the Korean War,* Lawrence, KS: University of Kansas Press, 2000.

31. Mark Clodfelter, *The Limits of Air Power*, New York: The Free Press, 1989, p. 21.

32. LeMay quoted in Thomas Hone, "Strategic Bombardment Constrained: Korea and Vietnam," in R. Cargill Hall, ed., *Case Studies in Strategic Bombardment,* Washington, DC: Air Force History and Museums Program, 1998, p. 517.

33. Clodfelter, *Limits*, pp. 39-56; also see Pape, *Bombing to Win*, pp. 174-210.

34. Hone, pp. 495-496.

35. The figure is from Earl Tilford, "Setup: Why and How the U.S. Air Force Lost in Vietnam," in *Armed Forces and Society*, Vol. 17, No. 3, 1991, p. 327. On Vietnam, see generally, Clodfelter, *Limits of Air Power*.

36. *Ibid.*, p. 205.

37. See Pape, *Bombing to Win*; also Pape, "Coercive Air Power in the Vietnam War," in *International Security*, Vol. 15, No. 2, Fall 1990, pp. 103-146.

38. Milton, quoted in Tilford, p. 335; see also Clodfelter, *Limits of Air Power*, pp. 206-208.

39. It is important to note that these were limited wars in the eyes of Americans. They were total wars for the Korean and Vietnamese peoples.

40. Richard G. Davis, *Decisive Force: Strategic Bombing in the Gulf War,* Washington, DC: "Air Force History and Museum Program," 1996, p. 20.

41. *Ibid.*, pp. 9-12.

42. John A. Warden, *The Future of Air Power in the Aftermath of the Gulf War*, Richard Schultz and Robert Pfaltzgraff, eds., Maxwell Air Force Base, AL: Air University Press, 1992, p. 65.

43. Davis, *Decisive Force*, p. 2.

44. *Ibid.*, p. 53; Michael R. Gordon and General Bernard E. Trainor, *The Generals' War*, Boston, MA: Little Brown, 1995, p. 474.

45. See Lieutenant Colonel David S. Fadok, "John Boyd and John Warden: Airpower's Quest for Strategic Paralysis," in Meilinger, ed., *The Paths of Heaven*, pp. 357-399; and John Andreas Olson, "Col. John A. Warden III: Smasher of Paradigms?" *Air Power Leadership: Theory and Practice*, London, UK: The Stationery Office, 2002, pp. 129-159.

46. Davis, *Decisive Force*, pp. 54-55.

47. Stephen Biddle, "Victory Misunderstood: What the Gulf War Tells Us about the Future of Conflict," *International Security*, 21, No. 2, Fall 1997, pp. 139-179.

48. David Deptula, "Effects-Based Operations: Change in the Nature of Warfare," Arlington, VA: Aerospace Education Foundation, pp. 3-5, 17.

49. For a good overview, see Eliot Cohen and Andrew Bacevich, eds., *War Over Kosovo*, New York: Columbia University Press, 2002.

50. Benjamin Lambeth, *NATO's Air War for Kosovo*, Santa Monica, CA: RAND, 2001, p. xiv.

51. Stephen T. Hosmer, *Why Milosevic Decided to Settle When He Did*, Santa Monica, CA: RAND, 2001, p. 94.

52. These included the following fallacious assumptions: 1) that the ethnic cleansing campaign might cause NATO to rethink the bombing; 2) that the elimination of the Kosovo Liberation Army would be swift and simple; 3) that the fallout from civilian casualties might break NATO; and 4) that Russia would provide steadfast support to the Serbs. See Hosmer, pp. 24-34.

53. USAF Basic Doctrine, *Air Force Doctrine Document 1*, November 17, 2003, available from *www.dtic.mil/doctrine/jel/service_pubs/afdd1.pdf*.

54. For examples from the Iraq War, especially between 2004 and 2005, see Colonel Howard D. Belote, USAF "Counterinsurgency Airpower: Air-Ground Integration for the Long War," in *Air and Space Power Journal*, Fall 2006, available from *www.airpower.au.af.mil*.

55. Major Jason M. Brown, USAF, "To Bomb or Not to Bomb? Counterinsurgency, Airpower, and Dynamic Targeting," in *Air and Space Power Journal*, Winter 2007, available from *www.airpower.maxwell.af.mil*.

56. Guidance on how to do this is offered in Alan J. Vick *et al.*, *Air Power in the New Counterinsurgency Era: The Strategic Importance of USAF Advisory and Assistance Missions*, Santa Monica, CA: RAND Corporation, 2006.

57. Stephen Biddle, "The Libya Dilemma: The Limits of Air Power," *The Washington Post*, March 25, 2011, available from *www.washingtonpost.com*.

58. See the November 17, 2011, speech given by General Norton Schwartz, USAF, to the Dubai International Air Chiefs Conference, on "Tailoring Airpower Capabilities for Joint Combat Operations," available from *www.af.mil/information/speeches/index.asp*.

CHAPTER 21

JOHN WARDEN'S FIVE RING MODEL AND THE INDIRECT APPROACH TO WAR

Clayton K. S. Chun

Military strategists and practitioners develop and execute campaign plans based on a host of factors. Experience, intelligence, force structure, technology, legal, the threat, and environmental factors are only a few elements that affect these decisions. Another key factor is theory. Theory attempts to explain and get a reader to understand the occurrence of an event or state of nature. Theory can provide a framework to consider how to approach a problem. It can help one consider issues or questions to solve before making detailed approaches toward developing a theater strategy or campaign plan. If a theory is sound, then one could use it to solve problems by predicting possible outcomes, identifying potential problems, and finding options to get an opponent to take certain actions or modify his behavior. Theory can provide a foundation to help military strategists contemplate or evaluate potential courses of actions.

Military theory is often criticized, not without justification, for being unrealistic or static. Theory may not seem relevant because it lacks details or does not adequately represent a situation. Additionally, a theorist may have created an appropriate theory for his age or historic context that does not seem to fit the contemporary environment. Societies, militaries, weapons, and political situations may evolve such that the theory may not be relevant. A theorist may have worked during a particular period with certain international conditions or technology available to fight a war. Over time, political relationships change, engineers replace technology, and the character of warfare evolves.

Although compared with other weapons like small arms, aircraft are relatively new weapons; they have changed significantly since the first Italian aircraft appeared in combat over Libya in 1911.[1] Aerial warfare has evolved from simple biplanes that dropped very limited bomb loads, which pilots hoped would land within miles of their targets. Today, aircraft using satellite navigation systems can place precision guided munitions within a few feet of the intended target. Air power theory has also evolved. Early air power theorists like Giulio Douhet developed ideas about aerial bombardment and predictions about its impact on the battlefield with particular technologies in mind. In hindsight, Douhet's theories on breaking the will of people through bombardment of cities lacked credibility. Douhet argued that the most humane way to end war was a swift attack on the most vulnerable element of society: the populace. Perhaps more of a vision than a theory, critics challenged his concept on moral, military, political, and technical grounds. For example, Douhet advocated that air forces could use poison gas against cities that "paralyzed all life" by killing civilians.[2] Still, Douhet's ideas had a great impact on future concepts and ideas during the interwar period and World War II. Many air forces developed bomber fleets with the thought that strategic bombardment would help destroy a foe's ability to fight a war. World War II demonstrated that breaking the will of individuals, let alone a society, by bombing was difficult. The United Kingdom, Germany, and Japan each suffered from massive bombing campaigns, but in each case strategic bombing alone proved inconclusive. Lack of information about targets, bombing effects, and the use of massive, indiscriminate attacks may have contributed to problems attacking the specific industrial and political centers of Germany and Japan.

Since the end of World War II, technology has changed significantly to include jet aircraft, radar, surface-to-air missiles, nuclear weapons, instant communications, improved reconnaissance and surveillance, improved bomb damage assessment, and precision guided munitions. Ideas that were once discounted as unrealistic might now find validity, due to improvements in fighting capability, increased urbanization, enhanced intelligence abilities to pinpoint key targets, and other changes. One recent air power theorist, John A. Warden III, believed that a state would collapse if sufficient pressure was placed on certain key elements of its government, economy, society, and military. Many World War II United States Army Air Forces (AAF) and British Royal Air Force officers agonized over what targets would accomplish this same goal. Eighth Air Force B-17 and B-24 bomber crews smashed industrial targets, while losing thousands of crewmembers and creating massive collateral damage, in search of a way to force Germany to capitulate. Warden built many of his ideas on concepts developed during the interwar period before World War II,

Warden believed that advances in technology—precision guided munitions and stealth had made revolutionary changes to the nature of warfare. Instead of using masses of bombers as in World War II, a single stealthy plane today, armed with precision guided munitions, could destroy a target. This fundamental change in aerial operations increased the options a commander had available in battle. Aircraft could attack several targets simultaneously with surprise. Precision guided munitions gave aircrews the ability to destroy or disable a target with a single mission instead of returning repeatedly to a target. Modern technology allowed air forces to avoid having to go to battle against the strength of most nation-states—their military. Attacks on several centers of gravity created more chaos and damage to an enemy than a single, direct clash between opposing militaries. Centers of gravity are targets that if destroyed or disabled have a significant impact on a nation's war-making capability. Warden thought that technology freed campaign planners to consider more options to strike an enemy. A main concern involved not how many aircraft or systems could attack a target, but what type of target should military forces damage or destroy? Commanders needed to consider what effects that strikes on the targets would have on the enemy. They also had to question whether a particular sequence of attacks made sense.

John Warden was able to employ his ideas directly in a campaign plan without the concern of interpretation or potential misapplication of his ideas. Unlike some theorists, Warden was able to translate his ideas into actual combat planning for operations in the 1991 Persian Gulf War. The use of his ideas and concepts for that situation is a prime example of how a military theory guided campaign planning and how to think about what targets to destroy or disable. Although geared toward a state-on-state confrontation, one might ponder how much of his theory may or may not be relevant to the rise of conflict with nonstate actors or states that do not have discernable centers of gravity.

THE ENEMY AS A SYSTEM

Colonel John Warden believed that nation-states operate like biological organisms composed of discrete systems. In a perfect world these systems function in harmony and the organisms survive and flourish. However, certain systems controlled other systems and were thus significant, while other elements might appear to be vital, they were actually not important for sustaining the organism. Warden believed that like a biological organism, a nation could be stunned. Military action could produce strategic paralysis. Strategic paralysis in Warden's terms would make an enemy incapable of taking any physical action to conduct operations.[3] The key was to think of the enemy as a related set of systems. By using this rationale, a strategist could distinguish the important systems and avoid wasting effort on less critical targets. How one can attack an enemy depends on the objectives being sought, the enemy's defensive capability and intensity of resistance, environmental conditions, and the effort and resources the attacker is willing to exert to attain his goals. But in every case, Warden believed a systematic approach would produce the most efficient use of air power. For example, striking targets essential to a nation's leadership or command and control functions might completely negate or at least inhibit the ability of an enemy to defend its cities or other locations. If a country could disable or destroy particular centers of gravity in an enemy nation, then it could stop that enemy from directing its political, economic, informational, and military elements of power. Victory was thus assured. Successful attacks on a particular hierarchy of systems might lead to a target country's downfall.

Warden believed that organizations from nation-states to terrorist organizations have a common critical feature: some type of leadership. An individual or a command group with control capability provides guidance and direction to that organization. Without this system, the organization would flounder and particular functions cease to exist or become severely limited. This leadership function has become a vital "center" of action against which an attacker should focus its military actions. Once an attacker neutralizes the "leadership" function, other systems become vulnerable for further assault or become neutralized. Ultimately, the goal of striking leadership targets was to destroy the psyche of the enemy's top command. Determining the level of success against the enemy's psyche is difficult, if not impossible. Warden reasoned that an attacker could only view the physical manifestations of the enemy that would help identify targets that would comply with this scheme.[4] A prioritized scheme of attacking leadership targets first; then others could provide a blueprint for a campaign plan.

Instead of attacking the "muscle" of the system, Warden advocated striking an enemy through a more indirect approach and creating a similar effect. A military force could clash directly in a conventional battle that could result in an attritional battle or a decisive encounter. However, if the leadership of the state was either disabled or unable to provide guidance to its forces, it might be possible to render those military assets useless much faster. Warden became an advocate for an indirect approach to warfare. This emphasis was developed while Warden was a graduate student at Texas Tech University, where he developed an affinity to British military theorist, Basil H. Liddell Hart.[5]

Liddell Hart, a land power theorist, focused on an indirect approach to warfare. A veteran of World War I, Liddell Hart saw the horror of trench warfare and the folly of direct attacks against entrenched positions. Instead of concentrating on an enemy's strengths, a nation's land power should focus on a foe's weakness and then exploit it. If a military force could find an unlikely avenue to approach and defeat a foe's military, then a country might achieve its objectives with fewer casualties quicker. Liddell Hart contradicted post-World War I conventional wisdom concerning a direct approach to warfare. His ideas clashed with existing approaches like Carl von Clausewitz's focus on trying to defeat an opposition's military forces first. Supporters of the "false doctrine of war" from Napoleon and Clausewitz, which saw enemy armies as the primary objective in war—created the vast carnage from World War I.[6] Liddell Hart believed a nation's will was subject to exploitation by attacking elements of the society where they were vulnerable. If the elements that created the country's peace and security were threatened, then the state could collapse.

Warden, a career Air Force fighter pilot, predicted that air power could play a pivotal role in conducting operations through an indirect approach. Given the nature of modern aircraft, support capabilities, and precision guided munitions, air power could destroy or disable systems that range from leadership to economic capabilities. Unlike the World War I and II aircraft that required a mass of inaccurate munitions to destroy a command and control center or other target, technology had improved, allowing a single aircraft to deliver munitions within a few feet of its intended target quickly. Aircraft, if a country attained air superiority, were free to attack several different types of targets simultaneously. This ability to strike many targets would confuse an enemy by not letting a foe determine the direction and focus of an attack. This approach allowed aircrews to conduct parallel warfare, and a commander could strike fast over a wide range of objectives. Other forces might need to attack in a slower, more linear manner. For example, ground forces would have to defeat a similar military force first, before proceeding to other targets like the rival's transportation networks or leadership. Aircraft could bypass the enemy's ground forces and strike directly against the capital, industrial centers, or other targets.

Although airplanes could attack most nation-states independently, Warden was careful to note that air power alone might not be sufficient or efficient enough to use exclusively to attack an enemy.[7] Warden is an air power advocate and stresses the value of using that means to achieve military and national objectives. However, commanders can use air power to support land and naval forces as part of a joint operation. Other military forces could also act as a supporting force for air power. Whether a commander uses air power in a supported or supporting role, Warden believed that one essential element is the attainment of air superiority. Air superiority allows control of the skies, which lets a military force attack from the skies while being protected from attack from the air by the enemy. An air force needs the ability to destroy enemy aircraft and support infrastructure, while protecting itself from similar enemy operations. Once a nation controls the air, it can conduct air and other operations without significant opposition.

Warden's theoretical blueprint for using air power would combine non-physical (or, in his term, "morale") and physical effects on warfare. Non-physical factors include the impact of fog, friction, and other psychological effects on national leadership, military, and civilian populations. Physical targets included military forces and means to fight war. Warden believed that the relationship between the two was defined by the equation Morale x Physical = Outcome. He realized that attacking morale was difficult. Modern technology could do much to reduce the impact of friction and fog through better communications and the availability of information; however, a military force could not completely negate friction, fog, or morale issues. A nation could not guarantee its ability to predict perfectly an enemy's intentions and actions. Unexpected enemy actions could also affect any outcome.

Physical damage to enemy forces or economic targets is easier to accomplish. If an attack could significantly reduce the enemy through physical damage, then morale considerations might be moot. This approach assumes that the nation can identify correctly the appropriate physical targets. Alternatively, "morale factors" could change the physical dimension of warfare. Leadership could exhort workers to produce more munitions or the populace to support the war effort better. Conversely, the attacks on physical targets could alter the morale of population and affect the ability of a rival to discern an attacker's intention; this may create the fog of war. Pressure on enemy leadership or the adversary's population, based on physical attacks, could affect morale and may change enemy behavior. For example, the relentless bombing of economic targets could cause significant disruptions in the everyday lives of workers. If conditions were bad enough, prominent members of the population might confront the national leadership with demands to negotiate or submit to the enemy. Short of such radical steps, opinion leaders and the general public might begin to openly question national policy.

JOHN WARDEN'S FIVE RING MODEL

John Warden selected five general areas or systems that he believed were key centers of gravity to exploit against any foe. This model provided a framework to analyze how to disable an enemy using strategic paralysis. The systems Warden picked were: leadership, organic essentials, infrastructure, population, and fielded military forces. One could envision this model as a series of five concentric rings, with the most important element in the center and progressively less important ones moving outward. A way to think about defeating an enemy was to attack the concentric circles from "inside out." That is, disable the most important center of gravity first, and work outward to less important rings, see Figure 21-1.

Leadership was at the center of Warden's ring model. In his biological system analogy, leadership equated to the brain of a living organism. The most important leadership in a state was the government, because it could ultimately decide to concede in a conflict to another state. Leadership, above all else, was the primary center of gravity in a state. If the national leadership was isolated, disabled, or destroyed, then the country could not function. Leadership requires an ability to gather, process, and act on information—all functions that an adversary might strike and affect the functioning of a nation-state. Direct attacks against enemy leaders, command and control structures, or headquarters could affect an opponent's ability to continue a conflict. The LINEBACKER II bombing campaign in December 1972 impressed Warden. In his opinion, the campaign forced the North Vietnamese government to return to peace negotiations with the United States.[8] Hanoi had broken off diplomatic efforts in the Paris Peace talks until LINEBACKER II. Air campaign planners directed these bombing attacks at Hanoi. Similarly, the combined Air Force and Navy attacks on Libya during Operation EL DORADO CANYON in April 1986 on Muammar al Qadhafi, who supported terrorist attacks on Americans, also impressed Warden. Neither attacks destroyed enemy leadership. However, actual destruction of leadership targets might not be possible, since political leaders might be highly mobile, operate in areas that are not conducive to military action, or are too diverse to damage effectively. Instead of direct attacks on leadership, Warden thought attacking other targets might produce enough internal pressure to force the leadership to capitulate.[9] Indirect attacks or effects against the leadership might produce the desired effect on the enemy.

Leadership targets can include executive, legislative, judicial, and other functions. Campaign planners could target physical governmental facilities. Attacking the means these targets use to coordinate or control activities within the nation requires a Herculean effort. Additionally, striking leadership targets of nonstate actors that do not have established facilities or locations can create problems. Conversely, foes with a loose confederation of leadership, such as a cartel or combined revolutionary movements, who are highly mobile, may not lend themselves to a rapid attack.

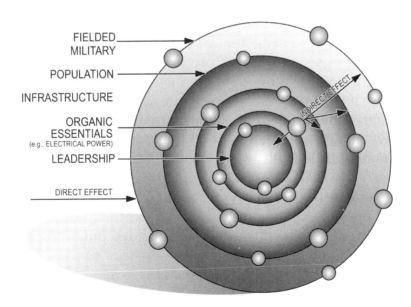

Figure 21-1. John Warden's Five Ring Model (adapted from "The Enemy as a System").

Living organisms do not exist on their brains alone. An organism needs certain raw materials to live. Organic essentials provide elements to function, grow, and replace damaged tissues. Similarly, a state cannot exist on leadership alone. It needs raw materials that include sources of energy, food, and financial resources to maintain its existence. These raw materials provide energy to the entire state. Attacking such targets, especially food sources, needs careful consideration because of ethical issues and other strategic implications like the national and international opinion. However, industrial countries require oil to fuel industry and transportation that, if effectively interdicted, could slow industrial and military operations to a crawl. The lack of energy can influence national leadership's behavior and limit severely actions by subordinate actors in the state. Warden believed that successive degradation of a state's organic essentials could lead to the collapse of the entire system; create conditions for a state that make it physically difficult or impossible for the state to continue a policy or fight; and force significant political and economic impacts due to damage to the ring.[10] He thought that destruction of key targets in the energy field, like petroleum refining stations or electric production facilities, could paralyze a modern state. Industrial production, transportation, economic activities, and people's lives would be altered suddenly, with massive disruptions rippling throughout the state. Pressure on national leadership to respond or mitigate the damages could force policy changes.

Warden's next ring is infrastructure. Infrastructure is like the vessels, bones, and muscles in the human body that allow an organism to move and take action. Society's infrastructure includes, among other things, road and rail networks, airports, power grids and factories. Potential infrastructure targets include a long list of activities—some of which are more valuable than others. Attacking rail lines may take months or years to destroy hundreds of thousands of miles of track. Destroying or disabling key infrastructure requires a careful analysis to find vital elements that, if struck, could disrupt operations. For example, instead of trying to bomb rail lines, a single bombing of a key bridge, tunnel, or rail junction might accomplish the same purpose. Commanders may need to consider the post-conflict impact of infrastructure attacks. Reconstruction of needed roads, rail lines, and other targets after the conflict may add time and cost to returning the nation to a normal state after the war. It might be wise to avoid destroying infrastructure you might need for your own purposes or will have to repair after the conflict.

The fourth ring is the population. Attacking the population does not focus solely on bombing civilians, but could also include using psychological warfare or other activities to reduce a populace's morale. Like an organism composed of millions of cells that can survive the loss of many of those cells, a nation can endure some loss of population. However, economic and military support might falter under air attack if the public perceives its losses are too high. The effect of bombing population is extremely unpredictable. Examples of increased morale under bombardment are numerous. Also, if organic essentials are limited, then a reduction in unessential parts of the population may actually improve the state's ability to operate by relieving pressure on limited resources.

The last ring comprises fielded military forces. Fielded military forces represent the "fighting mechanism" that protects the state from attack. Warden makes an organic analogy to leukocytes or white blood cells that ward off viruses.[11] If states lived in perpetual peace, they would not require a protective force like a military or even police. Although fielded military forces are a formidable foe, they depend heavily on the other rings for support. Instead of directly attacking this ring, strikes on the supporting rings could sufficiently weaken these forces to the point that they were incapable of resistance. Fighting through the fielded military forces—that is, making a direct military on military effort—could take much time and cause many casualties before breaking through to the other more important rings. Unhampered, the enemy leadership could operate normally and replenish fielded military forces with which to continue the fight.

Commanders should take a systems approach to warfare. Instead of destroying an entire foe, attacks on key system components could render a strategic effect. This type of approach forces one to consider how to derive a specific end—paralysis—using specific ways—attacks on subsystems or rings. John Warden's theory of identifying and creating a priority of subsystems allowed strategic planners the ability to attack in a specific order. However, Warden also stressed that a combination of varying size and scope of attacks could create certain vulnerabilities to the rings themselves. For example, attacking infrastructure, like transportation networks, could alter the ability of fielded military forces to move and engage against another military force. Likewise, striking industrial targets that manufacture weapons or munitions could also delay or affect the fielded military forces. Thus, selecting the correct targets and assessing the probable effect of their destruction on the system becomes a prime concern.

Many of Warden's ideas had surfaced earlier. Early air power theories and concepts in the United States were developed as a part of the Air Corps Tactical School (ACTS) at Maxwell Field in Alabama. ACTS writers had advocated the use of precision bombing to strike economic targets, to undermine the ability of a nation to sustain itself in war. Writing during the interwar period, the ACTS faculty was influenced by the brutality of trench warfare and the destruction during World War I. Perhaps by using strategic bombers that could hit and destroy specific targets, the nation could avoid another replay of a World War I type of conflict. Although ACTS writers also contended with issues concerning service independence and the tactical use of air power, the long-range, heavy bomber rose to prominence as a means of influencing events in a strategic manner. Army Air Corps bombers would selectively attack targets like transportation, steel plants, ball-bearing manufacturing, food sources, energy supplies, and especially, electrical production facilities.[12]

ACTS concepts focused on modern states. As a nation became more industrialized it generated complex economic interactions and increased degrees of specialization. Thus, modern nations became more susceptible to disruption by attacks on key nodes. A state could disrupt a foe more quickly, efficiently, and effectively through the air than by trying to conquer its fielded forces. Unfortunately, "precision" attack had not come of age. Low-altitude bombing risked the aircraft and crews to air defenses. High-altitude bombing forced crews to deliver their ordnance with great inaccuracy that would create collateral damage and cause massive casualties, a result ACTS faculty tried to avoid. Additionally, Air Corps pilots needed current target information. Given the lack of intelligence capabilities during the period, finding exact locations, functions, interrelationships, and impacts of destroyed targets may have overwhelmed the Army Air Corps' ability to accomplish actions ACTS had advocated. Technology was not available to either find the proper targets or to deliver munitions with "precision." However, today's aircrews have access to a host of precision guided munitions, navigational systems, weather reports, intelligence sources for targeting and bomb damage assessment, and other capabilities beyond the wildest imagination of the ACTS faculty.

Warden shared some of the ideas from the ACTS faculty. A common theme was the attack on targets using an indirect approach. Warden and ACTS concentrated on subduing an enemy through a particular center of gravity. Striking economic targets was the primary focus of the ACTS concepts. Warden used a series of targets to affect the will of national leadership. The ACTS approach of assaulting enemy targets by strategic bombardment alone created doubt in many minds throughout the 1930s and into World War II. Warden advocated the use of air power too, but also recognized the value of other military instruments.

AIR POWER'S VALUE

To Warden, air power offered many characteristics that could hasten the downfall of an adversary, especially if it were susceptible to his Five Ring model. Air power offered a number of characteristics that could serve a nation. Aircraft, by their very nature, could provide a very fast, long-range and flexible tool for commanders.[13] Given these characteristics, air power can conduct parallel attacks against an enemy that can hit simultaneously segments of all five rings. These multiple strikes can cause all types of second- and third-order effects and create pressures between rings. The leadership ring is especially susceptible to such pressures.

Air power allows a nation to conduct parallel attacks, since air power transcends geography. Aircraft can simply fly over enemy fielded forces and avoid marching through an enemy. Like other military forces, air power can mass against particular targets and is flexible enough to change targeting within minutes. The advent of stealth aircraft, improved battle management systems, precision guided munitions, instant information, and the growing capacity to integrate and use a combination of joint forces in combat operations simply enhanced this capability. Attacking in a parallel manner allows a nation to place demands on the enemy that can overwhelm an enemy's defenses. These missions create confusion and doubt for the enemy's leadership. Military force—air power, especially—can operate on several levels: strategic, operational, or tactical. Although these attacks could deal a direct blow against a foe, Warden recommended concentrated effort aimed squarely at a specific end—coercing the leadership to change its behavior.

For Warden, the destruction of key targets had secondary importance to the effects such destruction would have on the adversary's leadership. Since the United States can achieve almost unfettered air superiority and can deliver munitions accurately, the use of air power seemed logical. Countries around the globe did not have the capacity to challenge the ability of the United States to conduct air and space operations. Although Warden developed many of his ideas while the Soviet Union was a viable nation, his ideas about air power may have taken on more credence after 1991, when his concepts were tested in Desert Storm. In some respects, the focus on measuring the impact on a function instead of the physical destruction of a target forced a change in the way commanders viewed combat operations.

Effects-based operations became a key concern. Assessing particular targets for their impact on a larger scheme is not new. During the Combined Bomber Offensive in World War II, AAF pilots attacked ball-bearing plants to stop the manufacture of German industrial and military products. American officers believed that ball bearings were a crucial center of gravity in German industrial production. Reducing ball-bearing production would severely affect engine production that could limit aircraft and tank inventories. Unfortunately, German industrial production in some cases did not cease, but actually increased. For example, BMW 801 aero-engines manufacture jumped from 5,540 motors in 1943 to 7,395 units in 1944.[14] Perhaps due to a shift to full mobilization or use of methods to ameliorate ball-bearing shortages through alternative production or substitution, the predicted outcome did not occur despite its apparent plausibility. Still, strategic bombardment did disrupt the German economy and reduce production. By January 1945, German Ministry of Armaments officials claimed that strategic bombardment reduced aircraft production by 31 percent, tanks by 35 percent, and trucks a further 42 percent.[15] The Allies attacked targets such as oil, transportation nets, and other activities, but the selection of targets was difficult. Faulty intelligence, limited understanding of the German economy, and the changing nature of that economy made the feasibility of successful economic warfare questionable.[16] Although impressive in size and scope, the AAF bombing attacks could not stop German economic activities. The German juggernaut continued until its dying days of May 1945.

What has changed since World War II is vast improvements in technology that allow one to strike and make pre- and post-attack assessments against targets in a more effective and efficient manner than in the past. Could advances in aviation and other support systems today identify, find, and destroy targets that could cripple an economy or national leadership decisively? The dream of ending the war-making capability of an enemy, much like the hopes of AAF officers during the Combined Bomber Offensive during World War II, might come to fruition with these advances. Effects-based operations require a commander to predict accurately the impact of the destruction of specific targets and their eventual influence on an adversary. Economic activities today are even more complex than those in World War II. Suppose a country wanted to disable an economy. What targets should the nation bomb? With complexity and increased specialization from globalization, this task might actually be easier today than in the past. Many nations today require outside resources and components to take advantage of global markets and comparative advantages in prices, wages, and capital. Weakening key transportation nodes, energy sources, or assembly plants that focus on a few industries might shock a nation's economy. Especially in countries that have found their niche in the world economy due to globalization, John Warden's concepts might still work. However, issues still abound. Does the nation have alternative sources of products and services that can substitute for the target? Due to specialization of industrial products, would attacks on the economy create hardship on allies who trade with or produce products within the targeted areas? What amount of collateral damage will result from these actions? Suppose a country wanted to disable an economy, what targets should the nation bomb? Reducing electricity could force a slowdown in industrial production, but this could affect hospitals and other services that cause innocent lives to be lost. What if the country has few, if any, visible targets, like nonstate actors?

Warden's theory assumes that air power has almost unlimited access to attack enemy targets. To gain maximum efficiency and effectiveness, a nation must have the ability to gain air superiority. Warden takes great pains to ensure readers understand that air superiority is a "necessity" that allows air forces to conduct operations and allows them to conduct attacks on the centers of gravity that he believes would cripple a foe.[17] Given this assumption, Warden proceeds with his theory, but what if the nation cannot achieve air superiority? That condition may not be a problem for the United States in the near future, but it might not be the case for other states or in a particular region. Additionally, much of Warden's theory assumes a fairly static enemy. A rival can react and might modify its behavior to compensate for attacks on the ring structure. For example, instead of maintaining a strict chain of command leadership, what if a terrorist organization or state fragments its leadership or it dissolves into a loose confederation of leaders? Disabling one specific leadership center of gravity may not halt significant operations in the terrorist cell or a particular country.

Timing is also a concern. Warden assumed that a country's air force could strike the enemy at the onset of any hostilities.[18] Attacking an enemy at the very beginning of a conflict could produce significant shock value to an adversary. A tremendous level of parallel attacks could cause the foe's leadership to snap. Contrast this situation with one where an air force has a gradual buildup of attacks, as it shifts forces or tries to wrest air superiority from an enemy. A foe could attempt to disperse its economic centers of production (admittedly difficult), build redundant capabilities, or find alternative sources of production. Targeting information, like the flow of activities, could change and cause the air force to bomb unnecessary or counterproductive targets.

Warden's ideas were tested in 1990-1991. During Operation DESERT STORM, the United States executed a strategic air campaign plan that reflected much of Warden's theory. The uncontested use of American air power resulted in an asymmetric advantage over the Iraqi forces that pit U.S.

and coalition strength against Iraqi weakness. Iraq could not prevent the U.S.-led coalition from gaining air superiority. Strategic bombers, land-based tactical aircraft, cruise missiles, naval aviation, and multinational partners contributed to a massive attack on Iraq.

PLANNING AN AIR CAMPAIGN

During the 1991 Persian Gulf War, John Warden served in the Pentagon in the Air Staff's directorate of plans where he was deputy director for warfighting concepts. This position allowed him to experiment with many creative concepts of air power employment. During the opening days of the August 1990 during the Iraqi invasion of Kuwait, General H. Norman Schwarzkopf, commander of U.S. Central Command (CENTCOM), initiated planning activities that ranged from stopping a possible invasion of Saudi Arabia to immediately pushing Iraqi forces back into their own country. One area that Schwarzkopf found lacking in CENTCOM was the ability to conduct a strategic air campaign.[19] Schwarzkopf sought out the Air Staff. His request allowed Warden to work on a strategic air campaign against Saddam Hussein's government. The Five Ring model would be subjected to the test of action.

Warden proposed a number of approaches within the Air Staff. His final concept was presented as an Iraqi air campaign entitled Operation INSTANT THUNDER. The intent of INSTANT THUNDER was to conduct a very short, 6-day, intensive bombardment that would "incapacitate" the Iraqi leadership and destroy vital Iraqi military capability. It would not touch "basic" infrastructure that would create undue civilian hardship.[20] Warden cautioned that this action was not designed to be a long-term plan that would turn into an attritional campaign. INSTANT THUNDER would last days instead of the years of air operations by the Navy and Air Force over North Vietnam. The campaign plan seemed like a great opportunity to demonstrate his ideas. A rapid campaign could allow American air forces to isolate Hussein and attack systematically the centers of gravity of Iraq.

The Five Ring model capitalized on the strength of American air power. The United States could launch such an attack immediately as ground forces were building up in Saudi Arabia. If Schwarzkopf conducted the campaign as written, Warden predicted it would minimize United States and allied losses and could reduce Iraqi civilian casualties and collateral damage. This campaign, more importantly, could eliminate Iraqi military capability for an extended period.

Warden developed a set of specific targets that closely resembled his model. The first targets were designed to gain air superiority by destroying air defenses, airfields, and the Iraqi air force. After the coalition achieved air superiority, its air forces would concentrate on leadership, command and control, key internal production and distribution centers, weapons of mass destruction (WMD) production and storage facilities, and offensive air and ballistic missile capability. Warden did not include Iraqi fielded land power in the INSTANT THUNDER proposal. Instead, Warden proposed to incapacitate the Hussein regime and tie up its telecommunications, civil and military, in an effort to reduce national leadership effectiveness. The organic essentials ring had several potential targets to include electricity and petroleum and oil distribution and storage for domestic Iraqi use. Warden did not want to destroy the export capacity or damage Iraqi's long-term economic health. Aircraft would attack infrastructure targets that involved railroads and some bridges. Air forces would also use psychological warfare against the Iraqi population, foreign workers, and any forces in Kuwait to reduce Saddam Hussein and his Ba'ath Party's influence. The elements of the last ring—fielded military forces—which Warden addressed, were strategic air defenses and delivery systems like bombers and ballistic missiles that could use WMD or conduct strategic operations. The attacks would occur in parallel across all five rings from strategic air defenses to Saddam Hussein's palaces.

The key center of gravity was Saddam Hussein's ability to lead and control his nation.[21] Each target attacked by Coalition air forces would support this aim. The destruction of telecommunications and command and control capabilities would disrupt any connection between Hussein, his people, and Iraqi military forces. Striking at Iraqi strategic delivery capability would reduce any regional threat posed by Iraq at the time and into the future. Hussein had demonstrated his ability to use SCUD and modified ballistic missiles to hit targets in Tehran in the War of the Cities during his conflict with Iran in the 1980s. Hussein could use the same systems to attack south to Saudi Arabia or west to Israel. Eliminating Iraqi strategic air defenses would open Iraq to continual attacks and reduce a large threat to American air crews. A massive assault on electrical grids would cripple any industrial production and allow chaos to reign among the population. The lack of refined petroleum products could hamper transportation and paralyze civilian and military movements. These targets would underscore Hussein's weaknesses to his people and the world.

CENTCOM campaign planners modified Warden's original six-day INSTANT THUNDER campaign plan. Warden had used the idea of a six-day campaign as a device to sell the concept to Schwarzkopf.[22] When Warden was asked to develop a campaign plan, the Iraqis had just invaded Kuwait in August 1990. The original plan was an option to strike back at Baghdad. Fortunately, the United States and other powers had sufficient time to conduct an unmolested buildup of air, land, and maritime forces to eject Iraqi forces from Kuwait. The Coalition air forces did conduct a strategic air campaign, but planners dismissed the belief that air power alone could defeat Iraq. Top military leadership and CENTCOM planners did not believe Warden's idea that a week-long campaign that concentrated against 84 strategic level targets was credible. Instead, the Coalition conducted a four-phase campaign, after attaining air superiority, which included a longer strategic air campaign plan, followed by operations against Iraqi air defenses in Kuwait. The third phase featured air support of ground forces to attrite Iraqi forces and isolate enemy forces in Kuwait. The last phase used air and ground forces to push all Iraqi forces out of occupied Kuwait. The first two phases lasted 39 days. The Iraqi government did not capitulate, nor did the will of the people erode significantly enough to affect Hussein.

John Warden's theories had a major impact on Operation DESERT STORM and the air campaign. Warden's ideas on precision guided munitions, stealth, parallel attack, and other air power features did create some strategic paralysis among the Iraqi government. Although Hussein's government did not collapse, it was affected significantly during the strategic bombardment campaign. For example, air strikes disabled communications. In a centrally controlled state like Iraq, unimpeded communications was vital if Hussein expected to control every action in the country. Destruction and disruption of the center "ring" aided the Coalition efforts to reduce Baghdad's military capability and effectiveness. The destruction of key national leadership, command and control, communications, industrial sites, and other sites helped support Warden's ideas. However, Iraq was a nation-state with these types of targets, and American air superiority was not really challenged. In the future, enemy nations or nonstate actors may not present as lucrative a target to air forces as Iraq did in 1991.

JOHN WARDEN'S IMPACT

John Warden focused his ideas on getting commanders to consider attacking the enemy by measuring the impact of those strikes on the enemy's ability to wage war. His Five Ring model gave campaign planners the ability to focus on a framework to paralyze a foe. Warden linked his ring attack to a plausible scheme against a modern nation-state. The advent of advanced munitions and delivery systems created conditions in which these types of attacks might achieve what earlier air power theorists could only dream about.

Warden's ideas led to greater reflection among air power advocates not only on the planning and actual attack on targets, but also on the more complex factor of the effect of an attack on the enemy. Commanders needed to consider not only the primary, but also the secondary and tertiary effects on the destruction or temporary disruption of these targets. Commanders through the ages have planned campaigns to meet objectives that require a study of the effects and assessment of target destruction. The advent of greater precision, speed, and lethality has allowed unprecedented opportunities to strike targets that can cripple a nation. Calls to limit damage and reduce human suffering have forced commanders to operate under increased constraints as they seek ways to accomplish their aims. Careful consideration of targets becomes a prime concern. Additionally, the ability to conduct parallel attacks forces commanders to consider how to paralyze a foe arrayed as a network or a complex of indistinct relationships. All these considerations need detailed study as commanders plan operations.

In the future, can national and military leadership gather and analyze sufficient information to implement Warden's concepts on the battlefield? Adaptive foes, lack of understanding about complex economic relationships, and other factors can limit the ability of militaries to conduct set-piece operations. Adversaries who gather information and disseminate it quickly via the Internet or cell phones can thwart efforts to conduct parallel attack schemes even if the strikes occur almost simultaneously and are separated by vast distances. Technologies that enable air and space operations to make John Warden's ideas come true are also available for an enemy to exploit as he develops countermeasures. Similarly, foes who do not operate or react like a nation-state or mirror how this country might respond could make Warden's theories difficult to implement. Still, the focus on what factors make an enemy operate as a system is a valuable way to think about an adversary. Military commanders might not overlook targets or weaknesses that they could now exploit. Warden helped integrate technology and strategic concepts that supported a major change in how nations use air power in war.

ENDNOTES - CHAPTER 21

1. Bernard Brodie and M. Fawn, *From Crossbow to H-Bomb*, Bloomington, IN: Indiana University Press, 1973, p. 177.

2. Giulio Douhet, *The Command of the Air*, Washington, DC: Center for Air Force History, 1983, p. 58.

3. John A. Warden, III, "The Enemy as a System," *Air Power Journal,* Vol. 9, Spring 1995, p. 43.

4. Phillip S. Meilinger, "Air Targeting Strategies: An Overview," in *Air Power Confronts an Unstable World*, Richard P. Hallion, ed., London: Brassey's, 1997, p. 61.

5. Diane T. Putney, *Airpower Advantage Planning the Gulf War Air Campaign 1989-1991*, Washington, DC: Air Force History and Museums Program, 2004, p. 36.

6. Thomas Greer, *The Development of Air Doctrine in the Army Air Arm 1917-1941*, Washington, DC: Office of Air Force History, 1985, p. 19.

7. David R. Mets, *The Air Campaign: John Warden and the Classical Airpower Theorists*, Maxwell AFB, AL: Air University Press, 1999, p. 59.

8. Putney, p. 40.

9. *Ibid.*, 39.

10. Warden, p. 50.

11. *Ibid.*, p. 45.

12. Michael S. Sherry, *The Rise of American Air Power*, New Haven, CT: Yale University Press, 1987, p. 54.

13. David S. Fadok, "John Boyd and John Warden: Airpower's Quest for Strategic Paralysis," in *The Paths of Heaven The Evolution of Air power Theory*, Phillip S. Meilinger, ed., Maxwell AFB, AL: Air University Press, 1997, p. 371.

14. R.J. Overy, *War and Economy in the Third Reich*, New York: Oxford Press, 1994, p. 372.

15. *Ibid*, pp. 373-374.

16. Alan S. Milward, *War, Economy and Society 1939-1945*, Berkeley, CA: University of California Press, 1977, p. 301.

17. John A. Warden, III, *The Air Campaign*, Washington, DC: Pergamon-Brassey's, 1989, p. 10.

18. Richard T. Reynolds, *Heart of the Storm*, Maxwell AFB, AL: Air University Press, 1995, p. 17.

19. *Ibid., p.* 24.

20. John A. Warden, III, "Iraqi Air Campaign Instant Thunder," briefing, undated, slide 2.

21. Thomas A. Keaney and Eliot A. Cohen, *Revolution in Warfare?* Annapolis, MD: Naval Institute Press, 1995, p. 30.

22. Putney, p. 360.

CHAPTER 22

NAVAL THEORY FOR SOLDIERS

J. Boone Bartholomees, Jr.

Soldiers do not always know much about and often do not appreciate their seagoing counterparts in the Navy. For most of a typical career, that matters not at all, but once a soldier enters the strategic realm, understanding how sailors think about their environment and conducting operations in it becomes critical. One cannot understand naval strategy without understanding the sea. Sailors design naval strategy in harmony with their understanding of the sea and naval warfare. While this is certainly also true of strategy on land—soldiers design strategies in accord with their understanding of their environment and land combat—the differences in the mediums complicate mutual understanding. Soldiers and sailors think about their environments in fundamentally different ways, and that influences how they think about strategy. Thus, this paper will begin by examining how people have classically conceptualized the sea. Then it will discuss oceans as theaters of war and the general characteristics of navies. It concludes by examining classic naval strategic theories.

CONCEPTUALIZING THE SEA

The sea is a vast expanse of water. That incredibly obvious, even simplistic, statement is central to understanding how sailors think about their craft. The sea is a hostile and unforgiving environment, perhaps better suited to inspiring poets and artists than for other human activities. One does not hear sailors referring to the sea as their "friend"—they may love and respect the sea, but they approach it warily. Man needs specialized technologies just to exist at sea. Thus, people may live at sea for relatively long periods, but they almost always return to land. For mankind the sea is primarily an economic or communications medium.

In economic terms, the sea is a tremendous source of raw materials. Commercial fishing comes immediately to mind. Fishing vessels ranging from fairly small, individually owned, shrimp boats to enormous, corporately managed factory ships scour the oceans daily. In 2005, the world's catch of fish and crustaceans was estimated at 93 ¼ million metric tons plus another 1 ⅓ million metric tons of aquatic plants (seaweed).[1] One supposes that figure has not declined recently. Besides fish, the sea yields a significant and rising amount of mineral wealth. Oil and natural gas fields underlie many oceans, and active exploration continues to discover more offshore sources. For example, in May 2006, Mexico announced the discovery of an undersea oil field that may contain 10 billion barrels of oil, making it larger than Mexico's existing reserves. Located 60 miles off the coast of Veracruz, the field is 2 ½ miles beneath the seabed under 4,000 meters of water. Producing at least 3.4 million barrels a day, Mexico is already Latin America's largest producer, and this discovery will allow it to continue production into the foreseeable future.[2] Such economic activity is one of the major interests people have in the seas. Commercial recreational use is a subcategory of commercial uses of the sea. Activities like sport fishing, SCUBA dive charters, or the cruise industry extract commercial benefit from recreational activities. That does not count the economic aspects of standard recreational activities like personal boating or SCUBA/snorkeling, outside the guided dive industry. However, in the case of all the commercial operations, the home base and the final destination of all oceanic resources and even recreational activities is ashore. In the case of commercial products, only the largest factory ships process products afloat—the vast majority of resources from the sea are processed and consumed ashore.

Besides being a workplace, but equally significant in economic terms, the sea is a line of communications. It is a way to move people and goods cheaply from one place man lives to another. Since man learned to construct boats, he has used them in this manner. It was the sea as a line of communications that made such diverse phenomena as intercontinental commerce, immigration, and colonialism possible. Although the modern commercial airline industry has a near-monopoly on the intercontinental transportation of people, shipment by sea is still by far the most economical way to move bulk goods. One source estimated the total global maritime shipping tonnage for 2004 as 6.76 billion tons and total maritime activity as an astonishing 27,635 billion ton-miles. The same source gave the world's merchant fleet at 895.8 million deadweight tons in 2004.[3] Some of the world's important choke points—notably the Panama and Suez canals and the Straits of Malacca—handle impressive flows of commerce. For example, over 60,000 vessels carrying almost one third of the world's trade goods pass through the Straits of Malacca annually.[4] All that traffic has to go somewhere, so it is not surprising that, for example, the Port of New York and New Jersey alone handled 78.5 million metric tons of cargo valued at over a billion dollars in 2004.[5] Again, it is important to note that all that activity is between places on land, and the vast majority of cargo is intended for final consumption ashore.

If politically the world's seas are mainly of economic significance (overlooking the environmental aspects for the moment), what are the implications for strategy? In other words, how does conceptualizing the sea in economic terms influence or shape how statesmen use the sea or seaborne assets to achieve political objectives? The answer is obvious—at the strategic level, maritime warfare is primarily economic. Strategically, one fights war at sea to deny the enemy the economic advantages of the sea (sources of resources or lines of communication) and/or to secure those advantages for oneself. That analysis, while true, deserves one caveat about another important aspect of modern naval power. Nuclear-armed (as opposed to nuclear-powered) navies, and to some extent conventional navies, can deter based on their inherent power to inflict pain—a capability unconnected with the economic aspects of the sea. The deterrent utility of navies is enhanced by characteristics of the sea—like the difficulty of locating individual ships, especially submarines, because of the size and composition of the medium. However, because deterrence is a concept theoretically unrelated to medium or means, the fact that naval assets can do it is useful, interesting, and irrelevant to issues of general strategic naval theory. People interested in the theory behind sea-based nuclear weapons consult Schelling rather than Mahan or Corbett. Since we are interested in naval theory rather than deterrence theory, this essay will recognize the importance of, but dismiss discussion about, the strategic deterrent aspects of the Navy.

THE SEA AS A THEATER OF WAR

While most of the issues about the sea as a theater of war are arguably tactical in both nature and impact, they nonetheless influence how naval theorists and practitioners see the world. Every theory or strategy must consider and reflect the environment for which it is designed. In naval warfare the nature of the sea itself is the major environmental consideration. The sea is a vast and empty space. This has several implications for naval operations. First, identification of the players is fairly straightforward. In the modern world, friendly military ships and aircraft carry electronics that identify them and communications equipment to facilitate the exchange of information and data. They also look radically different from standard civilian vessels. Additionally, civilian ships over 300 tons are required to carry electronic identification systems so they can be identified and tracked; civilian commercial aircraft also carry transponders that show a flight number, airspeed, altitude, and destination when queried by radar. Even navigational aids like buoys and potential obstacles to navigation like offshore platforms carry radar beacons that function like transponders.

All these features were instituted for other purposes, but simplify identification of friend and foe (IFF) in the military sense. Of course, one might spoof the IFF system, turn off transponders or identification equipment, exploit stealth technology, or undertake other means to hide in the environment, but in general identifying the players at sea is much easier than on land.

If identifying the players at sea is generally easy, finding them has historically been a challenge. Unlike on land where road and/or rail networks tend to dictate possible lines of operation, a navy can go just about anywhere it wants using any of a multitude of possible routes. This was less true in the ancient world, where fleets had to at least touch shorelines frequently, and in the early age of steam, when the location of coaling stations tended to dramatically restrict options for naval lines of operation. But throughout the classic age of sail and since the introduction of diesel and nuclear power, fleets could and can use the entire ocean. Combining this fact with the enormous size of the earth's oceans, compared with the tiny size of vessels and the vagaries of weather, meant finding an enemy was problematic. Battles took place when both sides sought them or when operational necessities (like being tied to a convoy, nearing final destination, etc.) simplified the location problem.

However, the ability to hide at sea was totally dependent on the vastness of the environment, and as technology expanded situational awareness, that ability has dramatically decreased. Overhead and space-based systems have extended "vision" immensely. There are still occasional blank spots where surveillance is sporadic or uneconomical and a wily sailor might hide, but unless close to shore where vessels are vulnerable to other forms of detection, those surveillance voids are generally distant from anything of strategic importance. Surface clutter (unwanted surface echoes) can provide extremely small craft like Zodiacs concealment from distant detection by radar, but such vessels are still observable by the naked eye long before they can close to a distance where they might do damage. The USS *Cole* was attacked by two men in a small boat loaded with explosives while moored at a refueling point in Aden harbor in October 2000. Its lookouts carried unloaded weapons and had strictly defensive—fire only if fired on—rules of engagement.[6] Such an attack would not have come close to succeeding if attempted while the ship was at sea. In the subsurface arena, thermal layers and other oceanic conditions can hide submarines, and detection remains difficult. In relatively shallow waters like the Baltic, where the Russians are purported to use this technique, submarines can lay quietly and virtually undetected on the bottom (although, in such posture, all they can really do is collect information).[7] Researchers are actively searching for metamaterials, anechoic coatings, and other techniques that can acoustically cloak submarines from SONAR detection, but although there has been significant progress, efforts to date have not provided absolute protection from detection.[8] Still, the problem of hiding or detecting submarines is a technological issue that is amenable to solution given sufficient resources. Similarly, in the air, stealth technology provides a big edge against radar detection, but even that is not perfect, and is a classic example of a technology in search of a countermeasure.

To some extent because of the relative ease of IFF, but also based on independent factors related to the character of the naval environment, collateral damage at sea is generally a negligible risk. There are significantly fewer non-combatants at sea than on the world's land surfaces—unless, of course one happens to be in one of the world's congested maritime areas, and even there the numbers involved are low compared with typical modern ground combat environments. More importantly, virtually all the civilians at sea are contained on or inside easily recognizable vessels or aircraft. Civilian aircraft are usually readily identifiable and on well known, predetermined flight paths. Civilian commercial ships are also easily identifiable as such, with only a few military logistic and medical ships even remotely resembling a commercial vessel. Commercial maritime traffic, like its air counterpart, largely follows well-known trade routes, and choke points like the two great canals and the Straits of Malacca can become crowded; but, at its worst, maritime traffic still never approaches the density of automobile traffic around even a small urban center. Civilian cruise ships and other pleasure vessels, while they ply non-standard routes, are even more distinctive in shape and style. Civilian submersibles are exceedingly rare and would be difficult to confuse with a military submarine. People can make mistakes that result in tragic loss of innocent life—as when the USS *Vincennes* shot down an Iranian air bus in July 1988—but such incidents at sea are remarkable, specifically because they are so rare.[9]

The risk of collateral damage to property is equally minimal. The probability of damaging or destroying someone's house is nonexistent. There are no urban centers, churches, mosques, or sites of historical interest at sea. There are oil platforms, but they are all well known, completely immobile, and well marked. A few bridges span areas where a fleet might venture, but they are all so close to shore as to be of negligible impact on normal naval operations. A sailor has to engage targets ashore before he begins to worry about physical collateral damage—at least to the degree such considerations affect land combat.

A primary characteristic of the sea as a theater of war is that it includes two distinct liquid media and their intersection. One might say the same of land; however, because the earth is a solid medium, and movement through it is at least extremely difficult, the vast majority of land warfare occurs on the surface or within the first few feet of the surface even in complex urban terrain. The use of caves, mining, and other subsurface activity is uncommon enough to be exceptional. For thousands of years the same might have been said about the sea—only more so. All naval activity took place exclusively on the surface. However, the advent of the airplane and the submarine changed that. Now, naval warfare is truly three dimensional, while land warfare has become two dimensional. Second, the intersection of the media differs. Because water is liquid, the sea surface is essentially flat. Of course, one can argue that waves or man-made structures like oil platforms make the sea a highly textured surface, but that is at a micro level, which in no way compares in size, extent, or durability to the natural and man-made texture of the earth's land masses. Similarly, the phenomena of evaporative ducting, in which variable humidity near the surface distorts radar waves and can give false readings or readings at incorrect distances, is a pesky tactical issue, and one sailors know how to manage.[10] The junction of a liquid medium with a solid on the ocean floor provides texture similar to that of dry land, which can influence submarine/counter-submarine tactics in that it affects SONAR propagation. Sea-bottom terrain can also affect operations in extremely shallow littoral or gulf waters, but in general does not affect the overall nature of blue water naval warfare. Islands, of course, protrude in numerous places, but they are land rather than naval spaces.

The flat nature of the sea's surface has an impact on the medium as a theater of war. Visibility is limited by light or weather but not by obstacles to the line of sight as in land combat—the horizon is the only limiting factor in daytime and good weather at sea. Thus, for centuries detection of hostile forces at sea occurred long before engagement, and to hide, naval forces had to be over the horizon (six to ten miles away from a typical ship) from their opponent, use some fortuitous weather phenomenon like a fog bank or squall, or lurk behind the occasional island. Navies worked hard to increase effective engagement ranges and closing speeds. Modern technology and the ability to exploit air and subsurface media have fundamentally changed the nature of the problem. Modern navies are not surface entities—they are three dimensional. The horizon is no longer a constraint to either acquisition or engagement. In fact, a modern naval battle between world-class fleets would occur over hundreds of square miles of ocean, with the main-surface combatants almost certainly unable to physically see one another.

While distances in modern naval war might be enormous, the number of combatants is relatively small. The Naval Vessel Register lists 249 active commissioned U.S. Navy warships with a "battle force" that includes combat logistics ships of 283.[11] Even during the Cold War, the U.S. Navy typically comprised only around 600 vessels. A *Nimitz* class aircraft carrier has a complement of about 90 fixed and rotary wing aircraft, so if all the ships in the Navy's battle force were in one battle and all eleven carriers were flying all their assigned aircraft simultaneously (all of which is impossible, but makes a point), there would be 283 ships and 990 friendly naval aircraft somewhere in the battle space. A more reasonable estimate—although still very high for a real situation—would be half of the battle force, with two-thirds of five carriers' aircraft flying or 146 ships and 300 aircraft. That, of course, does not consider the land-based air that might be participating. Adding a reasonable figure for them (100 aircraft), the total number of friendly ships and planes would still be under 600. Estimating an enemy force at the same size would be generous, so the total number of combatants would be something under—and almost certainly very much under—1,200 combatants. The heavy brigade combat team (BCT) was designed to have about 220 combat vehicles, and the Stryker BCT to have about 282 combat vehicles.[12] That severely underestimates the total number of vehicles a BCT actually has, and does not include either type of BCT's supporting Army aviation, USAF land based air, or potential naval air assets. One heavy BCT in Iraq in 2008 had 871 total vehicles on hand (208 combat, 252 combat support, 395 combat service support, 6 engineer/material handling, and 10 operational readiness float).[13] None of that counts a single dismounted soldier or squad. A land battle as big as postulated for the naval example would include at least five or six BCTs and, if assumed to be half the available army, as was done with the maritime example, would be approximately twenty BCT's. Because sailors fight exclusively as the crews of ships and aircraft, while soldiers fight as crews of much smaller vehicles—dismounted in small teams, or in aircraft—ground combat will quickly dwarf a naval battle in terms of the number of discrete entities engaged. This comparison is in terms of numbers only, and is not intended to compare any other aspect of either force—which would, of course, be an exercise in apples and oranges.

Even in a huge modern naval battle between equivalent main battle fleets, one can identify and count all the participants. The number of aircraft (manned and unmanned) and missiles, which would easily be the largest numerical category of participants, is still a manageable figure. Given computers, one can reasonably hope to find, identify, track, and ultimately target and engage all the opponent's vessels and aircraft while simultaneously tracking and controlling all friendly assets. That is decidedly different than in land warfare, where we are only now reaching a stage where we can reliably identify and track friendly forces, and that is still at the combat vehicle degree of fidelity (not individual soldiers or small units), except in extraordinary cases with very small units. One can see why network-centric warfare appeals more to sailors, who would instinctively be amenable to the concept, than soldiers, who would tend to be more skeptical about its practicality.

Similarly, because navies are such technological, machine-based organizations and, because of the nature of their environment, tactical problems at sea differ significantly from their land counterparts. The most thorny naval tactical problems often lend themselves to technological solutions. Soldiers will be familiar with the technological measure-countermeasure struggle between armor and anti-armor systems. Take that kind of paradigm and impose it on the entire fleet in all its dimensions. Sailors do not worry about adapting tactical maneuver to the enemy and terrain the way soldiers do. Even classic tactical ploys like attacking out of the sun do not make any difference if we are talking about firing a smart, medium-range, air-to-air, active radar homing missile at a target beyond visual range.[14] It is not at all difficult to understand some sailors' faith in technological solutions to strategic problems.

Finally, unlike war on land where a commander can force combat, battle at sea does not have to happen. Naval theorists have pointed out correctly that both sides must agree to fight at sea. In

Julian Corbett's words, "In naval warfare we have a far-reaching fact which is entirely unknown on land. It is simply this—that it is possible for your enemy to remove his fleet from the board altogether. He may withdraw it into a defended port, where it is absolutely out of your reach without an army."[15] Of course, a modern sailor has means of attacking fleets in port that were unavailable in earlier ages, but obliterating a port to root out the fleet hiding there may not meet political acceptability tests. While one might intuitively suspect that withholding a fleet from battle by sheltering it in a port would be a terrible strategic move, it can theoretically have strategic benefits, as we shall see later.

NAVIES

The general characteristics of navies also influences how sailors think about maritime strategy. First, all navies are machine dependent. The ship is not simply a combat vehicle analogous to a big tank—it is essential to life at sea. A warship is a combination home, means of transportation, and combat platform. As a result, navies are now and have always been very technologically dependent; the best of them have been technologically proficient. A study of naval technology reminds one of how seemingly minor technological changes can have significant operational impact.

Certainly a product of the technological aspects of the job (skill requires long-term familiarity, practice, and study), but also reflecting the realities of life at sea, navies are almost exclusively professional in a way that has not been true of large armies since the French Revolution. The concept of a large, modern naval militia is untenable. While the Athenians might have been able to fill their triremes with citizen rowers for individual campaigns, modern navies are manned by long-service professional sailors. The belligerents in World War II drafted large navies, but they became effective only as they matured and became essentially professional sailors. The U.S. Navy Reserve today makes up only about 20 percent of the total Navy, and although it recruits directly from civilian life, many if not most of its sailors served previously in the active Navy.[16] One result of long-term professional service is almost invariably deeply held cultural norms based on historical tradition. These can be counterproductive if they fail to adapt to changes in the environment. Fortunately, and perhaps inevitably, although U.S. Navy culture is very traditional and conservative in some respects, it also tends to support and value technology. This natural and cultural reliance of sailors on machines and technology can influence their strategic thinking both in terms of process and content. For example, technology and machines often lend themselves to performance evaluation by quantifiable metrics, and it is logical to expect to gauge strategic performance similarly. There is nothing right or wrong about this; it is simply a learned way of thinking about problems.

Navies have historically performed a fairly consistent set of missions. These have traditionally been sea control, forward presence, blockade of enemy ports/coasts, coastal defense, commerce raiding, transportation and landing of ground forces, and maritime security actions like counter-piracy. The nuclear armed navy adds strategic nuclear deterrence to that list, and the modern navy has the engagement range and capability to strike targets ashore, either independently or in support of other operations. The modern U.S. Navy organizes those tasks under broad general headings and adds non-traditional tasks like humanitarian assistance and disaster relief, but those general categories still form the heart of any navy's mission. With the exception of deterrence, strike, and transporting and landing ground forces, all of those missions are at base economic in that their intended effect is to either facilitate or hinder trade directly or indirectly. That is understandable based on what we have said about the economic character of the sea, and is exactly in-line with what maritime strategists have traditionally theorized.

ALFRED THAYER MAHAN

The first original American military strategic theorist and the first famous maritime theorist was Alfred T. Mahan (1840-1914). An unlikely candidate for a theorist, Mahan's early career had been mediocre at best. He was rescued from obscurity by Stephen B. Luce, the self-taught, intellectual father of the U.S. Naval War College, who became the driving force behind military education in the Navy. In 1884, Luce invited Mahan to be the chair of military history and tactics at the new college, probably on the strength of *The Navy in the Civil War, The Gulf and Island Waters*—a forgettable volume that Mahan had just published.[17] Luce hoped Mahan would be "...that master mind who will lay the foundations of that science [of naval war], and do for it what Jomini has done for the military science."[18] Son of the influential West Point professor, Dennis Hart Mahan, the younger Mahan was nevertheless not particularly well prepared for an academic assignment, much less the lofty role Luce envisioned. Delayed at sea, Mahan was unable to join the faculty for the inaugural Naval War College class in 1885, and instead received permission to spend a year in New York studying his subject. He used that year to develop and refine his thoughts. Mahan determined that the theme of his history class would be the significance of the control of the sea or sea power and its relationship with other elements of national power. He joined the Naval War College faculty in 1886 and continued to refine his thinking and his classes until 1889, when he took the opportunity of a temporary suspension of the college to prepare his lecture notes as what was to become his most famous and important book—*The Influence of Sea Power upon History, 1660-1783* published in 1890. Two years later he published a second *Influence* book in two volumes—*The Influence of Sea Power upon the French Revolution and Empire*.[19] Mahan's *Influence* books made his name, and he became an instant literary success, especially in Great Britain. His books were politically timely because they both reflected the imperialistic ideas popular at the time and supported the advocates of a big navy in both Great Britain and the United States.

Using an historical approach, Mahan sought to expose "...the effect of sea power upon the course of history and the prosperity of nations." Further, he intended to demonstrate how dominating the sea had been the primary military factor that allowed Britain to dominate the world during the period he studied.[20] He thus approached sea power from the grand strategic level—at least theoretically; there remains significant tactical and operational detail in the *Influence* books. Mahan began with the assertion that the sea was a great highway or a wide common over which mankind could pass freely. Use of that common granted economic benefits, albeit at some risk. During wartime, merchant vessels needed secure ports and protection during transit. From this rose the requirement for a navy. "The necessity of a navy in the restricted sense of the word, springs, therefore, from the existence of a peaceful shipping, and disappears with it, except in the case of a nation which has aggressive tendencies, and keeps up a navy merely as a branch of the military establishment." Mahan made a distinction that still exists between sea power and naval power. Sea power described a nation's total capability at sea—"...not only the military strength afloat, that rules the sea or any part of it by force of arms, but also the peaceful commerce and shipping..." while naval power was the armed element of sea power.[21]

Some countries are better suited to be sea powers than others. Mahan listed what he considered the prerequisites for being a sea power; geographical position, physical conformation (primarily shoreline but including natural resources and weather), extent of territory, size of population, character of the people (seagoing vs. landlubbers), and character of the government.[22] He thought countries, like the United States, blessed with abundant potential sea power, should exploit that potential.

Mahan had distinct ideas about how naval warfare should be conducted. Although he modified his most extreme positions over time—for example, he admitted direct protection of ports and convoys and even commerce raiding might be appropriate in some circumstances—he has come to represent one school of thought in naval strategy. The school for which Mahan is the standard bearer believes the purpose of a navy is to fight the enemy navy in decisive engagements, the object of which is to gain command of the sea—that is, to establish such a dominant military position at sea that an opponent is incapable of effectively interfering with friendly operations.

Mahan's theory reflects the influence of Jomini, but he is more than Jomini at sea. Mahan believed that wars could be won by choking the opponent's maritime economic activity. To do that, one needed to defend one's sea lines of communication and threaten the enemy's. He believed the best way to protect sea lanes and economic activity at sea was by gaining command of the sea. The only certain way to secure command of the sea was by eliminating the enemy's fleet, and the best approach to that was by defeating the enemy's navy in a decisive battle or series of battles. Given that goal, as Jomini had advocated on land, Mahan advocated concentrating the fleet for the decisive naval battle. As long as the enemy's navy survived, it could contest use of the sea; when it was gone, friendly commercial activity could proceed, while the enemy's was stopped completely. Thus, defeating the enemy fleet to gain command of the sea was the overriding mission for the navy. Activities that detracted from concentration for the main fleet action were superfluous. There would be no need to protect merchant shipping directly or guard ports if the enemy's navy lay at the bottom of the sea. Trying to bypass the enemy's fleet and directly attack the commerce that was, after all, the ultimate objective, was total folly.[23] In fact, any action "…which subordinated the control of the sea by the destruction of the enemy's fleets, of his organized naval forces, to the success of particular operations, the retention of particular points, the carrying out of particular ulterior strategic ends" was folly.[24] Flowing from that basic thesis were derivates, such as: if the main fleet battle would decide the command of the sea, one should have a large, powerful fleet based on the capital ships of the day.

This line of reasoning flew in the face of traditional U.S. naval policy that—after 1814, when the nation was secure under the umbrella of Great Britain's command of the sea—had relied on small fleets and land fortifications for coastal defense, counter-piracy operations for merchant protection, and commerce raiding (especially in the case of the Confederacy) and blockade for offensive operations. Instead of that traditional small navy defensive policy, Mahan asserted that prosperity would result from developing a first-class fleet, acquiring the necessary coaling stations for worldwide deployment, and becoming a major maritime power capable of contesting control of the sea with the other major maritime powers. Mahan was an imperialist and wanted to position the U.S. to be an imperial power.

Mahan lived through a period of rapid and dramatic change in naval technology and warfare; he based his theory on the historical examination of the age of sail. His theories generated debate during their day, and to some extent, did not stand up well to changing political and technological times. For example he did not foresee the burst of anti-colonialism that would change forever the political structure he envisioned, nor the advent of effective aircraft and submarines that would do the same for naval tactics. Perhaps more damning, he overestimated the economic significance of sea power—most national economies, perhaps excluding island nations like Britain or Japan, do not depend on seaborne commerce to nearly the extent Mahan believed. At least by the early-20th century, domestic industrial capacity was far more significant to most countries than overseas colonies and trade. Additionally, as the geo-strategist, Halford MacKinder, noted, even as Mahan wrote the railroad was opening up the vast interiors of the continents in a way never before seen and was challenging sea- and river-borne transport as the cheapest and easiest way to move bulk goods over great distances.[25] Nevertheless, Mahan's was the first comprehensive study of naval strategic theory, and much of it is as current and applicable today as the day he wrote it. It is difficult to argue that command of the sea is not a desirable goal, especially for a nation with a coastline. And it is impossible to argue that naval combat has never produced decisive political results, even if one does not believe success at sea sufficient for all strategic success.

JULIAN STAFFORD CORBETT

The British maritime theorist Julian Corbett (1854-1922) was a contemporary of Mahan's. Like his American counterpart, Corbett was an unlikely naval theorist—in Corbett's case, because he had never served in the navy. Trained in law at Cambridge, Corbett disliked the legal profession and turned instead to a life as a writer. Several unsuccessful novels preceded his publication of popular biographies of the British admirals Monk and Drake. Those gave him the credentials and interest to join the newly formed Naval Records Society in 1893. His career as a naval commentator and theorist really began when the society asked him to edit some of the papers it was publishing. Corbett published volumes on *Fighting Instructions, 1530-1816* and *Signals and Instructions, 1776-1794*, which offered reinterpretations of naval warfare during those periods. He followed those with a series of books on British naval operations from Drake to Nelson that developed his controversial interpretation of sea power and naval history. Shortly after the turn of the century Corbett's reputation was such that he became the admiralty's chief unofficial strategic advisor. He was a strong supporter of Admiral Jackie Fisher's reforms as Second and later First Sea Lord. In 1911, Corbett published *Some Principles of Maritime Strategy*, which consolidated his thoughts and made them available to the general public.[26]

Corbett's strategic theory owes much to Clausewitz, whom he called "[t]he greatest of the theorists….", although it is more than a rehashing of the Prussian's work.[27] The Clausewitzian heritage led Corbett to think about naval warfare as political and as a branch of war in general, and thus only one part of the grand strategy of a nation. In fact, Corbett considered maritime operations less strategically important overall than operations on land "[s]ince men live upon land and not upon the sea, great issues between nations at war have always been decided—except in the rarest cases—either by what your army can do against your enemy's territory and national life, or else by the fear of what the fleet makes it possible for your army to do."[28]

Corbett recognized that the sea was an economic arena, and navies existed to protect or advance the national maritime interest. He differed with Mahan, however, in his thinking both about how wars might be won and how maritime contests should be fought. Corbett was convinced that maritime power was only part of national power. The nation's interests lay mainly ashore, and in only very specific cases could political objectives be achieved at sea. "The paramount concern, then, of maritime strategy is to determine the mutual relations of your army and navy in a plan of war. When this is done, and not till then, naval strategy can begin to work out the manner in which the fleet can best discharge the functions assigned to it." In some situations, command of the sea might be essential, and the army might have to assist the navy in that task. In other cases, the navy might have to devote itself to landing the army instead of fighting the enemy's fleet for command of the sea.[29]

Corbett believed that naval warfare was less likely to be decisive than land war. While navies might severely damage some enemies, they seldom could exert enough power to hurt or overthrow them decisively.[30] Even modern land armies had difficulty completely overthrowing nations, and modern war—especially at sea—was likely to be limited rather than total. In fact, maritime empires were ideally suited for limited wars. Corbett believed physical isolation was a prerequisite for truly limited war—if belligerents could expand commitment, they might, and thus escalate what was intended to be a limited engagement into a total struggle. Only island nations or nations separated from potential rivals by oceans could reliably elect to pursue limited wars. In a limited war, one had to both be able to isolate the enemy and prevent him from harassing or invading your homeland. That was the true value of command of the seas. It also modified in Corbett's mind Clausewitz's formulation that the value of the objective will limit the means employed to achieve it. Corbett believed that regardless of the value of the objective, if one could not physically employ force, one necessarily had to fight a limited war. Sea power could prevent the application of land power and thus limit war.[31]

Corbett also believed that other maritime theorists—including Mahan—got some fundamental things wrong. First, command of the sea was tremendously overrated. He agreed that command of the sea should be the objective of naval warfare; however, he believed the assumption that one belligerent or the other always had command of the seas was wrong. "The most cursory study of naval history is enough to reveal the falseness of such an assumption. It tells us that the most common situation in naval war is that neither side has the command; that the normal position is not a commanded sea, but an uncommanded sea."[32] Next, other strategists underestimated the power of the strategic defensive in naval war. Corbett believed naval action could produce political effect without decisive battle. This was related to his ideas about limited war. Corbett wrote:

> It [another reason for the strength of limited war] is that limited war permits the use of the defensive without its usual drawbacks to a degree that is impossible in unlimited war. These drawbacks are chiefly that it tends to surrender the initiative to the enemy and that it deprives us of the moral exhilaration of the offensive. But in limited war, as we, shall see, this need not be the case, and if without making these sacrifices we are able to act mainly on the defensive our position becomes exceedingly strong.[33]

Corbett believed that because objectives were limited—here he specifically meant seizing portions of an enemy's territory or his colonies rather than completely defeating his nation—the defensive made sense. Grab what you want and defend it. Finally, Corbett thought the emphasis on concentration of force was mistaken. To concentrate, one needed first to be dispersed, and in maritime war dispersion was essential. Corbett believed, "The degree of division we shall require is in proportion to the number of naval ports from which the enemy can act against our maritime interests and to the extent of coastline along which they are spread." This necessary dispersion had to be balanced with a degree of flexibility so "…any two parts may freely cohere, and that all parts may quickly condense…"[34]

Corbett had his supporters and critics. His analysis during the pre-World War I debate over naval policy and strategy proved to be correct; however, the large, traditional segment of British public opinion that expected the Royal Navy to sweep the seas clear of Germans took no solace in that. Corbett took the intellectual blame for the post-Jutland stagnation in the North Sea. Conversely, Corbett did not foresee the impact of the submarine on naval warfare, so he was not omniscient. His preference for limited over total war led to an overemphasis on amphibious operations and produced analysis that slighted the historic importance of Britain's contributions to operations on the European continent. Nevertheless, much of his thinking about maritime power and naval warfare remains relevant today.

JOSEPH CALDWELL WYLIE

Unlike Mahan or Corbett, Admiral J. C. Wylie (1911-1993) was a likely candidate for a military theorist. He graduated from the U.S. Naval Academy in 1932 and had a series of typical developmental assignments in the surface fleet through World War II. After the war, he had assignments in the Office of Naval Research and as both a student and on the staff at the Naval War College, as well as progressively responsible command and staff assignments at sea, before retiring in 1972.[35] He both earned the Silver Star for gallantry in two night destroyer actions off Guadalcanal and was "a rarity among American naval officers" for being the first since Luce and Mahan known for writing about naval history and theory. He wrote fairly sparsely, producing only a handful of articles before publishing *Military Strategy* in 1967—a book he wrote while commanding an attack cargo vessel in 1953 but did not submit for publication until 1966.[36]

Wylie's book presented a general theory of military strategy—one he hoped would be applicable to any conflict at any time or place, and one that subsumed what he called the four major theories of strategy (continental, naval, air, and Maoist). He looked at strategy in general as "[a] plan of action designed in order to achieve some end; a purpose together with a system of measures for its accomplishment." The purpose, then, of all military strategy was to establish some form of control over the adversary. In some few cases political pressure, bribery, revolt, etc., have produced political results akin to victory in war. However, usually wars are won by one of three means: military victory on land, military victory at sea that allows introduction of land forces to achieve victory on land, or military victory at sea that allows a sea power to apply economic forces to strangle the enemy.[37]

In terms of maritime strategy, Wylie combined aspects of both Mahan and Corbett. From Mahan he took the concept that "[t]he first, and it must be first, is the establishment of control of the sea"; from Corbett he took "…the exploitation of that control by projection of power into one or more selected critical areas of decision on land." Wylie did not accept that command of the sea need be total. He actually looked at the concept as a two-part proposition—ensuring one's ability to use the sea and denying the opponent use of the sea. He accepted the idea that the best one might be able to achieve was local or temporary control of the sea.[38]

Wylie also devised a way of categorizing strategies based on the sequencing of tactical events. He said some strategies were sequential in that they necessarily proceeded step by step to solve problems—one had to capture objective one before he could attack objectives two or three. Alternatively, in what Wylie called cumulative strategies it did not make any difference when, where, or in what sequence events occurred; it was the cumulative weight of their impact that produced eventual results. The classic example of a cumulative strategies, was a war against enemy commerce. It matters not at all when, where, how, or in what order vessels are sunk; strategic results flow from the cumulative impact of the loss of ships and cargoes.[39] Cumulative strategies make much more sense to a sailor or airman than to a soldier, whose significantly less relative mobility limits his possibilities and thus his thinking. Also, cumulative strategies are attritive (they work by grinding down the enemy), a style that to the soldier implies excessive loss of life and inelegant if not unimaginative strategic thought.

Wylie's work, although targeted broadly, became most influential in naval circles. Its meld of Mahan and Clausewitz makes it particularly attractive to modern sailors, and its recognition of the role of naval forces in overall national strategy makes it useful for all national security professionals. Both groups could benefit from reading Wylie's thoughts on grand strategy.

ALTERNATIVE NAVAL THEORIES

Mahan and Corbett (and to some extent Wylie) proposed strategic theory most suitable for large naval powers, yet most of the world's nations do not fit in that category. What is the small or midsized maritime nation to do if it gets involved in a war with the big boys? For example, how should France of Germany compete with Great Britain at sea? Since preemptive surrender is always an option, the smaller naval power may simply concede command of the sea with all its benefits to the large power and contest the issue strictly on land. That, however, is not the way it usually works, as a cursory look at the history of warfare between our example countries shows. There are other theoretical approaches for the small or midsized maritime powers to consider.

If Corbett was right and command of the sea is rare, then the weaker naval power has some options. One reason he may be a weaker maritime power than his adversary is that he depends less on the sea than does the adversary. Thus, while one might not be able to exploit the sea for his own benefit, denying its use to the enemy might be of disproportionate advantage. In modern terms, while one may not be able to adopt a sea control strategy, a sea denial strategy may still be appropriate. It follows that even if one cannot win the great naval battle to gain command of the sea, there are still useful missions for a navy. A well known, and often misunderstood, example of such a mission is the fleet in being. The theory behind the concept of a fleet in being is that a naval force can exert strategic influence on an opponent simply by existing. It need not leave port, and should not if there is a danger of its being caught and destroyed. A fleet's simple presence makes the enemy expend resources and allocate forces to watch or contain it. A fleet in being at least severely limits, if it does not eliminate, opposition merchant traffic in its immediate vicinity and those waters within its ready reach. Both strategically and ethically, a fleet in being is almost always a better, if less glorious, choice than a sortie against impossible odds. It may threaten a local coalition partner of its opponent even if it cannot beat the main opponent, but there again, the threat would be limited to cases in which it could isolate the ally, beat it, and escape the inevitable intervention of the stronger navy. Whatever its other possibilities, the strategist must remember that the fleet in being concept is mainly designed to deny or divert.

Other naval strategies can potentially achieve positive results for the underdog maritime power. The most common of these historically is probably the resort to *guerre de course*, or commerce raiding. That approach targets directly what is important about the sea—merchant traffic. If the sea is an economic commons, intercepting the opponent's seagoing commerce is a worthwhile enterprise. If one cannot win the great naval battle to gain command of the seas, then *guerre de course* allows you to skip that step and go straight for the ultimate objective of sweeping enemy commerce from the oceans. Hopefully, sinking enough commerce will cripple the enemy economy and produce surrender or political compromise; at a minimum, high risk of commercial loss at sea raises insurance rates and diverts warships from other duties. Through the 19th-century national navies conducted *guerre de course* in conjunction with licensed private vessels called privateers—a polite name for government-sanctioned pirates. The international community banned privateering in 1856, and the advent shortly thereafter of effective submarines fundamentally changed the conduct of *guerre de course*.[40] Submarines cannot capture an enemy vessel, take off the crew, supply a prize crew, sail the captured vessel to port, and have the vessel and its cargo condemned by a prize court—which had been the legal procedure for privateers and the way they made a profit. Submarines conduct *guerre de course* by sinking enemy merchantmen. Besides raising significant legal and moral issues, sinking enemy merchant vessels reduces by approximately half the economic impact of *guerre de course*, since the capturing nation no longer gets to add the value of the target's cargo to its economy while taking it away from the enemy. Still, *guerre de course* remains a very viable sea denial strategy for the small naval power.

Perhaps the most comprehensive approach to naval strategy for the underdog was a little-known 19th-century French school of strategic thought called the *Jeune École* (New School, or Young School), which combined a concept to address the issue of sea control with *guerre de course*. Even though France was a major naval power with significant maritime interests, it had always had difficulty competing effectively with British sea power. The development of torpedoes and large-caliber, flat-trajectory naval cannons seemed to argue for a different technological paradigm than the traditional navy. The *Jeune École* advocated numerous smaller, faster vessels armed with the new weaponry (100-foot-long torpedo boats and cruisers) as the technological counter to the battleship. For a period during the 1880s, battleship construction (even in Britain) almost stopped.

The French Minister of Marine, Admiral Théophile Aube, one of the sponsors of the Jeune École, in 1886 cancelled all French battleship construction and shifted funding into torpedo boats and cruisers. The *Jeune École* claimed that steam power and the new weapons combined to negate the ability of navies to do their traditional missions—battleship navies could not win command of the sea against an opponent armed with the new technology, and neither could they protect maritime commerce directly, since the volume was presumed to be too large to escort. Thus, command of the sea was meaningless. Instead, *guerre de course* by the same torpedo boats that doomed the battleships could inflict enormous economic penalties on powers like Britain that relied too heavily on maritime commerce. Technological problems with the torpedo boats, the development of the destroyer, and the publication of Mahan's *Influences of Sea Power Upon History* doomed the *Jeune École* concept. The 1889 British naval budget nearly doubled naval appropriations for battleships. The other powers followed suit, and the *Jeune École* receded into the footnotes of history.[41] Of course, significant progress in submarine technologies meant that during both World Wars I and II the Germans were able to use naval forces much as the *Jeune École* had advocated by substituting the submarine for the torpedo boat to put enormous pressure on the British economy. The general approach of the *Jeune École* remains attractive to smaller maritime powers today.

Modern naval underdogs retain all the options of their predecessors, but technology has increased and to some degree simplified those options. For example, mines of various degrees of sophistication can close or limit access to ports and waterways. These can be very cheaply and easily deployed; finding and counteracting them can be difficult, dangerous, costly, and time consuming. Huge modern container vessels and supertankers (as well as their cargos) are much too valuable to risk if even a minimal threat of mines exists, so even a poorly executed and perhaps technically ineffective harbor- or sea-lane-mining program can essentially shut down shipping until the mines have been swept and the confidence of shippers restored. This is a very attractive proposition for the underdog. It is cheap and easy enough for even a Third World country, yet potentially extremely effective.

CONCLUSION

The 21st-century U.S. Navy reflects the thinking of the classic naval theorists. As a the world's most powerful navy, it is more comfortable with Mahan and Corbett than the *Jeune École*; as a navy with no near peer competitor, it has the luxury of concentrating more on projecting effects ashore or even on humanitarian and disaster relief operations than on titanic naval battles between main battle fleets for the control of the sea. The U.S. Navy lists its core capabilities as forward presence, deterrence, sea control, power projection, maritime security, and humanitarian assistance and disaster response.[42] The main difference between that list and what Mahan and Corbett espoused is a modern expansion of the concept of military power beyond the immediate military realm. Forward presence, deterrence, and humanitarian assistance are non-military uses of naval power. The Navy today thinks of itself (as does the Army) as advancing the national interest beyond the narrow field of winning the nation's wars. Still, it reflects classic naval theory, which has not been replaced or even significantly modified in almost a hundred years.

The sea is still a vast expanse of water, and sailors still think about it and warfare afloat differently than soldiers think about land combat. The maritime theater will always be more transparent and susceptible to technological solutions than its land counterpart. The smaller number of combatants and the relative (as compared to the land context) ease of locating them simplifies all aspects of finding, identifying, targeting, and engaging the enemy—although one should not assume any of those problems are ever easy. The sailor will always think about war in his medium in a very logical, sensible pattern based on the characteristics of that medium. The soldier will not instinctively think about war in the same manner. Hopefully, this paper causes some soldiers to consider maritime strategic theory in a different light and produces increased understanding.

ENDNOTES - CHAPTER 22

1. Available from *ftp://ftp.fao.org/fi/stat/summary/summ_05/a1a.pdf* and *ftp://ftp.fao.org/fi/stat/summary/summ_05/a6.pdf*.

2. Available from *news.bbc.co.uk/2/hi/americas/4808466.stm*.

3. Available from *info.hktdc.com/shippers/vol29_2/vol29_2_trade02.htm*.

4. Available from *www.mima.gov.my/mima/htmls/papers/pdf/mokhzani/strategic-value.pdf*.

5. Available from *www.panynj.gov/abouttheportauthority/presscenter/pressreleases/PressRelease/index.php?id=501*.

6. Available from *www.al-bab.com/yemen/cole2.htm*.

7. Available from *www.hs.fi/english/article/Underwater+hide-and-seek/1135226965202*.

8. See, for example, of attempts to cloak, available from *blog.wired.com/defense/2007/11/invisible-subma.html*.

9. Available from *ocw.mit.edu/NR/rdonlyres/Aeronautics-and-Astronautics/16-422Spring2004/40763DF2-1797-48D5-9D5C-136DFE8D43C7/0/vincennes.pdf*.

10. Available from *spiedl.aip.org/getabs/servlet/GetabsServlet?prog=normal&id=PSISDG00588500000158850G000001&idtype=cvips&gifs=yes*.

11. Available from *www.nvr.navy.mil/nvrships/FLEET.HTM*.

12. PowerPoint briefing. "Modular Force Overview101 060523." In author's possession.

13. Data from BCT Combat Slant report, May 2008 in author's possession.

14. See, for example, the AIM-120 AMRAAM, available from *www.globalsecurity.org/military/systems/munitions/aim-120.htm*.

15. Julian S. Corbett, *Principles of Maritime Strategy*, originally published as *Some Principles of Maritime Strategy*, Longmans, Green, and Co., New York, 1911; reprint Mineola, NY: Dover Publishing Inc., 2004, p. 158.

16. Available from *www.navyreserve.com/about/*.

17. Azar Gat, *A History of Military Thought: From the Enlightenment of the Cold War*, New York: Oxford University Press, 2001, p. 443.

18. Stephen B. Luce, "On the Study of Naval Warfare as a Science," *United States Naval Institute Proceedings*, Vol. 1186, as quoted in *Ibid*., p. 446.

19. Gat, pp. 447-9.

20. Alfred T. Mahan, *The Influence of Sea Power Upon History: 1660-1783*, Boston, MA: Little, Brown and Company, reprint 1970, original publication, 1890, pp. v-vi, 63-4.

21. Mahan, pp. 25-26, and 28.

22. Mahan, pp. 28-89.

23. Gat, p. 465.

24. Mahan, p. 339.

25. Gat, p. 452.

26. Gat, pp. 480-483, 485-486.

27. Corbett, p. 2.

28. *Ibid.*, pp. 9, 13-14.

29. *Ibid.*, p. 14.

30. *Ibid.*, pp. 14-15.

31. *Ibid.*, pp. 54-56.

32. *Ibid.*, p. 87.

33. *Ibid.*, p. 68.

34. *Ibid.*, pp. 72-74, 150-152.

35. Available from *www.usni.org/navalinstitutepress/wylie.asp*.

36. J.C. Wylie, *Military Strategy: A General Theory of Power Control*, "Introduction," by John B. Hattendorf, Annapolis, MD: Naval Institute Press, 1989, original publication, Rutgers University Press, 1967, pp. xv, ix, xxxi-xxxii.

37. *Ibid.*, pp. 57, 14, 77, 129.

38. *Ibid.*, pp. 125, 127.

39. *Ibid.*, pp. 22-23.

40. On Paris Declaration of 1856, which outlawed privateering, available from *oll.libertyfund.org/?option=com_staticxt&staticfile=show.php%3Ftitle=1053&chapter=141126&layout=html&Itemid=27*.

41. Theodore Ropp, *War in the Modern World*, New York: Collier Books, 1973, original publication, Durham, NC: Duke University Press, 1959, pp. 208-9. For more detail on the *Jeune École* see Theodore Ropp, *The Development of a Modern Navy: French Naval Policy, 1871-1904*, Annapolis, MD: Naval Institute Press, 1987, pp. 155-180.

42. Department of the Navy and U.S. Coast Guard, "A Cooperative Strategy for 21st Century Seapower," October 2007, available from *www.navy.mil/maritime/MaritimeStrategy.pdf*.

CHAPTER 23

ON THE THEORY OF CYBERSPACE

Jeffrey L. Caton

Over the past 2 decades, many security professionals have declared cyberspace a new domain for warfare. More importantly, the ability to access and operate in cyberspace freely is considered a vital interest for the sovereignty and prosperity of the United States.[1] At a time when the federal defense budget is being reduced significantly, funding related to cyberspace is generally on the rise. Do these considerable investments in our nation's cyberspace capability reflect critical analysis and wise counsel? More specifically, is a domain approach to modeling cyberspace appropriate and sufficient for such applications as national policy and strategy, federal resource appropriation, and doctrine development?

This chapter argues the need for the development and adoption of theories of cyberspace that provide the context essential for informed decisionmaking for the full spectrum of cyberspace security issues. It will not offer a codified and refined theory. Instead, this chapter introduces the reader to the concepts necessary to develop theoretical frameworks (some of which already exist in limited scope); in essence, it offers the beginning of a broader dialogue. To accomplish this, we establish fundamental nomenclature and constructs in cyberspace to avoid potential debate over semantics. Next, there is a short survey of some existing theoretical frameworks that illustrate the utility of examining activities in cyberspace in a broader perspective. A more detailed examination of applying (by analogy) established naval theory is presented. Focusing on theory for the operational level of war, we offer for consideration examples of cyberspace manifestations for the principles of joint operations that include all nine classic principles of war. Broadening the scope again, the article then addresses the ontology of cyberspace itself, which includes its possible evolutionary paths. It concludes with implications for present strategic leaders and some of the fundamental questions that should guide how the nation will shape its interface with and activities in cyberspace. The thoughtful pursuit of answers to many of these questions is left to the readers.

FUNDAMENTALS

This section provides definitions as a baseline for evaluation of frameworks for cyberspace theory. Rather than debate the intricacies of these definitions, the domain approach is reconciled in the context of the cyberspace commons, which incorporates all instruments of national power. The section also presents key characteristics of cyberspace activities in general terms.

Definitions.

Currently, the Department of Defense (DoD) defines cyberspace as "a global domain within the information environment consisting of the interdependent network of information technology infrastructures, and includes the Internet, telecommunications networks, computer systems, and embedded processors and controllers."[2] Adding "and their operators" to this definition makes it consistent with the 2009 *Cyberspace Policy Review*, which notes, "Common usage of the term [cyberspace] also refers to the virtual environment of information and interactions between people."[3] In a broader sense that encompasses all elements of national power, cyberspace is "a new strategic common, analogous to the sea as an international domain of trade and commerce."[4] These are the working definitions for this chapter. From a more philosophical perspective, cyberspace is "a consensual hallucination experienced daily by billions of legitimate operators, in every nation."

This is the definition by William Gibson from his landmark 1984 novel *Neuromancer*.[5] Many other definitions of cyberspace exist, some of which are presented in works by Kuehl and Libicki and will not be addressed here.[6] It is important to note that not all countries use the term "cyberspace." While they may use similar terms that are largely the same, these terms may not be precisely interchangeable in usage for strategy, doctrine, and culture.

Consistent with current joint doctrine, cyberspace operations encompass the three dimensions of the information environment—cognition, content, and connectivity. *Cognition* centers on human perception, decisionmaking, and interaction in cyberspace. The proper study of it should include disciplines such as neurobiology, psychology, philosophy, and ethics. In today's broad discussion of national security, cognition is probably the least emphasized element of cyberspace. *Content* refers to the information that is created (and destroyed), transferred, and stored in cyberspace. It can take many forms, the vast majority of which currently involve digital representations transmitted via electronic means. It is probably the most emphasized element of cyberspace, with much focus on software programs that can create or destroy data at many levels. *Connectivity* represents the physical platforms and structures that facilitate the cognitive and content dimensions in cyberspace. It is the most visible dimension (e.g., personal computers [PCs], mobile devices, and cell towers) and thus probably the easiest for the average citizen to comprehend. As one might imagine, the boundaries between these dimensions are not discrete and inflexible but often overlap (e.g., consider social networking).

RECONCILING THE DOMAIN IN THE CONTEXT OF THE COMMONS

One can argue that most military professionals are comfortable with the concept of operational domains—land, sea, air, and space—and thus often look for cyberspace to be a logical extension or expansion of such familiar concepts. (Interestingly, there is no DoD joint definition for "domain.") In fact, the first strategic initiative of the 2011 *DoD Strategy for Operating in Cyberspace* is to "treat cyberspace as an operational domain to organize, train, and equip so that DoD can take full advantage of cyberspace's potential."[7] However, the strategy implies a broader scope in its text, which encompasses an interagency whole-of-government approach to cybersecurity that includes robust relationships with allies and international partners. From this, one can infer the need for a model that informs military planning and strategic decisionmaking with a holistic context—the commons. In simple terms, "commons" are areas not controlled or owned by any single entity, and states and nonstate actors use them to conduct commerce and communication.[8] Thus, the answer to the question: "Is cyberspace a domain, or a commons?" is yes—in short, selection of which framework to use depends on the level of application. For example, determining specific force structures and unit competencies may be best served by the domain view; examining the extent and priority of cooperative engagement with various countries may be best served by the commons view.

To illustrate this concept of domain in a larger commons better, consider Figure 23-1, which depicts cyberspace by access and operations. Access can be either open or limited, and operations can be either governed or ungoverned.[9] For purposes of this chapter, governance is any form of published rules or guidelines for operating in a given area of the overall commons. For the sake of discussion, the figure is populated based on the user's perspective. Thus, U.S. military operations exist mostly in a governed area with limited access (i.e., the global information grid or GIG), and thus its domain is one quadrant of the figure. However, overall mission requirements beyond mere network defense, such as network exploitation for situational awareness and perhaps even network attack, require activities outside the domain. The significant task of determining and maintaining the proper balance between security and personal privacy rights is always a consideration in such activities.

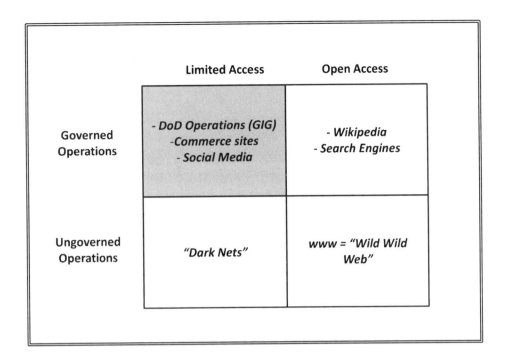

Figure 23-1. Cyberspace as Domain and Commons.

CHARACTERISTICS OF CYBERSPACE ACTIVITIES

As the development of cyberspace theory progresses, it should encompass all possible activities in cyberspace. The following is an attempt to identify some of the characteristics of such activities that are of high interest in today's security environment.

Physical versus Virtual.

Cyberspace enables the simultaneous manifestation of many planes of existence—some physical, some virtual, some a combination of the two. The term "virtual" usually refers to a computer-aided representation to simulate actual presence in the physical world. However, the concept of virtual reality has gone far beyond mere mimicry. For example, a single individual may have multiple personas in cyberspace. Conversely, a distributed group of individuals may collectively form a single persona. The virtual environment in which these personas reside may have no analog in the real world. Manipulating these embodiments may increase individual and group freedom to maneuver at various levels in cyberspace and presents challenges to others attempting to attribute specific activities to specific physical individuals.

Access and Creation.

Progressing through history, traditional domains required the use of technology to achieve access—carts on land, ships at sea, aircraft in the sky, and satellites in space. One could argue that such access did not create any new portion of the domain, nor significantly change the structure of domain itself. Cyberspace may be unique in that access and creation are almost synonymous or at least simultaneous—that is, the technology used to access cyberspace (e.g., computers and mobile devices) becomes an inherent part of the domain itself. Certainly, the growth of modern cyberspace from the infancy period of the ARPANET, with fewer than a dozen nodes of connectivity to the current Internet of more than six billion connected devices, demonstrates this concept. One should ponder if this will remain a constant relationship of creation nearly matching access, or if the balance will shift in the future until cyberspace becomes almost like the natural domains, and emphasis will be on access vice creation.

Reciprocity of Connectivity.

There has been much debate among cybersecurity experts regarding the ability to perfect defenses, encryption, and secure access in cyberspace. However, these debates often dive into the mundane, such as the speculated capabilities of organizations to "crack" passwords and thus ignore what the author posits as an axiom of cyberspace. That is, if a developer or user employs a device to connect to the cyberspace commons, then the *whole of the commons can connect to that device*. One must consider this a fundamental truth for the operator, since it defines the realm of the possible.

Thus, it is impossible to open a perfect one-way portal into cyberspace. This presents scenarios that may be unsettling to the uninformed. For example, all users of cyberspace must accept the fact that any messages or images they send or access over cyberspace *can be viewed by anyone in cyberspace*. Granted, such access may require illegal or unethical activity, but this does not change the fact that the action is in the realm of the possible.

With this in mind, cyberspace security cannot build a foolproof system, and thus should fall back on traditional risk management paradigms to design and prioritize security measures that punish potential adversaries with extreme costs for any benefits they may derive. In theory, this implies that anyone entering cyberspace to conduct attack operations can have these operations attributed to their point of origin.

Security, Freedom, and Privacy.

Achieving deliberate and conscious access to cyberspace continues to become simpler for the average citizen, but so does the access that is unconscious and perhaps unwelcome. The ubiquitous presence of cyberspace-connected devices is transforming the definitions and expectations of private versus public settings. Much friction is developing between the desire for freedom of action for all individuals in cyberspace and the desire for privacy and security of those actions. One end of the spectrum is the Orwellian view of a "Big Brother" government seeking to watch all activities and usurp all personal data. A recent demonstration of that perspective involved officials at high schools in Philadelphia who turned on cameras on laptops loaned to students without their permission.[10] The competing perspective reflects Huxley's view of a "Brave New World" dominated by materialism and hedonism where personal data is freely shared with little regard for negative repercussions.

Direct versus Indirect.

Internet-enabled communications have progressed to the point that most users consider them direct and instantaneous. This is largely an illusion derived from the shortcoming of human perception. For example, electrons traveling at the speed of light can circle the Earth in about 130 milliseconds, about one-third the time of a human eye blink. In the physical world, if one were to fire a weapon at a 10-meter target, the bullet would follow a largely predictable path, based on the gross properties of the air medium at the time (e.g., temperature, humidity, wind, etc.). Interactions at the molecular level are negligible compared with the momentum of the bullet; thus, it follows a direct path and achieves kinetic effects at the point of impact. That is not how things work in cyberspace.

Coupled with typical low-cost computer processing units that can accomplish billions of floating-point operations per second, the perceived transmission of a given data packet is assumed to follow a direct path in a stable environment. In reality, the configuration of cyberspace is constantly changing, such that, one could argue at the quantum level, it may change significantly in the milliseconds it takes for the human operator to press the "Enter" key. The illusion is that the effects and path appear to be direct from a physical perspective, but in the relative framework of cyberspace operations, they are indirect, inefficient, and slow to manifest. The author posits that projecting a guaranteed path in cyberspace is currently impossible, just as it is impossible to align all the molecules of air to accommodate a passing bullet. The goal of the cyberspace operator, then, is to determine the gross properties affecting cyberspace operations (if indeed they exist) as well as how to operate in them.

Kinetic versus Nonkinetic.

For discussion purposes, kinetic operations are those that occur in the visible physical environment and can be properly described using Newtonian physics. Operations in the traditional mediums (e.g., land, sea, and air) deal largely with kinetic means seeking kinetic effects, such as artillery barrages or bomb drops. These operations can have destructive immediate effects to facilitate beneficial changes to the localized medium—for example, the use of explosives during peacetime to carve out a highway tunnel or boat canal.

Consider nonkinetic operations as dealing with the unobservable exchange of information using various means in the electromagnetic spectrum. Figure 23-2 illustrates a simple model for analyzing possible scenarios for kinetic and nonkinetic methods used to create kinetic and nonkinetic effects. In general terms, nonkinetic means in cyberspace can produce kinetic effects in the real world. A dramatic example is the well-known experiment at the Idaho National Laboratories exploiting supervisory control and data acquisition (SCADA) systems. A large energy turbine was destroyed by sending it commands for performance that exceeded the design safety margins.[11] In contrast, cyberspace operations are vulnerable to disruption by kinetic attacks on the connectivity infrastructure—for example, dropping a bomb on a building that hosts Internet servers. Also, disruptions of the same node could be accomplished without physical destruction—for example, by sending a remote command that would turn the servers off.

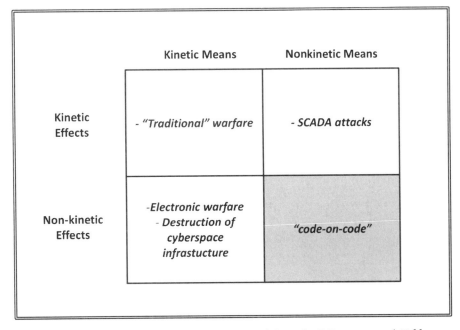

Figure 23-2. Kinetic versus Nonkinetic Means and Effects.

From the discussion of the indirect nature of cyberspace activities, one can infer that determining immediate nonkinetic effects resulting from nonkinetic means may be much more difficult to predict than the kinetic-on-kinetic case. In addition, when expanded to the second- and third-order effects, the task may be nearly impossible, since the effects will likely propagate at speeds well beyond human ability to comprehend.

Clearly, the separate quadrants of Figure 23-2 are ideal demarcations that in practice may be fuzzy. Phenomena such as electronic warfare using high-energy radio frequency or electromagnetic pulse means can be argued to straddle the kinetic/nonkinetic border. Although the specific role of such means is debatable, they should be included in dialogue that refines cyberspace theory.

Entropy in Cyberspace Operations.

Similar to other mediums, the active cyberspace environment has discernable structure that supports the disorderly movement of its contents. Classic thermodynamic modeling characterizes such random motion and disorder as "entropy." While some may offer cyberspace as an effective and optimized environment with little disorder, the truth is otherwise. In fact, cyberspace activity may actually be much more entropic than that of the physical world. The transmission of a data packet over the Internet may result in its division into many subpackets sent over different paths through an unknown number and type of processors and switches—this complexity may render tame by comparison the Brownian motion of air molecules colliding inside an inflated balloon.

Regardless of its relative scope of disorder when compared with the physical world, cyberspace is inherently complex and disorderly—the degree of which only increases as cyberspace continues to expand with the addition of new devices and connecting infrastructure. It is not logical to expect order to arise spontaneously out of such a cacophony, analogous to the second law of thermodynamics in the physical universe.[12]

The implications of the cyberspace entropy concept may be profound. In practice, it means that deliberate energy and effort are required to accomplish a specific task, and designers of content and connectivity may attempt to create structures that will decrease the entropy involved in their specific function. In a sense, one could consider the overlay of security measures as a way of purposefully adding entropy to a given system to thwart unauthorized use (e.g., passwords that use encryption to leverage the resulting disorder for security's advantage). An adversary may overcome this entropy, but must expend effort to do so.

The cyberspace entropy concept also offers a different paradigm on the concept of precision in cyberspace. One of the popular implicit promises of domain operations in cyberspace is that they will be clean, predictable, and repeatable. The author posits exactly the opposite—that operations in cyberspace are by nature not only disorderly and unpredictable, but also more difficult to characterize accurately in the realm of human cognition than traditional kinetic domain operations. This may have significant implications for the concept of precision engagement—the promise of some information technology enthusiasts is that cyberspace offers the ultimate form of achieving precision effects. The author asserts the opposite; that, in fact, achieving well-characterized and bounded effects in cyberspace is much more difficult to do than in physical space, and that the potential for unanticipated consequences is greater. Further, the means and methods used to achieve precision in cyberspace have limited utility, since their design is based on a configuration of cyberspace destined to change (by design or coincidence).

Siren Song of Certainty.

One of the most significant cautions for applications in cyberspace is to recognize that it is not a panacea for uncertainty. Implications stemming from the concepts of connectivity and entropy are that cyberspace is constantly changing in the microscopic sense—thus we will not soon resolve the vain pursuit of omniscience. The macroscopic features of cyberspace are also changing more rapidly than those of other domains, which, in operational terms, have reached a mostly steady state. The confluence of these changes may help to explain a common users' dilemma with computer activity that seems to both defy and comply with the definition of insanity attributed to Albert Einstein (i.e., doing the same thing repeatedly and expecting different results). Even though an operator may enter a command that fails on the first attempt, but succeeds on the second—the problem did not simply "go away"; the configuration of cyberspace changed. Thus, it may make perfect sense at the macroscopic level in cyberspace to expect different outcomes from the same input, since cyberspace at the microscopic level changes between the events.

EXISTING FRAMEWORKS

Now that the reader has an appreciation for the need to consider a context beyond the domain concept to evaluate activity in cyberspace properly, what are some of the practical methodologies for accomplishing this? While a holistic theory for cyberspace has yet to be offered, elements of such a theory exist, some of which we examine next.

Theory of Cyberpower.

In 2009, Dr. Stuart Starr of the National Defense University published an essay entitled "Toward a Preliminary Theory of Cyberpower," which offers a worthy framework to inform the dialogue regarding the national security aspects of cyberspace. He emphasizes the need for proper theory to address five key issues: definition of terms; categorization and structure of theory elements; explanation of the elements by analysis and example; connection of the elements for comprehensive examination; and anticipation of future activities and trends. He develops a three-layer pyramid model, with *cyberpower* sandwiched between the base section of *cyberspace* and the top section of *cyber strategy*. The article includes timelines illustrating the evolution of cyberspace over the past 50 years, and the evolution of cyberpower (military and economic elements) and cyber strategy over the past 30 years. Spread across all three tiers are institutional factors that theory must consider; these include issues of governance, law, information exchange, and civil liberties.[13] This model underscores the importance of pursuing overarching cyberspace theory as a foundation for developing derivative theories for cyberpower and cyber strategy.

Ecosystem Model.

In March 2011, a Department of Homeland Security paper proposed the concept of a "healthy cyber ecosystem" as a model for enabling future security in cyberspace. The article offers novel approaches, such as analogies based on the human immune system and the Centers for Disease Prevention and Control methods to achieve their three foundational building blocks of automation, interoperability, and authentication. The paper states the concept vision concisely:

> In this future, cyber devices have innate capabilities that enable them to work together to anticipate and prevent cyber attacks, limit the spread of attacks across participating devices, minimize the consequences of attacks, and recover to a trusted state.[14]

The proposed model uses mutually supporting healthy cyberspace devices working together proactively and dynamically to assess the severity of any "infection" and respond when an appropriate "alert threshold" is exceeded. It is prudent for further development along these theoretical lines to consider that anomalous and negative activities in cyberspace are not always attacks; they may be manifestations of complex interactions and the resulting entropy. Thus, designing systems where "automation allows the speed of response to approach the speed of attack" must strive to ensure that "attacks" are clearly distinguished from mere "alerts."[15] It is reasonable to assume that such measures may create an information environment that is largely self-regulating with respect to mundane threats. In addition, just as strengthening human immune systems may have the counterproductive effect of producing more virulent strains of germs, it is logical to ponder what new threats may emerge in response to a healthy cyberspace environment.

Service Models.

On October 31, 2010, U.S. Cyber Command achieved Full Operational Capability, with its mission to direct operations and defense of DoD networks, conduct full-spectrum military cyberspace operations, and ensure U.S. and Allied freedom of action in cyberspace and deny the same to adversaries.[16] The command structure includes service component elements from the Army, Marine Corps, Navy, Air Force, and Coast Guard. Not surprisingly, ingrained service cultures and doctrines significantly affect the lens through which each service views cyberspace.

A focus on applying traditional competencies in a domain environment, although it may be consistent with the *DoD Strategy for Operating in Cyberspace*, may run the risk of greatly underestimating the complexity of activities in cyberspace. The Army posits the cyber-electromagnetic contest as the third dimension of full-spectrum operations[17] led by a merged cadre of intelligence and signal operators. The Navy seeks information dominance that leverages the capabilities of their intelligence and communication personnel with support from space, information operations, and cryptology also being influential.[18] The Air Force has brought communication and computer specialties under the purview of their Space Command.[19] The result of these actions is that the inherent friction and conflict among these service subcultures may cause guidance from staffs and decisionmakers to seem unclear or self-conflicting. For example, the services acknowledge the role of the electromagnetic spectrum, but viewed it in vastly different ways.

In a recent *Survival* article, W. Alexander Vacca examines in more detail how the military cultures of the Navy (applying Mahan and Corbett's concepts) and the Air Force (applying Douhet's concepts) influence their approaches to cyber security. Vacca posits the Navy approach will more likely embrace the commons model and devise cyber operations to defeat enemy cyber operations. The Air Force will more likely be aware of the influence of popular will and morale in conflict, focus more on an effects-based view of cyber operations, and embrace a model of cyber deterrence. Vacca concludes that "given the proclivity of the services to consider threats and responses through different prisms, these inefficiencies seem preferable to potential blindness, especially as the nature of the threat continues to evolve."[20]

Given all this, can the DoD achieve a holistic and objective view and approach to cyberspace that allows it to perform its unique missions in concert with the activities of other U.S. Government players as well as those of private citizens, industry, and international organizations? Applying the domain in a greater commons view will help the process, perhaps through an expansion and enhancement of classic naval theory.

Naval Theory Analogy.

Traditional (i.e., Mahanian) naval theory provides an analogy to illustrate the value of modeling military activities as domain operations in a greater global commons. Part of the utility of the analogy is the difference between naval operations in the littoral area—the "brown water"—versus those in the broad ocean—the "blue water." When one connects the major ports in the brown water to other ports in the world, "sea lines of communication" emerge in the blue water that have strategic importance based on many factors, including geography and volume of traffic.[21] Similarly, one can map cyberspace to clearly show "cyber lines of communication" and critical nodes with tactical, operational, and strategic implications, perhaps even choke points—the "blue water cyberspace" equivalent of the Strait of Hormuz.

In a 2001 article in *Naval Law Review,* Lieutenant Commander Steven Barney added detail to such concepts by using the framework of the 1982 United Nations (UN) Convention on the Law of the Sea to examine issues related to routing information through cyberspace. He proposed the concept of national cyberspace as "the region of Cyberspace in which individual States require substantial sovereign rights to preserve the political and economic security of the State." He divided this region into internal cyberspace, "where a State may exercise complete sovereignty," and territorial cyberspace—the "portion of national cyberspace through which, and to which, governments, commercial enterprises, or private organization allow generally unrestricted access." Barney considers international cyberspace a region with no physical analogy to international waters. Rather, he offers that it "is not a physical place; it is a *characteristic* of cyberspace by which a data packet is not physically present anywhere but is merely in transit."[22]

Instead of ship traffic crossing oceans, it is useful to consider information traffic as packages of data moving across electromagnetic waves in cyberspace, and the principles of various types of passage over these waves are considered. The right of innocent passage provides "the right to traverse the territorial sea in a continuous and expeditious manner, so long as the passage is not prejudicial to the peace, good order, or security of the coastal State." The right of transit passage provides "freedom of navigation and overflight solely for the purpose of continuous and expeditious transit of the international strait between one part of the high seas or an exclusive economic zone and another part of the high seas or an exclusive economic zone." Both types of passages may be exercised by warships, but transit passage provides the advantages that "forces may transit in their normal mode of operation (i.e., warfighting) and bordering States may not suspend the right of transit passage through international straits." Applying these principles to his cyberspace scenario, Barney concludes that computer network attack (CNA) "may be lawfully transmitted through the international telecommunications infrastructure, including Internet routers physically located in neutral States." Further, he notes that such passage does not violate territorial sovereignty nor comprise an act of force in the intermediate territory. Since most states in his scenario lack the technical capability to detect the passage of a CNA, "neutral States had no obligation to prevent the transit of their national Cyberspace and their status as neutrals was not violated."[23]

Could it be possible to extend this framework further to have data packets be "nationally flagged" like ships—thus having the data itself represent sovereignty? Also, could diplomatic measures be developed between specific countries that allow (or deny) packet transit? How should the international community respond to unauthorized rerouting of packets through other countries via router disruption, as China is accused of doing in April 2010?[24]

This model may also facilitate development of theory related to virtual environments. One could argue that virtual reality exists as an immersion of the cognitive mind in nonphysical landscapes defined by codes often distributed among many machines. Perhaps we could use the naval concept of subsurface activity to model virtual activity. Arguably, from an operational aspect, it is more difficult to "track" individuals, groups, and activities when they go below the "normal surface" of cyberspace (whatever that truly is) into the potentially multidimensional subsurface virtual environment. Conversely, when they "resurface," their presence may be more readily acknowledged and attributed. The concept and doctrine of riverine operations—those that focus on a nation's inland waters—may also offer some useful models for devolved operations in the cyberspace "backwaters." This would focus on cyberspace activities that may use older technology, such as telephone modems and Disk Operating System (DOS)-based bulletin boards, instead of modern Internet connections.[25]

Regardless of how the packets travel, it is reasonable to posit that their movement through cyberspace may meet resistance in the same way ships must navigate through waves and currents. One implication would be the possible utility for "cyberspace weather" to model entropic effects—websites already exist that provide Internet "traffic reports."[26] Thus, ensuring freedom of navigation in cyberspace must necessarily include not only adversarial efforts to deny or disrupt, but also cyberspace entropy effects and possible physical environment impacts (e.g., power outages, solar storms, etc.).

APPLICATION: THE PRINCIPLES OF JOINT OPERATIONS

What are some of the implications for military operations in the cyberspace domain, and how do they relate to the greater commons context? To explore this question, let us address the nine classic principles of war as well as the additional joint principles of restraint, perseverance, and legitimacy. The discussion below is illustrative vice comprehensive and, by design, provides more questions than answers. The reader may note the implicit overarching assumption among the principles that achieving decisive results is possible in warfare—this notion reflects a domain-focused view. Another overarching domain aspect of note is that the time versus physical distance at which effects are manifested via activities in cyberspace operations may be significantly more rapid than activities in the other physical domains.

Objective.

The principle of objective strives "to direct every military operation toward a clearly defined, decisive, and achievable goal" with the understanding that these objectives "support attainment of the overall political goals of the conflict."[27] This reference to a scope beyond the military realm infers the need to consider effects beyond the domain view of cyberspace that, in turn, raises several fundamental questions. How do planners characterize and consider nth-order effects that propagate from their primary actions? How do they model possible interaction with effects in other domains and commons? Are they of significance if they do not translate into other domains? Will it be possible to achieve precise and decisive results through cyberspace operations?

Offensive.

The purpose of offensive action is "to seize, retain, and exploit the initiative . . . the most effective and decisive way to achieve a clearly defined objective" with such operations conducted "while maintaining freedom of action and achieving decisive results." Defensive actions are downplayed as "only a temporary expedient" until the offensive initiative is regained.[28] Such language strongly suggests a domain perspective in which physical terrain is taken and held—but can one occupy a specific area of cyberspace? Does a strategy that includes active defense with preprogrammed responsive actions blur the definition of initiative in the offensive? Traditional munitions (e.g., bullets and bombs) can be used in relatively predictable performance parameters. But, can cyberspace offensive measures based on specific exploitations of software be guaranteed to have a "shelf life" sufficient for a given conflict? When one pursues objective and offensive principles in military operations, what is the role and applicability of traditional conventions, such as the Law of Armed Conflict? What is the distinction or line drawn between what citizens or industry can do offensively in the cyberspace commons and what only nations can do?

Mass.

Mass means "to concentrate the effects of combat power at the most advantageous place and time to produce decisive results." One achieves mass in part through the integration and synchronization of capabilities.[29] This definition implies the feasibility of achieving asymmetric effects through the proper application of mass. However, how should mass be measured and compared in cyber operations? It could include factors such as the number of nodes of operation, computing power, speed, bandwidth, memory, and number of users and applications affected—possibly modeled using traditional munitions effectiveness analysis. Is it possible to weaponize malware to produce mass effects like those in chemical and biological attacks? Will this be easier or harder to produce in the future? As a unique challenge for cyberspace, botnets (robot networks) conducting distributed denials of service attacks[30] demonstrate the ability to achieve concentrated effects without concentrating forces. But in practical terms, how can a commander respond if an adversary is using a botnet to exploit innocent and unknowing third-party computers as part of its effort to achieve mass?

Maneuver.

Maneuver seeks "to place the enemy in a position of disadvantage through the flexible application of combat power" using "the movement of forces in relation to the enemy to secure or retain positional advantage," usually to facilitate the delivery of "direct and indirect fires of the maneuvering force."[31] While this principle infers the need to occupy or traverse physical terrain, it is possible to envision a cyberspace form of mass and maneuver using distributed botnets that shift their "fires" to multiple targets with shifting combinations and coordination with other botnets. This could introduce a concept of interior and exterior "cyberspace lines" that reflect the framework of Figure 23-1, with the interior operations being the GIG domain and the exterior operations being those in the broader commons (i.e., where the botnets exist).

Economy of Force.

Economy of force reflects "the judicious employment and distribution of forces" designed to expend minimum power on secondary effects and maximum power on the primary effect.[32] As with mass, a fundamental issue is defining forces and combat power in cyberspace. Once we delineate those, the challenge is to determine the ratio of cyber force allocated to various mission areas, such as exploitation (CNE), defense and active defense (CND), and attack (CNA).[33] From a cross-domain view, using nonkinetic cyber forces may free kinetic assets in other domains to pursue their primary effects.[34] For military operations in cyberspace, is asymmetry truly possible now or in the future?

Unity of Command.

The principle of unity of command endeavors "to ensure unity of effort under one responsible commander for every objective" possessing "the requisite authority to direct all forces employed in pursuit of a common purpose."[35] In operations involving multinational and interagency parties in traditional domains, this may be quite challenging; in cyberspace, it will be almost certainly more difficult, at least in the near term. Today, evaluating this principle is tricky, since the relevant force and command structures are still nascent for most military forces as well as their counterparts in civil and commercial operations. Efforts are underway to extend traditional kinetic command structures for collective defense, such as NATO article 5, to the cyberspace realm.[36] Because of its sensitive nature, sovereign states will most likely keep some aspects of their cyber capabilities and command structures undisclosed.

Security.

Security aims "to prevent the enemy from acquiring unexpected advantage"; it implements the tenets of enhancing freedom of action while protecting friendly forces. It embraces "prudent risk management, not undue caution,"[37] which implies consideration for cyberspace beyond the immediate domain view. How does one measure threat in cyberspace to conduct such risk management? Undoubtedly, the amount of malware present on the Internet has increased dramatically over the past decade—but is the overall threat increasing or decreasing when normalized against the equally dramatic growth of users, devices, and software resident? How does one distinguish deliberate negative effects from "natural" cyberspace entropy? Do the risk management assessments of current organizations—government or private—consider the two-way nature of security cameras based on the reciprocity of connectivity?

Surprise.

The purpose of surprise is "to strike at a time or place or in a manner for which the enemy is unprepared" with hopes of shifting the balance of power to "achieve success well out of proportion to the effort expended."[38] Certainly, activities in cyberspace appear to expend little effort if thought of as merely the transmission of "zeroes and ones." The potential application of unexpected combat power currently may be embodied in zero-day vulnerabilities or back doors built into devices during manufacturing or as part of the supply chain.[39] However, is achieving surprise in cyberspace easier or harder than in traditional physical domains? How do factors such as the proliferation of information, the layering of data, and the presence of multiple personas affect efforts for surprise?

Simplicity.

Simplicity aims "to increase the probability that plans and operations will be executed as intended by preparing clear, uncomplicated plans and concise orders" designed to "minimize misunderstanding and confusion" and address "stress, fatigue, fog of war, and complexities of modern combat."[40] Cyber devices promise to simplify execution, but do they also provide more complete knowledge of operations that facilitates agility and flexibility? Any examination to achieve simplicity of cyberspace activities must look beyond the domain to account for potential complicating factors in the commons. Even with this, is simplicity possible for the common user in cyberspace given the context of complexity and entropy?

Restraint.

The principle of restraint attempts "to limit collateral damage and prevent the unnecessary use of force" that requires instead the "judicious use of force."[41] As previously discussed, the unpredictable effects of entropy and emergence may make it difficult to achieve precision in cyberspace. Thus, during the development of rules of engagement for responding to perceived aggression in cyberspace, planners should question the wisdom of using active defense without proper limits.

Otherwise, restraint may unwillingly go by the wayside and open the door for ill-conceived notions such as "carpet bombing in cyberspace."[42]

Perseverance.

The principle of perseverance tries "to ensure the commitment necessary to attain the national strategic end state" that may include "preparation for measured, protracted military operations."[43] The current mission of military cyberspace requires sustained operations at a substantial level of effort. But will an increased use of cyberspace during conflict require significant increases in committed resources? Do cyber forces have the same logistical issues as forces in other domains? Will the methods of deploying and employing forces engaged in cyberspace activity place limitations on their endurance? What are the implications of possible operational effectiveness limitations of cyberspace weapons based on the "shelf life" of software flaws they may exploit?

Legitimacy.

Legitimacy endeavors "to maintain legal and moral authority in the conduct of operations."[44] Military and civilian experts around the world are evaluating the legal constraints related to cyberspace activity.[45] In addition, legitimacy is a burgeoning issue for cyberspace, especially with regard to morality and rightness in the many layers and persona of virtual cyberspace. How are such ethics created, and how are they evolving? How do these reflect the changing expectations of netizens (i.e., active members of the Internet community) and the evolving definition of fundamental human rights? What should be the balance between security and privacy from both the individual and collective perspectives?

ONTOLOGY AND EVOLUTION

The previous section examined some implications of the domain approach projected into the larger commons. The author posits that many of the activities in other domains (land, sea, and air) that led to the establishment of the principles of warfare deal with the attempts to gain local and temporal *control* of such domains. In contrast, cyberspace can be considered an artificial domain initially created for the purpose of *exercising control or governing activities*. This artificial domain requires energy to exist (e.g., use of the electromagnetic spectrum). Its control or governance can be first-order—conscious and deliberate—or various levels of nth-orders that may be unconscious, accidental, or emergent. This domain exists as part of a larger commons, both artificial and real.

However, for understanding that endures beyond our current technological manifestation of cyberspace, even the commons model is insufficient. To take a truly holistic view, one must deliberately examine the *ontology* of cyberspace to determine how its current form fits into its overarching evolutionary path. Ontology is the branch of metaphysics that studies the nature of existence or being; in this case, a study of the actual essence of cyberspace. As such, it is intimately connected with epistemology, which includes investigation into the nature of knowledge. A full discussion of such topics of philosophy is beyond the scope of this chapter, but we will examine several related issues for their relevance to developing cyberspace theory.

Cyberspace ontology must address many fundamental questions, some of which may be of particular importance for planning near-term cyberspace security. Is the balance of activity in cyberspace moving toward stability or instability, or perhaps dynamic stability? Will cyberspace become self-organizing and self-regulating in its function, perhaps similar to the processes in a living organism? If so, what are the implications? Will cyberspace reach a steady state of activity and scope; if so, what will be its limiting or defining factors? Can concepts such as complexity and emergence as well as convergence and divergence provide practical insight into the modeling of entropy in cyberspace? How is the cognitive dimension of the information environment changing based on the trend toward increased human-machine interface and the anticipated growth of neural prosthetics?[46] How will individual and collective ethics evolve in response to the increasingly blurred interface between human and machine?

At much deeper levels of theoretical physics, some may argue that the cyberspace ontology is but a subset of broader concepts such as "quantum reality" that strive to model the micro-to-macro structure of the universe itself.[47] Expanding the examination of individual cognition to the broader human condition, to include such concepts as morality and ethics, will eventually lead to discussions of epistemology and even theology. This presents an essential question: Is cyberspace merely an extension of existing technology, or does it possibly represent a fundamental step forward (or backward) in human evolution?

While there is much conjecture about the future of cyberspace, the author offers two concepts to consider regarding the potential role of cyberspace in human evolution. The first is the concept of "the singularity" explored in several books by futurist Ray Kurzweil as a "future period during which the pace of technological change will be so rapid, its impacts so deep, that human life will be irreversibly transformed." Specifically, the singularity refers to the inflection point at which the collective computational capability (*not* intelligence) of machines exceeds that of the human population. Kurweil posits three overlapping revolutions surrounding this event—genetics, as an intersection of information and biology; nanotechnology, as an intersection of information and the physical world; and robotics, as a growth of artificial intelligence.[48] The second concept is "the noosphere" developed and explored by Pierre Teilhard de Chardin as an extension of the concept of the biosphere to the realm of human thought.[49] In *The Phenomenon of Man*, he describes the noosphere as "much more coherent and just as extensive as any preceding layer, it is really a new layer, the 'thinking layer,' which, since its germination at the end of the Tertiary period, has spread over and above the world of plants and animals. In other words, outside and above the biosphere there is the noosphere." He extrapolated the evolution of the noosphere and envisaged the convergence of the human condition to a final stage that he termed "point Omega."[50] De Chardin posited some implications for humanity like those of Kurzweil, albeit through an approach of philosophy vice technology. Whether such predictions come to fruition is not the point; studying such concepts is essential to theory development because their outcomes influence the popular views of human behavior, which in turn influence activities of creation and utilization in the cyberspace commons and domains.

IMPLICATIONS FOR STRATEGIC LEADERS

Hopefully, the previous section broadened the reader's scope for thinking about cyberspace, and persuaded him/her that the true nature of cyberspace is more than analytical constants to be categorized, but rather, a developing enigma to be studied. However, current matters of international security include an abundance of "here and now" issues related to cyberspace. Balancing these practical demands while evaluating the rather esoteric aspects of cyberspace are challenges that strategic leaders should take seriously.

Despite some promising developments, it is risky to consider the current application of cyberspace operations as a "silver bullet." Developing theoretical principles for cyberspace may help to explore the opportunities as well as potential shortcomings that affect such operations. In a technical sense, planners and decisionmakers need to recognize that applications may be neither precise nor free from disorder, and that the cyberspace environment in which decisions are made may be significantly different from the cyberspace environment in which they are enacted. Thus, they should conduct critical, perhaps even skeptical, reviews of promised capabilities—especially when making resourcing decisions.

Because of the complex interplay of nonkinetic and kinetic forces that result in nth-order effects that are largely unknown, leaders need to adopt a holistic approach to planning that considers effects not only to other warfighting domains, but also to other instruments of power. To support such assessments, we must develop and quantify measures of power in cyberspace to help prioritize defense methods and investment; one should expect these values to be moving targets. We must exercise prudence and wisdom in the selection of areas to implement fully automated responses (e.g., active defense), since this represents a conscious abdication of the cognitive to the content dimension. While some measures of automated defense may require fully automated responses to preserve or protect critical functions, perhaps like reflexes in a human neural system to protect one's hand from a hot stove, the indiscriminate application could potentially create more problems than it solves.[51]

For future applications, we must continuously examine and refine theoretical models to reflect how the balance may shift among the cognitive, content, and connectivity dimensions in the information environment. This implies a departure from the current overemphasis on traditional information technology, which the author posits will have significantly less influence in the future. Leaders should anticipate significant blurring of the cognitive and connectivity dimensions as the human-machine interface becomes more engrained and pervasive, in the domain as well as the commons. Also, they should consider the possibilities presented by significant blurring of the cognitive and content dimensions as information is consolidated in cloud-type applications and collective computation and memory capacity of machines exceed that of humankind.

It is reasonable to assert that current and future embodiments of cyberspace will follow the model of human conflict described by the Clausewitzian trinity of emotion, reason, and chance. As witnessed in the so-called "Arab Spring" events such as those in Egypt and Tunisia, social media via cyberspace provided a conduit for raw human expression to force change on the world stage.[52] Governments and certain international organizations are wrestling with how best to apply reasonable and prudent measures to bring stability and justice to cyberspace as well as to foster its universal access. Finally, there is no evidence that cyberspace will lift the fog of war or make the application of force any less subject to chance, even though such chance may be much better characterized. Entropy and emergence simply cannot be eliminated in all circumstances—to have a military pursue such a goal as omniscience does not serve its mission for national security well. Current cyberspace strategies that anticipate flaws and failures, and thus emphasize the need for resilience by design, may provide enduring principles into the future.

CONCLUSION

While we can evaluate certain limited aspects of operations in cyberspace using a domain model, the proper examination requires a holistic approach that includes current concepts of the commons as well as those of a conscious future-directed model that recognizes the continuing evolution of cyberspace. In addition, cyberspace theory should embrace the potential for radical emergent behavior that may shift the balance of influence among the cognition, content, and connectivity dimensions. This requires the deliberate and thoughtful pursuit of cyberspace theory as a continuing dialogue that may include multiple frameworks for analysis. This pursuit of cyberspace theory will not occur unless we adopt a formal bifurcated approach to national efforts—one that is integrated to address both the pragmatic and urgent present challenge as well as a separately resourced effort dedicated to examining the changing nature of cyberspace itself. Without such a "big picture" view, planners and decisionmakers add risk in their activities by not characterizing the full spectrum of the interactions and effects of creation and use in cyberspace. Again, for the purist, the goal of this paper was not to prescribe such a theoretical framework, but rather, to begin a dialogue toward that end.

ENDNOTES - CHAPTER 23

1. Barack Obama, *National Security Strategy*, Washington, DC: The White House, May 2010, pp. 27-28. Also see *Department of Defense Strategy for Operating in Cyberspace*, Washington, DC: Department of Defense (DoD), July 14, 2011, available from *www.defense.gov/news/d20110714cyber.pdf*.

2. U.S. Deputy Secretary of Defense Gordon England, "The Definition of 'Cyberspace'," Memorandum for Secretaries of the Military Departments, Washington, DC, May 12, 2008, available from *integrator.hanscom.af.mil/2008/May/05292008/05292008-24.htm*.

3. *Cyberspace Policy Review: Assuring a Trusted and Resilient Information and Communications Infrastructure*, Washington, DC: The White House, May 2009, p. 1. In this document, the term "cyberspace" is often abbreviated to "cyber" when used as an adjective (e.g., cyber attack, cyber incident, etc.).

4. Arthur K. Cebrowski, "Transformation and the Changing Character of War?" *Transformation Trends*, June 17, 2004, p. 7.

5. William Gibson, *Neuromancer,* New York: Ace Books, 1984. Gibson is credited with popularizing the term "cyberspace" (*Neuromancer*, 1984) and the short story "Burning Chrome," for the purist. His full definition is: "A consensual hallucination experienced daily by billions of legitimate operators, in every nation, by children being taught mathematical concepts. . . . A graphic representation of data abstracted from the banks of every computer in the human system. Unthinkable complexity. Lines of light ranged in the nonspace of the mind, clusters and constellations of data. Like city lights, receding."

6. Daniel T. Kuehl, "From Cyberspace to Cyberpower: Defining the Problem," Chap. 2, *Cyberpower and National Security*, Washington, DC: National Defense University Press and Potomac Books, 2009, pp. 24-42; Martin Libicki, *Cyberdeterrence and Cyberwar*, Santa Monica, CA: RAND, 2009.

7. *Department of Defense Strategy for Operating in Cyberspace*, p. 5.

8. Abraham M. Denmark and James Mulvenon, *Contested Commons: The Future of American Power in a Multipolar World*, Washington, DC: Center for a New American Security, January 2010. This report lists four broad characteristics of commons, p. 7:

> 1. They are not owned or controlled by any single entity. 2. Their utility as a whole is greater than if broken down into smaller parts. 3. States and non-state actors with the requisite technological capabilities are able to access and use them for economic, political, scientific, and cultural purposes. 4. States and non-state actors with the requisite technological capabilities are able to use them as a medium for military movement and as a theater for military conflict.

9. Yochai Benkler, "The Political Economy of Commons," *Upgrade*, Vol. 4, No. 3, June 2003, pp. 6-7, available from *www.cepis.org/upgrade/index.jsp?p=2144&n=2179*. Of course, the full discussion of legal definitions of governance is beyond the scope of this chapter.

10. John P. Martin, "Another webcam claim settled in Lower Merion," *The Philadelphia Inquirer*, August 23, 2011, available from *articles.philly.com/2011-08-23/news/29917732_1_webcams-blake-robbins-school-issued-laptop*. "The district acknowledged that it had tracking software that let it remotely activate webcams on the laptops and view the images. In less than two years, staffers turned on webcams on more than 40 laptops, typically after students reported the computers lost or stolen."

11. "Experiment Showed Grid Vulnerability to Cyber Attack—Flaws Fixed," *Energy Assurance Daily,* Washington, DC: U.S. Department of Energy (DoE), September 27, 2007. The DoE reported on recommended changes to power-generation facilities resulting from a Department of Homeland Security (DHS) experiment in March 2007.

12. The second law of thermodynamics addresses how differences in temperature, pressure, and chemical potential equilibrate over time in an isolated physical system. From the state of thermodynamic equilibrium, the law

deduced the principle of the *increase of entropy* and explains the phenomenon of irreversibility in nature, e.g., the impossibility of creating a perpetual motion machine.

13. Stuart H. Starr, "Toward a Preliminary Theory of Cyberpower," Chap. 3, *Cyberpower and National Security*, Washington, DC: National Defense University Press and Potomac Books, 2009, pp. 43-88.

14. *Enabling Distributed Security in Cyberspace: Building a Healthy and Resilient Cyber Ecosystem with Automated Collective Action*, Washington, DC: Department of Homeland Security, March 23, 2011, p. 5.

15. *Ibid.*

16. U.S. Cyber Command Fact Sheet, Fort Meade, MD: U.S. Cyber Command Public Affairs, October, 2011, available from *www.stratcom.mil/factsheets/Cyber_Command*.

17. *Training and Doctrine Command (TRADOC) Pamphlet 525-7-8, Cyberspace Operations Concept Capability Plan 2016-2028*, Fort Monroe, VA: U.S. Army Training and Doctrine Command, February 22, 2010, p. iv, available from *www.fas.org/irp/doddir/army/pam525-7-8.pdf*. The Army view is that "The third dimension [of full spectrum operations] is the cyber-electromagnetic contest. . . . Trends in wired, wireless, and optical technologies are setting conditions for the convergence of computer and telecommunication networks."

18. "Information Dominance," *Rhumb Lines, Straight Lines to Navigate By*, Navy Office of Information, October 2, 2009.

19. *Air Force Doctrine Document 3-12, Cyberspace Operations*, Maxwell Air Force Base, AL: LeMay Center, July 15, 2010.

20. W. Alexander Vacca, "Military Culture and Cyber Security," *Survival*, Vol. 53, No. 6, December 2011-January 2012, pp. 159-176.

21. A. T. Mahan, *The Influence of Sea Power Upon History 1660-1783*, Mineola, NY: Dover, 1987 reprint, p. 30; also see pp. 31-32: "The geographical position of a county may not only favor the concentration of its forces, but give the further strategic advantage of a central position and a good base for hostile operations against its probable enemies."

22. Steven M. Barney, "Innocent Packets? Applying Navigational Regimes from the Law of the Sea Convention by Analogy to the Realm of Cyberspace," *Naval Law Review*, Vol. XLVIII, 2001, pp. 58-87, especially pp. 65-66, 71.

23. *Ibid*, pp. 77-82.

24. *2010 Report to Congress of the U.S.-China Economic and Security Review Commission*, Washington, DC: U.S. Government Printing Office, November 2010, pp. 243-244, available from *www.uscc.gov/annual_report/2010/annual_report_full_10.pdf*. In April 2010, a large number of routing paths to various Internet Protocol addresses were redirected through networks in China for 17 minutes, giving the network server operators the ability to read, delete, or edit e-mail and other information sent along those paths by U.S. Government, military, and business sites. This and other incidents raise questions about whether China might seek to leverage these abilities intentionally to assert some level of control over the Internet, even if only for a brief period.

25. "The 'Wild and Woolly' World of Bulletin Boards," *All Things Considered*, National Public Radio, November 21, 2009, available from *www.npr.org/templates/story/story.php?storyId=120649723*.

26. *Internet Traffic Report*, available from *www.internettrafficreport.com/*. This website monitors the flow of data around the world. It then displays a value between zero and 100, with higher values indicating faster and more reliable connections. The website's home page shows the current statistics (average response time in milliseconds and average percent of packet loss) for five regions: Asia, Australia, Europe, North America, and South America.

27. *Joint Publication (JP) 3-0, Joint Operations*, Washington, DC: Joint Chiefs of Staff, August 11, 2011, p. A-1.

28. *Ibid.*

29. *Ibid.*, p. A-2.

30. "Botnets" are virtual armies of compromised computers that can be controlled remotely over the Internet by a "botmaster." They may exploit hundreds of thousands of computers, usually without the owners' knowledge. An adversary with such capability, if coupled with a network structure, could achieve swarming attacks and defenses (such as distributed denial of service)—in cyberspace as well as other strategic commons—that challenge the "traditional mass- and maneuver-oriented approaches to conflict." See Clay Wilson, *Botnets, Cybercrime, and Cyberterrorism: Vulnerabilities and Policy Issues for Congress*, Congressional Research Service (CSR) Report for Congress RL-32114, Washington, DC: Congressional Research Service, January 29, 2008. Also see John Arquilla and David Ronfeldt, "The Advent of Netwar, Revisited," in *Networks and Netwars*, Santa Monica, CA: RAND, 2001, p. 12.

31. JP 3-0, p. A-2.

32. *Ibid.*

33. *JP 1-02, Department of Defense Dictionary of Military and Associated Terms*, Washington, DC: Joint Chiefs of Staff, November 15, 2011. *Computer Network Attack* (CNA) is "Actions taken through the use of computer networks to disrupt, deny, degrade, or destroy information resident in computers and computer networks, or the computers and networks themselves." *Computer Network Defense* (CND) is "Actions taken to protect, monitor, analyze, detect, and respond to unauthorized activity within the Department of Defense information systems and computer networks." *Computer Network Exploitation* (CNE) is "Enabling operations and intelligence collection capabilities conducted through the use of computer networks to gather data from target or adversary automated information systems or networks."

34. *Air Force Doctrine Document 3-12*, p. 16.

35. JP 3-0, p. A-2.

36. See "Defending the Networks: The NATO Policy on Cyber Defence," Brussels, Belgium: NATO Public Diplomacy Division, June 2011.

37. JP 3-0, p. A-3.

38. *Ibid.*

39. Zero-day vulnerabilities refer to software flaws that have been undiscovered or unresolved by the software developer. Back doors are methods of entering software programs through paths not envisioned by their creators for general use.

40. JP 3-0, p. A-3.

41. *Ibid.*

42. Charles W. Williamson III, "Carpet Bombing in Cyberspace: Why America Needs a Military Botnet," *Armed Forces Journal*, May 2008.

43. JP 3-0, p. A-4.

44. *Ibid.*

45. For examples, see Michael N. Schmitt and Brian T. O'Donnell, eds., *International Law Studies Vol. 76: Computer Network Attack and International Law*, Newport, RI: U.S. Naval War College, 2002.

46. Edward Skoudis, "Information Technology and the Biotech Revolution," Chap. 9 in *Cyberpower and National Security*, pp. 241-250.

47. For a brief survey of various philosophies and interpretations of quantum reality, see Shaun O'Kain, *Quantum Reality*, Bowmain Ltd., 2009, available from *www.bowmain.pwp.blueyonder.co.uk/QM/Quantum_Reality.pdf*.

48. Ray Kurzweil, *The Singularity is Near: When Humans Transcend Biology*, New York: Viking, 2005.

49. For a more contemporary examination of the term "noosphere" and its context related to cyberspace and the infosphere, see John Arquilla and David Ronfeldt, *The Emergence of Noopolitik: Toward An American Information Strategy*, RAND Monograph Report MR-1033-OSD, Santa Monica, CA: RAND Corporation, 1999.

50. Pierre Teilhard de Chardin, *The Phenomenon of Man*, Bernard Wall, trans., New York: Harper Brothers Publishers, 1959, pp. 18, 35-36, 182. Teilhard de Chardin wrote the original book in French during the 1930s. Since he was a Jesuit priest, his views were controversial in the Catholic Church, such as "The time has come to realize that an interpretation of the universe—even a positivist one—remains unsatisfying unless it covers the interior as well as the exterior of things; mind as well as matter. The true physics is that which will, one day, achieve the inclusion of man in his wholeness in a coherent picture of the world."

51. See Felix Salmon and Jon Stokes, "Algorithms Take Control of Wall Street," *Wired Magazine,* January 2011, available from *www.wired.com/magazine/2010/12/ff_ai_flashtrading/*; and *Findings Regarding the Market Events of May 6, 2010: Report of the Staffs of the CFTC and SEC to the Joint Advisory Committee on Emerging Regulatory Issues*, Washington, DC: Commodity Futures Trading Commission (CFTC) and Securities and Exchange Commission (SEC), September 30, 2010. This report examined a "flash crash" in the stock market that occurred due to the unanticipated interactions of automated trading algorithms. The report noted: "The interaction between automated execution programs and algorithmic trading strategies can quickly erode liquidity and result in disorderly markets."

52. Dr. Natana J. DeLong-Bas, "The New Social Media and the Arab Spring," *Oxford Islamic Studies Online*, June 2011, available from *www.oxfordislamicstudies.com/Public/focus/essay0611_social_media.html*.

ABOUT THE CONTRIBUTORS

JOHN J. ACLIN, JR. (M.Sc., National War College, 2008) is the Chair for Defense Intelligence at the U.S. Army War College (USAWC). He is a Senior Intelligence Officer with the Defense Intelligence Agency (DIA), where he has worked since 1989. Prior to his assignment to the USAWC, Mr. Aclin served as a senior briefer in the Pentagon, as Division Chief for both regional and functional analytic divisions, and as the DIA's Production Liaison Officer to U.S. Pacific Command. He has also served in assignments with the Office of Naval Intelligence and Central Intelligence Agency (CIA). A U.S. Naval Academy graduate, Mr. Aclin served in submarines and retired as a Captain from the Naval Reserve.

CHARLES D. ALLEN (MS-OR, Georgia Institute of Technology, 1986; MMAS, School of Advanced Military Studies, 1990) is Professor of Leadership and Cultural Studies in the Department of Command, Leadership, and Management at the USAWC. He is formerly the Director of Leader Development at the USAWC. He is a retired Army colonel who served in leadership and staff positions from platoon through Corps and in Army and Joint Commands. His recent works are published in *Joint Forces Quarterly, Parameters, Military Review*, and *Armed Forces Journal*. His areas of interest and authorship are strategic leadership, creativity and innovation, and organizational change. He is a frequent presenter on these topics for Senior Leadership Staff Ride and outreach programs for the USAWC.

J. BOONE BARTHOLOMEES, JR. (Ph.D., Duke University, 1978) is Professor of Military History in the Department of National Security and Strategy at the USAWC. He is the former course director for the USAWC core course, Theory of War and Strategy, and a former holder of the Dwight D. Eisenhower Chair of National Security Studies. He is a retired Army Colonel and the author of *Buff Facings and Gilt Buttons: Headquarters and Staff Operations in the Army of Northern Virginia, 1861-1865*. He edited *The USAWC Guide to National Security Policy and Strategy*, 2004, and the 2nd edition published in 2006, as well as *The USAWC Guide to National Security Issues* editions in 2008 and 2010.

TAMI DAVIS BIDDLE (Ph.D., Yale University, 1995) is the Hoyt S. Vandenberg Professor of Aerospace Studies at the USAWC. She was the 2005-07 George C. Marshall Professor of Military Studies at the College, and the 2001-2002 Harold K. Johnson Visiting Professor of Military History at the U.S. Army's Military History Institute. Prior to that she taught in the Department of History at Duke University, where she was a core faculty member of the Duke-University of North Carolina Joint Program in Military History. She received her Ph.D. in history from Yale, and has held fellowships from Harvard, the Social Science Research Council, and the Smithsonian Institution's National Air and Space Museum. Her research focus has been warfare in the 20th century, in particular the history of air warfare. She also studies military organization and leadership, civil-military relations, grand strategy and national security policy, and professional military education. Her book, *Rhetoric and Reality in Air Warfare: The Evolution of British and American Ideas about Strategic Bombing, 1914-1945* (Princeton, NJ: Princeton University Press, 2002) was a *Choice* Outstanding Academic Title for 2002 and was added to the Chief of Air Staff's Reading List, Royal Air Force. Some of her recent work includes, "Sifting Dresden's Ashes," *The Wilson Quarterly*, Spring 2005; "Sword and Shield: American Strategic Forces, 1945 to the Present," in Andrew Bacevich, ed., *The Long War: A New History of U.S. National Security Policy since World War Two* (New York: Columbia University Press, 2007); and "Leveraging Strength: The Pillars of American Grand Strategy in World War II," *Orbis*, Winter 2011, pp. 4-28.

JEFFREY L. CATON (MS, Air Force Institute of Technology, 1989) is the Associate Professor of Cyberspace Operations at the USAWC's Center for Strategic Leadership. Prior to his current position, he was an instructor in the College's Department of Command, Leadership and Management for over three years while also serving as the College's Defense Transformation Chair. He is a retired Air Force colonel having commanded units at the squadron and group level. His 28 years of service include space and nuclear missile operations, joint specialty operations and planning, acquisition engineering and test, program management, and foreign military sales. He has published on a number of cyberspace-, space-, and nuclear-related issues.

CLAYTON K.S. CHUN (Ph.D., RAND Graduate School, 1992) is chairman of the Department of Distance Education at the USAWC and held the General Hoyt S. Vandenberg Chair of Aerospace Studies. He was recently the Professor of Economics in the Department of National Security and Strategy. Dr. Chun is a retired Air Force officer with missile, space, command and control, strategy, and education assignments. He has published on a number of national security, economics, and space-related issues.

GLENN K. CUNNINGHAM (MA, Duquesne University, 2004) is Professor of Joint Landpower in the Department of Military Strategy, Planning, and Operations at the USAWC. He is also the Deputy Director for the Combined/Joint Force Land Component Commander Course. He is a retired Marine Corps colonel with a wide background of command and staff positions in contingency planning, joint operations, and interagency programs. He has written and presented on humanitarian demining operations, ethics, and critical thinking and was a military delegate to the Ottawa Convention on the prohibition of antipersonnel landmines. He is also an adjunct professor of leadership and ethics at Duquesne University.

REED J. FENDRICK (MA, Cornell University) is a senior Foreign Service Officer with the U.S. Department of State where he has served since 1974. He served with the Department of National Security and Strategy at the USAWC from 2002 to 2004. A graduate of the University of Wisconsin-Madison, he received the M.A. degree in Government from Cornell University. Among his diplomatic assignments, he has been Deputy Chief of Mission and Charge d'Affaires at the American Embassy in The Hague, the Netherlands; Political Counselor at the American Embassy in Pretoria, South Africa; Deputy Director of the Office of Central African Affairs; Pearson Fellow assigned to the Office of International Relations of the Governor of Hawaii; Political Officer in the American Embassies in Paris, France, Pretoria, South Africa, Bridgetown, Barbados, and the United States Mission to the United Nations; Deputy Principal Officer at the American Consulate-General in Alexandria, Egypt; Junior Officer at the American Embassy in Rabat, Morocco; and Staff Assistant to the Assistant Secretary of State for African Affairs. In July 2004, he joined the United States Mission to the United Nations, where he serves as Counselor for Political Affairs.

JAMES F. HOLCOMB (Colonel, Infantry, USA, Ret.) is a Faculty Instructor in the Department of Distance Education at the USAWC. Commissioned from the U.S. Military Academy at West Point, he served in a variety of Infantry, Special Forces and Russian/East European Foreign Area Officer assignments. Prior to his retirement from the Army in 2002, he taught for five years as Director of Military Strategy in the USAWC's Department of National Security and Strategy. He also teaches the elective in Grand Strategy and the Strategic Art to the Distance Education Course at the USAWC.

DAVID JABLONSKY (Colonel, Infantry, USA, Ret.) is the Professor of National Security Affairs in the Department of National Security and Strategy at the USAWC. A graduate of Dartmouth College and the USAWC, he received an MA from Boston University in international relations and holds MA and Ph.D. degrees in European history from Kansas University. He has held the Elihu Root Chair of Strategy, the George C. Marshall Chair of Military Studies, and the Dwight D. Eisenhower Chair of National Security Studies at the USAWC. He is the author of five books, eight monographs, and numerous articles and book chapters dealing with European history and international relations.

FRANK L. JONES (MPA, State University of New York at Albany, 1978) is Associate Professor of Security Studies at the USAWC, where he holds the General Dwight D. Eisenhower Chair of National Security. A retired member of the Senior Executive Service with more than 30 years of government service, he served in several positions within the Office of the Secretary of Defense, including Deputy Assistant Secretary of Defense for Special Operations Policy and Support and as Principal Director for Strategy, Plans and Resources in the Office of the Assistant Secretary of Defense for Homeland Defense. From 2006-2007, he was a fellow at the Homeland Security Institute, where he worked on national response planning and maritime security issues. He has written several book chapters and journal articles on such topics as national security policymaking, homeland defense, and terrorism.

DENNIS M. MURPHY (MS, Pennsylvania State University, 1984) is a Professor of Information Operations and Information in Warfare at the USAWC. Professor Murphy served in a variety of command and staff positions over his 27 years of U.S. Army service, to include command of a direct support artillery battalion forward deployed to Germany and an associate professorship at West Point. Professor Murphy was appointed as the first George C. Marshall Fellow for Political-Military and Diplomatic Gaming at the Department of State's Foreign Service Institute in 1999. His work in information operations (IO) and strategic communication includes a tour as senior observer-trainer for the Battle Command Training Program, Operations Group Delta (Joint Task Force and Combatant Command trainers), where he trained NATO multinational forces on IO prior to their initial deployment to Bosnia. He has written on information operations, strategic communication, and national security issues and published in *Military Review, IO Journal, Foreign Service Journal, Joint Forces Quarterly*, and *Parameters,* among others. Professor Murphy currently serves as the Director of the Information in Warfare Group at the Center for Strategic Leadership, USAWC, where he teaches information operations and strategic communication.

R. CRAIG NATION (Ph.D., Duke University, 1976) has served as Professor of Strategy and Director of Russian and Eurasian Studies with the Department of National Security and Strategy, USAWC, since 1996. His most recent major publication, a history of the Balkan conflict of the 1990s, is entitled *War in the Balkans, 1991-2002.*

LOUIS J. NIGRO, JR. (Ph.D., Vanderbilt University, 1979) is a career diplomat and a member of the Senior Foreign Service of the United States. From 2004-2006, he was seconded to the USAWC faculty as Professor of International Relations. In the Department of State since 1980, he has served overseas at U.S. Embassies in The Bahamas, Chad, Haiti, The Holy See, Guinea, and Cuba. He was Deputy Chief of Mission in the last three postings. In Washington, he has served in the Department of State's Operations Center, Policy Planning Council, Office of Western European Affairs, and Office of Canadian Affairs. For his service in Haiti, he earned the Department of State's Superior Honor Award. Before joining the Foreign Service, Mr. Nigro was a Fulbright-Hays Research Fellow in Italy and taught modern European history at Stanford University. He is the author of *The New Diplomacy in Italy: American Propaganda and U.S.-Italian Relations, 1917-1919* (New York: Peter Lang, 1999).

CONSTANCE PHLIPOT (MS, Industrial College of the Armed Force, National Defense University, 2000) is a retired Foreign Service Officer, now teaching and working as a consultant on international relations in Warsaw, Poland. She formerly served on detail to the Department of Defense as a professor of International Relations at the USAWC in the Department of National Security and Strategy. She spent much of her 30-year career focused on Eastern Europe and the former Soviet Union, including assignments as senior advisor on the former Soviet Union on the Policy and Planning staff of the Office of the Secretary of State; Deputy Chief of Mission in Minsk, Belarus; Deputy Economic Minister Counselor, Moscow; regional economic specialist and Deputy Director in the office of North Central Europe, Department of State; and Economic/Commercial Counselor, U.S. Embassy Riga, Latvia.

JOHN F. TROXELL (MPA, Princeton University, 1982) is an Associate Professor in the Center for Strategic Leadership at the USAWC and holds the General George S. Patton Chair of Operational Research and Analysis. Prior to assuming his current position he was the Director of National Security Studies in the Department of National Security and Strategy at the USAWC. He has also been a faculty member of the Department of Social Studies at the United States Military Academy. He is a retired Army Colonel and has served in a variety of operational and staff assignments to include the Department of the Army War Plans Division and as a force planner for the Assistant Secretary of Defense for Strategy and Requirements. He has published articles and monographs with the Strategic Studies Institute, *Parameters*, and *Military Review*.

HARRY R. "RICH" YARGER (Ph.D., History, Temple University, 1996) is a former faculty member of the USAWC and currently the Ministerial Reform Advisor at the U.S. Army Peacekeeping and Stability Operations Institute, USAWC, and a Joint Special Operations University Senior Fellow. A previous USAWC faculty member, he taught courses in: Fundamentals of Strategic Thinking, Theory of War and Strategy, National Security Policy and Strategy, and Terrorism. His research focuses on national security policy, strategic theory, stability operations, and the education and development of strategic-level leaders. Dr. Yarger has also taught at the undergraduate level at several local colleges. A retired Army colonel, he is a Vietnam veteran and served in both Germany and Korea.